EMPIRE AND THE
CHRISTIAN TRADITION

EMPIRE AND THE CHRISTIAN TRADITION

New Readings of Classical Theologians

Kwok Pui-lan, Don H. Compier, and Joerg Rieger

Editors

Fortress Press

Minneapolis

With gratitude to our teachers

and

for our students

EMPIRE AND THE CHRISTIAN TRADITION
New Readings of Classical Theologians

Copyright © 2007 Fortress Press, an imprint of Augsburg Fortress. All rights reserved. Except for brief quotations in critical articles or reviews, no part of this book may be reproduced in any manner without prior written permission from the publisher. Visit http://www.augsburgfortress.org/copyrights/ or write to Permissions, Augsburg Fortress, Box 1209, Minneapolis, MN 55440.

Cover image: © Kevin Jordan/Corbis
Cover design: Brad Norr Design
Book design: Brady Clark

Library of Congress Cataloging-in-Publication Data

Empire and the Christian tradition : new readings of classical theologians / edited by Don H. Compier, Kwok Pui-lan, and Joerg Rieger.
     p. cm.
  Includes index.
  ISBN-13: 978–0–8006–6215–8 (alk. paper)
  ISBN-10: 0–8006–6215–6 (alk. paper)
  1. Theology, Doctrinal—History. 2. Theologians. I. Compier, Don H. II. Kwok, Pui-lan. III. Rieger, Joerg.
  BT21.3.E47 2007
  230.09 —dc22
                                                                2007033275

The paper used in this publication meets the minimum requirements of American National Standard for Information Sciences — Permanence of Paper for Printed Library Materials, ANSI Z329.48-1984.

Printed in Canada.
  11   10   09   08   07   1   2   3   4   5   6   7   8   9   10

CONTENTS

CONTRIBUTORS

Edward P. Antonio was born and raised in Zimbabwe. He is Associate Professor of Theology and Social Theory at Iliff School of Theology in Denver, Colorado. He also serves as Iliff's Diversity Officer. He received his Ph.D. from Cambridge University and is editor of *Inculturation and Postcolonial Discourse in African Theology* (Peter Lang, 2006).

Anthony J. Chvala-Smith received his Ph.D. from Marquette University. He is Associate Professor of Early Christian Theology at Community of Christ Seminary, Graceland University in Independence, Missouri. With William W. Reader, he is co-author of *The Severed Hand and the Upright Corpse: The Declamations of Marcus Antonius Polemo* (Society of Biblical Literature, 1996).

Sathianathan Clarke is Professor of Theology, Culture, and Mission at Wesley Theological Seminary in Washington, D.C., after working many years as a social activist and liberation theologian at United Theological College, Bangalore, India. An ordained priest of the Church of South India, Clarke ministered among rural Dalit (untouchable) communities in Tamilnadu, India. He is the author of *Dalits and Christianity: Subaltern Religion and Liberation Theology in India* (Oxford University Press, 1998) and co-editor of *Religious Conversion in India: Modes, Motivations, Meanings* (Oxford University Press, 2003).

Don H. Compier is Dean of the Community of Christ Seminary, Graceland University, Independence, Missouri. He is a member of the Workgroup on Constructive Christian Theology and author of *What Is Rhetorical Theology? Textual Practice and Public Discourse* (Trinity Press International, 1999) and *John Calvin's Rhetorical Doctrine of Sin* (Mellen, 2001).

Reginald F. Davis received his Ph.D. from Florida State University. He has been an adjunct professor at Florida A&M University and Barry University at Tallahassee. He is a frequent guest and lecturer at colleges and churches across the nation. He served as Dean of Students at Garrett-Evangelical Theological Seminary and is the author of *Frederick Douglass: A Precursor of Liberation Theology* (Mercer University Press, 2005). He has published "African American Interpretation of Scripture" in the *Journal of Religious Thought*.

Wendy Farley is a Professor of Religion and Ethics at Emory University and the author of *The Wounding and Healing of Desire: Weaving Heaven and Earth* (Westminster John Knox, 2005) and *Eros for the Other: Retaining Truth in a Pluralistic World* (Pennsylvania State University Press, 1996).

David N. Field is Research Fellow at University of Zululand, South Africa and Coordinator for Theological Education in the Office of the United Methodist Bishop of Central and Southern Europe. He is the co-author with Ernst Conradie of *A Rainbow over the Land: A South African Guide on the Church and Environmental Justice* (Cape Town: Western Cape Provincial Council of Churches, 2000).

Michelle A. Gonzalez is Assistant Professor of Religious Studies at the University of Miami. Her research and teaching interests include Latino/a, Latin American, and feminist theologies, as well as inter-disciplinary work in Afro-Cuban studies. She is the author of *Sor Juana: Beauty and Justice in the Americas* (Orbis Books, 2003), *Afro-Cuban Theology: Religion, Race, Culture and Identity* (University Press of Florida, 2006), and *Created in God's Image: An Introduction to Feminist Theological Anthropology* (Orbis Books, 2007).

Marion Grau, a native of Germany, is Associate Professor of Theology at the Church Divinity School of the Pacific, a member school of the Graduate Theological Union in Berkeley, where she has taught since 2001. She is the author of *Of Divine Economy: Refinancing Redemption* (T.&T. Clark/Continuum, 2004) and co-editor with Rosemary Radford Ruether of *Interpreting the Postmodern: Responses to Radical Orthodoxy* (T.&T. Clark/Continuum, 2006).

Roger Haight, S. J., is a Jesuit priest and Visiting Professor at Union Theological Seminary in New York City. He received his doctorate in theology from the Divinity School of the University of Chicago in 1973 and is the author of *Jesus, Symbol of God* (Orbis Books, 1999) and *Christian Community in History, I-II* (Continuum, 2004-2005).

Theodore W. (Ted) Jennings Jr. is Professor of Biblical and Constructive Theology at Chicago Theological Seminary. He received his Ph.D. from Emory University. In addition to Emory and Chicago Theological Seminary he has also taught at the Seminario Metodista de Mexico in Mexico City. Among his books are *Good News to the Poor: John Wesley's Evangelical Economics* (Abingdon, 1990) and *Reading Derrida/Thinking Paul: On Justice* (Stanford University Press, 2006).

Mark D. Jordan is Candler Professor of Religion in Emory University. His recent books include *Blessing Same-Sex Unions: The Perils of Queer Romance and the Confusions of Christian Marriage* (University of Chicago Press, 2005) and *Rewritten Theology: Aquinas after His Readers* (Blackwell, 2006). He is now writing on queer adolescence within Christian churches.

David G. Kamitsuka, Associate Professor of Religion, teaches modern religious thought at Oberlin College. He is author of *Theology and Contemporary Culture: Liberation, Postliberal and Revisionary Perspectives* (Cambridge University Press, 1999), and is Chair of the Department of Religion.

Kwok Pui-lan is William F. Cole Professor of Christian Theology and Spirituality at Episcopal Divinity School, Cambridge, Massachusetts. She has published extensively in Asian feminist theology, biblical hermeneutics, and postcolonial criticism. Her most recent book is *Postcolonial Imagination and Feminist Theology* (Westminister John Konx, 2005). She is co-editor of *Off the Menu: Asian and Asian North American Women's Religion and Theology* (Westminster John Knox, 2007).

Rebecca Lyman is the former Samuel Garrett Professor of Church History at the Church Divinity School of the Pacific at Berkeley and a member of the Ancient History and Mediterranean Archaeology Group at the University of California, Berkeley. She is the author of *Christology and Cosmology: Models of Divine Activity in Origen, Eusebius and Athanasius* (Oxford, 1993) and *Early Christian Traditions* (Cowley, 1999).

Hjamil A. Martínez-Vázquez is an Assistant Professor at Texas Christian University. He has articles on postcolonizing criticism in anthologies such as *New Horizons in Hispanic/Latino(a) Theology* (Pilgrim, 2003) and *Her Master's Tools? Feminist and Postcolonial Engagements of Historical-Critical Discourse* (Society of Biblical Literature, 2005). Presently he is working on a book about Latina/o Muslims in the United States.

Ian A. McFarland is a Lutheran lay theologian and Associate Professor of Systematic Theology at the Candler School of Theology, Emory University. He is the author of *Difference and Identity: A Theologial Anthropology* (Pilgrim, 2001) and *The Divine Image: Envisioning the Invisible God* (Fortress, 2005).

James W. Perkinson is a long-time activist/educator from inner-city Detroit, currently splitting teaching responsibilities between Ecumenical Theological Seminary and the University of Denver. He holds a Ph.D. in theology/history of religions from the University of Chicago and is the author of *White Theology: Outing Supremacy in Modernity* (Palgrave Macmillan, 2004) and *Shamanism, Racism, and Hip-Hop Culture: Essays on White Supremacy and Black Subversion* (Palgrave Macmillan, 2005). He has written extensively in both academic and popular journals and is a recognized artist on the spoken-word poetry scene.

Jan H. Pranger is Assistant Professor of World Christianity at Concordia College, Moorhead, Minnesota. He is the author of *Dialogue in Discussion* (Interuniversitair Instituut voor Missiologie en Oecumenica, 1994) and *Redeeming Tradition* (University of Groningen, 2003). He is currently working on a manuscript on theology and postcolonial studies.

Inese Radzins, a Latvian-American, is Assistant Professor of Theology and Swedenborgian Studies at the Pacific School of Religion, a member school of the Graduate Theological Union, in Berkeley, California. She teaches in the areas of constructive theology, feminist theory, philosophy of religion, and Swedenborgian thought. Her current research explores the political and theological implications of Simone Weil's cosmology.

Shelly Rambo is Assistant Professor of Theology at Boston University. A constructive feminist theologian, she engages the textual tradition of Christianity with particular attention to literary analysis and criticism. In her current project, she is developing a theology of the Holy Spirit in light of contemporary studies in trauma.

Larry L. Rasmussen is Reinhold Niebuhr Professor Emeritus of Social Ethics, Union Theological Seminary, New York City. He is the author of *Earth Community, Earth Ethics* (Orbis Books, 1996) and editor of *Reinhold Niebuhr: Theologian of Public Life* (Fortress, 1991).

Darby Kathleen Ray is Associate Professor of Religious Studies and Director of the Faith & Work Initiative at Millsaps College in Jackson, Mississippi. Her publications include *Deceiving the Devil: Atonement, Abuse, and Ransom* (Pilgrim, 1998) and *Christic Imagination: An Ethic of Incarnation and Ingenuity* (forthcoming from Fortress Press).

Joerg Rieger is Professor of Systematic Theology at Perkins School of Theology, Southern Methodist University, Dallas. His books include *Christ and Empire: From Paul to Postcolonial Times* (Fortress, 2007), *God and the Excluded: Visions and Blindspots in Contemporary Theology* (Fortress, 2001), and *Remember the Poor: The Challenge to Theology in the Twenty-First Century* (Trinity Press International, 1998).

Cynthia L. Rigby is the W. C. Brown Professor of Theology at Austin Presbyterian Theological Seminary, where she has been teaching since 1995. She is the co-editor of *Blessed One: Protestant Perspectives on Mary* (Westminster John Knox, 2002) and the editor of *Power, Powerlessness, and the Divine* (Scholars Press, 1997). A specialist in Reformed theology, she is currently completing an introductory text in Reformed and feminist systematic theology.

Don Schweitzer is McDougald Professor of Theology at St. Andrew's College, Saskatoon, Canada. He is an ordained member of the United Church of Canada and active in the Canadian Theological Society. Together with Derek Simon he co-edited *Intersecting Voices: Critical Theologies in a Land of Diversity* (Novalis, 2004).

Deanna A. Thompson is Chair and Associate Professor of Religion at Hamline University in St. Paul, Minnesota, where she teaches courses in theology and ethics. Her most recent publications include *Crossing the Divide: Luther, Feminism, and the Cross* (Fortress, 2004) and "Becoming a Feminist Theologian of the Cross" in *Cross Examinations: Reflections on the Meaning of the Cross Today* (Fortress, 2006).

Tatha Wiley teaches courses in theology, social justice, and New Testament at the Metopolitan State University in Minneapolis and at the University of St. Thomas, St. Paul, Minnesota: She is the author of *Original Sin: Origins, Developments, Contemporary Meaning* (Paulist Press, 2002) and *Paul and the Gentile Women: Reframing Galatians* (Continuum, 2005), and editor of *Thinking of Christ: Proclamation, Explanation, Meaning* (Continuum, 2003).

Ellen K. Wondra is Professor of Theology and Ethics at Seabury-Western Theological Seminary. She is a member of the Anglican-Roman Catholic Consultation in the United States (ARCUSA) and is involved in other ecumenical work. She is the Editor-in-Chief of the *Anglican Theological Review*. Her research focus currently is the theology and practice of authority in the Episcopal Church and the Anglican Communion.

PREFACE

We, the editors, are most pleased to present this volume of outstanding and original essays about key figures in the history of Christian thought. The authors are experts in different disciplines, such as biblical studies, history, and theology. Some teach in departments of religious studies, others at seminaries and schools of theology. The contributors vary in their degree of personal religious commitment and come from a variety of religious backgrounds and cultural traditions—Asian, African, Baltic, Western European, African American, Asian American, Hispanic, Latino/Latina, and Euro-American. What all share, however, is a passionate concern for teaching and writing in ways that raise critical questions about the responsibilities of persons and institutions in the midst of contemporary imperial realities. All are convinced that religious beliefs and practices are always inescapably intertwined with the discourses and institutions of empires, capable of reinforcing and legitimizing domination, but also possessing the potential to raise and sustain counter-hegemonic challenges.

This volume came into being because we believe that there is no substitute for concrete historical examples of the relationship between religion and empire. Since the United States is currently the world's leading power, and its leaders often claim to represent the Christian tradition, we focused our investigations on representatives of that Christian religious heritage. Further, those of us who are personally committed to the Christian path believe that tradition is one of the principal sources informing contemporary theological reflection. We cannot imagine constructing responses to empire that would not involve comparing notes with and learning from the "great cloud of witnesses" (Heb. 12:1) that has preceded us. We believe that affirming the wisdom of ancient native traditions around the globe is a means of challenging the unrivaled sway of modern Western rationality. Incidentally, this approach in itself challenges the modernist myth of progress embedded in the current Western discourse of empire. As Catholic lay writer G. K. Chesterton asserted, the habit of making serious reference to the past is the most democratic of practices, since even the dead are given voice.

We aim, then, to contribute to multidisciplinary debates about empire, but we also have another audience in mind. We are convinced that this book will prove useful in classes about the history of Christian thought. We hope to supplement current textbooks in this field. By raising the issue of empire, we believe that we are suggesting a fuller, more robust portrayal of figures from the Christian tradition. Far too often theological concepts are presented with only bare hints about the concrete circumstances of the theologians who produced them. Ideas are discussed without sketching the wider political, social, and economic backdrop that locates them in proper perspective, and that could cause them to stand out in bolder relief. In short, students of the history of Christian theology are asked to consider interpretations of *texts* without an adequate sense of *contexts*. Even when writers and teachers attempt to pay attention to the broader setting, far too often our training predisposes us to exercises in rather abstract intellectual history. Hence texts may be compared to other texts written before, during, and after a particular author's life, but relationships to power dynamics and struggles tend to be obscured.

It is strange that leading proponents of a prophetic religion, which proclaims incarnation as its central revelation, have all too often been presented in such a disembodied fashion. Whatever the genesis and evolution of such academic practices may be, we believe that their continuance consciously or unconsciously supports empire. Current rulers always benefit when critical minds dwell only in a self-contained world of ideas, avoiding political connections. So we insist here that Christian thinkers should be rightfully regarded as what the Spanish Catholic philosopher Miguel de Unamuno called persons of "flesh and bones." We contend that no Christian thinker in any historical era lived or lives in an isolated ivory tower—the metaphor itself is a myth that obscures the fact that even the most arcane thinkers are connected to life and the flows of power. In these essays the authors demonstrate that theologians are multifaceted persons who live fully in their own times, often with significant pastoral responsibilities, and acutely aware of the realities of church and state, of work and cultural life. Their theologies influence us because they speak out of and to these concrete circumstances in compelling ways.

We hope these remarks indicate that this is not simply a book driven by current political issues. We are convinced that the type of inquiry modeled here will foster increased historical sensitivity in depictions of Christian theological traditions. We certainly do not wish to engage either in condemnation or hagiography. So these essays demonstrate that, in the famous phrase of Friedrich Nietzsche, each author discussed is "human, all too human." One concrete example of historical limitation is represented by the fact that past authors often did not have our sensitivity to gender inclusivity in the use of language. While none of the contributors to this volume would use terms that refer only to males, we have reluctantly decided not to edit exclusive phraseology found in historic texts. As much as possible, each predecessor has been allowed to speak in her or his own voice, even when our contemporary sensibilities make us uncomfortable with the form of their utterance.

In some cases, our forebears present an approach to empire that is profoundly ambiguous, both supportive and critical. Rather than denigrating our predecessors, we believe that frank acknowledgment of their humanity makes them more accessible and interesting to our students. We are confident that the approach followed here will facilitate a productive set of dialogues between the living and the dead that will bear active fruit as Christians and observers of their religion seek to find their bearings in today's often confusing and tumultuous debates about the relationships between Christian faith and empire. Only by laying open theology's ties to the powers of empire will we be able to identify the ways in which theology also provides alternatives.

We conclude with a few comments about the intent signaled in this book's title, and the realities presented by the table of contents. As an attentive reading of the various chapters will disclose, it does not make sense to speak of a single, unified Christian tradition stretching over more than twenty centuries. By using the word "classical," we are not subscribing to any literary theories about what makes certain authors or books perpetually more worthwhile than others. We are simply welcoming the many contributions of Christian authors prior to the current generation. We have focused mostly on theologians who have passed away, because some historical distance may be helpful to situate them in their contexts. We have also included the contributions of women as well as writers from Africa, Asia, and Latin America. We are sorely aware of the dominance of male and European voices from the past, but we are equally aware that these voices may need the most attention, because they and their readers are often least aware of their connections to empire, and because these theologians are also most widely taught in religious studies and theology and are frequently referred to when we discuss politics and Christian engagement with the world.

We certainly do not intend the table of contents of this volume to become the basis of a new canon! Part of our concrete historical reality is that—as we sought to produce a book in a reasonable period of time—a specific set of authors with particular interests and expertise was then free to contribute. We attempted to include new interpretations of most, but not all, of the commonly acknowledged "greats." We did our best to promote a broader sense of the genres of theological writing by deliberately blurring the lines between categories such as "theology," "missiology," and "spirituality."

We hope that the tools provided in the three introductory chapters will enable students to engage in similar studies of writers that we could not include here. And we are confident that the contributors to this volume have provided most helpful concrete examples of how such investigations may proceed. May this book signal only the beginning of a fresh approach to the study and teaching of Christian theology and history and its relevance to contemporary questions of global justice.

ACKNOWLEDGMENTS

From its inception this project has been a thoroughly collaborative effort. The idea was first broached at the 2004 meeting of the Workgroup on Constructive Christian Theology, coordinated by Serene Jones and Paul Lakeland. It was given clearer shape by the panel and discussion on "Globalization and the Classical Tradition" at the 2005 meeting. Members of the Workgroup became convinced of the utility of a book offering readings of a number of figures from the Christian past in light of issues raised by empire. All were supportive; many agreed to contribute an essay, and helped us recruit additional authors. This volume represents only one of the fruits of common labor regularly emerging from the Workgroup. We are most grateful to benefit from the encouragement of work like this.

We received immediate and enthusiastic support from editor Michael West. We thank him for guiding us in a way that enabled timely realization of our aims. It has been a delight to work with all of Michael's expert colleagues at Fortress Press.

Tammerie Day has offered extensive and skilled editorial assistance, efficiently preparing our manuscripts for publication. We are in her debt for such gracious service. We thank Perkins School of Theology, Southern Methodist University, for the funding to support Tammerie's work.

Last but not least we express heartfelt appreciation to all of the contributors to this volume. Their enthusiasm for the project, their prompt submissions, and their generous responses to suggestions made our work as editors very agreeable.

We have experienced the type of communal labor that overcomes the dominating, competitive dynamics on which empires thrive. We have therefore received the most important of all gifts in times like these: hope.

CHAPTER 1

Christian Theology and Empires

Joerg Rieger

WHERE WE ARE

Christianity can hardly be understood apart from empire. The Roman Empire was the context of the earliest beginnings of Christianity, and most of the subsequent major developments of Christian theology and the church are located somewhere within the force fields of empire as well. Unfortunately, theologians have rarely reflected on the connections and tensions between Christian traditions and empire. These connections were either taken for granted or simply overlooked. What was lost in the process was not only a clearer understanding of how the forces of empire affect us all, consciously or unconsciously, but also a sense of how Christianity can never quite be absorbed by empire altogether and which of its resources push beyond empire. One of the key purposes of the study of Christian theology in the context of empire has to do with a search for that which cannot be co-opted by empire, and which thus inspires alternatives to empire, based on what I have called a "theological surplus."[1] But these alternatives can only be seen in light of a clearer awareness of the impact of empire on theology, an awareness that points beyond the current situation where empire is either taken for granted or blended out.

Those who took the connections of Christianity and empire as a given often identified Christianity with empire in one of two ways: some welcomed this identification and assumed that it was positive, not least because it seemed to underscore and reinforce the greatness and the power of Christianity; others saw these connections of Christianity and empire as proof that Christianity was nothing but an epiphenomenon of a more powerful reality, namely empire, and thus mostly a

1

sellout. That both attitudes are deeply embedded in popular perceptions points to their pervasiveness. There is a widespread assumption among churchgoers that the Roman Empire was mostly beneficial for Christianity, because it reduced official persecution and because it supported the spread of Christianity through its infrastructures, like the roads on which missionaries such as the Apostle Paul traveled in order to spread the gospel. It is part of this assumption that Christianity was naturally poised to become the official religion of the powers that be. The same groups often also tend to see contemporary empire—when they see it at all—as beneficial for Christianity and its values, especially in its embodiment in the United States of America.

On the other hand, there is a widespread suspicion that the church's progress owed so much to the politics of empire and was so inextricably related to it that Christianity became simply another function of empire. Supporters of this position cite as evidence the Constantinian turn, when Christianity became the official religion of the Roman Empire, and prominent historical events like the Crusades in the Middle Ages and the Spanish Conquest of early modernity. To be sure, this position is held not only by well-known critics of Christianity but also by Christians (present and past, including for instance the Protestant Reformers of sixteenth-century Europe), some of whom would be quick to point out that there were other embodiments of Christianity that refused to give in to the lure of empire.

Unfortunately, however, both of these positions assume fairly straightforward relations between church and empire, an assumption that has prevented deeper investigations. The chapters in this book investigate the complex relations of church and empire, questioning whether there might be a theological surplus even in the theologies that shaped up under the conditions of empire, and whether there are traces of empire even in those theologies that consider themselves resistant to or independent of empire.

There are, of course, also those people who tend to overlook or blend out the relations between Christianity and empire. Some assume that Christianity and empire are totally incompatible because they are located in completely different conceptual realms; in modern times, this attitude has often been tied to the popular assumption that "religion and politics don't mix," or a pervasive and deep conviction that religion and politics have nothing to do with each other. Similar assumptions are embedded in the disciplinary divisions of modern universities, which study religion and politics in separate departments that rarely cross into each other's territories. Working along these lines, theologians have sought, for instance, to isolate what is political and what is religious in historical figures like the emperor Constantine or in historical events like the Council of Nicaea, which Constantine convened and chaired; the assumption is still prevalent that only if something can be classified as nonpolitical can it be seen as legitimately religious.

Others assume that empire and real Christianity are incompatible because they embody completely different realities and different ways of life. In this view, those who practiced real Christianity are free to carve out their own spaces and live authentic Christian lives; monastic communities or other intentional communities such as the Amish in the contemporary United States are often referenced as examples. Unfortunately, the representatives of all of these positions assume fairly straightforward separations and distinctions between Christianity and empire that cannot be sustained. When Constantine put his entire political fate and the future of the Roman Empire in the hands of the Christian God, was this a political or a religious decision? The separation of religion and empire, or more generally of religion and politics, does not make much sense in such a situation, and even clear-cut conventional disciplinary distinctions of the two categories must be called into question in light of this example. Likewise, when Amish farmers in the United States who reject many of the amenities that come with empire, such as electricity and motorized vehicles, then plow the fields that they own with five horses, how would the peasants of the world, past and present, who do not own their fields and who plow using their milking cows (who then produce less milk) or who push their own plows, judge their presumed independence from the benefits of empire?

What is new in this context is that we are beginning to understand that the relations of Christianity and empire are more complex than has been acknowledged to date. Christianity does not easily escape empire—understood as massive concentrations of power which permeate all aspects of life and which cannot be controlled by any one actor alone.[2] This is one of the basic marks of empire throughout history. Empire seeks to extend its control as far as possible, beyond the commonly recognized geographical, political, and economic spheres, to include the intellectual, emotional, psychological, spiritual, cultural, and religious arenas. The problem with empire is, therefore, that no one can escape its force field completely. Nevertheless, the good news is that at the same time empire is never quite able to extend its control absolutely. Whatever the extent of its influence, no empire has ever managed to co-opt Christianity entirely. Mindful of this fact, we embark on a search for theological surplus in the Christian tradition that resists empire and provides alternatives.[3]

There is much work to be done. Major representatives of the Christian traditions, and up until recently even Jesus himself, have hardly ever been considered in light of their deeper connections with the empires of their times. Assuming a strict separation of religion and politics, it has long been taken for granted that Jesus and Paul, for example, are religious characters who could not possibly have been concerned about politics. That Jesus did not engage in armed struggles of resistance like the Zealots of his time has commonly been interpreted as proof that he was not concerned about resisting the Roman Empire, as if armed struggle were the only form of resistance. That Paul preached the message of the cross was interpreted in similar fashion, as if the symbol of the cross in those days could have been separated from the fact that it was a colonial tool of execution for political rebels from the lower classes. That Anselm's notion of satisfaction presupposed the world of the Norman conquerors of England was (if it was noted at all) played down as if Anselm's references to feudalism were harmless sermon illustrations. Even if other theologians, for instance Bartolomé de Las Casas, were seen as opponents of empire, their resistance was often seen as an ethical choice, the deeper theological connections and motivations of which were rarely investigated. I could give many more examples, but it should already be clear that we must not continue with theology as usual.

METAMORPHOSES OF EMPIRE

Having defined empire as massive concentrations of power which permeate all aspects of life and which cannot be controlled by any one actor alone, let me hasten to add that the power of empire takes various different shapes and forms. Empires project their powers in many and often contradictory ways, and this complicates our work. The forms of power that proceed by open conquest, through fire and sword and other forms of open military aggression, always making use of the latest technologies of warfare in the process, are easily identified. The wars of conquest conducted by the Roman Empire, the Normans in England, the Spanish in Latin America, and even by the British in India (mostly fought vicariously through the East India Company) are not hard to spot, and there will be little disagreement about the fact that in these examples empire deploys overbearing pow-er and that this power has coercive traits. No wonder, therefore, that in the Unit-ed States, the Bush administration's twenty-first-century wars against Afghanistan and Iraq have unleashed a flood of debates about the U.S. Empire, a term which was mostly kept under wraps before.

Yet the fact that empires are expanded and stabilized by military means and by war does not mean that their power is always deployed unilaterally. While the Roman Empire, for instance, knew how to use its military force effectively, once its colonies were established Roman power tended to switch to economic, cultur-al, and even religious means of control (the latter embodied, for instance, in the emperor cult which was a phenomenon that went much deeper than has common-ly been noted).[4] In the aftermath of the Norman conquest of England, violence remained an effective means of control and was deployed strategically, but oth-er forms of power quickly became more prominent, including once again cultur-al and religious means. For example, Anselm of Canterbury was only the second archbishop instituted by the Normans after their conquest and he had to nego-tiate some of this power first-hand. Likewise, the largely failed military interven-tions of the Bush administration should not make us overlook the fact that other manifestations of U.S. power in economics and culture (often operating in com-bined fashion through the media, including Hollywood movie production and the advertising industry) are much more successful. This fact is not lost on those inside and outside the country who endure these pressures in their own bodies, but it is harder to see for those who are pressured to lesser degrees.

When it comes to the massive concentrations of power deployed by empire, open displays of power are commonly noticed but there are many other forms of power that are much more hidden and ambiguous. More than most other crit-ics of empire, Bartolomé de Las Casas openly opposed and deplored the Spanish conquest and the atrocities of the Spanish Empire in the New World, fully aware of the genocide that led to whole regions being stripped of their original inhabit-ants. At the same time, however, he himself did not entirely reject the rule and the authority of the King of Spain and the Roman Catholic Church over the inhabit-ants of the Americas; rather, he merely promoted more benevolent colonial mod-els. In fact, Las Casas's rejection of colonial violence and straightforward exploita-tion helped set the tone for later nineteenth-century colonial discourses in Middle and Northern Europe, allowing the Dutch and the English to congratulate themselves for their benevolent colonialisms.[5] In the eighteenth and nineteenth centuries, the Germans, who had been left out of the colonial race, would develop colonial fantasies that appeared to be yet more enlightened and benevolent than those of their Dutch and British rivals and that led to even more romanticized notions of colonial power. Such power, it was commonly held, was mostly interested in the welfare and betterment of the colonized.[6] What was understood as the "spread of civilization" was—and is—by and large exempt from the suspicion of empire.

The reasons for less violent forms of colonialism are many, but key among them is that some of the more violent forms of exploitation were no longer needed in situations where power differentials were more pronounced. The British settlement of Australia, for instance, had little to fear from the Aboriginals. Moreover, there was no pressing economic need for slaves in this situation, and thus changing economic modes of production also contributed to the development of less coercive and less overtly violent forms of colonization. The theological ramifications of these particular forms of colonization can be observed in the work of German theologian Friedrich Schleiermacher, whose imagination and curiosity were sparked by the British settlement of Australia and who shared in the German fantasies of developing more peaceful colonial relationships. Schleiermacher's vision of the power of Christ is shaped by notions like "attraction" and "persuasion." There is no need for violent and forceful images of power, given Christ's place at the very top of a colonial world that felt it could even do without divine miracles in view of its "great advantage in power."[7]

In general, nineteenth- and twentieth-century theologians reflected a much more benevolent sense of the goals of colonial systems, sometimes merely seeing them in terms of transnational trade, sometimes classifying them as the promotion of the benefits of modern culture (British culture, to be sure, in the later case of William Temple) or of "civilization." Unfortunately, these theologians were often lacking a deeper awareness that even the most benevolent moves on the part of those in power in fact continued to reflect a system of empire that was detrimental to the majority of those who were forced to endure it. While in the twentieth century the work of Dutch theologian Hendrik Kraemer, whose life spans the transition from a colonial to a postcolonial world, shows more sympathies for the independence of the colonies, Kraemer still tends to perceive the colonial other from the safety of his own perspective and without inviting an attitude of mutual critique. Kraemer also maintains the need for Dutch guidance in the independence process or, later, at least a sense of responsibility. As a result, Christian mission, one of the phenomena that have traditionally been closest to the benevolent exercise of colonial power, was not only not critiqued but allowed to continue to run in the old tracks.

Terms like "Orientalism," and "Occidentalism," coined by Edward Said and Walter Mignolo respectively, capture much of what is at stake in modern forms of colonialism.[8] Orientalism and Occidentalism refer to efforts (scholarly, literary, and others) to describe and understand the East and the (American) West but which, in the process, shape these places in their own image. As a result, empires used their grasp (a term that can be read both metaphorically and literally in this context) of others to expand their own power base and to boost their self image. The problem is not just a lack of understanding of the other but an often unconscious exercise of power over the other that is inextricably related to the massive concentrations of power of empire which permeate all aspects of life.

Unfortunately, while the more violent embodiments of empire did not often reach the level of theological awareness, the softer forms of colonialism and empire are even less reflected-upon theologically. For the most part, these forms of colonialism were not even recognized as such; small wonder, for example, that despite the vast amount of research dedicated to the work of Schleiermacher there are hardly any investigations of the colonial context of his work. While twentieth-century theology has been ambivalent at best in its awareness of empire—after all, most of the remaining colonies gained independence during that century—in the twenty-first century many people have completely lost track of the workings of the powers of empire. Talk about "postcolonialism" has at times contributed to this attitude, especially where the term is misunderstood to mean the end of all things colonial. And while the term *empire* has enjoyed a renaissance in the past few years in the U.S., there is sometimes a mistaken impression that the U.S. has become an empire only lately, through the aggressive foreign politics of the administration of President George W. Bush and its liberal deployment of military force.

AMBIVALENCE

We deal with empire and its metamorphoses in this book because we are convinced that in the midst of the various pressures of empire, Christian theology has the potential to make a difference. Not only can theology help us analyze what is going on, especially where empire assimilates concepts of the ultimate, theology can also point us in new directions and give us new hope. Nevertheless, such analysis and redirection always take place in the midst of ambivalence. Throughout its history, theology has often been employed in the support of empire and sometimes in the critique of it, and often there is only a thin line between the two. Nevertheless, the existence of ambivalence is itself a witness to the limits of empire. Postcolonial theorist Homi Bhabha notes how this ambivalence is disturbing to colonial discourse and how it "poses an immanent [*sic*] threat to both 'normalized' knowledges and disciplinary powers."[9] The challenge, he argues, is a "*double vision*, which in disclosing the ambivalence of colonial discourse also disrupts its authority."[10] Ambivalence is thus a welcome companion in the resistance against empire. At the same time, in this project more direct forms of resistance are investigated as well.

Enveloped in the multiple and complex relationships of theology and empire, the notion of ambivalence will be a helpful concept to keep in mind when reading the following chapters because many of the theologians presented in this volume did not directly oppose issues of empire and colonialism; more often than not, these issues were not even addressed. Of course, some theologians did pursue more direct challenges of empire, including the Apostle Paul, Bartolomé de Las Casas, and Dietrich Bonhoeffer, but these theologians often felt the repercussions of empire and had to bear the consequences of their critique: Bonhoeffer, and most likely Paul as well, were put to death for it. Those who remembered Jesus' injunction that "no one can serve two masters" (Matt. 6:24) stand out from the crowd as the ones who remained faithful to Jesus' own resistance to the powers that be in an extraordinary way, following him all the way into death. At the same time, the notion of ambivalence helps to remind us that the empire never managed to suppress completely even the work of some of those theologians who do not openly resist empire, which is the majority of theologians discussed in this volume. Though we can identify differing levels of ambiguity in the various theological models, there seems to be a residual spirit of resistance in many of them, so that theology is never altogether assimilated by the powers that be.

THEOLOGY AND EMPIRE

What should we be looking for in the relation of theology and empire? In some cases, it takes a fair amount of effort to read between the lines in order to see the contours of empire in the work of a theologian. In other cases, the evidence is right at hand, although it has been overlooked for a long time. Two prominent examples take us back to the beginnings of Christianity: the theological message of the life and ministry of Jesus, and the theological developments that found expression in the early councils of the church, particularly the Council of Nicaea and the Council of Chalcedon.

Already before the gospel accounts of Jesus' birth we can observe the entanglements of and tensions between the Christian tradition and the empire as they are reflected in the various gospels. Joseph and Mary's traveling to Bethlehem before Jesus' birth, reported in the Gospel of Luke, is set in the context of the Emperor Augustus's efforts to increase his tax base. The flight to Egypt, reported in the Gospel of Matthew, had to do with King Herod's efforts to get rid of even the slightest potential challenge to his rule by murdering all infant boys in Bethlehem; Herod, after all, was one of the vassals of Rome. The Gospel of Mark tells us that already during the earliest days of Jesus' ministry the Pharisees and the power brokers of Herod began to plot together to get rid of him (Mark 3:6). Even the temptations of Jesus, often interpreted in strictly religious terms, give us a glimpse of the temptations of the power of the empire, for instance when the devil offers Jesus unlimited power over all the countries of the earth, an offer that Jesus unambiguously rejects (Matt. 3:8-10, Luke 4:5-8). And despite all other efforts to explain the cross, it was ultimately the Romans who nailed Jesus to the cross. The Jewish masterminds who were also involved were closely connected to the Romans—the high priests, for instance, collected the taxes for the Romans and were selected either by Herod or by the Roman governors—and it seems to have taken a good deal of agitation to rally the common people against Jesus (Mark 15:11). We can conclude that Jesus' life and ministry were most likely too much of a challenge for the empire and its beneficiaries, a challenge summarized in statements that have lost nothing of their radical ring even today, such as that the last shall be first (Mark 10:31, Matt. 20:16), that the gospel implies the liberation of the oppressed (Luke 4:18), that no one can serve two masters (Matt. 6:24), and—expressed by Mary, Jesus' mother—that the hungry are being filled with good things and the rich sent away empty, to say nothing of the fact that the lowly are being lifted up while the mighty are brought down from their thrones (Luke 1:52-53).

By the fourth century, things had changed to such a degree that Christianity was now ready to be the official religion of the Roman Empire. At this time, it seems as if empire had completed the process of assimilating the radical traditions of Jesus and early Christianity. The most important councils of the early church, such as Nicaea and Chalcedon in the fourth and fifth centuries, were convened by the emperors and in part shaped by them. The emperor Constantine suggested the famous term *homoousios*, that made its way into the creed, holding that the first and second persons of the trinity are "of the same being." While Constantine's conversion to Christianity has often been considered superficial because it was inextricably tied to the politics of empire, it seems that Constantine put great faith in the Christian God and in the process was greatly impressed by what he identified as the power of this God at work. Efforts to separate religion and politics can only appear artificial in this case. The problem here is not primarily with the relation of politics and religion but with what kind of politics is supported by religion, and whether the politics of the Christian God supports the politics of empire.

In this context of empire it comes as a surprise that the Council of Nicaea rejects a hierarchical understanding of the relationship of Father and Son and that the Council of Chalcedon rejects a hierarchical relationship of Jesus' divine and human natures, despite general support for political and metaphysical hierarchies. Reading between the lines, we might thus find a latent tension between Christianity and empire, although it can be argued that this potential tension was not really dealt with until much later. The theological surplus contained in this tension harbors a possible correction to classical theistic notions of God, which are based on absolute hierarchies. The reception of Jesus into the divinity, that is the claim that Jesus was truly God, ultimately leads to challenges of empire and empire theology of which the fathers of the church were hardly conscious; it may be no accident that Constantine later reverted back from this position to his earlier appreciation of the Arian subordination of Jesus under God. Themes like God's omnipotence and immutability, which are only too easily applied to the politics of empire, can now be seen in a new light. And if equality is at the heart of the Godhead, on what basis can hierarchies in the world (or in the church) be justified? In addition, both Nicaea and Chalcedon left open many questions—perhaps another example of resistance against the kind of imperial control that cannot tolerate ambivalence. [11]

THEOLOGY AND EMPIRE TODAY

After exploring the various manifestations of empire and colonialism discussed in the chapters of this book, the reader might come away with the impression that these are mainly phenomena of the past. After all, the classical empires have withered away and formal colonial relationships have by and large ended as well; talk about "postcolonial times" is thus sometimes misunderstood to signify the end of power differentials and empire. Yet new forms of empire have arisen. In the U.S., there is a long tradition of rejecting the notion of empire: we have rarely understood ourselves as proponents of empire and we have often explicitly rejected the notion—until recently, when the policies of the administration of President George W. Bush have led to new debates about the United States as empire. Supporters of Bush and even members of his administration have taken up the notion of empire and given it a positive spin. In a Christmas card, Vice President Dick Cheney quoted Benjamin Franklin: "And if a sparrow cannot fall to the ground without His notice, is it probable that an empire can rise without His aid?" The administration's declaration of war against Iraq points to renewed imperial commitments, especially since the threat of weapons of mass destruction originally claimed as the main reason could never be verified and was perhaps never investigated with the required care. The fact that despite widespread initial support among the population some churches and bishops in the United States opposed this war might be seen as a sign that the empire can never completely control Christianity.

Yet this rejection of war is not enough because the methods of empire have changed dramatically. War is not the only problem and perhaps not even the primary one; war has not been particularly effective in recent history and many of its supporters have become disillusioned. The deeper problem has to do with more covert expressions of economic and cultural power which drive broad processes of globalization. The goal of the Iraq war, for instance, was not the establishment of traditional colonial relationships like those pursued by eighteenth- and nineteenth-century Europe; neither was it a conquest, such as the ones pursued by Portugal and Spain in the sixteenth century. Although many assume that the Iraq war had to do with oil, the goal was never to take direct possession of Iraqi oil. In the changed conditions of empire, direct U.S. rule in Iraq is not necessary, and even the oil continues to be owned by the nation of Iraq. What we get out of the relation are "production sharing agreements" (PSAs), according to which the oil remains in the possession of the nation but the fields are operated by U.S. companies, a deal that is ultimately more lucrative for the companies.[12] Politically, Iraq is supposed to govern itself, so the strings that now tie it to the United States will disappear from view again at some point in the future. Despite the more open displays of power that have now been seen for a while in this case, the less visible tactics of the postcolonial empire may be the more significant ones.

At first sight, talk about a "postcolonial empire" appears to be a contradiction in terms, since empire and colonialism are frequently seen as synonymous. But empire can exist without colonies, without overt violence, and without absolute, unilateral power. While the citizens of Iraq were not enslaved by the victors (although some are being tortured), and they retained ownership of their country and their oil this does not necessarily reduce the reach of the empire; in postcolonial times, this move can even reinforce empire. In the end, despite a somewhat hawkish administration in the U.S. (slightly less so with the departure of Secretary of Defense Donald Rumsfeld), empire today is more attuned to the approach of Las Casas and the softened kind of power as attraction, conjured up by Schleiermacher, than to the strict hierarchies of the Medieval and Roman Empires.[13] The more aggressive politics of this Bush administration may well turn out to be somewhat of an anomaly in the global empire building of the twenty-first century.

The church's links to these developments can perhaps best be seen in the history of Christian mission. While some of the problems of nineteenth-century missions have been identified, especially as they relate to colonialism and its clear structures of power, there is very little critical reflection about the current situation of missions. The major book on the subject assumes that today (in a "postmodern" world) we are free to pursue new and creative missionary encounters that are no longer hampered by power differentials.[14] Yet while power differentials may be less visible, they are still the heart of the problem. Plans that promote the "development" of other countries or that call for "social programs" remind us that if our goal is to make "them" more like "us," we continue to assume the inferiority of the other. This is true even for well-meaning notions such as the "inculturation" of the gospel in foreign cultures that are often promoted by more progressive missionary circles, because it assumes that acculturation has already been accomplished at home. Such a (hidden) sense of superiority has its oppressive effect even without colonies or the traditional kind of empire where the rulers pull all the strings. Economic and cultural structures are sufficient to maintain the differential of power, and those structures continue to reinforce even our most benevolent moves.

CONCLUSION

As we find ourselves at the intersection of theology and empire, we face two tasks: one is analytical and the other constructive. The analysis of how empire shapes theology not only consciously but especially at the deeper layers of our theological unconscious is no longer optional. If the power of empire is as widely dispersed as I have argued and if these powers are expanding not only geographically but also on many other levels—including those that shape our intellectual endeavors and our deepest personal identities—we need to investigate these powers if we want to understand ourselves and our own theological presuppositions and productions.

The constructive task depends on the analytical one. Without understanding how we are shaped by empire all the way into our deepest desires, we cannot properly identify the theological surplus, those intuitions and insights that point us beyond the horizons of empire. In other words, the purpose of the analytical task is not to assign blame (or to "foul one's own nest"—"*Nestbeschmutzer*" was a derogatory expression used in Germany for people who sought to remember the atrocities of Nazi Germany). Without the analytical exploration of theology and empire we will not be able to identify what is really path-breaking in theology, what it is that has the potential to shape truly fresh and constructive thinking about God and the world.

Further Reading

Cobb, John B., Jr., David Ray Griffin, Richard A. Falk, and Catherine Keller. *The American Empire and the Commonwealth of God: A Political, Economic, Religious Statement*. Louisville, Ky.: Westminster John Knox, 2006.

Hardt, Michael, and Antonio Negri. *Multitude: War and Democracy in the Age of Empire*. New York: Penguin Books, 2004.

Harvey, David. *The New Imperialism*. Oxford: Oxford University Press, 2003.

Horsley, Richard. *Jesus and Empire: The Kingdom of God and the New World Disorder*. Minneapolis: Fortress Press, 2003.

Rieger, Joerg. *Christ and Empire: From Paul to Postcolonial Times*. Minneapolis: Fortress Press, 2007.

Wood, Ellen Meiksins. *The Empire of Capital*. New York: Verso Books, 2003.

CHAPTER 2

Theology and Social Theory

Kwok Pui-lan

Long before the modern period, when the social sciences emerged as academic disciplines, theologians made efforts to connect themselves with the socio-political world of their times. Augustine's contrast of the two cities, Aquinas's just war theory, and Luther's view on church and state are examples that theologians in antiquity, the Middle Ages, and early modernity each had their own interpretations of society. With what Michel Foucault has called "the emergence of Man" in the human sciences since the Enlightenment,[1] theologians have had to converse with these critical new disciplines, in addition to philosophy, their customary dialogical partner.

Theologians have hotly contested the relationship between theology and social theory because of differing political commitments and divergent views of theology's concerns. On the one hand, political and liberation theologians have insisted that critical social theory is indispensable in theologizing. Political theologians have drawn insights from the Frankfurt School and the social theory of Jürgen Habermas.[2] From the beginning, Latin American liberation theologians, in particular Juan Luis Segundo, have famously argued that faith without ideology is dead. By ideology, Segundo means the bridge between the "conception of God and the real-life problems of history."[3] On the other hand, theologians who continue to do theology out of a metaphysical framework chastise such heavy borrowing from social sciences as reductionistic and overlooking the unique contributions of the Christian tradition and the church.

Such debates intensified in the latter half of the twentieth century because of the proliferation of theological voices, particularly those emerging in connection with people from marginalized communities. These interlocutors have brought to bear on theological reflection not only neo-Marxist analysis and theories that pertain to gender, race, and ethnicity, but also queer studies and postcolonial and postmodern theories. They have challenged the ideological assumptions of theology, critiquing its gender, race, and class biases, along with the complicity of theologians with colonialism and other forms of oppression. In the globalized world, in which religion has increasingly played a significant role in politics, there has been a renewed interest of philosophers and social critics on religion and theology, thus opening new avenues for fruitful dialogues.[4]

Theology and the Social Sciences

Theologians have looked at the usefulness of social sciences from different vantage points. I would like to contrast two distinctly different approaches—liberation theology and radical orthodoxy—and point out their blind spots. Liberation theologians propose a theological methodology based on commitment to social praxis and the transformation of history. In contrast to theology as wisdom or theology as rational knowledge, liberation theology is defined by Gustavo Gutiérrez as a "critical reflection on praxis."[5] In order to carry out historical praxis in terms of the preferential option for the poor, theologians need to analyze the social situation aided by the tools of the social sciences. Gutiérrez's work has been much influenced by the theory of dependency of Latin American nations, which argues that the exploitation of Latin America was exacerbated by its dependence on the more developed capitalist countries and by adopting their developmental model.

Gutiérrez says we need to maintain critical judgment in using social sciences because "to say that these disciplines are scientific does not mean that their findings are apodictic and beyond discussion."[6] Segundo also has consistently called attention to the dialogue between theology and social sciences because these disciplines can help to unmask unconscious or hidden "ideological infiltration of dogma."[7] However, Segundo is not blind to the fact that sociology has its ideological underpinnings as well, especially those types influenced by the United States, such as positivist or behaviorist sociology.[8]

Among the Latin American theologians, Clodovis Boff has presented a rigorous study on the epistemological foundations of liberation theology, including a detailed analysis of the relation between theology and the social sciences. If theology seeks to articulate praxis, Boff argues, it requires socio-analytical mediation, hermeneutical mediation, and dialectic of theory and praxis. He submits that social theories are not just tools for applying theology to concrete social circumstances, but are constitutive elements *of* theology:

> The sciences of the social enter into theology of the political as a *constitutive part* . . . .The text of a theological reading with respect to the political is prepared and furnished by the sciences of the social. Theology receives its text from these sciences, and practices upon its reading in conformity with its own proper code, in such a way as to extract from it a characteristically, properly, theological meaning.[9]

Theology, therefore, must be an interdisciplinary collaboration. Theologians have to respect that social sciences have their "scientificness," with their own methodologies, norms, and criteria. Boff is wary of the magisterium making pronouncements about the history and destiny of the world, often couched in religious terminologies, as if they were the authority on these matters. However, theologians must exercise their judgment and ethical choice in determining which social theory works best for liberation in a given situation.[10] He rejects the criticism that liberation theology is reductionistic, an "ideologization of faith" or a "socializing theology." While liberation theologians learn from Marxists' social theory to analyze the current socio-historical situation, they do not subscribe to its overall atheistic worldview.[11] Even as social sciences provide material raw data for theology, theology has its own proper subject, its own "theologicity," based on reflection on God as the object of faith and the praxis of the church.

Contrary to liberation theology's more positive assessment of the social sciences, radical orthodoxy, exemplified by the work of John Milbank, displays acute skepticism of modern, secular social theory. Milbank maintains that the "new science of politics" has its origin in theology and that "sociology is only able to explain, or even illuminate religion, to the extent that it conceals its own theological borrowings and its own quasi-religious status."[12] Even though sociologists reject the theological and the metaphysical and try to substitute supposedly "scientific" accounts of society, their secular theories leave much of the metaphysical framework intact. Sociologists have constructed the categories of "the social" or "social facts" as if they are more "real" than the religious, which is seen as arbitrary and irrational. Adopting a positivist stance, they commit the mistake of "socializing of the transcendental" (64) by reducing religious truth claims to statements about the social whole or the private life of an individual. Milbank therefore unveils sociology's theological presuppositions to show that "every secular positivism is revealed to be also a positivist theology" (143).

Milbank delineates the positive and negative contributions of Hegel and Marx. He finds Hegel's discussion of Christianity and his dialectics inadequate and Marx's anthropology and historical materialism wanting. Milbank suggests that only Christian socialism can offer the most incisive critique of the secular logic of capitalism (205). He criticizes the political and liberation theologians for relying on secular social theories for social mediation and thereby inheriting the shortcomings of those theories. The Latin American liberation theologians, in particular, have borrowed much from the humanist-Marxist tradition and erroneously equate liberation with salvation, he says. By doing so, they adopt a reductionist view of salvation that grounds ethics in the social and the political, separate from the religious. By splitting salvation into a transcendental and "religious aspect," which is fundamentally an individual affair, and a "social" aspect that is purely secular, liberation theologians are too ready to accept modernity and its secularization process as positive (244).

Milbank may have created a false dichotomy between the individual and the social as well as between the religious and the political, and superimposed that dichotomy onto the work of the Latin American theologians. His claims that the latter have not dealt adequately with grace, forgiveness, and the sacraments offered by the church sound less than convincing. After pointing out the errors of secular reason associated with modernity, Milbank and his colleagues propose a return to premodern sources, especially the work of Augustine, for the development of an adequate Christian social and historical critique.

Milbank's dismissal of liberation theology has been vigorously contested, with Marcella Althaus-Reid calling it a "colonial theology."[13] Here I would like to pinpoint some of the blind spots that both liberation theology and radical orthodoxy share. A critical blind spot is their Eurocentric bias in interpreting modernity and secularity. Philosophers and social theorists constructed secularity not only as a revolt against Christianity, but also as a demarcation of difference between Western societies and others. Richard King argues that "religion" is a category that plays a key role in the "imaginative cartography of western modernity."[14] The development of the secular West in modernity has been contrasted with the religious East, steeped in mysticism and traditional religions. In fact, much of modern social theories have been developed based on data drawn from the so-called primitive or less advanced societies, interpreted through Eurocentric intelligibility. Social theorists then proceeded to develop their theories of the origin of religion (Durkheim), the evolutionary narrative of history (Hegel), and modernity as disenchantment of the world (Weber). Neither the liberation theologians nor radical orthodox theologians have attended to the colonial collusion of these so-called "scientific" social theories.

Both sides frame the questions surrounding theology and social theory with the assumption that Christianity is the dominant religion. The relationship between religion and society in non-Christian societies has not been taken into consideration. As Christian demographics have shifted to the South, many Christians are living in a religiously pluralistic world, having to negotiate theology and praxis amidst this pluralism. Focusing on Western social theories, both radical orthodoxy and liberation theology are oblivious to theories developed by scholars not working with Christian societies, such as Talal Asad, C. K. Yang, Rey Chow, Harry Harootunian, Ranajit Guha, and Achille Membe, to name just a few. If the works of these scholars are consulted, the parameters of the discussion will be greatly expanded, in recognition that the relation between theology and the social varies from culture to culture.

Finally, these male theologians show a lack of sensitivity to issues pertaining to race, gender, and sexuality. The liberation theologians regard the male peasant as paradigmatic of the poor,[15] while the radical orthodoxy theologians try to restore faith in the postmodern age for urban, white, middle-class men. Even though both have criticized the injustice of capitalism, neither has analyzed the mechanisms that place the burden of capitalism disproportionally on people of darker skin colors and on the majority of women and their children in the world.

THEOLOGY AND POSTCOLONIAL CRITIQUE

Christian theology does not emerge out of a vacuum, but develops in constant negotiation with political and ecclesial empires and with other power dynamics throughout history. Postcolonial theory offers an invaluable vantage point on theology, because it interrogates how religious and cultural productions are enmeshed in the economic and political domination of colonialism and empire building. The postcolonial optic is quite different from that of the Latin American liberation theologies of an earlier era, which were keen on demystifying the ideological inscription in theology, seen variously as false consciousness, class interests, or the ideological apparatus of the state. Postcolonial critics, following Foucault, are concerned with how theological truth is made possible and how the regime of truth takes shape. Moreover, contrary to the radical orthodox theologians, postcolonial critics insist that the return to the Christian metanarrative and the language of transcendence overlooks how Christianity has colluded with colonial interests and camouflages contradictions in the postmodern world.

If postcolonial critics have learned from Foucault about the relationship between power and knowledge, they have also gone beyond him, because Foucault's study of the "emergence of Man" never broached the dimensions of race and ethnicity. Rey Chow has argued that, "If Man is an historical invention, it is because he is a Western invention, which relies for its inventiveness—its originality, so to speak—on the debasement and exclusion of others."[16] The work of the Subaltern Studies Group and postcolonial studies from a wide range of cultural backgrounds have provided much new data and challenged the politics of representation, disciplinary boundaries, and the knowledge-production process. In the discipline of theology, postcolonial critics are interested in how the Other has been represented in theological discourse as a boundary marker to secure Christian identity and to stabilize the theological subject.[17] In this anthology, we can see that the description of the Other—Jews, Muslims, Natives, women, and other marginalized groups—occupies not a marginal but a central position in theological imagining throughout the centuries. For every Las Casas who defended the rights of the Natives, there were countless others who justified the interests of colonial empires, arguing in theological terms that the Natives were not fully human. For every Matteo Rici who showed some respect for other peoples' culture, there were countless Hegels who could only see the development of the West as the fullest manifestation of the spirit and the culmination of universal history. In *Provincializing Europe*, Dipesh Chakrabarty argues that Europe has constructed itself as the center of the world from which all historical narratives evolve.[18] It seems to me that Christian theology has been part and parcel of the narratives of empire, and that it requires similar "provincializing" so that we can hear the pluriphonic voices coming out of the margins.

Postcolonial strategies of reading literary and cultural texts offer clues for developing critical theological hermeneutics. In *The World, the Text, and the Critic*, Edward W. Said discusses the "worldliness" or the circumstantial reality incorporated in the text, which forms "an infrangible part of its capacity for conveying and producing meaning."[19] It would be reductionistic to explain a text in terms of its historical context; but to overlook the circumstantial reality—which calls the text into being and to which the text responds—also hinders our understanding a text on its multiple levels.[20] Many authors in this volume have tried to read the world and the text in a dialectical way. They have elucidated the "worldliness" of the text by providing information about the political and cultural context of the theologian. Their use of "empire" as a heuristic key highlights historical data that were previously overlooked or seldom emphasized, such as Augustine's intercession on behalf of criminals or Julian of Norwich's testimony to the wounds of war and the crusades.[21] These dialectic readings show that theological texts constitute reality through the power of language and imagination, and have thereby affected the historical development of the church and the world.

Said also proposed a contrapuntal reading, which sees global histories as intertwined and overlapped. He demonstrates how the highly regarded novels of Jane Austen, Joseph Conrad, Rudyard Kipling, and Albert Camus, as well as the music of Verdi, inscribe empire. Said successfully shows that the justification of empire building was embedded in the cultural imagination of the age of empire.[22] Theologians were not immune to the ideas, thought patterns, and effects of the cultural productions of their time, and their respective responses were quite diverse. Edward P. Antonio finds that Søren Kierkegaard was virtually silent on empire and his philosophical concerns seemingly avoided political engagements, yet he had mounted an incisive attack on Christendom. Jan H. Pranger shows that Hendrik Kraemer, who had direct involvements in the Dutch colonial government, shifted his thinking on colonialism with the development of Indonesia's struggle for independence. Inese Radzins, in her chapter on Simone Weil, details the ways Weil was deeply moved by the plight of the colonized under the French, which led her to wrestle with the relation between Christianity and empire and the ideology of progress.[23]

Such a political reading of theological texts refuses to separate the center from the periphery and insists that the colonizers and colonized are mutually inscribed in the colonial process. It rejects a binary construction of center and margin, oppressors and victims, and the colonizers and their subjects. Using the theory of hybridity, which exposes the myth of cultural purity and colonialist disavowal,[24] postcolonial critics have shown how theologians from marginalized communities have creatively used elements from both the dominant and indigenous cultures in order to fashion their own theology. Korean American theologian Wonhee Anne Joh has said, "The power of hybridity is in the emergence of subjugated knowledge to enter into dominant discourses and thereby shift the basis of its authority."[25] Those situated closer to the center have often criticized these theological hybrids, but in fact there is no theology that does not borrow language, metaphors, and thought forms from its surrounding culture. When theologians use Plato or Aristotle, Heidegger or Derrida, they are touted as well-read and sophisticated, and if they dare to step outside the line laid down by the theological establishment and argue that Confucian teaching, African folktales, and slave narratives can provide theological data, they are considered less sophisticated or even accused of being syncretistic. Taiwanese theologian C. S. Song has said that resources for doing theology are unlimited: "What is limited is our theological imagination. Powerful is the voice crying out of the abyss of the Asian heart, but powerless is the power of our theological imaging."[26] This rings true for other contexts as well.

Postcolonial critics do not glorify the colonized, and speak of the collaboration of the colonized in the colonial regime and their divided and fragmented subjectivity. Theologians, as cultural and intellectual elites who have benefited from colonial education and enjoy the power and prestige provided by the church as a colonial artifact, must be vigilant about their own complacence. In the postcolonial period, theologians in many parts of the Third World have developed their indigenous or inculturated theologies. We must affirm the contributions of such theological movements to anti-imperialistic efforts by valuing the dignity and beauty of indigenous heritages and lifting up the voices of local leaders. However, we cannot be blind to the fact that there are shortcomings in these theologies as well, expressed for instance in the nationalistic fervor of some theologians, which has led some to construct theologies that dialogue only with elite culture, or which has presupposed a homogenous national culture that silences women, the dalits, and other marginalized groups.[27] It has been shown repeatedly that after the colonizers were driven away they were replaced by a national bourgeoisie that was not sensitive to the plight of the masses. In addition, colonization and globalization processes have changed indigenous cultures so much that it becomes difficult to speak of a clear divide between the local and the global.

One of the leading postcolonial theorists, Gayatri Chakravorty Spivak, has constantly cautioned us of the ambiguities of speaking for or representing the subaltern. She reminds intellectuals of the gulf between them and the masses, the poor, or the subaltern, and of the difficulties of recovering the subjectivity of the subaltern and documenting subaltern consciousness, as if their consciousness were unambiguous and transparent.[28] The same can be said for liberation theologies and political theologies of all sorts, which seek to work in solidarity with the oppressed and downtrodden. Some liberation theologians are careful to point out that they cannot speak on behalf of the poor because of their own class or educational privileges. They are aware that theologians must be self-critical of their own position and responsive to their communities of accountability. In our commercialized world, when identity can be commodified and people of color are rewarded not just for imitating the whites, but also lured into playing their assigned roles as "protestant *ethnics*,"[29] theologians from these communities can easily be co-opted into the multicultural theological marketplace or the carnival of postmodern difference.

THEOLOGY, EMPIRE, AND SOCIAL IMAGINARY

In their book *Empire*, Michael Hardt and Antonio Negri argue that the old form of imperialism, defined by military and political control of foreign territories, has been replaced by Empire: "In contrast to imperialism, Empire establishes no territorial center of power and does not rely on fixed boundaries or barriers. It is a *decentered* and *deterritorializing* apparatus of rule that progressively incorporates the entire global realm within its open, expanding frontiers."[30] With the decline of colonial regimes since World War II and the increasingly global reach of the neoliberal market economy, the nation-state is not as significant as before. The new Empire is defined more by economic power, secured and bolstered by military might; war becomes a continuation of politics by other means.

Hardt and Negri's theory has been criticized, because nation-states are reasserting themselves in global politics, in some cases to counteract globalizing forces, as in the Middle East and other Third World countries. Others have argued that territorial control is still important, as the United States seeks to exert its hegemony by using military force in its "grand imperial strategy."[31] However, Hardt and Negri's work is significant in calling our attention to reconceptualizing economics, the nation-state, and biopower in the age of globalization.

Another leading theorist of the cultural dimensions of globalization is Arjun Appadurai from India, whose work on "globalization from below" has captured the attention of both academics and social activists.[32] Globalization, he says, is characterized by disjunctive flows of people, capital, images and messages, technologies, and goods and services at enormous speed. Contrary to globalization from above, globalization from below depends on the coalition and collaboration of nongovernmental organizations, transnational advocacy networks, activists, public intellectuals, and socially concerned academics. He writes: "[O]ne positive force that encourages an emancipatory politics of globalization is the role of imagination in social life."[33] What can Christian theologians contribute to a social imaginary that will benefit the oppressed and marginalized?

In the Christian West, the ways people conceive human power, such as "will," "capacity," and "sovereign," are closely related to how divine power is imagined, as human beings are considered to be created in the image of God. As Milbank has argued, the "new sciences of politics" have their origins in theology, in that the basic characteristics of humanhood, such as private property, active rights, and absolute sovereignty, are rooted in Adam's *dominium*.[34] In past decades, the work of feminist theologians such as Carter Heyward has helped us to reimagine divine power not in terms of domination, but in terms of mutual relation.[35] Catherine Keller has linked the justification for preemptive force with the theo-logic of omnipotence that is influenced by Calvinism, an important component of the culture of Protestantism in the United States. Just as God, being omnipotent, does not need to wait to act, the United States, believing itself to be exceptional and innocent, can take preemptive action. Exposing such an imperial theo-logic, Keller calls for a new *theopoetics*, which reimagines and transcodes political power in terms of the *profundis* of creation and in service of counter-empire:

> God is called upon not as a unilateral superpower but as a relational force, not an omnipotent creator from nothing, imposing order upon chaos, but the lure to a self-organizing complexity, creation out of the chaos—the *tohuvabohu* of which Genesis 1 speaks.[36]

The reconceptualization of divine power and sovereignty is closely related to violence in the Christian tradition. While some parts of the Bible depict God as merciful and compassionate, God has also been described as the one who commands the Israelites to kill their enemies, including their children and livestock. Jesus met his death with nonviolence, but he also said that he came not to bring peace but a sword (Matt. 10: 34) and there are Zealots among his followers. While the early Christians adopted a pacifist approach in the first centuries, Ambrose and his student Augustine had begun to develop an ethic of war that considered war to be unavoidable because of fallen human nature and evil in the world. By the time of the crusades, Aquinas had developed a more detailed just war theory.[37] During the centuries of colonialism, violence and genocide were justified in the name of converting other peoples to Christ. Christianity both provided the religious sanction and justification of the colonial project and reaped the benefit. As political empires expanded, the ecclesial empire extended its global reach as well. After the September 11, 2001 incidents, some have sought to revive the just war tradition, though progressive Christian ethicists have strongly argued that the just war theory cannot be applied to our time. Because the technologies of war have changed so much and distinguishing between military and civilian persons and locations is so difficult, the ends can never justify the means.[38] At a time when violence and war are conducted in God's name, providing theological and moral imagination for building sustainable peace is a major challenge for theologians.

This theological rethinking has to start with none other than the central symbol of the cross. Feminist theologians have criticized classical atonement theories as "theological sadism" and divine child abuse.[39] Searching for a reinterpretation of the cross offers new possibilities for dialogue between theologians and critical theorists, since several of the latter have written explicitly on the cross. Julia Kristeva, for example, offers a psychoanalytical reading that the death of Christ expresses the melancholia of a subject ruptured from and longing for the maternal.[40] Slavoj Žižek reads the crucifixion through Lacanian lenses of a subject striking at himself to gain the space of free action.[41] A postcolonial perspective may find these theories unsettling as it is not clear how such psychoanalytical analyses will benefit those at the bottom of society.

Feminist theologians Rita Nakashima Brock and Rebecca Ann Parker take a different route and question if violence and redemptive suffering are key to salvation.[42] Their research has shown that in early Christian iconography and paintings, the dominant motifs had been on the resurrection, paradise, and fullness of life. The images of crucifixion appeared only after Christian violence erupted against the pagans. Anselm's satisfaction theory of atonement took shape during the First Crusade, when Jesus' death was seen as restoring God's honor. The symbol of crucifixion then becomes a justification for violence, which is remembered and re-enacted during Eucharist. Instead of glorifying suffering, Rita Nakashima Brock exhorts us to celebrate communal redemption: "Salvation comes from communal practices that affirm incarnation, the Spirit in life, and its ongoing promise of resurrection and paradise."[43]

Violence and salvation are closely related to the problem of evil. Womanist ethicist Emilie M. Townes breaks new ground in her exploration of race, gender, and the cultural production of evil. She is not satisfied with the objective and cool-headed studies of the "isms" which perpetuate oppression in society, and turns to narratives, especially those written by African-American writers, to probe "the deep interior material life of evil and its manifestations."[44] Building on and expanding Foucault and Gramsci's work, she elucidates how fantastic hegemonic imagination works to create caricatures and stereotypes of black people, especially black women, from the Black Matriarch to the Welfare Queen. She writes:

> This imagination conjures up worlds and their social structures that are not based on supernatural powers and phantasms, but on the ordinariness of evil. It is this imagination, I argue, that helps to hold systematic, structural evil in place.[45]

To dismantle the cultural production of evil, Townes returns to H. Richard Niebuhr's notion of social solidarity in his responsibility ethics. Individuals must work with their communities and social worlds, and increasingly in a global context. People of faith must respond to God's call to respect others and all of creation and to construct a countermemory that proclaims hope in the midst of evil.

An insidious cultural production of evil—to maintain a particular quality of life for a privileged few—has subjected people to slavery, colonialism, and genocide. Twenty percent of the populations in developed nations consume 86 percent of the world's goods, while a huge population, mostly people of color, is condemned to living in abject poverty. Half of the world's population subsists on less than $2 a day. The poor nations spend $13 on debt repayment for every $1 they receive in grants. The lives of millions of children are needlessly lost annually because of world governments' failure to reduce poverty levels.[46] The conditions that set liberation theology into motion have not gone away, but have actually worsened. After the disintegration of the Soviet Union and the realignment of Eastern Europe, theologians who supported the neo-liberal economy, especially from the North, were quick to declare that liberation theology was dead, passé, because Marxism was outdated. They appear not to be cognizant of the fact that liberation philosophers and theologians such as Franz Hinkelammert and Enrique Dussel continue to be deeply engaged with issues of the globalized market and postmodernity.

Liberation theologians from the South have made further investigations regarding the relationship between class oppression and the degradation of the environment. Leonardo Boff has argued for a broader understanding of liberation to include the nonhuman realm. The option for the poor, he says, must include the most threatened beings in creation, and democracy must include socio-cosmic democracy. He envisages that the concern for a more integral liberation of the human beings and the earth can open dialogues between the North and the South.[47] His colleague from Brazil, Ivone Gebara, has advanced an ecofeminist theology, which begins with criticizing the anthropocentric, patriarchal, and dualistic epistemology upon which traditional theology has been based. Instead of a salvation that focuses on humans, she argues for a biocentric understanding of salvation, which includes respect for the life of every being. Jesus does not possess a superior will, nor is he superior to other human beings. He is not the powerful "son of God" or the king who dominates. Rather, Jesus is reimagined as a symbol of our dream and our love, a model of communion with all things and of the vulnerability of love.[48]

Liberation theology meets postcolonialism and queer studies in the work of Marcella Althaus-Reid, born and raised in Argentina. By claiming that every theology is always a sexual theology, Althaus-Reid places sexuality firmly in a central position of the Christian imaginary. Contrasted with feminist theology's uncovering of the gender codes within Christian theology, Althaus-Reid's "indecent theology" reveals and undresses the sexual ideologies that pervade the assumptions and methodologies of theology. Sexuality is an integral part of liberation theology, she says, because there is no sexuality before society, and the poor are sexual beings as well as economic beings. She surmises:

> Sexual ideologies are foundational in economic and political structures of oppression, just as they remain foundational in our understanding of ourselves and ourselves in relation of God . . . only a political Feminist Theology has the capability of de-articulating the present gender ordering of the market system and liberating not only humanity but also God from the narrow sexual ideological confines in which God has been located.[49]

Shifting from gender to sexuality, with a perceptive understanding of the postcolonial condition, Althaus-Reid thus challenges both feminist theologians who dwell on gender and sexuality without talking about economics, and liberation theologians who dismiss women's and queer concerns as side-tracking from the "real" issues of liberation.

CONCLUSION

Jesus said, "Render to Caesar what is Caesar's and to God what is God's" (Matt. 22:21). What is due to Caesar and to God has become a critical question for Christians living in the age of empire, when the United States has become a super-power the likes of which human history has never seen before. By learning how those theologians who have gone before us dealt with this question in their time, we gain critical insights for engaging with the empire of our time. One lesson is that we must see theology and politics not as two separate spheres, but as necessarily interacting with one another. The issues of race, class, gender, sexuality, and colonialism are not added on or tangential to theology, as if they can be separated from discourses on God, Christology, ecclesiology, etc. Every discussion about God is also a discussion about power, about human relations, about sexuality, about our being in the world.

The New Testament closes with a powerful social imaginary—that of the new heaven and the new earth (Rev. 21:1). Writing on the island of Patmos, the author of the Book of Revelation articulates a counterhegemonic theo-logic radically different from that of imperial Rome. Today, the vision of the new heaven and new earth continues to inspire us in search for justice, peace, and reconciliation for the whole world.

FURTHER READING

Althaus-Reid, Marcella. *Indecent Theology: Theological Perversions in Sex, Gender and Politics*. London: Routledge, 2000.

Boff, Clodovis. *Theology and Praxis: Epistemological Foundations*. Translated by Robert R. Barr. Maryknoll, N.Y.: Orbis Books, 1987.

Browning, Don S., and Francis Schüssler Fiorenza, eds. *Habermas, Modernity, and Public Theology*. New York: Crossroad, 1992.

Gutiérrez, Gustavo. *A Theology of Liberation: History, Politics, and Salvation*, rev. ed. Translated by Sister Caridad Inda and John Eagleson. Maryknoll, N.Y.: Orbis Books, 1988.

Keller, Catherine. *God and Power: Counter-Apocalyptic Journeys*. Minneapolis, Minn.: Fortress Press, 2005.

Kwok, Pui-lan. *Postcolonial Imagination and Feminist Theology*. Louisville, Ky.: Westminster John Knox Press, 2005.

Milbank, John. *Theology and Social Theory: Beyond Secular Reason*, 2nd ed. Malden, Mass.: Blackwell, 2006.

Segundo, Juan Luis. *The Liberation of Theology*. Translated by John Drury. Maryknoll, N.Y.: Orbis Books, 1976.

Townes, Emilie M. *Womanist Ethics and the Cultural Production of Evil*. New York: Palgrave Macmillan, 2006.

Ward, Graham. *Theology and Contemporary Critical Theory*. New York, N.Y.: St. Martin's Press, 1996.

CHAPTER 3

The Christian Tradition and Empires: A Reader's Guide

Don H. Compier

In the two previous chapters my co-editors have described what empires are, how they function, and how diverse Christian theological perspectives seek to grapple with the related issues. They established the importance of empire as a key locus for contemporary theological investigation. In this chapter I contribute to these introductory reflections by further exploring two questions: (1.) Why should persons interested in fashioning theological, ethical, and political responses to imperial power dynamics bother to become familiar with thinkers from the Christian past? (2.) In approaching historical authors, what specific reading practices promise to inform transformative engagements with the many ways in which empires exercise extensive yet never total dominion?

Can historical work help to set loose the ever-present theological "surplus" of which Joerg Rieger speaks, and move theology closer to the truly postcolonial fruition for which Kwok Pui-lan calls? I believe the cumulative testimony of the chapters found in this volume offers a resoundingly positive answer. In this introductory essay, then, I hope to further orient readers to the riches contained in these pages. We do not aim to present the authors covered in this book in some definitive or exhaustive fashion. We have in no way sought to establish a new canon or a closed list of the "best" authors for tackling empire or any other issue. Nor do we wish to suggest that these chapters offer *the* final interpretation of any particular author. Instead we seek to present a set of case studies of concrete theological engagements with empire. I hope that the essays that follow will inspire persons to pursue similar studies of thinkers from the Christian past. I envision classes that would adopt this volume as a text and then assign students to write similar essays on figures not covered here, or on other aspects of the thought of persons discussed here. I offer this chapter as a methodological road map for persons pursuing further research of the type we have sought to exemplify here.

THE PAST MATTERS

As I imagine the diverse audiences likely to read this book and the different classrooms in which it may be used as a text, I offer two different but hopefully complementary answers to my first question: Why should we read texts from Christian history? The first answer, regarding the authority of tradition, primarily seeks to address persons committed to Christian constructive theology. The second answer, regarding rhetorical hermeneutics, may prove useful not only to Christian theologians but also to students in the disciplines of religious or cultural studies that do not assume personal commitment to Christian faith or, for that matter, to any other religious tradition.

The Authority of Tradition

In Christian constructive theology, appeal to the past has become standard practice. Contemporary theologians disagree about how particular authors should be read and how or even if their ideas are relevant today, but very few would argue against dialogue with predecessors.

Ever since the Reformation era, Protestants have disputed with Roman Catholics (and less directly, with representatives of Eastern Orthodoxy) about the extent of the influence tradition should exert over doctrinal formulations. Some expressions of Protestant Christianity contend that Scripture alone should exercise such authority. The rise of fundamentalism since the late nineteenth century represents a particularly extreme case of this tendency. Yet, on closer examination, no Christian theologian can dispense with appeals to the past. As Richard Hooker argued in Elizabethan England, many parts of the Bible simply do not interpret themselves. In deciphering what they mean, inherited hermeneutical approaches inevitably influence contemporary readings.[1] Scholars point out that the two most influential Protestant voices, Luther and Calvin, both read Scripture through lenses supplied by Augustine.[2]

The emergence of liberal theologies in the nineteenth century represented another challenge to the authority of tradition. These influences continue to resonate in the modern academy. Liberal theologians, offering a partial interpretation of the groundbreaking work of Friedrich Schleiermacher, argued that theology should reflect on Christian religious experience; however, these theologians tended to overlook Schleiermacher's insistence on the historically mediated nature of piety. Schleiermacher's questioning of some key traditions, most notably the doctrine of the Trinity, encouraged critical approaches to much of the Christian theological legacy.[3] His ambivalent Romantic response to the Enlightenment gave way to a fuller embrace of the values and epistemology of modernism.

The voluminous and highly influential work of church historian Adolf von Harnack (1851-1930) represents the high point of the liberal approach. Von Harnack deplored the political compromises of the post-Constantinian church, saw the decrees of the ecumenical councils of the first five centuries as capitulations to Greek philosophical categories, and in many other ways claimed that modern theology had the right to correct and—when necessary—discard much of previous Christian theology.[4]

Yet liberal theology did not obviate the resort to tradition. Like Scripture, spiritual experiences are not transparent or unambiguous but require interpretation. In fact, conceptions acquired from the past shape not only interpretations, but also the experiences themselves.[5] And as von Harnack himself demonstrated, critiques of past theological distortions depend upon the acceptance of religious norms derived from the breadth of Christian tradition, not simply from contemporary standards. He sought the "essence" of Christianity, the "kernel" enveloped in a variety of historical "husks," yet this essence was itself distinguishable only through historical investigation into the origins of Christianity and its preservation amidst centuries of cultural veiling and warping.[6] The liberal project, then, also depends upon the citation of precedents.

And so it has become common to pursue historical study of past theologians as part of the constructive process. However, we find ourselves less than satisfied with the manner in and degree to which theologians have thus far sought to accomplish this dimension of their labor. As Rieger noted in chapter 1, all too often theologians simply ignore the connections between empires and Christian doctrinal reflections. Even when sensitivity to contextual issues is present, a long-established penchant for generalization and abstraction can obscure fruitful connections and implications. For instance, I greatly admire the work of Canadian theologian Douglas John Hall. He points us in the right direction by seeking to construct a theology squarely in the context of the current empire.[7] Hall enshrines what he calls historical theology as the second step of his tripartite constructive method. He recognizes that when we are faced with contemporary challenges, we do well to inventory the resources offered by the Christian tradition. Yet when we examine his actual approaches to the Christian theological legacy, we find that he makes broad assumptions about the continuity of certain themes across centuries, thereby conflating discourses emerging from very different historical circumstances. Hall represents the common tendency to separate the legacy of ideas from the persons who fashioned concepts in the midst of historical struggles. And surprisingly, Hall only rarely offers explicit discussion of a particular thinker's reflections on imperial realities. As a self-proclaimed post-Constantinian theologian, he still seems guided by a liberal penchant to overstate the complicity of pre-modern theology with monarchical regimes. The theological "surplus" of resistances noted by Rieger thus fails to emerge with adequate concreteness. We contend that only sustained attention to particular cases of Christian theological negotiations with empire adequately informs fruitful contemporary reflections about appropriate responses to regimes of domination.

We will return to this theme when I elaborate upon my answer to the second principal question posed at the outset of this chapter. My main purpose in the preceding paragraphs has been to indicate why nearly all contemporary Christian theologians accept the necessity of historical study as a constructive endeavor. However, I believe that my discipline has not sufficiently appreciated how radical appeals to tradition can be, in and of themselves. We may come to a richer understanding when we realize the potential for resistance inherent in the central beliefs of ancient Christianity.

I particularly want to refer to the proclamation of the resurrection of the embodied dead. In her chapter in this volume, Tatha Wiley notes how this theme operated transgressively in Paul's first-century writings. In subsequent centuries, as martyrdom at various points became a real prospect faced by disciples, this doctrine in effect became a denial of the ultimate power of the empire. Even death could not defeat God's supreme purposes. Moreover, forebears who had entered into glory continued to inspire and somehow communicate with persons still enmeshed in life's struggles, a belief reflected in the Apostles' Creed language regarding the "communion of saints."

In our context, a determination to include the voices of the dead in discussions about the common good also undermines imperialistic pretensions. Today's global capitalist empire, chiefly centered in the United States, depends upon the modern myth of progress. It exalts an official story of steady growth in wisdom and knowledge culminating in the present state of affairs. Figures from the past, then, are only worth listening to if they can be cast as predictors and extollers of the current regime and its supposed virtues. Moreover, capitalistic consumerism depends upon an individualistic anthropology that denies the historical and social character of humanity. Its beneficiaries wish to maintain strict silence about the fatalities constantly created by global economic exploitation. Today's imperial legions do not want anyone to have encounters with or care about the dead as persons. Beliefs about solidarity with ancestors, which persist in all traditional cultures, are portrayed as demonstrative of the alleged inferiority and superstitious backwardness of non-Western peoples. Capitalism aligns itself with the supposed enlightenment brought by the culture industries, which include Western institutions of higher learning.[8]

In such circumstances, theologians are engaging in countercultural acts of resistance whenever we insist that deceased theologians should be given voice. We contend that the reading strategies demonstrated in this volume amplify the contributions predecessors make to contemporary debates about empire. We call for treating the dead as living interlocutors from particular lived contexts, not as wan, ghostly voices refracted through disembodied ideas. We also insist on the importance of multicultural dialogues about history. The contributors to this volume represent a considerable variety of perspectives, including German, Chinese, African-American, Indian, Canadian, Cuban-American, Dutch, Japanese, and Latvian. Moreover, this volume's chapters discussing living authors John S. Mbiti and Mercy Amba Oduyoye seek to point to an imminent future history of Christianity in which Western voices will no longer predominate. These strategies disrupt the ideologies of progress, individualism, and Western superiority that prop up today's attempts to achieve global dominion.

Sometimes we are surprised by the remarkable instances of resistance found in Christian history. At other times we experience deep pain as we become aware of the failures to act justly and the enormous suffering that resulted. Yet we are convinced that accepting the truth about our past leads to healing. When we face historical reality with courage, we develop an awareness that opens possibilities for a new and better future. We are not doomed to repeat past mistakes. We become makers of history in our own time.

Attending to the inescapably rhetorical nature of Christian theology benefits today's practitioners; we have only to gain by availing ourselves of the persuasive force of appeals to the past. Historical investigation can fund a variety of theological arguments, and all are strengthened by engagement with the work of predecessors. Naturally, the work of those not committed to the practice of Christian constructive theology can also benefit from appeals to history and its rhetorical underpinnings. In the next section of this chapter, I draw on the Greek and Roman tradition of rhetoric that predated the emergence of Christianity, which has continued to shape pedagogy, reading, writing, and speaking throughout the history of European culture.[9]

Rhetorical Hermeneutics

Aristotle defined rhetoric as "an ability, in each [particular] case, to see the available means of persuasion."[10] It is therefore an essential component of any human communicative act, including all attempts to address issues raised by empire. Rhetoricians insist that speech and writing can be transformative practices. Rhetorical wrestling with empire today would suggest that cogent analyses of imperial dynamics and well-constructed proposals for resistance are potentially effective practical forms of liberating social engagement. For orators, no communication can be counted as successful unless it inspires readers and hearers to act on behalf of the common good.

How does one learn to write and speak in ways that actually challenge systems of domination? From ancient times practitioners of the persuasive arts extolled the pedagogical utility of precedents. They required students to critically examine past rhetorical performances. Pupils learned valuable lessons from both successful and failed attempts to persuade. As apprentice rhetoricians read and discussed a wide variety of texts, they grew more confident in their grasp of essential rhetorical principles and were ready to begin making their own attempts to "teach, delight, and move."[11]

Rhetoric has been deployed on all sides of all power structures: emperors and their supporters have always deployed religious discourses to justify their rule, and imperial domination has always been challenged on religious grounds. As several essays in this volume demonstrate, the current U.S. administration certainly claims to represent Christian values (see the chapters by Deanna A. Thompson and Larry L. Rasmussen, for instance). Contemporary challengers of empire who are not theologians should therefore also benefit from perusal of the types of case studies presented in this text. Historical study of specific Christian engagements with various regimes may reveal unsuspected potential for resistance as well as blinders that obscure the vision of even the most well-intentioned persons enmeshed in imperial cultures. Even the latter sort of discovery has positive consequences, allowing us to acquire a humility that may help us to become conscious of the limitations of our own vision.

For both theologians and other practitioners of persuasion, examinations of individual historical figures offer irreplaceable benefits. In the preceding chapter, Kwok Pui-lan has made the case for employing various critical social theories as we seek to address imperial realities. The word *theory*, after all, derives from a Greek term denoting ways of seeing. Frequently, however, scholars too readily adopt a panoramic, bird's eye view and miss the trees for the forest. Only by using the lenses provided by theory in tandem with tradition to examine specific instances of thinkers negotiating with empire will our students acquire the skill to trace how the fine mesh of relationships of domination and resistance actually operate. From the perspective of the ground level we can detect what Michel Foucault called the "microphysics" or the "network of relations," the small channels through which power and resistance to it become specifically manifested.[12] In historical investigation we consider stories that have already concluded. Situations whose results are already known offer students more direct scenarios for analytical practice in the detection of power dynamics. Through examination of historical case studies students may therefore acquire a facility for critical perception while dealing with fewer variables and less fluid situations than those of the present.

In accordance with the tried and true principles of rhetorical pedagogy, we recommend exposure to a variety of examples provided by history. This method will in time enable adepts to apply concrete critical thought to the mapping of current power structures. The chapters on Mbiti and Oduyoye move in that direction. As Foucault's work illustrates, once we know the lay of the land, we can determine at what specific points to apply and support the most effective strategies of resistance.[13]

I hope the preceding reflections have persuaded diverse readers that contextual study of the past must inform current attempts to wrestle with imperial power. How then do we proceed?

Reading Christian Theologians in Context

1. Adopt an inductive approach.

As the table of contents of this volume indicates, we recommend that students begin by choosing a single Christian author. Comparisons of two or more thinkers should be left for more advanced study. Otherwise the apprentice researcher will invariably tend to take shortcuts, failing to appreciate the great complexity of each author's unique contexts. Skilled historical investigators generally avoid deductive methods, that is, approaches that primarily study individual writers by applying generalizations to them. Remember that we seek to hear out to the fullest possible extent each participant in the dialogue. We can only fruitfully note similarities and differences after having heard an interlocutor speak in her or his own voice.[14] In anti-hegemonic work we must constantly take care not to reduce persons to abstract categories. Treating individuals as means to an end, however enlightened, is a pro-imperial procedure.

2. Make free use of theory.

As already indicated, these cautions do not preclude employing a variety of theories as ways of seeing. I do recommend, however, remembering that theories are tools, and that no one instrument can perform all necessary jobs.[15] We should make free use of theories, gladly employing them when helpful, and leaving them behind when they don't seem productive in accomplishing the job at hand. We never study historical persons in the service of theory, but the reverse, for theories are means, not ends. The essays in this volume nicely illustrate appropriate use of theoretical tools. In fact, usually the perspectives that have informed the reading of an author are so thoroughly integrated that they will only be apparent to those well-read in critical theories. In other cases authors explicitly demonstrate the method being endorsed. In his essay on Hegel, for instance, David G. Kamitsuka exemplifies our approach through his deft handling of postcolonial discourse.

3. Avoid anachronistic reading.

As the investigator begins to approach a particular subject, he or she needs to make every effort to avoid projecting current realities onto persons from the past. The temptation of "presentism" constantly besets us. One form of this tendency has particular relevance for this volume.

We have well-developed notions about what theology is and what theologians do, even if we don't always consciously and clearly express these notions. In our modern academic context, theology is one of many highly specialized disciplines and professions. Its practitioners usually work for a university and/or seminary. Their authorship must satisfy the requirements followed by committees on tenure and promotion as well as the demands of publishing houses, which are in turn subject to current market realities. Normally this means that theologians must display considerable theoretical sophistication. Theologians may also be ministers or activists, but these endeavors are treated as avocational interests—we are usually not paid for hours thus spent. As Rieger suggests above, we assume a separation between church, interpreted as a private realm, and state, seen as the public sphere. I would point to a concomitant assumption of a split between our (subjective) spiritual life and (objective) intellectual life. Theologians generally operate on the church side, but as part of the academy they must favor intellect when engaging in teaching and writing. As a result, spirituality and theology are seen as separate enterprises.

If left unexamined, these presuppositions will prevent us from understanding the very different practices of the authors examined in this book. None of them understood theology as a specialized and self-contained field of study. The academic norms that we take for granted did not develop until the beginning of the nineteenth century at the earliest. And before and after that watershed, the work of the persons discussed here hardly conforms to narrow disciplinary boundaries. As Ian A. McFarland tells us, for instance, Theodore the Studite was primarily a monk, not an academic. According to Larry L. Rasmussen and David N. Field, Reinhold Niebuhr and Dietrich Bonhoeffer would certainly not accept any suggestion of discontinuity between their political involvements and their theological vocation. Few cultivated the intellectual life more than Thomas Aquinas, but he saw no divide whatsoever between his scholarly activity and his pursuit of mysticism. And many of the works now considered theological classics were written for popular audiences (those of Wesley studied by Theodore W. Jennings Jr., for instance). Before the invention of the printing press, they might, as in the case of Julian, be written for a rather small group, or even for specific persons. Wider distribution depended on decisions others might make to laboriously produce copies and perhaps read the ideas aloud to larger numbers of illiterate persons who formed the vast majority of the population.

The preceding reflections offer only one example of our need to strip away preconceptions as much as possible when we approach predecessors. We invite students to come to textual artifacts afresh. Sometimes we can only perform this task if we cultivate awareness of the complex reading histories that postdate the author's life yet tend to strongly color current reception of his or her work. Mark D. Jordan demonstrates this necessity in his treatment of post-Thomas Thomism. Conscious recognition of strongly established interpretational patterns helps us to acknowledge their presence even as we set them aside. As Jordan also illustrates, we should refuse to place our primary focus on a text's history of interpretation. We examine aftereffects only in order to find a way through them to more direct contact with the primary sources. In other words, we also aim to avoid the projections of other readers.

4. Broaden the definition of theology.
In accordance with the specialization of disciplinary labor I described in the previous section, modern scholars have formed canons of authors that exclude some of the most interesting ideas in Christian history. We have deliberately broadened our selection of authors for this volume. We include persons not usually covered in classes on the history of Christian thought. For instance, Wynfrith-Boniface and Hendrik Kraemer, and perhaps M. M. Thomas, might typically be covered in courses on missiology. Mechtild, Julian, and Simone Weil are usually considered the purview of instruction on spirituality. Some of our authors, notably Simone Weil, were not involved in the life of the church. Cultural and linguistic boundaries also shape canons. Bartolomé de las Casas, Sor Juana Inés de la Cruz, and Juan Luis Segundo, if considered at all, are normally relegated to classes on Latin American or Hispanic theology. These academic habits, of course, are themselves reflections of imperial distinctions between colonizers and the colonized. In this volume we aim to transgress both disciplinary and cultural boundaries. In the struggle with empire, why would we not wish to pay attention to a great variety of case studies? We have nothing to lose, and much to gain.

We believe that the focus on empire here discloses strategies of reading with broader application. In the past, classes on the history of Christian thought generally considered texts that could be read as philosophically sophisticated, at least in the sense that they displayed rigorous logical argumentation. As I suggested above, this practice displays the influence of a particularly modern academic definition of theology. If we recall that theology, *theo-logos*, is simply God-talk, or, to cite Anselm's famous formulation, "faith seeking understanding," there is no need to confine ourselves to any particular genre of writing. In fact, on closer examination we find that interpretations of theologians currently considered canonical can be distorted by adherence to the reigning definition. Luther, for instance, constantly displayed hostility toward overly systematic reflections. Many of the ideas we borrow from him were actually expressed in sermons, catechisms, and polemical appeals.[16]

Moreover, we will miss some authors altogether unless we adopt appreciation for a variety of genres. Michelle A. Gonzalez demonstrates that Sor Juana's skilled poetry and drama convey incisive theological lessons in forms that, let's admit it, tend to appeal to far more readers than do abstract theological arguments. In the selection of subjects for study, then, no writer in the Christian tradition should be dismissed as insufficiently theological. Human creativity finds expression in a multitude of ways, and all can prove instructive in the present task.

5. Assume holistic conceptions of human persons.
We believe that both the Christian tradition and the findings of recent critical theories call us to affirm the embodied nature of human persons. We eat, we sleep, we work, we constantly relate to other human beings and institutions, we receive news of events both near and far away. The production of texts represents only one dimension of our existence. While we may bracket it and other facets of our lives for analytical purposes, in daily experience all aspects of our lives are inextricably woven together.[17] The authors we consider here were bright and perceptive individuals. We may safely assume that they were well aware of what was going on in the world around them. All had deep concern for the welfare of others. Therefore, their texts inevitably addressed contemporary concerns, including the effects of systems and practices of domination. To suggest otherwise implies that they did not live in specific times and places. Separating authors from their contexts represents a reductionistic move, implying that human beings are only or primarily creatures of intellect producing isolated and abstract reflections for universal audiences.

It is sometimes easy to detect the ways in which texts reflect preoccupations that were current at the time the author was writing. As Larry L. Rasmussen shows, Reinhold Niebuhr was a particularly topical author. At other times we must dig deeper and venture hypotheses about the connections. Wendy Farley's chapter on Mechtild models such engagement, showing how this mystic addressed the realities of the crusades, even if power dynamics affecting the status of women required her to do so in indirect yet very effective ways. In fact, if an author does seem entirely silent on pressing issues of the day, this exceptional fact demands explanation. The study of such silences may tell us much about differing conceptions of the theological task. Silence may indicate that reflection on doctrine and political commentary were considered entirely separable discourses, or it may demonstrate just how enmeshed particular humans had become in systems of domination. Many Christian theologians living in the southern U.S. apparently never even questioned the validity of slavery or segregation. Attention to such cases may grant us the clarity to ask what wrongs lie right before our eyes while we fail to detect them.

Rather than dismissing such study as a reduction of theological writing to context, we should affirm holistic approaches as recognition of the full humanity of authors. Both Christian anthropology and critical theories accept the finitude or the historically and culturally conditioned character of human beings. We contend that the approach adopted here makes figures from other horizons more, not less, relevant. By seeing how they lived in their times and places, we can gain perspectives on how to make the best of our own geographical and historical location. Some persons prove capable of continually spurring fruitful thought and practice. But they do so because they effectively address their time, not all times.

6. Form a complex and broad sense of context.
If, as the preceding section argues, Christian writers always address current realities, then we must understand the context of their lives and times as best as possible. What was going on in the church? Did they or their contemporaries experience natural disasters, invasions, or other catastrophes? Did they live in times of war? Who were the rulers, and what were their policies? What contact did the chosen author have with these larger realities?

In this volume matters of context are addressed in the first section of each chapter. The endnotes reveal that our authors read widely in secondary sources. We did not confine ourselves to other theological examinations of the subject. Authors consulted the types of books and articles usually employed in departments of history and cultural studies. Note, for instance, how Marion Grau depicts the broader movement to Christianize Northern Europe at the beginning of the medieval period. Shelly Rambo shares her awareness of the impact of the devastating bubonic plague on Julian's city of Norwich. Don Schweitzer gives us a concise, comprehensive view of the life and conflicts of colonial America just prior to the struggle for independence from the British Empire. Inese Radzins points us to the realities of French colonialism in Indo-China and Northern Africa. In each case we find that our understanding of an author's work is enriched by this careful attention to larger contexts.

7. *Acquire a sense of the author's work in its entirety.*

In the second section of the chapters included here, our writers focus on primary sources. Authors addressing various specific situations may sound quite different, and even contradictory, from one text to another. As Anthony J. Chvala-Smith suggests, this problem has become acute as diverse aspects of Augustine's legacy have been variously interpreted across many centuries. Deanna A. Thompson notes that Luther himself had to contend with different readings of his texts during the peasant revolts. Especially for the beginning researcher, it therefore becomes essential to avoid partial depictions of an author's views. As Don Schweitzer shows in his discussion of Jonathan Edwards, sometimes one set of themes in a single author's work appearing to endorse or oppose empire may be significantly nuanced by other lines of thought coming from the same pen.

This approach may be easier to adopt with an author whose literary output is relatively small, like Boniface. However, when approaching more prolific legacies, one can sample a variety of texts and make judicious use of secondary sources, provided one is appropriately cautious in the face of well-established schemas of interpretation. Interpretive claims can then be stated with due reserve. When I teach historical theology, I ask my students to treat their study of other authors like a conversation. I counsel researchers to do all they can, within the limits of time and energy, to make sure that the voice of the other has been truly heard. Historical investigation is akin to spiritual discipline, placing a high premium on listening skills. When we share what we have heard from others, we do so in our own words and under our own authority. We do not speak *for* others. We remain open to correction and deepening insight as we become more familiar with an interlocutor.

These considerations are of particular importance because studies of the type gathered in this book are often dismissed as issue-driven grinding of axes. We must be ready to argue that our approach contributes to a fuller, more accurate historical depiction of texts. The mode of investigation promoted here will be much more persuasive if we can demonstrate our respect for commonly accepted standards of historical evidence and interpretation. I refer specifically to the injunction to avoid taking statements out of their broader literary context. And in any case I would remind readers once again that imposition of our concerns onto others is a form of interpersonal domination inconsistent with work seeking to question and challenge hegemonic regimes and practices.

8. *Cautiously draw implications for today.*

We can only live in our time. The contributors to this volume do not aspire to be antiquarians (though we are glad that some persons devote their lives to historical preservation!). We must therefore honestly acknowledge the interested character of our investigations. In the end our labor bears fruit when we have learned from the past in order to be more effective today. We must make the constructive move. As Foucault admitted, we are always writing the "history of the present."[18]

Yet we do well if we remember that we can only derive these benefits from the careful mode of inquiry I have sought to describe in the previous seven sections. Perusal of the third and final sections of the essays included here demonstrates that we virtually never draw direct lessons from the study of other situations. Instead we develop a healthy sense of the otherness of each historical horizon. We may find similarities and points of contact, but no two contexts are exactly alike. In this way historical study develops habits of mind that respect difference, and in so doing oppose the imperial logic of false similarities. Yet we do not need to resign ourselves to absolute incommensurability between past and present thinking, or between persons from different cultures. We have communicated, albeit in broken and incomplete words, with other human beings across the centuries, and we have been transformed in the process.

As should be expected, our authors draw both largely negative (Grau's chapter, for instance) and quite positive (like Gonzalez) lessons from their investigations. Often contributors offer a mixed assessment (as in the case of McFarland). Sometimes the predecessor's own thought provides the basis for both thorough critique and constructive retrieval (Schweitzer, Kamitsuka). We are not suggesting that we have the right to pass judgment on the virtues and vices of other theologians. Speaking as a Christian, I would reserve that prerogative to God alone. Instead we express the courage to take responsibility for determining what is useful in our own context, and what seems less helpful. We mean no disrespect. We simply acknowledge that we, too, must in the end offer our own voices to the ongoing dialogue. We listen first, and then we must speak. In this way we take part in what has been a very rich conversation.

Perhaps the steps I have enumerated sound like a lot of work, and they can be. But I hope that the essays included in this volume also bear traces of the sheer enjoyment, even exhilaration, we have felt as we have labored individually and collectively. I don't believe that I have the words to describe the personal significance I derive from my attempts to follow the paths of thinkers living in very different worlds than my own. Each of the essays in this volume has broadened my understanding and appreciation even of those figures I thought I knew quite well. Somehow my ever-broadening conception of the community that crosses centuries and spans the globe strengthens my hope and increases my energy to continue to strive for a postimperial world. I warmly second Kwok Pui-lan's evocation of the anxiously awaited new heaven and new earth. The collaborative work represented here has been most gratifying. I hope that others will join this discourse and enjoy themselves as much as I have.

FURTHER READING

Clark, Elizabeth A. *History, Theory, Text: Historians and the Linguistic Turn*. Cambridge, Mass.: Harvard University Press, 2004.

Compier, Don H. *What Is Rhetorical Theology? Textual Practice and Public Discourse*. Harrisburg, Pa.: Trinity Press International, 1999.

Eden, Kathy. *Hermeneutics and the Rhetorical Tradition: Chapters in the Ancient Legacy and its Humanist Reception*. New Haven, Conn.: Yale University Press, 1997.

Flynn, Thomas. "Foucault's Mapping of History." In *The Cambridge Companion to Foucault*, edited by Gary Gutting, 28-46. Cambridge: Cambridge University Press, 1994.

Lentricchia, Frank. *Criticism and Social Change*. Chicago, Ill.: University of Chicago Press, 1983.

Mailloux, Steven. *Rhetorical Power*. Ithaca, N.Y.: Cornell University Press, 1989.

CHAPTER 4

Paul and Early Christianity

Tatha Wiley

Paul was a citizen of the Roman Empire at the highpoint of its power. Throughout his life and ministry, he both benefited from Roman achievements and struggled with the oppressive consequences of Rome's domination of the Mediterranean world.

For their construction of free baths throughout the empire alone the Romans might be remembered with admiration.[1] While most were modest, the baths of the third-century emperor Diocletian covered thirty-two acres and included wrestling rooms, debating halls, reading rooms, and gardens. With some fifteen million subjects over a vast territory to keep calm, the Romans learned the political benefits of largesse. In addition to access to free baths, the lower classes were fed—at least at crucial times—on free grain and entertained by free games.

Even more famous than its baths was the Roman highway system of paved roads that unified the empire and enabled travel and trade. Moving troops quickly around the empire to quash rebellions was a major reason for construction of the roads. Once built, however, their use was open and diverse. Roman roads are often cited as a specific factor contributing to the successful spread of Christianity in its first centuries.

Roman innovations and achievements were also impressive. The skills that Romans brought to architecture and engineering produced both the practical and the splendid—roads, the aqueduct system, magnificent temples and palaces. Latin, the language of the empire, remained the language of diplomacy and scholarship until the modern era and remains that of official documents of the Roman Catholic Church today.

Rome permitted various levels of self-governance to the peoples under its rule. The distinctive religious nationalism of the Jews was acknowledged by allowing the aristocratic priestly class to govern religious matters through the Sanhedrin and by appointing Jewish political rulers. When not rebellious, Judaea was granted a degree of independence. At the first murmur of trouble, however, Roman military governors took over. Such a one was Pontius Pilate, the Roman procurator responsible for executing Jesus. Two great revolts in 70 and 131 C.E. resulted in massive human suffering. In the former the Romans destroyed Jerusalem and the Jewish Temple. Against the later rebellion, they waged a war of annihilation.

ROME FROM BELOW

The world of Jesus and Paul was Rome's world.[2] Conquered in 63 B.C.E. by the Roman general Pompey, the Jews suffered both defeat and the insult of Pompey's entering the most sacred space of the Jerusalem Temple, the Holy of Holies.[3]

The Romans were known for rebuilding what they destroyed. Their tactics of total destruction left much to rebuild. Imperial forces met opposition by burning entire regions, slaughtering men, and carrying women and children off into slavery. Repression of rebellious provinces was ruthless.

Imperial forces celebrated military victories in Rome by parading conquered peoples in chains and material spoils in carts. Images of enslaved subjects on Roman coins publicly noted their inferiority and reminded the colonized of their place in the empire.

For the colonized, Rome's achievement of peace, lauded by poets and politicians, was a welcome alternative to terror but still an enforced social and political calm of imperial domination. Sharing in the *Pax Romana* meant for them loss of their independence and subjugation to Roman rule with the requisite obedience and tribute. Peace also required weathering the rule of neurotic, not to say insane, rulers such as Nero (37-68 C.E.), emperor during the time of Paul's ministry and the one credited with Paul's death.

Rome's wealth was visible in its magnificent building projects, its vast legions, and the lifestyle of its elite classes. But for the subjugated, Rome's wealth represented theft on a massive scale. Plunder after battle was part of warfare, even of military pay. Anything and everything that could be carried was taken. Enslaved populations built the magnificent Roman structures, while those who were allowed to remain free paid for them with their taxes. What provinces produced, Rome exploited. The Book of Revelation captured this reality in a dramatic vision of ships sailing toward Rome with

> cargo of gold, silver, jewels and pearls, fine linen, purple, silk and scarlet, all kinds of scented wood, all articles of ivory, all articles of costly wood, bronze, iron, and marble, cinnamon, spice, incense, myrrh, frankincense, wine, olive oil, choice flour and wheat, cattle and sheep, horses and chariots, slaves—and human lives. (Rev. 18:12-13)

The imperial cult gave divine sanction to the politics of domination. Octavius, the first emperor, was given the name *Augustus*, exalted or holy one. Called "god on earth," he was worshiped in temples dedicated to his name. Subsequent emperors were divinized as god or sons of god as well. The emperor was Lord and his power absolute. Messengers delivered his announcements of good news, his gospel, to the ends of the earth. He embodied the empire. Refusing to offer sacrifices for the emperor raised suspicion of disloyalty to the empire itself. The *Pax Romana* was characterized as salvation for all.

As subjects of Rome, Jews were both pro- and anti-imperial. While the difference was based largely on class, it was not entirely so. The elite did have more to protect, and thus their orientation was usually pro-imperial. Expressions of opposition against the *imperium* arose along a broad continuum—there were bandits targeting Roman elites, assassins pursuing Jewish elites, charismatic leaders rousing communities, self-proclaimed messiahs announcing divine judgment, and full-scale revolutionaries. Resistance strategies were multiple.

Jesus' resistance strategy was straightforward: proclamation. His announcement of the beginning of God's reign was really a comparison of two radically different kinds of reigns, Rome's and God's. The Greek word *basileia* is translated *empire* when used with Rome and more often *reign, rule,* or *kingdom* when used with God. Replacing the latter terms with *empire* shows more clearly the obvious contrast Jesus was making.

The *basileia* of God is a Jewish eschatological symbol. Suffering and oppression generate hope for God's intervention and the replacement of the present oppressive reign with God's reign. The critique implicit in Jesus' appeal to *God's* empire would have been obvious to his hearers. In contrast to Rome's *basileia*, he held up an alternative *basileia* characterized by partnership, inclusion, and mutual respect between men and women. To the poor and powerless Jesus announced good news: *God is for us.*

For one reign to begin, another must end. For such a message, Jesus met imperial power's full force. Crucifixion was the empire's chosen means of public degradation and execution of those who resisted its rule. The Roman designation for Jesus, "King of the Jews," cynically captured the threat that Rome perceived in him. His execution confirms what kept the *Pax Romana* in place: violence.

THE IMPERIAL PAUL

What was Paul's attitude to the empire? Depending on the Paul we are talking about, he is both pro- and anti-empire. To determine the stance of the historical Paul, we have to clear away two other voices attributed to him. The first is the Paul created by the deutero-Pauline authors, that is, authors of letters written in his name after his death. The second is the Paul of the *adversus Judaeos* or anti-Judaic tradition.

These voices attributed to Paul have dominated the tradition. In varying degrees, they remain the Paul known by many today. They are the imperial Paul. This is the Paul whose authority is used to control subjects and to justify rule over them.

In the case of the deutero-Pauline letters, the subjects were within the church. These authors created an internal ideology of superiority that colonized women and slaves. Paul's word justified women's subordination to Christian men and the total subjugation of slaves—women, men, and children—to the rule of Christian slave owners.

The *adversus Judaeos* tradition created an external ideology. Paul's authority was used to control subjects outside the church. In the case of the religious other, especially Jews, Paul's proclamation of Christ was an expression of religious imperialism. The religious other was colonized by way of conversion to Christianity. To remain the other was often to invite Christian violence or, if not violence, marginalization and discrimination.

The third Paul is the postcolonial Paul, the historical figure whose proclamation of the crucified Jesus was made in the same empire that crucified him. To call him Lord was to challenge the lordship of the emperor. Neither Paul nor the imperial powers were unaware of the meaning of Paul's proclamation.[4] To us what sounds "religious" was, in the ancient world, quite political. Given the swiftness with which John the Baptist met the violence the regime used to keep peace, followed by the slightly longer time of Jesus' public ministry before he, too, met with violence, it is perhaps most surprising just how long Paul was allowed to engage in his resistance against the empire. Let us hear now from the imperial Paul, in each of his distinctive voices, and then from the postcolonial Paul.

THE DEUTERO-PAULINE PAUL

The Apostle Paul invited little suspicion upon himself when he encouraged Jesus' followers in Rome to be subject to authorities. His position appears unambiguously pro-imperial in his letter to the Romans: "Let every person be subject to the governing authorities; for there is no authority except for God, and those authorities that exist have been instituted by God" (Rom. 13:1).

The presumption of Pauline authorship for Colossians, Ephesians, and 1 Timothy reinforces this pro-imperial image. Writing in Paul's name, anonymous authors reappropriated the very patriarchal values for the Christian assembly that Paul had opposed. Imperial values of hierarchy, order, and obedience became Christian values. The assembly became the "household of God," patterned after the patriarchal household, in which relations of domination and subordination govern the place of each in the household (1 Tim. 3:15).

The authors Christianized patriarchal household codes by equating masters with Christ. The primary obligation under imperial rule, obedience, now constitutes the condition of justification and salvation for women and slaves. Their sin is disobedience of the one who rules over them. By fusing the structures and norms of the patriarchal world with the proclamation of Christ, the deutero-Pauline authors gave the secular ideology of male and class privilege the status of revelation. It is God who wills gender and class subordination. Christ does not liberate the subordinate but requires their acceptance of the status quo in the social order.

Paul's disciples became the dominant voice of Paul, overshadowing the distinctiveness of his own voice. The theological tradition reinforced their voice, thus identifying Christianity with a fundamental distortion of creation—the very forms of privilege that Galatians 3:28 identifies as sinful and "no longer" operative in Christian community. In the development of the theology of original sin during the church's first centuries, Christian theologians—on the deutero-Pauline Paul's authority—will take domination as the solution to fallenness rather than as its manifestation.

The close identification of Paul with the values and mandates of the deutero-Pauline writers remains strong today. Yet to see him either as authorizing patriarchal structures or as oppressive because he does so is to mistake a later post-Paul tradition for the earlier, authentic, historical Paul. Even the authentic Paul's challenges to women prophets in 1 Corinthians or the principle of headship (1 Cor. 11:3)[5] fall short of the confidence with which the deutero-Pauline writers appropriate the household codes and identify the master with Christ.

Paul's lack of success in Corinth also contrasts with the success of the deutero-Pauline writers. As Antoinette Wire points out, Paul was not successful in subduing the Corinthian women prophets. 1 Clement, a letter written at the end of the first century, shows that women remained important leaders in that community.[6] In contrast, Protestant ministers in the American South were still appealing in the nineteenth century to Colossians, Ephesians, and 1 Timothy to justify slavery as divinely willed. Likewise, taking the New Testament texts as divine revelation, Catholic theologians until the end of the nineteenth century described the "doctrine of slavery" taught by the Roman Catholic Church as an "unbroken tradition." Slavery was justified as "natural," following Aristotle, or "unnatural" (a product of original sin) following Augustine. Either way it was described as a permanent part of the created order. Christian ownership of slaves was understood to be morally acceptable. In response to a papal letter on the American situation in 1839, Catholic bishops argued that slavery was a political, not a moral, problem. The fact that many of the bishops owned slaves, as did the Protestant ministers in the South, had something to do with the effort they expended on justifying the validity of the institution.

THE PAUL OF THE *ADVERSUS JUDAEOS* TRADITION

From the early church on, Christians have taken for granted a basic set of judgments about the Jews.[7] Statements like the following were common:

- Jews forfeited their covenant with God by rejecting Jesus as Messiah. Because of their faith, Christians replaced Jews as God's elected ones. Christianity is the "new Israel."

- Judaism was a religion of "works righteousness." Jews thought that by observing religious rules and rituals they would merit righteousness before God.

- Obsessed with following the law to the letter, the spirituality of the Pharisees was legalistic.

- The suffering of Jews is God's punishment of them for not acknowledging Jesus as God's Son.

- The Jews crucified God. They are guilty of deicide.

The supercessionism of Christian theology was prevalent not only in the form of replacement statements—Christians have superceded or replaced Jews as God's chosen people—but also in numerous expressions of superiority: church over synagogue, gospel over law, faith over law. Christians assumed that "the Jews," collectively, could have known simply by looking that Jesus was the divine Son of God if they had not so resisted the knowledge. Until it was removed from the Good Friday liturgy in 1959, Catholics in services all over the world prayed that the blindness of Jews be overcome:

> Let us pray also for the unfaithful Jews, that our God and Lord may remove the veil from their hearts; that they also may acknowledge our Lord Jesus Christ. Almighty and everlasting God, Who drivest not even the faithless Jews away from Thy mercy, hear our prayers, which we offer for the blindness of that people, that, acknowledging the light of thy truth, which is Christ, they may be rescued from their darkness.[8]

Armed with the power of the state, Christian councils from the fifth through the seventh centuries decreed a variety of restrictions on Jews, including barring them from office, forbidding marriage between Jews and Christians, prohibiting them from eating together, and restricting Jews from being in public during Easter. Later councils required Jews to adopt a distinctive dress and Jewish neighborhoods to be enclosed with gates locked at night. In the sixteenth century Martin Luther put this question to the German princes: "What then shall we Christians do with this damned, rejected race of Jews?" He answered his own question for them in a litany of actions:

> First, their synagogues. . . should be set on fire. . . . Secondly, their homes should likewise be broken down and destroyed. . . . Thirdly, they should be deprived of their prayer books and Talmuds. . . . Fourthly, their rabbis must be forbidden under threat of death to teach anymore. . . . Fifthly, passport and traveling privileges should be absolutely forbidden. . . . Sixthly, they ought to be stopped from usury. All their cash and valuables of silver and gold ought to be taken from them.[9]

Modern biblical scholars brought Christian anti-Judaism into their critical work, going so far as to separate Jesus from his own people. The Hebrew Bible scholar Martin Noth wrote: "Jesus himself, with his words and his work, no longer formed part of the history of Israel. In him the history of Israel had come, rather, to its real end."[10] Even liberation theologians—champions of unmasking the political and social ideologies of their own cultures—did not recognize their own inherited religious ideology of superiority. Gustavo Gutiérrez, the architect of liberation theology, reinforced the invalidity of Judaism, writing in 1973 in his now-famous *Theology of Liberation* that the "infidelities of the Jewish people made the Old Covenant invalid. . . ."[11]

Leonardo Boff, another influential liberation theologian, eloquently expressed the meaning of Christian discipleship shaped by the crucifixion of Jesus. Such commitment, he writes, involves "taking up a solidarity with the crucified of the world—with those who suffer violence, who are impoverished, who are dehumanized, who are offended in their rights."[12] Yet, turning to the Jews, arguably one of the most visible groups to suffer horrific genocidal violence in the twentieth century, Boff repeats the themes of the *adversus Judaeos* tradition in his 1987 work *Passion of Christ, Passion of the World:*

> Observance of the Mosaic law had become the very essence of postexilic Judaism. Sophistical interpretations and absurd traditions had caused the law to degenerate into a terrible slavery, imposed in the name of God…the law had become a prison with golden bars. Instead of being an aid to human beings in the encounter with their fellows and with God, the law shut them off from both, discriminating between those whom God loved and those whom God did not love, between the pure and the impure, between my neighbor whom I should love and my neighbor whom I may hate. The Pharisees had a morbid conception of God. Their God no longer spoke to human beings. Their God had left them a Law.[13]

A small, marginalized religious group, such as the early Christians, could engage in polemic and hate-mongering without too much effect in the real world. But with the conversion of Constantine in 311 C.E., Christianity became the imperial religion and remained dominant for the next 1500 years—surviving even the empire itself. Given its imperial context, Christianity's religious polemic carried real and often lethal consequences for Jews in the form of social, religious, and political discrimination, violent pogroms, and forced exile. Writings of the early church theologians "against the Jews" vilified and demonized the Jews. Medieval stories of Jews as agents of the devil fueled massacres.

The religious imperialism of the *adversus Judaeos* tradition claimed to find its justification in Paul. Here the problem was not the subversion of his thought by authors with very different interests than his but a selective reading of the authentic letters. Early Christian theologians took Paul's references to "new creation" and "new Israel" as confirmation that the old (Jews) had been replaced by the new (Christians) in the covenantal relation God had formed with humankind. They saw in Paul's harsh words about the law a divine rejection of the Jewish covenant. They read in Paul's description of the law as a "curse" sufficient evidence that Judaism was spiritually dead. Paul's conversion proved the superiority of Christianity. God revealed the risen Christ to Paul and, in response, Paul abandoned the spiritual darkness of the law for the light of the gospel. The "truth of the gospel" encompassed both the truth of Christianity and the falsity of Judaism. Paul's "one Lord, one faith" became the underpinning of an anti-Judaism, a position that, after the conversion of Constantine, had the backing of the *imperium*.

The deutero-Pauline Paul and the Paul of the *adversus Judaeos* tradition have both served imperialist interests. The former gave sacred status to pagan social institutions of gender and class oppression by militating against acceptance of women's equality with men and the freedom of slaves. Likewise, the supercessionist interpretation of Paul militated first against recognition of the authenticity of Jewish faith and the way of the Torah and, second, against affirming the salvific value of any non-Christian religion.

The Paul read by early Christian theologians as being in conflict with flourishing synagogues served imperial interests. The Paul of Ephesians and Colossians who Christianized patriarchal social institutions also served imperial interests. At the heart of imperialism is the denial of rights and even humanness to those made subject to another's rule. The appeal to Paul has justified Christian teachings on the legitimacy of slavery, male domination, the exclusivity of salvation, and the subjugation of peoples. The imperial Paul is no friend of freedom—for slaves, for women, or for Jews. But the authentic Paul identifies Christ quite explicitly with freedom: "For freedom Christ has set us free" (Gal. 5:1).

THE POSTCOLONIAL PAUL

After the Holocaust, biblical scholars began to question the *adversus Judaeos* tradition and turned to the New Testament with new questions: Did Paul really reject

Judaism? Did he pronounce the law spiritually dead? Does Paul's theology generate contempt for Jews?

Situating Paul in his social and historical context, a different picture began to emerge than the Paul seen by theologians in the early church.[14] Recent scholarship has concluded:

- Paul's conversion did not take him from one religion to another but from one Jewish party to another, from Pharisaic to Messianic Judaism.

- "The truth of the gospel" denoted for Paul not Christianity's superiority but God's inclusion of Gentile women and men in Israel's salvation "as they were," on the basis of their faith in Christ, not by becoming Jewish.

- Paul's diatribes against the law were not about Jews living the way of the Torah but about the need for Gentiles to become Jews to share in Israel's salvation.

- "Works of the law" was not Paul's short-hand for "works righteousness" but for "living as a Jew."

- "Faith in Christ" was not a theological proposition for Paul but an existential orientation toward the God of Israel.

- Paul's contrast between "faith" and "works" was not one between superior and inferior religions but between opposing conditions for membership in the covenant people of Israel.

- The law was not the norm for justification because God had validated one who had died "outside the law," that is, a death designated in the Torah as that of a sinner (Deut. 21).

- Paul was not the silencer of women we find in 1 Timothy—although he was not above trying with the Corinthian women prophets— but the friend and co-worker of Phoebe, Prisca, and Junia of Romans.

What did this Paul think of empire? If the Paul of Romans and Galatians did not have the imperialistic tendencies of the deutero-Pauline tradition or the *adversus Judaeos* interpretation, did he engage in a resistance strategy?

Yes. We know that he did not choose the way of bandit or assassin nor even that of a self-proclaimed messiah. The strategy he chose was the same that Jesus chose: proclamation. His proclamation of Christ destabilized and decentered the empire's claim to absolute power.[15]

Given an empire whose signature was violence, religious language mediated opposition through a kind of code language. Would the Roman emperors Domitian or Trajan have recognized that the author of the Book of Revelation was talking about *Rome* when an angel with great authority calls out with a mighty voice, "Fallen, fallen is Babylon the great! It has become a dwelling place of demons..." and another voice from heaven declares, "and she will be burned with fire; for mighty is the Lord God who judges her" (Rev. 18:2, 8)?

Using terms that echoed imperial self-designation, the effect of Jesus' and Paul's proclamation was subversion of the imperial ideology. Jesus and Paul both saw the social order through what scholars today call Jewish restoration eschatology. What is to be restored is Israel—its land and independence—and right relations between human beings and between God and human beings. Sin has distorted creation. Redemption is the righting of what sin has distorted.

In contemporary terms, Jewish eschatological thinking "beyond occupation" is an example of postcolonial thinking.[16] As is always the case, the *post-* is misleading. The colonizing power is still very much present. A chief feature of postcolonial thinking is its seeing beyond the oppressor's self-proclaimed right to rule, exploit, and destroy in the name of a natural superiority.

The new studies emphasize that the overriding context for Paul's ministry was the imperial order. What his proclamation opposed was the empire, not Judaism and the Jewish law. The challenge that the gospel of Christ makes is to the gospel of Caesar. Paul's emphasis on the sovereignty of God over the sovereignty of kingdoms means just that: the sovereignty of the empire is limited. Further examples reinforce this:

1. Crucified Jesus

A prime example of this resistance strategy is in Paul's proclamation of the crucified Jesus. "We preach Christ crucified" (1 Cor. 2:2), said Paul. Crucifixion was used for political executions by the Romans. To say that this man crucified by the state was raised by God undermines the power of the state. The Roman claim is that the empire's power is absolute. The resurrection undoes that claim.

Today we may easily miss the offense given by preaching the crucified Christ in the empire that crucified him. In effect Paul was saying that Caesar has been superceded by a crucified Messiah. The powerless one, executed by the Romans, is now proclaimed transcendent over them.

2. Resurrection

Proclamation of resurrection gave similar offense. In Jewish restoration eschatology, resurrection signaled the beginning of God's action against evil in history. Prime candidates for judgment were foreign rulers and occupiers. The beginning of God's reign implies the end of Rome's. It also signals the restoration of a distorted creation; Galatians 3:28 points to sites of distortion in the created order and envisions their transformation.

3. Lord

In imperial ideology, the emperor is Lord. He has absolute power over everything and everyone. Total submission and tribute are required from all. Paul's proclamation of "Lord Jesus Christ" (1 Thess. 1:1) unmasks imperial pretense and challenges the status quo. In fact, Paul's frequent fulminations against immorality and fornication may be allusions to imperial misconduct. Rome will not establish the ultimate kingdom, says Paul. Christ will do so at his return.

4. Ekklesia

The ancient Greek notion of *ekklesia* as the assembly of free citizens was, by Paul's time, a distant memory, a nostalgic anachronism. Paul's emphasis on *ekklesia* was a stubborn invocation of an ideal that the imperial order wanted to diminish. But further, Paul's communities are a genuine alternative social order. With Christ, the world will not be a field for conquest, possession, and exploitation. As Paul says, "When anyone is united to Christ, there is a new world; the old order is gone, and a new order has already begun" (2 Cor. 5:17).

5. Imperial cult

Beginning with the first emperor, imperial rulers were proclaimed Son of God or God. The Roman imperial cult was thus deeply offensive to the Jewish people. Participation in it through worship in temples dedicated to the emperor's name and his status as Son of God posed a strong threat to Jewish identity. Paul not only challenges this false God with the true God, he also appropriates the title Son of God for one who *gives up* honor, who "takes on the form of a slave" (Phil. 6:11). Jesus as Son of God reverses a whole system of honor-grabbing that goes right up to the emperor's arrogation of divinity to himself.

6. Gospel

The term *evangelion* was identified in the Roman world with imperial announcements, such as of the birth of a new royal child, an imperial military victory, or the ascension of a king. But "the gospel of God" (Rom. 1:1), by contrast, offers the good news of Jesus, who preaches that God is for the poor and marginalized and whose arrival has set in motion a transformation of values in the whole social order.

7. Salvation

Salvation was presented by the empire as the *Pax Romana,* a purportedly benign peace that was actually achieved by military conquest and kept in place by military violence. By contrast, the "Day of the Lord" (1 Thess. 5:2), says Paul, will mean deliverance for the faithful, even as it spells destruction for those who say "there is peace and security" (a Pauline allusion to the *Pax Romana).* Paul believes that the return of Christ will radically change the world, bringing about the end of empire and restoring creation's right relations. In Paul's eschatological perspective, Christ will destroy every ruler, power, and authority (1 Cor 15:24), and all things will be subject to him.

PAUL'S IRONIC LEGACIES

For the postcolonial Paul, then, Christ will destroy "every ruler, every authority and power" (1 Cor. 15:24). For much of the tradition Paul's statement was read abstractly, as if rules and powers and authorities did not have names. But in the first century all authority, power, and rule were Rome's. Rome is the empire that God will judge and that Christ will destroy. The reign of God will end the reign of Rome. Paul's execution by the Romans offers some evidence that his disruptive use of imperial language was not entirely lost on the authorities. Yet in succeeding generations, the interpretation of Paul's encounter with empire was to take three distinctly ironic turns:

First, with the deutero-Pauline distortion of Paul's message, freedom was returned to its place as a male elite privilege. The "household codes" would be considered God's will for women and slaves—women and men—until twentieth-century suspicion that the codes reflected interests more economic than divine.

Second, Paul's appropriation of imperial language contributed to Christian exclusivism. Did clothing the message in imperial terms make the message itself imperialistic?[17] Paul's emphasis on Christ as the sole and exclusive mediator of salvation was soon coupled with the church's claim to be the sole and exclusive mediator of Christ. To these christological and then ecclesiological layers was added an anthropological one: because of original sin, all are in need of Christ's grace of forgiveness mediated through the church's sacrament of baptism.

Defining salvation in terms of Christ and the church assured the inadequacy of other ways to God. If these other ways cannot meet these basic conditions for salvation, they cannot be a means of salvation. Once the church became an insider to the empire rather than a marginalized outsider, after Constantine's Edict of Milan in 311, the same empire that executed Jesus will require belief in him, and theology will take on a decidedly imperialist tone with Cyprian's principle, "Outside the church there is no salvation."

Third, once the exclusivist and imperialist interpretation was enthroned, the violence rejected by Jesus and Paul was justified in their names against non-Christians. Jews especially would suffer from the Christian indulgence in the human impulse from which religion is rarely free: claiming superiority for oneself and punishing the inferior for their difference.

Because of this legacy and the ongoing discovery of Paul's true meaning, the alternative he posed to empire is as relevant to the church as to the world, to today as to yesterday, to the individual person as to the whole social order. We can see, perhaps more clearly than other generations, the extreme challenge of Paul's momentous discovery of "the truth of the Gospel"—God's reign as the redemptive space of inclusion and freedom, repudiation of privilege, the compassionate befriending of those in bondage, the affirmation of the dignity and equality of all, and the experience of God's liberating humans from all forms of slavery, evil, and death. Recovering an authentic Paul is key to forging an authentic personal religious life today and an authentic Christian witness against the demonic imperialisms of our time.

FURTHER READING

Crossan, John Dominic, and Jonathan L. Reed. *In Search of Paul: How Jesus' Apostle Opposed Rome's Empire with God's Kingdom*. San Francisco, Calif.: Harper SanFrancisco, 2004.

Dunn, James D. G. *The Theology of Paul the Apostle*. Grand Rapids, Mich.: Eerdmans, 1998.

Elliott, Neil. *Liberating Paul: The Justice of God and the Politics of the Apostle*. Maryknoll, N.Y.: Orbis Books, 1994.

Horsley, Richard A., ed. *Paul and Empire: Religion and Power in Roman Imperial Society*. Harrisburg, Pa.: Trinity Press International, 1997.

CHAPTER 5

Athanasius of Alexandria

Rebecca Lyman

Athanasius (c.300-373), the bishop of Alexandria and defender of orthodoxy as defined by the Council of Nicaea in the fourth century, has been a lightning rod for historians and theologians. Described by some as a "gangster" for his use of force to advance his theological beliefs and revered by others as a "saint and martyr" for his unwavering opposition to heresy, he became bishop before he was thirty, at a time of tremendous social and religious change in the Roman Empire. Even Edward Gibbon conceded that Athanasius rather than the weak sons of Constantine was better qualified to rule an empire.[1]

In Athanasius's lifetime Christians went from their worst persecution under the reforming Emperor Diocletian to lavish patronage from the Emperor Constantine and his successors. Christian churches received unprecedented amounts of financial resources and political power as they were first raised to equal status with traditional religion and then increasingly favored as the central religion of the empire. At the same time many in the East and West were drawn into the complex and seemingly interminable Nicene controversy, which debated the divinity of Jesus through a new structure of state-sponsored ecumenical councils. Finally, in the countryside and cities, a spiritual revolution was taking place in which increasing numbers of women and men withdrew from the world to become ascetics. Athanasius's life and thought was therefore defined by incessant conflict and change as he found himself, by position as much as temperament, in the center of a new Roman Empire and a new Christian community.

THE CONSTANTINIAN SHIFT

In 312 Constantine, the son of a former ruler of the western Roman Empire, defeated his rival at the Milvian Bridge. Years later, according to his Christian friends, Constantine claimed that this victory had been given by Christ as a means of ensuring his rule. In 313 Constantine together with his co-ruler Licinius issued a statement that recognized Christianity as a legal religion, restored confiscated property, and asked for their prayers for the benefit of the empire. As Constantine's political power increased, he granted authority to bishops to act in legal cases and gave vast financial gifts to dioceses, attempted to mediate theological conflicts, and built monumental churches, especially in his new Eastern capital, Constantinople. Although Theodosius I would designate Christianity as the sole Roman religion in 395 and close down traditional temples, Constantine is usually heralded or vilified as the originator of the union of political power and Christian people which laid the foundations for the later "Caesaro-papism" of Western Europe and the union of church and imperial power in Byzantium.

This "Constantinian shift" has been regarded as a mixed blessing within the Christian community. For many Protestant Christians, both liberal and conservative, the events of the fourth century mark "the fall of the Church" since the patronage of Constantine hopelessly mixed the will of God with the will of the state and compromised the prophetic nature of the gospel by putting the church on the government payroll. Creeds should have no credibility since they were enforced by state power when Christian belief became a matter of citizenship rather than conviction.[2] However, for Christians in Orthodox traditions the age of Constantine marks the "baptism of Hellenism" and the regeneration of ancient culture through Christianity into the new society of Byzantium. This era sets the stage for the growth of a new Christian state in which bishops became integral social and political reformers and emperors were joined in solidarity to the poor through their common religious convictions. Bishops were to decide doctrine, but the emperor was to enforce it; educated laity had an active role within theological disputes. The prophetic voice was preserved in the monks, whose spiritual and social independence led them to challenge bishops and emperors alike.[3] Finally, for Roman Catholics the conversion of Constantine marks the uneasy alliance of church and state during which the church must vigilantly assert its moral ascendancy and spiritual superiority over the lay power of the ruler. Peter Brown described this attitude of the Western church as "twice born," since its leaders faced the barbarian invasions and the need for constant Christianization of new tribal rulers, in contrast to the cultural continuities of the East.[4]

Historically, this ecclesiastical and spiritual watershed is linked to the profound crisis of Roman power in the third century. After two centuries of political and economic expansion around the Mediterranean basin, Roman military strength had begun to stumble under the pressure of continuing wars. Roman power in the early empire had operated ideologically from Rome through the use of local leadership for the collection of taxes or military enlistment. Citizenship had been extended to all free men by Caracalla in 212; this move attempted to soften the earlier dichotomy between citizen and alien, though it did not eliminate and may have exacerbated the economic and social hierarchy of *honestiores* and *humiliores*.[5] However, the expense of debilitating border wars in the North with various tribes and in the East with Persia led to economic strain and political instability. Generals seized power in rapid succession. Rather than the aristocracy of the senate leading the empire, provincial men of humble background but superb military skill became emperors. The demand and costs for a larger army increased the bureaucracy and created an administrative centralization for the first time. When Diocletian, a freedman from Dalmatia and victorious general, became emperor in 284, he accomplished an entire series of administrative and economic reforms. He divided the unmanageable empire into two sections with two co-emperors. Within these halves, he doubled the number of provinces and then divided these smaller units into "dioceses" in order to have accountable administration and financial management. With the luck of a long reign, he instituted monetary reforms, tax reform, and new law codes to stabilize the "crisis of the third century."[6]

Religion was an important aspect of the political and social reorganization of the third century. While Christians had experienced local persecution occasionally in the first two centuries, imperial and systematic persecutions now emerged. In 250 for the first time the Emperor Decius required that all inhabitants sacrifice to the gods, perhaps to show the unity and piety of the empire. This was not directed particularly at Christians, but their refusal to sacrifice to idols created a number of new martyrs. At this time the emperor began to acquire divine titles as his power was identified with a growing henotheism that honored one god above all as the head of the universe; the cult of *Sol invictus* became a symbol of imperial unity and power.[7] Diocletian included religion in his plans to unify and restore the fortunes of the empire. In 295 he banned Manicheanism, a Persian form of Christianity, and ordered their sacred writings to be burned. In 303, in response to economic problems and advice from a group of philosophers wishing to revitalize traditional religion, Diocletian issued a series of edicts against Christians. He ordered that the books of Christians be destroyed, church buildings leveled, and clergy imprisoned. Eventually, all Christians were required to sacrifice or be executed. This last and most fierce of the ancient persecutions was particularly destructive in Egypt and Palestine. Especially in the Eastern cities, the Christian movement had matured from the scattered and charismatic house churches of the second century to episcopal structures of settled authority and power. When Diocletian began his attack, churches and clergy were easily identifiable. He watched a church burn the first night from the balcony of his palace in Nicomedia.[8]

The reversal of Christian persecution ten years later by the victorious Constantine was hailed by the beleaguered Christians as a miracle. He eventually refused to attend the traditional blood sacrifices and instructed that no new temples to traditional gods were to be built in Constantinople. Calling himself a bishop to those outside the church, Constantine through councils, consultation, threats, and exiles sought to have the bishops find solutions to their theological difficulties and become faithful citizens promoting the peace and stability of the empire. As Richard Vaggione pointed out, the emperor had a pressing need to control or co-opt a pre-existing system of power parallel to the state.[9] The third century had seen many aristocrats withdraw to their country estates, leaving the traditional civic offices and services vacant, and the fourth century was a period of rebuilding leadership. Bishops and deacons had become effective and unique urban mediators between the elite and the poor. Because bishops were elected for life, unlike Roman offices filled for set terms, and were protected from execution, they possessed an unusual longevity, influence, and cohesion with other leaders through councils. Large basilicas modeled on Roman assembly halls gave their liturgies and consultations a central place in the ancient cities. Bishops would become almost a parallel senate with significant influence on the emperor.[10]

In Egypt, Alexandria had been home for Christianity for several centuries when Athanasius was born around the turn of the century. Established by Alexander the Great as his namesake capital at the head of the Nile delta, Alexandria was the second city of the empire with great economic and cultural importance. The grain fleet carrying between four and eight million bushels was the lifeline of food and therefore domestic tranquility in Rome and later Constantinople as the source of the public dole. Alexandria was also the hub of trade and ideas flowing from the East. The city was polyglot with Roman power imposed over the Greek ruling families originally imported by Alexander, and with fewest rights going to the native Egyptians or Copts. Divided into ethnic quarters, the city often witnessed violence between Jews, Christians, and Greeks. Intellectually, its library and museum had been until recently a center for philosophical and philological study, influencing such famous scholars as Philo, Origen, and Plotinus. Christianity in such a context was deeply engaged with self-definition in regard to Greco-Roman and Jewish culture and extremely sophisticated in philosophy and exegesis. As with the Donatist controversy, the church had been divided as a result of the Great Persecution over the question of church discipline. Melitius of Lycopolis objected to Peter of Alexandria's restoration of those who had sacrificed, and a separate group was formed that persisted for several centuries.[11]

With the patronage of the emperor, the bishop of Alexandria in the fourth century became immensely powerful. Over the third century, episcopal power had concentrated over other church offices; traditional charismatic privileges such as the laity's right to preach, the teaching authority and mobility of widows, or the forgiveness of sins by confessors, were limited. In Alexandria the bishop's jurisdiction now extended beyond the city to the whole of Egypt, including another one hundred bishops. The Council of Nicaea would affirm Alexandria's broader jurisdiction and pre-eminence among the Eastern churches. Due to the wealth of the city, the resources of the church had been increasing even before Constantine's largesse. Bishops could influence the grain shipments, and could demand obedience from captains of ships. As the Christian population increased dramatically in Egypt from 310 to 360, the power of the bishop as patron within the society and politician among other bishops of the East also increased.[12]

For the most part, Christians welcomed the patronage of the emperor when it worked to their own advantage but could easily draw on older images of martyrdom and opposition to political power when they disagreed. For example, the Donatists initially hailed Constantine's mediation. But when the state opposed them, they compared themselves to martyrs who had always resisted Roman power. Eusebius of Caesarea was the most fulsome in his celebration of the saving moment of salvation history in which the Roman state was now brought under the rule of God, but this was also to ensure state enforcement and leadership of a Christian agenda. Like other bishops, Athanasius spoke against state coercion as a religious policy, but he welcomed its application toward those he considered to be heretics. He judged emperors by their theological choices rather than by any blind loyalty. The murder of Athanasius's patron, the Emperor Constans, for example, could be considered a martyrdom; Constantius could be a Christian ruler or Pharaoh depending on the most recent ecclesiastical council.[13]   For ordinary people on the ground the new imperial structures and political role of the church created a new access to public participation. Theological groups and class concerns were increasingly mixed in unprecedented ways.[14]   Ideologically, the transition from a persecuted sect rooted in an apocalyptic language of opposition and martyrdom to a church that was integral to the administration of a new society could not be an easy or an obvious one. Ambrose successfully called the emperor to account and repentance as a layman; John Chrysostom was deposed as an idealistic nag. If bishops became adept at imperial politics, bribes, and free transport, emperors also began to adopt Christian tones and manner in order to communicate to and control their restive populations.[15]

ATHANASIUS *CONTRA MUNDUM*

The valorization of Athanasius as standing alone "against the world" of heretical bishops and emperors has turned his life into an ecclesiastical *Odyssey* in which the wiley bishop defeats various obstacles and monsters before being able to return home to his faithful household in triumph. Since we receive his story framed by the normative theology of the Council of Nicaea, we may find it difficult to imagine him less a solitary hero than one of the most powerful of many wiley bishops engaged less in a journey than an all-out war for theological and ecclesiastical dominance in the eastern part of the empire. Traditional accounts, which had leaned heavily on Athanasius's extensive—and defensive—histories of the Nicene conflict, naturally adopted his view of a binary struggle between truth and error. Recent histories have softened this opposition of "orthodox" and "Arian" to show the multiple theologies and shifting alliances that developed over the fifty-six years from the Council of Nicaea in 325 to the Council of Constantinople in 381.[16] The Nicene orthodoxy adopted by Theodosius was in fact neo-Nicene; it was actually developed by the Cappadocians and other second-generation thinkers rather than Athanasius.[17] His innovative actions in establishing the Egyptian church and his devastating theological polemics remain his greatest legacy.

Like the generals who became emperor or the provincial *honestiores* who formed

Constantine's new Senate in Constantinople, Athanasius was another socially modest man who achieved great power through patronage and ability. With a basic rhetorical and biblical education, he was groomed by Bishop Alexander as a promising and brilliant young deacon to be his successor. Scholars disagree as to whether he was in fact Egyptian or perhaps was a mixture with Greek inheritance, as was Origen. But he was certainly able as bishop to inspire the broader population of Egypt in a way not previously done.[18] Several scholars would now date his apologetic work *De Gentes—De Incarnatione* to his twenties along with a letter previously attributed to his predecessor, Alexander, *Henos Somatos*. These writings exhibit a robust celebration of the paradox of the transcendent creator God taking suffering flesh to enter into the world. This incarnation reversed the terrible decay and mortality initiated by the fall, so that human beings were now restored and delivered from death and history into divinization. If mummy portraits eroded, the new resurrection body did not. Incarnation as celebrating the transformation of passive and enslaved material human nature by divine intervention remained axiomatic to Athanasian spirituality and theology: "He became human that we might become divine; and he manifested himself through a body that we might receive the conception of the invisible Father."[19]

This early dating allows Athanasius to be active in the first stages of the Nicene controversy and therefore perhaps a more obvious candidate for the bishop of Alexandria. The Nicene controversy began around 318 when Arius, a popular presbyter and ascetic, and Bishop Alexander argued about the origin and status of the incarnate Son: could he be from the essence of the Father and if not, how could he be divine? Alexander defined the Son as the essential image of the Father who had been begotten eternally and mysteriously from him in order to show and communicate to humans the divine essence. Since his works were largely destroyed, all reconstructions of Arius remain controversial; but he seemed to argue that since the Father was by nature unbegun and therefore unable to share his essence by definition, his Son should be defined as coming into existence by the will, not generation. The Son possessed a direct and derivative divinity, so that he could act as a revealer of God and exemplar for humans in the incarnation, but he did not share the same nature as the Father. The conflict rapidly escalated as both men enlisted allies from around the Mediterranean. Arius appealed to the tradition of Lucian of Antioch and enlisted support from such powerful allies as Eusebius of Caesarea and Eusebius of Nicomedia. In Alexandria there seem to have been popular demonstrations including women ascetics, lawsuits, and separate meetings. This exegetical and cosmological question on the origin of the Son somehow touched a nerve in the early fourth century concerning monotheism, salvation, and Christian identity.

When local synods failed to quiet the participants, Constantine summoned a council at Nicaea to sort out the problem, rebuking them for publicly quarrelling like philosophers over obscure points and disrupting the peace of the church. If Arius was present at the council, he was a nonvoting figure, as was the deacon Athanasius, since bishops alone were voting representatives. The term *homoousios* (of the same substance or being) seems to have been included only because it was rejected by Eusebius of Nicomedia and others. Two bishops from Libya who refused to sign the statement and Arius were exiled. Eusebius of Nicomedia signed the creed but was later exiled because he gave hospitality to followers of Arius. A number of important matters of ecclesiastical jurisdiction were also agreed upon, including allowing the Melitians back into the Alexandrian church. Alexander signed the creed but did not make peace at home with the Melitians.

In 328 Alexander died. But like his precedessor, Peter, he designated a successor: Athanasius. He was opposed by the Melitians as being too young, and probably also because of his association with Alexander. At some point Athanasius and a small band withdrew, and he was elected in secret. For the next seven years he attempted to retain power through what often appears to be rough means and to continue the policies of his patron, Alexander. He refused Constantine's request to receive Arius in Alexandria after a small council in Nicaea determined his theological orthodoxy. In 331 he was formally accused by the Melitians of an uncanonical election, extortion, bribery, and sacrilege. Constantine dismissed the charges. In 334 sacrilege and murder as well as sexual impropriety were raised. But the murdered man turned up alive and the prostitute could not identify him, so he was again acquitted. In 335 he was called to appear before a hand-picked council of his episcopal enemies in Tyre to answer again to charges of violence. He appeared with forty-eight Egyptian bishops who were not allowed to participate. When convicted, he fled to Constantinople to plead directly to the emperor. Constantine granted him a pardon but later sent him into exile when the charge surfaced that he was inhibiting the grain shipments from Egypt. His accusers declared that he was "rich, powerful and capable of anything," but he pleaded that he was only a poor man.[20] These events seem to be a combination of rough urban tactics by supporters, continuing theological divisions in Alexandria, lingering resentments from many Eastern bishops over the theological formula at Nicaea (which seemed to obscure the traditional distinction of two *hypostases* or persons in the Godhead), and the desire of Eusebius of Nicomedia to control the events in the East by crippling his most significant rival from Alexandria.[21] Everyone was learning how to play theological hardball.

With the death of Constantine in 337, this period of "enforced encounter" and managed peace through exile ended, and a new era of "personality" and "identity creation" began. The battles became increasingly heated and technical not because of profound theological differences but rather because in fact so much was shared in common and progress occurred only incrementally.[22] The new emperor, Constantius, enjoyed theological debate and found the views of the Eusebian party in the East the most hopeful for ecclesiastical peace. In 339 during his third exile, Athanasius enlisted the support of the Bishop of Rome, Julius I. Here he composed his first polemical works in concert with another exiled bishop, Marcellus of Ancyra. Marcellus was a controversial ally due to his assertion of only one *hypostasis* and no eternal distinction between the Father and Son. When asked about associating with such a potential heretic, Athanasius reportedly only smiled. Together they turned the alliances of the Eusebian bishops into a single heretical party of "Arians." Arius and his original theology became irrelevant except as a heretical category to be attached to opponents of Nicaea.[23] Using conventional heresiological categories, a "school" was created based on a demonically inspired teacher, and diverse opinions could be melded into a coherent sect relentlessly opposed to the apostolic truth of the orthodox. To be an Arian was no longer to be a Christian, and the designation came to be associated with outsiders such as Jews, Greeks, or Manichees. Portrayed as philosophical not biblical, political not holy, and effeminate not masculine, Arians opposed the "holy" Alexander and the decisions of Nicaea.[24] This binary opposition in the extensive works of Athanasius over the next thirty years turned Arius from a historical opponent into a mythological heresiarch and the shifting theological alliances into a vast imperial and demonic conspiracy. Constantius's support of the Eusebian theology in the East made him a forerunner of the Antichrist in Athanasius's eyes.[25] In reality the polemical title of "Arian" did not figure in all controversies of the fourth century, nor was it used as a theoretical boundary in contradistinction to Modalism; Athanasius himself modified the term, using it later only for the most extreme non-Nicenes, the "Neo-Arians," and upholders of the Homoian creed of 359.[26]

In 346 Athanasius returned to Alexandria. During this time as well as a later period of hiding in the desert (356-361), he built alliances and ties with the many monks and bishops outside the city which created a cohesive identity of Nicene Egyptian Christianity with personal ties to the Bishop of Alexandria. Each Easter Athanasius had issued a Festal letter that celebrated Christian endurance over against pagans, Jews, or heretics. They are based primarily on Scripture and exhort a life modeled on ascetic practices of obedience, humility, and faith. [27] The church under the direction of the bishop was the sole and unified home for all Christians, lay or ordained, urban or rural. Athanasius also appointed reluctant monks as bishops, arguing that public service overrode personal perfection. One of these Festal letters contained the first direction concerning appropriate private reading, and the list of books that Athanasius considered to be canonical.[28] His famous account of the *Life of Antony* is another example of his blend of religious instruction and ecclesiastical cohesion. In the story, Antony is portrayed as a simple Egyptian whose spiritual power comes from his direct encounter with Christ, not from education or worldly status. Antony is also an enemy of Arians and a supporter of the Alexandrian bishop. Indeed Athanasius can claim a sheepskin bequeathed to him from the holy man.[29] Egyptian Christian identity therefore was forged around Scripture, episcopal loyalty, and Nicene belief.

Upon the ascension of a new emperor, Julian, Athanasius returned from the desert to Alexandria. Julian had rejected his Christian upbringing—perhaps due to the high rate of murder among heirs to the throne—and was determined to restore the dominance of traditional Greco-Roman religion. He cut off funds to the Christians, and recalled all parties of bishops from exile. Athanasius acted quickly to begin reconciliation among competing alliances. A new generation of thinkers, the Neo-Arians, now opposed Nicaea and *homoousios* by a dependence on "exact" language. By his willingness to reconcile with former opponents at a council in 362 and include "inexact" language, Athanasius forged a new, broader consensus that acknowledged shared orthodox intentions. Exiled by Julian in 363 and again by Valens in 366, Athanasius died in Alexandria in 373 after an unprecedented forty-five years in office, including fifteen years and ten months in exile.

ORTHODOXY AS A POLEMICAL DISCOURSE

According to Edward Gibbon and many others since, the decline of reason and civilization began with the rise of Christianity, whose violent monks and dogmatic bishops eventually overwhelmed the skeptical Greek academies and the reasoned tolerance of Roman law. The persistent violence and sectarian politics of the theological controversies of the fourth and fifth centuries do provide a convincing amount of evidence as to an essential intolerance within Christianity. The valorization of theological conflict in church history has created the heroic "fathers of the church" who saved the apostolic faith from demonic and intellectual heretics to create a moderate and populist orthodoxy. If the historical means were shocking, the theological results were justifiable.

To our modern eyes the development of orthodoxy in the imperial church has all the attributes of a "totalizing discourse" with both political and spiritual power.[30] The earlier theological diversity of Christian house churches was now disciplined by local bishops who represented their regions at councils. Public orthodoxy created an official and public topography of authorized meeting spaces and holy places. Just as Athanasius wished to regulate private reading or ascetic households, other bishops banned private gathering or worship spaces.[31] The binary categorization of the world into orthodox and heretical provided a clear map for discerning not only theological formulas but later, with the legislation of Theodosius, civil rights as well. If the empire was protected by correct worship and belief, then the enforcement of theological decisions became a matter of public safety. The exile of deviant thinkers and the suppression of their works was a public duty that constructed the unified and holy world. Equally important, violence itself as a defense of Christ and Christianity can be easily justified within the apocalyptic discourse of demonic error and holy truth.

For many ancient historians, the problem with emerging Caesaro-papism is not therefore the emperor, but the church. According to Richard Lim, the Christian propensity for debate and division left over from sectarian origins was simply exacerbated by imperial power. Christian fractiousness perpetuated civil war within the empire as the rational traditions of political debate were erased by an appeal to intellectual obfuscation and passion.[32] More sympathetically, Hal Drake argued that violent sectarianism was not necessary to ancient Christianity per se, but the fear of heresy overrode even Christian traditions against religious coercion and allowed theological militants to gain an upper hand.[33] Others have noted that a focus on Christian violence in late antiquity without a corresponding attention to pagan or routine state violence can easily distort our historical evaluation. Both apologists and critics can separate an "essential" Christianity from culture, which allows either a secular discourse (where religion or passion is inevitably a source of disunity at the expense of rational statecraft) or a religious whitewash (which attributes all misbehavior to secular politics).[34] Unquestionably, the continuing theological debates in the fifth century—especially between the episcopal rivals of Alexandria, Antioch, and Constantinople—weakened the later Roman Empire. As Michael Gaddis commented, the religious violence was the clash between the authorities' determination to preserve unity and the extremists' vision of absolute truth, both of which were deeply rooted in Roman Christian tradition.[35] The ultimate legacy of this clash was a variety of Christianities separated by language, culture, and theology. The Muslim empire offered repressive pluralism in place of imperial Christian coercive harmony.[36]

CONTEMPORARY ASSESSMENTS

Recent studies of the Roman Empire in light of postcolonial theory and new theories of globalism may help us to re-evaluate some common assumptions about the rise of councilor orthodoxy. For the most part, Roman political structures have received a positive evaluation, especially by Western scholars concerned to defend their own European imperialism or Enlightenment values rooted in classical antiquity.[37] Now, Romanization is seen as a less uniform or even desirable process but rather a means of "structuring a system of differences" through local adaptation of certain cultural values to achieve a "general Mediterranean language of success."[38] Admittedly, in contrast to elite literary culture like the Greek *paideia*, Roman *humanitas* through behavior or action could be absorbed by all, although class and economic distinctions were never erased. Identity was increasingly expressed by degree or common behavior rather than a binary opposition of citizen or alien.[39] Romanization could be seen not as a centrally imposed or a binary system but rather as a discourse among elites with an emphasis on connectivity. These recent interpretations focus on the adaptation and negotiation of Roman values by locals for their own advantage. Indeed "glocalization" describes the use of outside objects to reassert local self-identity.[40]

In this framework, the conflicting interpretations and interests of bishops in the imperial councils could be seen as an interesting example of glocalization in which urban leaders sought to assert local identities through their control of imperial instruments of unity. Orthodoxy itself has long been seen by sympathetic interpreters as focused on "connectivity" rather than uniformity, since creeds were public theological compromises to include multiple rather than technical interpretations. The importance of local tradition can explain the historical negotiation and ambiguity that lie beneath the binary discourse of orthodoxy and heresy. Like the empire itself, Christianity remained pluralistic in local practice and interpretation. And, like the empire itself, enforcement of external boundaries through categories such as Arians or Manichees actually offered little help when fresh internal controversies began. Whose theological ancestors would end up as icons of error and whose would feature in the diptychs of orthodoxy? In the Monophysite controversy Egypt and Syria could not be reconciled to the christological formulas.

Imperial Christianity attempted to construct an unprecedented demographic and geographical unity yet with the potentially apocalyptic language of heresiology ever-present in instruments of unity. Orthodoxy was inherently unstable as a disciplining hybrid of positions that increasingly suited no one. Michel Foucault commented in *Discipline and Punish* that the new social technologies of the body in the transformation of penal institutions in Europe were best enforced by internal cognitive constructions: "The soul is the effect and instrument of a political anatomy; the soul is the prison of the body." We may reflect that the discourse of heresiology paradoxically performed a similar function in the imperial church, in which doctrinal obedience to regulate episcopal authority or ascetic practices increasingly made "orthodoxy" a prison for the church.[41]

CONTEMPORARY IMPLICATIONS OF ATHANASIUS'S THEOLOGICAL WORK

On his deathbed, John Wesley wrote to the weary William Wilberforce to encourage him to continue his decades-old fight in the British Parliament against the African slave trade: "Unless the Divine Power had raised you up to be as Athanasius *contra mundum*, I see not how you can go through your glorious enterprise. . . ."[42] The Christian valorization of theological heroism can be a powerful stimulus for prophetic political action. Yet it has idolatrous potential when theology is defined as a static discourse and negotiation treated as apostasy. Athanasius and Wilberforce achieved their goals by negotiation as much as by tenacity; Wesley, we must remember either proudly or sadly, was a schismatic. Edward W. Said commented shrewdly that the disenchantment of Western intellectuals with narratives of emancipation is the other side of the nostalgia for empire: no one wants to be "outside" the comfort of essentialism and without special historical privileges to confront the discrepant experiences of diverse cultures and experiences.[43]   In contemporary global Christianity, the polemical categories of heresiology and appeals to essential orthodoxy continue to have irresistible power, especially in addressing ideas that challenge the political or ecclesiastical status quo.

Athanasius's attack on his opponents was rooted in a defense of the essential Fatherhood and the Sonship within the Trinity, yet deconstruction of this masculine imagery by theologians has evoked much "nostalgia" for empire on the part of even liberal thinkers. The unique authority of the revealed masculine names of the Trinity has been not only a theological building block but also an important piece of the construction of male power within Christianity. An affirmation of materiality and body that focuses only on a passive recipient with absolute exclusion of any feminine imagery can hardly be considered theologically adequate.[44] Even historical challenges to the necessity of the Alexandrian incarnational model that attempt to reconstruct an alternative ancient Christology focused less on human passivity and more on cooperative grace can be dismissed as "liberal" or "modern."[45]

Ecumenism and ecclesiastical apologies have begun to break down the triumphal history of orthodoxy for a larger embrace of a diverse Christian community. The ancient schism between the Egyptian and Greek churches has been slowly mended through concentration on their common theological ancestor, Cyril of Alexandria. The Roman Catholic Church has issued several apologies for the condemnation and persecution of innocent persons labeled as heretics, such as Galileo. These events are steps toward a sort of restorative justice, famously used in South Africa, to mend a community by remembering and repenting difficult history rather than separating. Historians have noted for decades that the theological icons of error that define the boundaries of traditional orthodoxy are false: Arius, Nestorius, and Pelagius either did not teach what was accused of them or later changed their position. Whether this acknowledgment of demonization and labeling can be extended to interfaith relations to affirm context and negotiation rather than abstraction and negation remains to be seen. Rising conflicts in global Christianity over "orthodoxy" and "culture" seem to indicate the language of heresiology is too useful and powerful to abandon just yet.[46]

Finally, the construction of a dynamic and interdependent spiritual world in Christian antiquity offers an intriguing resource for current thinking on dialogue and authority. However cynical we may be about the relation of bishops to ordinary believers, the acknowledgment of spiritual power in holy men and women, places, objects, and eventually icons can be the source of a fresh vision, especially for the secularized Western view. An acceptance of the in-breaking of the holy from marginal and unexpected voices was an important balance to political and ecclesiastical power in the East. The belief that simple monks could outdebate philosophers or ordinary married people humiliate monks by their hidden righteousness could now be retrieved less to support professional holiness than to affirm the authority of the trickster or the prophet to challenge global or racial bias in Christian theology. Theological tradition should valorize the Syrophoenician woman as well as Athanasius. Beneath the ritualized foot washing of Christendom lies the human commonality of the beggar and the king, which gated communities of democratic affluence have effectively destroyed. Retrieving the immanence of the divine image in the physical human being is therefore a needed corrective to the often dualistic traditions of the West; using Emmanuel Levinas to expand Athanasius's passionate defense of incarnation to embrace the inassimilable other might be the most redemptive exercise.[47]

FURTHER READING

Primary Sources

Antatolios, Khaled, ed. *Athanasius*. London: Routledge, 2004.
Gregg, Robert, ed. *The Life of Antony and the Letter to Marcellinus*. Classics of Western Spirituality. New York, N.Y.: Newman Press, 1979.

Secondary Sources

Antatolios, Khaled. *Athanasius: The Coherence of His Thought*. London: Routledge, 1998.
Barnes, Timothy. *Athanasius and Constantius: Theology and Politics in the Constantinian Empire*. Cambridge, Mass.: Harvard University Press, 1993.
Burrus, Virginia. *"Begotten, Not Made": Conceiving Manhood in Late Antiquity*. Stanford: Stanford University Press, 2000.
Burrus, Virginia, ed. *Late Ancient Christianity*, A People's History of Christianity, vol. 2. Minneapolis, Minn.: Fortress Press, 2005.

Drake, Hal. *Constantine and the Bishops: The Politics of Intolerance*. Baltimore, Md.: Johns Hopkins University Press, 2000.

Gaddis, Michael. *There Is No Crime for Those Who Have Christ: Religious Violence in the Christian Roman Empire*. Berkeley, Calif.: University of California Press, 2005.

Rapp, Claudia. *Holy Bishops in Late Antiquity: The Nature of Christian Leadership in an Age of Transition*. Berkeley, Calif.: University of California Press, 2005.

Vaggione, Richard Paul. *Eunomius of Cyzicus and the Nicene Revolution*. Oxford: Oxford University Press, 2000.

Chapter 6

Augustine of Hippo

Anthony J. Chvala-Smith

At Easter in 387 a former pagan orator from North Africa, recently converted to Christianity, came to the church in Milan to receive baptism from Ambrose, the bishop of the city. The orator's name was Aurelius Augustinus. Western theology since has stood under his shadow. Augustine of Hippo (354-430), rhetorician turned Christian bishop, became for the medieval church *the* authoritative theologian, whose interpretations of scripture and creed were benchmarks for over a millennium.[1] Both Reformation and Counter-Reformation theologians assumed him to be the champion of their positions and strip-mined his writings to buttress their opposing claims.

For moderns and postmoderns, Augustine's heritage has become more like an intellectual aquifer: an underground source that silently forms and informs life, and sometimes deforms it. Whether Christian or not, we still drink from Augustine's well. *The Confessions*, the narration of his journey to Christian faith, is a Western classic: not surprisingly, psychotherapy, which arose on Western soil, is hard to imagine apart from Augustine's legacy of self-analysis. Many of our experiential and theological categories—guilt, sin, grace, anxiety about sexuality, freedom, predestination, just war, selfhood—owe something to him. This figure from late antiquity has a curious power to address and move readers still.

Augustine's Context: The Vulnerable Empire

With Augustine, theology and biography are inseparable. It is helpful that he left a colossal amount of information about himself.[2] From his letters, sermons, treatises, commentaries, and books; from the biography of him by his contemporary, Possidius; and from a vastly improved critical knowledge of the later Roman Empire, contemporary scholarship has ably charted the contours and textures of his life and times.

Augustine's theology is profitably understood in relationship to three major contextual factors: the Roman Empire, the cultural setting of North Africa, and the Constantinized situation of the church in the late fourth century.

We consider first how the all-pervasive social and political reality of the Roman Empire shaped the world in which Augustine grew up. Even in a Christianized Roman Empire, school children—like the precocious North African youth Augustine—still memorized the poetry of the ancient pagan author Virgil, with its lyric myth of Rome's vocation: "be thy charge, O Roman, to rule the nations in thine empire; this shall be thine art, to ordain the law of peace, to be merciful to the conquered and beat the haughty down."[3] Romans remained in awe of their achievements. Augustine could speak of the "terrestrial glory of that most excellent empire."[4] To land a position in the imperial bureaucracy, or better, at the imperial court, was the hope of educated youths. The pre-conversion Augustine had, while in Italy, come up to the edge of such greatness, having received appointment to serve as court orator. In the late-fourth century C.E., the empire and its symbolism remained, to use Peter Berger's expression, the sacred canopy of Mediterranean life. A world apart from Roman domination was conceivable only negatively, as imperial rhetoric termed those outside of Roman control "barbarians."

At the same time the empire was undergoing far-reaching transformations. When Constantine died in 337, there would never again be a sole emperor of a united Rome. By 340, the Empire was split between Constantine's two sons, Constans and Constantius.[5] Henceforth there would be two empires: a western, Latin-speaking one, and an eastern Greek-speaking one. In Augustine's day Rome, though symbolically weighty, was no longer functioning as capitol, that honor being shared by Milan and then Ravenna in the West, and Constantinople, the "New Rome," in the East.

Notwithstanding widely held convictions regarding Rome's permanence, Augustine's theology emerged within a radically endangered empire. Constant warfare, economic woes, internal cultural shifts, and the increasing incursions of barbarian tribes along the imperial frontiers led Peter Brown to describe Augustine's world as "on the edge of dissolution."[6] The nomads of Africa's Saharan border and the once-suppressed tribes of the European hinterland now roamed freely, striking where they would. As the center of political gravity shifted to the East, the last two decades of Augustine's life brought two catastrophes that transformed the West: the sack of Rome and the fall of North Africa.

In 410 Alaric's Gothic army stormed into the Eternal City and devastated it. Refugees brought the news to North Africa, recounting the horrors of the assault. Africa, once secure from such threats and already imperiled by incursions of desert tribes, was swiftly becoming vulnerable to Rome's fate. In 428 the unthinkable happened again. Possidius recounts that "a vast army...came by ship from Spain across the sea and poured into Africa."[7] This army of Arian Vandals, Alans, and Goths swept along the coast of North Africa. They reached the gates of Hippo in 430, penning in its citizens and refugees. The tale of slaughter that had come before them left Hippo's bishop, Augustine, grief-stricken: "the part of his life that he endured almost at the very end was thus the bitterest and saddest of his old age."[8] He died during the siege.

The second contextual factor that influenced Augustine's theology was his African cultural setting. Apart from a single trip to Italy, Augustine spent his life in North Africa within one hundred miles of his childhood home. He was born in Thagaste, some fifty miles from the Mediterranean, in that area of Roman North Africa today called Algeria. This fertile strip of land along the coast was the bread basket of the empire. Home to Latin-speaking descendents of Roman colonists, Greek-speaking sailors and merchants, Punic-speaking descendents of the Phoenicians, and the indigenous Berber-speaking peasants, the Africa Augustine knew was of mixed cultures.[9] And so was Augustine himself. As a *Roman* African, Augustine was by birth and his parents' ambitions for him allied with imperial interests. His father Patricius, a city counselor who possessed some land and slaves, insisted his son be educated for a public career.[10] Augustine's devoutly Christian mother, Monica, bears a name of Berber origin, and following Berber custom, Augustine named his own son Adeodatus ('Godsend'). It remains an open question whether Augustine was fluent in either Punic or Berber, though in this multi-lingual environment, Augustine clearly preferred Latin. As a trained rhetorician Augustine the African was literate, articulate, and polished: at once unlike many people among whom he ministered, and yet, also one of them. Indeed, Augustine always thought of himself as an African, and recent research into his ethnicity has shown rather convincingly that he was part Berber.[11]

The Christianity of Augustine's homeland was fervent, at times even fanatical.

The same North Africa that produced Augustine had, in the second and third centuries, bequeathed two brilliant, if rigorist, theologians to the church, Tertullian and Cyprian. Unlike Hellenized Alexandria, Christianity in North Africa hesitated to cultivate intellectual points of contact with pagan philosophy. Further, North Africa had contributed its share of martyrs in the great persecutions of the third and early fourth centuries, its numerous shrines to the martyrs attesting the cost of being Christian. And it was North Africa that birthed Donatism, a separatist Christian movement that was to split the African Church until the Islamic conquest in the seventh century.

Understanding Augustine's thought requires recognition of both its distinctive African hues and its striking independence. Rooted in North Africa, Augustine developed a theology of marked universality. While he shared North African Christianity's preoccupation with ecclesiology and biblical interpretation,[12] he did not share in its sectarianism. This was partly due to his sustained engagement with non-Christian literature. His education and his long pre-Christian quest for truth left him deeply respectful of the pagan classics, and willing to seek and acknowledge insights from outside his Christian convictions. He remained in dialogue with Roman literary and philosophical traditions until his death. Admiration for such voices as Cicero, Sallust, Varro, and Plotinus saved his theology from the regionalism and narrowness it might have had. In this he departs dramatically from the religious culture that shaped him.

The third contextual factor vital for understanding Augustine's theology is the Constantinization of the church. The church that baptized him was far from being the bizarre, antisocial sect Romans had once thought it to be. In the fourth century, the Emperor Constantine's formal endorsement of Christianity rendered it the only *religio licita.* The church's life became interwoven with the empire's in intricate ways. Paganism persisted, but Christianity's eclipse of it would soon be total: during Augustine's life pagan worship was finally declared illegal. Augustine was baptized in a setting in which the large-scale social revolution effected by Christian faith during the previous century had created a new, complex relationship between church and empire.

One cannot overstress that the church Augustine joined was already a Constantinized institution. Its legitimacy in Roman society was assumed and assured. Unlike his North African counterparts a century earlier, Augustine could take for granted the idea of a Christian emperor and even hold up Constantine and Theodosius as exemplars of piety.[13] Augustine also assumed the long-standing right of the empire to intervene in church matters, first asserted by Constantine at the Synod of Arles in 314 and again in 316, at the start of the Donatist controversy.[14] As civil society disintegrated in North Africa, Augustine would plead with Count Boniface to stay a soldier, and not become a monk, so that he could serve God by protecting the church from marauding desert barbarians.[15] The picture of a Christian bishop encouraging a Roman general to stay at his post to protect church and society reveals the radically different situation of Christianity in Augustine's time.

The imperial church context shaped, to some extent, the sources of Augustine's theology. His ministry, first as a presbyter (391-395) then as bishop (395-430), occurred between the Council of Constantinople (381) and the Council of Ephesus (431), and therefore at a time when the Church's canon and doctrine of God had stabilized.

Augustine's setting made him *de facto* an expounder of creed and sacred text. When he was born in 354, the contours of the New Testament were still porous. Cyril of Jerusalem's *Catechetical Lectures* (c. 350), for example, did not include the Apocalypse of John in its canonical list. But by the early fifth century, custom and conciliar decision had fixed the New Testament at twenty-seven books. Moreover, when Augustine was born, the Nicene solution to the question of the nature of God was still widely contested, many preferring instead some version of Arianism, the doctrine that the Son of God was not of the same substance as the Father, but a kind of lesser deity. But by Augustine's death, Arianism had receded into the shadows, except among Goths and Vandals, to be replaced in the mid-fifth century by new christological controversies. While Augustine's theology manifests creativity, even novelty, it is important to see him as the interpreter of a theological consensus he inherited and accepted. In this sense, he was quintessentially Catholic.

Nevertheless, the Catholic Church Augustine joined in North Africa was an embattled minority.[16] When he became Bishop of Hippo, Christians in North Africa had for over eighty years been bitterly divided into Catholic and Donatist factions. The otherwise orthodox Donatists rejected the authority of Catholic clergy and the validity of Catholic sacraments. They charged that during the persecution under Diocletian (c. 303), some North African clergy had handed over the Scriptures to Roman authorities. By this act they forfeited their sacramental authority, and Donatists believed that any subsequent ordinations and baptisms performed by these *traditores* were invalid. The efficacy of the sacraments depended on the purity of the officiants, the Donatists claimed. Since they could only be sure of the purity of their own clergy, they maintained that they alone, in all the empire, embodied the true church. Even with their charges and claims rejected by earlier councils, the Donatists persisted and thrived. In 347 at the behest of North African Catholics, Count Macarius used force against the Donatists.[17] Compulsion only hardened their resolve, and the hostility it fomented created the intractable situation Augustine inherited as bishop: decades of allegations, hatred, and violence between two otherwise nearly identical Christian communities.

AUGUSTINE AS INTERPRETER OF THE GOSPEL COUNTER-NARRATIVE

Readers of Augustine, both friend and foe, have habitually expected him to be a timeless figure, unconnected to any specific context. His traditional status as a doctor of the church, the far-reaching influence of his theology, and the authority with which his writings have been vested contribute to perennial difficulty in seeing him for who he was: a North African pastor struggling to proclaim the drama of redemption amid the moral ambiguities and brutal realities of a disintegrating Roman Empire. Failure to contextualize him has allowed his thought to be pressed into the service of ends for which it was not suited, judged by values he could not have considered. Nowhere has this been truer than with his views on women, sexuality, and marriage. Before considering his negotiations of the power realities of the late Roman Empire, it will prove helpful to understand him on these related issues.

Augustine has been variously accused of misogyny, sexual repression, and being the wellspring of the West's ambivalence about human sexuality. Indeed, not all his utterances on the subject of women, marriage, and sex are salutary, and it is right to be critical of his and the church's negative legacy in these matters. At the same time, he deserves here, as much as in any area of his thought, to be read in light of his own setting. In Augustine's world marriage was typically viewed as a property arrangement, and sexual expression in marriage a means of domination and of raising offspring to perpetuate civic life.[18] Marriage, in the church of Augustine's time, could occasionally be treated as if a necessary evil, as in Jerome's hostile treatise titled *Against Jovinian*. In the late imperial period, sexuality itself was already viewed with deep ambivalence: eroticized and on display in the public shows,[19] yet still seen with jaundiced eye by some of the philosophical traditions. Augustine's commitment to celibacy predates his conversion: his choice to be sexually continent reflects his attraction to Neoplatonism.

Moreover, four centuries of interaction with Greco-Roman culture had transformed Christianity's early egalitarian impulses to the point where some Christians wondered if women were actually made in the image of God in the same way men were.[20] Even Augustine can speculate on whether, except for the purposes of reproduction, another male would have been a better companion for Adam.[21] In an Imperial Church, celibacy and sexual renunciation, not the radical equality of the earliest Christians, had become a kind of higher morality, as well as a form of protest against the social order.[22] What we rightly name and reject today as the subordination and subjugation of women were simply accepted as the common coinage of male-female relationships in Augustine's social world.

This framework shaped Augustine. Nevertheless, on occasion he rose significantly above this framework and saw marriage and sexuality in a more positive light.[23] Experience surely helped him. Unlike some of his ecclesial contemporaries, Augustine had been, prior to his adoption of a celibate lifestyle, in a monogamous, fifteen-year relationship with a woman, with whom he had had one child.[24] In his short treatise titled *The Excellence of Marriage*, Augustine rejected Jerome's denunciation of marriage, refusing to see it as the lesser of two evils, the greater evil being fornication. Rather, he argued that marriage promotes three social goods: procreation, mutual fidelity, and the bond of union (*sacramentum*).[25] He even boldly affirmed that "the marriages of the faithful are superior to the virginity of irreligious women."[26] In *The Trinity*, Augustine further argues that women and men both have the same rational mind, that women are "together with us men . . . heirs of grace," and that they possess as fully as males the image of God and the ability to contemplate eternal ideas.[27] Furthermore, in *The Literal Meaning of Genesis*, Augustine dismisses a popular interpretation of creation that held that Eve's soul was not made directly by God but fashioned out of Adam's. He even imagines that if they had not fallen, the first humans would still have had sexual relations in Paradise.[28] Sexuality and sexual activity are thus not intrinsically sinful in Augustine's thought.

Augustine did not accept every aspect of the patriarchal culture that shaped him. Importantly, it was his own close reading of the Bible that helped him glimpse these different ways to construct sexual realities. Measured by extremes of his era, he exemplified moderation. His views on sex and marriage will be misunderstood if they are treated merely as a foil against which to display the hard-won convictions of our own time. Rather, he is best and most compassionately read against his own horizon, where he sought to interpret the gospel amid the complexities of life in the late Roman Empire.

How, then, did he respond to the power dynamics of this political setting? As befits a trained rhetorician, Augustine's most potent weapon was speech. Oratory was the chief medium of power in antiquity, and some of Augustine's moral and spiritual authority was linked to his mastery of language. Words were for him "finely-wrought, precious vessels"[29] with the power to lift and turn the soul. His notable eloquence got Augustine—recently converted and newly returned to Africa from Italy after resigning his post as court orator—ordained a presbyter, quite against his will.[30] Always the conversationalist, Augustine's preferred method for dealing with opponents was reasoned debate.

Augustine's relationship with his craft was paradoxical. As one who stood in the ancient tradition of Cicero, he knew well the dangers of rhetoric. "When the principles of speaking are taught to fools, they are not made into orators, but weapons are put into the hands of madmen," he cautions a father who had sent him a sample of his son's declamations.[31] Nevertheless, Augustine never ceased being an orator. Dealing with imperial officials required the delicate touch of the diplomat, but sometimes Augustine could be blunt, as when he confronted Count Boniface with his sins and called him to do penance.[32] With verbal command of the Bible and classical authors, church tradition and Roman law, and with devastating mastery of every turn of phrase, Augustine was an imposing interlocutor. Ironically, this orator, trained for the public square, had withdrawn from public after his conversion and returned to Africa seeking the contemplative life. But his ordination thrust him into the public rhetoric and reality of the church's precarious situation in North Africa. Like Ambrose before him, circumstance made Augustine a public theologian.

Augustine saw plainly that caring for souls and preaching the gospel were not only theological but political activities. Later, as bishop of Hippo, he often turned his rhetorical ability to the work of Christian diplomacy on behalf of those who were powerless before the machinery of the empire. For the welfare of souls Augustine willingly confronted this machine. Two sets of letters are illustrative. In the first, Augustine intervenes in the case of Faventius, who for unknown reasons had claimed asylum in Augustine's church.[33] When after some days Faventius incautiously stepped out of the church, he was arrested and detained. The next morning he was secreted away, and Augustine feared some harm might come to him.

Augustine's concern is clearly not with Faventius's guilt or innocence (Augustine claims not to know). It is with due process. He reminds each official to whom he writes of an imperial law that allows the accused, once publicly arraigned before the magistrate, to have thirty days' leave, under some surveillance, to set his case in order. In Faventius's case, the law has been conveniently ignored. He asks Cresconius, Hippo's harbor tribune and a Catholic, to present his petition to the magistrate. "What shall I say," writes Augustine, "to the Lord our God and what account shall I give him if I do not do as much as I can for the safety of one who entrusted himself for protection and help to the Church I serve . . . ."[34] To Florentinus, the arresting office and another Catholic, Augustine sends an actual copy of the text of the law, "not in order to threaten but in order to plead and to intercede for a human being in a human way and with the mercy of a bishop, to the extent that humanness itself and piety permit."[35] Augustine deftly appeals to Florentinus, recalling the obedience this Catholic official owes both church and empire: "Be so good, my lord and son, as to add this to your reputation and grant my request, and do not hesitate to do on the occasion of my intervention and petition what the law of the emperor, whose country you serve, commands."[36]

In the second set of letters, Augustine and Macedonius, vicar of Africa, discuss Augustine's reasons for interceding for a condemned criminal.[37] The letter that contained Augustine's initial appeal is lost, so the exchange begins with Macedonius's statement of the issues. Augustine had requested clemency for a condemned man, in whom there was no sign of remorse. "How can we claim in the name of religion that we should forgive a crime, no matter what sort it is? And when we want it to go unpunished, we of course approve it," comments Macedonius.[38] Pardon is deserved when a criminal promises correction, but intervening for one who makes no such promise seems immoral. Macedonius is accusing Augustine of being soft on crime and easy on sin. Augustine's penetrating reply still merits attention:

> In no way, then do we approve of the sins that we want to be corrected, nor do we want the wrongdoing to go unpunished because we find it pleasing. Rather, having compassion for the person and detesting the sin or crime, the more we are displeased by the sin the less we want the sinful person to perish without having been corrected. For it is easy and natural to hate evil persons because they are evil, but it is rare and holy to love those same persons because they are human beings. [39]

Augustine's intercession is grounded in God's Christ-shaped mercy and in the common humanity both the innocent and the guilty share. Those who care for the sick do it not to keep them sick, but so that they become well; likewise, the church must love the bad in hope that they become good.[40] Moreover, Augustine maintains, "there is no other place for correcting our conduct save in this life."[41]

Augustine assumes the authority and value of Roman law, and uses it against imperial officials who wink at injustice. Nevertheless, both sets of letters show that whatever old narratives about Roman legitimacy are in his head, he cedes primary authority to another narrative: the story of God's mercy made known in Christ. Augustine's primary weapon against the dehumanizing forces at play in the dissolving empire is the *theo*-logic of the gospel, which alone secures the dignity of persons.

How, then, shall we understand the logic Augustine used to justify imperial suppression of the Donatists? His support of state coercion to end the Donatist schism has earned him the unfortunate title "first theorist of the Inquisition."[42] Is this the same Augustine who sought clemency for condemned prisoners?

To begin, we recall that Donatists were the religious majority in North Africa throughout the fourth century. Moreover, long before Augustine became bishop, the Donatists had perfected their own forms of coercion. Roving bands of militant vigilantes, nicknamed "Circumcellions," had for decades waged a dirty war of terror and intimidation against Catholics and their own folk who dared convert. Their strategy included burning churches and maiming or killing Catholic priests.[43] One of their tactics was to throw lime mixed with vinegar into the eyes of a captured priest, blinding him.[44] Augustine once barely escaped an ambush when his guide took a wrong turn.[45] Ultimately, the Circumcellions succeeded in provoking an imperial response: the forced closing of Donatist churches, fines for Donatist bishops, and execution for any involved in violence.

"Augustine hated violence."[46] As noted earlier, he ardently opposed the death penalty. When a group of Circumcellions and Donatist clerics had been convicted of murdering a Catholic priest and tearing out the eye of another, Augustine petitioned the Imperial Commissioner not to employ the *lex talionis*. Instead, he requested a commutation of sentence, because "we still do not want the sufferings of the servants of God to be avenged by punishments equal to those sufferings."[47] A Christian magistrate's tools against violence were clemency and gentleness. When the case was sent on to a Christian proconsul, Augustine becomes bolder: "in order that [the death penalty] may not happen, I as a Christian beg the judge and as a bishop warn a Christian."[48] Donatists, he knows, would welcome their own executions, and yet Augustine does not base his appeal on a utilitarian desire to avoid creating new martyrs. The crux of his appeal is the cruciform logic of the gospel: "They spilled Christian blood by their impious sword; on account of Christ hold back from their blood even the sword of judgment."[49]

Augustine long opposed the idea of forcing the Donatists into the Catholic Church. His primary strategy was theological debate with them and organization of the Catholic clergy. However, as new peaks of Circumcellion cruelty led many African bishops to appeal to the emperor for help, Augustine changed his mind about force.[50] Finally in 412 an imperial edict made Donatism illegal.[51] Several years later, Augustine, in a letter to the Tribune of Africa, subsequently re-titled *On the Correction of the Donatists*, articulated a theological justification for suppressing Donatists.[52] They, like the people in Jesus' parable of the banquet, must be "compelled to come in" (Luke 14:23). It is hard not to see his use of Scripture as a kind of exegetical *Realpolitik* and a violation of his best hermeneutical principles.[53] Yet throughout the letter pulses Augustine's underlying concern about ending the Donatist violence, not only against the Catholic minority, but against themselves: Donatists sometimes committed suicide as a form of self-produced martyrdom. Not to seek state help, Augustine says, would have been negligent.[54] But while Augustine changed his mind about force, he never changed his opposition to the death penalty for Circumcellions, and even held that Donatist clergy should retain their offices and Donatist baptisms be accepted as valid. Augustine wanted bloodshed in his beloved Africa to stop.

Augustine's theological arguments against Donatism remain persuasive. He saw that the church is not, in the words of Jaroslav Pelikan, "a moral all-star team . . . [but] a moral hospital. . . ."[55] His justification of imperial coercion, though, is another story. He could not control what others would do centuries later with arguments shaped by his concerns. As Chadwick maintains, the much later idea of burning heretics had nothing in common with his situation and would have horrified Augustine.[56] In the conflict with Donatism, he was no mouthpiece of the empire, but a pastor seeking to stop a spiral of violence. Yet Augustine's theological justification of imperial intervention against Donatism raises permanently urgent questions. When the situation is already violent, how will those who live by the counter-narrative of the gospel act, not just to avoid violence, but to limit it? Is coercion always wrong, especially when it may create relatively more justice? Can forced union ever yield a truly *Catholic* unity?

However morally ambiguous Augustine's support of the forced correction of the Donatists, he clearly did not base his argument on a presumption that the Roman Empire had a divine stamp of approval on it. Here, he can still be our guide.

The destruction of Rome in 410 led many thoughtful pagans to wonder aloud if Christianity had, by its rejection of the traditional gods, brought about the destruction of the city. As news of the disaster and of the pagan critique of Christianity reached Africa, Augustine responded with his monumental book *The City of God Against the Pagans.*

Augustine set out to prove the charges against Christianity baseless. What began as a defense of Christianity against pagan accusations, however, became a work of grander scale. Using the biblical imagery of the city, Augustine articulated a theology of history in which two opposed realities, symbolized as Babylon and Jerusalem, are at work in human experience. "Two cities have been formed by two loves: the earthly by the love of self, even to the contempt of God; the heavenly by the love of God, even to the contempt of self."[57] The Earthly City, characterized by the violence of its founder, Cain, is not eternal; the City of God, distinguished by divine love, is eternal and is both a present and future eschatological reality. In the first city, human beings pursue their desires for earthly things; in the second, human beings live by faith and seek eternal things. Within human experience, however, these two cities are "entangled" and "intermixed," their separation occurring only at the last judgment.[58] Part of the City of God is a "pilgrim city," exiled in history. Its exact contours do not equal the visible church, for not every member of the church belongs to the elect, and among the present enemies of the church are those destined for citizenship in the City of God.[59]

What does this mean for the empire? Empires are expressions of the Earthly City; they serve the definite purpose in history of helping human beings pursue and achieve a limited justice and peace under the rule of law. The Roman Empire was thus not unambiguously evil.[60] But even at their best, all of history's "excellent empires" are based on the love of power, which reveals not love of God but love of self. Constituted by self-love, they share in the Earthly City and its destiny. For Augustine, even a presumed Christian empire still belongs to the *genus* "empire," and could not possibly be identified with the City of God. "Justice being taken away," Augustine writes, "what are kingdoms but great robberies?"[61] As Chadwick points out, Augustine uses the phrase "Christian Empire" only once in all his writings.[62] An empire run by Christians remains an empire, still governed by the

Earthly City's deformed logic of self-interest. The City of God, however, is governed solely by divine love. While the City of God remains in its earthly pilgrimage, it will obey the laws of the Earthly City, so long as these promote justice and well-being and do not infringe upon the worship due God alone. But the City of God will not balk at dissenting, if Babylon makes demands that trespass on ultimate loyalties.[63]

This possibility, along with Augustine's belief that *no* empire is the City of God, is a seminal moment in his theology and in the post-Constantinian church. What he accomplishes in the *City of God* is the final de-divinization, and hence relativization, of the Roman Empire. No earthly dominion, even one ruled by Christians, has claim to ultimacy; there is no "Eternal City," except God's. Augustine is here the antithesis of Eusebius, who in the fourth century had extolled Constantine and the new Christian Empire as earthly reproductions of the heavenly kingdom.[64] Eusebius created a theology of empire that Christianized the old imperial rhetoric so as to re-absolutize both the emperor and the empire. Nothing could be further from Augustine's thought, for the *City of God* strips imperial rhetoric of its divine pretensions.

Implications

How can Augustine address those who live in another era of failing imperial narratives? Quite specifically, he offers twenty-first century American Christians a profoundly theological critique of our theocratic instincts. To that unself-critical American propensity to imagine our institutions and our national and religious life as a "city on a hill," Augustine proffers a stern rebuke. Within human history, Augustine would not identify even a "Christianized" empire as the City of God. God wisely and lovingly leaves the just and the unjust bound together in a complex web of life until final judgment. Theocrats, though, wish to do the sorting for God in the here and now, whether by coercion, conquest, or capital punishment. But through the lens of the gospel counter-narrative, Augustine reveals this for what it is: a form of idolatry in which the creature claims the prerogatives of the creator. Augustine's theological vision exposes as lethal self-deception the belief that individuals and nations can use the tactics of Babylon to impose on others the virtues of Jerusalem.

He would warn us that the oft-imagined ideal of the "Christian Nation" is a morally hazardous mirage. The nation and the culture (and even the church) are always penultimate realities, of limited and finite goodness, hence *never* to be unambiguously equated with the City of God. Augustine's theology unmasks exceptionalism as a dangerous myth: no nation is the City on a Hill, since every nation's founder is Cain. Insofar as nations use power to serve their self-interest, they will always have their feet stuck in the Earthly City's muck. Egotism and the love of domination are Babylon's engines, whether Babylon goes by the name of Rome or some other superpower. But the supra-national City of God runs solely by faith, hope, and charity.[65]

Within a few centuries of his death, a sainted but decontextualized Augustine had become rather like the "official" theologian of the Holy Roman Empire. This ironic and dubious honor is instructive in its own right: self-interest always tempts human beings to use a limited good for self-assertion and the domination of others. Sadly, the Augustinian West forgot a great truth about Augustine, articulated brilliantly by Edmund Hill: "All his life Augustine was a powerful seeker. He always asked far more questions than he answered; he was never easily satisfied that he had found what he was looking for, never lazily took anything for granted—not even his faith."[66] His ongoing quest to understand the meaning of human life under the mystery of God-in-Christ—ever a threat to empires, which thrive on the myth of their own permanence—remains Augustine's living legacy to the postmodern world.

FURTHER READING

Primary Sources

Augustine. *The City of God.* 1.33-36; 4:3-4; 14.28; 15.1-4; 20:1-2. Translated by Marcus Dods. Introduction by Thomas Merton. New York, N.Y.: Modern Library, 1993.

———. *The Works of Saint Augustine: A Translation for the 21st Century.* Edited by John E. Rotelle, O.S.A. II/1. Hyde Park, N.Y.: New City Press, 2001. See especially letters 33 and 88, translated by Roland Teske, S.J.

———. *The Works of Saint Augustine: A Translation for the 21st Century.* Edited by Boniface Ramsey. II/2. Hyde Park, N.Y.: New City Press, 2003. See especially letters 152-153, translated by Roland Teske, S.J.

———. *The Works of Saint Augustine: A Translation for the 21st Century.* Edited by

Boniface Ramsey. II/3. Hyde Park, N.Y.: New City Press, 2004. See especially letter 185, translated by Roland Teske, S.J.

_____. *The Works of Saint Augustine: A Translation for the 21st Century.* Edited by Boniface Ramsey. II/4. Hyde Park, N.Y.: New City Press, 2005. See especially letter 10* (Divjak Letters). Translated by Roland Teske, S.J.

Secondary Sources

Brown, Peter. *Augustine of Hippo: A Biography*, 2nd ed. Berkeley, Calif.: University of California Press, 2000.

Chadwick, Henry. *Augustine: A Very Short Introduction.* Oxford: Oxford University Press, 1986.

Wills, Gary. *Saint Augustine.* New York, N.Y.: Viking, 1999.

Chapter 7

Wynfrith-Boniface

Marion Grau

Boniface and Middle Europe's Early Medieval Transformations

Wynfrith-Boniface (675-754) was an Anglo-Saxon monk, teacher, missionary, ecclesial intellectual, and bishop who struggled to organize Germanic churches in the Hessian-Saxon borderlands. He was born as Wynfrith in Wessex in 675, spent most of his first forty years in monasteries there, and the next thirty-six years as missionary and reformer on the European continent in the Frankish church. He took on the name Boniface later in his life. When he was 74, he and his companions were killed by robbers in 754 in Dokkum, Frisia. Boniface is often referred to as the "apostle of the Germans," though this title is somewhat misleading. Though he did in some sense function as apostle or missionary, his main work was in the reorganization of the church in an emerging Carolingian Francia rather than the actual conversion of Germanic peoples.[1] Hence, much of his work consisted in teaching, fortifying a Roman-centered monastic infrastructure, enforcing Roman ecclesiastical canons, church discipline, synods, annual episcopal visitations, and the general disciplining of laity, clergy, and nobility.

Whom the ancient people called "Germans" has been a notoriously vexed issue. What the Romans called *Germania* was located predominantly east of the Rhine, between the Northern Sea and the Danube to the south.[2] Hence, his sphere of influence did not correspond to any of the incarnations of modern Germany, but rather primarily to central Germany and the regions of Hesse, East- and Westphalia. Other Irish and Anglo-Saxon missionaries worked in adjacent areas on the continent.

The Europe of the time saw the slow decline of the Roman Empire, only temporarily delayed through the unifying influence of the Christianization of the empire. The empire had exposed much of western and middle Europe to Christianization by a slow and partial assimilation that had allowed for a variety of hybrid versions that combined local religious sensitivities with Christian practices. The age of migrations had started with the pushing of a variety peoples into Western Europe, ceding to the pressures of central Asian steppe people pushing west.[3] Migrating Visigoths and Ostrogoths had become Christian centuries before Boniface's time and had created an indigenized version of vernacular Gothic Christian culture with the help of the Gothic bishop Wulfila (d. 383). Doctrinal and credal developments had overtaken some of these peoples remote to the centers of imperial power and they were retrospectively declared "Arian" and hence effectively "heretics" or "pagans."[4] The Frankish lineage of the Merovingians had been brought into increasing conformity with the Roman Catholic version after the baptism of Clovis and his army in 508.[5] Hence, at Boniface's time, the Frankish rulers as well as most peoples located within the direct Roman sphere of influence claimed at least nominal allegiance to the Christian God and the terms of Nicene-Chalcedonian orthodoxy.

Prior to the Anglo-Saxon missions, Irish-Scottish monasteries had sent numerous missionaries to the continent, and had many points of presence in Alamannia and Bavaria, south of the location to which Boniface migrated. The age of migrations sped the decline of the Roman Empire—but not of *romanitas* as the cultural ideal to aspire to—and the splitting of the Christian lands into two distinctly separate regionally dominant cultures, the Western Latin tradition and the Eastern Greek Byzantine tradition. Over time, close ties between the Latin West and the Greek East unraveled, due to increasing theological differences and rivalries but also due to the beginning invasions of Arabic peoples, which diverted much of the attention and energy of Byzantium.

The invasions of Arab armies into southern Europe and northern Africa led to the fall of Visigothic Spain to the Umayyad dynasty in 711. By 718 most of the Iberian Peninsula was under Muslim rule and in 733 Charles Martel ("the Hammer") stopped a Muslim raiding party on its way to loot Tours. Subsequently, he gave new meaning to the expression "terror of the Franks" as he embarked on a series of invasions into areas around and south of Tours and Poitiers and with much violence imposed his hegemony over local people.[6] Under Charles Martel and his successors, the Frankish warlords of his fledgling dynasty began to command increasing power beyond their traditional tribal lands. They were the regional rising power to reckon with. The emerging Carolingian dynasty lacked dynastic legitimation, and so—once they finished off the shadow reign of the Merovingians—they offered themselves as supporters to the papacy in return for its willingness to recognize their claim to rule and to endow that rule with sacral qualities.

This bond led to a realignment of the papacy toward the West, and toward the rising imperial powers to its north.[7] Boniface was a crucial broker in solidifying and extending this bond as the papacy found itself in need of powerful military supporters to shield it from the threat of invading peoples such as Lombards and Muslims.[8] This tie was sealed in 751 through the crowning of Pippin the Younger (III) as the first "king" of the Franks with the consent of Pope Zachary.[9] Consequently, Boniface sought papal recommendation letters that would secure the protection and support of the Frankish kings for his plans to convert the "savage" Saxons. The military expansionism of the Franks led to the establishment of Charlemagne's (747?-814) Frankish kingdom only a few years after Boniface's death and inaugurated a long-lasting, if vigorously embattled, Frankish-Germanic Christian monarchical rule that was expanded throughout the following centuries. Charlemagne's eventual crowing as *imperator augustus* and protector of the Western church by Pope Leo II paved the way to a "Holy Roman Empire" (later with the addition "of the German nation") that lasted for many centuries in its various incarnations. It is this second *Reich* that Hitler aimed to tragically and perversely recreate in the Third Reich.

BONIFACE'S AMBIVALENT POSITION IN THE FRANKISH WORLD

> Boniface, having sought and received both a blessing and letters from the Apostolic See, was sent by the blessed pope to make a report on the savage peoples of Germany. The purpose of this was to discover whether their untutored hearts and minds were ready to receive the seed of the divine word.[10]

Written sources about Boniface's life are limited. The main source about the dates and events of his life is the biography written by a monk named Willibald a few years after his death. At the behest of Lullus and Megingoz, his former protégés and now successors as bishops in Mainz and Würzburg, Willibald committed to writing Boniface's life and events so that later generations may be "instructed by

Boniface's model and led to better things by his perfection."[11] A collection of his correspondence with abbesses, bishops, Frankish rulers, monks, nuns, and popes also was preserved.[12] Both sources are laced with numerous conventions of time, place, and genre. His hagiography repeats previous models of sanctity, and embellishes when portraying him as "having brought light and order to a wild country." This grandiose contrast was far from reality, as "what he found, instead, was much Christianity, and almost all of it the wrong sort."[13]

Wynfrith grew up in monasteries and made a name for himself as a talented grammarian, a teacher knowledgeable in matters of scripture and doctrine. He gained some popularity among the ecclesiastical elite there, including a number of nuns and abbesses who formed part of his spiritual and material support system during his time abroad. To flee his increasing popularity, he crossed the English Channel in 718 and tried to convert the Frisians in the northern coastal plains. Without social standing and support, he gave up after a year and returned to Britain. From there he departed to Rome in order to beg the current pope for support and recommendation letters to the representatives of the rising power of the region, the Frankish rulers.

During his first visit to Rome, Pope Gregory II asked him merely to "make a report on the savage peoples of Germany."[14] The Christian Anglo-Saxons of his time thought of the continental Saxons as their relatives, close enough to feel sent to bring them the faith.[15] While Christian missionaries were ready to go to the "savage peoples" at the boundaries of Frankish rule, they did not entertain thoughts about moving to Arab-Islamic religions. The same was true of Muslim missionaries. Despite the tempestuous expansion of both religions in the early Middle Ages, they generally did not compete on the same territory. Rather, these religious worlds remained largely separate.[16]

After challenges to Boniface's mission in Frisian and Saxon territories proved insurmountable at that point in time, his main goal became to uproot the various kinds of symbioses between indigenous and Christian beliefs and practices he found in places where Christianity had been present for some time. Pope Gregory II, who was little aware of the regions north of the Alps, took note of these circumstances when he endowed the new bishop with a new name and a mission:

> Hearing, to our great distress, that certain peoples in Germany on the eastern side of the Rhine are wandering in the shadow of death at the instigation of the ancient enemy and, as it were, under the form of the Christian faith, are still

in slavery to the worship of idols, while others who have not as yet any knowledge of God and have not been cleansed by the water of holy baptism but as pagans, to be likened unto the brutes, do not acknowledge their Creator, we have determined to send the bearer of these presents, our brother the reverend Bishop Boniface, into that county, for the enlightenment of both classes, to preach the word of the true faith. . . . If perchance he shall find there some who have wandered away from the true faith or have fallen into error by the cunning persuasion of the devil, he is to correct them and bring them back into the haven of safety, teach them the doctrine of this Apostolic See and establish them firmly in that same catholic faith.[17]

Hence, Boniface set about to remedy the under-education of clergy and the decline of the catechumenate for laity; he disciplined several bishops and clergy who had overstepped their bounds of authority, while denouncing others as heretics and apostates to the papacy. His stridency, obsessive adherence to canon law, and willingness to publicly criticize anybody, including popes, who would not adhere to Christian law and values as he understood them, assured that he was a controversial figure. While some of his critiques may seem justified and even courageous as they challenged the status quo, many saw him as an interloper who habitually interfered with local authorities, and many Frankish and Bavarian bishops resented his tendency to run interference with the pope, overriding others' areas of power.[18] It seems, however, that he chose to refrain from interference in some other regions, such as that of the Irish-Scottish monk Pirmin in Alamannia, presumably out of respect for his work.[19]

Boniface had grown up in a British monastery shaped by the enduring Irish-Scottish tradition of the *peregrinatio* that motivated many of the Anglo-Saxon and Irish intellectual elite to travel abroad to found new monasteries and spread Christian life practices. The particular shape of Christian practices Boniface knew were those of an Anglo-Saxon Christianity that had kept close ties with Rome since Gregory the Great (540-604) had sent the monk Augustine (d. 605) to become the first Archbishop of Canterbury. The resulting cultural clash between local Irish-Scottish indigenized Christianities and the exported local Roman traditions had been shifted toward Roman liturgical and canonical traditions through a synodal decision at Whitby (644) and the solidifying influence of the archbishopric of Theodore of Tarsus (668-690) at Canterbury. The bond to Roman tradition and influence was dominant and travels to Rome were becoming more frequent.[20] Subsequently, Roman liturgical and canonical traditions came to dominate, though some Irish elements endured. It is during one of these travels that he was consecrated bishop by Pope Gregory II and renamed Boniface.[21] His oath of loyalty tied Bishop Boniface closely to Rome, with an oath that omitted the oath of allegiance to the Eastern Emperor.[22]

Like any monastic, missionary, or church official of the time, Boniface needed to secure the favor of the powers that be in the region in which he intended to work. Those powers were less and less those of the Roman Empire and increasingly those of the rising regional powers. The Franks had strong ties to Rome that preceded Boniface and hence it was between both of these centers of worldly and sacral power he had to map out his role and function.[23]

For the next decades he worked under the protection of Charles Martel, Pippin, and Carloman. Consequently, his work among Saxons and Frisians was quite limited, as they were resisting these Frankish rulers' expansionism and considered the fact that Boniface received Frankish protection and support as an impediment to their adoption of the Christian faith. It is perhaps also because of this ambiguous alliance with Frankish power that we hear virtually nothing from Boniface about the atrocities they committed in war or their treatment of the populace. On the contrary, Frankish expansion was expected to lay open "heathen" lands (the lands of the heath dwellers) to Christian mission and hence was both in Boniface's and in the papacy's interest. Difficult negotiations with the Frankish rulers and the needs of the local churches were a constant factor in Boniface's long presence in Francia, especially since the Franks focused their Christian adherence on cultic reverence and tribal loyalty to a powerful deity, rather than on ethical behaviors emphasized by church officials at the time, such as monogamy, for example.[24]

When it came to the sphere of church canons, correct doctrine, and marital ethics, however, Boniface showed no inclination to hold back in his duty as disciplinarian empowered not least by his ordination to the bishop's office by Pope Gregory II himself during his journey to Rome in 722. Boniface's critique of Frankish rulers' behavior, it seems, was mostly limited to a critique of adultery and other personal habits, rather than their treatment of subjugated peoples or slaves. In the texts and sources that remain today, the subaltern, whether "pagan," or subaltern of any other sort, cannot speak. The borderlines between Christian Francia and the tribal religions of the Saxons also demarcated the boundary between civilization and savagery in some of Boniface's rhetoric, even though his letters and hagiography show that a hybridized Christianity remained intermingled with local religious loyalties to sacred springs and trees both in Boniface's native lands and in Franco-Germanic regions for centuries to come. Yet, for Boniface, a recognizably Christian life and worship had in some places, as in Thuringia, been repressed by negligence and oppressive rulers. When Boniface arrived there,

> he addressed the elders and the chiefs of the people, calling on them to put aside their blind ignorance and to return to the Christian religion that they had formerly embraced. . . . Thus, when the power of the leaders, who had protected religion, was destroyed, the devotion of the people to Christianity and religion died out also, and false brethren were brought in to pervert the minds of the people and to introduce among them under the guise of religion dangerous heretical sects.[25]

This powerful statement about the connection between a ruler's patronage of Christianity and its proper shape and strength illustrates well the concerns of Boniface. In the wake of the declining Roman Empire, power had increasingly returned to more local entities. Many of the semi-romanized societies throughout Europe at the time showed increasing community formation around charismatic individuals enforced by strong bonds of honor and shame. Some of the culturally specific Germanic customs included a "sacral kingship" that required as its highest value an unquestioned loyalty to the military leader of the community.[26] Loyalty to a male leader in war often transitioned toward a permanent rule over increasing facets of life, attempts to establish a dynastic rule and emulate the greatness of the Roman Empire through the local adaptation of romanesque customs and laws. These military leaders united several offices, including some forms of religious leadership; their conversion had been a main objective of missionaries.[27] Since these were men who knew best how to respect a coercive power that was greater than theirs, and, what is more, could potentially crush missionary efforts, missionary tactics focused on demonstrating the superior power of the Christian God. Hence, much of the missionary rhetoric presented a version of "muscular Christianity," emphasizing a strong, male God and targeting an audience of military rulers who needed to be convinced that shifting allegiances both politically and spiritually would enhance their power, welfare, and influence. What is understood as conversion of the heart in the history of missions is often as much a conversion in the economy of power, influence, and status.

Boniface, as obsessive in seeking advice from ecclesial mentors and power holders as in attempting to discipline each expression of Christianity he encountered, did eventually adopt a missionary strategy of gradualism as proposed by Gregory the Great in his letter to the Abbot Mellitus. The pope had recommended:

> that the temples of idols in that nation should not be destroyed, but that the idols themselves that are in them should be. Let blessed water be prepared, and sprinkled in these temples, and altars constructed, and relics deposited, since, if these same temples are well built, it is needful that they should be transferred from the worship of idols to the service of the true God; that, when the people themselves see that these temples are not destroyed, they may put away error from their heart, and knowing and adoring the true God, may have recourse with the more familiarity to the places they have been accustomed to. . . . For it is undoubtedly impossible to cut away everything at once from hard hearts, since one who strives to ascend to the highest place must needs rise by steps or paces, and not by leaps.[28]

What we read here represents a marked shift in the mental horizons of the church. Boniface is a representative of what took place during his time: Christianization was less and less perceived as a clash between supernatural powers as the victory of Christianity over the gods became taken for granted. Now, the "real task of the Church, there was a *mission civilatrice*. Education was as important as miracles."[29] The letter Boniface received from his episcopal mentor Daniel of Winchester thus encourages him to make the following point:

> If the gods are all-powerful, beneficent, and just, they not only reward their worshipers but punish those who reject them. If, then, they do this in temporal matters, how is it that they spare us Christians who are turning almost the whole earth away from their worship and overthrowing their idols? And while the [Christians] possess lands rich in wine and abounding in other resources, they have left to the [pagans] lands stiff with cold where their gods, driven out of the world, are falsely supposed to rule. They are also frequently to be reminded of the supremacy of the Christian world, in comparison with which they themselves, very few in number, are still involved in their ancient errors.[30]

The "civilizing mission" loomed large in the modern history of Western Christianity and its reach around the globe. The most remembered and depicted event of Boniface's life was his well-orchestrated felling of an ancient sacred oak tree: Boniface's publicity stunt in felling the sacred Oak of Geismar exemplifies this "shock and awe" missiology. Yet the incident at Geismar is an exception to his generally more realistic stance, likely enforced by encountered reality and necessity. A more regular sight would have been the missionary entering the market places and delivering a standardized sermon in the local language. This occurred with the support of the local power holders and included attempts to reform the local clergy and monasteries.[31]

From what we can tell, the event represents the challenge of Christianity to indigenous powers of life and strength as experienced by locals especially in old, large trees. The incident was intended to demonstrate the impotence of local deities and spiritual presences in nature and claim the omnipotence and universal presence and relevance of the Christian deity. It was located in a liminal space, an intertribal sanctuary at the border between the nominally Christian Hessians, and the pagan Saxons to the north.[32] Willibald, the writer of his hagiography, indicates that many of the Hessians who had acknowledged the "Catholic faith" continued, secretly or openly, "to offer sacrifices to trees and springs," and engage in divination, incantations, and "other sacrificial rites; while others, of a more reasonable character" had abandoned these activities. Boniface, "with the counsel and advice of the latter persons" attempted to cut down "a certain oak of extraordinary size called in the old tongue of the pagans the Oak of Jupiter."[33]

> Taking his courage in his hands (for a great crowd of pagans stood by watching and bitterly cursing in their hearts the enemy of the gods), he cut the first notch. But when he had made a superficial cut, suddenly the oak's vast bulk, shaken by a mighty blast of wind from above, crashed to the ground shivering its topmost branches into fragments in its fall. As if by the express will of God (for the brethren present had done nothing to cause it) the oak burst asunder into four parts, each part having a trunk of equal length. At the sight of this extraordinary spectacle the heathens who had been cursing ceased to revile and began, on the contrary, to believe and bless the Lord. Thereupon the holy bishop took counsel with the brethren, built an oratory from the timber of the oak and dedicated it to Saint Peter the Apostle.[34]

Though the hagiographer heightens the dramatic effect by stressing the anger of the "pagans," the Frankish garrison nearby would have been enough of a presence to keep Boniface safe without direct divine intervention.[35] Much could be said about this highly loaded passage, and much of what seems to carry significant spiritual meaning can only be guessed at due to our ignorance about pre-Christian Germanic religions. Simon Schama's reading points to a theological reinscription, a wooden palimpsest, inscribed on material too valuable to destroy:

> It is often said that the source of Boniface's determination was his own native landscape of Devon, dotted with obstinate tree cults, not least that of the Celtic yew, which still decorates Devonian churchyards as an emblem of immortality. But it's at least as plausible to offer an opposite interpretation, namely that his familiarity with local animism may have given him a healthy respect for its power. After all, Willibrord's story, ostensibly a conversionary miracle, actually demonstrates the ways by which pagan beliefs could be turned to Christian ends. The "divine blast" that helped Boniface fell the oak is identical with the pagan lightning bolts which in Celtic and Germanic lore mark the tree as the tree of life. . . . So Boniface's axe transformed rather than destroyed. The spiritually dead pagans were turned into living believers. The rotten (perhaps hollow) trunk of the idolatrous tree was turned inside out to reveal four perfect, clean timbers, from which a house of the reborn and eternally living Christ could then be constructed.[36]

Schama sees the felling of the oak as a transformation rather than a destruction, and makes much of the seasonal life cycles of a tree and their similarity to the life of Christ and the ensuing iconography of the verdant cross, symbolizing the death as well as the resurrection of Christ. However, the continuation of place and substance of the wood also irrevocably indicates the merging rather than the outright replacement of a tradition that would continue to contribute its own share of meaning and symbolism to the mix. Boniface was unable to eradicate the mutual transformation of Christian and pagan practices that had already been occurring in the centuries before his arrival, for example in his homeland, where many famous monasteries and churches are located on sites of pagan reverence. This repressed history of their own tradition's "symbioses" haunted Boniface and many modern European missionaries who followed in his ideological footsteps.

Others see this meeting of metal and wood as the prelude to the clear-cutting of the Germanic forests that heretofore had been left untouched because of their sacral quality.[37] This episode is also symbolic for the foundations of monasteries Boniface introduced throughout his area of influence. At least some of them seem to have been built intentionally in sacred groves or clearings, with the logged timber used to erect the monasteries. Hence, there is more than an exchange of spiritual economies at work here; this event also symbolizes the beginning change from forest foraging economies to expanding agricultural societies.

With the *Concilium Germanicum* in 742, Boniface was able to step up the reform program. Boniface and Carloman rewrote the Frankish Church in the Anglo-Saxon image, reorganizing it as a Rome-oriented episcopal union. Yet, eventually, his reform program was slowed by the resistance of the locals to the recovery of church property and the gradualist policy of the king. Frustrated, Boniface removed himself from this particular context, and headed off to Frisia.[38]

Boniface's relationship to women is, unsurprisingly, ambiguous. In some ways his activities contributed to the further marginalization of women in Europe, as he was intent on enforcing the papal tradition of monastic, and hence celibate, clergy. Yet monastic women were arguably some of the closest friends and supporters of Boniface. The abbess Eadburga sent him important supplies for this work, for which an exhausted Boniface shows himself very grateful:

> To his beloved sister, the abbess Eadburga . . . May he who rewards all righteous acts cause my dearest sister to rejoice in the choir of angels above because she has consoled with spiritual light by the gift of sacred books an exile in Germany who has to enlighten the dark corners of the Germanic peoples and would fall into deadly snares if he had not the Word of God as a lamp unto his feet and a light upon his path.[39]

He assigned some of his female relatives to posts on the continent. Thus he called on the noblewoman Saint Leoba of Wessex (702-782) to become the abbess of the German nunnery of Tauberbischofsheim, Thecla (d. 790) became the abbess at Kitzingen and Ochsenfurt, and Walburga (d. 790) in Heidenheim.[40] Toward the end of Boniface's life, as he left for Frisia, he entreated Leoba to stay in her adopted land and gave orders that "after his death, her bones should be placed next to his in the tomb, so that they who had served God during their lifetime with equal sincerity and zeal should await together the day of resurrection." He left her with his cowl, thereby demonstrating that in his absence she was his delegate. She was in charge of all the nuns that worked for Boniface, and was the only woman with access to male monasteries in Fulda, where monks consulted her.[41] Hildegard, the wife of Charlemagne, considered her a friend, and she was held in high esteem at the court of Frankish ruler, Pippin III. The presences of Leoba, Walburga, Thecla, and others on the continent emphasize the important role played by women in the establishment and management of monasteries.[42] Hence, Boniface's mission was not only partly funded and supported by Anglo-Saxon women, but they themselves were crucially involved in bringing Anglo-Saxon Christian practices to women in Germanic territories. There, along with other Anglo-Saxon abbots and bishops, they formed and educated a literate diasporic elite.

Traveling in Frisia, his earliest missionary field, where "the faith had been planted strongly ...and the glorious end of the saint's life drew near," Boniface and his party were killed, most likely in order to steal potential valuables they carried. Though his companions aimed to defend themselves and him against the attackers, Boniface is reported to have encouraged them "to accept the crown of martyrdom":

> Sons, cease fighting. Lay down your arms, for we are told in Scripture not to render evil for good but to overcome evil by good. . . . Brethren, be of stout heart, fear not them who kill the body, for they cannot slay the soul, which continues to live forever.[43]

A box they had carried was found broken, and its contents, perhaps some of the "sacred books" Eadburga had sent him in years past, were found strewn around and torn apart. One book in particular, known as *Codex Ragyndrudis* (its contents are a collection of mainly anti-Arian texts), sustained a severe cut and was thought to be the book Boniface used to protect himself from the sword of his killer. Some hagiographic depictions from the ninth through twelfth century thus show him with a book in his hand as the sword comes down on his head, while others show him with a book only, or with a sword in one hand and a book in the other. Sometimes, he holds a sword with a book impaled upon it.[44]

His hagiographer reports that at least two monasteries, Mainz and Fulda, contended for Boniface's relics, as they represented a powerful local presence of sacrality.[45] For a church or monastery to have its own relics gave it significance and meaning in the local sacral landscape. Rome continued to solidify its own power by gifting pilgrims to Rome with relics, which they then deposited in local sanctuaries upon their return.

THE AMBIVALENT INHERITANCE OF GERMANIC CHRISTIANITY

Today, around 25,000 persons make the pilgrimage to the site of Boniface's death and his relics each year. There is a pilgrimage path that follows the route on which his relics were taken from where he died to Fulda. For his 2004 anniversary, a musical was created and performed.[46] In counterpoint to Boniface's hatchet job on the oak in the aftermath of "Waldsterben" or the dying of forests in Germany, avant-garde artist Joseph Beuys started planting 7000 oaks to counter the results of deforestation and environmental degradation in twentieth-century Germany.[47]

Popular opinion of Boniface has varied between outright hagiography and cult for his efforts in "converting the Germans," to criticism for bringing Christianity at all (the neo-pagan version of Nazism), or for bringing a nonindigenous ultramontanist version of Rome-enslaved Christianity (opinions predictably more prevalent on the Protestant side of things, as well as among German Christians during the Nazi reign). The changes wrought by the rise of industrial capitalism and fears of modernity's challenges led in some German contexts to the desire for a nationalist romantic recovery of an imagined pure Germanic past, or a particular contribution to Christianity that could be accredited to Germans.[48]

These highly problematic claims must fail, because it is virtually impossible to try to map anything approaching a German specificity or identity. We know next to nothing about pre-Christian Germanic religions; attempts to deduce them from Icelandic Nordic myths ignore the fact that those represent a far later version, put in writing in an already Christian nation.[49] The modern German obsession with establishing Germanic origins and purity was reinforced by a passionate literary relationship to Tacitus's *Germania* and its ambivalent discourse of the Germans as indigenous noble savages, as the "better Romans" of the time.[50] These notoriously vague and biased reports have incited a proliferation of searches for origins rather than an ability to be satisfied with only traces of a largely mute past: multiethnic groups of people with both large continuities and discontinuities with their neighbors multiply throughout the ages of migration.[51] The different designations given to "Germanic peoples" by their neighbors—"Deutsche," "Teutonen," "Tyskere," "Allemands," "Tedesci," and "Germans"—to this day remind us that this region has been profoundly multiethnic.

The economies of exchange in power and meaning-making between the centers of Roman, Anglo-Saxon, and German locales allow us to contemplate contemporary struggles over center-periphery alignments, centralization of religious power in a particular location empowered by the history of tradition in that location, the reversal of center-periphery, and the questioning of that dichotomy as the "islands" of the barbarians become revalued as the new centers of earthly and sacral power (e.g., the struggles over power and tradition in the Anglican communion).[52]

The shifting of centers is an important reminder that all traditions are local customs first and that as foci and attention shift, local traditions shift in significance for other regions.

In the wake of modern Western nation-states, the postcolonial phenomenon of the creation of new nation-states out of former colonies carries the ambivalent heritage of communities that form themselves around perceived ethnic commonalities in the wake of being ruled by a foreign center and by a "comprador" class that inserts itself between foreign rulers and local peoples. How do such searches for a tribal or national identity play out today, as Europe and many places around the globe develop new forms of transnationality, while other societies and groups refocus on local indigenous identities in an attempt to preserve their distinct languages, practices, and beliefs?

The Anglo-Saxon and Irish-Scottish traveling monks and nuns were the diasporic intellectuals of their time. Their willingness to travel to the liminal spaces of Christian influence made them powerful brokers between local and Christian brokers between cultures; indigenous power holders and the claims to the power of Christian God and church; and the founders of centers of education for royalty, nobility, and other local elites. As foreigners they were yet woven through with an understanding of a universal Christian community that transcended ethnic boundaries. What is the position of contemporary postcolonial intellectuals, writing from locales outside their homelands, ambivalently placed in positions of power and privilege, estranged from the populace by in-group language, culture, and education? What is their "mission" in the world?

Valuable future explorations of this topic might include an investigation of how Christianity benefited from the unifying aspect of empire, and how it facilitated Christianity's transethnic shape and development. Christian theology today might consider how it can be shaped to avoid false alternatives: the universalism of an imperial Christianity, the xenophobic ethnocentrisms that must dismiss, dominate, or destroy the other. How can we facilitate having many spaces for Christian theologies that are translocal and transcendent of each particular context, while relevant to local settings, respectful and inclusive of the sacred truths and sites of all our ancestors?

Boniface's presence meant the loss of more indigenized religious options. This loss of a pre-Christian past in Europe has sparked a variety of movements. Among the more harmless are neo-pagan attempts to resuscitate an imagined past Germanic religion. But the focus on local, tribal, and supposed national pasts has also resulted in nationalist and xenophobic attempts to recover the figment of an essential tribal, national, or racial identity. Boniface's context reopens for us the possibility of reconstructing our own ideas of mission, inculturation, the relation between Christians and power, and the attendant ambivalence of trying to negotiate these economies of exchange.

The symbolic event of the felling of the oak at Geismar contributed to shaping later missionary attitudes toward indigenous peoples of the land and sacred groves during the times of European colonial empires. Hence, Nobel laureate Wangari Maathai has argued that missionary policies against sacred groves are part of the cause of deforestation in Africa.[53] Such fears of "syncretism" and "nature worship" are hardly issues only of the past. The resurgence of neo-pagan practices runs up against the violent fear of many conservative Christians that environmental action and protection equals nature worship. This conflict feeds on ancient stereotypes of iconoclast missionaries whose actions exacerbated the split between nature and culture, with "nature-worshipping pagans" as the paradigmatic uncultured human. As these conceptions were solidified, hostility to nature religions often accompanied ecocidal tendencies, prying the people of the land away from the land and toward a God who was claimed to be both universal and hence placeless, and omnipresent and hence in all places.

Remembering the wisdom of indigenous peoples throughout the world as a wisdom related to that of European ancestors could be a far more helpful reconnection to a lost past than xenophobia and ethnic violence. Contemporary reconstructions of transcendence and immanence and the rise of ecological theologies are attempting to mend this split in the Western mindset. As constructive theologians rediscover the local and contextual nature of all theology, a reassessment of intercultural encounter between gospel, the culture of the missionary, and local religious culture becomes crucial. The heuristic epistemology that might well accompany such investigations centers around what are appropriate mixtures of local and translocal culture, what are elements of compromise (*adiaphora*), what elements can take local shape—and who makes these decisions.

FURTHER READING

Primary Source

Boniface. *The Letters of Saint Boniface.* Introduction by Thomas F. X. Noble.
Translated by Ephraim Emerton. New York, N.Y.: Columbia University Press,
2000.

Secondary Sources

Brown, Peter. *The Rise of Western Christendom: Triumph and Diversity, A.D. 200-
1000.* 2nd ed. Malden, Mass.: Blackwell, 2003.
Willibald. "The Life of Saint Boniface." In *Soldiers of Christ: Saints and Saints'
Lives from Late Antiquity and the Early Middle Ages*, edited by Thomas F. X.
Noble and Thomas Head, 107-40. University Park, Pa.: Pennsylvania State
University Press, 1995.
Proksch, Nikola. "The Anglo-Saxon Missionaries to the Continent." In *Monks of
England: The Benedictines in England from Augustine to the Present Day*, edited
by Daniel Rees, 37-54. London: SPCK, 1997.

CHAPTER 8

Theodore the Studite

Ian A. McFarland

Along with his contemporary, Patriarch Nicephorus of Constantinople (758-828), and John of Damascus a generation earlier (c. 675-749), Theodore the Studite (759-826), abbot of the monastery of Studius in Constantinople, was one of the three great defenders of icons during the controversy over their veneration that rocked the Byzantine Empire for over a century, from 726 to 843. Though the conflict between iconodules (who supported the veneration of icons) and iconoclasts (who opposed it) tends to be little known by Western (especially Protestant) Christians, few theological debates in the history of the church are more closely bound up with the politics of empire. From beginning to end, the fortunes of Byzantine iconoclasm depended on the support of the imperial court, and the arguments deployed by Theodore and other iconodules in the face of iconoclastic policy may correspondingly be seen as symptoms of a broader political struggle over the control of the sacred.

THEODORE'S CONTEXT: BYZANTINE ICONOCLASM

Icons—liturgical portraits of Christ, Mary, and the saints—were not an original feature of Christian piety. On the contrary, the principled rejection of images from worship was one of the chief ways in which the earliest generations of Christians distinguished themselves from the pagan cults that dominated the civic life of the Roman Empire. By the eighth century, however, the veneration of icons was well-established as a central feature of Christian piety, especially in the Greek-speaking areas of the eastern Mediterranean. The practice was widely believed to be of apostolic origin, to the extent that in 692 the Qunisext Council explicitly commended the depiction of Christ in human form for devotional purposes.[1]

As it happened, however, this official endorsement of iconography coincided with a period of unparalleled turbulence in the Byzantine Empire. While the western half of the old Roman Empire had long since succumbed to successive waves of barbarian invaders, the eastern half, ruled from Constantinople, had been much more successful in maintaining its political integrity. Yet as the seventh century drew to a close, various pressures were straining it to the breaking point. Arab armies, fired by the new faith of Islam, had overrun Byzantine territories from northern Africa to Syria. While they had been turned back from Constantinople itself in 678, they continued to make frequent incursions in the Byzantine territory. To the north, the Bulgars posed still another military threat, while in the far west Germanic tribes were challenging Byzantine power in Italy.

Things came to a head with the overthrow of the Emperor Justinian II in 695, setting off a period of political instability that witnessed no fewer than six occupants of the imperial throne over the next twenty years. During this period Arab pressure on Asia Minor resumed, leading to a second assault on Constantinople in 716; and while the capital was not taken, many other cities were—notwithstanding repeated attempts to invoke divine protection by means of solemn processions of icons around the city walls. Many interpreted the various catastrophes overwhelming the empire as evidence of God's judgment, and it was largely in an effort to appease what was perceived as divine wrath that the Emperor Leo III issued the first imperial proscription of icons in 726.

Leo's decision to focus on icons as the cause of political turmoil and military defeat is not especially strange in context. While later iconodule writers attributed his iconoclastic policies to Muslim and Jewish influence, the Christian tradition—for the temporal welfare of which he, like other Byzantine emperors, saw himself responsible—provided no shortage of reasons to turn against the veneration of icons. Aside from the anti-pagan polemic of the early apologists, well-known figures in the history of the church had explicitly condemned the manufacture of images of Christ and the saints.[2] Given the string of disasters that were afflicting the empire and the apparent inability of icons to protect so many Byzantine cities against the Arab onslaught, it is easy to understand why the emperor might have been open to the idea that the popular enthusiasm for religious images was misplaced and in need of correction.

At the same time, it would be a mistake to see iconoclasm as the linchpin of Leo III's reign. His iconoclastic policy was not pursued with particular ferocity, and it was just one component of a broader program of reform. During the course of his reign, Leo completely reorganized Byzantine naval command and also initiated an extensive restructuring of land forces in order to weaken the power of individual commanders as possible sources of political instability. On the civilian front Leo instituted legal reforms to restore stability and uniformity of juridical practice after years of disruption, as well as monetary reforms designed to stimulate trade and stabilize prices. Iconoclasm was thus just one component of military, political, and economic reorganization that continued on all fronts under his successors.

Together these policies proved successful in restoring the empire's fortunes: both Leo III and his son, Constantine V, had long reigns characterized by order, prosperity, and success in securing the empire's borders. Their achievement in bringing stability to the empire at a time when it stood on the brink of collapse goes a long way to explaining the popularity of their iconoclastic policies among some segments of the population—especially the military. Indeed, it has been argued that iconoclasm was only able to become a significant theological issue in the first place because Leo and Constantine's combined success at home and abroad gave the voice of the emperor genuine credibility in matters of faith.[3]

As tenacious as iconoclasm proved, however, it was always a highly centralized policy that depended on imperial support.[4] While individual bishops pursued iconoclast policies prior to Leo III's edict, and while there were isolated milieus in which it was received with comparative enthusiasm, iconoclasm was at no point a broad-based movement in Byzantine society. Indeed, so little was it connected with the internal dynamics of church life that only after a quarter century of state iconoclasm was the attempt made (at the Council of Hieria in 754) to give this piece of imperial policy formal ecclesiastical validation. Though this attempt was backed by theological arguments of considerable sophistication, however, it did little to consolidate support for the iconoclasm in church or society.

The reason for this lack of popular appeal is not hard to fathom. Iconoclasm may have been just one part of a broader program of imperial reform, but it was also the element with the most immediate impact on the life of the typical Byzantine. What evidence we have about origins of icon veneration suggests that it was driven by popular piety: people wanted to have immediate, visual, and personal access to what they worshiped. The proscription of icons thus cut against an intensely personal dimension of popular religious practice.

Underlying iconodule practice was the implicit theological claim that the material could mediate the divine, and it was this claim that constituted the flashpoint of the Byzantine debate over icons. Given the central role of matter in the church's sacraments, the claim that icons provide a further instrument of communion with the divine might not seem especially controversial—yet there was an important difference between the two sets of practices. For while the performance of the sacraments was strictly limited to (and therefore subject to control by) the church hierarchy, the mediation of divine presence through icons was not subject to clerical regulation. The veneration of icons did not require the mediation of a priest, and their portability meant that icons could be accessed completely independent of centralized ecclesiastical control.

The problem for the iconodules was that the very features of icons that assured their popularity could be seen as substantive theological reasons to object to them. Wasn't the desire to hold or possess the divine in a physical object the mark of paganism? Hadn't God explicitly proscribed the manufacture of images in the Decalogue precisely to forestall this temptation (Exod. 20:4-5; Deut. 5:8-9)? And hadn't no less a figure than Paul argued that the manufacture of images was the principle cause of God's wrath against the nations (Rom. 1:23-25)? Against these charges, John of Damascus, writing during the first period of iconoclasm in the eighth century, had deployed three main arguments in defense of icons:

1. The veneration (*proskunesis*) shown icons is not the same as worship (*latreia*), which is rightly given to God alone.[5]

2. Images have pedagogical value, and were so used even in Old Testament times.[6]

3. The fact that God took material form in the incarnation supersedes the biblical prohibition against physical depictions of God.[7]

While the first two arguments have antecedents in earlier, pagan apologies for the use of images, the third is uniquely Christian and is the linchpin of John's iconodule theology: because God has taken material existence in the incarnation, *all* matter has been vindicated as a potential vehicle of encounter with the divine.[8] Christology thus became the central justification for Christian iconography.

John's specifically christological defense of the icons set the stage for the transformation of iconoclastic polemic in the period after 750. The initiative was taken by the iconoclasts, who argued against John that icons of Jesus actually *under-mined* the commonly accepted principles of orthodox Christology, according to which the divine and human natures were united in Christ "without confusion or change, without division or separation."[9] The iconoclasts maintained that insofar as Christ's divine nature is, by common consent, uncircumscribable (and therefore incapable of representation), an icon of Christ *either* depicts only Christ's human-ity (thereby dividing the natures), *or* presumes to depict both natures together (thereby confusing them).[10] In short, icons had be rejected because they could not depict Christ correctly (i.e., as both fully human *and* fully divine). It followed that the incarnation, far from vindicating the revelatory possibilities of matter, only re-enforced its dangers as a potential source of apostasy.

THEODORE'S RESPONSE TO ICONOCLASM

Theodore the Studite was by no means the first to face the christological arguments of the iconoclasts, nor were his counter-arguments especially original.[11] Theodore was still a young monk when in 787 the iconodules achieved temporary victory at the Second Council of Nicea. In response to the iconoclast charge that icons failed to represent Christ in both natures, iconodule theologians retorted that in the same way that the whole Christ, divine and human, was encountered in the flesh, so the whole Christ, divine and human, could be contemplated in an icon depicting his flesh.[12] Yet this triumph proved ephemeral. In 815 the Emperor Leo V summoned another council condemning II Nicea and reaffirming the iconoclas-tic theology of the Council of Hieria. It was at this point that Theodore the Stu-dite emerged as a leading figure among the iconodules.

By this point in his career, Theodore was intimately familiar with imperial court politics, having already been exiled twice for political resistance in a matter having nothing to do with icons.[13] This history should not be taken to imply that Theo-dore subscribed to anything like modern notions of the separation of church and state. He inherited from earlier Byzantine theologians a fairly high estimate of the theological significance of the emperor. Nevertheless, he had a clear sense of the limits of imperial power in ecclesiastical matters:

> It is the duty of Emperors and governors to offer assistance, to approve things that are decreed and to reconcile differences arising out of secular concerns. But God has given them no power whatever over the divine dogmas, and any-thing they do in that realm will not last.[14]

The iconoclast controversy was for Theodore a clear case of the emperor hav-ing exceeded his authority. In this respect, his view of the separate (though closely related) competencies of secular and ecclesiastical authority gave him grounds for resisting the kind of centralization of power iconoclasm represented. At the same time, he also recognized that questions of jurisdiction were only part of the prob-lem. If the challenge to imperial policy was to prove effective, Theodore needed to show that iconoclasm was bad doctrine—and that meant defending matter's capacity to mediate the divine.

Before exploring Theodore's arguments, however, it is important to recognize that the iconoclasts' opposition to materiality as a mediator of the divine was far from unqualified. As adherents to Chalcedon, they were, as we have seen, commit-ted to the full humanity of Christ, and they demonstrated a genuine appreciation for the need for some enduring witness to Jesus' materiality by affirming the bread of the Eucharist as the one genuine icon of Christ. Moreover, they also accepted the cross as a legitimate object of Christian veneration. It therefore seems that their objection was not to ascribing a place to matter as such in Christian devotion, but rather to the veneration of matter in specifically human form.[15] Thus, in addition to objecting to portraits of Christ, the iconoclasts rejected images of saints on the grounds that depictions of earthly bodies misrepresent the essentially unrepresent-able character of glorified humanity. In short, whether their subject matter is the saints or Christ, icons are held to depict what cannot in fact be depicted and thus must be regarded as idols.[16]

Building on the line of argument developed during and after II Nicea, Theo-dore's counter to this iconoclast logic rests on his understanding of the significance of the body as a mediator of personal identity. He thus insists that to deny that Christ can be circumscribed in painting is to deny that he is human, since human bodies (whether or not they are united with the divine nature) are, as human, cir-cumscribed in the same way that every other material body is. In this way, Chris-tology is turned to the iconodules' advantage by arguing that it is the iconoclasts who confuse Christ's two natures by suggesting that the properties of the divine nature (*viz.*, its essential uncircumscribability) change those of the human nature (which is inherently circumscribable).[17]

The real center of Theodore's argument, however, is the claim that the iconoclast focus on Christ's natures completely fails to reckon with the central role of the per-son (or, to use the technical term of the period, hypostasis) as the object of iconodule veneration. Theodore points out that just as the agent of salvation is not either the divine or human natures in the abstract, but rather the particular person in and as whom they are united, so it is the person—and not one or both natures—who is the one depicted in the icon. To be sure, the person of Jesus is encountered by us through his human nature, since it is that nature which, by virtue of its capacity to be circumscribed, can be seen, heard, and touched; but what counts soteriologically and devotionally is the one who is present in the natures and not the natures themselves.[18]

The particular properties of the human nature therefore have significance because they are the way in which Jesus' personal identity is mediated to us. Theodore explains his position as follows:

> When anyone is portrayed, it is not the [universal] nature but the [individual] hypostasis which is portrayed. For how could a nature be portrayed unless it were contemplated in a hypostasis [i.e., in a particular, concrete instance]? For example, Peter is not portrayed insofar as he is animate, rational, mortal, and capable of thought and understanding; for this does not define Peter only, but also Paul and John, and all those of the same species. But insofar as he adds along with the common definition certain [individual] properties such as a long or short nose, curly hair, a good complexion, bright eyes, or whatever else characterizes his particular appearance, he is distinguished from individuals of the same species.[19]

This perspective allows Theodore to challenge at its root the iconoclast contention that icons are inherently idolatrous because they presume to portray a reality that is inherently incapable of being portrayed. He does this by arguing that while one's hypostasis (or concrete personhood) is not visible in itself, it is nevertheless present in and through the body, such that one can legitimately point to a particular body and say, "That is Peter," or (in the case of the incarnate Word), "That is the Son of God." In short, Theodore's position is that insofar as personal identity is truly mediated by human bodies (such that I can rightly identify any human person by reference to her body), it may be communicated in icons that depict those bodies.[20]

In this way Theodore argues that the relation between the image and original (or prototype) in an icon reflects the mysterious relation between the body and the self in a living human being.[21] Thus, to deny that Christ can be represented in an icon is necessarily to compromise confession of his genuine humanity.[22] At the same time, the acknowledgement that only the material is capable of physical representation does not convict the iconodule of idolatry, because what is venerated is not the matter in itself (whether the body of the historical Jesus or an iconic depiction of him), but the hypostasis recognized in and through the matter.[23] In short, over against the iconoclast charge that attention to the physical form of Christ or the saints invariably impedes encounter with the person, Theodore argues that the incarnation confirms an inalienable (if mysterious) link between them, such that the "what" of the physical form—whether living or depicted in an icon—is a genuine marker of and point of contact with the "who" of the person.

Once these points have been secured, the iconoclast attempts to limit acts of veneration to the nonhuman forms of the Eucharist and the cross appear arbitrary. With respect to the Eucharist, Theodore argues that for the iconoclasts to allow that any matter can mediate Christ's presence is effectively to undermine their contention that to point to the circumscribable as an icon of Christ necessarily either divides or confuses Christ's divine and human natures.[24] Likewise, the fact that liturgical crosses vary among themselves and all differ from the true cross in dimension and composition simply confirms that what counts in the manufacture of an image is not a complete identity according to which the nature of the original is repeated in the image. Rather, what counts is the commitment to represent a particular subject—the fact that the two are "called by the same name" and are thus identifiable as the image of that particular reality.[25]

In concluding his defense of iconodule practice, Theodore ventures what is perhaps his most surprising contention of all. Not only is it the case, he argues, that icons of Christ are permissible; they are mandatory. "Otherwise," he claims, "He would lose His humanity if he were not venerated through the production of the image."[26] Theodore seems to be building here not only on the assertion of the necessity that Christ's humanity, if real, must be circumscribable (and thus capable of physical representation), but also on a theory of human knowing according to which visible encounter with a person is a prerequisite even for proper knowledge of her words.[27] From this perspective the veneration of icons, far from promoting idolatry, actually serves as a safeguard against it by providing new insights capable of correcting our potentially idolatrous constructions of who Christ is. As Theodore puts it, "Christ's image becomes more conspicuous to all when it appears by imprinting itself in materials."[28]

CONSTRUCTIVE IMPLICATIONS

In 815 Theodore was arrested for his iconodule convictions. There followed six years of imprisonment, including periods of severe deprivation and torture. In 821 the Emperor Michael II released him from confinement but did not allow him to return to the capital. When Theodore died five years later, still in exile, iconoclasm remained official state policy. Its final defeat did not come until 843, when the Empress Theodora, acting as regent for her three-year-old son, convened an assembly at which the Second Council of Nicea was confirmed as the seventh ecumenical council and the last of the iconoclast patriarchs was deposed. The event is still commemorated in the orthodox churches on the first Sunday in Lent as the "Feast of Orthodoxy."

Though Theodore's defense of the icons was thereby vindicated, the implications of his theology for broader questions of Christian faith and practice are mixed. For example, given the very strict conventions that govern the manufacture of icons in the orthodox churches, it is open to question whether the proliferation of liturgical images of Christ has actually deepened the church's Christology in the way that Theodore believed it would.[29] Even as otherwise conservative a theologian as Hans Urs von Balthasar has registered his concern about the validity of the iconodule position, arguing that iconoclasm remains "valid at least by way of a permanent warning against allowing the Image of himself that God made to appear in the world—the Image that is his Son—to be extended without any critical distance whatever into other images."[30] While von Balthasar is far from defending iconoclasm as such, he does identify it as a "warning corrective" against what might be seen as Theodore's overly optimistic supposition that physical depictions of Christ invariably make the divine image more conspicuous.[31]

Yet the dangers in the iconodule position should not be allowed to obscure its genuine contribution to Christian reflection on God's relation to the created order. If the iconoclasts cannot fairly be accused of an ontological dualism that denies the goodness of matter, they nevertheless can be charged with a dualist epistemology according to which the fundamental identity—and thus the saving presence—of Christ is fundamentally separate from his body. So, too, they maintain that the bodies of the saints give only an imperfect access to their persons. It was Theodore's merit to have pointed out that only such a dualism can explain the iconoclasts' resistance to the idea that icons of Christ and the saints can mediate encounter with them. In the final analysis, their position implies that persons' bodies somehow impede their presence to one another rather than serving precisely as the mode by which such presence is experienced.

Against this view of the material as a mask that must be penetrated in order to arrive at the underlying reality, Theodore insisted that what the incarnation implied was precisely God's availability in a human body. If this bodily presence was real—if the Word truly took flesh and not just its appearance—then Jesus' body must have the same properties as other human bodies, including the property of being subject to physical representation through painting, mosaic, or sculpture. To be sure, any given representation may be false, and even a true portrait may be misinterpreted or otherwise misused; but that is no more an argument against icons than poor sermons are an argument against proclaiming the gospel. Matter is, of course, not inherently revelatory, and (though Theodore seems loath to admit this for Christian iconography) the idolatrous confusion of creature and creator remains a genuine possibility. But the incarnation reveals a further possibility: that matter, for all its ontological difference from the divine, can nevertheless serve as a medium of communion with the divine.

Although the theological principles behind the veneration of icons are important in their own right, it is crucial to note that the defense of the revelatory capacity of matter also had significant political implications. Unlike the sacraments, which were under the exclusive control of the ordained priesthood, icons represented a material point of contact with the divine that was more free-floating: they could be venerated anywhere, by anyone, without the mediation of a third party. In this context, it is vital to recall once again that Byzantine state iconoclasm was part of a wider program of political centralization that sought to eliminate any source of power capable of weakening the state by serving as a competing focus of loyalty.[32] Icons were a just such a power source, and the fact that the most famous collections were housed in monasteries—the most decentralized and autonomous Christian institutions within the Christian Empire—helps explain why monks like Theodore were at the center of resistance to imperial iconoclasm. By insisting that icons were worthy of veneration, iconodules were effectively engaged in a struggle with the state over the control of sacred capital within the empire.

With the "Triumph of Orthodoxy" in 843, the state effectively gave up on the goal of complete control over access to the divine that was a definite implication (if not a stated aim) of the iconoclast emperors. Given the role of the monasteries in the resistance to state iconoclasm, it is interesting to note that when the Byzantine Empire finally collapsed in 1453, the monasteries continued to be centers of popular piety that survived throughout the subsequent period of Muslim hegemony. And while the presence of vibrant monastic communities did not prevent the virtual extinction of Christianity in the formerly Byzantine territories in Africa and the Near East, it is perhaps not altogether irresponsible to suggest that the prospects for the survival of Christianity in the Balkans and the Aegean basin would have been less likely if the iconoclasts had won, and orthodox identity had been more tightly fused with the structures of Christian Empire. As it was, the piety of the icon helped provide a framework within which Orthodox Christianity could survive even where the ruling powers embraced a different (and, ironically, profoundly iconoclastic) faith.

FURTHER READING

Primary Sources

St. John of Damascus. *Three Treatises on the Divine Images*. Translated by Andrew Louth. Crestwood, N.Y.: St. Vladimir's Seminary Press, 2003.

St. Theodore the Studite. *On the Holy Icons*. Translated by Catharine P. Roth. Crestwood, N.Y.: St. Vladimir's Seminary Press, 2001.

Sahas, Daniel J. *Icon and Logos: Sources in Eighth-Century Iconoclasm*. Toronto: University of Toronto Press, 1986.

Secondary Sources

Alexander, Paul. J. *The Patriarch Nicephorus of Constantinople: Ecclesiastical Policy and Image Worship in the Byzantine Empire*. Oxford: Clarendon Press, 1958.

Cholij, Roman. *Theodore the Stoudite: The Ordering of Holiness*. Oxford: Oxford University Press, 2002.

Cormack, Robin. *Writing in Gold: Byzantine Society and Its Icons*. New York: Oxford University Press, 1985.

Gardner, Alice. *Theodore of Studium: His Life and Times*. London: E. Arnold, 1905.

Giakalis, Ambrosios. *Images of the Divine: The Theology of Icons at the Seventh Ecumenical Council*. Rev. ed. Leiden: Brill, 2005.

Meyendorff, John. "Vision of the Invisible: The Iconoclastic Crisis." Chap. 9 in *Christ in Eastern Christian Thought*. Crestwood, N.Y.: St. Vladimir's Seminary Press, 1987.

Parry, Kenneth. *Depicting the Word: Byzantine Iconophile Thought of the Eighth and Ninth Centuries.* Leiden: Brill, 1996.

Pelikan, Jaroslav. *Imago Dei: The Byzantine Apologia for Icons.* Princeton, N.J.: Princeton University Press, 1990.

CHAPTER 9

Anselm of Canterbury

Darby Kathleen Ray

Anselm of Canterbury (1033-1109) lived during a period of stunning change. The breadth and depth of the transformation routinely prompt historians of the West to compare the period (c. 1050-1300) to the Reformation or the Industrial Revolution. In nearly every area of life—politics, economics, social relations, and religion—Europe was dramatically transformed. Amid the torrents of unprecedented change that rocked Anselm's world, the imperial experiences and desires of church and state and of Christianity and Islam formed a constant undercurrent whose own not-infrequent turbulence was both a catalyst for and an obstacle to change. Anselm's relationship to the imperial power dynamics of his day was unquestionably complex.

As a philosopher and theologian, Anselm's creativity of method and content mark him as a key transitional figure that transgressed centuries-old norms and initiated or embraced new trends that would characterize scholarship and piety for generations to come.[1] As we will see, Anselm's conceptions of God and the divine-human relationship are potentially subversive of imperial pretensions and violence. At the same time, the root assumptions and many of the conclusions of his scholarly work are profoundly conservative of imperial values and hierarchies. As a monk, abbot, and archbishop, moreover, Anselm appears to have been an often-willing participant in the empire building moves of both ecclesial and secular authorities; at other times, he seems astonishingly oblivious to such moves. In the final analysis, Anselm's life and writings reflect an ambivalent relationship to the imperial powers of his day. Nevertheless, when considered in light of the imperial dynamics of our own twenty-first century world, Anselm's theological proposals have the potential to function as part of a larger theology of resistance to empire.

Anselm's Context

We cannot understand the complexity of Anselm's thought and actions, nor assess their fruitfulness for our contemporary situation, unless we view them in historical context. One way of approaching medieval European culture is to consider that at its heart, and circulating throughout its varied discourses—including Neoplatonism, feudalism, monasticism, patriarchy, church-state conflict, chivalry, scholasticism, anti-Semitism, and crusade against Islam—is what we might call an imperial spirit. That spirit or *Gestalt* is characterized by a thoroughgoing, if occasionally flexible, embrace of hierarchical or top-down power and an unflagging commitment to the expansion of that power. The imperial spirit takes purest form in formally recognized empires and dynasties but is also at work in more diffuse constellations—such as in social relations and rituals, in an institution's self-understanding or objectives, or in particular ways of viewing reality. During Anselm's lifetime, the imperial spirit was especially evident in the Neoplatonic philosophy that ordered conceptual and intellectual life, the feudal relations that ordered social existence, and the vision of unrivaled power that motivated both church and state. Each of these "imperial" discourses left its mark on Anselm.

The medieval Western thought of Anselm's day was saturated with Neoplatonic assumptions of the superiority of the spiritual, intellectual, immutable, and rational, and the concomitant inferiority of all things material, earthly, bodily, and mutable. The created world was assumed to be a poor imitation of the pure realm of perfect forms. As Anselm affirms, "[I]n the things created, there is not a simple and absolute essence, but an imperfect imitation of that true Essence."[2]

The metaphor of the great chain of being was an organizing idea of immense power and persuasion. It told the individual how he or she was related to other people; explained and legitimated class distinctions; and provided a compelling conceptual framework that encompassed the realities of both this world and the transcendent realm. According to this worldview, God and other spiritual beings such as angels and saints are at the top of the hierarchy; humans, who are part material and part spiritual, populate the middle tier; and nonhuman beings and nature comprise the bottom layer. Within each tier, hierarchy is again the ordering principle: God is above the angels, men are above women, and sentient beings are above nonsentient beings. In every case, that which is thought to be more spiritual or heavenly ranks above and is seen as superior to that which is less spiritual or more earthly.[3] Not surprisingly, given this hierarchy of values, it was widely assumed in the medieval West that monasticism was the earthly institution and calling that most closely approximated Neoplatonism's ideal world of forms and universals and that had the best chance of taming or holding in abeyance the chaos of change. Despite his rise to significant ecclesial power, Anselm seems to have understood himself first and last as a monk. He was, insists R.W. Southern, more at home with the clarity and certainty of monastic rule than with the ambiguities and uncertainties of the wider church and of secular society.[4] As we will see, this monastic self-understanding, undergirded by a fundamentally Neoplatonic way of viewing and valuing reality, undoubtedly contributed to Anselm's ambiguous response to the imperial dynamics of his day.

In addition to Neoplatonism, another defining feature of Anselm's world was feudalism.[5] While the earliest forms of feudal relations may have been "loose alliances between equals or near-equals instead of hierarchically determined and legally precise arrangements between superiors and inferiors," by Anselm's time, flexibility of relations had largely given way to a relatively rigid system of roles and rules around which public life was ordered.[6] The key to the system was hierarchy. Those with relative social power in the form of wealth, social standing, or political might had authority over those who lacked such power. In exchange for the lord's protection and access to basic necessities, vassals were obliged to serve and defend the lord's economic and political interests. Submission to the will of the lord was the vassal's most important job; without it, the lord's honor and the wider social order were jeopardized. When insubordination did occur, a precise system of redress commonly known as "satisfaction" was put into action to restore the offended lord's honor and, by extension, the order and rightness of the social whole. Importantly, honor and its associated social expectations and rituals were defined by one's position vis-à-vis the overall social hierarchy. So just as lords were above vassals in this hierarchy, kings outranked lords and emperors outranked kings. The particular form of redress required to respond appropriately to a dishonorable act depended upon the social roles of the parties involved. A king who accidentally killed a peasant, for example, might pay a fine, while a peasant who accidentally killed a lord would forfeit his life.

Feudalism was a powerful imperial discourse in the Middle Ages. Its system of hierarchically defined social roles and carefully prescribed rituals for inscribing and restoring those roles was part of the *habitus* of medieval Europeans. It was an unquestioned, commonsense feature of reality, assumed to be divinely ordained and hence constitutive not only of "secular" relations but of the church as well. No wonder, then, that its impress on Anselm's life and thought is clear.[7] Our question, to be taken up shortly, is whether Anselm managed in any ways to resist or talk back to feudalism's imperial *Gestalt*.

A third imperial discourse circulating through the veins of Anselm's culture was the church-state conflict of the eleventh to twelfth centuries. Given the complexities of church-state relations in this time we must be content, once again, with a mere sketch of the situation. Nevertheless, even that should give us an appreciation of the turbulent forces of competing imperial desires with which Anselm, willingly or not, had to contend.

Anselm's context has been described as one of "medieval empire formation—the Norman conquest of England, the First Crusade, the expansion of the lands of 'Latin Europe,' and the extension of the power of the pope."[8] Behind practically every event, text, controversy, council, and building project, one can discern the watermark of imperial power or desire. For most of Anselm's life, church and state were locked in a protracted ideological battle for control of Europe—a Europe each fought to expand. Since the Council of Nicaea in the fourth century at which Constantine established his authority over the church, the state had controlled the church to one extent or another. By the tenth century, the church had become thoroughly corrupted by what historian Clifford Backman describes as a constellation of "greedy warlords, petty princes inheriting ever smaller pieces of patrimonies, and urban magnates feeling the pinch of economic hard times."[9] With its wealth being plundered, its clerical appointments employed to shore up secular authority and curry favors among the elites, the papacy being treated like "a political plaything" by aristocratic families, and its moral authority plummeting to an all-time low, the church was fighting for its life. The struggle was occasionally bloody, but more often it was a jurisdictional war of words and rituals.[10] It was, moreover, a war that by the end of Anselm's life the church appeared to be winning, prompting one eminent historian of the period to describe the church as "an empire spiritual in nature but political in action, which was more powerful and more rapidly expanding, more loyal to its ruler and richer in resources for future development, than that which any Western ruler including the ancient Roman emperors had ever commanded."[11] In the attempt to wrest control away from the state, the church underwent radical reform, a main result of which was the centralization of power in the papacy. No longer merely the "Vicar of St. Peter" or the head of the Christian communion, the pope was now known as the "Vicar of Christ," the universal sovereign and sole imperial power.[12] With the power tables turned, it was the church that could control the monarchy, declare crusade against Islam—another imperial power in the mix—decide all important disputes, and confidently claim supremacy over the secular world, at least for a time.

Anselm's role in and attitude toward the clash of imperial titans evokes little scholarly consensus. At times he appears to stand boldly in favor of ecclesial rule; at the very least he submits himself to papal authority and is at one point a fiercer advocate of papal doctrine than the pope himself. Anselm also expresses vociferous resistance to the king's interference with church business. At other times, he pays dramatic homage to secular powers even in the face of ecclesial decrees forbidding such homage, and he commands troops on the king's behalf. Interpretations of these apparent inconsistencies range widely. R.W. Southern, for instance, argues that even as the influential Archbishop of Canterbury—a position with authority over England, Scotland, and Ireland—Anselm is properly understood as a monk who "felt no call to entangle himself in the ecclesiastical-political questions of his day" and hence who showed little interest in and remained surprisingly ignorant of many of the controversies and decisions of his day.[13] A quite different appraisal is offered by Sally Vaughn, who emphasizes Anselm's political savvy and strategic maneuvering despite his well-known demonstrations of political disinterest and public humility.[14] When we turn away from the more political side of Anselm's life to take up the question of whether and how his *theology* either supported or resisted the imperial desires of his day, we encounter a similarly complex scenario.

ANSELM'S THEOLOGY

Anselm's theological method was at the same time both transgressive and reiterative of the rigidly hierarchical norms of his day. For Anselm as for Augustine, theology was always "faith seeking understanding"—a matter of using reason to clarify and interconnect the claims of faith rather than to call them fundamentally into question.[15] At the same time, by not continually founding his reflections and proposals on the authority of earlier texts from Scripture and tradition as Augustine and other forebears did, Anselm broke new methodological ground, effectively expanding the house of Christian authority.[16] Marilyn McCord Adams portrays Anselm as deeply collaborative in method and theological vision. She emphasizes, for instance, his frequent use of the dialogue—a discourse of mutuality rather than hierarchy; his view of Scripture as "a tutor" rather than a top-down authority; and, according to Adams, his understanding of "the human search for God as throughout, in all its dimensions and phases, a matter of divine-human collaboration, involving initiative on both sides."[17] By contrast, Southern presents a picture of a thinker who "reached his conclusions in private" rather than in collaboration with others and whose use of the form of dialogue is "deceptive"— useful with those who already agreed with him but dropped when true opposition appeared.[18] Despite the pretense of mutuality, says Southern, "in all his writings, [Anselm] appears on the field already a victor, ready to explain, perhaps to demonstrate, but not to fight."[19]

Anselm's God is always already a victor as well. And here, in the content of Anselm's theology, is where the complexities of his relationship to the imperial *Gestalt* are perhaps more intriguing than even the ambiguities of his theological method and ecclesial-political life. Here we see him both defying the idolatry, arrogance, and violence of empire *and* reinscribing them.

In the *Proslogion* Anselm articulates his famous definition of God as "that than which nothing greater can be conceived."[20] God is for Anselm not only of unsurpassable greatness but also perfectly powerful, just, good, true, wise, immortal, incorruptible, beautiful, and eternal. These divine attributes, moreover, are intrinsically constitutive of God's being. They are not, insists Anselm, "accidental" or "relational." They do not require that God undergoes or is subject to change, and they do not emerge from or imply a necessary connection of God to anything else. God is not, in other words, needful of or substantively affected by anyone or anything. God is perfectly self-producing, -sustaining, and -fulfilling, "individually and apart from association with [God's] creatures."[21] The "supreme Essence," says Anselm, created the world and its multitude of beings "from nothing, alone and through itself."[22] As "a supreme Spirit," moreover, God is not subject to the vagaries of corporeal existence but is rather "superior to body." God "feels," admits Anselm, but only inasmuch as God perfectly "cognizes" or knows "all things in the highest degree."[23]

Let us pause to consider what Anselm's concept of God, presented in condensed form in the preceding paragraph, implies about his relationship to the imperial powers of his day. I have suggested that Neoplatonism can be considered an imperial discourse insofar as it constitutes a pervasive and expansive conceptual framework that organized the medieval Western worldview along powerfully hierarchical lines. So influential was this conceptual grid that no alternative was imaginable, much less practicable, by the vast majority of medieval men and women. Clearly, Neoplatonism's root assumptions both reflected and buttressed the power of the ruling class, which was comprised of men who had the luxury of largely avoiding manual labor and the bodily, earthly associations it connoted. These were men for whom the great chain of being was, indeed, a great thing. In relation to them and the Neoplatonic worldview, Anselm's all-powerful God, who is pure Spirit and perfect cognition, seems a perfect match.[24]

A God-concept like this one was surely invoked by those in Anselm's day who argued, sometimes violently, for the superiority of the church over the state. From their standpoint, the state was a troublingly "worldly" institution whose grasping for power was nothing short of idolatry. To pay homage to it, as in the practice of lay investiture, was to reverse the proper order of the universe, the divinely ordained hierarchy of authority. Just as God depends on no associations or relationships for His inconceivable greatness, so must the church lay claim to its absolute independence from the state. Pope Gregory VII's bold declaration in 1075 of the *Dictatus Papae* ("Dictates of the Pope") is a dramatic example of this sentiment. Its twenty-seven statements of papal power express not only a clear refutation of state claims to authority over ecclesial appointments ("The pope alone has the power to instate and depose bishops."), but also an unprecedented assertion of the church's authority over the state ("The pope has the power to depose emperors.").[25]

The church in Anselm's day seems to have been blind to the degree to which its own practices and pretensions were no different than the state's.[26] Each institution sought to rule; each wanted absolute power and unrivaled authority. Perhaps the perfect example of this ironic doubling occurred in 1076 when Pope Gregory VII and King Henry IV anathematized each other, each declaring the other excommunicated and deposed from office. Anselm himself seems to have missed the sad irony, despite the fact that his own most fundamental understanding of God as "that than which nothing greater can be conceived" offered him the firmest possible ground on which to take a stand against the imperial desires of both church and state.

Anselm took no such stand, either publicly or in any of the multitudinous letters he wrote to friends. Why did his own deep convictions about the absolute *uniqueness* of God's being and power not inspire him to question those people and institutions that claimed such power for themselves? Was he protecting his own interests as one who benefited from such claims? Surely that was an inevitable causal factor, but an even greater one likely came from the double-edged nature of his notion of God. Regardless of the intent behind Anselm's emphasis on divine aseity, simplicity, and omnipotence, the cumulative effect within an imperial context is the affirmation—nay, the divinization—of top-down, hierarchical power. No wonder, then, that Anselm embraced what might be called a politics of quietude. Where he could have used his powerful theological conviction of God's incomparable greatness and absolute power to relativize and criticize monarchical and papal pretensions to greatness and power, Anselm was apparently either too embedded within the church-state power structure to recognize or refute its idolatrous dynamics, too saturated by Neoplatonic assumptions of hierarchical power to consider their theological shortcomings, or too paralyzed by the conflict between his own God-concept and the world in which he lived to take action. Whatever its cause, Anselm's inability to connect his theology to his politics is both a moral failure and, we must admit, a theological one as well, calling into question his most basic assumptions of divine omnipotence and aseity—a question we will consider again in the third section of this chapter.

The question of how Anselm's theology relates to the imperial *Gestalt* of medieval feudalism is also worth considering, especially given its powerful influence in Anselm's day and his own frequent theological use of feudal language and analogies. Here, our focus is not only Anselm's doctrine of God but also his understanding of the creaturely realm and, in particular, divine-human reconciliation, or atonement. Not surprisingly given the ambiguity of his theology's relationship to the imperial dynamics of the Neoplatonic philosophy and church-state conflict of his day, we find that Anselm's theology fits ambiguously with the dominant (and dominating) discourse of feudal relations.

Perhaps the first thing to note is that the main tenets of Anselm's theology could be expounded without recourse to feudal concepts or analogies. As R.W. Southern proposes, "Everything of importance in Anselm's argument can survive the removal of every trace of feudal imagery and the supposed contamination by elements of Germanic law."[27] That said, we should also admit that absent the feudal concepts and connotations, Anselm's theological proposals lose a good deal of their force. These proposals rely, if not necessarily then at least aesthetically and rhetorically, on the feudal context in which they were originally articulated. Anselm's concept of God, for instance, takes for granted and resonates deeply with the feudal "lord" who commands the honor and obeisance of his vassals and who, in return, provides the basic provisions and protection needed for daily living. Just as transgressions of the lord-vassal hierarchy were socially frowned upon by medieval Europeans, so too does Anselm take very seriously the transgression of human sin. Indeed, compared to theologians of any era, his awareness of and repulsion toward the heinousness of human sin are notably acute. The gap between human being and God is, to Anselm's mind, enormous.

However, given God's incomparable greatness and power, Anselm is quite certain that God's dignity is ultimately inviolable, even by the horrible breach of human sin. As we have seen, according to Anselm, God's perfect being is not relational; it is self-caused and self-sustaining, in need of no one or thing. Even so, Anselm insists, human sin creates a situation that must be addressed, a transgression that must be counteracted. This is the challenge Anselm takes up in his famous account of atonement, written during the more politically aware and active years of his life.

Anselm's atonement thinking seems actually to have begun in response to criticisms of Christian doctrine raised by "Jews" and "unbelievers." While there is evidence that a number of learned Jews had recently moved to London and were raising hard questions about the Christian doctrine of the incarnation—in particular the logic and prudence of claiming that the all-powerful God of the universe took on the debasement of fleshly existence and death—Jews were nevertheless hardly a major force in Anselm's England. By contrast, his mention of "unbelievers" (sometimes translated "pagans") as a catalyst for his atonement thinking was likely a veiled reference to the Muslim Empire, which was in Anselm's day thought to be a clear and present danger to Christendom. As Joerg Rieger suggests, it may well be that what Anselm ultimately accomplished in his *Cur Deus Homo*—to his own satisfaction, at least—was a robust affirmation of Christian identity and logic in the face of "others" who either symbolically (Jews) or literally (Muslims) threatened the authority and power of the Christian Empire. With his forceful logic of the atonement, Anselm "achieves by intellectual means what the Crusades achieve only through fire and sword—a victory over the Muslims."[28]

Whether the problem is the transgression of human sin, the apparent humiliation of the incarnation, or the threat of an imperial rival, Anselm's response is to emphasize the unparalleled honor, power, and justice of the Christian God. At the same time, these are precisely the things that appear to be at stake in Anselm's conception of atonement. According to this conception, human sin constitutes an affront to God's honor and, by extension, a disruption of the proper order of things.[29] In line with Norman understandings of law that prevailed in his day, Anselm assumed that a violation of the lord's or king's honor was, at the same time, a disruption of the larger imperial order. According to Rieger, what was at stake in transgressions of the ruler-ruled hierarchy was not simply one's personal reputation or esteem but the "ontology of the empire" itself—that is, the logic of a forcibly hierarchical social order.[30] In this context, Anselm's stubborn insistence that human beings offer some kind of recompense to God, some "satisfaction" for the wrong done to a superior, does not reflect a tyrannical God-king so much as a precarious social order in constant need of reiteration. An affront to the infinite God would have meant an intolerable violation of that order—a violation that had to be undone. The problem, as Anselm saw it, was that finite human beings could not possibly offer adequate recompense for an infinite affront. Hence the necessity of the incarnation, for only one who is human *ought* to offer satisfaction, but only one who is divine *can* offer such satisfaction. Clearly, Jesus the Christ, fully human and fully divine, is the only possible solution to the problem of human sin and the breach of social and cosmic order it produces.

As the incarnate one, Jesus *can* pay humanity's debt, and through his voluntary death, reasons Anselm, he does just that. Because it was widely assumed that death was the result of human sin, and because Jesus was wholly without sin, his innocent death is of infinite worth; therefore, it can and does reconcile human beings to God.[31] Thus, to those Jews and "pagans" who object to the idea that the incomparably great and powerful God would take on the humiliation, weakness, and mutability of finite, fleshly existence, Anselm responds that such a move is in fact perfectly, wondrously, salvifically reasonable—a testimony to God's wisdom, justice, and goodness. What appears to some to be weakness is actually a brilliant display of power—the power to conquer human sin and reestablish cosmic order.

In Anselm's day, this construal of atonement made immediate good sense, especially to those who were most invested in preserving the hierarchically arranged social order. While the medieval masses held on for generations to the earlier explanation of the incarnation as God's ingenious strategy for tricking the devil into defeat, Anselm's logic gradually eclipsed the old mythology and soon became the dominant interpretation of the meaning and efficacy of the incarnation and the death of Christ.[32] In all likelihood, the deception of the devil motif had been losing ground ever since Constantine and Justinian made Christianity the religion of the Roman Empire; it was, after all, essentially an "underdog" narrative and hence ill-suited for an increasingly imperial religion. Seen in this light, we might entertain the possibility that Anselm's contemptuous dismissal in the *Cur Deus Homo* of the popular deception of the devil trope underscores his own embeddedness in the imperial dynamics of the day, his own investment in a hierarchically ordered society. We might, moreover, interpret his theology's unrelenting emphasis on God's incomparable greatness and power and on humanity's thoroughgoing sinfulness as a (probably unconscious) theological enabling of an imperial *Gestalt*. Finally, we might see in Anselm's logic of atonement a not-very-subtle reinforcement of feudal hierarchies and their ritualized restoration and reiteration.

At the same time, however, we should acknowledge the ways in which Anselm's construal of the divine-human relationship appears to resist those same imperial dynamics. Within the context of feudalism's hierarchical social grid, and particularly in light of the pervasiveness in medieval Europe of armed violence as a response to social tension and conflict, it is possible to appreciate Anselm's approach to divine-human reconciliation as a judicious and even peaceable approach. In the face of a transgression of the hierarchical bond—as when a vassal disobeys or otherwise dishonors his lord—the choice for satisfaction as a means of conciliation was, in a sense, a choice for nonviolence (where violence means physical violence).[33] As Gerd Althoff explains, satisfaction "apparently consisted in a demonstrative act of public, unconditional subordination" aimed at regaining the lord's favor. This public ritual was often accompanied by a compensatory payment of money or fiefs to the injured party. The exact details of the ritual and payment depended on the social status of those involved in the dispute and were typically negotiated in advance by a mediator.[34] Anselm's own thinking about atonement appears to fit this interpretation of conflict resolution like a glove. Because the damage is infinite, Christ fulfills all three roles: He publicly demonstrates his subordination to God; he offers his innocent life as compensatory payment; and he even plays the role of mediator between the two interested parties.

By employing the satisfaction model to understand the reconciliation of God and human being, Anselm avoids a violent resolution—in this case, the physical or eschatological punishment of the human sinner—and he offers a compelling explanation for why the incarnation was a perfectly logical and "fitting" response to the ugly reality of human sin. Furthermore, Anselm's model of atonement emphasizes that regardless of their considerable differences, God and humans are inextricably connected to each other, bound in a reciprocal relationship and hence mutually responsible to each other. Unlike Anselm's empire-hungry contemporaries, his God does not anathematize the opponent, much less declare warfare. One might even suggest that in Christ, human being meets God no longer as vassal or subject but as partner or even friend. Despite the fact that human being's dishonoring of God *should* meet with total rebuke and punishment, instead God in effect abdicates God's social position at the very top of the hierarchy and voluntarily assumes a far lower position in order to come to human being's aid. In so doing, God defies the hierarchy at the heart of the imperial order. One could argue, in sum, that given the powerful constraints of feudal society, Anselm opted for the most peaceable, magnanimous, even radical solution possible to the divine-human conflict. Perhaps those of us who live outside his constraints have a difficult time appreciating that Anselm's theory of atonement resisted in important ways the hierarchy and violence of his age's imperial spirit.

Nevertheless, questions linger: If God is truly "that than which nothing greater can be conceived," then why should God be hamstrung by the norms and rituals of human society? Why, for instance, must God make a relatively narrow construal of justice (satisfaction, compensation) the precondition of God's mercy (forgiveness)?[35] Moreover, why are mercy and compassion treated by Anselm as "secondary" attributes of God—subsets of God's "goodness" but always at the mercy, so to speak, of justice, order, and power?[36] Despite his boundary-bursting notion of God and the hierarchy-subverting potential of his conception of atonement, we might still worry about the extent to which Anselm's theology reiterates feudal conventions. True, we could remove the feudalisms from his theology and still *have* a theology, but it would be a theology that depended in important ways for its logic and beauty on *some* system of hierarchical order and top-down power (if not feudalism then something similar). Anselm's God may be the "lord of lords," but does he transcend in a robust way the imperial *Gestalt* embodied in the system of feudal relations? Particularly when viewed in light of Anselm's failure in his own life to oppose the imperial designs of church and state in any clear or consistent way, we may conclude that despite Anselm's best intentions, his theology was at best ambiguous in its relation to the imperial spirit of his day.

IMPLICATIONS

But what about our own day? What can we glean from Anselm's theology that might be useful or instructive for our twenty-first century context? Limitations of space permit only a few brief reflections.

On the surface it appears that we live in an entirely different world than did Anselm. In many ways, of course, we do. And yet we share a common and vitally important challenge: the navigation of turbulent imperial waters. In Anselm's eleventh-century Europe, rival would-be empires clashed mightily: church and state, Christianity and Islam. In our day, there is arguably but one empire, one superpower—the United States of America—but imperial desire swells in many places, from the boardrooms of multinational corporations to the caves of Afghanistan. Many of us suspect that while the U.S. carries the scepter of empire, it is global capitalism that actually rules the world. There are those who resist these awesome imperial forces, including those who wish to replace the current "evil" or "fallen" empire with a new and improved imperial model—Islamism? A truly Christian empire?—as well as those who yearn for a wholly different, counter-imperial paradigm. What can we learn from Anselm about how (or how not) to navigate theologically the imperial tensions of our day?

We might begin by acknowledging those Anselmian theological assumptions or claims that appear in our own day to undergird or enhance imperial desires. We should, I believe, continue to worry about assumptions of divine omnipotence and aseity. While these claims certainly have the potential to relativize human grasping for power, they seem too often to have the opposite effect. Consider the extent to which a theology of power has been used effectively by the White House in the post-9/11 era to authorize a heroic national identity. Without the backing of a theology of unilateral power, would the Bush administration's promulgation of unilateral military action in Iraq, despite the lack of evidence of weapons of mass destruction or a clear connection to Al-Qaida, have found such widespread and deeply rooted public support?

In our context, Anselm's Neoplatonic assumptions of divine aseity and immutability are troubling. If we conceive of power in more expansive and life-giving terms than the power to control, we can appreciate as an essential divine attribute the power to relate to and be affected by others. Recognizing the wisdom of process theology, we might acknowledge that precisely because God *is* "that than which nothing greater can be conceived," God cannot be imprisoned within the abstract realm of Neoplatonic forms or universals.[37] That which is both the ideal form *and* the concrete actualization of that form is greater than that which is only one or the other. Anselm's interest in defending the incarnation, God become flesh, should have led him to this insight, but his vision was no doubt clouded by the Neoplatonic lens through which he gazed as well as the felt need to defend God's impenetrability against the threat of non-Christian assault. Had he seen his way clear to a thoroughly expansive, or genuinely incarnational, notion of divinity, Anselm might have been suspicious of the tendency of unilateral power to obliterate relationship and destroy concrete connections that are part of the complex but fragile web of created life. Reversing the order of his main concern in the *Cur Deus Homo,* he might have defined human sin primarily in terms of destruction of this intricate web (a truly cosmic order of things rather than merely an imperial order) and then, by extension, in terms of resistance to (or dishonoring of) God.

We get a hint of this broader, more symbiotic God-world relationship in Anselm's earlier considerations of God's nature. Written when concerns about Christianity's superiority vis-à-vis Judaism, Islam, and a secular Europe had probably not yet captured his interest or even awareness, Anselm affirms that God "dost permeate and embrace all things."[38] More boldly still, he identifies God as "Being itself . . . [who] supports and surpasses, includes and permeates all other things." "[I]t is," he says, "this same Being which is in all and through all, and from which, and through which, and in which, all exist."[39] When *this* theological sensibility is given credence, Anselm's keen interest in the "beauty" and "fittingness" of right relationship (what he typically refers to as "order") has the potential to transform his notion of justice in an anti-imperial direction.

Instead of reading justice as a gloss on omnipotence and as mainly concerned with the restoration of divine-human hierarchy, it could be defined as the restoration of the beauty of right or fitting relationships between God and creatures as well as among creatures themselves. Anselm gestures in important ways toward a theological anthropology of interconnection when, in his *Cur Deus Homo,* he affirms that compensation or satisfaction is necessary not for God's benefit but because of human being's deep need for right relationship to God and to the larger world.[40] Yet Anselm fails to consider the possibility that God, too, might be in some sense constitutively relational, claiming instead that relationality is for God merely "accidental." Had he pursued the relational instinct at the heart of his notion of satisfaction, Anselm might have emerged with a notion of atonement, and indeed of God, that was married not to hierarchy but to mutuality. He might then have affirmed that while a healthy relational "fit" (between God and human, human and human, or human and nonhuman) will sometimes include hierarchical dynamics, these will be contingent and always in service of the overall aim of the mutual flourishing of those in relationship. Within this connectional cosmic order, mercy will be understood as a primary means to justice rather than a mere consequence of it.

In considering the implications of Anselm's theology for our own imperial context we might, finally, acknowledge appreciatively the seriousness with which he takes human sin. The dismantling of our culture's habits and systems of greed and oppression will no doubt require powerful theological concepts, such as a robust notion of sin. With that in mind, we will want to emphasize the ways in which Anselm's understanding of sin pushes beyond the individual and interpersonal realms to recognize the societal and even cosmic frames within which sin works. To take sin as seriously as Anselm does—that is, to insist that sin be not only acknowledged but also actively addressed—would mean individual repentance, *metanoia,* and interpersonal mediation; it would also require concerted communal efforts to oppose the fracturing of human lives and spirits along lines of race, gender, religion, economics, nationality, and sexual orientation. It would mean working to end human exploitation of nonhuman beings. It would mean living lives and building institutions and communities that "honor" the beauty, complexity, and rightness of a truly cosmic "order." Nothing less, in the final analysis, would offer "satisfaction."

FURTHER READING

Primary Sources

Anselm of Canterbury. *Anselm of Canterbury: The Major Works.* Edited by Brian Davies and G. R. Evans. Oxford: Oxford University Press, 1998.

_____. *Complete Philosophical and Theological Treatises of Anselm of Canterbury.* Edited by Jasper Hopkins and Herbert Richardson. Minneapolis, Minn.: Arthur J. Banning Press, 2000.

_____. *Trinity, Incarnation, and Redemption: Theological Treatises*. Edited by Jasper Hopkins and Herbert Richardson. New York, N.Y.: Harper & Row, 1970.

_____. *The Prayers and Meditations of Saint Anselm with the Proslogion*. Translated by Benedicta Ward. Harmondsworth: Penguin Books, 1973.

Secondary Sources

Davies, Brian, and Brian Leftow, eds. *The Cambridge Companion to Anselm*. Cambridge: Cambridge University Press, 2004.

Southern, R.W. *Anselm and His Biographer: A Study of Monastic Life and Thought 1059-c.1130*. Cambridge: Cambridge University Press, 1966.

_____. *Saint Anselm: A Portrait in a Landscape*. Cambridge: Cambridge University Press, 1990.

CHAPTER 10

Mechthild of Magdeburg

Wendy Farley

Mechthild of Magdeburg (1208-1282 or 1294) lived in a time of enormous cultural creativity and conflict. Her one text, *The Flowing Light of the Godhead*, was translated from the vernacular Low Middle German not long after her death into Latin and High Middle German but virtually disappeared from view soon afterwards. The recovery of her text for a more general readership allows us to rediscover a creative theologian as she encounters the paradoxes of an ecclesia struggling with the possibilities and temptations of wealth, political power, war, innovation, and dissent.

Little is known about Mechthild, beyond what might be inferred from her writings. In general, she is thought to have come from a reasonably wealthy family, since she can read and write and is familiar with courtly love poetry and imagery. She was first "greeted" by God at twelve and as a young adult moved to Magdeburg where she lived as a beguine. In about 1250 she shared with her confessor, a Dominican friar, an account of the extraordinary richness of her contemplative practice. He insisted that she write down her experiences, which she did in a series of seven books over a period of several decades. The last years of her life were spent in the Cistercian convent at Helfta, whose nuns credit the flourishing of their own contemplative life to her presence among them.[1] Beyond indications in her writings that she was sickly and experienced conflict with the clergy, the real reasons for her move to a convent are impossible to know.

Mechthild was in many ways an outsider to the structures of institutional power. She vowed herself to a life of poverty and deprived herself for most of her life of the support of a family or monastic order. But pausing to identify some of the features of ecclesial and secular authority that shaped her world may help us to interpret her writings and their significance for us.

MECHTHILD'S SOCIAL CONTEXT: "A DISTANT MIRROR"

Not unlike our own era, the thirteenth century was a time of great cultural and technological creativity as well as one of imperial ambitions and tumult. We might get a sense of the cataclysmic cultural shifts of the thirteenth century by comparing them to those of the twentieth, which traversed the distance between a farmer without electricity and a wage earner surrounded by computers, iPods, and cell phones. These changes occur against the background of two world wars, the second of which introduced into modern consciousness the techniques of genocide and weapons that continue to haunt us with the possibility of annihilation. Similar juxtapositions of creativity and destruction provide the context for Mechthild's writings.

Mechthild's is a century of intellectual and spiritual flowering, of wave upon wave of crusade, and of incessant local warfare.[2] In the decade of Mechthild's birth, the great Jewish philosopher Maimonides had just died. Constantinople had been sacked. Dominic and Francis of Assisi preached and the first Latin translations of Aristotle, Galen, and Archimedes were brought to Europe.

The thirteenth century saw the development of much of the best of European culture. The poetry of courtly love continued to flourish and Dante was born. The gothic cathedrals of Chartres and Rheims were built. The Universities of Paris, Oxford, Salamanca, and the Sorbonne were created. The triumph of academic methods nourished Dominican (Albert Magnus and Thomas Aquinas) and Franciscan (Bonaventure, Robert Bacon, Duns Scotus) theologians whose writings remain deeply influential. Dialogues with Muslim scholars made possible advances in mathematics, including the use of Arabic numbers and the first use of the number zero in Europe. The invention of the keel, rudder, and compass, together with advances in ironmongering and stonemasonry, transformed possibilities for daily life, trade, and warfare.

Naturally all of this intellectual and technological creativity contributed to significant social change. Mathematical innovations facilitated the calculation of interest and thus the transition to a profit economy and the use of money. One aspect of these changes was a restlessness in cities that chafed under the constraints of feudal relations. The development of the Hanseatic League reflects the increased power of towns against imperial and ecclesial authorities, though this power was often dearly bought.[3] The wealth which was displayed in both ecclesial and secular society reflected a materialism that troubled some. St. Francis's love affair with "Lady Poverty" is only one example of a thirst for an antidote to the opulence that profit made possible.[4]

Magdeburg represents a microcosm of these changes. As a thriving urban center, it was one of the first cities to enjoy the acquisition of rights known as the *Magdeburger Recht*. Its position on the banks of the Elbe River made it a natural launching point for the colonization of the east. Through this city poured the tribute and slaves that were the fruit of the trade and warfare that constituted relations between Germanic and Slavish peoples. In 1193 this low-level conflict was upgraded to the status of a crusade.[5] This meant that "troops fought under vows of fidelity which freed them and theirs from secular cares and vexation, and obtained remission of sins for their souls."[6] St. Bernard of Clairvaux, whose beautiful interpretations of the "Song of Songs" inspired so many, "urged crusaders to fight the heathen 'until such time as, by God's help, they shall be either converted or wiped out.' There was to be no truce, no taking of tribute from the unconverted; baptism or death were the only alternatives."[7]

In 1199, Albert of Buxhoeuden, Archbishop of Bremen, organized monastic orders of soldiers to augment crusaders as a permanent and dedicated fighting core. Although they were "accused of every crime," these warrior monks greatly contributed to the pacification of pagans.[8] But this Northern Crusade relied also on entrepreneurs, whose participation was encouraged by the indulgences Pope Innocent IV granted to anyone who moved to the Eastern colonies or contributed money to the cause. These colonists brought cultural goods eastward while carrying profit westward.

The use of Arabic numbers improved the logistics of investing in things like crusades and colonialism. The invention of cogs made it possible to carry unprecedented numbers of warriors and goods in and out of Slavic territory. This, together with the crossbow, decisively tipped the balance in favor of the Western armies. The passion of the Dominicans to purify the church and spread the gospel could be diverted from its attention on the corruption of the clergy and directed to the mission against the godless. The outrageous violence of criminals was likewise absorbed by the creation of orders of warrior monks. Towns like Magdeburg thrived on the wealth produced by crusading colonialism and were able to secure greater independence for themselves, creating mechanisms that would allow capitalism to displace feudalism. This interweaving of economic, military, civil, and ecclesial interests underlies the creativity and violence of religious movements of the thirteenth century.

MECHTHILD'S RELIGIOUS CONTEXT: "WHEN THINGS OF THE SPIRIT COME FIRST"

The crusading impulse that one sees turned against Slavs, Muslims, dissenters, and occasionally peasants is not among Christianity's noblest expressions. But the religious spirit of the thirteenth century is also evident in the spectacular explosion of spiritual innovation and diversity. It is difficult to capture the bubbling, brilliantly creative, horrifically contested landscape of thirteenth-century religion in a few paragraphs. Christians fought with Muslims with a ferocity that remains legendary, but also profited from a slave trade with them and benefited from their enormous learning. Jews were expelled from Spain, England, and France. Movements for spiritual purification and renewal caught hold of women and men, who flooded the ranks of Albigensians, Cathars, and the Waldensians. Dominicans and Franciscans shared their fervor for renewal but (usually) found ways of remaining within the fold of orthodoxy. Both orthodox and dissenting movements extended Christian practice to the laity.[9] But it was the beguines who proved to be particularly well suited to provide women such as Mechthild with opportunities to express themselves spiritually and theologically.

The beguines were not a uniform movement but rather women who sought a contemplative life independent of marriage and monasticism. There was no rule or doctrine that bound them to a single form of life. But in ones and twos, in small or large communities, women carved out ways of life characterized by commitment to chastity, poverty, and contemplation. The period of the movement's greatest flourishing lies between 1215—when Jacques de Vitry obtained papal dispensation for women to live together in chastity and poverty—and 1311-12, when the Council of Vienne all but abolished this right.[10] Some beguines practiced works of mercy among the sick and poor. Some supported themselves through their own work; others depended upon alms or family dowries. Their religious practice generally included observation of the seven canonical hours of prayer; penitential acts including fasting and vigils; mantric prayer, and forms of meditation that included visualization.[11] This movement gave rise to some of the most creative and beautiful theological writing done by women, including the works of Hadewijch in Belgium and Mechthild in Magdeburg, both of whom participated in the innovation of writing theology in the vernacular. Marguerite Porete, another brilliant writer, was burned at the stake in 1310. She represents the dangers encountered by the beguines and her death is a dramatic illustration of why the movement withered after only about one hundred years.

While some women continue to pursue this way of life even up to the present day, the vibrancy of the movement was dramatically curtailed during the thirteenth century, when the fate of the beguines exposed some of the fault lines of Christianity. It is not surprising to find the papacy of that century struggling hard to find ways to supervise, incorporate, and extinguish various aspects of these dynamic religious movements.[12] It assimilated some of the dissenting energies of the mendicant movement by recognizing the new Dominican and Franciscan orders. It extended its care and supervision of the laity through innovations of pastoral care. This care was accompanied by a concern that the laity not get too close to the sources of authority and in fact "opening scripture to the unworthy" was punished as heresy.[13] By contrast, the penitential system was refined and extended. One aspect of the system was the requirement instituted by the Fourth Lateran Council of 1215 that "[e]very believer, male and female, was now required to confess sins 'faithfully' at least once a year to his or her own priest."[14] This in turn required the construction of confession manuals to guide the confessor in his uncovering of sin.[15] The uncovering of sin required an antidote in the form of penances. In these refinements of the penitential system, the church offered a "moral and spiritual discipline that gave them [the laity] hope for salvation."[16] But this system also functioned as "a weapon in an on-going, and hotly contested, ideological struggle."[17]

The mechanism of inquisition arose to address those religious movements that appeared recalcitrant to the ministrations of the church. We recall that this is a society "which expressed its endemic tensions in religious terms," so strictly separating religious from secular motivations is difficult.[18] But since the conflicts manifested theologically, manuals were created to guide inquisitors in identifying doctrinal error. "Much of the thirteenth century can be seen as the continuation and ever increasing proliferation and expansion of these genres."[19] This includes the production of a technical literature to more systematically define and treat persons as heretical, which occurred "under the influence of the theology of the universities. The most elaborate were now written by members of the new mendicant Orders of Dominicans and Franciscans."[20] Dominicans were also charged with hunting out heretics and displaying the cost of dissent: yellow crosses worn on clothing, destruction of homes, compulsory pilgrimages, as well as the "terror and drama of burning."[21] The Dominicans and Franciscans remind us of the ambiguity that haunts religion: they ignited much of the energy for spiritual and intellectual creativity. They nourished women's spiritual independence through their support of beguines and tertiaries. At the same time their "scientific" scholarship and passion for reform are implicated in the escalating violence over theology, money, and power.

We remember the writings of Aquinas (a Dominican) and Bonaventure (a Franciscan) as monuments of beauty and wisdom, and yet the religious movements they helped invent contributed to the development of a "vast and intricate system of social control" that invaded even the most intimate details of human life.[22] Likewise, in the writings of women contemplatives and the preaching of the mendicant friars we see resistance to whatever contributed to theological and institutional violence. Interpreting the interdependences of these riptides of ecclesial innovation is complex, but for the participants it could be extremely hazardous. In the midst of this volatility, Mechthild felt compelled to set the fruit of her contemplative practice onto paper.

MECHTHILD OF MAGDEBURG'S *THE FLOWING LIGHT OF THE GODHEAD*

In the prologue to Mechthild's book, the reader is advised to read the book nine times if they wish to understand it. Although this may seem excessive, it is a highly condensed work, almost each page opening onto an implicit systematic theology of extraordinary subtlety. One can get a general overview of some of her basic themes fairly quickly: the utterly dependable love of God; the dialectic between yearning and contentment; the role of suffering in contemplative practice. In particular the bold imagery with which she describes the intimacy between God and the soul might stand out at first.

> What do you bid me, Lord
> Take off your clothes
> Lord, what will happen to me then
> Lady Soul, you are so utterly formed to my nature
> That not the slightest thing can be between you and me...
> And so you must cast off from you

Both fear and shame and all external virtues....
Then a blessed stillness
That both desire comes over them.
He surrenders himself to her,
And she surrenders herself to him. (1:44)

It is possible to avoid the challenging implications of contemplative theology by dismissing it as "merely" subjective or affective.[23] But Mechthild's vivid prayer life is interwoven with strong criticisms of the church and this invites us to interpret her practice in light of Christianity's perennial struggle to define itself. She is, after all, *writing down* her poetry and visions. She is allowing her writings to be circulated in a context that makes her vulnerable to "all my Christian torturers" (5:34). She may have been willing to do this because she shared the missionary zeal of the Dominicans; both she and her confessor believed her message to be relevant beyond the confessional. "Aligning herself with the Dominicans, Mechthild takes up their mission to reform erring members of the Church."[24] Although she was excluded from the academy and from the priesthood, her writing provided her with a way to participate in the reform of the church. This mission of the book is evident in the prologue, added by the anonymous translator. He quotes from a passage in Book 5 in which Jesus and Mechthild are discussing the appalling state of Christianity. Christ explains to Mechthild the significance of her writings: "I hereby send this book as a messenger to all religious people, both the good and the bad; for if the pillars fall, the building cannot remain standing" (5:34; 1:1). Mechthild and her translator believe that the pillars (the clergy) are falling, and this book is meant to protect the building (Christianity) from its own disintegration. As we have seen, part of the Dominican understanding of reform included heresy-hunting, inquisition, and crusade. Mechthild felt a particular closeness to St. Dominic but it is not clear what draws her to him. Some Dominicans, including her confessor, were supporters; others apparently put her in danger (7:4l). She does not mention the Inquisition or crusades so it is difficult to know exactly how she interpreted those aspects of reform that have become symbols of ecclesial violence. We cannot really know her views on the issues of her day, but her writings invoke a renunciation of power that is very much at odds with the kinds of theology that undergird imperialism.

Mechthild's criticisms of the church are accompanied by a vision of Christian life in which Love (*Minne*) is personified as the motivating source of divinity and love is the fundamental practice of Christian life.[25] Love is, of course, the rhetoric of virtually all Christians, who can burn one another's mortal bodies out of love for the immortal soul. Mechthild, like other beguines and contemplatives, used this personification of *Minne* to express a distinctive understanding of what Christian life looks like, who God is, and what salvation means. The practice of love occurs as prayer, as service to the sick, and as intercession for sinners. But what is more distinctive about *Minne* is that it requires an abjuration of power, honor, and even justice.[26] Perhaps the most radical aspect of her theology is that she understands renunciation not as a way of ascending to God but as participation in the practices which the Godhead itself engages.

This renunciation of authority is modeled in the opening passage of Mechthild's book. In this initial appearance, Lady Love occludes the infinite superiority of her divinity by employing the deferential language of a courtier speaking to royalty.[27] But Mechthild, "mistress and queen" of divine Love, is called upon to perform her own renunciations. Mechthild castigates Love as a robber who has defrauded the Soul of youth, possessions, friends, relatives, honor, riches, and health. Lady Love is rather blithe about these accusations, merely pointing out that these trifles have been exchanged for Love herself and "in addition you may demand God and all his kingdom" (1:1). Mechthild loses everything in the exchange for Love and yet she gains access to a divine kingdom, one run by an entirely different logic from the kingdoms of the world. God and Mechthild alike must renounce self-will in order to become naked to desire; it is only in this self-emptying, kenotic desire that "love is perfect" (7:16).

For Mechthild, renunciation is not merely play in the game of love. It is a model for the way authority is really intended to work in the world, as we see from her advice to priors and prioresses. They should count among their key responsibilities daily comfort to the sick, carrying away their waste, and standing by them in their most private infirmity. "Then God's sweetness will flow into you in marvelous ways." She further advises these leaders that "When a person prays in Christian faith with a heart so humble that one cannot endure a single creature to be beneath one, and with a soul so detached that all things but God alone disappear when one is praying, then a person is a divine God with the heavenly Father" (6:1). It is hard to envision a model of authority more at odds with that of empire than one in which tenderly caring for the plumbing needs of the infirm becomes not the path to but unity with the divine. This contrasts with the machinery of power that Mechthild identifies with the church. In a vision in which she sees God castigating the pope she hears this condemnation of the priesthood: "You have nothing left but your trappings; that is, ecclesiastical authority with which you war against God and his chosen intimates" (6:21).

Like many, even most, contemplatives, Mechthild understands the fundamental religious practice to be renunciation of self-will. She extends this to apply to the way religious superiors relate to their charges, even to the way the pope and the clergy are supposed to exercise their authority. But it is when she extends this practice of renunciation to the Godhead itself that her theology more dramatically undermines the logic of empire.

Mechthild has repeated visions in which members of the Holy Trinity renounce power in order to permit the flow of love to proceed unimpeded *even by the Godhead itself*. Sometimes this takes the form of a kind of pillow talk between divine and human lovers. In one passage Mechthild begs for the soul of a condemned sinner and God answers: "Indeed, when two wrestle with each other the weaker must lose. I shall willingly be the weaker, though I am almighty" (6:10). When preparing for the Eucharist, Mechthild invited God to share her bed of suffering and then almost tricks him, in the manner of Esther:

> Now if Lord, you wish to soothe me,
> Then do my will
> And give me those sinners
> Who are in a state of mortal sin . . .
> Lord you can satisfy me in no other way. (7:21)

God is love, as God himself tells Mechthild: "That I love you passionately comes from my nature, for I am love itself. That I love you often comes from my desire, for I desire to be loved passionately. That I love you long comes from my being eternal, for I am without an end and without a beginning" (1:24). At the same time, Lady Love personifies the energy that animates divinity and connects the members of the Trinity with one another and with humanity. It is only through the deferral of certain kinds of power to Love that divinity emerges in its most authentic form. This deferral is central to the narrative of creation lost and found as retold by Mechthild. She describes an egalitarian Trinity self-enclosed in "indescribable bliss": the Father adorned with omnipotence, the Son with wisdom and the Holy Spirit full of generosity. The Father, importuned by the Spirit and the Son, agrees to depart from their barren bliss: "a powerful desire stirs in my divine breasts as well and I swell in love alone . . . I shall make a bride for myself who shall greet me with her mouth and wound me with her beauty. Only then does love really begin." Love so beautifully begun is quickly challenged when the beloved falls into sin and the Father regrets his work. But the Holy Spirit and the Son implore the Father on behalf of bloody and disgraced humanity to forsake his wrath. Again the "Father then bowed to the wills of them both with great love" and assists them in carrying out their plan for redemption (3:9).

Mechthild displays for us the characteristically all-powerful and just Father eager to renounce these features most associated with God the Father. The Father longs for Love to persuade him to renounce his wrathful desire for punishment. His reluctance to carry out his prerogative for punishment combines with his eagerness to renounce omnipotence: Mechthild, most worthless of sinners, *demands that the Father do her will*. God agrees to exchange almighty power for weakness so his beloved can secure the release of sinners. Renunciation allows God to be the kind of God he longs to be, but which is possible only through his eagerness to be persuaded by the importunities of love, personified in Lady Love, manifest in the second and third persons of the Trinity, and mediated by Mechthild's prayers and importunities on behalf of sinners.

Renunciation of power is not without painful costs. Mechthild and even God must bow to the painful reality that if Love is to enjoy a beloved, humanity must be granted free will. "Knowledge" (*Bekantnisse*) acknowledges the anguish Mechthild feels on behalf of sinful religious people: "They have freedom of choice to go to heaven or to hell or to a long stay in purgatory. That is a heavy burden for you" (7:17). This is apparently a heavy burden for God as well. God "considers the sinner as a converted person" (6:17) and cries out: "My soul cannot endure that I banish the sinner from me. And so I pursue many of them on and on till I have them in my grasp" (6:16). But even God cannot invalidate the consequences of free choice. God agrees to heal hell-bound sinners, personified in a vision of a sick and bloody child: "I shall heal the sickness of this child. Arise, my dear child, you are healed! Free will I have given you and shall never take it away, for according to it all your dignity shall be measured, like that of the saints, in the beautiful heaven." But this healing by God the Father remains insufficient: "Alas, this child still lies motionless upon its own selfish will" (5:8). God can lend grace to sinners, but cannot by a simple forensic act free them from their distorted desires.

MECHTHILD AND CONTEMPORARY THEOLOGY

It is hard to know exactly what Mechthild thought of pagan Slavs who had been dragged through Magdeburg's marketplace to be sold as slaves or the bloody crusade against the Albigensians which was preached by her beloved Dominic. We know almost nothing about her, really.[28] But her writings reveal a determined struggle to remain faithful in the midst of disorienting conflicts, betrayals, and disillusionments. As a theologian who had to find her feet amidst some of the church's most terrifying displays of violence, she teaches us something about power. Christianity suffers an enduring temptation to deify might. Notwithstanding the magnificent display of the kenosis of this power in a stable and on a cross, divinity is typically presented in mimicry of empire. A.N. Whitehead notes that the depiction of God acting by fiat and imposing obedience has infused a tragic history into Christianity. "When the Western world accepted Christianity, Caesar conquered; and the received text of Western theology was edited by his lawyers . . . . The deeper idolatry, of the fashioning of God in the image of the Egyptian, Persian, and Roman imperial rulers, was retained. The Church gave unto God the attributes which belonged exclusively to Caesar."[29] The degeneration of pastoral care into the machinery of a "police state" is the particular version of this idolatry characteristic of the thirteenth century. But it is well known in our own time, too. Its symptoms are the perennial henchmen of idolatry: the approval of violence, hostility toward others, and fluctuation between arrogance and apathy in the face of the environmental and political disasters that threaten to overwhelm us.

But if Christian history has always been deeply shaped by this idolatry of power, it has also been haunted by an unsentimental vision of a kind of love that demands an excruciating renunciation of might. Mechthild's writings remind us both that this living stream has not been entirely extinguished by mechanisms of power but also that it is present only on the most obscure fringes of history and theology. It is important to incorporate her writings into a broader canon of Christian theology because she pursues the logic of love with rare intensity and single-mindedness. She witnesses to the astonishing kenosis of might that occurs within the Godhead itself. She articulates the implications of the divine kenosis for the practice of prayer and the exercise of authority. She pursues the implications of renunciation with a thoroughness and integrity that is difficult to sustain. It is perhaps here that her wisdom is most important. She does not understand the gospel of love and its abjuration of might either as a doctrine or as an accomplishment. It is a *practice*.

Learning a Christian way of life is something that unfolds over a lifetime, perhaps over centuries. It is worked out through the details of what we eat, what we buy, how we raise children, the work we do, the social world we create, and the ecclesial movements in which we participate. This ongoing practice has as its handmaid a kind of humility that recognizes the partiality and imperfection of every moment on this path. This humility in turn liberates the generosity of love so that it can extend even to hell-beings and purgatory mates. Mechthild's theology encourages practices ever more passionate in their devotion to the Holy Trinity and ever vigilant against the securities of might.

Mechthild witnesses to an ideal of ecclesia that does not require consoling fictions or ideological allegiances. She reminds us that it is possible to see the worst of the church and of humanity and remain dedicated to the practice of renunciation. She knows that her candor is getting her into trouble when church officials threaten to burn her book; she even accuses God of leading her astray by requiring her to write. But God answers:

> My dear One, do not be overly troubled.
> No one can burn the truth.
> For someone to take this book out of my hand,
> He must be mightier than I." (2:26)

We can see how mighty the forces of history are in the invisibility of *The Flowing Light of the Godhead* in Christian history and theology. But these are not mightier than God and so we again have a chance to explore her bold imagery, her ruthless honesty, and her undying allegiance to Lady Love.

FURTHER READING

Primary Sources

Mechthild of Magdeburg, *The Flowing Light of the Godhead.* Translated by Frank Tobin. New York, N.Y.: Paulist Press, 1998.

Beguine Spirituality: Mystical Writings of Mechthild of Magdeburg, Beatrice of Nazareth and Hadewijch of Brabant. Edited by Fiona Bowie. Translated by Oliver Davies. New York, N.Y.: Crossroad, 1990.

Secondary Sources

Hollywood, Amy. *Soul as Virgin Wife: Mechthild of Magdeburg, Marguerite Porete, and Meister Eckhart*. Notre Dame, Ind.: University of Notre Dame Press, 1995.

McGinn, Bernard. *The Flowering of Mysticism: Men and Women in the New Mysticism (1200-1350)*. New York, N.Y.: Crossroad, 1998.

Murk-Jansen, Saskia. *Brides in the Desert: The Spirituality of the Beguines*. London: Darton, Longman and Todd, 1998.

Poor, Sara S. *Mechthild of Magdeburg and Her Book: Gender and the Making of Textual Authority*. Philadelphia, Pa.: University of Pennsylvania Press, 2004.

CHAPTER 11

Thomas Aquinas

Mark D. Jordan

Any discussion of Thomas Aquinas (1225?-1274) and political power faces the necessity and the impossibility of separating him cleanly from imperial uses made of him after his death. Because "St. Thomas" or even "Divine Thomas (*Divus Thomas*)" was for long periods and in many places the emblem of the most aggressive Roman Catholic orthodoxy, his name authorized countless exercises of imperial enforcement, both inside and outside the Roman Catholic church. That church privileged his works (if sometimes only superficially) both by underwriting them and by monitoring their study. Those outside the church frequently responded by condemning him not for what he said, but for how he was being used. In these and other ways Thomas's historical identification with authoritarian Catholicism has made it more difficult both to understand him and to assess him apart from institutional consequences. Here the main effort will be to read Thomas so far as possible before imperial Thomism. Only then will attention turn to the ways in which Thomism blocks constructive retrievals of Thomas in resistance to empire.

THOMAS'S LIFE IN ITS CONTEXTS

Biographical evidence easily misleads theological reading. For older authors, like Aquinas, the evidence is often fragmentary, and so its reconstruction invites projection or fantasy. Even if the evidence for his motives and choices were a hundred times greater than it is, it could only provoke more questions—for example, about the relations of religious upbringing to theological insight, about the psychological location of the "author," or about the limits of the stories scholars construct around human lives. These problems are real, but they do not render biographical

153

evidence useless. Thinking biographically can help a reader to listen for elements in a text that she might not otherwise hear—as it can save her from imagining that an author invented certain topics or doctrines when they were in fact clichés.

Thomas was born, most probably during 1225, into an imperial struggle. His birthplace was a family castle in Roccasecca, about half way between Rome and Naples. Thomas's family, members of the minor nobility, occupied the disputed borderlands between the domains ruled by the papacy and the "Kingdom of Two Sicilies," which Frederick II, the "Holy Roman Emperor" of German lands, continued to rule in defiance of the pope. Thomas's father held an office from the emperor and remained loyal to the cause. His brothers took higher posts, but switched sides. One of them was killed by the emperor as a traitor for allying himself to the papacy.

Thomas was born as well into the crusades. "Crusade" is not here a weak metaphor. It refers literally to a war waged under the sign of the cross to defend or regain "Christian" territories from perceived enemies of the faith. Recruits for these wars evidently had mixed motives, but some of the strongest were religious. Becoming a crusader was a religious act that brought spiritual blessings, including the forgiveness of penalties owing to sin (the so-called crusader's indulgence). The crusades had begun more than a century before Thomas's birth. They had mostly failed, but the call to undertake a crusade retained its power. Only twenty years before Thomas was born, crusaders caught in a dynastic struggle over the Eastern Christian throne turned aside from Jerusalem, their intended target, to Constantinople, the Byzantine capital. Once their candidate was deposed, the supposed defenders of Christianity sacked the most civilized of Christian cities to set up their own kingdom. Constantinople would remain in Western hands until Thomas was in his thirties.

More important, the papacy had discovered that crusades did not have to be directed outwards. Ten years before Thomas's birth, crusading rhetoric had been turned on perceived enemies within Western Christendom. The Albigensian "heretics" in southern France were ruthlessly repressed in a military campaign that promised its warriors the crusader's indulgence. This was late legitimation of the internal violence that had accompanied crusades since the first one was preached in 1095. Along the routes of armies (or mobs) marching to the Holy Lands, the crusaders regularly committed atrocities against Jews. When the crusaders conquered Jerusalem in 1099, they burned Jews in their synagogues and butchered Muslim prisoners after using them to bury the mounded corpses.

Thomas, born into these imperial struggles and crusades, was destined for a career in the church as the family's youngest son. At 5 or 6, he was sent as an "oblate" or living donation to the important Benedictine center at nearby Montecassino. (Under prevailing church law, Thomas would have to confirm his dedication to monastic life when he came of age or else return to the world.) Perhaps the family hoped to bring the abbey closer to itself and so to the emperor. Eight years later, in 1239, as political tensions flared, Thomas was sent with his parents' permission to the university in Naples. He would have been around 14, not an unusual age to enroll in the faculty of liberal arts at a medieval university. Frederick II had founded the university a few years before to train professionals for the Italian portion of his empire, but it also served as a multilingual center for importing knowledge from Byzantium and the Islamic Empire. Much of the imported knowledge was scientific and philosophical, but it could also be religious. One of Thomas's teachers, Peter of Ireland, figures years later in a Jewish-Christian group studying Moses Maimonides and then as an expert in the biology of organ formation.

For Thomas, the most important figures at Naples were Dominicans, members of the new Order of Preachers. The order won papal approval in 1215 as an outgrowth of efforts by Dominic of Guzman to combat the spread of popular heresy by turning the heretics' own techniques against them. Dominican preaching would be frequent, accessible, and well-informed, but most of all it would be backed by Dominican lives of poverty, simplicity, and holiness. From early on, Dominic wanted his preaching brothers theologically educated, so he sent them to study theology at universities. Once there, the Dominicans recruited other students and faculty. Professors of theology joined the order and brought their university positions with them. The order soon had a growing network of its own teachers—and a reputation for intellectual achievement. Perhaps Thomas was drawn to the order by this fusion of academic and apostolic ideals. We know only that he joined the Dominicans in Naples, taking the habit in April 1244, probably at the age of 19. His choice put an end to his family's plans for him. As a Dominican, Thomas would stand in the papal camp—and serve under others' commands.

His family reacted as families often do. When Thomas headed north from Naples in a small group of Dominicans, the family intercepted him and took him by force back to Roccasecca, where it used various means to persuade him to change his mind. His stubbornness, supported by protests from the Dominicans, convinced his family after a year or so that nothing was to be done. They let him go—and this time the Dominicans moved him quickly out of the family's reach. Thomas himself has left us no account of his motives for joining the Dominicans. It looks like a decision for a fresh form of religious life actively engaged in current intellectual struggles. It was also a choice against dynastic ambitions and imperial service. Of course, Thomas's entry into the Dominicans hardly cut his connection with politics; it only changed his position within contending political networks.

"Empire" is an analogical concept: it has a range of related meetings that are held together around notions of standardized centralization, boundless annexation, and managed exploitation. If his family served what the medieval Europeans called "the empire," Thomas's vocation took him into another sort of empire, one with more demanding and universal ambitions. The Dominicans were identified with an expanding papacy as it experimented with new forms of control, including the inward crusade. The order already had a reputation as a papal vanguard by the time Thomas joined them. The reputation would increase as they were attached to the several institutions, local and international, called "the Inquisition."

Within the order, Thomas was put on a less directly political track: he would be a theologian who trained preachers rather than a preacher himself. He spent about half his Dominican life studying or teaching at the University of Paris. The other half he spent studying at Cologne under his Dominican mentor, Albert the Great, and teaching at Dominican houses of study within Italy. In Italy, Thomas's first obligation was to form other Dominicans at the order's various kinds of study houses. Twice Thomas was asked to head up new Dominican schools, in Rome and in Naples. In Rome, he experimented with curricula and forms of writing that could bridge the gap between university theology and the pastoral formation needed by ordinary Dominicans. The structure of Thomas's *Summa of Theology* (*Summa Theologiae*) shows the results. It inserts an extended consideration of the moral life between accounts of the Trinitarian God as creator and Jesus Christ as redeemer and sacramental pastor. But the interests of the order were not merely local—or confined to the borders of Christendom. Its program of preaching and pastoral care now included missions to Byzantium, Islam, and barely Christianized territories in Northern and Eastern Europe. There is a legend that Thomas wrote his (so-called) *Summa against the Gentiles* for the use of Dominican missionaries. The legend is a pious fiction, but it is true that parts of *On the Truth of the Catholic Faith* (its more probable title) were quickly reworked by Dominican experts in proselytizing Muslims and Eastern Christians. They had to rework the text because Thomas was not particularly well-informed about the religious content of Islam. He studied the arguments of Muslim philosophers and theologians carefully, but he describes the religion on hearsay as a debauched fiction.

For some years, the Dominican order also placed Thomas at the papal court as a resident theologian. There Thomas provided expert advice on a range of topics, but perhaps especially on how to engage Eastern Christianity and Islam. Communities that spoke Greek or Arabic had access to philosophical and scientific works that were known to the Latin-speaking West poorly or not at all. The crusades, expanding trade, and other contacts brought this knowledge within reach, but they could not make it easy to absorb into existing frames of reference. The early history of the university at Paris, Thomas's own school, is marked by struggles over the teaching of the new translations of Aristotle and other Greek philosophers. It is no coincidence that Thomas wrote literal expositions of many Aristotelian texts: they offer accessible readings that mostly harmonize with Christian views, though not always. Thomas struggles particularly to understand Aristotle's descriptions of Greek social and political customs—and to restrain his judgment on them. Sometimes he cannot keep silence. When Aristotle reviews Cretan legislation that encouraged homosexual activity as a mean of population control, Thomas adds that the activity is "wicked."

Other shocks were produced by the translation of Greek Christian texts coming out of Byzantium. It was awkward to realize that the Eastern churches, which were judged heretical by Latin speakers, had much greater access to authoritative texts from the early Christian centuries. Thomas was asked by the pope to respond to charges that the Easterners were actually more faithful to original Christian teaching. He replied with detailed interpretations of contested passages, but he also proposed a model for thinking about theological translation in relation to history. His model stressed the differences among languages and the local context of theological polemic. Thomas's own hunger for Greek texts was legendary. While in Italy, he led a team of scholars in preparing a verse-by-verse patristic commentary on the New Testament.

However much the papal court may have appreciated Thomas's energy for imported learning, other institutions and other scholars remained doubtful. After a decade in Italy, Thomas was sent back to resume his chair in Paris, at least in part to defend Dominican interest in Aristotle's texts from the charge that some Aristotelian tenets were dangerously anti-Christian. Three years later, Thomas returned to Italy—though not because his efforts had been particularly successful. After his death, indeed, some of his views would be condemned, without naming him, in a lengthy list of errors prepared by Parisian theologians and published by the Bishop of Paris. Thomas was spared that embarrassment. He returned to Naples in 1272 as leader of a new Dominican school. He died less than two years later at a Cistercian monastery, on the way to a church council that he was to advise. Before the last journey, the testimony of his companions tells us, Thomas stopped writing in response to a vision. According to another legend, he died dictating to the Cistercians a commentary on the *Song of Songs*, the biblical charter for Christian contemplation.

POLITICS IN THOMAS'S THEOLOGY

There have been many efforts to extract a political theory from the works of Thomas Aquinas. Once he became a central authority for Catholic thinkers, some thought that he needed to be an authority in every possible field. So they tried to make him speak to every topic, including modern political circumstances. The writings Thomas left do not offer anything like a finished political teaching. His exposition of Aristotle's *Politics* only covers a portion of that text. Its content cannot be considered Thomas's own thought so much as his best reading of Aristotle. On another occasion, the Dominicans asked Thomas to compose a treatise on good government as a gift for a king. Thomas left only fragments, many borrowed from earlier compilations.

To find Thomas's teaching on politics, a reader has to go to the large-scale theological works, especially the *Summa of Theology*. In them, political topics appear not in a separate treatise, but as part of a larger moral teaching. If there is any one starting point for Thomas's reflections on politics, it is the inseparability of politics from ethics. Political regimes exist in order to prepare human beings for their created end, which is reunion with God. Because human beings are embodied rational creatures, they reach that end using both body and soul. Politics must care for both. So far as it recognizes that the body is hierarchically subordinated to the soul, while other faculties in the soul are subordinated to the interlocking command of will and intellect, politics must nurture especially the rational faculties. Will and intellect are best addressed not by coercion or brute force, but by education and reasoned persuasion. Politics is fundamentally charged with ordering human communities so that human beings can flourish as moral learners.

One consequence of this view is that a reader cannot isolate politics within a single part of the *Summa of Theology* or any other of Thomas's large-scale theological works. Virtues and vices important to political life are scattered throughout the second half of the moral heart of the *Summa*, the so-called "second part of the second part" (*secunda secundae*, abbreviated here as 2-2). Each of these sections must be read back into the overarching plan of the whole part, which makes no special place for political virtues. The virtues needed for politics are included within the virtues of human life simply. There are some questions that modern readers tend to categorize as political, but they are widely scattered—and approached by Thomas under very different headings. Thomas asks, for example, whether human beings have power or dominion over each other only as a result of original sin, but the context is a discussion of the sinless state before the fall (*Summa* part 1 question 96, abbreviated here as 1.96). Much later, Thomas reviews the "judicial precepts" of the Old Law, that is, the biblical descriptions for Israelite government (1-2.104-105), but his main interest is to defend revelation from charges of irrationality. Thomas's influential discussion of the criteria for morally permissible war falls within an analysis of sins against peace considered as an effect of love (2-2.40): his question is whether war is *always* sinful.

The best place in the *Summa* to get a sense of Thomas's views on politics is the long series of questions on the various meanings of law, near the end of the part devoted to the grounds and elements of moral action. Three sections in the series show Thomas's characteristic views of political power. The first has to do with human law, the second with the political regimes that God instituted for Israel, and the third with natural law.

All of the questions on law consider variations of one basic definition: a law is a reasoned arrangement for promoting the common good, devised by someone having authority over the community, and properly promulgated (1-2.90). Thomas extends each element of the definition analogically. Natural law, for example, is "promulgated" only in the sense that it is part of human capacity at creation. The New Law, the content of Christian revelation, is promulgated by the infusion of grace into human hearts. If the definition of law ranges widely, it still yields definite conclusions, especially in the case of human law, where the analogical stretch is shortest. A human law may be unjust because it is not for the common good, but only for the ruler's advantage; or because it exceeds the legislator's power; or because it distributes burdens unequally and irrationally. A citizen is not bound in conscience to obey such a law, which is to be regarded not as a law, but as an act of violence (1-2.96.4).

Thomas keeps the basic definition of law in mind when he turns to Israelite regimes (1-2.105.1). He asks in effect whether we can find reasons to explain why God revealed particular political arrangements in the Hebrew Scriptures. Thomas argues that the so-called "judicial precepts" were reasonable provisions for the practical and moral needs of the Israelites, but he denies that they are universally binding because God revealed them. They do not bind in virtue of God's command, since the legal force of the Old Law was abrogated with the New Law of Christ. There is no direct inference from what God did for Israel to what a Christian ruler should do for another people in another place and time. A king in Thomas's time could choose without sin to imitate Israel's regime; he would sin if he pretended that the regime were obligatory because legislated by God. For Thomas, the test of a government—as of any law—is whether it provides citizens what they need in order to flourish as rational beings at a given level of moral education.

When it comes to justifying God's choice of regime, Thomas argues that a rightly ordered government balances the participation of all with the selection of those best suited to rule (1-2.105.1). The Israelite regime accomplished this by mixing monarchy, aristocracy, and democracy: the people had the right of choosing from among themselves a ruler who governed with the aid of others, according to their virtue. A monarchy is the most effective regime so long as the monarch is virtuous. For a vicious people, monarchy turns quickly to tyranny. God had to educate the Israelites morally before they could be trusted to have a monarchy (1-2.105.1 reply to obj. 2). With another people in another time, God might have chosen other political arrangements. There is for Thomas no best regime, simply speaking. The wise legislator allocates power in view of the character of the particular people to be ruled.

It is in this context that the reader can make sense of Thomas's famous teaching on natural law. Thomas is often cited to support the claim that every human being carries around a full set of moral regulations that she or he need only consult in order to act rightly. On this view, a legislator looks up an answer in the inner book of natural law, passes appropriate legislation, and then enforces it with the power of the state—fully confident that it is in accord with divine purposes for creation. Nothing could be further from Thomas's understanding of political history or of the limits on moral knowing. For Thomas, God reveals so much moral and political teaching in the Old Law precisely because individual sin and community corruption have obscured the natural law, have buried it within human minds. Even under the best circumstances, human beings need human law and human communities in order to specify and complete the impulses of natural law (1-2.91.3 reply to obj. 1). Sinful humanity needs more: the detailed presentation of moral precepts in divine revelation and the power to accomplish them in divine grace (1-2.100.1, 107.1 and 2).

The content of natural law, to the extent that it can be written out, starts from the most basic teaching or precept: "the good is to be done and pursued, and evil is to be avoided" (1-2.94.2). There are different kinds of goods, and Thomas gives a few examples for each. He does not pretend to deduce a whole set of specific laws under each heading. He argues to the contrary that a complete deduction of the natural virtues cannot be performed (1-2.94.3). Natural law directs human beings to act rationally, virtuously, but it does not enumerate all virtuous acts they ought to perform. Communities have to discover particular virtuous acts through their political experience (1-2.94.3). In no way does Thomas's account of natural law provide a legislative code for all of humanity. Much less does it authorize any one nation to impose that code on the planet by conquest—though some later "Thomists" have offered this sort of argument in order to justify colonization. Thomas himself imagines politics locally, regionally, in terms of a tightly knit community at a certain stage of its historical maturation. Thomas denies that the Christian bible offers a universal blueprint for perfect government. He also denies easy certainty about political questions. For him, morality and therefore politics are forms of practical knowledge, which is intrinsically more limited than theory.

Once a reader sees human politics and divine revelation as progressive moral teaching across history, she can make better sense of Thomas's more particular political arguments. For example, when Thomas tries to imagine human life before sin, he sees some form of government in it. Communities of sinless human beings would still have needed rulers to achieve their common good; power would have gone naturally to those superior in moral knowledge or the exercise of virtue (1.96.4). For Thomas, governments ought to reflect the natural hierarchy of human beings, a hierarchy of sex, age, knowledge, virtue, and physical attributes—but especially of moral excellence. He finds the hierarchical principle written everywhere in creation. Graded difference is not a tragic flaw; it is a created beauty. Here too, the political order must mirror the cosmic order.

This may sound foolishly optimistic—not to say dangerously supportive of prevailing prejudices about which human qualities are "higher" than others. There is indeed both naïveté and cultural blindness in Thomas's political views, but he never loses sight of the ways in which political regimes can go badly astray. He repeats from Caesar's account of German history the claim that a whole society can forget so basic a moral lesson as the prohibition against stealing (1-2.94.4 and 6). In other works, such as *On Kingship*, Thomas raises the possibility that it might be necessary to kill a tyrant for the common good. Thomas also concedes the necessity of warfare in human history as a defense against unjust attack from without or within (2-2.40). He argues that a Christian community may legitimately engage in war so long as the authority for it is legitimate, the cause is just, and the intention is to preserve the common good while restoring peace (rather than carrying out vengeance, say).

The remarks on war may provoke a sharp question: Aren't the scattered things Thomas has to say about politics in the *Summa* dangerously naïve—or simply complicit with imperial evils? They seem to take no account of realities he must have known—of crusaders sacking Constantinople or killing heretics. The best reply would concede that Thomas treats political matters with a certain optimistic abstraction. This is due in part to a lack of specialist knowledge or interest: Thomas is much more concerned with other moral topics. But there is also a striking limitation to the form of political analysis that he knew. Latin-speaking theologians of Thomas's generation did not have access to the most scathing of the ancient indictments of tyranny: Plato's *Republic*, Thucydides, Tacitus. They also did not know the sophisticated political philosophy of Islamic cultures, which were better read in ancient political sources and more alert to conflicts between politics and philosophical or theological inquiry. Thomas inherited instead a tradition of "mirrors for princes," idealizing and flattering depictions of princely duties. Thomas writes about politics in idealistic abstraction partly because that is the model of political discourse that he inherited. The narrow view of political teaching reinforced his own indifference to the acts—and the horrors—of imperial history.

Something more striking occurs in relation to church power. As a Dominican theologian, Thomas might seem to have a declared and detailed interest in church governance and its relation to civil power. It can be surprising to discover that he wrote less deliberately about church than about state. Even in his large-scale theological works, there is no section devoted to church structure. Most of what he teaches about the church concerns the sacraments. Thomas knows, of course, about disputes between church authorities and secular rulers. He is also familiar with the most important

sources of church law, some of which he quotes in the *Summa*, but he does not repli-
cate their extended discussions of church structure and jurisdiction. He tends to treat
church governance in passing. To take a small example from the *Summa*: in discussing the object of the divinely infused virtue of faith, Thomas considers who has the
authority within the church to publish creeds (2-2.1.10). He argues that the pope has
been charged with preserving the unity of the church's faith by settling disputes about
it. Since the pope has authority over whatever affects the whole church, it belongs to
him to convene church councils and to confirm their rulings. Further into the discussion of faith, Thomas will emphasize again that the authority for settling doctrinal debates resides "principally" in the papacy. Once a doctrinal issue has been settled, anyone who stubbornly contradicts it becomes a heretic (2-2.11.2 reply to obj.
3). These are strong views of papal primacy, but they are much weaker than modern
Catholic claims for universal papal jurisdiction and doctrinal infallibility under certain conditions. They are also weaker than some views of papal supremacy circulating
during Thomas's life. If he treats worldly politics abstractly and idealistically, he treats
church politics hardly at all—leaving the topic to the canon lawyers.

Should Thomas be blamed for failing to treat secular or ecclesiastical politics real-
istically and critically? Does his relative silence implicate him in the crimes of the
institutions within which he taught? Such questions set a severe standard for judgment. Few theologians have become martyrs of conscience, and most martyrs have
evaded capture for as long as they could. It is also true that writers write the thoughts
they have—not the ones later generations wish on them. To insist that Thomas be a
critical theorist of institutional injustice is to treat him as cavalierly as those zealous
neo-Thomists who demand that he answer all our questions whether he wants to or
not. Still I think that it is fair to ask of Thomas—as of any other writer—whether he
enjoyed the profits of empire without attending enough to the costs. He got his new
translations of Aristotle. Did he ask what getting them implied for the conquered?
He dismissed Islam contemptuously on little evidence. Did he ask what the dismissal might authorize once it fell into other hands? These questions lead us to turn in
conclusion from Thomas's texts to the uses that have been made of them.

THOMISM AND THOMAS FOR CONTEMPORARY READERS

When Thomas died, he was a famous Dominican theologian—personally revered
by many, but also suspected by some of having gone too far in appropriating new
learning. In the decades after his death, his views were implicated (as noted) in

official condemnations and publicly corrected by rival schools (especially the Franciscans). In the same decades, and for mixed reasons, the Dominicans began to gather support for him as an emblem of the order's orthodoxy. They worked to have him declared a saint by the papacy and prohibited their members from attacking him. Thomas was canonized in 1323, in part because his teaching appeared to favor papal positions on some contested points. Over the next centuries, Thomas's importance grew within the Dominican order and at the papal court, though more as a common language or standard of reference than as an absolute authority. At the Council of Trent, convened to counter Protestant movements, Thomas's *Summa* was prominently displayed as a reference book for all. In 1567, while the council was still in progress, Thomas was declared doctor of the church by the (Dominican) pope, Pius V. Much of Thomas's language was incorporated into the extensive conciliar legislation that defined modern Roman Catholicism.

More important for the contemporary reception of Thomas is the movement of "neo-Thomism" from the middle of the nineteenth century. This began as a philosophical program to combat the perceived liberalism and relativism of modern Europe. Thomas seemed to offer the basis for a Catholic philosophy and theology that could resist the revolutionary disruptions of the Enlightenment and its successors, of socialism, secularism, and nihilism. The program of neo-Thomism received decisive backing from Pope Leo XIII in the encyclical, *Aeterni patris* (1879). The encyclical led to the institutionalization of a certain kind of Thomism in Catholic universities and seminaries from the end of the nineteenth century until the mid-1960s, when the intellectual climate shifted significantly at the Second Vatican Council. Between those two dates, there were a number of efforts to make Thomism into a viable political platform. Notable among them is "Christian Democracy," which saw in Thomas a groundwork for a Christian doctrine of human rights, but also a guide for reconstructing morally decadent societies.

In his writing, Thomas did not mean to provide anything like a complete political philosophy, much less a political platform suitable for use in a pluralistic democracy. Thomas's importance for contemporary reflection on politics lies in other directions. He resists the claims for any totalitarian regime. He denies as well the basic notion of empire—of a universalized regime or economy imposed across national differences. For Thomas, politics is a form of moral education. It depends on a view of the human end beyond this life, but also on recognition of historical differences in how communities will approach that end.

These are important lessons for our present. Still it may be that Thomas's greatest lesson is something else again: the survival of an anti-imperial teaching in his texts despite centuries of imperial efforts to claim him. Thomas's texts have been regularly appropriated by the ideologies of one empire or another, secular or ecclesiastical. Despite centuries of efforts to make them repeat lessons agreeable to an emperor's ears, Thomas's texts continue to teach *against* the delirious epistemology of empire—against the feverish science that pretends to universal control over human lives. The texts are powerfully misread—and still the texts just as powerfully offer contrary readings. Thomas's authorship offers remarkable hope for the persistence of theological writing even in the hands of an empire's police.

FURTHER READING

Primary Sources

Thomas Aquinas. *Summa theologiae*. Cambridge, U.K.: Blackfriars, and New York, N.Y.: McGraw Hill, 1964-73 . A bilingual edition in sixty volumes with extensive notes and appendices.

_____. *On Kingship, to the King of Cyprus*. Translated by G. B. Phelan, revised by I. T. Eschmann. Toronto: Pontifical Institute of Medieval Studies, 1982.

_____. *Political Writings*. Edited and translated by R. W. Dyson. New York, N.Y.: Cambridge University Press, 2002. This anthology excerpts a number of passages on political topics. It is best used to find passages that can then be read in the original contexts Thomas crafted for them.

Secondary Sources

Finnis, John. *Aquinas: Moral, Political, and Legal Theory*. New York, N.Y.: Oxford University Press, 1998. This is a recent overview, in the style of analytic philosophy.

Maritain, Jacques. *Scholasticism and Politics*. New York, N.Y.: Macmillan, 1940. This is a classic neo-Thomist effort to deploy Thomas as a critic of modern regimes and advocate of a return to Christian governance.

Torrell, Jean-Pierre. *Thomas Aquinas*. Vol. 1: *The Person and His Work*. Translated by Robert Royal. Rev. ed., Washington, D.C.: Catholic University of America, 2005. This is now the standard biography.

CHAPTER 12

Julian of Norwich

Shelly Rambo

Just blocks away from the central market in Norwich, England, Julian (1342-c.1416) recited her daily prayers. Locked away in a small cell adjoined to the main sanctuary of St. Julian's Church, she lived the life of an anchoress, a life of solitary prayer and devotion to God. We know little of Julian's life. From the parish logs, we know that she inhabited St. Julian's; from the *Book of Margery Kempe* we know that she provided spiritual counsel between 1412 and 1413; and from the *Ancrene Riwle,* the thirteenth-century guidebook for anchorites, we know something of her daily life and practices. We know her primarily as a writer: her text, *The Revelations of Divine Love,* is considered one of the most stunning works of Christian theology in the medieval period. There, she gives an account of a series of visions that she receives from God. On May 13, 1373, at the age of thirty, she writes, God revealed to her multiple mysteries of the faith.

She records her visions in two versions. The Short Text is a brief account of the sixteen visions. On her deathbed, Christ appears to her sixteen times, each time revealing something of the nature and meaning of his sufferings. Showing Julian his bleeding face and his sagging, dying body, Christ speaks to her about the nature of sin, the goodness of creation, and the love of God for humanity. The Long Text, the product of twenty years of contemplation, develops both the spiritual and theological dimensions of the mysteries that Christ revealed to her. She identifies herself in Chapter 2 of the Long Text as "unlettered" (2.177),[1] indicating that she is lacking in literary skills. Yet the text itself appears to contradict this claim, displaying the rhetorical and theological acumen of this anchoress. Given the depth of insight and skilled prose of the Long Text, there is much speculation about her literary and theological education. The Long Text, as Grace Jantzen notes, "requires a great deal of theological chewing."[2] Within these reflections lie profound affirmations about creation, the incarnation, the Trinity, and the passion.

The question here is to what degree her writings engaged the world around her. Through this text, does Julian address the issues of the city surrounding the anchorhold? Given her status as an anchoress, it may seem unfitting to claim that she is engaged in a lively conversation with the external world. In fact, the very term "anchorite," meaning "to retire," indicates her retreat from the outside world. Like others entering the anchoritic vocation, Julian was to physically and publicly embody the Pauline proclamation in Galatians: "It is no longer I who live, but it is Christ who lives in me"(Gal. 2:20). In the ceremony ushering her into the religious life, an officiating priest administered extreme unction, sprinkled ashes over her, and recited the last rites before she stepped over the threshold into the cell. The door closed behind her, and she was forbidden to exit the cell, except upon her own death. Considered "dead to the world," her enclosure was seen as an awakening to a new life of contemplation and devotion to God. Yet that awakening, as recent scholarship indicates, did not mean that she knew nothing of the happenings of the outside world. The *Ancrene Riwle* warns of the temptations of the world that continue to threaten the anchoresses, even after they cross the threshold. The outside world will still enter, even if they are physically prohibited to exit.

This worldly interaction can be symbolized through the architecture of the anchorhold. Inside the anchorhold there are three small openings, in most cases, windows, to the outside. One window looked onto the Mass, in which Julian would have been able to see the priest administer the Eucharist. Another window opened out to the servants' quarters. Through this window, she would be able to receive food and speak with the young woman assigned to take care of her daily needs. There, she could learn something of the domestic life of Norwich. The young woman would come and go to market, tend to the wash and the daily cleaning of the cell, and she, herself, would be dedicated to holy living in order to honor the intense spirituality of her anchoress. The third window is the window through which she would offer spiritual counsel to those who sought it. Julian counseled people within the city of Norwich and those on spiritual pilgrimage to the city. Through these three windows, Julian would not only be versed in the ecclesial, domestic, and civic life in Norwich; she, as an anchoress, actually participated in these dimensions of life.

I want to highlight one instance of her participation, revealing the ways that these three windows interact within her writings. I will focus on one event, the Crusade of 1383, and one vision, the sixteenth, to display Julian's engagement with issues of empire in her time. Steeped in meditation on the cross, Julian interpreted the events around her through the lens of Christ's suffering and wounds. What could her meditations on Christ's wounds mean for the wounded soldiers returning to Norwich? What could they mean for the less visible but daily wounds resulting from the economic and social realities of empire? In this essay, I will examine Julian's sixteenth and final showing for its potential to address the realities of war in late-fourteenth-century Norwich and, in turn, to provide a theological vision for living within our contemporary context of empire. In a context in which salvation was purchased in exchange for bodily sacrifice, Julian's theology overturns this notion of salvation, therein resisting the justification of wounds in God's name. She, in turn, provides a vision of persistent witness to the wounds suffered at the hands of those in power.

Julian's theology provides critical testimony to the wounds of war in a context in which the reality of these wounds are increasingly obscured. By "wounds of war," I refer to both the immediate situation of military combat and the ongoing and even less visible wounding of persons and communities who are deemed powerless and politically dispensable within empire. Reinterpreting her vision of the city in light of empire, I will reveal her resistance to the religiously sanctioned militarism of imperial powers. Although this final vision is often interpreted as a crowning vision of the triumphant city, I argue that the power of Julian's final showing lies in its radical call to witness amidst the war-torn city.

Highlighting here the potential of her visions to counter the political and ecclesial injustices of her time, it is equally important to note the ways in which Julian participates in these systems. As evidenced in her frequent assertions of doctrinal obedience to "Holy Church," she is continually aware of where she is situated and, like many of her female contemporaries, faces the burden of legitimating her writings. Lynn Staley notes that Julian's "talent for negotiating among the various expectations and concerns" is evident, but it is important to be aware of the potential dangers of these negotiations.[3] Although it is tempting to emphasize her rhetorical strategies of indirection and resistance, it is also important to note the blind spots operating within her own theology. For example, her reading of "Christ as Mother" appears revolutionary for its introduction of a feminine aspect of the divine, yet the attributes of the mother as nurturing, patient, and longsuffer-ing reinforce essential gendered roles of the medieval period. To read both the ways that she resists *and* concedes to those in power in her writing is, as I suggest later in the essay, a way of reading religious texts that prepares us for strategic thought and action within a contemporary context of empire. It is a practice of reading that sharpens our ability to see the realities of our own situation: that we are complicit in the structural realities that we often seek to transform. How do we theological-ly reckon with this complicity?

THE CRUSADE

At the time of the Crusade of 1383, Julian was writing the Long Text. She was appointed to the anchorhold by the Bishop of Norwich, Henry Despenser.[4] Renowned for his skill in battle, he is often referred to as the *episcopus martius*—the martial bishop. Despenser had caught the attention of Pope Urban VI during the peasant uprisings just a year earlier, when he had come to the rescue of a fel-low bishop, who was marked for death by a leading rebel army. While rescuing the bishop, Despenser killed a large number of rebels and marched back to Nor-wich, looking very favorable in the eyes of the pope. Urban VI appointed him to head the crusade.

The pope had called for the Crusade of 1383 to secure support for his papa-cy against his rival, Pope Clement VII.[5] In exchange for military service, Urban VI and Despenser offered young male recruits indulgences, assuring them salva-tion, both for themselves and their family members, even those deceased. The six-month campaign leading up the crusade was extremely successful, drawing a record number of enlistments and extravagant financial gifts from patrons who believed that the more they gave, the more they would receive from God. Though the British Parliament was ambivalent about the pope's appointment of Despens-er and the religious aims of the war, they had an economic stake in going to war in Flanders. The English wool industry relied heavily on production centers based in Flanders, and with France's increasing dominance in Flemish commercial regions, the English economy was threatened. After months of impassioned debates, Par-liament finally decided that the church's war would be beneficial: not only would the church help fund the war, but a war fought in the name of religion would ensure a greater numbers of recruits.

In May of 1383, soldiers from Norwich joined the nearly five thousand soldiers making their way to the border of Flanders. At the beginning of the crusade, the English troops experienced a great deal of success. But as they moved deeper into Flanders, the casualties began to mount. When news of the crusade reached France, King Charles VI flooded the region with troops. The English army was unprepared for the onslaught. Despenser had anticipated an early victory and had not planned for sustained fighting. By the time he called for his own reinforcements, it was too late. The French forces crushed the English army, and less than four months into the crusade, the English were forced to surrender. It was a virtual slaughter.

Inevitably, Julian witnessed the defeated soldiers' return to Norwich. With the anchorhold located just blocks from the center of Norwich, news of the war would have been difficult to escape. Reading Julian's text in light of these events reveals theological reflections rife with social and ecclesial commentary.[6] Julian's constant wrestling with church teachings about sin and salvation was also her way of wrestling with a bishop and pope who used salvation to pursue a military agenda. Promising victory to the city in the form of salvation, these promises would later appear empty in the face of the wounds of war. Norwich, at the time that Julian was writing, had already suffered a great deal of death. The bubonic plague had wiped out one third of the population in the city, killing most of the livestock as well. Barely recovering economically from the radical impact of this death-toll on the labor force, the daily realities of economic life were further threatened by the prospect of more lives lost in war. Though the crusade was argued as necessary for England's economic success as a nation, the costs of war were experienced much differently at home.

THE WOUNDED SERVANT

To interpret the final vision, it is important to briefly emphasize Julian's significant reworking of familiar understandings of sin and salvation through the lord and servant parable, presented in chapter 51. Aware of the dominant conceptions of human sin and the judgment of God, in the Long Text she develops a stunning counter-picture to the reigning paradigm of Anselmian satisfaction.[7] She claims, in chapter 50, to receive a vision that answers her most compelling question: "What is sin?" (11:197) Her desire to reconcile the church's teaching about sin and salvation with her understanding of God's nature fuels her reflections in the Long Text, and she devotes a great portion of the later chapters to developing the images of the lord and the servant. The central plotline is this: a lord summons his servant to do a task. The servant, desiring to fulfill the will of the lord, runs eagerly to meet the lord's request and, in the process, falls into a ditch, known in Middle English as a dell. The servant, wounded from the fall, is unable to get out of the dell. Bruised, weak, clumsy, blind, and all alone, the servant's greatest predicament is that he is unable to see the gaze of the lord, who looks on him with love and tenderness.

Julian begins interpreting the parable by identifying the figures and then moves to attributing particular characteristics to each. She writes:

> I understood that the lord who sat in state in rest and peace is God. I understood that the servant who stood before him was shown for Adam, that is to say, one man was shown at that time and his fall, so as to make it understood how God regards all men and their falling. (51:270)

The lord, God the Father, is full of mercy. The servant is both the first and second Adam, representing both fallen humanity and the God-man who restores humanity from its fallen condition. The dynamics between the lord and servant display, at center, the incredible love and desire that the two have for each other. The eagerness of the servant to do the will of the lord and the loving gaze of the lord toward the fallen servant refute the typical depiction of the guilty sinner before a judging God. Julian describes sin as woundedness and weakness as opposed to defiance and disobedience. Rejecting a conception of sin rooted in human disobedience, Julian presents the problem of sin and evil as a central challenge to the divine nature. Sin was often regarded as the problem of humanity that must be rectified in the face of a God who calls human beings to judgment. Although Julian is familiar with this paradigm and wrestles with it in her continual conversations with Holy Church, she casts the problem of sin in terms of God's nature.

What is stunning about this parable is that the lord is featured more than the servant. And this, I claim, is linked to Julian's visions on the cross. In the visions, Julian is no longer standing at the foot of the cross gazing up; instead, she is transported onto the cross. What she sees there is the world from a radically different perspective. In the Long Text, her theological reflections continually suggest this change of position. The mysteries of God unfold to her, as she gazes at humanity through the eyes of the suffering Christ. She experiences an intense, almost unbearable, awareness of the problem of evil and human suffering. But she cannot, from this perspective, see the weight of the problem on humanity. This would only intensify the existing suffering. She calls the lord to task in a way that would not only have been perceived as audacious for a woman in her time, but that would have challenged the relationship between lords and servants as they existed in Norwich.

There are two aspects of Julian's theological development of this parable that inform our reading of the final vision and its contributions to issues of empire. First, she challenges social and economic structures through her reading of the lord and servant. Although it may be easy for us to read references to lords and servants as parabolic, these titles would have been live and operative in late-fourteenth-century Norwich.[8] As an analogy of the divine-human relationship, this illustration would not only be accessible to the reader, it would also have the potential of critiquing the existing structures in which people lived and worked. The lord and servant relationship is not presented as one in which the lord acts for his own material gain at the expense of the well-being of the servant. Instead, the lord seems uncharacteristically attentive to the plight of the servant. Aligning God with the lord, she presents an example of lordship that potentially critiques rather than reinforces power-seeking, hierarchical lords. Note, in line with earlier comments about Julian's strategic rhetoric, that she keeps the feudal relationship in place. What we have is a more beneficent lord, but a lord nonetheless.

The second aspect of Julian's theological interpretation of this parable is her resistance to militaristic images. Julian contrasts the religious and political disregard for space and the abuse of territorial boundaries by resituating the activity of God elsewhere. She counters terms like occupation and overcoming, used to describe the devil's attacks, with references to home and dwelling, used to describe God's relationship to the soul. Under the rule of Henry Despenser, homes would not be created but, rather, destroyed. Christopher Abbott notes that Julian's descriptions of God's restoration of the soul do not contain the language of force. He writes: "Militaristic metaphors do not find a place in Julian's store of tropes and she prefers the language of transformation to that of annihilation."[9] She does not simply shift images from battleground to home. Instead, she introduces another image—the city.

THE VISION OF THE CITY

Julian first presents the image of the city in the context of the lord and servant parable in chapter 51. The lord, understood to be God, sits on the ground, in the barren and waste wilderness, awaiting the restoration of the human soul through the toil and labor of the Son. Julian explains that God is preparing the soul "to be his own city and his dwelling place" (51:272). The Son labors in order to make the city into a beautiful dwelling place for the divine. In a strange sense, God is depicted as homeless until the soul is tended to, healed, and made into something beautiful again. She uses both images of landscaping and of child-rearing to describe the process of restoring the city. Militaristic images are not employed. Note that this labor on behalf of the soul is not aligned with fighting; the Son is not a soldier going out to war, to bring back a victory for the city. It is the Son's work to bring about the soul's restoration, and yet he does so through labor, not conquest; he works the land.

Within the parable, Julian identifies the city with the sensual nature of the soul. Two natures, according to Julian, constitute the human soul—the sensual and the substantial nature. Grace Jantzen differentiates them as follows. The substantial nature is our created nature that is rooted in God; therefore, it is the essence of our humanity. The sensual nature represents our physical and psychological existence as individual human beings. She writes: ". . . sensuality refers to our existence as psychosomatic beings in a physical world."[10] Julian identifies the root of sin in the sensual nature. Given that she identifies the problem of sin (the sensual nature) with woundedness, the restoration of the sensual nature to the substantial ties the city to woundedness. The wounded soul, when reunited with its substantial nature, is like a wounded city restored to a place of beauty. Joan Nuth writes:

> While Julian sometimes calls the soul without qualification the city of God, the fact that she often specifically designates sensuality as God's city shows that she was conscious of the historical and bodily implications of the term as employed by Augustine.[11]

For Nuth, Julian is not just employing the image of the city to demonstrate an abstract spiritual concept. It has all the dimensions of a real city. Nuth highlights the power of Julian's theological interpretation within her context. Could Julian be considering, when writing the Long Text, the wounded city of Norwich and, more specifically, the wounded soldiers returning home? The wounds of Norwich are war wounds, received by soldiers who believed that they were going out in the name of God to bring back victory to their city. God's aim, Julian says, is to heal the city-soul in order to reside in it. Healing the city involves patient waiting (the Father) and hard laboring (the Son) on its behalf. In the sixteenth showing a full

Trinitarian vision unfolds, revealing another dimension of the restoration of the city—the presence of the divine Spirit. Central to the promise and presence of the Spirit is an imperative to witness wounds. The showing provides a strategy for existence within the earthly city that testifies to the underside of empire building: the reality of wounded soldiers.

THE RETURN OF THE WOUNDED

> And then our good Lord opened my spiritual eye, and showed me my soul in the midst of my heart. I saw the soul as wide as if it were an endless citadel, and also as if it were a blessed kingdom, and from the state which I saw in it, I understood that it is a fine city. —The Sixteenth Showing (68:312-313)

The revelation of the soul as a city is Julian's final vision. Earlier in chapter 51, this vision is anticipated; God waits for the return of the city. Now in chapter 68, the waiting ends. God not only awaits the city; God makes a home in it. Looking into her heart, Julian sees the Lord Jesus sitting in the midst of the city. He is robed in fine, colorful linen, and he is sitting peacefully there. She uses all of the powerful figures that one would expect in a royal city—wealthy lords, kings, bishops, and guards are all present. It is the picture of perfect sovereignty and total control. All is at rest, because the city, it seems, is completely secured against all outside forces. She writes: "And the soul is wholly occupied by the blessed divinity, sovereign power, sovereign wisdom and sovereign goodness" (68:313). A surface reading of this sixteenth showing reveals a picture of God establishing a kingdom in the soul. The soul has been made worthy to house the divine. God is the highest ruler and is the most powerful of all political and religious leaders. The soul is transformed into a royal palace, and the transformation bears all the marks of an imperial takeover. Victory is won; the city and soul are secured and are at rest.

But Julian does not leave us with this. The positioning of this final vision and her additions to the Long Text are critical to interpreting the city-soul. This vision is positioned between two instances in which the devil—the fiend—attacks Julian. Her vision is grounded in witnessing woundedness, and, more concretely, in witnessing the reality of wounds that imperial forces continually dismiss, manipulate, or actively deny.

First, the devil, depicted as a fierce warmonger. The fiend appears in chapters 67 and 69-70, immediately before and after the vision of the city-soul. In the first visit, the fiend appears while she is sleeping and he attacks Julian's throat. She writes: "His body and his hands were misshapen, but he held me by the throat with his paws, and wanted to stop my breath and kill me, but he could not" (67:312). His face thrust against hers, he attempts to silence her by grabbing her throat. Others are gathered around her bed and part of Julian's struggle is to verify what is taking place. She experiences an onslaught of the devil; his touch, smell, and appearance are shockingly vivid and horrifying. Yet those around her feel, smell, and see nothing. This is a great deal of the disorientation of the devil's attacks for Julian. The devil not only cuts off speech, but any testimony that she would give would not be understood by those around her.

The second attack occurs after her spiritual vision of the city-soul. The heat and smell return with oppressive force, signaling the devil's presence, but now they are accompanied by noise. He tries to confuse her through his mutterings. The fiend is multi-vocal in the second visit. She writes:

> . . . and I could also hear in my ears a conversation, as if between two speakers, and they seemed to be both talking at once, as if they were conducting a confused debate, and it was all low muttering. (69:315)

"Confused debate" is a translation of the Middle English term *parliamente/perlement*.[12] Julian maintains the word from the Short Text. It is clear that the mutterings of the devil directly refer to Parliament. In arguing for reading Julian in context, Lynn Staley references this particular word choice to make her case: "[Julian] retained almost verbatim from the Short Text this analogy between hearing someone talk at cross-purposes and the sound of a parliament."[13] Using this term, Julian intends to link readers to their context, inviting them to imagine the devil's activities as similar to the activities of Parliament. The sounds of the devil are like the politicians whose barrage of words does not lead to resolution but to greater confusion. The sounds appear to mock her and move her to despair.[14] This is not just spiritual despair but, instead, the despair of living within a city in which those in power launch assaults with their rhetoric, overwhelming and confusing citizens.

Julian experiences an underlying uncertainty in the presence of the devil's attacks. Is she really seeing what she is seeing? Her fears lead to her second-guessing what she knows to be true. This is countered, in chapter 70, by Jesus' assuring words: "Know it well now; it was no hallucination which you saw today" (70:317). The hallucinations and the indiscernible mutterings that Julian experiences suggest that one of

the ways that coercive power manifests itself is in blurring the truth and getting people to mistrust the things that are most fundamental to them. The clarity of seeing,
hearing, and speaking is undermined. Within her context, political and ecclesial figures like Pope Urban VI, Henry Despenser, and members of Parliament were strat-
egizing about the extension of power through military invasion. Those under their
rule are not only confused by their mutterings, their voices are silenced by those
in power. Julian likens these activities to the devil as they play on the weakness of
human beings, break down human resistance, and lead to pursue military pursuits.

Second, Julian draws on the Johannine farewell discourse to interpret the final
vision. The picture of God's waiting and laboring in the lord and the servant parable is now placed within a Johannine context, giving way to Julian's alternative
vision of the city-soul. God is not only expressed in Trinitarian terms at this point
in her text; God is presented in radical relationship with the disciples. Significant
additions to the Short Text emphasize the Trinitarian nature of God's residence in
the soul. Julian immediately follows the images of Jesus occupying the soul with
reflections on the Trinity:

> The place which Jesus takes in our soul he will nevermore vacate, for in us is
> his home of homes and his everlasting dwelling. And in this, he revealed the
> delight that he has in the creation of man's soul; for as well as the Father could
> create a creature and as well as the Son could create a creature, so well did the
> Holy Spirit want man's spirit to be created, and so it was done. (68:313)

Following her "final" vision of God and the soul, Julian references the dynamic
engagement of the Trinity in creation. Julian, at this ultimate point, draws us back
to see God's original intention for soul. She centers her comments on delight. The
divine intention at creation is not about power or victory. Instead, it is imaged in
the rhetoric of celebration and delight. The insertion of Trinitarian images here and
in the chapters that follow provide a counter-image to that of unilateral power and
sovereign control over the city. There is no single ruler wielding power. When Julian
identifies Jesus within the city, she does not refer to one occupant. Instead, she depicts
God as three, celebrating and delighting in creation. Just as the three delight in what
they make, they also delight in making a home in the soul. This delight would not
be the typical mark of a powerful leader in Julian's context. Instead, the divisions in
the papacy stem from two powers vying for singular control over the church.

Given the Trinitarian additions, she also presses us to think about the figure
of the Holy Spirit in connection to the vision of the soul as a city. Although

three-fold Trinitarian patterns appear throughout the *Showings*, the Spirit is unfigured, unlike the Father and Son. In developing this final vision within a Johannine and Trinitarian context, the question of the presence and role of the Spirit arises: Where is the Spirit in this final vision? Although the Spirit is not figured, the heavily Johannine language employed by Julian following this final showing reveals the presence of the Paraclete-Spirit.[15] A figure in the Johannine text who remains, abides, advocates, and comforts the disciples in Jesus' absence, the Paraclete-Spirit operates in the disciples as witness to God's continued presence in the wake of the divine death. In a context of uncertainty and change, one of the primary roles of the Paraclete-Spirit is to testify to the reality of God when this reality is contested. The disciples will receive, through the Spirit, both the power to discern and to testify to the truth. With God's spirit dwelling within them, they will now be the ones waiting and working for the restoration of the city.

Both the Johannine gospel and the Julian text seek to orient believers in the midst of forces that undermine their testimonies to Christ's passion. Julian continually comments on clinging or fleeing to the passion in the midst of the attacks. The powers of the world will seek to threaten that testimony, the Johannine writer warns; they will seek to silence you in order to cut off your testimony. Here, the attacks of the devil in Julian's text take on Johannine significance. The vision, placed in the midst of the attacks of the devil, is intended to both comfort and instruct the readers in the midst of warring presences. With competing claims to occupation of the soul, by God and the devil, the disciples are placed in a vulnerable yet critical position. The chapters that follow focus on the relationship between love and fear. Julian, like the Johannine writers, recognizes that fear will be the central obstacle to those who seek to live faithfully in the wake of Christ's passion. The powers of the world will appear insurmountable in relationship to the message of the gospel. The powers will, both writers acknowledge, play on people's fears in order to lead them to despair and keep them under control.

The powers of the world attempt to prevent this faithful witness. The Johannine text depicts the cost of truth-telling in John 16. Jesus prepares his disciples for the hostility that they will face for speaking truth to power. What truth are they speaking? What is the message they bear, and why is it so threatening to the powers?

Julian's answer is unrelenting. Love. Love is the threatening message.[16] This message comes for her inarguably from the mouth of the suffering Christ. The message is connected to his wounds. This is one of the most puzzling and contested aspects of Julian's theology. The message of divine love emerges from the suffering and bloody Jesus on the cross. This is often misinterpreted as Julian sanctioning the blood and violence of the cross. But the pneumatological focus of the final vision resists that interpretation. The central message of love, if read in light of the final vision, comes through *witness* to this suffering and, in turn, to the imperative, implicit throughout the entire text, to witness the wounds, both divine and human. Julian pleads with God, at the beginning of the *Showings,* to allow her to witness the sufferings of Christ. Granted this request, she unfolds a theology of witness that involves looking straight into the wounds. Her persistent focus on the wounds may function powerfully, in this context, to warn against the propensity of the powers to deny or dismiss them.

If the vision of the city-soul is read in light of the devil's attacks and the Johannine spirit, then it is not a conclusive vision of God's sovereign rule in the city. Instead, it is a vision handed over to the Johannine disciples and to Julian's readers in the context of death. It is a vision of witness and truth-telling in the face of imperial and ecclesial powers. The truth-telling of the disciples yields a beautiful and gutsy picture of people witnessing to the wounds of war in the name of God. If sin is described in terms of woundedness, then salvation can only come through attention to those wounds. This is the challenge that Julian poses to empire. As the soldiers return to Norwich, Julian calls those faithful to the gospel to witness the wounds in their midst. As the political and religious powers wage their wars, Julian envisions Christians standing as witnesses to the wounded city, waiting, longing, and resisting the forces of the world in order to testify to the truth of war. It is this third element that is unique to the final vision. Drawing on the power of the Paraclete-Spirit in the Johannine text, Julian envisions God dwelling in the human soul in such a way that the disciples carry on the vision of God's restoration of the wounded city. This restoration comes about not through coercion or force but through faithful witness to the reality of human woundedness. This is the texture of love as Julian portrays it.

WOUNDS AND EMPIRE

> We need to bear witness, compassionately, to the destructive events of our era
> if we are to embark on a more humane course. —Robert Jay Lifton[17]

At the end of the *Showings,* Julian writes: "The book is begun by God's gift and his grace, but it is not yet performed, as I see it" (86:346). Over six hundred years after Julian writes these words, the question arises: What would it mean to perform Julian's text? Interpreting the final showing, I suggested that this performance takes the form of witness. There are many efforts to analyze and diagnose the American form of empire emerging in the twenty-first century, but what is startling about these analyses is the sense that war, in this context, is inevitable, that it is constitutive of empire. Instead of the exception, war is the constant. "In an era of armed globalization," Michael Hardt and Antonio Negri claim, "a false pretense of peace . . . merely presides over a state of constant war."[18]

In this new era of global civil wars, there is greater risk of leaving the wounds unwitnessed. Without clear enemies and clearly stated aims, estimating the cost of war is somehow threatened as well. The greater access to war in the media and the resulting consumer packaging of war makes it difficult to see the wounds as real wounds. Robert Jay Lifton, in his book *Superpower Syndrome,* claims that any superpower has a great stake in presenting an image of invulnerability. A nation's military is the chief means of constructing and maintaining this image. Although the soldier is the principal figure preserving this image, the *wounded* soldier is most threatening to this image. The wounded soldier physically bears the marks of the nation's vulnerability. These wounds must be "bandaged" in such a way that they do not threaten, but rather serve, national interests. As a chief extension of the superpower's image, they literally guard what Lifton identifies as the "illusion of invulnerability" globally.[19] The real experience of the soldier stands to threaten that image, both by reminding the superpower that it is susceptible to wounding and by communicating to the outside world this vulnerability.

The image of the soldier must be carefully constructed by the superpower. This construction, what I will call "packaging," places soldiers in a dangerous bind: they bear the marks of war but cannot speak them. Lifton and others who work with veterans testify to the fact that this unspeakability deepens the trauma of war. Part of the unspeakability comes from the trauma of war itself. But another is the threat that speaking poses to the nation. These truths are not meant to come into speech, because, if they do, they threaten to reveal the complexities and ambiguities of war, thereby calling the workings of empire into question. The silencing (in service of the invulnerable image) compounds the trauma of the soldier because the soldier is permitted to tell only one version of the story—the one that serves national interests. To speak otherwise deems them unpatriotic, cowardly, and weak. There is no room for telling the truth of one's experience, a practice that fosters healing in the case of trauma. Not only are soldiers attacked by memory and the complexity of speaking about the traumas of war, they are gripped by an imperative to keep silent. Like Julian's fiend, the powers have them by the throat.

Through greater technology, media access, and marketing strategies, we have better means of maintaining the illusion of invulnerability. In short, we have a greater ability to package war. However, this packaging belies the realities of war and its true toll on human lives. Bearing witness to the truth of war is even more difficult yet even more essential in the new form of American empire. One of the challenges to bearing witness is that although we *see* more of the war than we did before, we do not see any more of its reality. With cell phones, video technology, and endless media access, we can be present with soldiers in a way that makes us feel as if we are on the front lines. Yet watching the war is not the same as witnessing the war. We *see* more, yet our ability to discern truth from fiction, real story from constructed narrative, is increasingly dulled. Virtual reality gives us the illusion of participation that, strangely, meets the needs of empire. If the viewers, the citizens, feel a greater sense of control over what is happening to them, then they present less resistance to those actually making decisions about the war.

Additionally, what we see in the media is carefully packaged to persuade. With consumerism at the heart of American identity, packaging war is inevitable. There is an increasing economic element operating, not just in the pursuit of war for economic ends but, rather, in the packaging of it. War itself becomes a commodity at play in the global market. For example, the language of coercive force, unpopular and bad for America's image, can be packaged in terms of America's extension of "influence" in the global pursuit of freedom and liberation for all.[20] This packaging sells the war to viewers. The marketing mindset runs the risk of making the ugliest of war somehow beautiful, a synonym, perhaps, for justifiable. The greater sophistication in marketing does not alter the inevitable outcome of any war—human casualties. Just as the religious rhetoric of the crusade broke down in the wake of the 1383 crusade, the rhetorical justifications of empire seem vapid in view of human wounds. If packaged well, however, this human cost can be rendered invisible.

Bearing witness is an even more dangerous and necessary act in the face of the new era of empire. Distinguishing between watching and witnessing is essential. To witness requires critically discerning the places where the rhetoric of empire and human experience cannot be reconciled. Probing empire through the lens of human woundedness, we expose the illusion of invulnerability by pointing, again and again, to the wounds of war. Unwrapping the layers of packaging involves training ourselves to discern truth apart from the media sea of virtual images. To *really* see the wounds would be to acknowledge that a life is changed and, in many cases, marked by a profound encounter with death. Any "victories" leave physical and psychological wounds, and they remain as signs that violence has a human cost almost unspeakable in the aftermath of the war.

The wounds of empire, however, are not always and only war wounds. And although Julian was aware of the collusion of military and ecclesial powers affecting life in Norwich, she was perhaps more attuned to the ways in which power operated more subtly in daily life. The windows of the anchorhold allowed her to see the three dimensions of life in Norwich—the ecclesial, the domestic, and the political. Although Julian's textual engagement with Despenser reveals the power of her gaze through the first window, the second window is perhaps the least studied in her work. The second window of the market and the maidservant reminds us that her spirituality was also informed by those who did not bear any ecclesial or political power. In this sense, Julian witnessed the domestic realities around her.

But she also, as I said before, participated in them. What we see in her text are images that can both witness and wound; the image of Jesus as Mother can both subvert patriarchal claims *while* reinforcing prescribed roles for women. The servant, in her writings, remains a servant. And outside the second window, her maidservant would come and go, tending to her daily needs. There are many ways that the devil has you by the throat. And in reading Julian's text, it is important to see the hold that grips these texts as well. While there is a temptation to read her toward liberative ends, her charge to witness also asks us to be aware of the ways in which her own text is domesticated.

Perhaps Julian's two decades of meditation on her visions reveal the long and arduous task of discerning truth. At every turn in the Long Text, she insists that everything in the visions points to God's love. This simplicity and clarity reveal the great gift that Julian receives from her spiritual reflections. But forged amidst the attacks of the devil, the texture of love is neither trite nor sentimental. Instead, genuine love refuses the packaging of wounds. Her Johannine vision of the soul's return to God bears, within it, the imperative to witness wounds and to resist the powers that cover the wounds and deny their reality. Witnessing wounds exposes the vulnerability that lies beneath the shiny packaging of imperial power. For Julian, vulnerability is a mark of our humanity. It is neither blameworthy nor judged by God. Neither should it be evaded or manipulated. Instead, it is the soil of God's careful tending and patient waiting. This tending and waiting are now tied to the act of witnessing. To witness the reality of war, to speak about the marks of war on human bodies, is to speak a truth that those in power do not want to hear. In fact, Julian shows us, the powers will attack your throat, cutting off your attempts to speak. To attest to the reality of the wounds is a Christian act of resistance amidst the powers.

FURTHER READING

Primary Sources

Julian of Norwich. *A Book of Showings to the Anchoress Julian of Norwich.* 2 vols. Edited by Edmund Colledge, O.S.A., and James Walsh, S.J. Toronto: Pontifical Institute of Medieval Studies, 1978.

_____. *Showings.* Translated by Edmund Colledge, O.S.A., and James Walsh, S.J. Classics of Western Spirituality. Mahwah, N.J.: Paulist Press, 1978.

Secondary Sources

Anchoritic Spirituality: Ancrene Wisse and Associated Works. Translated by Anne Savage and Nicholas Watson. Classics of Western Spirituality. Mahwah, N.J.: Paulist Press, 1991.

Aers, David, and Lynn Staley. *The Powers of the Holy: Religion, Politics, and Gender in Late Medieval English Culture.* University Park, Pa.: Pennsylvania State University Press, 1996.

Georgianna, Linda. *The Solitary Self: Individuality in the "Ancrene Wisse."* Cambridge, Mass.: Harvard University Press, 1981.

Jantzen, Grace. *Julian of Norwich: Mystic and Theologian.* 2nd ed. New York, N.Y.: Paulist Press, 2000.

Nuth, Joan. *Wisdom's Daughter: The Theology of Julian of Norwich.* New York, N.Y.: Crossroad, 1991.

CHAPTER 13

Martin Luther

Deanna A. Thompson

The Muslim Martin Luther may be living among us and his name actually may be Osama bin Laden.[1]

This flippant comment made by a political scientist may be intended to illumine the character of Osama bin Laden, but what does it say about the sixteenth-century Reformer Martin Luther? Scholars continue to debate the legacy of Luther, who, by his resistance to the medieval church, changed the course of Christianity and, many argue, of society and politics as well. But the above comparison takes the debate to new depths. While those who invoke this comparison of bin Laden and Luther suggest a shared commitment to religion as personal and interior rather than as an "ascriptive social condition,"[2] it is precisely on the issue of how religious conviction is manifest externally where bin Laden and Luther differ pointedly. For bin Laden, the alleged mastermind of the 9/11 terrorist attacks, religious convictions lead to blatant disregard for state, national, and international law. His brand of religious resistance pays little heed to temporal rules and rulers.[3] Luther, on the other hand, upheld the institution of government as God-ordained and worthy of obedience. But as we will see, Luther's reimagining of religious freedom leads to a theology of resistance with respect to ecclesial and even imperial authority in ways that differ from the outright rebellion, revolution, or terrorism that radical leaders like bin Laden invoke today.

THE CONTEXT

Martin Luther was born and raised in the complex political system of late medieval Europe. In the early sixteenth century, Germany was comprised of disparate territorial powers. While the emperor reigned over all the territories, local authorities actually controlled more of the day-to-day affairs of the people. The sixteenth century also brought growth in urban centers, and the presence of numerous universities in the empire introduced a growing critical awareness into the atmosphere of the time. Within German lands in particular, one target of this growing critical capacity was the Church of Rome. Large numbers of Germans believed their nation to be "most richly exploited" by the papacy.[4] By the beginning of the sixteenth century, many German princes saw church control as a matter of great political urgency.

Thus Martin Luther did not ignite a movement of reform *ex nihilo*. Clearly he was a product of the higher education ushering in this new critical awareness. After receiving a university education and briefly immersing himself in the study of law, twenty-one-year-old Luther entered the order of Augustinian monks. Within the walls of the monastery, Luther devoted himself to serious theological and philosophical study. Captivated by the power of the biblical text, Luther earned his doctorate in Old Testament, and began lecturing and preaching at the University of Wittenberg.

It was there, in his post as professor of biblical theology, that Luther began to envision a theological universe quite different from the one in which he had been raised. His famous breakthrough with Romans 1.17 ("The righteous will live by faith") shattered the view that being a Christian was about following all the rules and regulations of the Roman Church or of Scripture. For Luther, a true theologian is a theologian of the cross, one who understands Christ's death as securing freedom from all attempts to see oneself as better than another or to make oneself worthy before God. Equipped with this new vision, it did not take long for Luther to find fault in church practices and make such grievances public. And it did not take long for German princes to embrace this outspoken theologian as a central weapon against what they saw as overzealous control of their territories by the church.

JUSTIFIED, FREE, OBEDIENT, AND RESISTANT

In 1517 Luther penned his famous *Ninety-Five Theses*, detailing what he considered abuses of papal authority, particularly the practice of indulgences. Due to the important development of the printing press, copies of this document circulated throughout Germany, making it into the hands of Emperor Maximilian I. At that time, the empire was feeling the effects of defiance not just from Luther but also from the German Estates in their insistence on the primacy of territorial needs over imperial demands. In hopes of containing this outspoken monk, the emperor summoned Luther to Augsburg and exhorted him to recant his criticisms of the church, but Luther would not. Over the next several years, Luther continued his offensive against the church and his advance of a new theological vision. Martin Brecht observes, "Luther had been able to transform the new experience of justification by faith alone into a thoroughgoing alternative conception which extended across the entire breadth of religious and ecclesiastical life."[5] Luther's position gathered momentum, and the church knew it needed to respond.

In June 1520, Pope Leo issued Luther an ultimatum: either recant or be denounced as a heretic. Yet again, however, Luther went on the offensive. He did this through publishing three of the most significant treatises of his career: *Appeal to the Christian Nobility, On the Babylonian Captivity of the Church*, and *On the Freedom of the Christian*, all in 1520. In his *Appeal to the Christian Nobility*, Luther directs his remarks to the German aristocracy and to the emperor, arguing vigorously that the papacy should have no jurisdiction over secular authority. Luther insists that Christ did not involve himself in temporal affairs; therefore, neither should the pope. He appeals to the German princes to protect the German people "from these rapacious wolves in sheep's clothing" who "thieve and rob" by selling indulgences.

In *On the Babylonian Captivity of the Church*, Luther seals his fate as a heretic by reimagining the authority and power of God's Word through his vision of baptism. Luther accuses the Romanists of virtually destroying the power of baptism and subverting the power of God's Word. For all Christians, Luther proclaims, are baptized "with the same baptism, have the same faith and the same gospel."[6] In baptism, we die to our sinful selves, and through the righteousness given by Christ's death, all are freed to live a new life in Christ. Going even further, Luther insists that every baptized Christian belongs to the royal priesthood of all believers. Contrary to claims of power by the Roman hierarchy, Luther insists that according to scripture, all are one body (1 Cor. 12). The priest, then, differs from the laity only with regard to office. To claim otherwise, Luther insisted, was to embrace a theology of glory caught up in earthly prestige and power. As a theologian of the cross, Luther adamantly rejected the view that exalted a few over the majority of Christians, for that countered what he saw as the radical equalizing of Christ's death for all on the cross.[7]

After his attacks on church practices, Luther penned the third treatise, *The Freedom of the Christian*, which takes a conciliatory tone, focusing more intently on how justification frees up Christians to live a dramatically altered existence in the world. "A Christian is free lord of all, subject to none. A Christian is a perfectly dutiful servant of all, subject to all."[8] This dialectic encompasses for Luther "the whole of Christian life." Paradoxically, Christians stand before God in a sinful state, and yet God's gift of justification frees them from having to perform works to gain God's favor. At the same time, however, this freedom from a preoccupation with self-concern manifests itself in a life of "works of freest service, cheerfully and lovingly done, with which a [person] willingly serves another without hope of reward."[9] To embrace the role of servant means living as Christ did, and rejecting all claims to power over others, as the world constantly tempts us to do. Luther believes this gift of Christian freedom from requirements and freedom to serve others is the locus of Christian hope, hope in God's power to transform our current condition of selfishness into one of true love of neighbor.

In response to these treatises, Rome sent Luther a papal bull of excommunication. In response to Rome, Luther and his supporters burned the papal bull. His opponents then set his writings ablaze. In just a few years, what had begun as a regional dispute about indulgences had grown into a situation of national significance.[10] The situation demanded that the new Emperor Charles V summon him to a diet in Worms, setting the scene for Luther's "famous appearance on the imperial stage."[11]

In 1521, public support for Luther was at its height. As he traveled to Worms, the German people cheered him on. When he faced the emperor and church authorities, it was clear they expected him to recant. But this monk, one who, by his own admission, was accustomed "not to courts but to cells of monks" gave this response: "I am bound by the scriptures I have quoted and my conscience is captive to the Word of God. I cannot and will not retract anything, since it is neither safe nor right to go against conscience." Then he added, "Here I stand. I can do no other. God help me! Amen."[12] Walther von Loewenich frames the significance of Luther's words: "For the first time, the principle of freedom of conscience was exposed publicly before the highest ranking representative of the church and the world. One could make demands of everything else, but not of faith, for faith was a matter of conscience, [and conscience was] bound to God's Word."[13] For Luther, the transforming claim of the gospel—that we are saved by faith—becomes so deeply engraved in one's being that conscience can and must go against earthly authorities who threaten the gospel's proclamation. It is difficult to overestimate the force with which this vision of freedom and resistance permeated the imaginations of the German people, from the monasteries to the farmlands. Many were captivated by the image of freedom, and as we will see, understood its relevance to their lives in ways that would shock even the Reformer himself.

Fearing for his safety, Luther's political allies staged a friendly kidnapping and hid him in the Wartburg castle following the Diet of Worms. About a month after the diet, Emperor Charles issued the edict, declaring Luther a heretic and an outlaw of the empire. The edict charged that Luther be taken prisoner, his books burned, and that his allies lose all their property as well. It was a potentially fatal threat to Luther and his movement. While princes decided whether or not to enforce the edict in their territories, Luther fought loneliness at the castle by immersing himself in writing before learning that radical forces were taking hold of Wittenberg.

When he caught wind of the rioting that was visited upon Wittenberg, Luther risked his life to return immediately, where he preached against violent uprisings for eight consecutive days. While he calmed the university and surrounding town, significant pockets of unrest remained beyond the reach of his preaching. Heiko Oberman places this dynamic in context, noting that "the roots of unrest had long been present . . . as a nonviolent impulse for reform. . . . The new foment of the reformation proved to imply political radicalization by a biblical-spiritual opposition to the secular power of the church."[14] It was clear to Luther that he needed to clarify his own position on the relationship between reform of the church and reform of the state, for he resisted seeing his reformation theology as a template for political and economic reform.

In 1523, Luther published *Temporal Authority: To What Extent It Should Be Obeyed.* In it we see his vision of the two kingdoms at work, setting out the parameters of authority within each kingdom. According to Luther, God ordained three natural orders at creation: the family, the church, and the state. Only the state, Luther suggests, has any legal authority. And yet God stands as the ruler of both the earthly and spiritual kingdoms; neither is sufficient in the world without the other.[15] We do not exist bodily in a profane realm, cut off from God. Rather, God governs the earthly realm with the left hand, which in Luther's view, should never lead to a theocracy, for the gospel governs the spiritual realm only. "It is out of the question that there should be a common Christian government over the whole world, or indeed over a single country or any considerable body of people, for the wicked always outnumber the good."[16] Clearly, Luther's opposition to theocracy is strong and passionate, and it is rooted in the necessity of the distinction between the two realms, where the spiritual governs the internal life while the earthly governs the external life.[17]

In this treatise Luther also articulates what he sees as the limits of temporal authority. Rulers of the temporal realm possess authority to legislate behavior and action, but it is beyond their authority to legislate beliefs. Matters of faith belong to the spiritual kingdom; "thoughts are free," Luther insisted.[18] With this vision, Luther "allowed for the possibility of refusal to obey in cases where the princes trespassed upon the jurisdiction belonging only to God."[19] As we will see, this principle remains a significant component of Luther's understanding of resistance and its limits.

In addition to overstepping their authority regarding matters of faith, Luther also strongly admonishes the princes for their over-taxation and harsh treatment of the peasants under their rule. Here he sounds a prophetic note about the bloody Peasants' Uprising looming on the horizon:

> The common man is learning to think, and the scourge of princes . . . is gathering force among the mob and with the common man. I fear there will be no way to avert it, unless the princes conduct themselves in a princely manner and begin again to rule decently and reasonably. Men will not, men cannot, men refuse to endure your tyranny and wantonness much longer.[20]

Princely rule, Luther made clear, stood in need of serious reform. But before the peasants could use his words as a rallying cry for social change, Luther quickly invoked the biblical imperative of "turning the other cheek" when encountering abuse. Likely Luther called for such restraint in order to "[strengthen] the state, the instrument he relied on for reform of the church, against the secular powers of the papacy."[21] The significance of this perspective is crucial to understanding Luther's relationship to the rulers. Without temporal power on his side, his words might have incited uprisings, but dramatic reform would have come much more slowly. But Luther repeatedly cautioned princes against their abuse of power, imploring them to "mete out punishment [of evildoers] without injuring others."[22] Nevertheless, in all earthly matters, Luther insisted that Christians are obligated to obey and follow the laws of the state.

Despite Luther's efforts to preach reform and passive resistance around Germany, "the fundamental Reformation concepts, such as freedom and the priesthood of all believers, became slogans that electrified and mobilized peasants everywhere."[23] While Luther's defiant stance against Rome (and consequently, against the emperor) did not by itself create the unrest that led to violence, it can be argued that Luther functioned as a "symbol, a beacon, a sign of the times" for the peasants,[24] and that his theological vision equipped them with a lens through which they could interpret and protest their experience of oppression at the hands of temporal authorities. Although Luther preached submission to earthly rulers on earthly matters, his noisy disobedience in the ecclesial realm fueled the imaginations and religious zeal of the peasants and radical reformers set on ushering in the reign of God on earth.

The years 1524-25 were a bloody time. In 1524, the peasants issued their *Twelve Articles*, using Luther's theology to bolster their demand for free use of woods, pasture, and water, and their refusal to accept new taxes. As priests and lords of all, they argued, should they not have the right to control their economic and social affairs as well? Luther responded quickly with his *Admonition to Peace Concerning the Twelve Articles*, which he addresses to "my dear brethren." In it he admonishes both peasants and lords to practice restraint. To the peasants he reiterates his sharp delineation between the spiritual and the earthly realm, insisting that "the fact that the rulers are unjust and wicked does not excuse disorder and rebellion."[25] Luther's admonition did not have the calming effect he had hoped, and the peasants became more violent. Many followed the rallying cry of radical reformer (and former student of Luther) Thomas Müntzer, who proclaimed, "Kill a prince for Christ!" Müntzer and others were fighting for revolution and calling for a theocracy, where their version of the gospel would be wedded tightly to the sword. Such a vision not only thoroughly confused the two realms, Luther believed, but it—not unlike the medieval church—held the gospel captive to a dangerous form of glory theology that emphasized freedom without any thought to sin and the necessity of external restraint.

These developments pushed Luther over the edge. He produced a vitupera-tive pamphlet entitled *Against the Robbing and Murdering Hordes of Peasants.* In it Luther positions himself squarely behind the princes, berating the peasants for stopping "at nothing short of revolution and overthrow of the existing social order."[26] Because the peasants committed violence in the name of Christ, Luther accuses them of "blaspheming God." While such a response is consistent with his understanding of the two kingdoms, Luther needlessly rants against the peas-ants, arguing that "a pious Christian ought to suffer a hundred deaths rather than consenting to the peasants' cause."[27] Luther also emboldens the princes by rec-ommending that they punish peasants without a trial, in order to hasten the end of the ordeal. This pamphlet was not published until after the uprising had been quelled. Nevertheless, the rulers invoked Luther's words and plundered the peas-ants brutally.

As many as one hundred thousand peasants lost their lives in the uprising.[28] Amidst the bloodshed Luther intoned that "God would save the truly innocent." In the wake of continued atrocities committed by the rulers in the revolt's after-math, Luther's position came under attack by friends and foes alike. He finally published what was supposed to be a retraction of his position toward the peas-ants. But in *An Open Letter On the Harsh Book against the Peasants,* Luther stood firm in his unrepentance. He insisted that "anyone who knows how to distinguish rightly between the two kingdoms will not be offended by [the earlier tract]."[29] He refused to accept any responsibility for the behavior of the rulers, depicting their actions merely as proof of the reality of God's wrath. If Christians acknowledge the distinction between the two realms, he argued, they will understand the earth-ly realm as the realm of wrath, and the heavenly realm as the realm of mercy. This, we can argue, was Luther at his worst.

What are we to make of this transformation of Luther the proclaimer of free-dom of the Christian to Luther "the hammer of the poor"?[30] Peter Matheson offers one approach, observing that "when a great shattering takes place and an enchant-ed world is lost, it can free us up to step out in new directions but can also toss us into the abyss. Dreams and nightmares frequently interweave. There is a nightmare dimension to the Reformation, too."[31] From our vantage point, Luther's stance against the peasants qualifies as one of the nightmarish aspects of Luther's life. He refused to rein in his rhetoric and disregarded his own admonition to rulers that they must "deal justly with evildoers."[32] Why couldn't the Reformer see what seems so clear to us? Jürgen Moltmann faults Luther for his inability to see that "church and society were too closely bound for the church to be reformed without consequences for society as well."[33] A key insight of the Reformation, Moltmann continues, is communicated through Luther's vision that the reformation of life necessarily follows from the reformation of faith. Despite his continued insistence that faith transforms the sinful self, altering the way the believer acts in the world, in the context of the Peasants' Uprising this sheltered monk could not yet envision a more nuanced relationship between the limits of temporal rulers and the limits of citizenly obedience.

It is not surprising that after Luther's brutish opposition to the peasants and their concerns, popular enthusiasm for his program began to wane. At the same time, "[t]he Reformer lost his confidence in the common people and went forth to build the new Church with the help of the territorial rulers."[34] Even as the 1520s brought significant unrest, the Reformation continued to expand and take hold throughout Germany, largely through the efforts of the princes. Although the emperor attempted to implement the Edict of Worms, practically speaking, the "notion of empire had little effect on political practice."[35] For the reformation of ecclesial life in the territories was ultimately a political decision, enacted by local political authorities and guided by aspirations of a new relationship between church and state.[36] Nevertheless, public support by the princes for Luther was relatively slow to develop, for supporting the Reformer was officially a crime. Thus, backing for Luther's position had to be rendered in political terms.

This leads us to the 1530 Diet of Augsburg. Emperor Charles V had actually been quite lenient toward the growing evangelical territories,[37] for he needed their support to counter the Turks, who were advancing toward Vienna. After attaining a victorious peace with France and receiving the imperial crown from the pope (which was to be the last crowning of an emperor by a pope), Charles returned to the empire to preside over the proceedings at Augsburg.[38] The goal was to bring religious unity to Germany, which would aid further in fighting against the Turks. In 1521 Luther, an accused heretic, had stood alone before the emperor; in 1530 a large group stood together before Charles, including many powerful princes.[39] Since Luther remained under the ban of the empire, he was forced to remain a safe distance away.

Although the emperor set a conciliatory tone for the diet, he was determined to proceed against the evangelicals "with fire and sword," should they not yield to his kindness."[40] At this point, the future of the Reformation was uncertain, for even though Luther doubted imperial support for the Reformation would emerge from the diet, he regarded the movement's survival to be at stake in Augsburg. Housed in a nearby town, he remained close by and influenced the proceedings through frequent correspondence with his evangelical colleagues.

At Augsburg, just as at Worms and other diets, the evangelical perspective itself was put on trial. Luther feared that Philip Melanchthon, his friend and primary negotiator for the evangelical position, would compromise their core beliefs in attempts to appease the emperor, whose insistence on agreement was backed by military threat. The Augsburg Confession, penned largely by Melanchthon, did not contain all that Luther had hoped. Nevertheless, it was the first written synthesis of the evangelical faith. And when Luther heard it was read at the diet, he exclaimed, "I rejoice mightily that I have experienced this hour, when Christ is publicly proclaimed through this glorious confession by such men in an assembly!"[41]

Despite the rigorous defense mounted by the evangelicals within and outside the proceedings, the edict of the diet ruled against them. Evangelical territories within Germany quickly rejected the edict out of protest, and the Reformers at Augsburg refused to admit any error, further undermining the imperial authority and continuing to erode people's trust in their rulers. Amid the unrest, Luther and the evangelicals participating in the diet were ordered to silently accept the edict. Not surprisingly, Luther actively rejected both commands. Robert Bertram sets Luther's and the other evangelical leaders' refusal in context:

> Whatever suffering befell the confessors they themselves had occasioned by what *they first refused to suffer*, the subversion of the gospel in high places. . . . Directly by the act of submitting their teaching, the confessors were nonetheless teaching, probably more publicly than ever and now in conscious defiance of ecclesiastical policy and, soon after, of imperial policy as well. . . . Whatever suffering the confessors were willing to endure was only consequent, rooted in this prior refusal to suffer. In refusing that, and in refusing to cease refusing, they were both ecclesiastically and civilly disobedient. [42]

Indeed, Luther's supposed acquiescence to civil authorities is more complex than it appears at first glance. On the one hand, he claims that "obeying the emperor is the same as obeying the ordinance of God";[43] while on the other, he openly disobeys imperial orders. This tension finds its genesis, it seems, not only in the delineation of power within the two kingdoms, but also in his view of the human being as both sinful and justified. Not only does he insist that "sinners like myself . . . need repentance every day,"[44] but he knows that those in power are no different, and must also "begin with repentance" before they act, whether in war against the enemy[45] or in action against the evangelicals. And Luther informs pastors that their office affords them "very wide admonitory power" to call temporal authorities to account when their actions reflect self-serving motives rather than the good of the citizens under their care.[46] Thus Christian freedom is manifest in bold action of obedience to God's Word, which at times requires active disobedience with respect to the edicts of particular rulers.

Likely influenced by the Reformers' disobedient stance, the evangelical princes began after the Diet of Augsburg to seriously consider military alliance against imperial forces. Not long thereafter, the evangelical territories formed the League of Schmalkalden and became a new political power within the empire.[47] For Luther, admonishing rulers was one thing, but supporting any kind of military action against the emperor and the Catholic territories was another matter entirely. He was faced with a painful choice: if he did not speak out publicly, his silence would appear as a tacit endorsement for the Catholic position. Further, when he realized that the ability to practice an evangelical faith was likely at stake, he did set forth what some would call a theory of Protestant resistance.[48] In his *Warning to my Dear German People,* Luther insisted, "I will convince you that it is God's command to disobey" the emperor's edict.[49] During the Peasants' Uprising, Luther had called for passive endurance of suffering by those who insisted the gospel was on their side. But now, Luther opens the door to the possibility of armed defense of evangelical territories.

In the charged atmosphere following the Edict of Augsburg, Luther concluded that he would have to respond to the prevailing political reality of the threatened evangelical estates. He begins his *Warning* quite cautiously, saying "Assuming there is no God," as if to alert his readers that this theologian was wading into civil and legal waters that take him far afield from theology. He confesses that it weighs heavily on his conscience as a pastor, a "mouthpiece of God's Word," to "counsel war." But Luther immediately distinguishes his call for the evangelicals to defend themselves from the insurrectionist position of the peasants in 1525: "He is an insurrectionist who refuses to submit to government and law . . . that is the true definition of a rebel. . . . In accordance with this definition, self-defense against the blood hounds cannot be rebellious."[50] Luther is clear: the evangelical estates are not trying to establish a new government. Rather, Luther "let it pass as self defense"[51] to protest against possible imperial takeover of the evangelical regions, which would lead to repression of their faith. He realized that this civil predicament required a civil response.

But Luther's argument is more than merely a civil one. Not only are Germans permitted to resist the emperor, they are duty-bound to resist—even to the point of (suffering) violence—in defense of the gospel. Luther reminds people that in baptism they "vowed to preserve Christ's gospel and not to persecute or oppose it."[52] If they do not resist the emperor, they "would also lend a hand in overthrowing and exterminating all the good which the dear gospel has again restored and established."[53] We must be clear, however, that Luther is *not* advocating armed defense in support of a theocracy, or in support of the expansion of the gospel.[54] Rather, he advocates defending the freedom to proclaim the gospel as evangelicals in their own territories. Here we see strong affinity with Luther's claims in his treatise on *Temporal Authority*, where he insisted that "thoughts are free" and that earthly authorities have no jurisdiction over spiritual beliefs. Eventually the emperor did fight the Schmalkaldic League, and even though he defeated their army, he nevertheless came to realize that the evangelical presence in German territories was ultimately too strong to overthrow.

This analysis of Luther's relation to imperial politics cannot come to a close without addressing an issue where Luther transgresses his anti-theocratic stance: that is, in his writings against the Jews. Although Luther confessed that the chief doctrine of his theology was "that God is the God of the Jews and the Gentiles, rich toward all," he quickly added that "because of their pride, the Jews lost their promise which was theirs and was due them."[55] Earlier in his life, Luther had adopted a more compassionate stance toward the Jews, arguing that Christians had treated them too harshly, thus discouraging conversion. Therefore, Luther's earlier writings took on a conciliatory tone.[56] But when mass conversions failed to materialize, Luther went on the offensive. In the 1530s-1540s, many of his writings were commissioned by political leaders, including those against the Jews. In what is perhaps the most loathsome text of Luther's entire corpus, *On the Jews and Their Lies*, he insists that the Old Testament tells the story of God's rejection of the Jews as the chosen people. "[O]ne dare not regard God as so cruel that he would punish his own people so long, so terribly, so unmercifully, and in addition keep silent. . . . Who would have faith, hope, and love toward such a God?"[57] Some scholars suggest that Luther's verbal assaults on the Jews are no more (or less) venomous than those he launched at other enemies, such as the papists. But for those of us reading Luther on this side of the long and painful legacy of violence done to Jews, we cannot neglect that such venomous rhetoric was also tied to blueprints for civil action. In *On the Jews and Their Lies* Luther prods earthly rulers to take violent action against the Jews—not because they are insurrectionists, not because they threaten the existence of the evangelical states, but simply because they fail to believe rightly. He instructs Christian rulers and laypersons alike to set fire to Jewish synagogues, destroy Jewish homes, and forbid Jews safe passage anywhere. Those admonitions counsel a dangerous kind of theocratic rule and should haunt those of us living in the shadow of the Holocaust. When Luther calls on rulers to treat the Jews with "harsh mercy" he eerily foreshadows much modern oppression of the Jewish people.

Again some scholars suggest that we must keep in mind that Luther is writing here on behalf of the civil authorities, and that such writings may not always accurately reflect his own views. After the first printing of *On the Jews and Their Lies*, however, a second printing was forbidden out of fear the treatise would incite considerable violence.[58] It must be acknowledged, then, that even though he writes on behalf of the civil authorities, he advances a vision of a violent theocratic approach to the Jews that makes even the authorities nervous.

Almost a decade after Luther's death and some twenty years after the Diet of Augsburg (with the bloody Schmalkaldic War in between), the Peace of Augsburg was finally achieved (1555), where both the evangelical and Catholic faiths were granted legal standing in the German lands of the empire. The medieval idea of a monarchy, where one religion and one man rule, was no longer a possibility.[59] What Luther had started with his appearance on the imperial stage at Worms came to fruition through the Peace of Augsburg, which authorized evangelical territories as a constitutional force. While Luther spent much of his life actively supporting temporal rulers, he nevertheless proffered a theology of resistance that advocated defense against individual rulers when they attempted to coerce in spiritual matters.[60]

CONSTRUCTIVE IMPLICATIONS

"If things in this world were in the same state now that they were then, I would still have to hold to and defend [my previous position]."[61] Here Luther refers to his evolving position regarding war against the Turks. But this statement also highlights a crucial characteristic of Luther's thought: his views were based not on abstract concepts but on specific encounters with actual events. Luther's comments above serve as a caution against taking his words from one context and merely setting them down unaltered in another. Luther's world of imperial politics differs significantly from our contemporary political context. Yet there are ways in which Luther's words can influence current conversations on how Christians relate to rulers and their claims to power.

George Lindbeck has observed that modernity offers significant talk of freedom; following in the tradition of Luther, however, Lindbeck worries that it is "explosively dangerous" to talk of human freedom in the absence of any talk of human sinfulness.[62] In the midst of a bloody war in Iraq, where our president sent troops to fight under the banner "Enduring Freedom," we must ask whether our leaders and our citizens have spent adequate time in "national repentance and repentant prayer."[63] Just as Luther criticized the hastiness of his leaders in their war with the Turks by saying, "Nor did I like that Christians and princes were driven into attacking the Turk before they had amended their own ways,"[64] so too must we hold our leaders accountable, insisting upon reflection and confession of our country's own missteps, flaws, and imperfections.

We also have in Luther an understanding that support and cooperation with rulers is necessary unless the proclamation of the gospel is at stake. Even though Luther's theology of resistance was much more finely honed when it came to abuses in the ecclesial realm, he nevertheless offers insight into the freedom of the Christian to resist the policies of our government when the gospel is threatened. If we look to the current context, we see that President Bush uses biblical and religious language when explaining and justifying U.S. actions. While this is certainly the president's prerogative, some Christians have critiqued the administration for wrapping national ideology in a veneer of religious language. For instance, as Jim Wallis points out, in the 2003 State of the Union speech,

> the president evoked an easily recognized and quite famous line from an old
> gospel hymn. Speaking of America's deepest problems, Bush said, "The need

is great. Yet there's power, wonder-working power, in the goodness and ideal-ism and faith of the American people." But that's not what the song is about. The hymn says there is "power, power, wonder-working power *in the blood of the Lamb*" (emphasis added). The hymn is about the power of Christ in salva-tion, not the power of "the American people," or any people, or any country. Bush's citation was a complete misuse.[65]

To portray a nation as having salvific power would certainly qualify in Luther's mind as a threat to the gospel proclamation that God alone has the power to save. The wonder-working power of Christ's going to the cross represents a radical alter-native for resisting the powers and principalities that want to supplant God's real-ity with their own counterfeit reality, like the one currently offered by our govern-ment. When such an abuse of the gospel occurs, Luther believed, Christians are duty-bound to resist. And while Luther's own life represents a flawed attempt to live out his own theology, his insistence that resistance to both ecclesial and polit-ical authorities is a faithful response to God's free gift of righteousness can prod contemporary Christians into debate and even protest of the misuse of power among our political leaders.

FURTHER READING

Primary Sources

Luther, Martin. *Luther's Works*, American ed., 55 vols. Philadelphia, Pa.: Fortress Press (vols. 31-55); St. Louis, Mo.: Concordia (vols. 1-30), 1955-1986. Here-after *LW*.

_____. "To the Christian Nobility of the German Nation Concerning the Reform of the Christian Estate" (1520) *LW* 44: 115-217.

_____. "On the Freedom of the Christian" (1520) *LW* 31:327-376.

_____. "Temporal Authority: To What Extent It Shall Be Obeyed" (1523) *LW* 45: 74-128.

_____. "On War against the Turks" (1529) *LW* 46: 154-204.

_____. "Dr. Martin Luther's Warning to His Dear German People" (1531) *LW* 47: 3-54.

Secondary Sources

Dixon, C. Scott. *The Reformation in Germany*. Oxford: Blackwell, 2002.

Matheson, Peter. *The Imaginative World of the Reformation*. Minneapolis, Minn.: Fortress Press, 2001.

Simpson, Gary. *War, Peace, and God*. Minneapolis, Minn.: Fortress Press, 2007.

CHAPTER 14

Bartolomé de Las Casas

Hjamil A. Martínez-Vázquez

In recent years Chiapas has been the place where the most disdained, most humiliated, and the most offended people of Mexico were able to recover intact a dignity and an honor that had never been completely lost, a place where the heavy tombstone of an oppression that has gone on for centuries has been shattered to allow the passage of a procession of a new and different living people ahead of an endless procession of murders. These men, women, and children of the present are only demanding respect for their rights, not just as human beings and as part of this humanity but also as the indigenous who want to continue being indigenous. They've risen up most especially with a moral strength that only honor and dignity themselves are capable of bringing to birth and nursing in the spirit, even while the body suffers from hunger and the usual miseries. —José Saramago[1]

On January 1, 1994, we heard a scream from the mountains of Chiapas reminding us that indigenous communities are human beings who have human rights. These voices keep reminding us today about land, justice, and equality. They have been crying out against their annihilation since 1492. We heard the scream in 1994 because it was accompanied by what the U.S. Empire called a "transgression." In other words, we heard their voices because it affected the livelihood of those in power. These voices that have been silenced by history, by guns, by indifference, by injustice, and by truth have been speaking for more than 500 years, but still colonial discourses, accompanied by violence, have manage to cover them. However, voices of revolution and hope, like the one from Chiapas, still break through these colonial discourses in order to challenge and transform the unjust social conditions. Thus, it is important to understand these voices as foundational for the construction of new theologies, as they illuminate the challenge of justice for indigenous communities. One of those voices is Bartolomé de Las Casas (1484-1566).

Las Casas, who served as Bishop of Chiapas and was known as one of the most adamant defenders of indigenous rights, serves as a prophetic voice in the struggle to confront the empire with new theologies. While the situation today is different from the one Las Casas found in 1502 when he arrived in the Americas, colonial discourses still govern the status quo. Accordingly, his voice and his message are relevant today for those who seek to confront unjust systems of power. In this article, I will not only look at this man's voice and life but I will try to put it in a contemporary perspective, to connect Las Casas with the present struggle of indigenous communities all over the world. As a historian, I in no way imply that his message is fully anti-colonial, but it can serve as ground for the construction of new theological discourses.

LAS CASAS'S CONTEXT: RISE OF A MODERN/COLONIAL SYSTEM

Bartolomé de Las Casas was born in 1484 in Sevilla, and came to the "newly discovered Indies" in 1502. At the time of his arrival at La Española, "still a teenager, he was apparently going to help in the family business, which seems to have involved farming and trading."[2] This family business had to do with some land his father acquired after he came with Columbus on his second voyage to the "Indies." Upon his arrival he became a witness of the treatment the enslaved indigenous population was sustaining at the hands of the Spanish *conquistadores*. Still, Las Casas became a colonist and within his first years in the "new world," "he was given an *encomienda* in Española and had participated in expeditions to eastern Española to seize Indians."[3] Although he participated and benefited from it initially, the *encomienda* system would later become a central target of Las Casas' confrontation of the Spanish conquest and evangelization of the Americas. As George Sanderlin states, "An *encomienda* was a tract of land or village whose Indians were entrusted to a Spanish settler who, in return for instructing the Indians in Christian doctrine—or promising to instruct them—had the right to their forced labor in fields and mines."[4]

After being ordained as a priest in Rome in 1507, Las Casas returned to the new world to continue with his *encomienda* in La Española. In 1513, he was given another *encomienda*, but this time in Cuba, and after making this *encomienda* a prosperous one, he started to question the actions sustained against Amerindians. Las Casas was not the first one to do so, as Pedro de Córdoba and Antón de Montesinos had already started to speak against injustices being committed by Spaniards. In 1514, after some personal soul-searching, he was convinced of the importance of the struggle against the unjust treatment of Amerindians, and he decided to give up his own *encomienda*. On August 15 of that year, he preached his first sermon denouncing the mistreatment of Amerindians, and from that day on he fought the colonial power of the time on this issue. But, in order to comprehend Las Casas's long and hard struggle it is vital to understand the colonial system he was standing against, the colonial system responsible for the colonization and evangelization of Amerindia, the "destruction of the Indies."

To go back and read the historical accounts regarding the colonization of Amerindia by the Iberian countries is to re-visit one of the most violent and deathly enterprises in the history of humanity. Various books and articles have been written about these events, and it is not my intent here to narrate a different story regarding the particulars of these colonial enterprises. In this sense, I am not interested here in re-visiting the events or challenge their occurrence. Instead, following a postcolonizing perspective, I analyze the discourses that lie behind these events and help to construct an imperial power, in order to understand Las Casas's message. I argue that while control over the land and the geopolitics of imperialism caused the solidification of Spain as an imperialistic power, it is its location within the development of modernity that helps explain the colonial discourse employed in the conquest of Amerindia.

Modernity, understood as a period in time, emerged with Columbus's voyage to the Amerindian territories, and developed through the period of the Reformation, the Renaissance, the scientific revolution, and the Enlightenment. This contradicts the common understanding, which situates the development of modernity, as Enrique Dussel argues, "from the Italy of the Renaissance to the Germany of the Reformation and the Enlightment, to the France of the French Revolution."[5] Dussel challenges these common interpretations because it leaves Spain and the ideology of conquest and colonialism out of the development of modernity. And as Walter Mignolo argues:

> By locating the emergence of modernity toward the end of the fifteenth century and the European "discovery" of a "New World," Dussel places the accent on the Early modern/colonial period when Europe moves from a

peripheral situation in relation to Islam, to a central position in relation to the constitution of the Spanish Empire, the expulsion of the Moors, and the success of trans-Atlantic expansion. In that configuration, the Americas become the first periphery of the modern world and part and parcel of the myth of modernity.[6]

It is important to see modernity not as simply an epoch or a period in time, but as a discourse, "a highly complex yet coherent narrative containing assumptions about how it is possible to represent the state of nature as supported by a new realist historical consciousness of change over time."[7] In other words, beliefs, characteristics, cultural trends, and rules defined modernity. The period of the conquest and colonization of the Amerindian territories gave Europe, represented by Spain, a reason to locate itself in the center of a world system, the modern/colonial system. Subsequently, events like the Enlightenment and the scientific revolution helped northern Europe displace Spain as the center of the system. The Reformation was also part of this process of displacement and marginalization since it relocated Catholicism to the periphery of the Christian world. The discourse of modernity, then, locates Europe, which becomes the West, at the center of the modern/colonial system and the rest of the world at the periphery.

Thus, Spain becomes the initial location for the construction of the modern/colonial system. These events put Spain in contact with an Other, different than Islam, who could provide a sense of comparison and a continuation of the *reconquista*. What this means is that Spain could build an identity itself in the light of this Other, and for that matter it could position itself at the center, even when it was marginalized later by the rest of Europe. Colonialism is, then, the mechanism used to define and support this relationship of center/periphery. The modern/colonial system is built upon not only the assumed superiority of Europe, but also on the subjugation and oppression of the periphery, both physically (by political and economic control) and intellectually (by controlling history). Colonialism coerces a territory and its people in order to maintain control over them. As Albert Memmi argues, "Colonization is, above all, economic and political exploitation."[8] This process develops a relationship of colonizer/colonized in which the colonizer names, defines, and speaks for the colonized. Through this process of construction of the Other, Spain constructed Amerindians in order to dominate them by identifying them as "less than human," and this became Bartolomé de Las Casas's major issue to address.

Spain followed this modern/colonial model to conquer Amerindians and their lands, which created the imaginary of what Luis Rivera Pagán calls providential messianism. Thus, this colonial enterprise "was guided by a strong Spanish mentality of providential messianism that perceived historical events in the context of a cosmic and universal confrontation between true faith and infidelity."[9] This religious impetus (providential messianism) is critical because it is at the core of the rationale behind the colonial enterprise. As Rivera Pagán argues,

> It was ideologically impossible for the Spanish crown to conceive the conquest and colonization of America in terms other than missionary evangelization. It could not articulate the legitimacy of its colonial dominion exclusively from a political or economic perspective. What for other modern empires might be possible, namely, to control the instruments of political and economic power allowing the dominated peoples spiritual solace for their troubled subjectivity in their native religiosity, was absolutely out of the question for the sixteenth century Spain. The spiritual conquest, and the "extirpation of idolatry" were essential elements of the Spanish conquest and colonization of the Americas. They constituted their ideological matrix and symbolic configuration.[10]

This means that the colonial discourses and the representations of the Other were based upon the religious understanding of the Spaniards. The construction of the Other was based upon religious identity and superiority. This representation of indigenous religious inferiority helped built the scaffold of providential messianism that gave Spaniards the notion that they were an elected nation and that God had given them a providential and transcendent mission.[11] God was behind the construction of a political empire. "To Spaniards of that time there was no clear distinction between political and religious motivations; they tend to assume that political advance automatically served religion by extending religious frontiers and that religious expansion strengthened political positions."[12] Las Casas, as mentioned below, will challenge these religious motivations by stating that Spaniards were more concerned for the economic and political benefits and that these guided their rationales, away from any religious justification.

The myth of superiority enabled the *conquistadores* to represent the Amerindians as barbaric, spiritually deficient (idolatrous), irrational, naturally inferior, and created to serve. John Major, a Scottish Dominican, developed a philosophical discourse that "proved" the conquest and the domination over Amerindians as justified. Paul S. Vickery's recent work on Las Casas, while locating Major's arguments within "the continuance of medieval thought," provides a succinct explanation of his discourse:

> Major not only wrote concerning the spiritual justification for conquest, but also, quoting Aristotle, expanded this reasoning to include a secular justification. Aristotle reasoned that, by nature, some individuals are free to determine their own fate, while others, also by nature, are born to be servants. Since this was true, Major reasoned, it was only right and proper that those born servile should willingly submit, in their own self-interest, to those possessing natural authority and command. Thus, Major became the first to apply Aristotle's views of natural servitude to a specific and entire race of people.[13]

This discourse was followed and validated by other scholars of the time, like Juan Ginés de Sepúlveda, who—based upon Major's writings and Aristotelian philosophy—justified the war against Amerindians on the basis of the existence of two different kinds of human beings.[14] Gustavo Gutiérrez, regarding this issue, references the work of Ginés de Sepúlveda when he writes:

> Those born to be slaves must be subjected to those destined to dominate. This will be one of the justifying reasons for the wars against the Indians. The purpose of these wars is regarded as the guarantee that they are waged "with rectitude, justice, and piety, and that, while affording some utility to the people that conquer, they provide a much greater benefit to the barbarians that are conquered." The Indians gain in humanity by being subjugated to the Europeans, even by means of war.[15]

These "barbarians" needed the help of rational human beings in order to acquire any type of humanity, and most of all the true monotheistic religion of Christianity. Following this idea, Amerindians were enslaved and placed within the *encomienda* system, which was designed to give Spaniards tutelage over them with the principal objective being their Christian conversion.[16] In other words, the *encomienda* system served as a colonial tool of the Spanish empire to maintain control over the Amerindians, who were subject to hard labor for the economic benefit of those in power, and, for that matter, the time for spiritual guidance was limited. Thus, the politico-economic motivations win over the religious motivations, even when the basic discourse supporting the enterprise was religious.

The colonizer gained control over the colonized through violence, but it is because of the colonial discourse of superiority, providential messianism, and call to evangelization that the former finds ideological support for its enterprise. In this sense, violent acts could be denounced, but the colonial discourse that supported these acts itself needed to be decolonized through alternative discourses. The work of Bartolomé de Las Casas became foundational among these alternatives discourses. While the colonial discourse finds its source within modernity, Las Casas's alternative discourse finds its source in what Rivera Pagán calls "prophetic indignation." He goes on to say that it is only through the interplay of these two discourses that we could understand fully the history of Christianity in Latin America. He writes:

> Latin American Christianity—as well as Latin American cultural identity and national consciousness—was born in the midst of the encounter and clash between two paradigmatic and paradoxical sources—the messianic providentialism guiding the violence of the *conquistadores* and the prophetic indignation reacting in the name of the biblical God of mercy and justice.[17]

LAS CASAS'S RESPONSE TO AMERINDIAN OPPRESSION

In *The Devastation of the Indies*, Bartolomé de Las Casas narrates the violence and describes the atrocities committed by the *conquistadores*.[18] In this work, Las Casas not only engages in a description of the actions but also in a condemnation of Spaniards' actions and the killings of Amerindians. He writes:

> Their reason for killing and destroying such an infinite number of souls is that the Christians have an ultimate aim, which is to acquire gold, and to swell themselves with riches in a very brief time and thus rise to a high estate disproportionate to their merits. It should be kept in mind that their insatiable greed and ambition, the greatest ever seen in the world, is the cause of their villainies. And also, those lands are so rich and felicitous, the natives peoples so meek and patient, so easy to subject, that our Spaniards have no more consideration for them than beasts. And I say this from my own knowledge of the acts I witnessed. But I should not say "than beasts" for, thanks be to God, they have treated beasts with some respect; I should say instead like excrement on the public squares. And thus they have deprived the Indians of their lives and souls, for the millions I mentioned have died without the Faith and without the benefit of the sacraments.[19]

In the eyes of Las Casas, the economic reasons supersede the religious/missionary motivations within the conquest, and he argues further that this economic

greed is guided by the representation of Amerindians as less than beasts, as excre-
ment. By looking at this situation, Las Casas understood that it was not just about
challenging the actions of the *conquistadores* and the *encomenderos*, but mostly
about challenging the ideology behind them, the colonial discourse. So, he decided to challenge the common colonial understanding regarding the nature of Amerindians, even if it meant speaking against his own people.

Bartolomé de Las Casas saw himself from a providential perspective, as did the
conquistadores involved in the colonial enterprise itself. But unlike the ideology
behind the conquest, his providentialism, as Rivera Pagán explains, came from a
prophetic indignation.[20] He sees himself as a messenger of God not only in defense
of the Amerindians, but also in the defense of his fatherland, as he wants to prevent God's punishment for the destruction of Amerindia. He writes:

> I, Fray Bartolomé de Las Casas (or Casaus), a Dominican friar, through the
> mercy of God, was induced to come to this court of Spain to bring about the
> ending of that inferno in the Indies and the irremediable destruction of souls
> that were redeemed by the blood of Jesus Christ; and to set up a work that
> would bring about those souls to know their Creator and Savior. I am also
> here because of the compassion I have for my native land, Castile, that it not
> be destroyed by God as punishment for the great sins committed by Spaniards
> devoid of faith.[21]

In order to fulfill his mission, Las Casas uses his personal experiences to put forward
a hermetic defense of Amerindians. He is not only interested in talking theologically or even philosophically about the natural humanity of peoples in the new world,
but also speaks in "anthropological" terms by carefully describing their daily life and
civilization, in terms of religion and institutions, among others.[22] These descriptions
have the purpose of providing enough information about these communities to complement the philosophical and theological approaches to the discussion. As Gutiérrez acknowledges, "He tells us of the social, cultural, artistic, and ethical achievements
of the native populations."[23] Ultimately, he wants to locate this population among
humanity and dispute the colonial discourse of there being two types of humans.

For Las Casas, all humans were created equal; to say that there were different
types of humans was to imply that the divine providence somehow failed in the
creation.[24] Referring to those "who proclaimed that these were not peoples possessing sound reason by which to govern themselves; that they lacked well-ordered

republics and the human life," Las Casas argues that, "They proclaimed this simply because they found these peoples so gentle, patient, and humble, as if Divine Providence had been negligent in the creation of innumerable rational souls and had allowed human nature to [go] astray."[25] Thus, arguing for a second type of humanity was second-guessing creation, and Las Casas argued against that. He believed that humanity should be seen as a process of progression; so even the "defects" found in Amerindians should be seen as part of the maturing process of a human being. So, while many focused solely on the "defects," Las Casas "dismissed the Indian's defects as accidents; the favorable characteristics were the substance."[26] For example, people like Juan Ginés de Sepúlveda declared that war could be waged against Amerindians since—because of their condition as barbarians and incapables—they "fell into the classification of slaves by nature according to the Aristotelian doctrine."[27] Bartolomé answered this and other arguments in his famous debate against Ginés de Sepúlveda in 1550.

In this debate, "the basic point Las Casas made was that not all barbarians are irrational or natural slaves or unfit for government."[28] He wanted to locate Amerindians among humanity and as being comparable to other societies, not as outside of the realm of human nature. In his *Apologética Historia*, written right after this debate, he develops further his defense and his proof of the humanity of Amerindians. Proving his own competence in Aristotelian philosophy, which was used against Amerindians, Las Casas would argue that these peoples not only "have excellent, subtle, and very capable minds," but that "They are likewise prudent, and endowed by nature with the three kinds of prudence named by the Philosopher [Aristotle]: monastic, economic, and political."[29] He goes further to situate them within the spectrum of history, as he argues:

> As for political prudence, I say that not only have the Indians shown themselves to be very prudent peoples, with acute minds, having justly and prosperously governed their republic (so far as they could without faith and knowledge of the true God), but they equaled many diverse of the past and present, much praised for government, way of life, and customs. And in following the rules of natural reason, they have even surpassed by not a little those who were the most prudent of all, such as the Greeks and Romans.[30]

Locating Amerindians within the history of humanity challenges the colonial discourse of representation of the Other. Thus, Amerindians acquire agency, and they must be seen not as objects but as subjects of their own history: they move from being considered no-persons to historical human subjects. But still, it is important to address the fact that while Las Casas provides an argument for Amerindian agency, he still finds this population in need of the true faith in order to acquire higher standards.

Las Casas, while admitting that Amerindians' way of life differs from the European one, "emphasized the Indian's rationality, as shown in his domestic, religious, and political life—above all, his potentiality to rise in the scale of civilization and to assimilate Christian values."[31] He furthers this argument in chapter 263 of *Apologética Historia* by highlighting that these populations are as capable of "receiving the Gospel" as any other nation.[32] Here lies Las Casas's major concern: the evangelization and salvation of the Amerindians. This evangelization should be guided not by violence and war but by persuasion. He wanted to enforce a missionary enterprise among Amerindians, based upon their freedom as human beings.

In his book *The Only Way*, Las Casas discusses the biblical and adequate method for this missionary enterprise. Here, Las Casas concludes, "The form Christ, the Son of God, set His apostles for preaching His gospel everywhere, before His death, after His resurrection, was one and the same, to win the mind with reasons, to win the will with attractive, compelling motives."[33] In this sense, Las Casas not only uses philosophical arguments to provide proof of the Amerindian's humanity, but also focuses his attention on the example provided by Christ in order to confront the religious motivations behind the war against this population. For him, Christ set the example of how to treat others with dignity, as he "would not stoop to using war as a way to gain a people, nor war to expand, enrich, ensure a kingdom."[34] Thus, war, in this case, not only goes against the Christian imperative of justice, but clearly goes against the way of Christ.

Following this argument, we can see how Las Casas understood Amerindians not only as human beings but also as people in need of the true faith, Christianity. This concern for the evangelization of this population guided Las Casas's work against the colonial discourses of representation and the politics of war, but was also the reason why he supported the general enterprise of colonization. As I mentioned earlier and as Gutiérrez acknowledges, "The salvation of the new infidels, through their incorporation into the church, was to be the primary motive advanced to justify the European presence on this continent."[35] Las Casas was not against that motive, but thought that the missionary endeavor should be the only motive for the colonization. In this sense, his challenge was not aimed at the enterprise in itself but at the violent way it was being conducted, and the ideology through which such violence was supported. He never talked about ending the colonial enterprise in Amerindia.

Following a utopic idealism, Bartolomé de Las Casas defended tutelage because it would be to the temporal and spiritual benefit of the natives in the new world.[36] God ordained the Spanish crown to this tutelage, so his discourse was directed to the crown in order for them to stop the violence and establish a real missionary enterprise. He writes:

> Since certain kingdoms and their peoples, solely because they are pagans and need to be converted to our holy faith, have been committed and entrusted by God and by the Holy Apostolic See in his name to the sovereigns of Castile and Leon . . . so that the sovereigns may attract and persuade them to come to the knowledge of Jesus Christ, . . . no one is qualified to have the care of those souls who is not the king of Castile.[37]

Not only was it God's mission to help the natives, but also most importantly it was the responsibility of the crown to fulfill that mission. That mission all but called for imperial dominion over the Amerindians. So, although Las Casas's discourse confronts the rationale behind the violent actions against Amerindians' human rights, it nonetheless supports the missionary aspects of the colonial enterprise. In this sense, Las Casas should be seen as an *indigenista*, not as an anti-colonialist, by which I mean that we should understand his discourse in light of human rights discussion, not as anti-imperialistic discourse.[38] In other words, he challenged the colonial representation, but supported the colonial power because this population, while being human, still needed to be persuaded not only to the true faith, but also "to order and reason and laws and virtue and all goodness."[39]

CONSTRUCTIVE IMPLICATIONS: LAS CASAS'S THOUGHT TODAY

While many scholars still debate the importance of Bartolomé de Las Casas, "the majority view, at least in the western hemisphere, is that which pays tribute to Las Casas as the representative *par excellence* of a New World ideal of liberty and justice for all men."[40] His influence is evident within liberation theology, especially in the work of Gustavo Gutiérrez.[41] Stephen Judd recognizes that, "For Gutiérrez and others identified with liberation theology, Las Casas's words—the poor of Latin America are a 'people who die before their time of an unjust death'—still ring true in the present context."[42] In this sense, Las Casas's message of human rights, agency, and historical subjectivity resonates with the language of the preferential option for the poor. In the present day Las Casas's message becomes even more essential to ensure attention to a resurgence of indigenous voices in Latin America. "From Mexico to the Andes, indigenous peoples have aggressively stepped forward to demand their long-denied cultural, political, and economic rights."[43] This resurgence has been accompanied by a theological discourse called *teología india*.

Indigenous theology, although brought up in the tradition of liberation theology, should not be categorized as being within any particular theological canon. "This theology from the underside of history looks at 'balance, complementarity, identity, and consensus' as alternative ways of understanding people's relationship with the transcendent and with each other respecting the quality of difference."[44] While a formal and extended discussion about *teología india* lies beyond the scope of this article, it is important to mention some key aspects of it and how Las Casas's legacy can be located within this theological movement.

Teología india moves beyond the Eurocentric models of theology and erupts from the ability of indigenous communities to see themselves as part of creation, not as a separate kind of humanity. In this sense, it is not only about recognizing their humanity, as Las Casas established, but also recognizing that indigenous people can think about God within their social context. As Judd states, "This theology is a reflection of how indigenous peoples express their relationship to God and each other in varying historical circumstances."[45] This entails self-respect for the local culture, tradition, and history, which the colonial discourses tried to erase by labeling them less than human, a move Bartolomé de Las Casas challenged. Thus, Las Casas's message, while not directly reflected within the discourse of *teología india,* is still prevalent in the underlying aspect of construction of the discourse.

Las Casas, as an *indigenista*, put forward a prophetic discourse of hope, a vision that is being recovered through *teología india*. We should not see Las Casas's influence only as part of a theological discourse but also as a symbol of resistance, memory, and hope. The consciousness the memory of Las Casas raises in the indigenous movements in Latin America is more important than the constant presence of his message.

In the article "Mayan Catholics in Chiapas, Mexico: Practicing Faith on Their Own Terms," Christine Kovic talks about the Indigenous Congress of 1974 celebrated in San Cristóbal de Las Casas, and how "an organization named after Fray Bartolomé de Las Casas was formed to continue the congress's work."[46] She writes:

> In 1977, one of the advisors to this group asked, "Who will be the new Fray Bartolomé de Las Casas?" The Indians answered, "We will. We are Bartolomé. We needed one before because everything was decided in Spain, where we couldn't go and where we didn't have a voice; then they spoke for us. Now we are beginning to speak for ourselves."[47]

The memory of Las Casas results in a postcolonizing ideology and provides indigenous populations a source of empowerment in order to become agents and subjects, and acquire a voice. Thus, the colonial system that promotes the silencing of indigenous voices, as the Other, is confronted by the voices of those who believe that *otro mundo es posible*. So, while Bartolomé de Las Casas may have not acted as an anti-colonial agent, his legacy as an *indigenista* has become a source for transgression against the empire. The words of José Saramago at the beginning of this article are proof that his voice still speaks to us today in the form of transgression.

FURTHER READING

Primary Sources

de Las Casas, Bartolomé. *Historia de las Indias*, 3 vols. México: Fondo de Cultura Económica, 1951.

_____. *The Devastation of the Indies: A Brief Account*. Translated by Herman Briffault. Baltimore, Md.: Johns Hopkins University Press, 1992.

_____. *Obras Escogidas*, Vol. 3. Edited by Juan Pérez de Tudela. Madrid: Biblioteca de Autores Españoles, 1958.

_____. *The Only Way*. Edited by Helen Rand Parish. Translated by Francis Patrick Sullivan. New York, N.Y.: Paulist Press, 1992.

Ginés de Sepúlveda, Juan. *Tratados Políticos de Juan Ginés de Sepúlveda*. Translated by Ángel Losada. Madrid: Instituto de Estudios Políticos, 1963.

Secondary Sources

Gutiérrez, Gustavo. *Las Casas: In Search of the Poor of Jesus Christ*. Translated by Robert R. Barr. Maryknoll, N.Y.: Orbis Books, 1993.

Rivera Pagán, Luis. *Evangelización y Violencia: La Conquista de América*. San Juan: Editorial CEMI, 1990.

Sanderlin, George. *Witness: Writings of Bartolomé de Las Casas*. Edited and translated by George Sanderlin. Maryknoll, N.Y.: Orbis Books, 1971.

Sullivan, Francis Patrick. *Indian Freedom: The Cause of Bartolomé de las Casas, 1484-1566*. Kansas City, Mo.: Sheed & Ward, 1995.

Traboulay, David M. *Columbus and Las Casas: The Conquest and Christianization of America, 1492-1566*. Lanham, Md.: University Press of America, 1994.

Vickery, Paul S. *Bartolomé de las Casas: Great Prophet of the Americas*. New York: Paulist Press, 2006.

CHAPTER 15

Jean Calvin

Don H. Compier

Several well established myths stand in the way of a proper appreciation of Calvin's life and work in its own historical context. While scholars of the sixteenth century have persistently labored to dispel these misconceptions, stereotypes continue to have amazing influence on the popular imagination. Persons who have never read a page of Calvin's voluminous writings are convinced that he exercised a theocratic dictatorship in Geneva. In fact, he was never even a citizen of the town and never sought or obtained secular power. For most of his career he and his allies struggled with the magistrates of Geneva. Calvin certainly did share the then-common belief that heretics, since they threatened public safety, could not be tolerated; but his only power to enforce this conviction was that of persuasion. Calvin did consistently campaign to establish the principle that the reform of the church required the pastors to regulate the moral conduct of parishioners. He sought to make Geneva a secure base for his European-wide operations, and hoped that the city would be a shining example of the virtues of reformed religion. Yet when compared to other cities of the time, actual punishment of wrongdoers was more lenient in Geneva than elsewhere.[1]

Calvin has also been blamed (or praised, depending on one's point of view!) for creating a religious worldview conducive to the rise of capitalism. Even the controversial book most often cited in defense of such claims, Max Weber's *The Protestant Ethic and the Spirit of Capitalism*,[2] suggests that the critical steps in the acceptance of market principles were taken long after Calvin's death. Concerned about the survival of Geneva's economy (including its publishing business, so vital to his program of reform), Calvin endorsed the charging of interest on loans and the relaxation of other strictures on commerce. He supported challenges to the monopoly that vested interests, often allied with the medieval church, exercised over economic life. However, it is entirely anachronistic to suggest that he could have anticipated the economic developments of the next several centuries. Seemingly pro-capitalist passages in Calvin's works are counterbalanced by demands for social justice and welfare.[3]

Finally, we should exercise great care not to equate Calvin's own views with those of later Calvinists. Popular disapproval of the Puritan colonizers of New England, for instance, too often leads to ready dismissal of Calvin's theology. We have reason to suspect that the common perception of Puritans is also contradicted by a nuanced historical understanding of their thought and aims. In any case, however, these opponents of the Anglican establishment reached their own conclusions on doctrine, morals, and church government, because their contexts differed widely from those of Calvin. And while later Calvinists did hold the Reformer of Geneva in special regard, many other theologians shaped their outlook as well.[4]

In this essay, then, I ask the reader to lay aside preformed judgments about the Frenchman Jean Calvin and to consider him afresh. Read against the backdrop of his own time and place, how did he respond to imperial dynamics?

CALVIN'S CONTEXTS

The life of the French Reformer Jean Calvin (1509-1564) coincided with the emergence of the first transatlantic empire centered in Europe. In the fateful year of 1492 Spain, newly united by the marriage of Ferdinand and Isabella, conquered the last Muslim foothold on the Iberian Peninsula, expelled the Jews, and celebrated the "discovery" of the "new" world by the expedition commanded by its envoy, Christopher Columbus. Between 1521 and 1544 Spanish adventurers conquered the mighty empires of Mexico and Peru. Vast quantities of gold and silver began to flow from the Americas into the coffers of the Spanish crown, and forced labor on haciendas produced additional wealth.[5]

At the same time the power of Spain's Hapsburg dynasty threatened to dominate the entire European continent. Charles V (1500-1558), King of Spain and ruler of the Netherlands as heir of the house of Burgundy, was also elected Holy Roman Emperor in 1519. He thereby became the ultimate authority over most of Central and much of Eastern Europe. Large portions of Italy also fell under his control. Like Ferdinand and Isabella before him, Charles considered himself the chief defender of the traditional faith. He sought to assure the election of popes meeting with his approval, and he waged a series of wars with the Lutheran principalities and the Turks. When Charles retired in 1556, his son Philip II (1527-1598) would not inherit the throne of the Holy Roman Empire, but the election of Charles's brother Ferdinand I (1503-1564) assured that Hapsburg interests would continue in the ascendancy. Philip's devotion to the Catholic cause was more fanatical than that of his father. He waged an unrelentingly harsh campaign against what he considered heresy. He therefore became the embodiment of the Counter-Reformation.[6] In the Netherlands, for instance, the authorities he set up to persecute Protestants would become popularly known as the Council of Blood.

Calvin personally experienced the threat of Spanish imperial power. The city of Geneva, the center of his work for the last half of his life, was located along the path followed by Hapsburg troops on their way between Spain and Italy to the south and Germany and the Netherlands to the north. In fact, the movement of such armed forces unexpectedly produced his arrival at Geneva in the first place. Calvin was bound for Strasburg when, hearing that the road ahead was blocked, he made an unscheduled stop in a city that had just undergone religious reformation. Interpreting this surprise visit as an act of providence, the fiery preacher Guillaume Farel managed to convince Calvin to stay and minister in Geneva. The Reformer could never feel entirely safe in this new home. On several occasions large armed hosts passed near the city, alarming the populace. In hindsight we know that Spanish reliance on Swiss mercenaries prevented them from taking actions that might alienate their recruitment base.[7] To Calvin and his contemporaries, however, it appeared all too possible that at any time the Spanish forces might veer off course and lay siege to their city.

Spanish militarism inflicted a very personal loss on Calvin. What he called his *patria*, the town of Noyon and its environs in the province of Picardy (near the frontier with the Spanish Netherlands), was twice subjected to devastation by the advancing forces of the Hapsburgs. Extant letters reveal his profound grief over the ruination of the place of his birth and childhood.[8]

Noyon's fate was representative of a byproduct of Spanish imperialism that affected Calvin's fate much more than direct manifestations of Hapsburg power. The monarchy of Calvin's native France felt surrounded by the ascendancy of Charles V and his son, and determined to fight back with every means at its disposal. Francis I (1494-1547) and his son Henry II (1519-1559) therefore engaged in nearly three decades of intermittent warfare with their hated continental rivals.

Italy became the primary battleground for this grand contest, but the French also sought to outmaneuver Charles and Philip in papal elections and attempted to found their own colonies in the Americas. Both Francis and Henry would from time to time seek alliances with the Lutheran princes of the Holy Roman Empire. And as in Picardy, sometimes war ravaged parts of France itself.

The house of Valois also contested the Spanish claim to leadership of Christendom. The French monarchs proudly used the title of "most Christian king" and extolled the religious superiority of their realm. Their apologists would claim, for instance, that no heresy had ever originated on French soil, and that France had produced more saints than any other land. The coronation of French monarchs clearly indicated adherence to a notion of sacral kingship. The new king was anointed all over his body and permitted to take communion in both kinds as if he were a priest. The next day he exercised the king's touch, believed to miraculously cure scrofula. Moreover, in the Concordat of Bologna (1516) the papacy gave the French monarchs wide discretionary powers over religious affairs, especially in the selection of bishops.[9]

Francis's early support of reform-minded humanist scholars, the need for an alliance with German Lutherans, and ongoing tensions between him and the papacy gave some hope that he might become a supporter of Protestant reforms in his kingdom. With the benefit of historical hindsight, however, we can see that the religious status quo perfectly suited the ambitions of French monarchs. The established faith provided powerful legitimation for royal power, while the Concordat meant that papal interference in the affairs of the French church would never become too irritating.[10]

And so when the rector of the University of Paris, Nicolas Cop, offered an address in 1533 too reminiscent of Lutheran ideas, the intense reaction of the conservative faculty of theology persuaded Francis to crack down on proponents of rather moderate reform. As a suspected supporter of Cop, Calvin's apartment was ransacked by the police, and he was forced into hiding and then exile. The subsequent Affair of the Placards (October 1534), when leaflets attacking the mass were posted even in the royal bedchamber, greatly hardened the lines. The denial of Christ's real bodily presence in the host implied that in fact God did not regularly take up residence in France and that the French body politic did not enjoy a quasi-divine status conferred by partaking of Christ's true body. The "sacramentarian" views expounded in the placards and other tracts thus undermined a religious ideology supportive of the monarch's claims to privilege and power as the representative of the entire society. Francis quickly acted to reaffirm the king's traditional role as defender of the mass. He intensified the persecution of those suspected of Protestant sympathies. While Calvin would craft a less extreme doctrine of the Eucharist, he also firmly rejected what he considered the idolatry of the mass. To his lasting regret, he soon realized that he could never return to France. The fate of friends left behind was of grave concern to him, acting as a chief motivator of his theological work.

In 1559 France and Spain finally made peace in the treaty of Cateau-Cambresis. It now seemed that the powerful defenders of the established church would join forces to extirpate the growing Protestant movements. The accidental death of Henry II that same year, however, weakened the French monarchy and created new prospects for Calvin and his allies. They organized their forces for resistance that would eventually lead to religious wars in France, the Netherlands, and Scotland. In that process theological articulation played a pivotal role.

CALVIN'S THEOLOGICAL NEGOTIATIONS WITH EMPIRE

Calvin always sought to avoid direct confrontation with imperial power. His basic political instincts were profoundly conservative. He abhorred the prospect of popular revolt and social unrest. This careful exegete always defended the precepts of Romans 13 and 1 Peter 2:13-14, calling for submission to temporal authorities. Adherents of the Reformed religion were often charged with sedition. Calvin repeatedly offered strenuous rebuttals of this accusation. To do so he appealed directly to royal persons.

The first edition of the *Institutes of the Christian Religion*, considered by many to be Calvin's masterpiece, appeared in 1536. It opened with a letter to Francis I, begging him to carefully study the matters under dispute. The Reformer passionately argued that the ecclesial program he promoted was in no way subversive or novel. Lamenting the persecution to which his co-religionists had been subjected, Calvin attempted to demonstrate that their faith was firmly based on Scripture and on the best traditions of the church universal. Therefore, he argued, his brothers and sisters in France deserved royal protection, not imprisonment, exile, and execution.[11] In spite of changing circumstances and the death of Francis, all subsequent editions of the *Institutes* retained this dedicatory preface.

In 1544 Calvin wrote a treatise addressed to Charles V and the imperial diet meeting at Spires, "The Necessity of Reforming the Church." This work labored to prove that by promoting reforms, Calvin and his collaborators were not schismatic. Citing much precedent, the author insisted that actions taken by the Protestants were actually prophetically upholding and defending true apostolic worship and doctrine.[12]

Calvin's attempt to make a favorable impression on another monarch reveals further dimensions of the Reformer's essential conservatism. In 1559, shortly after Elizabeth I's accession to the throne of England, Calvin sent her a copy of the new edition of his commentary of Isaiah, with its dedicatory preface addressed to the new queen.[13] His gesture received a rather cold reception, because the Scottish Reformer John Knox had defended his rejection of female rule by citing Calvin. Writing to the queen's principal counselor, William Cecil, Calvin made an unusually clumsy rhetorical attempt to repair the damage. He professed that God sometimes graciously chose female leaders, yet admitted that in his view such exceptions represented "a deviation from the primitive and established order of nature" and "a judgment on man for his dereliction of his rights, just like slavery." Similarly, on other occasions Calvin seemed willing to accept the possibility of the ordination of women in theory, but never in practice.[14]

At least Calvin heard of Elizabeth's reaction, and the general cause of Protestantism remained safe in her reign despite her offense at his appeal. He failed to persuade Francis I, Charles V, or their successors. We can't even be sure that they ever read his earnest, carefully argued petitions. Throughout Calvin's life persecutions would continue with varying degrees of intensity. His profound sympathy for his martyred, struggling, and exiled co-religionists is constantly apparent in his voluminous writings. Geneva soon became the center of a robust printing industry, turning out a multitude of texts effectively smuggled to Protestants all over Europe, and most notably in France.[15] When we realize that suffering members of religious minorities were Calvin's primary audience, we learn to appreciate how their plight shaped his thought, and we read his theology in light of its pastoral intent. Calvin abhorred abstract, speculative theology. His aim was more practical, seeking to offer comfort, hope, edification, encouragement, and support to the defenders of what he considered the true Christian faith.

Calvin is best known for his controversial advocacy of double predestination, understood as "God's eternal decree, by which he determined with himself what he willed to become of each man [sic] . . . eternal life is foreordained for some, eternal damnation for others" (*Inst.* 3.21.5). He believed that this doctrine offered profound consolation. Strange as this may seem to contemporary readers, that is precisely how it was received by anxious sixteenth-century Protestants, as extant diaries and letters demonstrate.[16] Persons feared that under threat and even torture they might renounce their convictions and betray the gospel, losing their salvation in the end. By stressing God's inalterable election, Calvin offered the spiritual antidote to this preoccupation. He wrote:

> here is our only ground for firmness and confidence: in order to free us of all our fear and render us victorious amid so many dangers, snares, and mortal struggles, [Christ] promises that whatever the Father has entrusted into his keeping will be safe. (*Inst.* 3.21.1)

As this important example suggests, the Reformer's primary intent was not to overthrow or politically resist empire, but rather to offer resources that would permit the faithful to persevere and retain their integrity in spite of the state's violent attempts to root out the Reformed religion. During the first half of his career at Geneva, Calvin counseled those who could to follow him into exile. Losing one's homeland was deemed preferable to remaining in situations in which persons would be coerced into participating in officially sanctioned rites and confessions that Calvin considered idolatrous. He strenuously condemned "Nicodemism," or a split between private convictions and public observance. In his view true Christians could never take part in the abominable papal mass and related devotions. In order to preserve both life and integrity, he counseled his brothers and sisters in the faith to emigrate to places such as Geneva, where they could freely participate in the pure worship of God. Barring that possibility, he always felt that martyrdom was preferable to participation in idolatry.

The 1550s, however, witnessed the explosive growth of Calvinist congregations in France, and soon Scotland, the Netherlands, and certain German and Eastern European territories saw similar developments. Some members of the nobility began to protect the adherents of Protestantism. In this changing atmosphere Calvin now altered his policy, encouraging those influenced by his writings to remain where they were and build up the Reformed cause. While he thereby in effect justified disobedience to the religious laws of Catholic empires, he continued to denounce and discourage seditious tendencies. In spite of his great prestige in Reformed circles, however, the developments leading to the outbreak of the first religious war in France in 1562 demonstrated that events had slipped beyond Calvin's control. In the next several decades Calvinists all over Europe would begin to articulate theological grounds for the right to renounce their allegiance to Catholic sovereigns and to take up arms in defense of their religious liberty. Moreover, in so doing they proclaimed their fidelity to the theology of their revered Genevan mentor. We must ask, then, what features of Calvin's own thought would encourage the development of aggressive resistance to the Catholic empires.

First, Calvin's virulent attack on what he considered the idolatry of the mass and his uncompromising opposition to any participation in the ceremonies of the traditional faith inevitably fostered acts of rebellion. Again and again he returned to the subject of the Eucharist. Good arguments can be made for its centrality in his thought. His Christology, for instance, seems governed by his insistence on a real (spiritual) but not corporeal (physical) presence of Christ in the bread and wine (see *Inst.* 4.17.30). In his numerous denunciations of Catholic sacramental observance Calvin uses scatological language that would be entirely unacceptable to most religious people today. He wrote that papal rites harm as much as snakes' venom. He suggested that persons that attended Mass, the "Table of Demons," committed a sin equivalent to fornication; worshipped a god "extracted from a cook shop" or "a missal-god of wafer"; venerated "the foulest and most pestiferous of all Idols"; and were still "wallowing in the old sty," "the mire of Sacrilege."[17] Little wonder that persons exposed to his writings frequently engaged in acts of iconoclasm. They sometimes showed utter disrespect for the host by feeding it to dogs, throwing it out in the street, etc. When reports of these graphic protests reached Calvin, he usually condemned extremism and counseled restraint, but the violence of his own rhetoric made these appeals sound hollow. Catholic controversialists writing in defense of the mass constantly accused Calvin and his colleagues of spreading seditious doctrine. They certainly had a point, because as noted above, the "royal theology" had made defense of the sacred host a critical part of the foundation of the reigning political order.

Second, Calvin is well known for his absolute insistence on the supreme sovereignty of God. Yet interpreters often fail to note how his extreme theocentrism in effect relativized all claims to temporal authority. Calvin frequently referred to God's operation in the world by using the Latin phrase *imperium Dei*, or God's empire.[18] True to the language attributed to Jesus in the gospels, Calvin can be read as saying that only God, and no earthly emperor, deserves ultimate allegiance. He clearly stated that whenever fidelity to human authorities interferes with our principal duty to submit to God's will, we must, in the words of Acts 5:29, "obey God rather than men [sic]." This biblical text is cited in the last paragraph of the *Institutes*, which was expanded in the 1559 edition by using sharp phrases such as "As if God had made over his [sic] right to mortal men [sic], giving them the rule over mankind [sic]!" (*Inst.* 4.20.32). When we understand the rhetorical conventions regularly employed by Calvin, we come to see that the importance of this paragraph is heightened by its position as the peroration, or closing argument, of the *Institutes*—the last word Calvin hopes his readers will remember.[19] Calvin's theocentrism was more a prophetic than a philosophical stance.

Similarly, his descriptions of the "secret" or "hidden" providence of God suggested another order both metaphysically and morally superior to present reigns. Without the "spectacles" of the Scriptures, working in tandem with God's spirit, we are blinded by the glitter of worldly power, caught in mirages. They deceive us into acceptance of the tyranny of the status quo. By divine grace we are freed to understand that in spite of all appearances, the majestic and just creator is in fact in charge of the entire cosmos, including humankind and the church. By faith we perceive and trust in the invisible work of God, whose purposes cannot fail. Calvin linked providence to our future hope.[20] I would therefore suggest that his doctrine of God functions as a prophetic eschatology. By giving persecuted believers another way to imagine the world, as John the Revelator did on Patmos, Calvin undermined the absolute power of empires over the minds of their subjects. Initially Calvin was clearly pursuing a pastoral strategy, allowing Protestants under intense pressure to persevere in faith, even if it led to martyrdom. As the prospects of active resistance increased, however, it is not hard to see how these doctrines fomented organized civil disobedience and even rebellion against those seen as lying usurpers of God's prerogative.

Third, Calvin himself smoothed the way for these developments by subtly yet surely shifting his teaching on temporal authority during the last five years of his life. The final Latin edition of the *Institutes* appeared in 1559, the same year that Henry II's death following a jousting accident created a royal power vacuum in France. The new king, Francis II, was only fifteen and died in December 1560. His mother, Catherine De Medici, served as regent, weakened both by her status as a foreigner and by the French prohibition of rule by queens. Catholic and Protestant noblemen were now vying for influence over the weakened monarchy.

And precisely at this point the final chapter of Calvin's master work suggested that lesser magistrates may sometimes need to take control to defend true religion! The same chapter still counsels obedience to human authority, and certainly provides no justification for popular revolt. Yet its acknowledgement that sometimes officials "of the people" are "appointed to restrain the willfulness of kings" represents a significant step toward the development of full-blown Calvinist resistance theories. Moreover, Calvin reminded his readers that in the past God "broke the bloody scepters of arrogant kings" and "overturned intolerable governments. Let the princes hear and be afraid!" (*Inst.* 4.20.31).

In the early 1560s Calvin sharpened these arguments by preaching sermons in which he criticized the specific behaviors of royal persons. He had always used the pulpit to attack his opponents in Geneva and beyond, but from 1550 on the ever more bold inclusion of monarchs in these diatribes represents a significant new departure. Calvin's public exegesis, for instance, employed the prophetic narratives of the Old Testament to suggest that God rejects impious rulers. Some argue that the sermons on 2 Samuel, preached from May 1562 to February 1563, offer a complete theory of political resistance. Calvin's principal tenet was that defense of idolatry invalidated the authority of monarchs.[21]

Finally, Calvin's suggestions for the organization of the Reformed movement and his doctrine of the church (*Inst.* 4) consistently demonstrated a preference for collegial structures of shared leadership and a distrust of authoritarian rule in the hands of a single individual. In the church, a council of Presbyters oversaw discipline at the congregational level. Deacons deliberated on how best to provide for the worthy poor. Calvin battled with the Genevan magistrates to grant the council of pastors the right to approve new ministerial colleagues and to determine church policies without interference from the secular authorities. In France and elsewhere these principles were soon extended to regional, national, and even international levels as representatives were sent to synodical gatherings. Particular circumstances and different readings of Calvin's teaching would lead to interminable debates about polity, but nowhere did the Reformed movement adopt structures that fostered the concentration of power.[22]

By the force of example Calvin's form of church government constituted a powerful critique of the growing absolutism of imperial monarchies. In practice, he thereby strongly reinforced his stated reservations about monarchy as the best model for human governance (see *Inst.* 4.20.8). In a time when the modern separation of church and state did not yet exist, his followers' experience in shared governance made them ever less willing to accept royal dictatorships.

CONTEMPORARY IMPLICATIONS OF CALVIN'S THEOLOGICAL WORK

Calvin was a man of his own time. His rhetorical preparation disposed him to find contextually appropriate verbal weapons suitable for resisting the specific imperial abuses of power he knew so well. His example should not inspire us to slavish adherence to a discourse forged in the past. We face our own forms of empire in a very different age. Calvin himself made rather free use of theological precedents; in our time, Calvin's tools are unlikely to work for us without significant modification. Yet his example may raise productive questions for us to ponder as we prepare our own strategic responses to oppression and exploitation.

Calvin suggests that certain historical situations demand combative, partisan theology. In the last phase of his life he demonstrates that theologians may at times even be called to become subversives. In spite of his own conservative tendencies, then, his Reformed theology anticipated the theologies of liberation of our era. Calvin may even help sharpen the focus of contemporary anti-imperial theology by raising the critical rhetorical question of audience. Who, specifically, are we addressing, and how must our arguments be tailored to persuade these particular hearers? Calvin's example urges us not to forget to speak to both rulers and their victims.

Few today would defend Calvin's doctrine of double predestination. Yet we overlook its pastoral intent at our peril. Those who resist must find grounds for comfort and assurance. Perhaps today's critiques of God's power and our endorsements of human self-determination have gone too far. Can human community adequately fill the void? While avoiding the abhorrent implications of Calvin's solution, we must articulate a sense of the sacred "beyond" that can anchor revolutionary hope.

We also recoil at Calvin's seemingly exaggerated depiction of God's almost micro-managing style of sovereignty. Yet we must find equally cogent ways of providing new imaginative possibilities. Our critical social theories show how empire colonizes the mind and creates thick ideological fog. The renewal of eschatological ways of thinking in recent theology offers new and perhaps improved ways of pursuing Calvin's goal of correcting the vision of imperial subjects.[23]

Calvin challenges us to consider the extent to which we can make compromises with empire. He suggests that rulers always find ways to use piety to advance their own domination. Today we must also analyze and fiercely critique the rituals through which tyrants seek sacred sanction for their realm. The all-too-frequent equation of American (actually, U.S.) exceptionalism with Christianity, evident in some evangelical circles today, should raise serious concerns. Unlike Calvin, however, we should exercise greater care to avoid elitism. Calvin understood what the mass meant to kings, but may have been oblivious to its significance for peasants. Sacred symbols and rites have an amazing capacity to escape any one interpretation. The poor can creatively employ the very images and practices given by the powerful to subtly yet surely critique and resist subjection.

The marginalized, then, must always be part of the deliberation appropriate to shared governance. While Calvin's polity represents a significant advance over royal autocracy, his exclusion of women and the less educated is now indefensible. Anti-imperial forces must always be on guard against the many subtle ways in which democracy can be undermined and co-opted. Modernism constantly promotes hyper-individualistic competition and self-sufficiency that is inimical to true community. Theologians must never forget that when all is said and done, our work must promote the formation and maintenance of genuine human collaboration, mutuality, and intimate connection. Calvin was always first and foremost a servant of the church. He too struggled with and against that vocation, yet stayed at his post. However church may be defined in our post-denominational age, we too must exercise constant loyalty to the public good.

FURTHER READING

Primary Sources

Calvin, Jean. "On Shunning the Unlawful Rites of the Ungodly and Preserving the Purity of the Christian Religion" (1537). In *Selected Works of John Calvin: Tracts and Letters*, Vol. 3. Edited and translated by Henry Beveridge, 359-411. Reprint, Grand Rapids, Mich.: Baker Book House, 1983.

————. *Letters of John Calvin, Selected from the Bonnet Edition*. Edinburgh: Banner of Truth Trust, 1980.

McNeill, John T., ed. *Calvin: Institutes of the Christian Religion*. The Library of Christian Classics 20-21. Translated by Ford Lewis Battles. Philadelphia, Pa.: Westminster, 1960.

Secondary Sources

Cottret, Bernard. *Calvin: A Biography*. Translated by M. Wallace McDonald. Grand Rapids, Mich.: Eerdmans, 2000.

Gilmont, Jean-Francois. *Calvin and the Printed Book*. Kirksville, Mo: Truman State University Press, 2005.

Oberman, Heiko. *The Two Reformations: The Journey from the Last Days to the New World*. New Haven, Conn.: Yale University Press, 2003.

CHAPTER 16

Sor Juana Inés de la Cruz

Michelle A. Gonzalez

Sor Juana Inés de la Cruz (1651-1695) is a compelling seventeenth-century Mexican scholar and writer whose work deserves a significant place in the history of Christian thought. Scholars who study her religious writings consider her to be the first female theologian of the Americas. Her poetry and dramas offer a theological voice through the medium of literature. While relatively unknown in the field of theological and religious studies, Sor Juana is considered one of the greatest writers of the Spanish language. A study of her writings reveals a substantial resource of creative thought and also provides a window into a better understanding of colonial Mexico (New Spain). The colonial era in the Spanish-speaking Americas is a fundamental moment in the construction of an American voice distinctive from the Spanish Empire. This is thus a time of struggle and negotiation. Perhaps no other colonial Latin American figure embodies this struggle more than Sor Juana Inés de la Cruz. Her biography and corpus attest to the conflicts that accompanied the meeting of indigenous, African, and European peoples in the painful birth of the modern-day Americas. Her theological contribution is found in the methodological and contextual nature of her work. The aesthetic form (poetry, drama) of the majority of her writings offers an alternative to modern conceptions of theological expression. As a Latin American figure, and a woman, she contests patriarchal Eurocentric constructions of Christian history.

SOR JUANA'S CONTEXT

An attempt to portray Sor Juana's life accurately is a daunting task, for what the modern-day scholar knows about Sor Juana is very sparse. A spectrum of interpretations of her life, piety, and sexuality abound, and any effort to claim an accurate depiction risks staunch criticism from opposing camps. Diego Calleja, S.J. has written the only biographical account of her life, but it is framed as a spiritual biography that mythologizes Sor Juana in a manner similar to hagiography. In addition to this biography scholars have the scattered comments Sor Juana herself wrote as another primary resource. Juana Ramírez de Asbaje, the daughter of unwed parents, was born in the town of Nepantla, Mexico between 1648 and 1651. Her mother was a *criolla* and her father a Spanish military officer.[1] At a young age Sor Juana developed a passion for the intellectual life. She was an avid reader, primarily self-taught, and by her mid-teens she was recognized as the most erudite woman in New Spain. At the age of thirteen she joined the court of the Viceroy Don Antonio Sebastián Toledo and the Vicereine Doña Leonor Carreto as a lady-in-waiting. Her reputation as a scholar was a crucial factor in her gaining a position in the viceregal court. She stayed there for three years.

The viceroyalty was a temporary governing position in New Spain, with each leader intended to rule for only a short period of time. Sor Juana saw four viceroys in her public lifetime.[2] Of the four, Don Tomás Antonio de la Cerda, the Marquis de la Laguna, and his wife, María Luisa Manrique de Lara y Gonzaga, Countess of Paredes de Nava, would have the greatest impact on Sor Juana's career as an author. Sor Juana had the most fruitful and public period of her writing career during their reign. A patron of the arts who developed a close relationship with Sor Juana, María Luisa secured the publication of Sor Juana's writings in Spain.[3] The first volume of Sor Juana's works was published in 1689, the second in 1692, and a third volume was published posthumously in 1700. Today her corpus stands with sixty-five sonnets, sixty-two romances, a prolific amount of poems in other forms, two comedies, three *autos sacramentales* (allegorical dramas), sixteen sets of *villancicos*, one *sarao*, and two farces.[4]

During her time at court, the Jesuit Antonio Núñez de Miranda encouraged Juana to enter the convent. Aware of her academic gifts as well as her distaste for marriage, he felt the convent was the best venue to monitor Sor Juana's growing public notoriety and intellectual aspirations.[5] Sor Juana hesitated to take the veil, fearing that convent life would impede her studies. Around the age of sixteen Juana entered the Order of the Discalced Carmelites as a novice. After three months she left that order due to health complications stemming from the Carmelites' ascetic lifestyle. In 1669 she took the veil in the convent of San Jerónimo, to the order of the Hieronymites, known to be a bit more lenient than the Carmelites. Núñez de Miranda would become Sor Juana's confessor for a significant portion of her cloistered life. Sor Juana dedicated her life to intellectual study and scholarship in the fields of literature, philosophy, theology, and science. Her library was the largest in New Spain, and she also amassed scientific and musical instruments. Her poetry and plays were in high demand for both ecclesial festivities and court occasions. The majority of her corpus was written by request and for commission. During her lifetime Sor Juana's work was known throughout Spain and New Spain. She was a cloistered nun yet simultaneously a very public and recognized writer.

After enjoying a public life as an intellectual, Sor Juana's situation took a dramatic turn when in 1690 her critique of a cleric's analysis of Christ's greatest demonstration of love was circulated without her authorization. The critique was circulated with a letter written under the pseudonym Sor Filotea, criticizing Sor Juana's intellectual pursuits. Sor Juana scholars agree that the author of the letter was the Bishop of Puebla, Manuel Fernández de Santa Cruz, and that Sor Juana was aware of this. Fernández names the object of Sor Juana's critique as a fifty year-old sermon written by the prominent Jesuit theologian Antonio Vieira. Though the actual object of Sor Juana's critique is a matter of debate amongst *sorjuanistas* (Sor Juana scholars), the perceived target in the eyes of her contemporaries was Vieira.[6] Her response to that publication, *La Respuesta* (*The Answer*), an autobiographical defense of women's right to intellectual pursuits, was completed the following year. Within four years of the production of *The Answer,* Sor Juana renounced her public life. The reasons behind this renunciation are also the subject of much contemporary speculation. She died in 1695 during a cholera outbreak in the convent.

New Spain

Sor Juana's life and corpus are marked by the contours of her socio-political context as a *criolla* living in a Spanish colony. The colonial era was a time when the *criollo/a*, the "American"-born Spaniard, was developing his or her consciousness and identity. Within literary circles it is often referred to as the Baroque period. The seventeenth and eighteenth centuries are an extremely formative time for identity in the Americas, as it distinguished itself from European Spanish culture. Racial, biological, and cultural mixture characterizes the Latin American colonial subject. Depending on one's skin tone and ancestry one could fall into different levels of the colonial social hierarchy. Some colonial subjects, for example Spanish-born elites living in the Americas, did not experience colonialism in a manner similar to subjects of African and indigenous descent, or even *criollo/as*. In New Spain the top of the social hierarchy was the European-born Spaniard. Below them were the *criollo/as*, who rarely held positions of power and were extremely resentful of the Spanish. *Mestizo/as* and *mulato/as* came next, and their skin color often determined their social standing, with light-skinned peoples able to have more opportunities than darker peoples.[7] Blacks, also depending on their skin color, were able to exist on varying social levels, though always submissive to the *criollo/as*, *mestizo/as*, *mulato/as*, and Spaniards. The indigenous were the lowest rung of the social ladder.

Latin American scholar Irving Leonard emphasizes the social immobility of this era. "This blending process in a relatively immobile society placed so indelible a stamp on Hispanic America that the Baroque pattern lingered long after the close of the colonial period and traces of it are visible today."[8] Latin American literary scholar Yolanda Martínez-San Miguel interprets the colonial era as a time when the modern colonial subject was in the process of developing his or her consciousness, at the intersection of the European and the American. It was a subject that was always attempting to legitimate its voice in the face of the European-born Spaniard.[9] This is an important historical moment in the constitution of an "American" subjectivity, found at the intersection of Spanish, indigenous, and African cultures, religions, and worldviews.

New Spain was a courtly culture, and the viceroyalty was the center of society. The viceroy of New Spain was also the governor, captain general, and presiding officer of the *real audencia* (court of appeals). In order to maintain the loyalty of the viceroy to the Spanish court and curb personal ambition, their appointments were for very short terms.[10] All these checks and monitors were placed in order to control the local power of the viceroy and ensure his loyalty to Spain. While Spain could attempt to control the viceroy through governmental constraints, it could not control the influence the viceregal court had upon the broader colonial society, setting its moral and aesthetic tone. In addition to offering a connection to European culture, the court also served as the secular alternative to the other dominant institution in Sor Juana's time, the Roman Catholic Church, the other center of power in New Spain. The intermeshing of politics and religion that characterized the Spanish Conquest continued in Sor Juana's era. Within her lifetime Sor Juana gained intimate knowledge of both these institutions, participating in courtly and convent life.

Corpus

A brief introduction to Sor Juana's corpus does not do justice to the complexity and depth of her writings. For one to truly engage Sor Juana's body of work, familiarity with philosophy, theology, Spanish letters, and mythology are mere entry points into her writings. In style she both mirrors and transcends the Spanish greats that she emulated. My emphasis here is on the manner in which her writings demonstrate the birth of an "American" consciousness in colonial Mexico, interweaving the voices of Africans and indigenous people in her writings. This consciousness is exemplary of the broader struggles of American peoples as they sought to define themselves as different to the Spanish. Sor Juana's voice is distinct, however, in that while many *criollo/as* distinguished themselves as particularly American, they did so in a manner that emulated European culture and society. Sor Juana, in contrast, offers an American voice that does not negate but instead embraces the racial and cultural hybridity that constitutes the Americas.

I would be remiss if I did not mention the importance of gender in Sor Juana's writings. In the past twenty years there has been a rediscovery of Sor Juana's work, particularly through the lens of feminist theory. *Sorjuanistas* are very clear in stating that Sor Juana's recognition of the social construction of gender is what distinguishes her from other Baroque figures.[11] Electa Arenal and Amanda Powell depict Sor Juana as a proto-feminist. "Because she wrote as a woman aware of her gender status and because she intended her arguments to be applied on behalf of other women *as women*, she is certainly a precursor to worldviews and activities we call feminist."[12] Arenal and Powell bring forth a persuasive point. Sor Juana does, at times, not only argue on her own behalf, but on behalf of all women. This is seen in her prose piece *La Respuesta* and in various poems.[13] However, Sor Juana does not have the systemic analysis or the link with a broader social movement that defines feminism. With some hesitancy, therefore, I agree that her writings can be characterized as proto-feminist. This is a heuristic device, for the term proto-feminist borders on implying continuity of thought between the writings of Sor Juana and contemporary academic feminists today. Sor Juana's concern for gender, one that is pervasive throughout her body of work, demonstrates her awareness of power and the function of social location within her milieu. Sor Juana's writings clearly depict a notion of gender as a social construction that limits her voice and her options. Among the proto-feminist themes found in her work are: her catalogs of women that justify women's intellectual endeavors; her emphasis on women known for their intellectual gifts; her critique of the construction of silence and authority imposed on women; and her defense of women's right to education.

Yolanda Martínez-San Miguel sees Sor Juana's writings as constituting a discourse with a concern for subjectivity, especially with regard to a feminine, colonial, and *criolla* consciousness. Sor Juana, Martínez-San Miguel contends, fashions an "American" subject at the intersection of gender and colonial society, creating an alternative discursive space within a discourse that is exclusively masculine.[14] Her writing is also a point of intersection between epistemology, gender, and the colonial condition. Martínez-San Miguel sees *La Respuesta* and the poem *Primero Sueño* as two places where Sor Juana defines rationality as a human capacity, not a gendered one, thus refuting the male philosophical constructs of her day. She also simultaneously argues against women's marginalization.

> Far from self-marginalizing herself through the creation of "feminine writing" or in the postulation of a world of knowing that was specifically feminine, Sor Juana leans towards amplifying the intellectual space of her era through the inclusion of women in the epistemological and theological debates within the University, religious centers, and other educational and intellectual institutions in New Spain.[15]

Sor Juana does not argue for a particular space for women's contributions. Instead, she wants the current discourse expanded to include women's voices. Sor Juana is not critical of masculine discourse; she is critical of her exclusion from it.[16] She does not argue, for example, that women would somehow make a different sort of contribution. Instead, she holds that women and men should be playing on the same field within the constructs of knowledge in her day.

A key feature of Sor Juana's justification in *The Answer* of her study and writing is grounded in her belief that her desire to study was a gift from God, which she must use in order to serve.

> For ever since the light of reason first dawned on me, my inclination to letters was marked by such passion and vehemence that neither the reprimands of others (for which I've received many) nor reflections of my own (there have been more than a few) have sufficed to make me abandon my pursuit of this native impulse that God himself bestowed on me. His Majesty knows why and to what end He did so, and He knows that I have prayed that He snuff out the light of my intellect, leaving only enough to keep His Law. For more than that is too much, some would say, in a woman; and there are even those who

say that it is harmful. His Majesty knows too that, not achieving this, I have attempted to entomb my intellect together with my name and to sacrifice it to the One who gave it to me.[17]

Elsewhere in *The Answer* she describes her intellect as that which proceeds from a force beyond her. In a thoughtful study of the rhetorical practices of *The Answer* and its connections to the accepted forms of Christian women's writings, especially Teresa's *Vitae*, Kathleen Meyers emphasizes that Sor Juana both adopts and revises the tradition of women's spiritual autobiography.[18] This is especially seen in her revision of the call to vocation reinterpreted as a call to intellectual study. "Sor Juana extends this to include the highest authority, God, as she weaves it together with the convention of the Divine call. Sor Juana locates the need for her writing and desire to pursue intellectual life in God's will."[19] The religious vocation is transformed to include an intellectual vocation. Through this rhetorical strategy Sor Juana defends her intellectual pursuits as motivated by a divine force beyond her control.

In addition to the emphasis on gender, the growing body of scholarship exploring the role of indigenous and black peoples in Sor Juana's corpus links this emphasis to both her context as a *criolla* and her concerns for social justice. Within Sor Juana's dramas one finds the foregrounding of marginalized voices, namely the indigenous. In her *loa* (theatrical prologue) to the allegorical drama *El Divino Narciso,* she argues for the value of indigenous religions as precursors to Christianity and critiques the militaristic arm of the Conquest. *El Divino Narciso* reinterprets the Ovidian myth of Narcissus into an account of Jesus' passion, death, and resurrection, highlighting the dramatic character of humanity's relationship with the divine. The internal plot of its *loa* revolves around the instruction of the indigenous concerning Catholic doctrine. However, the *loa* is in fact a means of demonstrating to the Spanish audience the dignity and complexity of indigenous peoples through its exposition of their history and customs. This is based on its intended performance in Madrid, as noted in its closing scene. *El Divino Narciso* is written for performance in Spain, not colonial Mexico. As Pamela Kirk has noted, "Though the fiction at the preface of the play is that the sacramental drama, *El Divino Narciso,* will teach the Indians the mysteries of the Catholic doctrine of the Eucharist, it is again clear that the play is really intended to convince the audience at the Spanish court of the dignity and piety of the Indians and of the complexity of their history, customs, and religion."[20] While the *loa* seems to address the evangelization of indigenous peoples, it is in fact the Spanish audience that will be "evangelized" by Sor Juana's *loa*. Comparing Sor Juana to Bartolomé de las Casas, Kirk highlights Sor Juana's suggestion that indigenous religions are of equal merit to Greek and Roman sources as vehicles for divine truths.[21] Sor Juana creates a space where marginalized truths are able to enter into the discourse of Christian truth.

The Christology that emerges from *El Divino Narciso* is one where Jesus is depicted as the embodiment of divine "Beauty." Unlike the Ovidian Narcissus, in Sor Juana's version the Christ-Narcissus figure looks at his reflection in a fountain, but instead of seeing himself he sees humanity blessed by God's grace. He falls in love with this image and the incarnation occurs. The Beauty of Christ becomes the foundation of the *imago Dei* and the glory of all humanity. The play affirms Beauty as the primary attribute of God. Created in the image of God, "Human Nature" also embodies this Beauty. The *imago Dei* is defined as Beauty, the incarnation a result of love and attraction. Christ-Narcissus's incarnation is a result of this: his captivation with humanity's Beauty as reflective of him, and his consequent desire for her as a result of it. However, humanity's Beauty is impermanent and fragile, and will never truly reflect the divine perfectly. Narcissus articulates this in his realization that he must die for his love. While his love for Human Nature is great, and her Beauty through her accompaniment by grace is similar to his, it is not identical. Sor Juana bases the incarnation on Christ's desire for the human. A major emphasis in her christological reflections is the primacy of Christ's universal salvific will. While this insight may seem dated to modern ears, in her explicit incorporation and emphasis on the indigenous of the Americas, Sor Juana was a pioneer. She affirmed the very humanity of those who were systematically dehumanized and oppressed.

Sor Juana had an awareness of some indigenous practices and beliefs. Her inclusion of these rites, as well as African cultural symbols, is yet another way Sor Juana includes marginalized voices. Her *villancicos* offer a literary device for this endeavor. While these poems do not include systematic analyses as one finds in the *loas*, in their use of indigenous and black voices Sor Juana creates a space for their experiences and concerns. In addition, as publicly sung and performed poems, they offer a public theology that allowed Sor Juana to share her worldview with a broad audience, including the educated elite and the larger population. Contrary to her *loas*, which are dominated by indigenous concerns, the presence of African voices in Sor Juana's poetry is more prominent. Marie-Cécile Bénassy-Berling grounds the privileging of African voices in the Spanish literary tradition of the early seventeenth century.[22] The originality of Sor Juana's thought lies in the valorization and defense of Africans within her writings. This includes, for example, adopting typically African themes into her poetry. In the ninth poem of the 1686 series of *villancicos* written in celebration of Mary's assumption, Sor Juana includes African dialect as the language of over half the poem. This language can be juxtaposed to the Latin of the earlier poems in the series. By incorporating their voices and even their language, Sor Juana creates a public forum for African concerns.

In addition to African language, this poem even goes so far as to describe Mary as a "*Nenglita beya.*" In describing Mary as a beautiful black woman, this *villancico* is in sharp contrast to the white European theology of the colonial clergy. This is also not an isolated incident. In the 1689 *villancicos* on Mary's conception, Mary is described as "Negra, la Esposa" and "Morenica" (Dark).[23] By providing imagery of Mary as nonwhite, Sor Juana valorizes the humanity of those peoples that are at the very bottom of the social hierarchy within her era. Her 1676 *villancicos* on the assumption include a section sung by indigenous and African voices. The indigenous section is written in Nahuatl, the language of the Aztecs, and includes an Aztec ritual dance as part of the poem's performance.[24] Yet another *villancico* includes Nahuatl and Spanish words interlaced together.[25] It is interesting to note that many of the instances of her inclusion of African and indigenous voices occur in her Marian poetry. Also, in her *Ejercicios de la Encarnación* Sor Juana encourages her audience to pray the *Magnificat.*[26] One can perhaps find a connection in her work, therefore, between Mary and social justice.

In nine of the thirty-two poems written for the dedication of a new church for the Bernardine sisters (1690) Sor Juana emphasizes Marian themes. This should not surprise us, for Sor Juana states in the first lines of the series, "In Mary is the best Temple of God, when one dedicates a Temple to God, it can only be in the name of Mary."[27] The twenty-fifth poem of the series offers one of the more creative images of Mary, where Sor Juana compares the womb of Mary to the harvest of the Eucharist. She continues by describing Mary's pregnant stomach as the monstrance of the Eucharist.[28] The Beauty of her stomach is found in the divine presence filled with the host. Mary clearly holds a privileged role in Sor Juana's theology as the mother of God and consequently the reflection of Beauty. The source of her Beauty is her motherhood. The ornate Baroque language that surrounds Sor

Juana's depictions of Mary is grounded in a clear Christology. When one links this to her imaging of Mary as dark-skinned, one finds yet another affirmation of the universal beauty of all of God's creation.

The frequency of the inclusion of indigenous and African voices, as well as the more refined arguments presented in her *loas*, demonstrate that Sor Juana protested the injustices she saw around her. As Jean Franco notes, "She was uneasy about black peonage, and her poems written in Nahuatl suggest a respect for indigenous culture that others certainly did not share."[29] Sor Juana could not protest in a straightforward and outright manner. Such a thing would have made her the object of critique and ridicule. The Conquest was a recent memory in the minds of colonial Mexicans. However, in her own subtle manner, Sor Juana gently reveals her discomfort with some of the practices of her government. Subtlety is perhaps the best word to embody Sor Juana's writings on marginalized peoples. Her writings on gender are understandably more direct and passionate at times, fueled by her own personal persecution in light of her biological sex.

Her corpus exemplifies a negotiation of identity that marks the colonial era. This time period is definitive for understanding contemporary Latin American identity. The overwhelming majority of independence movements within Latin America were led by *criollos*. This signifies that the true subalterns of Latin American societies, namely indigenous, black, and darker-skinned mixed peoples, were not the leaders or in power during and after struggles against colonialism. Even when there was participation of these groups, once former colonies gained independence from the Spanish, the lighter-skinned *criollos* seized power. Sor Juana's privileging of the marginalized presents a prophetic voice in terms of contemporary academic and political struggles within the Spanish-speaking Americas.

CONTEMPORARY CONTRIBUTION

Sor Juana's life and work exemplify the negotiation of power within colonial Latin America. *Sorjuanistas* have established that Sor Juana was never persecuted by the Inquisition; as many detractors as she had, she also had supporters.[30] However, as Elias Trabulse indicates in his recent interpretation of Sor Juana's last years, her bishop had the authority to sanction her without the tribunal of the Inquisition. The same month when Sor Juana turned from her pursuit of letters, Antonio de Aunsibay y Arena, a vicar general for the Episcopate who was also in charge of the bishop's local branch of the Inquisition, visited Sor Juana's convent. The proceedings that followed this visit are unknown today, though shortly after Sor Juana took her vow of silence. The contents of her cell at the time of her death reveal that her renunciation was directed at the public dimension of her writing.[31]

In Sor Juana's era the sphere that was the most monitored was women's access to and participation in the public realm, especially with regard to preaching, publication, and participation in debates. Sor Juana did all of these things, in her own way, through her publicly performed pieces and her circulated writings. Being a cloistered woman writing in colonial Mexico is not what sets her apart. There were, in fact, many cloistered nuns writing in colonial Mexico. What sets Sor Juana apart is the subject matter, namely theology and philosophy. The majority of nuns writing in New Spain wrote spiritual pieces that were characterized by their visions of God and their mystical tone.[32] In the hierarchical and rigidly compartmentalized culture of New Spain Sor Juana defied social norms and gender constraints. She contested her society and church's rejection of women's abilities to claim an authoritative voice. Her life is representative of an era when the Spanish Empire and the Catholic Church sought to constrain any voices that challenged the status quo.

Through her introduction of the aesthetic within the theological task, Sor Juana makes the symbolic a privileged form of theological expression. She goes so far as stating that the aesthetic is *the most appropriate form* of theological expression. Pamela Kirk highlights certain connections one can make between Sor Juana's writings and Latin American and Latino/a theologies precisely on this topic. She highlights, for example, an explicit link between Sor Juana's writings and Latina feminist theologian María Pilar Aquino's. "Yet even the literary form of her theological production corresponds to what María Pilar Aquino, building on María Clara Bingemer, has described as the 'primacy of desire' over the purely rational in the theology of Latin American women."[33] Sor Juana argues for the aesthetic as a form of theological expression. Accompanying the aesthetic form of her theology is an inter-disciplinary understanding of theology that saturates Sor Juana's corpus. Theology is not merely limited to what contemporary scholars deem today "theological" texts. Instead, literature, poetry, and drama become central forms of theological expression.

Mary becomes a key figure in Sor Juana's theological anthropology. Not merely a passive object of devotion, in Sor Juana's theology Mary is a theologian, "Mother of the Word," and advocate for the marginalized. It is no accident that Sor Juana's defense and validation of the humanity of indigenous and African peoples occur most frequently in her Marian poetry. Sor Juana's defense of Africans and the indigenous includes her use of non-Christian sources within her theology and her emphasis on the validity of their humanity and religious practices.

Sor Juana's corpus expands the traditional sources for theology and philosophy. Accompanying her incorporation of African and indigenous sources is her use of song and dance as part of her theological expression. Linked to this is her emphasis on *lo cotidiano* (daily life) as a vital intellectual resource.[34] Sor Juana taps into the popular imagination. She offers a public theology that was known to the elite of the court and the popular masses. The public performances of her writings and plays allowed her voice to reach a broad and mixed audience. The public nature of her work, coupled with her self-proclaimed intellectual authority and her subject matter set her apart from other women religious writing in her era. As Kirk notes, "Sor Juana writes with the authority that comes from her intellectual and literary talents. Neither does she need to appeal to the mystical experience of the reader as a basis for understanding what she writes. Because she draws on both intellectual and devotional traditions, her religious writing is open to the educated reason of the elite, as well as the imaginative intuitive understanding of the uneducated populace."[35] In an era where the contributions of certain theologies are becoming increasingly isolated and irrelevant, the inter-disciplinary project of recovering Sor Juana's voice seeks to rectify the seclusion of theology while simultaneously recovering a marginalized woman's voice.

Sor Juana's life and corpus disallows a simplistic read of the construction of empire within colonial Latin American society. She was, for a significant portion of her career, supported by the colonial government, primarily through the patronage of the vicereine and other wealthy patrons. Sor Juana used the often public platform of her work to include the voices of the marginalized and challenge the construction of colonial women's identity. However, within this ethos it was not only the government that ruled, but also the church. While the details of the final years of Sor Juana's life remain unknown to us today, what is clear is that she came into conflict with ecclesial authorities. Whether it was the content or style of her writing, or merely the fact that she became such a well-known public intellectual, Sor Juana and her work came under fire. Clearly she challenged and threatened the ecclesial status quo. Through her writings it would appear likely that her biological sex played a huge factor in this condemnation. Sor Juana dared to write in a style that was deemed unacceptable for women. Her eventual silencing reveals to us the power of the church in New Spain, where Sor Juana's secular viceregal connections could not protect her.

The inclusion of Sor Juana's voice in the canons of Christian theological history expands the very nature and writing of Christian history. Most often, when one reads introductory texts on Christianity, the Third World is an afterthought. Usually tied to more recent missionary activity or inculturated Christian expressions, those peoples who are the children of Africa, Asia, and Latin America are relegated as the "Others" of Christianity, relatively "new" arrivals with very little Christian history. As Dale Irwin notes,

> The vast majority of Christian historical and theological writings continue to assume that the history of Christianity prior to the modern period was exclusively European. Thus the history of European Christendom continues to function as a master narrative of Christian tradition, legitimating European or Western theological domination in all its diverse forms and de-legitimating traditions that cannot be articulated through this narrative history.[36]

This "master narrative," Irwin argues, is an idolatrous universalization of one particular strand of Christian history as representative of the entirety. It affects every dimension of Christian theology, functioning as an unspoken mythology that shapes the sources and methods of all theological disciplines. Unchallenged, it is a working ideology that reaffirms European and Euro-American dominance. The Christian tradition becomes exclusively incarnate in those cultures that inform the master narrative.[37] This ideological erasure of non-European contributions to Christian history must be recast into a more inclusive vision of the Christian tradition.

This radical re-writing of Christian history has profound implications on Christians' self-understanding. As Albert J. Raboteau thoughtfully writes, "History, especially religious history, because it touches on the deepest myths, beliefs, and values of our society, is personally important to us all. To change our view of history changes our view of ourselves."[38] We must re-evaluate the manner in which we write Christian history and construct contemporary identity. Those "marginal" stories within the metanarrative of Christianity must be brought to the center of Christian identity, such that all racial-ethnic groups share equal weight. For Latin Americans this is particularly significant. Too often the theological history of Latin America begins with the twentieth century explosion of liberation theology, a practice that implies that no theological word was uttered in Latin America prior to the late 1960s.

A serious consideration of Sor Juana's life and corpus has implications for the process of Latin American identity-making. She offers a window into the often ignored colonial era within this region. Her life attests to the precarious negotiation of power that was operating as Spain struggled to remain in control of its colonies. Her silencing demonstrates the manner in which an astute theological contribution by a woman undermined male clerical authority. She presents a theological alternative to the patriarchal, Eurocentric construction of Christian identity. The aesthetic form of her theology provides an alternative understanding of theological expression, one that broadens contemporary understandings of theological discourse. In her autobiographical defense Sor Juana describes her writing as "drafts and scratches."[39] She then describes herself as "a poor nun, the slightest creature on earth and the least worthy of drawing your attention," and "an ignorant woman."[40] These self-deprecating remarks could not be further from the truth. Poet, dramatist, theologian, and philosopher, Sor Juana is a Latin American Church Mother and a key figure in the history of theology.

FURTHER READING

Primary Sources

Juana Inés de la Cruz, Sor. *Obras Completas*. Edited by Alfonso Mendez Plancarte and Alberto G. Salceda. 4 vols. México: Instituto Mexiquense de Cultura; Fondo de Cultura Económica, 1995.

_____. *The Answer / La Respuesta*. Edited by Electa Arenal and Amanda Powell. New York, N.Y.: Feminist Press at the City University of New York, 1994.

Secondary Sources

Gonzalez, Michelle A. *Sor Juana: Beauty and Justice in the Americas*. Maryknoll, N.Y.: Orbis Books, 2003.

Kirk, Pamela. *Sor Juana Inés de la Cruz: Religion, Art, and Feminism*. New York, N.Y.: Continuum, 1998.

Martínez-San Miguel, Yolanda. *Saberes Americanos: Subalternidad y epistemología en los escritos de Sor Juana*. Pittsburgh: University of Pittsburgh, 1999.

Some of the material for this chapter has been drawn from Michelle A. Gonzalez, *Sor Juana: Beauty and Justice in the Americas* (Maryknoll, N.Y.: Orbis Books, 2003). Used by permission of the publisher.

CHAPTER 17

Jonathan Edwards

Don Schweitzer

Jonathan Edwards (1703-1758) lived in colonial New England at one edge of the British Empire, where it clashed with Native American cultures and the imperial forces of France. Edwards's relationships to the empires of his day cannot be easily categorized. In some ways his theology and pastoral practices served and reflected British colonial imperialism. In other ways he resisted and transcended imperialism. Socially Edwards was a conservative who attempted to uphold a passing colonial culture. Yet his thought included ideas and supported practices which undermined colonial ideologies in his time and which had a revolutionary influence afterwards. His theology continues to have critical potential in relation to empires today.

EDWARDS'S CONTEXT: COLONIAL NEW ENGLAND

Edwards was born and raised in East Windsor, Connecticut, the fifth of eleven children born to Esther Stoddard and Timothy Edwards. He was educated to follow his father into the Puritan clergy. After two brief pastorates and a stint as a tutor at Yale, he went in 1726 to Northampton, where he first assisted and then succeeded his grandfather, Solomon Stoddard, as pastor of the prestigious church there. This helped him attain status and exercise leadership as a member of colonial New England's cultural elite. In 1727 he and Sarah Pierpont were married. They had eleven children. Edwards was dismissed from his position at Northampton in 1750. He moved to become a pastor and missionary to Native Americans at Stockbridge, in what is now Massachusetts. In January of 1758 he left Stockbridge to become president of the College of New Jersey, now Princeton University. He died shortly thereafter of smallpox contracted through inoculation.[1]

Throughout these transitions Edwards produced a steady stream of theological writing in the Reformed tradition. His thought was influential during his lifetime and immediately afterwards in Reformed churches in Europe and colonial New England. It continued to be influential in Reformed churches in the United States in the century after his death, and then suffered eclipse. Since World War II it has attracted increasing attention, as historians have found in his writings a window on colonial New England, and theologians have discovered him to be a fruitful conversation partner in relation to contemporary issues.[2]

New England was being transformed during Edwards's lifetime by economic and population growth. Communities that had been largely based on subsistence farming, mutual trade, and aid, were developing competitive and differentiated economies, politicized factions, and a culture of competitive individualism. This growth was due partly to the industry and high birthrate of colonists, but also to the expropriation of Native American lands, the destruction of their way of life, and the labor and suffering of African American slaves. Edwards lived on the edge of the British Empire but not in isolation from it. From Northampton and Stockbridge he participated in a transatlantic community of trade, politics, religion, and letters, with centers in Boston, England, and Scotland. Naval transport moved people, goods, letters, and books between Britain and New England, and brought slaves from Africa to New England. Edwards kept several slaves during his lifetime.

For Edwards, physical realities were always representative of greater and more encompassing spiritual realities. He located himself and the world in which he lived within the framework of God's work of redemption that reached from the beginning of the world to its end and beyond. Edwards understood this work to be an apocalyptic struggle between God and the forces of evil, unfolding as foretold in the Bible, particularly in the book of Revelation. Edwards identified himself and Protestant churches with the faithful elect. Roman Catholicism, Islam, other religions, and the political powers aligned with them were "Satan's visible empire upon earth."[3] In this struggle between the two, God's truth, which Edwards identified with Protestant Christianity, was arranged against a variety of material and intellectual foes, all of which served Satan and the Antichrist. Edwards's theology was developed in the service of this struggle: to defend Reformed Protestantism against its critics, and to give it guidance and understanding by illuminating what he believed to be the truth and refuting what he believed to be pernicious errors.

As Edwards speculated on the meaning of past and current events in light of the prophecies of Revelation, interpreted natural phenomena as types of spiritual realities, involved himself in the events of his own or neighboring parishes, and corresponded with church leaders in Scotland and England, he used insights from John Locke to reinterpret Calvinism in relation to Newtonian physics and to defend it against the challenges of deism and Arminianism.

EDWARDS'S THEOLOGICAL VISION

Edwards's engagements with the empires of his day were shaped by his theological vision and the circumstances in which he found himself. However, his theological vision was itself shaped by forces of empire. As a member of New England's colonial elite, Edwards shared the assumptions typical of his class that some were born to rule and others were born to serve; that political authority was divinely instituted; and that the hierarchical social institutions and relationships of his time were divinely willed and should be preserved. These assumptions led him to seek the improvement of individuals within the social structures of his day, but not a change in the social structures themselves. His ultimate loyalty lay not with the British Empire, but with the transatlantic network of evangelical Protestantism that his writings were meant to guide and direct. Yet on a number of occasions when his evangelical Protestantism clashed with these assumptions, he denied its socially disruptive implications and defended the existing colonial social order instead.[4]

Edwards's theological vision can be divided into his metaphysics and his apocalyptic view of history. In his metaphysics, it was the energy of God's goodness and the inclination of God's will to further express this that gave rise to creation and redemption.[5] These are outward expressions or repetitions of the communication and celebration of God's goodness that occurs eternally within God's triune being. According to Edwards, God creates and redeems the world in order to communicate God's beauty and goodness to others. Doing so leads to an increase of God's own joy and being. As people come to know and love God's beauty and creation as God's work, and as they give thanks to God for these, there is a repetition in time and space of the communication of God's goodness and the praise of God for this that constitutes God's being in eternity. The increase to God's being that occurs through this and the further expression of God's love in peoples' own lives is the reason for creation and redemption. This metaphysical vision forms one basis for

Edwards's ethics. For Edwards, true virtue consists in consent to God or to being-in-general, expressed in benevolent love for God and all of God's creation. Within history, people participate in God's great work of redemption by evangelism, which seeks to bring more people to an awareness of God's love and beauty, and by pastoral and communal practices that deepen the appreciation and expression of this in their lives.

In Edwards's mind, this conception of God as infinitely beautiful and good dovetailed with a view of God acting directly in all events and judging humanity, condemning the unconverted/unrighteous to an eternity of torment and elevating the elect to an eternity of joy. In line with this, evangelism that led to another person's conversion and salvation was the greatest act of caring and solidarity that any person could offer another. While a person's physical well-being was a genuine concern, care for their own or their community's spiritual well-being should always be predominant, as the latter ultimately determined the former. Like the classical Hebrew prophets, Edwards believed that the political success or well-being of a community was related to its moral condition. Historical and natural events were seen by Puritan clergy like Edwards to be communications from God in this regard. Earthquakes, military defeats, or other disasters were often interpreted as calls to the elect to repent and renew their commitment to God.

Such communications were part of God's great work of redemption, in which all of creation was involved. Though God's work was resisted by Satan's powers and God's church was persecuted and suffering, God's sovereignty and transcendence meant that the final victory of good over evil was never in doubt. Warfare, trade, philosophical ideas, scientific discoveries, and mechanical inventions: all served in one way or another to move history toward its predetermined, and for the elect, glorious end. Edwards's theological work was intended to demonstrate how this was so, and to guide people in participating in God's work.

Edwards and the Empires of his Day

Edwards's apocalyptic view of history led him to judge the British and French empires in terms of how he saw them serving or opposing God's work of redemption. He interpreted the disruption of French and Spanish trade by British forces as the drying up of the river Euphrates prophesied in the book of Revelation.[6] Such interpretations were born of Edwards's belief that the millennium might come soon, possibly beginning with events in colonial New England. While Edwards tended to keep his eschatological speculations to himself, they were the private side of an evangelical and eschatological outlook that he helped foster though his writings and pastoral activities. This evangelical outlook led Edwards to support the British Empire over against the French. Yet this same evangelical outlook, promoted by Edwards and others "almost entirely within the church and through 'the ordinary means'" became a significant factor in colonial resistance to the British Empire, for it functioned as "the avatar and instrument of a fervent American nationalism."[7] Edwards also emphasized, following Moses Lowman and others, that the millennium, the thousand years of peace prophesied in the book of Revelation, would come before the return of Christ. This position, known as postmillennialism, meant that the actions of ordinary Christians could contribute to the reign of God being progressively realized, though not fully consummated, in history.[8] This meant that the actions of ordinary human beings could be a means by which God brought radical change and definite though not final improvement to history. By propagating these ideas Edwards helped create an ideology of independence and expectation that became an important inspiration behind the American Revolution. Here one can see the ambivalence of his theology in relation to the empires of his day. It led him to support the British Empire. It also helped create an ideology of independence that contributed to the overthrow of British rule in the American colonies.

Edwards's theological vision could do this partly because though he aligned the British Empire with the cause of God, he never fully fused the two. His sense of divine transcendence and his eschatological outlook relativized all social orders and political outlooks, judging each in terms of how they served what he saw to be the cause of God. Edwards's eschatology looked for the coming of a future that would be greater than the present, and so this eschatology could be a source of critique as well as encouragement to colonial New England. His apocalyptic vision linked political powers to spiritual realities: the empires of his day were but instruments in God's hand. Political alliances and military engagements were a means by which God worked, and Edwards paid attention to them. But they were not as powerful or important as the outpourings of the Holy Spirit that occurred in revivals and awakenings. In his view, the central locus of God's redemptive activity in history lay in the converting and sanctifying work of the Holy Spirit in the hearts and minds of common people.[9] Edwards's view on this was clearly stated in a letter he wrote in 1752, where he argued "if ever North America is regained from a subjection to Antichristian powers, it must be more by the spreading of the light of the gospel than by any policy, wealth or arms of the British Empire."[10] The military force of the British Empire might protect a space in which this work of the Holy Spirit could go forward, but it could never equal or replace it.

Edwards's metaphysics and apocalyptic vision similarly relativized the value of patriotism. For Edwards a virtuous citizen must be actively concerned with the public life of their community and country. But for Edwards, particular countries and nations, including his own, could never be more than "limited" parties.[11] Devotion to them could never be the highest virtue. Patriotism was only praiseworthy if it expressed benevolence and care directed toward the good of all. Furthermore, for Edwards, the true home of the converted, to which they owed final allegiance, lay in the future, in the coming reign of God. While the particular places in which the converted lived were to be cherished and cared for, these should never take the place in their hearts of their true home, which was yet to come. Edwards did support some colonial military expeditions. But in his view, the claims of empire to loyalty and support were always to be judged by how they served the greater good that far exceeded the self-interests of his own community and nation.

Edwards was essentially conservative in regards to the social stratifications and hierarchical institutions of his day. He labored to restrict many of the democratizing economic and cultural forces undermining these. He also shared many British colonial prejudices, viewing Native and African Americans as "little more than children in the extent of their innate capacities."[12] Yet Edwards did see revolutionary social change that would bring an end to slavery and oppression for all to be part of God's work of redemption, and thus to be inexorably on its way. At one point he wrote of how in the future,

> liberty shall reign throughout the earth. And every nation shall be a free people, not only with a freedom from spiritual slavery, but from civil too, from the tyrannical and absolute power of men, as well as from the power of the devil.[13]

Edwards may have been able to reconcile this with his social conservatism in part because he did not share the modern notion of society as a human project that people can create through their common action. Instead he tended to see this glorious future as coming through the dramatic work of the Holy Spirit, and he envisaged it as the perfecting and spreading of the British social institutions of his day, rather than as their reformulation or overthrow. He thought this realm of freedom that the future would bring would be ruled by "kings" who would be "as the judges were before Saul (which government was that which was best pleasing to God), and as the kings of England now are in civil matters."[14]

Thus an impulse toward freedom for all peoples lay at the heart of Edwards's vision. Wherever this aspect of his theology took hold in subsequent generations, it had a revolutionary influence. But Edwards himself did not envisage pursuing this impulse by seeking structural changes in his society, or through freeing the slaves that he owned. He saw himself to be called to work toward this only through leading and supporting evangelistic revivals, and working to deepen the piety of those he pastored. He critiqued many social evils of his day, but his solution to them was conversion or deepened piety on the part of individuals and communities. He looked for radical change to be effected by God in the future, but not for a political revolution designed and carried out by human hands.

The contours of Edwards's engagement with the forces of empire in his day were also shaped by the different ways in which his theology led him to view societies and humanity. First, on an ontological level, Edwards viewed humanity in essentialist terms. Regardless of their cultural, racial, or ethnic differences, all people were essentially the same in needing conversion to a Protestant expression of faith in Jesus Christ. This essentialism led him to recognize the humanity of Native and African Americans in a limited but real way. Edwards shared the bigotries of the colonial elite to which he belonged toward cultures and peoples other than his own. But his underlying vision of the ontological oneness of humanity led him to recognize that the glory of God was increased through the conversion of Native and African Americans just as much as through the conversion of those of British descent. Edwards did not see peoples of other cultures and ethnic origins as equals, but he did see them as destined ultimately for freedom and as having a place in God's work of redemption. Those who were other by race or culture were still members of the human community to whom a fundamental recognition and justice was due.

This belief was evident in his missionary work at Stockbridge. Here he encountered the Native Americans he worked with as people who could win his affection, and it pleased him that to some degree, he and his family won theirs. Edwards invested considerable time and energy in defending their interests against the predations of other colonists. He was also "the first minister at Northampton to baptize blacks and admit them into full membership" in the church.[15] Edwards's notion of the oneness of humanity before God never overcame all his inherited colonial assumptions. But it did challenge some, and it led him to speak and act in ways that often subverted colonial and imperial hegemonies, despite his social conservatism.

This ambivalence between the then socially revolutionary aspects of Edwards's thought and practice and his social conservatism is particularly evident in his relationship to slavery. Edwards's position on this changed over the years and is difficult to assess. He called for an end to importing slaves from Africa, but defended the keeping of slaves born in North America. He can be indicted for having kept slaves throughout his lifetime. However, his admission of slaves to full membership in the church worked against the social denigration that enslavement brought with it. In his relations with both African and Native Americans, Edwards frequently displayed a combination of deep insight and naïveté. He naïvely viewed missionary efforts under the umbrella of the British Empire as a benefit to Native Americans, remaining oblivious to how these were inevitably part of an expansion of the British Empire that aimed ultimately at displacing Native Americans from their lands and ways of life.[16] Similarly, Edwards seemed to believe that belonging to Christian owners was a spiritual benefit to African American slaves, without considering the suffering that enslavement entailed.

Insightfully though, Edwards could see that those who refused to own slaves in colonial America were "partakers" of slavery even without keeping any themselves, for they enjoyed the benefits of a society built in part upon slavery.[17] While Edwards recognized that African and Native Americans belonged essentially to the moral community that included all human beings and expressed this belief on numerous occasions, he frequently failed to fully grasp the implications of this, and he never promoted this idea with the intention of directly challenging colonial social structures in light of it. When he called church members to live in loving and harmonious relationships with each other, he failed to see keeping slaves as a violation of this ethic.

Edwards's perspective on humanity shifted as he moved from the ontological to the historical level. Ontologically, all were one in Adam and their need for Christ. Yet Edwards's apocalyptic outlook led him to interpret history in conflictual terms. People belonged either to the forces of light or the forces of evil. Through conversion their position might shift. But as France and Spain were officially Roman Catholic, their populations, economies, and military served the Antichrist. This justified opposing them violently. The evangelical outlook that led him to a limited recognition of the humanity of African and Native Americans and to oppose the overseas slave trade also found expression in the demonization of Roman Catholicism and of countries like France and Spain where Catholicism was the established religion. But Edwards's eschatology also imparted a pragmatic element to his evaluations of empires and their actions. He could recognize how the industry of the French was winning the allegiance of Native Americans, while the sloth and vice endemic in British colonial relationships to Native Americans was losing it. The question of how empires were serving the Protestant cause was always on his mind and was the overriding criterion by which he judged societies. His conflictual reading of history never became an ontological dualism on the level of nationalities and cultures, as he recognized the possibility that conversion could occur at any time in a person's life. It led him to support the military interests of the British Empire and its North American colonies, but this support was never unconditional. However his historical dualism did continue into his view of eternity, where he believed the redeemed and the nonredeemed would be forever separated.

Edwards also analyzed society on a third level. While his apocalyptic outlook led him to view history in conflictual terms, he viewed the Protestant community, locally or internationally, in organic terms. The redeemed community was essentially one in Christ, and should be bound together by bonds of love and forgiveness expressed in common practices. But by 1740 colonial New England had become a society based on economic competition and self-interest.[18] The economy of the present-day American empire was taking shape here in embryonic form. This was challenging and undermining the formative influence of Edwards's church on the community of Northampton. Edwards interpreted the transformation of values and the changes in practices occurring here as destroying the ethos of common care and concern that should have characterized Northampton, and directly opposed them.[19] He called for a renewed commitment to the common good and denounced self-interest as greed. Partly in response to this, a majority of his parishioners had him removed as their pastor.

Each of Edwards's approaches to social analysis caused him to resist or support the empires of his day in different ways. His ontological analysis of all humanity as being one in Adam led him to a limited recognition of the humanity of African and Native Americans over against the exclusionary colonial prejudices of his time. His conflictual historical analysis led him to support the British Empire and denigrate the French and its Native American allies. His organic vision of Northampton led him to oppose the emerging social and economic forces that would give rise to modern capitalism and its attendant empires.

Relevance of Edwards's Vision for the Present

In the years following his death, Edwards's ideas played crucial roles in the thought of his New Divinity followers like Samuel Hopkins, who developed a critique of slavery and British colonialism out of Edwards's notion of disinterested benevolence. African American and white Christians devoted to abolition interpreted this notion as an obligation to free those who were enslaved, giving it a further and more concrete application than Edwards had himself. Their use of Edwards's ideas to call for an end to slavery contributed "to an unbroken American rhetoric of emancipation that would eventually triumph in the Civil War."[20]

As previously noted, Edwards's evangelical thought and practice also had an indirect anti-imperial effect in helping give rise to the American Revolution. His view of history as moving toward something dramatically new, the socially leveling influence of the awakenings, his notion that human activity could contribute to the progressive realization of the reign of God in history, and his notion of true virtue as consent to being in general, all helped shaped an evangelical outlook and piety that in the 1770s became an impetus for revolution. Even as Edwards sought to uphold the hierarchical social structure of the preceding century against liberalizing developments of his time, this social structure was being undermined by the democratizing effects of the religious revivals he helped lead. Although Edwards was socially conservative in many ways, these aspects of his theology had a revolutionary influence and continue to have an emancipatory potential today.

Perhaps the most important contribution of Edwards's theology for a critique of empire lies in his doctrine of God and his understanding of God's relationship to the world. Responsible resistance to empire always requires immanent and transcendent principles of expectation that social change is possible.[21] Immanent expectation involves concrete and rationally defensible strategies for change in relation to the possibilities present in a given situation. Transcendent expectation lies more on the level of religious or prophetic faith. The two are distinct and yet always intertwined. Edwards's understanding of God and God's relationship to the world provides a particularly powerful and focused transcendent principle of expectation for social change.

As noted earlier, according to Edwards, God's actions in creation and redemption are a repetition in time and space of the communication and celebration of divine beauty and goodness that characterize God's triune being in eternity. Edwards was careful to argue that God's goodness is already fully communicated amongst the three persons of the Trinity, so that God is not ontologically dependent upon creation for fulfillment. But while God's nature has no ontological need of further expression, the inherent dynamism of God's disposition to beauty remains open and oriented to it. In Edwards's conception, God's decision to create and redeem the world is free but not arbitrary, because it is grounded in God's nature as love and leads to an increase in the divine being through the further expression of God's goodness and beauty in time and space.

This understanding of God's relationship to the world provides a particularly powerful and focused principle of transcendent expectation for social change because it combines a radical sense of divine transcendence with a genuine sense of the meaningfulness to God of what happens in history. The self-sufficiency or transcendence of God to creation means that God's creative power is ultimately greater than that of any evil or opposition to it in history. If God wills that "liberty shall reign throughout the earth . . . and every nation shall be a free people,"[22] then in the fullness of time this will happen, and one can work toward it with hope.

However, Edwards's affirmation of divine transcendence does not undermine the meaningfulness of human action because it is paired with the affirmation that God is also affected by what happens in history. God's being is increased through people repeating in their own time and place the sharing and communicating of love and joy that characterize the trinitarian relationships of the divine being, and this activity can contribute to the progressively greater realization of the reign of God in history. This reinforces the meaningfulness of ethical behavior, of human action and commitment, even as God's transcendence provides a basis of hope for the overcoming of radical evil. In this way Edwards's understanding of God provides a transcendent source of hope that imperial oppression can be overcome and an affirmation of the meaningfulness of resistance to it.

Edwards's vision of divine transcendence also had a particular focus. His eschatological vision for the future reign of God on earth was one of liberty being enjoyed by every people and nation. For Edwards the glory of God was not demonstrated or repeated in history by acts of brute power as much as by the establishment of loving and harmonious relationships among people or peoples, and between people and creation. Edwards failed to effect such relationships inasmuch as he kept slaves and defended slavery as an institution. But his vision of the coming millennium had a decidedly anti-imperial cast in his expectation that it would bring freedom from tyranny and oppression that would be enjoyed by all.

For Edwards, God's work of redemption aims at an increase of God's being. But the nature of God's being is such that it increases through a corresponding increase in the love and joy that God shares with others, and thus through an increase in their being as well. The focus of Edwards's eschatological vision was not simply the increase of God's being, but the increase of the beloved community that God shares with humanity and all of creation. This is part of a strain of humanism running through Edwards's thought, which celebrated human life and achievements in their many different forms. While Edwards at times played the glory of God off against human finitude and frailty, more frequently he portrayed God's glory as exhibited in the healing, comforting, protecting, and fulfillment of human lives and communities. The beloved community that Edwards expected would be structured by love and mutual respect. Its order would arise out of consent to the wellbeing of each other that would be present in the hearts of all its members, including God. This ideal was to be lived out in history. For Edwards as for Irenaeus, the glory of God is seen in humanity fully alive. Though Edwards did not recognize the implications of this for the institution of slavery, many of his followers did.

By developing a coherent affirmation of both God's sovereignty and the meaningfulness of creation and human activity for God, Edwards developed an understanding of God's relationship to the world in which the divine creativity became a principle of expectation for the overcoming of imperialism and oppression. Edwards's relationships to the empires of his day, as expressed in his own practices and value judgments, were ambivalent. Yet in his ethical writings, in his sense of history as moving even through disasters and suffering toward the triumph of good over evil, in his conception of God's relationship to the world and how ordinary people can contribute to a greater realization of God's reign on earth, Edwards provides some key resources for theologies that seek to engage the life-destroying forces of empires in the present.

FURTHER READING

Primary Sources

Edwards, Jonathan. *The Works of Jonathan Edwards*. Vol. 5, *Apocalyptic Writings*. Edited by Stephen Stein. New Haven, Conn.: Yale University Press, 1977.

_____. "Concerning the End for Which God Created the World," and "The Nature of True Virtue," in *The Works of Jonathan Edwards*. Vol. 8, *Ethical Writings*. Edited by Paul Ramsey. New Haven, Conn.: Yale University Press, 1989.

_____. *The Works of Jonathan Edwards*. Vol. 9, *A History of the Work of Redemption*. Edited by John Wilson. New Haven, Conn.: Yale University Press, 1989.

Secondary Sources

Lee, Sang Hyun, ed. *The Princeton Companion to Jonathan Edwards*. Princeton, N.J.: Princeton University Press, 2005.

Marsden, George. *Jonathan Edwards: A Life*. New Haven, Conn.: Yale University Press, 2003.

McDermott, Gerald. *One Holy and Happy Society: The Public Theology of Jonathan Edwards*. University Park, Pa.: Pennsylvania State University Press, 1992.

Pauw, Amy Plantinga. *The Supreme Harmony of All: The Trinitarian Theology of Jonathan Edwards*. Grand Rapids, Mich.: Eerdmans, 2002.

CHAPTER 18

John Wesley

Theodore W. Jennings, Jr.

The imperial designs of the nineteenth century were significantly based upon national interests as the great nation-states of Europe sought colonies in Africa and Asia. However, in the eighteenth century, the lineaments of empire were already beginning to become manifest, including the economic bases of an imperial order that would entail economic exploitation, international "trade," the economic rights of the strongest being protected by national military forces, and cultural expansions that threatened the integrity of outlying cultures. These forces continue to operate as key ingredients of what Hardt and Negri have famously characterized in our time as today's new form of empire.

In this emerging world stage of empire, the English evangelist and church reformer John Wesley (1703-1791) took a number of positions that may be understood as a critique of empire. Wesley had been an instructor in Greek and classics at Oxford University where, with his brother Charles, he founded a "holy club" of young men devoted to achieve entire holiness of life. Soon after his father's death he had undertaken the work of missionary and priest in the English colony of Georgia for what was to be the only time he accepted the duties of a parish priest. After his return to England from Georgia (where his ministry among the English colonists had met with no success), he became persuaded that scriptural holiness was not something to be restricted to a spiritual elite but was a divine gift freely bestowed even upon those excluded from society and church. Thus he launched into his life work of proclaiming the gospel to the marginalized and impoverished of British society and of organizing those who responded to his message into bands and societies to encourage one another to grow into the life of holiness. From these seeds grew the Methodist movement and the variety of Methodist and holiness denominations that have spread across the globe.

While Wesley is most remembered as a tireless evangelist and organizer, he was also a trenchant critic of those who held wealth and power, and he regularly lifted his voice on behalf of the poor and excluded among whom he worked and lived. It was this combination of suspicion directed against the powerful and his identification with those who were the victims of power that brings Wesley into contact with the question of nascent empire.

Many years ago Franz Hinkelammert indicated that the two main pillars of the emerging British Empire were the slave trade and the franchising of India under the East India Trading Company.[1] After a consideration of the use to which Wesley put the reports of other cultures that came to his attention, we will turn to an examination of his perspective upon these main pillars of emerging empire.

WESLEY'S EXPLORATION OF OTHER CULTURES

Wesley was an avid reader of travelers' reports on distant lands as an extension of his insatiable curiosity about the world, a curiosity that extended into all the sciences.[2] Given that some contemporary reflections upon empire—especially those developing through post-colonial studies—consider the drive to explore and report on distant places an essential part of the colonial apparatus and one that inevitably produces colonialist perspectives and practices,[3] it is important to notice how Wesley appropriated these early forays into what would eventually become cultural anthropology.

Wesley did not normally read these reports with an eye to discovering signs that the peoples of distant cultures needed the civilizing mission of Christian Europe, a motive that would eventually become one of the legitimating strategies of imperial ambition. On the contrary, Wesley generally emphasized those chronicles and descriptions that contrasted favorably with a supposedly Christianized Europe. Wesley read with an eye to emphasizing the superior values that were embedded in non-European cultures.[4]

Wesley did not suppose that the Christian West was the repository of wisdom for how to live in harmony with nature and with one's fellow human beings. He remarked that his goal in going to Georgia was to learn from the native peoples how to live in accordance with the prescription of Acts 2 and 4 concerning the community of goods. Thus on October 10, 1735, in a letter to a friend, he identifies his reasons for going to Georgia, a colony of England administered by General James Oglethorpe. He admits that his chief desire is to "save my own soul" and expects that by living and working among the Native Americans he will be able to attain a simplicity of life that he regards as essential to the attainment of holiness. He supposes that "it will be no small thing to be able, without giving offense, to live on water and the fruits of the earth" and hopes to banish from his thoughts the desire for externals that everywhere beset him in England. He remarks: "an Indian hut affords no food for curiosity; no gratification of the desire of grand, or new, or pretty things." His principal goal is to learn from the Native Americans how to live in accordance with the Pentecostal community's community of goods:

> The same faithfulness I hope to show, through his grace, in dispensing the rest of my Master's goods, if it please him to send me to those who, like his first followers, have all things in common. What a guard is here against that root of all evil, the love of money, and all the vile attractions that spring from it![5]

As it happened Wesley was not able to fulfill his dream of living among the Native Americans. Oglethorpe, the head of the Georgia colony, insisted that he devote his time to the spiritual direction of the English colonists in Savannah and to serving as Oglethorpe's own assistant in the management of the affairs of the colony. Nevertheless, many years later, in one of his homiletical reflections of the Sermon on the Mount, he would still recall this feature of Native American life that had first drawn him to journey to Georgia:

> It is not easy to say, when we compare the bulk of the nations in Europe with those in America, whether the superiority lies on the one side or the other. At least, the American has not much the advantage. But we cannot affirm this with regard to the command now before us. Here the Heathen has far the pre-eminence. He desires and seeks nothing more than plain food to eat, and plain raiment to put on; and he seeks this only from day to day: He reserves, he lays up nothing; unless it be as much corn, at one season of the year, as he will need before that season returns. This command, therefore, the Heathens, though they know it not, do constantly and punctually observe. They "lay up for themselves no treasures upon earth;" no stores of purple or fine linen, of gold or silver, which either "moth or rust may corrupt, or thieves break through and steal." But how do the Christians observe what they profess to receive as a command of the most high God? Not at all! not in any degree; no more than if no such command had ever been given to man.[6]

Much later in his career Wesley would turn to accounts of the peoples of Africa in order to insist upon the virtues of their societies, virtues that would serve to undermine the cogency of arguments for the slave trade. Thus Wesley writes in his "Thoughts upon Slavery" of Guinea (then the name of the entire central western coast of Africa): "It appears that Guinea, in general is far from a horrid, dreary, barren country, —[it] is one of the most fruitful, as the most pleasant, countries in the known world."[7]

Wesley speaks of the Fulani of Senegal and Nigeria: "They desire no more land than they use, which they cultivate with great care and industry."[8] Noting the remarkably just customs of the people and of their general regard for the poor and the ill, he concludes:

> Upon the whole, therefore, the Negroes who inhabit the coast of Africa, from the river Senegal to the southern bounds of Angola, are so far from being the stupid, senseless, brutish, lazy barbarians, the fierce, cruel, perfidious savages they have been described, that, on the contrary, they are represented . . . as remarkably sensible . . . as industrious to the highest degree, perhaps more so than any other natives of so warm a climate; as fair, just, and honest in all their dealings, unless where white men have taught them to be otherwise; and as far more mild, friendly, and kind to strangers, than any of our forefathers were.[9]

But now Wesley turns to a comparison not with European forebears but to the existing state of affairs in the presumably enlightened West: *"Our forefathers! Where shall we find at this day, among the fair-faced natives of Europe, a nation generally practicing the justice, mercy and truth, which are generally found among these poor Africans?"*[10] It is especially important to note Wesley's reference to "justice, mercy and truth" for these are the very characteristics that Wesley often associates with the renewed image of God.

Wesley's evident appreciation of the virtues of Native American and African cultures undercuts what would become one of the principal legitimations of emergent empire: the civilizing mission of Europe, or what in England would be termed the white man's burden. In today's new form of empire, this rationale has become the mission of extending freedom (of the financial market) and "democracy" (as the politics of marketing) to other nations and cultures.

CRITIQUE OF EMERGENT EMPIRE

Wesley's appreciation for the virtues of other cultures, combined with his keen sympathy for the misfortunes of those who were the victims of avarice and violence, made him a critic of the imperial ambitions of the great European nations, including his own. Thus, in the 1750 sermon "A Caution against Bigotry"[11] Wesley can be seen both to emphasize the limitations of "heathen" cultures in his attack upon deism, but also to issue the following broadside against the imperial designs of the great nations:

> It were to be wished that none but heathen had practiced such gross, palpable works of the devil. But we dare not say so. Even in cruelty and bloodshed, how little have the Christians come behind! And not the Spaniards or Portuguese alone, butchering thousands in South America. Not the Dutch only in the East Indies, or the French in North America, following the Spaniards step by step. Our own countrymen, too, have wantoned in blood, and exterminated whole nations: plainly proving thereby what spirit it is that dwells and works in the children of disobedience.[12]

Despite this rare foray into a critique of other nations, Wesley is most concerned with the emerging imperial designs of England. Interestingly he does not pay much attention to Britain's colonial expansion into North America, although he does remark upon the depopulation of the Americas in his sermon "The Imperfection of Human Knowledge":[13]

> How little better is either the civil or religious state of the poor American Indians! That is, the miserable remains of them: For in some provinces not one of them is left to breathe. In Hispanola, when the Christians came thither first, there were three millions of inhabitants. Scarce twelve thousand of them now survive . . . [.] Therefore are they decreasing daily; and very probably, in a century or two there will not be one of them left.[14]

In the same sermon he also points to the suffering of the peoples of India and Africa in order to indicate the limits to our understanding of God's providential ruling over history. "In what condition, in particular, is the large and populous empire of Indostan! How many hundred thousands of the poor quiet people have been destroyed, and their carcasses left as dung of the earth!"[15] And of Africa: "And who cares for thousands, myriads, if not millions, of the wretched Africans? Are not whole droves of these poor sheep (human, if not rational beings!) continually driven to market, and sold, like cattle, into the vilest bondage, without any hope of deliverance but by death?"[16]

But Wesley's characterization of these vast continents of suffering has a somewhat different edge than a simple recognition of the (apparent) contradiction between the belief in a benevolent and ruling deity and the magnitude of human suffering. For this is not suffering that is basically inscrutable; it has a direct human cause: British policy regarding the mercantile subjugation of India and the conduct of the slave trade.

In order to understand the significance of Wesley's argument here it is helpful to return to the characterization of Wesley's England offered by Franz Hinkelammert. He points out that England's nineteenth-century predominance in the Industrial Revolution as well as in the construction of empire depended upon two closely related ventures, which had their origin in the beginnings of the eighteenth century and which were the principal political-economic realties with which Wesley had to contend. These were the transfer of the monopoly of the slave trade from Portugal to England by trade treaty in 1703, and the fostering of the East India Trading Company, which developed as a result of the same trade agreement. We will come back to the slave trade in the next section, but here deal with the emergence of Britain's role in India.

In 1703, England acquired from Portugal the right to conduct the textile trade with India. This was a potentially lucrative trade since India produced cotton cloth, a commodity very much desired in Europe as well as in Africa (in exchange for slaves), and in the American colonies which otherwise had to rely on wool for clothing. However, the inherent problem in this trade was that Europe produced virtually nothing that India wanted in exchange for its cloth. As a result, gold poured into India in exchange for its cotton cloth, setting up not only a huge trade imbalance but also a loss of Europe's currency reserves (the gold and silver coming from Spain's New World colonies).

Both England and France realized that a remedy for this situation would be to acquire not only the trade rights but also the production rights for the cloth. This meant subjugating the Indian subcontinent in order to take over the production of cloth. In the race to subjugate India, England had the advantage in that it was able to first make use of mobile artillery,[17] which not only vanquished the French but made it possible for relatively small numbers of British soldiers to destroy vast numbers of

Indian troops. In the end textile production was stopped in India and moved to England in what would become the basis of England's Industrial Revolution.

Against this background we must read Wesley's outraged remarks on British policy in India. For example in his journal entry for November 13, 1776, we read one of his responses to Bolt's account of India:

> What consummate villains, what devils incarnate, were the managers there! What utter strangers to justice, mercy, and truth; to every sentiment of humanity. I believe no heathen history contains a parallel. I remember none in all the annals of antiquity: Not even the divine Cato, or the virtuous Brutus, plundered the provinces committed to their charge with such merciless cruelty as the English have plundered the desolated provinces of Indostan.[18]

Subsequently, in a sermon from 1783, we read:

> Look into that large country, Indostan. There are Christians and Heathens too. Which have more justice, mercy and truth? The Christians or the Heathens? Which are the most corrupt, infernal, devilish, in their tempers and practice? The English or the Indians? Which have desolated whole countries, and clogged the rivers with dead bodies? "O sacred name of Christian! How profaned!" O earth, earth, earth! How dost thou groan under the villainies of thy *Christian* inhabitants.[19]

In 1776, in his seasonable address to the inhabitants of Great Britain (after excoriating the slave trade) Wesley writes:

> And is the East-India trader a jot better? I fear not. They seem very nearly allied. For though here is no leading into captivity, as in the former; yet the refined iniquity practiced there, of fomenting war amongst the natives, and seizing the chief of the plunder, has been as conspicuous to the serious and attentive. What millions have fallen by these means, as well as by artificial famine! O earth, cover not thou their blood! It will speak to heaven and to the inhabitants of the earth to the latest posterity.[20]

But Wesley does not merely sound a prophetic protest against this injustice. He also supposes that God will judge England for these unspeakable crimes:

> . . . [W]e may call the myriads that have been murdered happy, in comparison of those that still groan under the iron yoke. Wilt not thou visit for these things, O Lord? Shall the fool still say in his heart, "There is no God?"[21]

In these texts we see a Wesley who has moved from being an observer of human misery who must simply have recourse to the inscrutable providence of God to one who finds the causes of human misery in the imperial policies of his own nation.

THE SLAVE TRADE

This transformation is even more evident in Wesley's perspective on the other main pillar of British economic prosperity, the slave trade, the monopoly rights to which England had also acquired from Portugal in 1703. Although in his sermon on "The Imperfection of Human Knowledge"[22] he seemed to simply point to the apparent contradiction between this suffering and what one might expect to be the case if a good God presided over the affairs of human history, already by the 1770s Wesley was placing the blame not on inscrutable providence but on English greed. Moreover, in Wesley's thinking the activity of God has now been transformed from that of inscrutable providence to that of one who acts in history to punish those who cause great suffering in the world. One might say that his general orientation has changed from that of a Roman stoic to that of a Hebrew prophet.

In his "Thoughts upon Slavery" of 1774 Wesley not only writes of the prosperous, peaceable and indeed just character of the African cultures that had been devastated by the slave trade, he also indicts the injustice and cruelty of those who foment and conduct this trade. Thus he writes of the injustice of the manner in which slaves are acquired: "It was some time before the Europeans found a more compendious way of procuring African slaves, by prevailing upon them to make war upon each other, and to sell their prisoners."[23]

He then turns his attention to the horrors of what has come to be known as the Middle Passage:

> But in what numbers and in what manner are they carried to America? . . . So many are taken on board our ships; but at least ten thousand of them die in the voyage; about a fourth part more die at the different islands, in what is called the seasoning. So that at an average, in the passage and seasoning together, thirty thousand die; that is, properly, are murdered. O Earth, O Sea, cover not thou their blood![24]

After considering the miserable conditions of those slaves who finally arrive at the plantations Wesley exclaims: "Did the Creator intend that the noblest creatures in the visible world should live such a life as this?"[25] He summarizes this whole saga of monstrous suffering:

... [W]here is the justice of taking away the lives of innocent, inoffensive men; murdering thousands of them in their own land, by the hands of their own countrymen; many thousands, year after year, on shipboard, and then casting them like dung into the sea; and tens of thousands in that cruel slavery to which they are so unjustly reduced?[26]

But Wesley is not content to denounce the horrors of this unjust suffering. He also goes to the economic roots of the problem and to an identification of the avarice that propels this violence. He addresses himself to the merchants who profit from this trade:

This equally concerns every merchant who is engaged in the slave-trade. It is you that induce the African villain to sell his countrymen; and in order thereto, to steal, rob, murder men, women, and children without number, by enabling the English villain to pay him for so doing, whom you overpay for his execrable labour. It is your money that is the spring of all, that empowers him to go.[27]

Wesley then turns his attention to the plantation owner:

Now, it is your money that pays the merchant, and through him the captain and the African butchers. You therefore are guilty, yea, principally guilty, of all these frauds, robberies, and murders. . . . Therefore, the blood of all these wretches who die before their time, whether in their country or elsewhere, lies upon your head.[28]

For Wesley, however, this is not merely a matter of individual or even corporately organized greed and violence on the part of those who take part in, or profit from, this trade. It is also, as he begins to see, a matter of national policy. Thus Wesley writes of the Caribbean colonies that at that time received the main number of slaves to work the sugarcane plantations:

First, it were better that all those islands should remain uncultivated for ever; yea, it were more desirable that they were altogether sunk in the depth of the sea, than that they should be cultivated at so high a price as the violation of justice, mercy, and truth.[29]

Wesley then attends to the ways this entire system of international trade was alleged to benefit the English people and the prosperity of the nation as a whole:

266 EMPIRE AND THE CHRISTIAN TRADITION

First, wealth is not necessary to the glory of any nation; but wisdom, virtue, justice, mercy, generosity, public spirit, love of our country. These are necessary to the real glory of a nation; but abundance of wealth is not. . . . Better is honest poverty, than all the riches bought by the tears, and sweat, and blood, of our fellow-creatures.[30]

As he was to do with respect to the colonial policies in India, so also here Wesley further moves toward a claim that God will punish England for its complicity in this human suffering. He takes as his point of departure the uprising of the British colonies on the North American mainland:

. . . [A]nd as we are punished with the sword, it is not improbable but one principal sin of our nation is, the blood that we have shed in Asia, Africa, and America. Here I would beg your serious attention, while I observe, that however extensively pursued, and of long continuance, the African trade may be, it is nevertheless iniquitous from first to last. It is the price of blood! It is a trade of blood, and has stained our land with blood![31]

As we have seen, this in turn is linked to what he has said about the colonial policies in India.

And is the East-India trader a jot better? I fear not. They seem very nearly allied. For though here is no leading into captivity, as in the former; yet the refined iniquity practised there, of fomenting war amongst the natives, and seizing the chief of the plunder, has been as conspicuous to the serious and attentive. What millions have fallen by these means, as well as by artificial famine! . . . O ye Governors of this great nation, would to God that ye had seen this, and timely done your utmost to separate those tares from the wheat of fair and honest trade! . . . "There can be no peace, saith the Lord." While "the voice of thy brother's blood crieth unto me from the ground," . . . "Shall I not visit for these things? Shall not my soul be avenged on such a nation as this?" Yes, my brethren, we have much reason to fear and tremble, as upon the brink of fate.[32]

Thus Wesley has moved from thinking of suffering as fate in the hands of the inscrutable providence of God to thinking of it as having specific economic and political causes. God then becomes not some mere spectator to this suffering but rather one who rises up to overthrow those who inflict that suffering upon their fellow human beings.

The move that Wesley does make in relation to slavery that he does not in relation to India is to support those who purposed to abolish the slave trade. Thus he lends his support to the work of Lord Wilberforce in ending the African slave trade.[33] A similar move does not seem to have been made in relation to India; indeed it would have been difficult to find allies in government to stop the juggernaut of emergent empire. After all, it did, as Wesley himself acknowledged, seem to contribute, at least at that stage, to the potential prosperity of the working poor.[34]

However, Wesley does realize that the gospel itself contains the impetus for a very different sort of economics than that instantiated in the slave trade or the East India Trading Company. Instead of an economy based upon greed and violence, he articulated the vision for one based upon open generosity. Moreover it is this economy of communal sharing of goods with all who have need that Wesley imagined would be the force that could transform the earth from a scene of suffering usually augmented by so-called Christians into a new world in which so much unnecessary suffering would be abolished. This at least is the vision implicit in his sermon on "The General Spread of the Gospel."[35]

CONCLUSION

In evaluating Wesley's views on empire we note a number of important ways in which he comes into opposition with the emerging empire of his own day. To be sure, this opposition has very real limits. When combating Deist views, he occasionally falls into the sort of negative assessment of other cultures that would ultimately become a legitimation for empire. Although he is critical of the brutal suffering caused by proto-imperialist extensions into South America, India, the East Indies, and Africa he is not critical of the planting of England's North American colonies. And, finally, he stops short of a direct appeal for the reversal of England's designs on India. Thus when, in the century following his death, Britain undertook in earnest the task of constructing and extending the British Empire, it was possible for many of those associated with the movement he had initiated to become apologists for empire.

Just as many "Methodists" lost contact with Wesleyan devotion to the improvement of the condition of the impoverished (and the condemnation of the snares of prosperity) and sought instead to gain respectability among the emerging middle classes of Britain and America, so also the imperial search for new colonies in Asia and Africa often went hand in glove with an evangelical missionary zeal that had lost contact with a critique of the nation's putative innocence. Wesley had not developed a systematic critique of European ambition, any more than he had developed an economic theory that would have exposed the roots of an industrial capitalism barely in its infancy in his own day. However, within these limits, Wesley's critiques of the emerging policies of empire can be quite instructive for those who take on a similar stance today.

Wesley is not persuaded by those who suppose that other cultures require the intervention of the West in order to acquire virtue or civilization. Whether this intervention be couched in terms of a "civilizing mission" as happened in the nineteenth century, or in terms of extending the blessings of the free market as happens today, Wesley was not taken in by the pretensions to social virtue that too often serve as a cloak for naked self-interest on the part of stronger nations at the expense of weaker ones.

Wesley is quite clear that the principal cause of human suffering is Western avarice and violence and he is unrelenting in his critique of the supposed superiority of a society or civilization for which these become the main motivators of imperial ambition. In terms of our own situation it is noteworthy that Wesley keenly diagnoses the economic interest that is the chief animator of those policies that cause human suffering on a stupendous scale.

As a theologian and reader of the Bible, Wesley also knows how to call upon those who profit from systems of exploitation to turn away from injustice in order to avert the judgment of God. For Wesley, the practice of injustice on such a scale must necessarily result in the destruction of the perpetrators of such terrible suffering. And this must be true not only for the individuals who directly promote and profit from such policies but also for the nations that are enriched and corrupted thereby. Although Wesley did not have the benefit of more recent critiques of imperialism and of empire, he offers perspectives that continue to be useful in the critical understanding of the ways in which empire is related to the magnitude of human suffering which is its cost.

FURTHER READING

Primary Sources

Welsey, John. *John Wesley's Sermons: An Anthology*. Edited by Albert C. Outler and Richard P. Heitzenrater. Nashville, Tenn.: Abingdon, 1991.

_____. *The Works of John Wesley*. 14 vols. 3rd ed. 1872. Reprint, Grand Rapids, Mich.: Baker Book House, 1979. Esp. "A Seasonable Address to the More Serious Part of the Inhabitants of Great Britain," 11:119-28; and "Thoughts upon Slavery," 11:59-79.

Secondary Sources

Hinkelammert, Franz. "Las condiciones económicos-sociales del Metodismo en la Inglaterra del Siglo XVIII." In *La tradición protestante en la teología latinoamericana: Primer intento: lectura de la tradición metodista*, edited by José Duque, 21-29. San José, Costa Rica: DEI, 1983.

Jennings, Theodore W, Jr. *Good News to the Poor: John Wesley's Evangelical Economics*. Nashville, Tenn: Abingdon, 1990.

Maddox, Randy L. *Responsible Grace: John Wesley's Practical Theology*. Nashville, Tenn.: Abingdon, 1994.

Runyon, Theodore. *The New Creation: John Wesley's Theology Today*. Nashville, Tenn.: Abingdon, 1998.

CHAPTER 19

Friedrich Schleiermacher

Joerg Rieger

Modern theology has come under increasing criticism from various directions in recent years. The challenges range from postliberal and conservative charges of an undue emphasis on human experience and a related neglect of the authority of the texts of the church, to postmodern charges of a lack of appreciation for otherness and difference, and the more general impression fostered by critics informed by liberation theologies that modern theology is plagued by self-centeredness and narcissism. None of the standard critiques of modern theology, however, give much consideration to the colonial character of modern theology and its relations to empire.[1] Yet modernity, colonialism, and empire are not only simultaneous and parallel developments; they actually reinforce each other. What does this mean for our understanding of modern theology?

As a theologian whose work was shaped by the emergence of the modern middle class, Friedrich Schleiermacher (1768-1834) presents a useful case for our examination of these questions.[2] This arising middle class is represented, for instance, by the members of the salons of Berlin at the beginning of the nineteenth century. In these salons, an emerging class of wealthy citizens would open their homes to young intellectuals, prominent scholars, and other interested observers. These groups showed progressive tendencies; here diversity was appreciated, women played important roles, and other religions were tolerated, highlighted by the prominence of Jewish participants. And while political critique was discouraged by the Prussian government, these circles refused to set aside political interests; Schleiermacher himself was quite active at times in political matters and even played a role in the resistance against Napoleon and the French.[3] Nevertheless, the

271

wider horizon of the context of the modern middle class and of its cultural and political production is hardly noted. Key to our investigation is that the middle class takes shape not in isolation but in close relation to (and on the back of) the lower classes both domestically and abroad.

In Schleiermacher's time, Germany as a nation did not yet exist, and hence was not a colonial power; nonetheless, Schleiermacher's Prussia had expanded its territory toward the East, and there was great excitement about the colonial spirit, which preceded sustained colonial action (in the years 1884-1919). Schleiermacher himself was drawn into this excitement about colonial interests, which were being manifested in various ways. Individual Germans had participated in colonial enterprises as far back as the Spanish Conquest. Trade relations with the colonial powers and some of their colonies flourished in Schleiermacher's time.[4] In the sixteenth century Bartolomé de Las Casas denounced a group of German merchants whom he, playing with words, calls the "*animales alemanes*" (German animals) for being crueler than the Spaniards. This denouncement had a strong impact on later generations of Germans, at a time when Las Casas's work had become widely known. Yet, while the denouncement of violent colonialization was common in Schleiermacher's time, it was being projected on the other colonial powers, thus opening the way for alternative German colonial fantasies.[5]

Schleiermacher and Australia

Schleiermacher's interests in external colonial affairs can best be seen in what has survived of an extensive work on the British settlement of Australia, which he produced for the greatly expanding market of travel writings. Part of Schleiermacher's work consists of a translation into German of a popular book published in London in 1798 by David Collins, entitled *Account of the English Colony in New South Wales*, but Schleiermacher supplemented it with his own research. He worked on this project, which was under contract but never published, between 1799 and 1802. It has been characterized as a major project among his literary endeavors of that time.[6] This work resembles other German scholarship of that era in that it does not gather first-hand knowledge through travel and immersion, but relies on the reports of others, particularly British, French, and Dutch explorers. Nevertheless, as Edward Said has pointed out in regard to Orientalism, "what German Orientalism had in common with Anglo-French and later American Orientalism was a kind of intellectual *authority* over the Orient within Western culture."[7] German thinkers conceived their interpretations of the Orient and of other colonized parts of the world, we might add, precisely because they could bring to it a more detached and objective perspective which was not tainted by the messiness of colonial power struggles.[8] Of course, rather than following the "Orientalist" trajectory, Schleiermacher follows "Occidentalist" impulses.[9]

As recent research has shown, the general German interest in these matters was driven by secret colonial fantasies[10]—envisioning that Germany too could become a colonial agent. When Schleiermacher himself remarks on the unusual nature of the project which is new and strange to him, he notes that he has a special desire to do this work and that he does not know where this desire comes from.[11]

What remains of Schleiermacher's appropriation and interpretation of the descriptions of New South Wales and its original inhabitants is interesting on various levels and will help us take another look at his theology. The descriptions of nature which he selects from his sources have factual character but always usher in a discussion of their utility to the colonial project. The climate is not only identified as "healthy" (for the colonizers) but allows for year-round agricultural use; animals such as sheep, pigs, and goats can easily be raised in that locale.[12] The products which are named as giving the place its "greatest importance" are fir trees and flax, both of which are useful primarily for further colonial exploration in other parts of the world. Flax can be used for sails and ropes, and fir trees as masts for the British fleet in East India.

Schleiermacher's descriptions of the original inhabitants of Australia, which he develops further in his own research, are even more telling and help us dig deeper into the underlying colonial mentality. He describes the Aboriginals as barely human—or human at the very lowest rung of human civilization. The Aboriginals, he continues, are worse off than the ants which live in the same area; at least the ants have housing. There is no trace of law or civil order to be found, not even of religion or superstition.[13] In an earlier section of the project, Schleiermacher notes that the only act of submission—obviously a sign of civilization and order in his eyes—is a certain level of respect that the younger pay the older.[14] Furthermore, there is neither agricultural nor artisanal capacity of any kind. The Aboriginal people are described as "completely naked"—a statement which reflects Schleiermacher's prejudice about clothes since he notes in the next passage that they wear adornment and color their skin. A country populated with such people, he concludes, was of no use to the Dutch, and thus they abandoned it.

Hierarchical thinking provides the underlying structure of Schleiermacher's seemingly objective comparisons of different tribes, some of whom "seem to deserve more the sparse adornments" than others. Comparing the inhabitants of Australia to the inhabitants of Africa, he notes their black skin and "wooly hair" which, in his opinion, lacks "the peculiarly repulsive facial expressions of the negro."[15] Schleiermacher's colonial mentality is displayed here in raw force.

Nevertheless, the colonial attitudes which come through in Schleiermacher's descriptions differ in some fundamental ways from the earlier and more violent colonialisms of the Spanish and Portuguese in Latin America. He rejects the slave trade, which is still going on, and he praises the efforts to live in peaceful relationship with the natives.[16] Yet a closer look reveals the reasons. Peaceful coexistence was called for neither primarily because of an enlightened "feeling of original equality" which was indeed displayed by the colonizers, nor because of a "more noble feeling of honor" which entails a refusal to repeat the atrocities of earlier colonial histories. Peaceful coexistence is called for on the basis of a "natural rule," according to which there was simply nothing to be gained from exploitation or any other relationship. There was absolutely no use for these natives to the colonial system, not even as labor force. Schleiermacher also notes that they owned virtually no property; all they possessed was the original "spark" which set in motion the progressive civilization of humanity, without any noticeable progress. These natives, arrested at the "lowest rung of pleasure and action," would not pose any threats or prevent the colonizers from owning the treasures of the land.[17]

Consciously or unconsciously, Schleiermacher's interpretation is based on a position of colonial power and a sense of cultural and religious superiority. Said's summary of the attitudes of Orientalism applies to Schleiermacher as well: "Even as Europe moved itself outwards, its sense of cultural strength was fortified. From travelers' tales, and not only from great institutions like the various India companies, colonies were created and ethnocentric perspectives secured."[18] In Germany, travel writing and other literature dealing with colonial fantasies and "the other" helped generate a sense of self-identity and unification that was not available otherwise and that could not easily be examined because it was based on others who were not only different (as in the case of Jewish neighbors)[19] but also very far away (as in the case of the Australian Aboriginals). As Susanne Zantop has argued, against Said, the fact that Germany lacked colonies made German colonialist discourse not less but more powerful; this lack created a "pervasive desire for colonial possessions and a sense of entitlement to such possessions" which could develop without being challenged by colonial subjects. More than mere "intellectual authority" (Said), a "mythological authority over the collective imagination" (Zantop) evolved.[20] The modern European self affirms its own value and superiority over against the different other. In the case of Germany, this self-affirmation was connected also to a sense of moral superiority over the colonizing nations.[21] Could this be at the root of Schleiermacher's inexplicable desire to explore these matters?

THEOLOGICAL IMPLICATIONS

Schleiermacher's colonial mindset has parallels in his theological thought. It is increasingly recognized that European intellectual movements are tied to colonial relationships. This is true also for Romanticism, the intellectual environment of Schleiermacher, which was influenced among other things by the writings and drawings of German explorer and scientist Alexander von Humboldt, informed by his travels in Latin America from 1799-1804. Humboldt produced, in the words of Mary Louise Pratt, "his own journeys and subject matters and spent a lifetime of energy promoting them."[22] Schleiermacher knew him from his early days in the Romantic networks of Berlin. Schleiermacher's own study of the Aboriginal other, as Stephen Prickett has argued, had an important impact on at least two areas of his work. If the notion of religion were to include Aboriginals, religion could not be a matter of knowing or doing but only of feeling or intuition, one of the notions at the very core of Schleiermacher's work.[23] Likewise, if the huge gap that separated Europeans from these Aboriginals was to be bridged, hermeneutics would be a necessary tool. Prickett's conclusion is that had "Schleiermacher not begun to read of the English settlement at Sydney Cove, the history of Romanticism, and indeed of Western culture, would have been profoundly different."[24] Along these lines, it might perhaps be argued that the awareness of the Aboriginal other had a positive influence on the development of modern theology and thought, but the problems in this relationship must not be overlooked.

Schleiermacher's Christology, in particular the classical Reformed doctrine of the three offices of Christ, provides an example. It is developed in relation to a colonial order—in this case mostly in relation to what might be called "internal colonialism," i.e., the relation of Christians to the Jewish other.[25] Similar to other modern colonial relationships, Schleiermacher does not perceive the relationship of Judaism and Christianity as antagonistic. In the *Speeches* he is "charmed" by Judaism's "beautiful childlike character"[26] although later he utters harsher criticisms of what he perceives to be the limits of the Jewish religion, expressed for instance in the statement that "by its limitation of the love of Jehovah to the race of Abraham" it "betrays a lingering affinity with Fetishism."[27] Schleiermacher's 1799 stance on the place of Jews in Germany mirrors his complex position on colonial matters. Supporting the equality of Christians and Jews in civil matters, he rejects the idea of a Christianization that enforces baptism and only leads to a "judaizing Christianity." Assuming support from his Jewish friends and Reformed Judaism, he nevertheless demands that Jews should subordinate their ritual laws to the laws of the state, and that they should give up their hope for the Holy Land.[28] His ultimate goal, in keeping with the spirit of his work as a whole, is to seek "harmony."[29]

A link between these colonial perspectives and theology can perhaps best be seen in Schleiermacher's description of the work of Christ in human beings. He rejects interpretations of the work of Christ in terms of coercive action. Schleiermacher's Christ is not at work like the Spanish colonizers with fire and sword, overwhelming people by sheer force and coercing them into his kingdom. Rather, Christ is at work through "attraction" and "pervasive influence." Schleiermacher describes Christ's work as "impulses [that] flow to us from Him," that operate to pull us into "His sphere of living influence" through "attractive power."[30] At first sight this is a much more liberating understanding of Christ than a view that identifies Christ's power with the top-down coercions of crude military and political power; yet the colonial context raises questions. Are the oppressive relations between colonizers and colonized really overcome in this more enlightened colonial setting?

In his *The Christian Faith*, Schleiermacher draws on the example of teacher and student when he talks about the "attractive power" of those "to whose educative intellectual influence we gladly submit ourselves," an influence which is not only "person-forming" but also "world-forming."[31] Here this attractive power operates under the assumption of a clear hierarchy of teacher and student. This hierarchical difference is also reflected in Schleiermacher's taxonomy of religion. While he acknowledges the validity of other religions outside of Christianity—just as modern thought following Las Casas acknowledged the basic humanity of non-Europeans—he also insists on a classification which allows for "different states of development,"[32] with European Protestantism being at the highest level. Elsewhere in *The Christian Faith* he talks about a "most manifold gradation of life, from the lowest and most imperfect forms up to the highest and most perfect"; a gradation which is willed and put in place by God, "the divine good-pleasure" which is to be received in "quiet acceptance." Both human nature and the "sphere of spiritual life" are permeated by this gradation.[33]

This same logic applies to the colonial enterprises of the British in Australia. If the colonizers are superior in relation to the colonized, and if they are representatives of the "attractive power" that is a mark of those higher up, the colonized have no choice but to "gladly submit" to the colonizers. Anything else would be irrational. Christ's own attractive power models this superiority, and the differential between Christ and the Christian gets translated into the differential between colonized and colonizers. Nevertheless, one might wonder which differentials are ultimately greater, the ones between Christ and the European Christians, or the ones between European Christians and native Australians who even lack religion.

Another example of how colonial attitudes shape theology can be seen in Schleiermacher's discussion of Christ's miracles. The individual miracles of Christ, Schleiermacher argues, do not necessarily distinguish him from other miracle workers. Our advantage over the contemporaries of Christ is that we can see beyond individual miracles to the "general spiritual miracle, which begins with the person of the Redeemer and is completed with the completion of His Kingdom." Christ transcends both the Jewish limitations and the limitations of the present, and is both the "climax" and the "end of miracle."[34] Everything that might be perceived as miraculous is now simply the further development of Christ's work. This could be an instance of a counter-colonial moment in Schleiermacher's work because this move shuts out extreme forms of top-down religious domination that claim a special connection to the miraculous. At the same time, however, Schleiermacher's conclusion on miracles firmly reestablishes the colonial framework in another way: "Even if it cannot be strictly proved that the Church's power of working miracles has died out," he states, "it is undeniable that, in view of the great advantage in power and civilization which the Christian peoples posses over the non-Christian, . . . the preachers of to-day do not need such signs."[35] Miracles are unnecessary because of the "power and civilization" of the Christian nations compared to the non-Christians. In other words, Christianity itself appears to be the divine miracle and its colonial triumphs are the proof. Even the Jewish-Christian relationship testifies to this. While Christ is the climax and end of teaching, prophecy, and miracle, European Christianity is closest to Christ—closer than the Jewish religion and certainly closer than any other.[36]

Interesting parallels can be seen among the transformations that bring about modern colonial societies. Already in the eighteenth-century transitions from feudalism to capitalism, the notions of power and force change. Power is transferred from the hands of the noble ruler into the hands of a more democratically organized bourgeois state. Even in Prussia, while the kings retain power, there are moves to distribute power and authority more broadly. Gunther Pakendorf finds a striking parallel to Michel Foucault's analyses of the prison system, where power is gradually transformed from public and physical forms to a form that is hidden and internalized socially and psychologically; in a situation of surveillance in a panopticon, where prisoners can be watched but never know whether they are being watched or not, no strong physical acts of coercion are necessary since power is internalized. The top-down powers of the feudal rulers become more dispersed in the modern world and can thus afford to be less severe without losing force. The field of Christian mission parallels these developments: power that used to be expressed through physical coercion is increasingly internalized. In the Protestant missions of Schleiermacher's time power is expressed less and less by force but more and more through language.[37]

Related to this use of language is the power of knowledge; as Homi Bhabha, in reference to Foucault, has pointed out: "the late eighteenth century . . . could not tolerate areas of darkness and sought to exercise power through the mere fact of things being known and people seen in an immediate, collective gaze."[38] The development of modern theology needs to be seen as part of these processes. In Germany, the study of theology and religion became one of the outlets for intellectuals to participate in the exercise of power, since there were few opportunities to influence politics directly.

THEOLOGICAL RESISTANCE TO COLONIALISM

Reading Schleiermacher in light of the colonial spirit of his age puts his work in a new light. That he shares these sentiments does not come as a great surprise—in fact, we continue to share a few of them in our own times. The challenge for us, though, is to become aware of these (often unconscious) biases and to overcome them.

There are instances where Schleiermacher's work pushes beyond the limitations of the colonial mindset, and perhaps we can take some of our own constructive cues from them. It is noteworthy that Schleiermacher does not promote the rugged individualistic ideologies of other modern forms of colonialism, like the ones modeled by the emerging business interests of the early capitalism of his day or the ones that eventually found expression in the pioneer spirit of the expanding United States. The reconciling activity of Christ brings about a "corporate feeling of blessedness," he claims, an experience of relatedness and community within Christianity. In this community the Christian's "former personality dies, so far as it meant a self-enclosed life of feeling within a sensuous vital unity, to which all sympathetic feeling for others and for the whole was subordinated."[39] Unfortunately, however, this community appears to be fairly homogeneous, without much use for outsiders and with little sensitivity to those in its midst who do not fit in. There is no constructive place for suffering either.[40] Suffering in such a community would not be a sign that something is wrong with the community; it would merely signal that someone is not yet fully integrated and it can thus be overcome by pulling people more fully into the community's "corporate feeling of blessedness." By the same token, the existence of outsiders would not be seen as a sign of a problem; it would merely be a reminder to the community of the need to be more inclusive.

Still, there is a material quality to Schleiermacher's reflections that might lead to a different kind of appreciation of the world and of history: "From all finite things we should see the Infinite," he claims. This might allow for the possibility to find God in unexpected places, including unexpected places in the colonial system, even though Schleiermacher does not emphasize this.[41] In addition to this attention to the world, there is an attention to history which introduces a self-critical moment: Noting that "religious men are throughout historical," religion cannot be perceived apart from its particular history, although religion must not be confused with this history; not "everything found in the heroes of religion or in the sacred sources" should be considered as decisive sources of religion.[42] This insight makes us take another look at the colonial history of Christianity. What if we look at history and finite things differently than Schleiermacher, waiting for a different set of what he calls "new ambassadors from God" and another kind of rebirth of Christianity in "a new and more beautiful form"?[43] What if we developed, for instance, a more historically informed view of Christ, which would appreciate factors like his Jewishness and his solidarity with the "least of these"?

We might take Schleiermacher's ambiguity about the colonial as a cue and appropriate it in a different way. After all, the younger Schleiermacher of the *Speeches* is hopeful that "younger, and, if possible, stronger and more beautiful types of religion arise outside of this corruption," and he refrains from colonial uniformity: "as nothing is more irreligious than to demand general uniformity in mankind, so nothing is more unchristian than to seek uniformity in religion."[44] The question might be raised on the basis of these reflections: what if colonial Christianity is not the highest stage of religion?

Perhaps Schleiermacher's approach could even help restrain colonial expansion. Christian action is not self-empowered expansionism but rooted in Christ's own actions, Schleiermacher notes. What moves us is Christ's spirit.[45] Patterned after Christ's power, which works through attraction rather than sheer force, Schleiermacher identifies both a Christian desire to act in broadening ways and a desire to receive (the latter manifest especially in those who do not yet know Christ).[46] This alone is the basis for Christian mission; Schleiermacher connects the subject of mission to the idea of progress within the church as well: just like mission ultimately grows out of the strength of the personal conviction of individual Christians, so each member of the church should have "freedom of judgment, freedom of communication even of those things which might look like a deviation," because such freedom might lead to progress within the church.[47] In this way the church is like a school which continuously educates itself "in and through" its members in whom it seeks to infuse its basic principles.[48] In this context, Schleiermacher even compares the church to a language, in which and "into which" everyone has to form his own thinking but which is still open to being perfected.[49]

Depending on how this moment of integration into a language takes place, Schleiermacher's approach contains some real potential for resistance. Due to his concern for the openness and perfectibility of Christianity and Christian language, Schleiermacher's approach may be more promising than some of the current cultural-linguistic models in theology. While authority is rooted in education (i.e., the transmission of language) and in the level of peoples' consciousness, it is also tied to the "diversity of experience."[50] The latter category is of special interest in the resistance to the status quo; it potentially pushes toward a greater sensitivity for the colonial other who, forced to live a hybrid existence which pulls together the reality of colonizer and colonized, displays the greatest diversity of experience.[51]

Schleiermacher concludes his *Christliche Sitte* by returning to his particular notion of "feeling," and thus to the core of his theology; feeling, rather than knowing or doing, brings together self and other and enables understanding (in its ultimate form, as "feeling of absolute dependence," feeling brings together humanity and God). Communication with those who are different cannot happen without "greatest toleration" and "the most determined respect for the modifications of feeling in other people"; no one can contribute to the "purification and perfection" of others except those who are able to put themselves into the feelings of the other. This brings us back to where we started—the growing sense that modern theology and hermeneutics are inextricably connected to the encounter with the colonial other. Schleiermacher's focus, however, is here not negative but positive: he is not searching for the shortcomings of the others but for their achievements; the one who is pure, he says, will be able to identify what is pure in others as well.[52] Here is real potential for overcoming some of the more blatant colonialist enterprises, even though we need to keep in mind that Schleiermacher does not give up his position of superiority.

James Brandt has highlighted Schleiermacher's notion of love as key to his concern for the transformation of society.[53] Schleiermacher broadens Christian love so as to include all of humanity.[54] Yet, as Zantop reminds us, love was a favorite metaphor in eighteenth-century colonial discourse: love could establish natural boundaries, improve the races that needed improving, and even let the colonial enterprise appear in the light of "legitimacy and mutuality." One of the prominent colonial fantasies of love was the educational and patriarchal relation between father and child.[55] The notion of love as such, therefore, does not necessarily overcome the colonial system. Yet there is a sense in which Schleiermacher's categories push beyond some of the incarnations of colonialism in his day. Challenged with digesting the heritage of modern theology, we need to pursue this trajectory further.

FURTHER READING

Primary Sources

Schleiermacher, Friedrich. *The Christian Faith*. Edited by H. R. Mackintosh and
　　J. S. Stewart. Edinburgh: T. &T. Clark, 1986.
　　_____. *Die Christliche Sitte nach den Grundsätzen der evangelischen Kirche im
　　Zusammenhang dargestellt*. Waltrop: Spenner, 1999.
　　_____. *On Religion: Speeches to Its Cultured Despisers*. Translated by John Oman.
　　Louisville, Ky.: Westminster John Knox Press, 1994.

Secondary Sources

Brandt, James M. *All Things New: Reform of Church and Society in Schleiermacher's* Christian Ethics. Louisville, Ky.: Westminster John Knox Press, 2001.

Mariña, Jacqueline, ed. *The Cambridge Companion to Friedrich Schleiermacher.* Cambridge: Cambridge University Press, 2005.

Redeker, Martin. *Schleiermacher: Life and Thought.* Translated by John Wallhausser. Philadelphia, Pa.: Fortress Press, 1973.

CHAPTER 20

G. W. F. Hegel

David G. Kamitsuka

There is both an audacity and candor to Georg Wilhelm Friedrich Hegel (1770-1831) that can take the contemporary reader's breath away, for good and ill. The job of the philosopher is "to comprehend what is," Hegel writes in the preface to the *Philosophy of Right*. He was not one to worry about setting the bar of his own or the reader's expectations too high! He understood the task of the theorist to be the thorough illumination of the broader and deeper meanings of the cultural, spiritual, and political moment, and, as any reader of novels knows, you need a sense of the beginning, middle, and end—*what is*—before you can make sense of the events narrated on any single page.

Hegel could also be candid. In the very next sentence, he observes that "every individual is a child of his time; so philosophy too is its own time apprehended in thoughts."[1] In saying this, Hegel was being candid about the limitations of philosophy. Hegel took the political, economic, cultural, military, and religious events up through the early nineteenth century and developed an audacious meta- or master-narrative, an overarching story intended to account for all of reality. His metanarrative recounted the movement of "spirit," Hegel's richly multifaceted concept encompassing individual and communal self-consciousness culminating in freedom. That Hegel's discourse on spirit and freedom is marked by Germanic ethnocentrism and Orientalism will become clear.[2] What is perhaps not self-evident is the extent to which the colonialist flaws of Hegel's project find echoes even today.

HEGEL'S TIMES AND INTELLECTUAL PASSION

Hegel was born into the Holy Roman Empire in 1770 and it was gone well before he died in 1831. So Hegel was born into a world of unprecedented change in

283

Europe, caused by conflict within the collapsing Holy Roman Empire and by the subsequent seizure of German territory by French Republican armies under Napoleon. He writes to a colleague: "I am about to be fifty years old, and have spent thirty of these fifty years in these ever-unrestful times of hope and fear."[3] These times began shortly after Hegel enrolled in seminary at the University of Tübingen where in 1789 the French Revolution changed everything for him. There is truth in the observation that "there is no other philosophy that is a philosophy of revolution to such a degree and so profoundly, in its innermost drive, as that of Hegel."[4]

This drive is evident from his early seminary days where he was as consumed with the French Revolution and concepts of freedom as he was with his theological studies. He followed closely the events in France and longed for similar revolutionary expression in the German population. Although perhaps more legend than fact, fellow students at Tübingen recount Hegel and his friends erecting a "freedom tree" on the fourteenth of July in commemoration of the storming of the Bastille. Throughout his life he celebrated Bastille Day—that "glorious dawn"—much to the astonishment of his fellow Germans.[5] For Hegel, the French Revolution represented a decisive historical moment because it embodied the initial political attempt to achieve consciously the freedom of every individual.

Like other German intellectuals during this period, Hegel associated the spirit of freedom of the French Revolution with the Protestant Reformation (with its emphasis on subjective inner freedom) and saw both as crucial moments of spiritual renewal and social betterment. However, Hegel eventually became disillusioned with French culture and enamored of his own German culture. As one postcolonial cultural critic has written, "the narrative of 'German' cultural representation, within the Western European context, is ...one of difference."[6] Hegel plays out this notion of German difference (and preeminence) by contrasting the development of spirit in Germany not only with European colonies but also the rest of Western Europe, and especially France and its revolution. Ultimately, it rests with "the German Spirit" to be the bearer of spirit in its fullness. The service of the German culture to the "World-Spirit was that of not merely possessing the Idea of Freedom ...but of producing it in free and spontaneous developments," reaching the highest period of spirit from the time of the "Reformation to our own times." While non-Germanic Europe of the sixteenth century was preoccupied with economic and political expansion, Hegel argues that

Martin Luther took the lead in matters of spirit, discerning that Christ "is not to be regarded as merely a historical person," but that "*all mankind*" has "*an immediate relation to him in Spirit.*" The "essence" of the Reformation was that "Man is in his very nature destined to be free," or, put differently, "Christian Freedom is actualized" in principle.[7]

In light of Hegel's estimation of the German Protestant Reformation, along with his youthful hopes of the French Revolution, the brutal and repressive "reign of terror" that followed the Revolution was deeply sobering for Hegel. In the name of freedom, frenzied revolutionary agents tore down the civic structures that made civic freedom possible. What was left, Hegel tells us in the *Phenomenology of Spirit* (1807), was an undeveloped form of freedom whose "sole work and deed" was "the coldest and meanest of all deaths, with no more significance than cutting off a head of cabbage,"[8] suggesting the horrific yet indifferent image of the guillotine.

Reflecting on this passage from the *Phenomenology* some seven years later, Hegel observed that the "Absolute freedom—which I had previously described as the purely abstract formal freedom of the French Revolution . . . —passes out of its own self-destructive actuality over into *another land,*" namely Germany.[9] One biographer restates Hegel's point nicely when he comments that in this crucial section of the *Phenomenology,* "the Revolution had now officially passed to [Germany] that would complete 'in thought' what the Revolution had only partially accomplished in practice—as it were, that the 'novel of the Revolution' was to be completed by German philosophy, not by French politics."[10] Hegel was not giving up on politics in favor of philosophy; rather he concluded that the aftermath of the French Revolution proved that the French lacked an adequate philosophical principle to serve as the basis of civil society and the state. Hegel was convinced that "the consciousness of the Spiritual" must be "the essential basis of the political fabric."[11]

With this full "consciousness of the spiritual," we have as close as anything to the lifelong heart of Hegel's intellectual passion—namely, developing a system of thought that united the best of religion and philosophy with the best insights about socioeconomic and political life. The first thing to observe about this system of thought is that God is everywhere related to it, as Hegel describes in this mind-blowing introduction to his 1824 *Lectures on the Philosophy of Religion*:

> God is the beginning of all things and the end of all things; [everything] starts from God and returns to God. God is the one and only object of philosophy. [Its concern is] to occupy itself with God, to apprehend everything in God,

to lead everything back to God, as well as to derive everything particular from God and to justify everything only insofar as it stems from God, is sustained through its relationship with God, lives by God's radiance and has [within itself] the mind of God.[12]

Elsewhere Hegel describes this going forth and returning of the divine as spirit (*Geist*): "an eternal process of self-cognition, dividing itself into the finite flashes of light of individual consciousness, and then re-collecting and gathering itself up out of this finitude—inasmuch as it is in the finite consciousness that the process of knowing spirit's essence takes place and that the divine self-consciousness thus arises."[13] God is the beginning (premise) of all things and the end (telos) of all things as spirit. The eternal essence of God as eternal idea (abstract spirit), manifested concretely in human subjectivity (finite subjective spirit) and society (finite objective spirit), moves toward fullness and reconciliation in the sublation of difference (absolute spirit). As one commentator describes it, the "emergent subjectivity of both individual human beings and the human community are elements in the becoming of the divine (inter)subjectivity."[14] This emergent subjectivity is the process of becoming more and more explicitly self-conscious and self-determining in history. Hegel's overarching philosophical project is squarely theological—namely, to render the relation between both eternal idea and finite spirit in the reality of God as absolute spirit. Hegel interprets finite spirit's rise to the absolute in terms of the Christian trinitarian imagery of Father (identity), Son (difference) and Spirit (identity-in-difference). The essential truth of the Christian Trinity discloses in image or representation *(Vorstellung)* the truth of life itself—a truth that philosophy grasps fully in terms of its essential concept or idea *(Begriff)*. Hence Christianity is the "consummate" or "absolute" representational fulfillment of religion, just as "absolute knowing" is the conceptual fulfillment of reason. As such, philosophy and consummate religion are, for Hegel, the final standards by which to evaluate the development of spirit in religions, cultures, and emerging self-consciousness generally—because philosophy and consummate religion also are the inner spiritual and rational principle at work in the world.

The philosopher's task of comprehending "what is," as Hegel put it, entails identifying this emergence of self-consciousness and freedom in individual human beings and community. The bulk of Hegel scholarship has focused on this vast intellectual project, but we should also linger a bit on Hegel's other observation that every philosopher is a "child of his time." Even the concrete shape of Hegel's intellectual ambition—the modern metanarrative form it takes—very much reflected his European and particularly German cultural milieu (and he unabashedly admitted that). Moreover, as I will develop in the rest of this chapter, Hegel's Eurocentrism suffused his developmental schema of the unfolding of spirit that served as a broad conceptual framework for his interpretation of the "Other" in religion, history, and politics.[15] This Eurocentric account of the movement of spirit conveniently fits with his forthright justification of colonialist economic and political interests.

SPIRIT'S MOVEMENT FROM EAST TO WEST

Armed with the metanarrative of absolute spirit and the category of "universal history," Hegel sets out to evaluate religions and cultures more generally in terms of their contribution to the development of spirit. In his *Phenomenology of Spirit,* along with his *Lectures on the Philosophy of Religion* and *Lectures on the Philosophy of History*, Hegel endeavors to show "the development of the consciousness of Freedom on the part of Spirit, and the consequent realization of that Freedom." Moreover, this "development implies a gradation—a series of increasingly adequate expressions or manifestations of Freedom, which results from its Idea."[16] Given the close association of the history of religion and the history of cultures, it is not surprising that the concrete gradations of the consciousness of freedom on the part of spirit present themselves similarly in both historical accounts.

Roughly speaking, Hegel envisions the gradations of the development of spirit as a movement from east to west: China, India, Persia, Israel, Egypt, Greece, Rome, Western Europe. Within this geographical movement, Hegel identifies shifts in the development of religious consciousness and culture more generally. Hegel offers a phenomenology of the development of religion from primitive magic and more sophisticated "nature religions" of the East to the higher religions of spiritual subjectivity (Jewish, Greek, and Roman) in the West, ultimately consummated in the religion fully revelatory of spirit, namely Christianity. This evolutionary and hierarchical development interprets non-Christian religions as inadequate realizations or prefigurations of true religion itself, which Hegel defines as "the idea of spirit that relates itself to itself, *the self-consciousness of absolute spirit*" or, put differently, "the self-knowing of divine spirit through the mediation of finite spirit." In other words, religion is not simply finite consciousness of the infinite but also the self-consciousness of absolute spirit mediated through finite consciousness—

only fully represented religiously in the Christian trinitarian and incarnational language. Non-Christian religions "are not indeed *our* religion," Hegel suggests to his Christian audience; "yet they are included in ours as essential though subordinate moments. . . . Therefore in them we have to do not with what is foreign to us but *with what is our own*, and the recognition that this is so is the reconciliation of true religion with false."[17]

Hegel begins with the lower stages of the development of spirit in Asia wherein, he explains, "arose the Light of Spirit," and where he believes "the history of the World" began. The so-called Oriental World—"antique as well as modern"—has as its "inherent and distinctive principle" what Hegel describes as the "Substantial" or "Prescriptive" in ethos. By this he mean that we have the "first example" of the subjugation of arbitrary will expressed in laws. However this first example is not conscious of the subjectivity of spirit and, hence, "Oriental" law is but an external force: "[n]othing subjective in the shape of disposition, Conscience, formal Freedom, is recognized." To clarify this point, Hegel tells his German students that "[w]hile *we* obey, because what we are required to do is confirmed by an *internal* sanction, there [in the Orient] the Law is regarded as inherently and absolutely valid without a sense of the want of this subjective confirmation."[18] Since spirit has not yet attained subjectivity, it remains bound to the conditions of nature. Hegel associates this form of spirituality with "immediate religion" or "nature religion."[19]

While Hegel presents the Oriental World as characterized as a whole by "nature religion" and the nonrecognition of the absolute as free spirit, he generates comparisons that reveal the evolutionary and hierarchical development of culture within his philosophy. The Chinese culture is the least developed and its "distinguishing feature" is that everything associated with spirit properly so-called (unconstrained morality, inward religion, science, art) "is alien to it." Individuals attain no subjective freedom because there is no freedom of separation. In this respect, Hegel identifies an "essential advance" made in India where individual differences emerge but the distinctions themselves "are referred to Nature" (as in a system of castes).[20] As such Indian culture represents a step toward but still falls short of self-consciousness of subjective freedom or inward morality.[21]

In contrast to the "Asiatic" character of the Chinese and Indians ("Farther Asia"), the Near East ("Hither Asia"), in Hegel's reading, belongs to "the Caucasian, i.e., the European Stock." The European visiting Persia finds himself to be "somewhat still at home, and meets with European dispositions, human virtues and human passions." Depending upon the iteration of Hegel's lectures on the philosophy of religion, Zoroastrianism is placed under the category of religions of nature or as a religion of transition from nature religion to spiritual religion and closely associated with Judaism. In Persia and its "religion of the Good" (Zoroastrianism), humans become subjectively free, occupying for the first time "a position face to face as it were with the Highest Being, the latter being made objective for him" in the form of the "Abstract Good" available to all. Hence, Hegel believed that in Persian culture, one can find "the principle of Free Spirit as contrasted with imprisonment in Nature."[22]

Virtually absent from Hegel's lectures on religion and history are both Islam and Africa, but for different reasons, both illuminating. Islam gets very little treatment in Hegel's lectures and plays a different role in his philosophy of religion than do the other historical religions. Hegel refers to "Islamic doctrine" as containing "merely the fear of God," as Islam was often described in modern Europe. Unlike other historical religions that foreshadow elements of Christianity as consummate religion, Islam is seen as something more akin to a deformation of it.[23] Islam, Hegel tells us, "is tolerated only in one corner of Europe through the jealousy of Christian Powers . . . and has retreated into Oriental ease and repose."[24] Africa and African religions get relatively more treatment than Islam but only to clarify that Africa does not belong to history and that African *religion*, "if we are willing to call it that," is hardly worthy of the designation religion.[25] What for Hegel constituted "Africa proper" was land "south of desert Sahara" (the rest of the continent being too associated with Europe or Asia). Africa did not make the grade of history and religion because Hegel deemed it to be almost completely associated with "nature" to the exclusion of spirit.[26] The African "character" has not emerged from nature in its "completely wild and untamed state," knowing nothing of "*our* ideas—the category of Universality." The African has realized no "substantial objective existence—as for example, God, or Law—in which the interest of man's volition is involved and in which he realizes his own being." Since the "basis of religious conceptions is the consciousness on the part of man of a Higher Power," Africa proper is not part of the world history of religion. [27]

As many Hegel scholars point out, Hegel may well have made more of an effort to learn about religions of the world (however misinformed he was about them) than other European thinkers of his day.[28] Nonetheless, it is evident, as one critic writes, that any "adequate analysis of Hegel's posture on history"—and I would add religion—needs to take into account "his prosecution of an ethnocentric perspective as if it were universal. To claim, as he did, that Africa, the birthplace of the oldest human civilizations, was devoid of morality and consequently ahistorical, was to demonstrate both an aggressive Eurocentrism and an ignorance of Africa."[29] Moreover the idea that world history and the history of religions can be viewed as a single process is profoundly suspect for all the reasons that metanarratives more generally have received philosophical and more generally cultural critique.[30]

That this evolutionary and hierarchical model is partially driven by Hegel's philosophical interests in grasping the development of spirit from the perspective of its consummation in Christianity and the German people is not in question.[31] Hegel's characterization of world religions is arguably also what one critic refers to as an "imperial/colonial model of religion." This colonialist model of religion means that "conquest provides the historical context for the emergence of a theory of religion that models the hierarchical, sociopolitical relations with native peoples in the Americas, Africa, Asia, Australia, and the islands of the Atlantic, Pacific, and Indian Oceans."[32] That colonialism does indeed provide the context for Hegel's broader discussions of cultures and religions is where we need to turn next.

COLONIALISM AND FREEDOM

Spirit, for Hegel, imbues all of life, not simply religion and culture understood in generalities. "Civil society," comprised of the institutions and practices entailed in the production of goods and services ("the *System of Needs*") and including the necessary protections of freedom required for that orderly production, is the social locus for the actualization of freedom and therefore is at the historical heart of spirit.[33] Hegel knew that for a philosophy of spirit to be at all relevant, it must take political economy into account, and especially the middle class as a crucial foundation of any modern state both in commercial enterprise and civil service.

In progressive liberal fashion, Hegel upheld the principles of individual autonomy, the rule of law, and the private ownership of property.[34] Freedom entails the right of property—one's body and possessions—because "a person must translate his freedom into an external sphere." Possession of property is essential for the satisfaction of needs, but its "true position," namely "from the standpoint of freedom," is that "property is the first embodiment of freedom." Given that the actualization of one's freedom is always in relation to the freedom of others, property-related "contracts" in which parties enter and, hence, recognize each other as persons and property owners (by virtue of "participation in a common will") are essential. A central aspect of the administration of justice in civil society involves the protection provided by the state of rights of private property.[35]

Hegel's theory of private property and civil society has been of central concern to "left-wing" Hegelians (e.g., Karl Marx), but for our immediate purposes we can grant his theory in order to examine critically the colonialist ramifications Hegel himself drew from it.[36] Socioeconomic inequality was a vexing problem for Hegel and he saw it as inevitably flowing from inequality of skill and inequality of unearned capital leading to extreme class divisions.[37] Hegel explains that the "inner dialectic" of civil society is such that its unimpeded domestic activity leads to expansion of population and industry wherein the "amassing of wealth is intensified" and the "largest profits are derived" resulting in "the concentration of disproportionate wealth in a few hands" and deep "distress" of the working class in the form of poverty and the "inability to feel and enjoy the broader freedoms and especially the intellectual benefits of civil society." Hence, a materially impoverished working class leads to an ethically impoverished "rabble."[38]

Hegel reflects upon ways to mitigate this structural inequality in Germany and Europe generally through the private and public sectors (e.g., private charity and philanthropy and public works projects for the unemployed), only to conclude that none provides a viable long-term solution to the problem of poverty whose root causes include economic unsustainability and the loss of "the feeling of individual independence and self-respect in its individual members." Hegel concludes that the only solution is for the state to turn outwards—that is, "to push beyond its own limits and seek markets, and so its necessary means of subsistence, in other lands which are either deficient in the goods its has overproduced, or else generally backward in industry, etc."[39] In short, the development of spirit in terms of socioeconomic freedom leads inevitably to colonialism.

Given Hegel's account of the development of spirit in religion and history, it should not be surprising that his account of the international dimension of the state resonates with his imperial/colonial model. Among the "civilized," states ought to respect treaties and, in principle, "one state should not meddle with the domestic affairs of another." This imperative applies to intra-European international relations because "[t]he European peoples form a family in accordance with the universal principle underlying their legal codes, their customs, and their civilization."

When it comes to "any people of a low level of civilization," however, Hegel tells us that "[t]he question arises how far" such a people "can be regarded as a state." His answer is consistent with his theory of the development of religion and history and the need for economic colonialism by European powers. "Civilized" European nations are justified in "treating as barbarians those who lag behind them. ...The civilized nation is conscious that the rights of barbarians are unequal to its own and treats their autonomy as only a formality."[40] As some critics have rightly observed, "[i]t is impossible ...not to link both Hegel's philosophical recuperation of the Other within absolute Spirit and his universal history leading from lesser peoples to its summit in Europe together with the very real violence of European conquest and colonialism."[41]

But that is not the end of the story. Political and economic colonialism, so Hegel suggest, leads (albeit indirectly) to the development of spirit in the colonized Other. This brings us back to Hegel's evolutionary and hierarchical model of religion and cultures. To the extent that Hegel thought that modern Europe was the purveyor of the fullness of spirit in religion and culture more generally, "commerce of this kind" (i.e., European colonialism) "is the most potent instrument of culture."[42] One critic has remarked that what is "silently left out of Hegel's assessment . . . is the fact that colonialism is . . . grounded on the destruction of non-European civilizations."[43] I would go even further. The notion of the destructiveness of colonialism per se is not "left out" by Hegel; within the framework of his metanarrative, it cannot actually even be logically thought. Recall Hegel's comment to his Christian audience regarding non-Christian religions (and we can add cultures more broadly): "we have to do not with what is foreign to us but *with what is our own,*" to the extent that non-Christian religions or cultures are partial realizations of spirit. As such, Western cultural imperialism cannot be thought of as destructive but only instructive—a potent catalyst for the full spiritual development of the undeveloped nations. With Hegel, one is candidly supplied with as totalizing and consistent a Eurocentric imperialist vision as one finds in the early nineteenth century.

IMPLICATIONS

From our historical position we can only assess Hegel's evolutionary, hierarchical, and colonial system as evidence of his own assertion that "every individual is a child of his time" and so "philosophy too is its own time apprehended in thoughts." We began by noting Hegel's audacity and candor. Indeed he articulates both his genius and the colonialist and Christocentric ethos of his age forthrightly. This could be seen as grounds for dismissing Hegel, but I contend that we should not because there are lessons we can learn from reading Hegel. Many postmodern critics have noted how deeply problematic Hegel's totalizing project is on both epistemological and ethical grounds.[44] Yet for all his totalizing ambitions driven by his need for making overarching sense of his chaotic historical moment, and for all his ethnocentric conviction that German culture's prized export to the rest of the world was the fullness of spirit, Hegel remained convinced of the philosopher's need for self-critique. Every thesis generates its antithesis; every synthesis is yet another thesis. What we get with Hegel, one might say, is totality but not finality.[45] Even his own vision of spirit must be submitted to a deconstructive moment that he calls "dismemberment": Spirit "wins its truth only when, in utter dismemberment, it finds itself."[46] This is the ironic dimension of Hegel's legacy for our postcolonial times. As left-wing Hegelians (including literally his own students as well as contemporary students of Hegel) recognize, his philosophical, cultural, political, and economic vision must also give way to his dialectical method.[47] I believe it is consistent with Hegel's method for us, as children of our own times, to continue the task of critical dismemberment vis-à-vis his conceptualization of spirit in world history.

Hegel on North America can be read as an illustration of this nonfinality. Unlike Europe, America was exempt, at least for the time, from the negative effects of private property "for it has the outlet of colonization constantly and widely open, and multitudes are continually streaming into the plains of Mississippi." (Presumably, Hegel did not consider the appropriation of Native American lands and the decimation of Native American peoples and cultures to be negative effects.) America thus presented for Hegel something of a mystery that exceeded the bounds of his conceptual frame of reference. North America, he concludes, is thus "the land of the future, where, in the ages that lie before us, the burden of the World's History shall reveal itself."[48] Hegel did not conceive of socioeconomic freedom in such a way that it could avoid colonialism, but he did seem to recognize that a modern society that generates a different economic dynamic might well present one with currently unimaginable possibilities.

Tarrying one final moment with Hegel, there is also a lesson that we—in Hegel's land of the future—can learn from reading Hegel. The challenge Hegel raises for those of us disturbed by his religious hierarchicalism, Orientalism, Eurocentrism, colonialism—in short, his imperial/colonial model—is that although our early twenty-first century high cultural veneer of political correctness keeps us from the audacious and forthright advocacy of this model, we often nonetheless continue to live by it in many spheres. The inordinate wealth of the United States exists by virtue of the economic and political colonialism of late capitalism, as we are reminded by contemporary left-wing Hegelians. Contemporary Christian theology remains, for the most part, even more exclusivistic than Hegel's. Orientalist Western imperialism is the cultural basis of much of our foreign policy (e.g., the Bush administration's Iraq policy or U.S. foreign aid policy generally). The irony is that any critical judgment we cast on Hegel—and no doubt we should—comes back doubly as a critical judgment on ourselves.

FURTHER READING

Primary Sources

Hegel, G. W. F. *Lectures on the Philosophy of Religion*. Edited by Peter C. Hodgson. Berkeley, Calif.: University of California Press, 1988.

———. *The Philosophy of History*. Translated by J. Sibree. New York, N.Y.: Willey Book Co., 1944.

———. *Philosophy of Right*. Translated by T. M. Knox. Oxford: Clarendon Press, 1942.

Secondary Sources

Avineri, Shlomo. *Hegel's Theory of the Modern State*. Cambridge: Cambridge University Press, 1972.

Hodgson, Peter C., ed. *G. W. F. Hegel: Theologian of the Spirit*. Minneapolis, Minn.: Fortress Press, 1997.

Pelczynski, Z. A., ed. *Hegel's Political Philosophy: Problems and Perspectives*. Cambridge: Cambridge University Press, 1971.

Pinkard, Terry. *Hegel: A Biography*. Cambridge: Cambridge University Press, 2000.

Taylor, Charles. *Hegel*. Cambridge: Cambridge University Press, 1975.

Chapter 21

Søren Kierkegaard

Edward P. Antonio

Søren Aabye Kierkegaard was born on May 5, 1813 in Copenhagen, Denmark. He died on November 11, 1855. He was the last of seven children. His father, Michael Pedersen Kierkegaard (1756-1838) was a wool merchant. In 1830 Kierkegaard entered the University of Copenhagen, where he studied theology, philosophy, and literature. His literary output was enormous. It included an assortment of topics and subjects ranging from theology, literature, aesthetics, and philosophy to what today would be described as psychology. His methods of writing and communication were also hugely varied and included polemic parody, humor, rhetoric, irony, satire, and the famous method of "indirect communication." As we shall see later, he employed some of these methods in his critique of Christendom.[1]

At the time of Kierkegaard's birth, Denmark had long been a part of the economic, religious, and political culture of Europe. Economically, like other European nations, Denmark was mercantilist in outlook and practice. The extensive overseas trade of the Danish East India Company served as one example of this. Politically, though initially neutral, by 1810 Denmark had become an important part of the continental system contrived by Napoleon.[2] Denmark fully participated in the imperializing and colonizing activities, which characterized much of Europe's relationships to non-Europeans. Driven by the desire to expand its overseas trade, it acquired territories and established colonies in India at places such as Tranquebar (Fort Dansborg) (1620), Balasore (1763), Serampore (1755), and the Nicobar Islands, also known as *Frederik Øerne*. Within Europe itself, at first with Norway and later on its own, Denmark had an imperial or colonial relationship with the Faroe Islands. From the seventeenth to the early part of the twentieth century, Denmark held the Caribbean islands of St. Thomas (1671), St. Jan (1718) and St. Croix as imperial possessions. St. Croix was bought from France in 1733. In 1917 the islands were sold to the United States and became part of the Virgin Islands of the United States.[3] Denmark may have had no economic or political need for these islands (and others of her imperial colonies), and acquired them largely to imitate Holland and England.[4] Yet it is clear that all three were essential to the trade in sugar and the supply of slave labor. In this, Denmark was like other imperial powers such as France, Spain, England, Holland, and Portugal.[5] If we add to this both the presence of Christianity at home and the missionary factor in the imperial expansion of Denmark, then the list of the elements which helped to integrate Denmark into the culture of Europe is complete.

Kierkegaard lived during the Danish Golden Age, a period of great literary and artistic production which witnessed the works of such figures as Adam Oehlenschläger, Thomasine Gyllembourg, J. L. Hiberg, Hans Christian Andersen, Nikolai Frederik Severin Grundtvig, and many others including Kierkegaard himself. Many of these leading literary and cultural figures were conservative.

Given this background, the problem is how to deal with Kierkegaard's silence on imperialism. To resolve this, I offer an interpretation of some of Kierkegaard's works, which suggests an understanding of aspects of his thought, which may be construed as to imply a critique of empire. True, Kierkegaard had nothing directly to say about empire, but his work is interesting not only because it took place against the background of an imperial nation, but also because it contains a trenchant critique of modernity taken by some to represent an incipient "social critical theory," which culminated in his famous attack upon Christendom. It is this critique of modernity I want to explore here as a basis for arguing that some of Kierkegaard's ideas might be relevant for a critical analysis of certain social features of empire.

Kierkegaard's "critical social theory" performed at least three functions: First, he used it to uncover, reveal, and contest the problematic aspects of modernity and its impact on Danish society. Second, he used it to analyze the barriers modernity threw in the path of social transformation. Third, because it was inspired by a deep religious and moral vision of the world, Kierkegaard used his critical theory to articulate and promote a vision of Christianity as a viable alternative to the social malaise of modernity.

There are three areas of his thought and work that illustrated the development of his critical social theory: his assessment of the press in modernity, his critique of the public or of mass society, and his attack upon Christendom. Accordingly, I first look at his *Early Polemical Writings*, which express his initial view of the press. I also briefly examine the *Corsair Affair*, perhaps representing the most decisive moment in Kierkegaard's view of the press. Then I make some remarks on Kierkegaard's examination and critique of modernity in the *Two Ages: The Age of Revolution and the Present Age, a Literary Review* (1846). This is followed by a short discussion of his theology of love in *Works of Love* (1847) and two crucial texts, which anticipate a full, systematic, and sustained critique of Christendom made in *Attack Upon "Christendom"* (1854-55). These texts are: *Concluding Unscientific Postscript* (1846), considered by some the greatest of his works, and *The Point of View* (written in 1848 but published posthumously in 1859). I conclude by looking at *Attack Upon "Christendom"* and by suggesting some of the ways in which, while deeply ambiguous, Kierkegaard's critical social theory provides hints for a method of identifying and examining modernity's problematic social and political formations, including those that inhabit and sustain empire.

THE EARLY POLEMICAL WRITINGS AND THE *CORSAIR AFFAIR*

Kierkegaard was concerned about social and political issues from very early on as his *Early Polemical Writings,* (1834-1838) illustrate. As a student in the mid-1830s he was already critically addressing issues pertaining to journalism, literature, women, equality, freedom, and idealist philosophy, issues that continued to preoccupy his mind in later years. Although there was little by way of theology or religious commentary in these early works, Kierkegaard's emerging "ethical" voice was clearly unmistakable. Of course, for Kierkegaard, theology is inseparable from his consideration of social problems. Below I shall discuss aspects of his theology of love, which are relevant to his critique of modernity. Here I see journalism as an important entry point into a discussion of his social critique.[6]

The clearest example of his critique of the press is doubtlessly contained in his reaction to the *Corsair Affair*. The *Corsair* was a satirical journal that lampooned prominent members of society, the King, government officials, clergy, and intellectuals. Being a supporter of cultural elitism and of the monarchy, Kierkegaard disliked both the journal's lack of respect for public figures and its liberalism. He regarded it as immoral and was not happy that his own work had been positively reviewed in its pages. He had not himself been subject to the journal's satire but the public expression of his displeasure precipitated a feud with the "editors" of the journal, which started in late 1845 and continued for months. The journal subjected Kierkegaard to continuous ridicule through cartoons, innuendo, and outright mockery. His personality, physical appearance (one of his legs was shorter than the other), and his dress, especially his trousers, were singled out. He became an object of public derision.

The *Corsair Affair*, as it has come to be called, "had momentous effects on his life and work."[7] What exactly was the nature of Kierkegaard's critique of the *Corsair* and of the press? Kierkegaard's critique of the *Corsair* was fourfold: first, because it attacked, vilified, and defamed people it had no conscience or moral scruples. Second, that as "the most widely read paper in the country" it abused its popularity.[8] Third, Kierkegaard worried that the paper was causing great public damage by "seducing the innocent," the "unstable," the "sensate" and the "irresponsible." Fourth, Kierkegaard was critical that the paper was driven by commercial interest, by "the rattle of money in the cash box."[9]

He thought of all this as literary prostitution representing national demoralization, public indifference, and lack of depth. Concern over public indifference was part of his critique of the very notion of "the public." Indeed, one of the profound aspects of his denunciation of the press was the connection he made between the press and the emergence of "the rabble," "the multitude," "the crowd," "the mass," and "the public." Kierkegaard picked this up in the *Two Ages* published in March of 1846 during the time of the *Corsair Affair*, and around the same time when one of his major works, *Concluding Unscientific Postscript* (which began to systematize his attack upon Christendom), came out.

TWO AGES

I said earlier that one of the tasks Kierkegaard assigned his social theory was that of identifying and diagnosing his social and historical situation. This is clearly apparent in the *Two Ages*. The book is an extended review of *Two Ages*, a novel by Thomasine Gyllembourg, a leading conservative literary figure of the Danish Golden Age.

In his review Kierkegaard compares the age of revolution (the French Revolution) and his own (present age). His preference is clearly for the former. What he admires about the age of revolution is not its politics, its appeal to human rights, freedom, equality, and its violent methods (regicide, for example), but its passion and zeal. Passion is an important theological and philosophical category in

Kierkegaard's thought. It stands for his view of subjectivity (the self) as well as his understanding of the nature of ethics; it is as much a function of knowledge as it is about faith understood as suffering passion.[10] Passion, then, has many dimensions. In the *Two Ages,* passion—which Kierkegaard defines as, among other things, "the tension and resilience of the inner being" or as "essential inwardness"— is what endows the age of revolution with form and dynamism, it is the expression of the essence of its culture. It is a source of cultural refinement, personal development, moral stamina, and social propriety. Although the age of revolution was marked by violence and brutality (and went astray in this sense), it is the *idea* behind passion that defines the latter's true identity and not these outward or external aberrations. "However externally oriented his ambitions, the person who is essentially turned inward because he is essentially impassioned for an idea is never crude."[11] In the age of revolution it is still possible to take a principled stand against social evil or to be under the claim of an idea for which it is worth dying. In contrast, however, the present age is "essentially a *sensible, reflecting age, devoid of passion, flaring up in superficial, short-lived enthusiasm and prudentially relaxing in indolence.*"[12] Here Kierkegaard expresses his opposition to the increasing colonization of everyday life by reflection or reason, the "rational" calculus of official, pragmatic rules.[13] The "calculating shrewdness," inventive, and technical skills of modernity produce dizzying "mirages" and "flares of enthusiasm," which feed upon a negative use of power hiding behind "proposed formal changes" in society. For Kierkegaard, there is no aspect of life, not even suicide, which is not subject to reflection. Perhaps anticipating Max Weber's notion of the iron cage, Kierkegaard describes this aspect of modernity as a prison in which the individual and the age are incarcerated.[14]

Furthermore, reflection breeds indolence, inaction, and misplaced pleasure, and diversionary entertainment. The immediate cause of indolence and social inaction is characterized in the *Two Ages* in terms of indecision. The idea of decision, to which the notion of indecision is obviously related, is central in Kierkegaard's thought. He says of it: "decision is the little magic word that existence respects."[15] The idea of "decision" is crucial to his critique of Christendom and is a key element in his understanding of the nature of authentic Christianity. In *Two Ages,* however, he is concerned with indecision. Indecision is a function of both "reflection" and modernity's obliteration of what he calls the "principle of contradiction." This is the principle that enables recognition of good and evil and thus ethical decision. Something is either good or it is evil. There is no middle ground.

A striking aspect of Kierkegaard's analysis of modernity is his critique of money. He writes: "But an age without passion possess no assets; everything becomes, as it were, transactions in *paper money*," or again, "So ultimately the object of desire is money, but it is in fact token money, an abstraction."[16] The manner in which *paper money* dominates and controls life, observes Kierkegaard, has become the model on which conversation, human relationships, and ethical values are all based. Terms like *paper money* or *token money* describe a situation in which the true nature of ethical value is overturned by being traded for money and thus evacuated of all content.[17] In addition to being dominated by money, this is also an age of envy, which fails to recognize the hero, the knight of faith, and the great humanitarian.[18]

This, then, is an age under the rule of reflection, envy, and money. To be sure, these are not the only defining characteristics of the age. Indeed, the *Two Ages* provides a long list of many other features such as the public, leveling, etc., illustrating lack of passion and inwardness in religion and politics.[19]

Let me conclude this section by briefly looking at the three markers of modernity just mentioned. All three are closely related to each other in Kierkegaard's thought. However, envy is the key to understanding the operations of all the other defining traits of modernity.[20] Kierkegaard says that "*envy* becomes the *negatively unifying principle in a passionless and very reflective age*."[21] Envy is the principle through which reflection organizes human relationships. Its opposite is admiration. In an age of passion the crowd is able to admire those who take risks and display their courage and skill in the face of danger or those who have made some great achievement. Relationships in this environment are driven by the ethics of understanding, sympathy, and the ability to participate in and celebrate the achievements of others.[22] In modernity, by contrast, relationships are defined by competition and resentment against excellence.

The logic of envy consists in the requirement to reduce all human effort to one common denominator so that no one single achievement is judged superior to any other. Since reflection, inaction, and indecision are everywhere, the age no longer privileges ethical and religious striving. It puts everyone and everything on the same level. It homogenizes and equalizes all relationships by making them interchangeable. Kierkegaard writes: "Envy in the process of establishing itself takes the form of leveling . . ."[23] For Kierkegaard, leveling "is a quiet, mathematical abstraction," which leads to depersonalization and loss of individuality and character.

"The trend today is in the direction of mathematical equality, so that in all classes about so and so many uniformly make one individual."[24]

Kierkegaard stressed the abstract nature of this process, the fact that it was not the work of any particular individual but the result of "a negatively superior force," which Kierkegaard describes as a demon. It is a runaway process, which no one can stop, not even society itself, since it is already in the service of leveling. To emphasize the point one more time Kierkegaard holds the idea of the "public" responsible for the logic of leveling. The public, itself a phantom or abstraction and the motivating principle of leveling, is the condition of possibility for the manifestation of envy as a demand for sameness. Kierkegaard's complaint against the public is that it is nothing and everything, all at once. It is the most dangerous and the most vacuous creation of modernity. Kierkegaard's assault on the notion of the public here recalls his attack on the press during the *Corsair Affair*. In the *Two Ages* he singles out the public as a creature of the press, i.e., as a phenomenon produced by the press or by the age of publicity. He availed himself of an assortment of terms to describe the public, terms such as "the herd," "the crowd," "the multitude," "the assemblage," etc. Of course, these are terms that even as he was diagnosing and criticizing the reality he thought they represented, were increasingly gaining critical currency in political theory and were becoming associated with the notion of democracy.

In this part of the discussion, I have dwelt at length on various aspects of Kierkegaard's critical social theory and have not said much about his theology or his understanding of Christianity. It is not easy or even possible to separate Kierkegaard's critique of modernity from its religious moorings. Nevertheless, Kierkegaard has a clear theological response, which is scattered throughout his writings and takes many different forms. Here I focus on his book *Works of Love*. This book is interesting because it deals theologically with some of the same themes Kierkegaard addresses ethically in the *Two Ages*, themes such as love, change, and interpersonal relationships.

In this book Kierkegaard presents his view of true, authentic love as the principle of stability, the anchor against the shifting sands of modernism and ultimately as the only secure mode of comporting oneself in the face of the modernist onslaught. In developing his theology/ethics of love Kierkegaard begins from an exposition of Matthew 22:39, which is Christ's command to love one's neighbor as oneself. The book opens with a prayer in which he identifies God as the source of all love. God, for Kierkegaard, is eternal love. He says that outside of God it is not possible to speak of love. His reference to the eternal character of this love will emerge as a serious theological critique of temporal or preferential love. In his exposition of the above Scripture Kierkegaard makes it clear that Christ's command involves a basic symmetry. One is to love oneself as one's neighbor. The first part of this is not about self-love precisely because this is what is excluded by the second part of the command—to love the neighbor as oneself. By the same token, love of neighbor as oneself is not an invitation to love the neighbor more than oneself. This too is a distortion of the command.

Kierkegaard warns against mistaking this love of the neighbor for erotic love or the love one has for one's friends and family. He calls this preferential love.[25] The trouble with this kind of love is that it is subject to temporality and thus is always vulnerable to change. This is love without "enduring continuance."

Over and against change and changeability Kierkegaard posits eternity as the source of true love. Kierkegaard repeatedly contrasts a love that is subject to temporality and one that is secured by eternity.[26] His point is to establish that true love for self and neighbor is a duty (as in Christ's command "thou shall . . ."), which becomes so by undergoing the change of eternity. Thus he writes: "But the love that has undergone the change of eternity by becoming duty does not know jealousy . . ." or again, "Only the eternal and, therefore that which has undergone the change of eternity by becoming duty is the unchanging. . . ."

It is important to point out here that Kierkegaard is not rejecting or criticizing change because he thinks it is inherently destructive. He is not criticizing some metaphysical idea of change. Rather the repeated and ubiquitous contrasts between temporal change and "the change of eternity" have a specific historical and social target. In these statements Kierkegaard is reacting to the manner in which the forces of modernity imposed destructive changes on every aspect of life. He is after a theology/ethics that will provide endurance and security in the midst of radical social or historical change. That this is not a far-fetched reading of Kierkegaard can be seen from how he makes love that has become a duty through the change of eternity a critique of jealousy (recall his critique of the role of the parallel concept of envy in modernity) or how such love dislodges habit (he describes the obsession with principle in modernity much along the lines of his description of habit in *Works of Love*).

But the clearest application of his theology/ethics of love to a concrete social problem he has already discussed in the *Two Ages* is his critique of equality. In the latter work Kierkegaard has complained against the leveling effects of modernity; he has rejected its creation of false equality, and he has denounced the idea of mass society or the many. However, *Works of Love* provides a different picture. Here Kierkegaard poses the question, "Who is my neighbor?", and answers it in a way that reconstitutes the "many" and redefines equality. Once again, the neighbor is not just one's beloved, one's family, or those in one's spatial proximity. The neighbor is a "multiplicity" (this is Kierkegaard's term); it is "all people." One of the striking features of this is that Kierkegaard makes the neighbor endure through space and time. Friends and family come and go but the neighbor remains constant. Furthermore, in *Works of Love* Kierkegaard arrives at a theological anthropology according to which the temporal differences of rank, status, gender, and wealth are matters of outward appearance and thus conceal the essential humanity of each person. Because of Christ's command to love the neighbor "we are all unconditionally like each other" or again "Dissimilarity is temporality's method of confusing that marks every human being differently but, the neighbor is eternity's mark on every human being."[27] How is this relevant to our discussion of empire? It is relevant because the new global imperialism has given rise to enemy combatants, to a grammar of "us" and "them"; it is marked by the presence of "terrorists" and other politically criminalized groups. Ours is also a world marked by genocide, xenophobia, and hatred of gays and lesbians. In this context Kierkegaard's theology of love raises the question of how to apply such love socially and politically. Is love not the basis of any genuine social and political Christian commitment to change the world?[28]

Attack Upon Christendom[29]

Before concluding this essay by looking at what Kierkegaard's critique might teach us about how to think ethically and theologically or religiously in an age that fancies itself as an imperium, let me briefly consider how he implemented his social critique in a specifically Christian or theological direction. He did this in his famous *Attack Upon "Christendom"* (1854-55), a series of writings carrying that title. It is important to emphasize here that *Attack Upon "Christendom"* is an extension of his social critique. In it he applies to the church and to church politics the same diagnosis he has already applied to society. In other words, he interrogates the impact of reflection, publicity, money, envy, leveling, in short, the impact of modernity, on the church. What this means is that we should not attempt to read the "attack" outside of the overall structure and development of Kierkegaard's thought. Moreover, because of its explicitly "theological" orientation the attack reminds us that Kierkegaard is not just a "negative" diagnostician of the present age: in between his diagnoses he produced works—such as *Edifying Discourses, Works of Love, Practice in Christianity, The Gospel of our Suffering, Either/Or* and *Concluding Unscientific Postscript*—in which he put forward his own answer or solution to the problem of modernity.

The particularities that precipitated Kierkegaard's final attack do not concern me here.[30] My interest is in his view of the true nature of Christianity. For in the end, that is the larger context within which the particular controversies that launched the attack must be placed. Kierkegaard thought that true Christianity is a matter of "inwardness" involving the decisive conversion of the individual to Christ, a conversion in which one gains a new existence lived in and through the intensity of passion. But this view turned out to be at odds with the self-understanding of the Lutheran church which held that one was a Christian merely by being born Danish and baptized Lutheran. For Kierkegaard such a view was against New Testament Christianity and could be possible only because the church had become too identified with the Danish state and with Danish society. It was this unity of church and state which produced a kind of civil religion in which to be a citizen of Denmark automatically meant to be Christian. In *The Point of View for My Work as an Author* (written in 1848 but published in 1859) Kierkegaard complains that all manner of people—"all these thousands and thousands," "[t]hese many many people"—including those who do not believe in God, call themselves Christian and are recognized as such by both the church and the state. He describes this situation as Christendom and attacks it as a prodigious illusion.[31] In Christendom one can live as a pagan (Kierkegaard's term) and still claim to be a Christian.[32] In the *Concluding Unscientific Postscript*, Kierkegaard described the idea that one was a Christian by simply being born Danish as "childish Christianity" or "childish orthodoxy." He reproaches "childish Christianity" because it is not based on any resolve to *become* a Christian. It is not a product of passionate, decisive commitment but the expression of being externally recognized by church and state.

Given all this, Kierkegaard's topmost task is that of reintroducing Christianity into Christendom. The basic question that drives his authorship in *The Point of View* and in *Concluding Unscientific Postscript*, is how to become a Christian in Christendom.[33] The structure of the attack consists of several things.

First, although the main thrust of the attack is religious it, nevertheless, is thoroughly situated in the context of his social critique of modernity. If up until now that critique has seemed to have no explicit theological or religious basis, in *The Point of View* Kierkegaard is clear that throughout the range of his work he has been concerned with not just the "aesthetic" or the "cultural" but that the "religious" has all along been the ground-motive of his analysis of modernity. In other words, Christendom was a religious figure standing in for modernity. Thus, for him, the problem of modernity was essentially a religious problem requiring a religious solution. What this tells us is that Kierkegaard saw reproduced in the church many of the very problematical contents of modernity he critiqued in his social polemic.

Second, Kierkegaard singles out the following features as being basic to Christendom and thus to modernity: the loss of passion, personal autonomy, individuality, and decisiveness. He sees this as a major consequence of the absence of true Christianity in Christendom. This loss of individuality is confirmed in his critique of mass society. The church has succumbed to the "multitude," it is a church of the "crowd," made up of the "herd," and as such, has been radically assimilated into the "public" or into society, more generally. It has become indistinguishable from the culture and social norms of Danish society.

Third, precisely because the public is an abstraction, by becoming so fully identified with it, the church itself becomes an abstraction. Again, to be an abstraction means to be without inner life or vitality. But a church that lacks these attributes can only be focused upon pure formalities and the external trappings of empty religious rites and practices. This is a reflection of three things; the bureaucratization of Christianity in which the church has become a social organization like any other with all the appurtenances of organizational rule, regulations, and hierarchy; the identification of church and state; and the lack of pathos or passion as consequences of all this. It is the totality of this situation that Kierkegaard attacked as Christendom.

Kierkegaard's concern was how to be truly Christian in this context. For him true Christianity, which he repeatedly identified with the teachings of the New Testament,[34] was incompatible with Christendom.

KIERKEGAARD AND EMPIRE TODAY

I now want to turn to the question of the relevance of all this to the problem of empire. Though Kierkegaard is silent on this problem it is nevertheless possible to make connections among aspects of his historical context on the one hand, and his social critique on the other, in such a way as to enable the application of his analysis and criticism of modernity to empire. I will briefly comment on three basic historical moments—Christianity, Christendom, and modernity—that formed the structural context of his work. Then I want to recover specific features of Kierkegaard's social critique in order to indicate some of the ways in which they may be applied to an analysis of empire today. With regard to these three moments of Kierkegaard's historical context mentioned above, it is important to emphasize the structure of the historical relationship of these three ideas: Christianity, Christendom, and modernity in nineteenth-century Europe. Kierkegaard's treatment of both Christianity and Christendom takes place against the background of modernity; in turn, the problem of modernity dialectically unfolds against the background of empire, and the problem of empire against that of modernity.

Given Kierkegaard's silence on imperialism, how do we apply his social critique to empire today? Two aspects of his critique can be recovered as a possible critique of empire: his critique of the press and his critique of illusion (ideology). However, in mentioning only these two aspects, it is important to remember that because Kierkegaard himself applied his social critique to a wide range of social phenomena, its extension to empire today need not be limited to an analysis of the role of the press or the media or just to "critique of ideology," narrowly understood.

Kierkegaard saw the press as an agent of modernity. But if modernity was itself implicated in imperialism, then it seems possible to extend this to the claim that the press was also an agent of empire and has continued to be such. Many people have noted how our so-called global era is dominated by the Western media. Films, newspapers, television, the internet, videos, and so forth are all largely in the hands of powerful Western corporations such as Disney, AOL Time Warner, Sony, Viacom, Vivendi, Bertelsmann, the BBC, and so on. This can be described in terms of "media imperialism." Central to the operation of the Western media in both Western and non-Western countries is the vigorous promotion of certain values linked to neo-liberalism and market capitalism. The imperialist dimension of the Western media is clearly evident in the manner in which, in the name of globalization, it markets these and other Western cultural values.

In his criticism of the *Corsair*, Kierkegaard identified several important features associated with the press of his day, which can be found also in today's media: the media is driven by logic of capital, or "commercial interest" as Kierkegaard called it, and the media plays an important role in creating and manipulating "public" opinion and thus the public itself. Furthermore, in his quarrel with the *Corsair*, Kierkegaard complained about the media showing disrespect through mockery and derision. This is not unlike the politics of representation practiced by much of the Western media today, involving the insulting, negative, and derogatory portrayals of others, such as Muslims, Africans, and other people.[35]

The second component of Kierkegaard's social critique that can be appropriated for an analysis of empire is his critique of "ideology." This refers to the role of "reflection" and of how the theological beliefs or teachings of the church had become distorted by being so totally integrated with the secular and political ideals of the state. Although Kierkegaard does not use the term "ideology," throughout his attack upon Christendom, he speaks of the state "misleading the people,"[36] "the optical illusion" (which gives the appearance of serving a nobler purpose when, in fact, it does the opposite), "seducing the youth,"[37] "newfangled religious assurances,"[38] and the "illusion of Christendom," and so on. What is noteworthy here is that, at least since the publication of Marx's *German Ideology* in 1845, some of these terms have in one way or another been associated with definitions of ideology in social and political theory. How does this apply to empire today? Imperialism today operates through a contorted logic in which moral beliefs, and political and legal ideas (our values or way of life) are thoroughly identified with Christianity. The nonsense about the so-called clash of civilizations belongs to this logic.[39] The lying, dissimulation, and misinformation that justified the invasion of Iraq are the clearest and most brazen examples of the operations of ideology of imperialism.

I could give more examples and discuss this at length. My point here is that Kierkegaard's "critique of ideology" reminds us that no meaningful criticism of social structures can be formulated if in the end it has no room for a critique of ideology. Indeed, the tasks that Kierkegaard assigned his social criticism would not have been possible without such a critique of ideology.

Further Reading

Primary Sources

Kierkegaard, Søren. *Attack upon "Christendom."* Translated by Walter Lowrie.
New Introduction by Howard A. Johnson. Princeton, N.J.: Princeton University Press, 1968.

_____. *Concluding Unscientific Postscript to Philosophical Fragments.* Kierkegaard's
Writings 12. Edited and translated by Howard V. Hong and Edna H. Hong.
Princeton, N.J.: Princeton University Press, 1992.

_____. *The Point of View.* Kierkegaard's Writings 22. Edited and translated by
Howard V. Hong and Edna H. Hong. Princeton, N.J.: Princeton University
Press, 1998.

_____. *Two Ages: The Age of Revolution and The Present Age, A Literary Review.*
Kierkegaard's Writings 14. Edited and translated by Howard V. Hong and
Edna H. Hong. Princeton, N.J.: Princeton University Press, 1978.

_____. *Works of Love: Some Christian Reflections in the Form of Discourses.* Translated by Howard V. Hong and Edna H. Hong. New York: Harper and Brothers, 1962.

Secondary Sources

Elrod, John W. *Kierkegaard and Christendom.* Princeton, N.J.: Princeton University Press, 1981.

Hannay, Alistair. *Kierkegaard: A Biography.* Cambridge: Cambridge University
Press, 2003.

Hannay, Alistair, and Gordon D. Marino. *The Cambridge Companion to Kierkegaard.* Cambridge: Cambridge University Press, 1998.

Rée, Jonathan, and Jane Chamberlain, ed. *Kierkegaard: A Critical Reader.*
Oxford: Blackwell, 1998.

CHAPTER 22

Frederick Douglass

Reginald F. Davis

Frederick Douglass (1818-1895) was one of the most conspicuous advocates of human rights in the nineteenth century.[1] He rose from obscurity as a slave to an awe-inspiring career as an eloquent national and international abolitionist lecturer, newspaper editor, successful author, recruiter for the Union army, statesman, and women's rights advocate. His biting jeremiads were directed not only toward the political platforms that kept the machinery of oppression operating, but also the hypocrisy of the church that was complicit in maintaining it.

DOUGLASS'S EARLY CONTEXT

Born in Tuckahoe, Maryland, in February 1817, Frederick Augustus Washington Bailey, later known as Frederick Douglass, was raised and nurtured in one of the most reprehensible institutions of crime known to humanity—slavery. Douglass was the son of an unknown white father and Harriet Bailey, a slave. His mother was never granted the opportunity to raise him herself and would walk several miles to visit him in Talbot County, Maryland. When Douglass was around seven, his mother died, and his grandparents became his caretakers. Around the age of eight, learning that his grandmother, her children, and he himself were not autonomous, but the possession of "Old Master," was psychologically distressing for Douglass. Douglass later wrote:

> The very first mental effort that I now remember on my part, was an attempt to solve the mystery, Why am I a slave? . . . When I saw the slave-driver whip a slave-woman, cut the blood out of her neck, and heard her piteous cries, I went away into the corner of the fence, wept and pondered over the mystery.[2]

Douglass experienced a major turning point in his life when he went to Baltimore, Maryland, and his new owner Sophia Auld began to teach him to read. Douglass quickly perceived that education and freedom were somehow related. Oppressors must control the thinking and actions of the enslaved if oppression is to survive. With this insight, Douglass wrote, "To make a contented slave, you must have a thoughtless one."[3]

At the age of thirteen, Douglass's religious thinking began to develop, and he sought to learn more about human freedom and bondage and why the two coexisted. A white Methodist minister convinced him that all human are sinners. Since all humans are sinners, why is it that one group of sinners are slaves to another group of sinners that are slave masters? Through critical reflection and analysis, Douglass concluded that God does not favor one human group over another; therefore, to accept slavery because all humans are sinners is to fall prey to paternalistic manipulation.

When the Aulds sent Douglass to Edward Covey, the "Negro-breaker," he was beaten, cut, and tormented. Douglass wondered if there was a God and questioned the providence of God. He decided his destiny would be in his own hands. His theistic posture of total dependence upon God gave way to a human-centered codetermination, a belief that humans work with God in deciding the course of events in history as a consequence of their freedom, which is endowed by God. Douglass resolved to defend himself against the brutality of Covey. Thus, he discarded the slave theology that yielded a quietist response: "My religious view on the subject of resisting my master had suffered a serious shock by the savage persecution to which I have been subjected, and my hands were no longer tied by my religion. . . . I had backslidden from this point in the slaves' religious creed."[4]

Though it was a risky venture, Douglass escaped from slavery in 1838 by impersonating a black sailor who had the permission to move about the country. Traveling by train to the free soil of the North, he contacted Anna Murray, a free woman from Baltimore whom he had met earlier. They married and moved to New Bedford, Massachusetts, and Douglass held various jobs to support the family. Soon Douglass met William Lloyd Garrison, the editor of the weekly journal *The Liberator*, who had spoken out against slavery and oppression. Before long Douglass was introduced to the abolitionists and for a while traveled with them and narrated his story of slavery. Crowds would gather to hear this black man speak on behalf of his cause. Douglass eventually parted with the Garrisonians for he desired to start his own anti-slavery newspaper. From Douglass's perspective, the time had come for the oppressed to speak for themselves. A group of British anti-slavery women raised funds that enabled Douglass to purchase a printing press. Relocating to the city of Rochester, New York, he prepared to establish his own publication, the *North Star*, and subsequently published a series of papers.

In July 1852, Douglass had the opportunity to point out America's inconsistency in religion and politics, and he did so with great passion and eloquence. Speaking on the fourth of July in Rochester, New York, Douglass said:

> Americans! Your republican politics, not less than your religion, are flagrantly inconsistent. You boast of your love of liberty, your superior civilization, and your pure Christianity, while the whole political power of the nation is solemnly pledged to support and perpetuate the enslavement of three million of your countrymen. . . .The existence of slavery in this country brands your republicanism as a sham, your humanity as a base pretense and your Christianity as a lie.[5]

Through his newspaper publications, autobiographies, and public speeches, Douglass seized every opportunity to crush the Christian enterprise of slavery and the theological, philosophical, and scientific rationale for maintaining it.

CIVIL WAR AND AFTERMATH

The Civil War was one of the darkest periods in American history. The divide over slavery set the nation at odds with itself. Paternalism and its religious justification were now threatened. Christian abolitionists vigorously stepped up their attack on slavery through literature and public discourse. Douglass was at the forefront of this atmosphere of militancy. The war he advocated would be long and bloody. Nevertheless, Douglass urged President Lincoln to draft and sign the Emancipation Proclamation. Without freedom for all, there could be no nation. The legislation was signed into law, bringing an end to legalized slavery. But Douglass was not satisfied with the abolition of slavery; he wanted the full citizenship rights of black people. Simply turning people loose after 200 years of slavery was not enough. Social programs needed to be put in place to lift up the enslaved from their long years of oppression.

Douglass held several important positions after the Civil War; among others, he was President of the Reconstruction-era Freeman's Savings Bank, marshal of the

District of Columbia, and counsel-general of the Republic of Haiti (1889-1891). He moved to Washington, D.C., in 1872 after his house on Rochester, New York was burned down—possibly due to arson. Throughout his career, he was an eloquent speaker and staunch supporter for women's rights and befriended such leaders as Ida B. Wells and Elizabeth Stanton. After Anna Murray Douglass died, Douglass married a white feminist, Helen Pitts, and their interracial marriage stirred quite a controversy. In February 1895, after returning home from a meeting of the National Council of Women in Washington, D.C., Douglass died of a sudden heart attack. Headlines around the country carried the news. A once obscure slave had risen to the status of a national symbol.

An Eloquent Voice against Oppression

Douglass's constant reading and reflection revealed how grossly Christianity was being used as a tool of oppression. He heard Southern ministers preach that it was the arrangement of providence that one group of people was made to do the thinking and another group the working. This arrangement, of course, meant that the black race was not on an equal ontological status with the white race, which Douglass saw as nonsensical, a religious maneuver to keep slaves docile. The great scheme was clear to Douglass: the slave masters and their divines perpetuated the horrible system of slavery. Religion and slavery for him were interlinked with each other.

The church could not be trusted; as Douglass witnessed, the church was the guarantor of the system of oppression. It abetted the entrenchment of a racialized society in which blacks were discriminated against in every way. Oppression formed America's religion, and Douglass was able to comprehend the particular tilt of American Christianity. It certainly was not neutral and impartial; in fact, as Douglass saw it, the church was on the side of the oppressors. He saw how American Christianity was contaminated by fraud, deception, and hypocrisy. Its whole theoretical framework was designed to perpetuate oppression. As a man in search of a theological perspective conducive to liberation, Douglass labored tenaciously to show that American Christianity was anti-human and diametrically opposed to the prophets of old and the gospel of Jesus Christ. He knew the biblical message meant liberation not only from the chains of slavery, but also from the functional theological framework of a religion that splits humanity into two groups and arranges them into a hierarchy of masters and slaves, males and females, superior and inferior, with the claim that God instigated such a dichotomy and, therefore, it is right, moral, and just.

Equally important is Douglass's understanding that the true gospel of Christ is for the poor and the oppressed. They are the object of God's love and concern, as embodied in the great redeemer who preached the gospel to the poor and came to set the captives free. Douglass's life was consumed with replacing the American Christianity of human captivity with the biblical gospel of human liberation. He would not accept any rationalization for slavery and oppression. American Christianity was too corrupt, too bloody, too racist, too sexist, and too filled with iniquity to be accepted as a compromise of the truth of the gospel of Christ. The two are incompatible, and Douglass hated with a passion "the corrupt, slaveholding, women-shipping, cradle-plundering, partial and hypocritical [religion] of this land"[6] because it advocated keeping the slave chains on rather than taking them off.

Douglass saw that human activity is central for one's salvation or liberation. Divine power has never removed evil from the world. Without human activity, the low and the vile in this world will continue to gain victory over the good and the spiritual side of humanity. Human progress and liberation have never been achieved apart from the actions and struggles of humans, and Douglass realized that slavery would not end by some divine power that would force people or nations to chart another course. Therefore, Douglass opted for counter-violence as a liberation tactic to stop human tyrannical force. He was convinced that counter-violence in defense of liberty is justified. Resistance to evil is a moral obligation. Those who believe in justice and don't wage any action to stop the evil that is destroying the republic are actually cooperating with it. Douglass was convinced that radical revolutionary activity was the only option left if the oppressed were to achieve freedom and justice. In fact, he saw revolution in this instance no differently than the revolution the founding fathers waged when they were oppressed by the British government.

Because of his philosophy of social reform, Douglass was often critical of the black church and its ministers. He thought that the energy put into spiritualizing oppression was a diversion of the energy needed to correct the present situation of oppression. The black church was too adapted to oppression, and it relegated liberation to an eschatological orientation that caused the black church to conform to rather than transform the present situation. Douglass saw that the black church "valued strong lungs rather than higher learning"[7] in its ministers. For Douglass, the black church had not done the necessary theological reconstruction that would free them from the stronghold of their psychological enslavement. Many of the ideas that the black church held about God were distorted and unrealistic in various respects. Douglass viewed the church and its idea of God in the same vein as Benjamin Mays later observed: "The Negro's social philosophy and his idea of God go hand in hand. . . . Certain theological ideas enable Negroes to endure hardship, suffer pain and withstand maladjustment, but . . . do not necessarily motivate them to strive to eliminate the source of the ills they suffer."[8]

Lost in an otherworldly or eschatological view of a better world, the oppressed neutralize any idea that promotes confrontation with oppressive structural institutions. Political encounters and social and economic challenges are discouraged due to the feeling of trepidation that things may get worst or that these activities are going against God's design and purpose. By believing all things are in the hands of God, the oppressed portray themselves as totally helpless, and view God as an almighty bellhop who is summoned to do for the oppressed what they choose not to do for themselves. Douglass felt that the black clergy had not done enough for social reform and had not been delivered from the priest-craft and superstition that had instilled a counterrevolutionary spirit, stifling social reform. Douglass understood that in order for a people to free themselves, they must first be freed from the conceptual system that controls their thinking. Until a reconstruction and decodification of the values that served to maintain oppression occurred, Douglass could not see the black church serving as an autonomous, viable institution that would uplift the downtrodden.

In addition to his criticism of the black clergy and their traditional religious beliefs, another thing that further alienated the clergy from Douglass was his stand for the equal rights of women. As an advocate of human liberation, Douglass fought just as hard for women's liberation as he did for black liberation. The same argument that justified the inferiority and enslavement of blacks was used to keep women oppressed and disenfranchised. Douglass knew that the liberation of women would require the same persistent agitation and organization as black liberation.

Douglass attended the Seneca Falls Convention in 1848, and was a signatory of the Declaration of Sentiments, which argued for the full rights of women as American citizens. He was far ahead of his contemporaries in understanding oppression and its effects on people, regardless of their race and gender. From the inception of his first publication, the *North Star* carried the slogan, "Right is of no sex." Douglass understood that sexism and racism were twin evils, one no less ominous than the other. Douglass saw the abolition of sexism as just as integral to the human rights struggle as was the abolition of racism. Rejecting traditional religious beliefs that supported male supremacy, Douglass accented that the struggle for women's rights "is the cause of human brotherhood as well as the cause of human sisterhood, and both must rise and fall together. Woman cannot be elevated without elevating man, and man cannot be depressed without depressing woman also."[9]

As a liberation visionary, Douglass perceived siding with oppressed women for their liberation as a moral duty. When no one else pleaded the cause of women's equality and justice, Douglass stood firm with the oppressed women. When others neglected to acknowledge women in the struggle for human liberation, Douglass did not fail to recognize them. In a letter to Harriet Tubman, Douglass honored her for her superior labors in the struggle against inhumanity:

> I have had the applause of the crowd and the satisfaction that comes of being approved by the multitude, while the most that you have done has been witnessed by a few trembling, scarred, and foot-sore bondmen and women, whom you have let out of the house of bondage, and whose heartfelt "God bless you" has been your only reward. . . . It is to me a great pleasure and a great privilege to bear testimony to your character and your works, and to say to those to whom you may come, that I regard you in every way trustful and trustworthy.[10]

It was no wonder that those who fought for women's rights and dignity mourned Douglass's death and paid tribute to him. Elizabeth Stanton's letter shows the loss that many felt at the passing of this great man:

> He was the only man I ever saw who understood the degradation of the disenfranchisement of women. Through all the long years of our struggle he has been a familiar figure on our platform with always an inspiring word to say. In the very first convention, he helped me to carry the resolution I had penned demanding woman suffrage. Frederick Douglass is not dead. His grand character will long be an object lesson in our National history. His lofty sentiments of liberty, justice, and equality, echoed on every platform over our broad land, must influence and inspire many coming generations.[11]

Frederick Douglass is a towering figure in American history. His influence and tenacity for justice and equality for all people cannot be forgotten.

A PRECURSOR TO LIBERATION THEOLOGY

Given the use of religion as a tool to oppress, no one can blame Douglass for his mistrust of it. And yet many of themes found in liberation theology are also found in the thinking of Frederick Douglass. As Douglass tried to rescue his people from misreligion, liberation theology is trying to rescue Christianity from the exegetical hermeneutical interpretation of oppressors. Douglass's life and thought represent what it means to struggle against oppression and the religion that holds it in place. We can see in his life a precursor to liberation theology.

Liberation theology is not formed in a vacuum. It came forth as the longing of oppressed people to have meaning in the midst of being treated meaninglessly. The indignities the oppressed suffered through the misuse of Christian religion as practiced in America left them with no hope or frame of reference that would release their reality as human beings. The theological consciousness of the oppressor was so deeply embedded in the American culture that every move toward "setting the captives free" was met with harsh resistance by many whites. But Douglass knew that he had to recover the meaning of the gospel of Jesus Christ if there was to be a bursting forth of a fuller humanity for the oppressed. We can see two themes that Douglass lifted up and how these two themes have influenced other thinkers in the formulation of liberation theologies. These two themes are *the point of departure for theological discourse* and *the cooperation between God and humanity for social reform*.

To break the chains of oppression, Douglass had to first break the psychodynamics of racism that held him in bondage. Douglass knew that the oppressed were defined by the theological and anthropological idiosyncrasies of white racism, and he was determined to define himself and help free the oppressed from their false consciousness. Once the oppressed free themselves from false consciousness, then they can counter the racist presuppositions and stratification in ways necessary for their liberation. In July 1859 Douglass wrote about his understanding of Christ's religion and its particular tilt. The religion of Christ "was for [humanity], . . . and for the poor, especially and particular for the poor. . . . The religion of Jesus is like himself, a copy of himself. His heart is with the bleeding heart of humanity."[12]

Douglass understood Jesus' statement that "you cannot serve two masters. You must love one and hate the other." Allegiance must be given to one and total rejection to the other. The oppressed must reject the ideological or cultural hegemony at the heart of the matrix of domination. They must go through a process of deconstruction and reconstruction to refute institutional mechanisms that are used to point out their subservient place in the world, and to thereby create a space for themselves with the education, ideas, beliefs, and values that would enhance and maintain their total liberation. In this process, Douglass saw how religion was a main factor in the enslavement of his people. The church was serving the maintenance needs of oppression by converting religion into a tool to legitimate oppression.

Douglass asserted that the gospel of Jesus was not intended as a postponement of justice, and the release of the captives was more than an eschatological salvation. The gospel of Jesus Christ speaks of salvation in terms of a present reality. There are needs on earth that cannot be met by waiting for salvation outside of human history. Douglass firmly believed that the liberation of the oppressed would come only with their participation. He believed it superstitious to think that God would do everything for the oppressed: "It is idle, a hollow mockery, for us to pray to God to break the oppressor's power, while we neglect the means of knowledge which will give us the ability to break this power."[13]

To understand Douglass's view of God in the liberation struggle and why he moved from a God-centered stance to a human-centered stance, stressing the power and ultimacy of humankind, it is necessary to compare and contrast traditional concepts of God and what is advanced by a liberation theology. We shall treat the concept of God and the different positions of liberation theologians who have a theological concern for theism, but who stand at opposite poles of the theological spectrum in the struggle for liberation. On the one side of the theological pole is the position of theocentric-Christocentric theism, which depends upon God through Christ to liberate the oppressed. The opposite side of the theological spectrum is that of humanocentric theism, which depends upon humans to liberate themselves. Douglass's position was more akin to the latter. His humanistic worldview influenced and inspired subsequent thinkers to explore, interpret, and develop a theology of liberation.

The concept of God is difficult and complex, but in the traditional classical view, God is viewed as omnipotent and utterly transcendent to finite human beings; nevertheless, God directs and controls every event. In contemporary thought, liberals view God as the "Sovereign Ground of Hope" who identifies with the weak and suffering people of the world. Liberals are compassionate but passive toward evil. Liberationists take action to end evil. They echo God's partiality to the poor and oppressed, making them the object of God's liberation. The God who freed Israel from Egypt is the same God who acts on behalf of blacks suffering from white oppression and on behalf of women suffering from patriarchal oppression. But just how God will act or is acting on behalf of the poor and the oppressed is not clear, and this is a challenge and often a theological impasse for liberation theologians, as it was earlier for Douglass.

Douglass asserted that the belief that God will free people from oppression in God's own good time had been used to promote the miseducation and misreligion of the oppressed. Contemporary theologian James Cone addresses this theme:

> Black theology rejects the tendency of classical Christianity to appeal to divine providence. To suggest that black suffering is consistent with the knowledge and will of God and that in the end everything will happen for the good of those who love God is unacceptable to black people. The eschatological promise of heaven is insufficient to account for the earthly pain of black suffering.[14]

Though liberation theologians agree that compensatory beliefs about God and the idea of evil as divine purpose must be discarded by the oppressed if liberation is to become a reality, they find the inquiry into just how God is acting on behalf of those who are suffering to be problematic. The claim that God is good, just, and a liberator must be supported by empirical evidence.

James Cone asserts that God is credible through Jesus Christ. What God has done through Christ makes God not only credible, but the true liberator of the oppressed. Cone states that "Christianity begins and ends with the man Jesus— his life, death, and resurrection. He is the Revelation, the special disclosure of God to man, revealing who God is and what his purpose for man is. In short, Christ is the essence of Christianity."[15] Cone believes that Christ is the decisive event of liberation, and the resurrection is the victory over sin, death, and oppression. And though suffering is still with us and "is wrong, . . . it has been overcome in Jesus Christ."[16] Through Christ, God has shown love for us. God has sided with the oppressed for their liberation, and they have been made free to fight along with God in the struggle. The liberating act of God is clear in the resurrection of Jesus Christ.

William Jones believes that the crucifixion is not necessarily a sign of God's love for humanity; it could be interpreted as divine malevolence against humanity.

We must admit that this historical event is certainly paradoxical, in the sense that God's love for humanity is demonstrated by divine hostility. But whatever position we embrace, Jones believes that the suffering of Christ as a symbol of God's salvation for humanity plays a major part in helping the oppressed to reconcile to their suffering. He writes: "By arguing that human suffering should be endured and accepted because God Himself has suffered even more, the strategy is laid to keep man, particularly the oppressed, docile and reconciled to his suffering."[17]

Therefore, Jones rejects Cone's theocentric and Christocentric theism and asserts what he calls humanocentric theism as the most appropriate vehicle for treating the suffering of the oppressed. Humanocentric theism claims the cosmic freedom and autonomy of humanity. It is grounded in the anthropological functional ultimacy of humankind, rather than the ontological superiority of the transcendent. Humanocentric theism eliminates the allegation of divine racism and elevates humans to areas of control "that previous theological traditions reserved for God alone."[18] To transfer areas of control to humans is to affirm their authentic created freedom.

What Douglass and others have said is that freedom is God's will, and God does not interfere in the affairs of humanity when the affairs are grievous to God. Since events are produced by humans, then God is vindicated. What has happened in human history has been the result of the conscious decisions and choices of human beings. This is why the positions of Douglass, Jones, and others are at variance with Cone's theocentric and Christocentric theism, which argues for God's controlling influence and sovereignty over the human situation. Though Jones's theistic framework has a secular flavor that places him outside the mainstream of American religion, especially black religion, his position cannot be dismissed. Not only did Douglass displayed similar insights during the horrible days of slavery, but other African Americans, such as Robert Alexander Young and David Walker, have asserted features of humanocentric theism in the struggle for freedom.

Just how much influence Douglass has had on the formulation of a liberation theology cannot be measured. But anyone who is serious about liberating the oppressed, especially using a Black Theology of liberation as a tool, cannot undervalue the influence Douglass has had on those shaping such a theology. The creators of black theology linked the liberation struggle with the gospel of Jesus Christ, thus mixing religion and politics. This linking of religion and politics was viewed as outside of the norm by the great majority of white churches and theologians who thought that the two should be kept in splendid isolation from each other. This is the same reason that Douglass broke with the Garrisonians. Douglass saw the need to wed the two, and he knew that if the struggles of the people produced any gains, those gains had to be secured by legislation. This finally took place in the twentieth century when the political process was linked to the social disruptions taking place in the 1950s and 1960s, enabling changes in American society that benefited the oppressed. Here Douglass and Cone share a common perspective: "Black Power and black religion are inseparable. Both seek to free black people from white racism. It is impossible for Black Power to be effective without taking into consideration man's religious nature."[19]

The criticism that Douglass and Cone have of Western theology and its point of departure is that the cultural elite's theological framework was structured toward maintaining an unjust situation. Western theology has been unmistakably partisan, in that it did not take into account the wretchedness of the oppressed. From the sixteenth century to the mid-nineteenth century, with the exception of some Quakers and a few other Christians, the white church never championed the cause of black people. After the Civil War, white church interpretation of the gospel message was quiet on the subject of racial oppression. In the same vein as Frederick Douglass, James Cone said that white theologians never made the oppressed their theological point of departure; therefore, they "missed the decisive ingredients of the gospel message."[20] Their overall theological concern was "with the universal dimension in the gospel, which transcends the particularities of the Black experience. The particular concerns of Black people, they contended, were at best an ethical problem or even a pastoral problem and thus more appropriately belonged in the 'practical' department."[21] Concomitantly, from Jonathan Edwards to Walter Rauschenbusch and the social gospel movement, all neglected to see the problem of black oppression. The churches and governments of the United States were united in their dismissal of black suffering and in their refusal to come to grips with it.

Not until the Civil Rights Movement, led by a brilliant young minister by the name of Martin Luther King Jr., do we find the United States confronting black suffering seriously. King took black suffering to the streets to show the world that America has not lived up to its promises of democracy and fair play. Participating in the Civil Rights Movement, black theologians knew that their theology had to reflect the needs of the great masses of black people both inside and outside of the Christian Church. Their theology had to become more clearly a theology of the people, rather than an academic theology that makes no connection with black peoples' suffering.

In 1970, James Cone published *A Black Theology of Liberation*, in which the suffering of the oppressed was his point of departure. His book gives justification to blacks struggling against nonbeing in a context of oppression. As Cone stated, "Theology can never be nonpartisan. . . . It is either identified with those who inflict oppression or with those who are its victims."[22] Cone expresses the same sentiment driving Frederick Douglass's earlier claim: "My hands were no longer tied by my religion."[23] Cone's Black Theology of liberation was no longer tied by the white religious interpretation of the gospel, which left black people despised and degraded. It was the long-awaited point of reference that the oppressed people needed in order to affirm their humanity and release their reality. A Black Theology of liberation opened up a way for other people who found themselves in a context of oppression to do liberation theology. Whatever else can be said about liberation theology, it is certain that Frederick Douglass helped to lay the groundwork for this type of theology to emerge.

CONCLUSION

A prophet and visionary of his time, Douglass continues to inspire us in our struggle against rising American imperialism. Oppressed people of the world must understand that their liberation is contingent upon purging their consciousness of their oppressors. When the oppressed are intentional about this process, the hegemony of the oppressor is seriously threatened and the possibility of liberation is at hand. Centuries ago God spoke through Moses to Pharaoh saying, "Let my people go." God is now saying to the oppressed, "Let Pharaoh go." Only when the oppressed reject their oppressors' beliefs, values, and manipulations can they experience authentic liberation.

FURTHER READING

Primary Sources

Douglass, Frederick. *The Life and Times of Frederick Douglass*. New York, N.Y.: Pathway, 1941.

_____. *My Bondage and My Freedom*. New York, N.Y.: Arno Press, 1969.

_____. *Narrative of the Life of Frederick Douglass, an American Slave*. New York, N.Y.: Penguin Books, 1982.

Secondary Sources

Cone, James. *A Black Theology of Liberation*. New York, N.Y.: Lippincott, 1970.

Foner, Philip S. *Frederick Douglass on Women's Rights*. New York, N.Y.: Da Capo Press, 1992.

Jones, William R. *Is God a White Racist? A Preamble to Black Theology*. Garden City, N.Y.: Anchor Press, 1973.

Martin, Waldo E. *The Mind of Frederick Douglass*. Chapel Hill, N.C.: University of North Carolina Press, 1984.

Mays, Benjamin E. *The Negro's God*. New York, N.Y.: Atheneum, 1969.

CHAPTER 23

William Temple

Ellen K. Wondra

Theologian, social ethicist, ecumenist, and Anglican archbishop, William Temple (1881-1944) was one of the most influential church leaders of the first half of the twentieth century. For Temple, Christ's incarnation, the inalienable dignity of every human person, and the coming of God's reign were the ground of human existence, however much they might be obscured in the conditions of history. The mission of the church and of its members is to embody the continuation of the incarnation persistently until the kingdom comes. Faithful pursuit of this mission through the transformation of persons and policies will gradually strengthen and deepen a worldwide Christianity in which all persons will live together justly and peaceably, each in the full dignity of the image of God. In these convictions, Temple reflected the confidence of late Victorian Britain as it passed the height of its empire.

In the last few years of his life he went beyond this optimism to speak more directly about the pervasiveness of sin and evil in the world, expressed through injustice and despair. This shift in Temple's thought was brought on not by the horrors of World War I—as had been the case for his contemporaries Karl Barth, Reinhold Niebuhr, and Paul Tillich—but by the effects in Britain of the world-wide depression of the 1930s and by the spread of fascism and Nazism. Temple died before he could fully work out the implications of this shift in his thought.[1]

CONTEXT: THE BRITISH EMPIRE, INDUSTRIAL EUROPE, AND WORLD WAR

Temple's persistent personal and theological optimism is often attributed in large part to his family situation: Frederick Temple, his father, was already Bishop of

Exeter when William was born, and soon after went on to become Bishop of London and then Archbishop of Canterbury. William's mother Beatrice Lascelles was a member of the hereditary aristocracy. William himself was educated at Rugby and Balliol (Oxford) and held highly prestigious posts, culminating with the archepiscopates of first York and then Canterbury.

Temple's larger social and historical context played a large part in his formation as well. Temple was born at what would subsequently be seen as the height of the British Empire which, by 1914, covered about one quarter of the globe. The British justification of empire was three-fold. First, conquest and settlement provided both materials and markets for industrializing Britain, and ensured free trade that would not necessarily be possible with other sovereign nations such as the United States and France (a traditional rival). Second, imperial expansion provided military protection from Britain's perceived enemies, both in Europe and abroad. Third, and perhaps most significant for our consideration of Temple, the expansion of British holdings meant an expansion of British culture, a development that was widely viewed in Britain as the working of divine providence. In this, the spread of Christianity was both crucial and ambiguous.

Although Temple was a national leader in Great Britain during a crucial period in the history of the British Empire, his work shows little concern with the global reality of the British Empire. However, his concern with economics and human degradation in Great Britain itself—factors aggravated by empire—was lifelong.

Before the nineteenth century, Britain had held lands beyond the British Isles for centuries. Imperial expansion involved emigration, trade partnerships, slave trading, piracy, and military action. Violence and conquest were more or less constants as the empire was built, though Britons saw themselves as protecting vulnerable peoples through the spread of British civilization.[2] From the British point of view, the spread of empire vindicated the British system of government and trade: imperial expansion was successful because of the obvious merits of British culture and civilization. That view was largely held in Britain into the twentieth century, despite growing dis-ease in the imperial possessions themselves.

One of the great motives for the expansion of empire was the growth and support of industrial commerce. Raw materials from British territories and trade partners were sent to Britain's industrial centers and their products subsequently sent throughout the empire for purchase. Thus, empire fueled the prosperity of middle- and upper-class capitalists, industrialists, merchants, and officials. At the same time, prosperity rested on the exploitation and continued impoverishment of the colonized and of the poor in Britain itself.

The plight of the British poor occupied much of Temple's attention and energy, and significantly shaped his social ethics. Throughout the seventeenth and eighteenth centuries, land reforms and industrialization had changed the social and economic fabric of British life. Urban poverty became an intractable problem, increasing as some of the colonies and territories developed industrial centers that surpassed those in Britain. From the middle of the nineteenth century, labor unions and political action groups became more and more organized, vocal, and influential. Well-meaning individuals and groups—many of them church-related—launched efforts aimed at amelioration and social transformation. However, the investment in empire was such that even liberal governments were unable to effect domestic social reforms and were forced into positions supporting imperial policy. By the 1880s, the empire presented to poor workers in Britain the possibility of economic advancement overseas, with emigration acting for Britain as a social safety valve that could "check [the working poor's] potentially destabilizing effects or divert them into more beneficial channels."[3]

Imperial expansion was supported by most Britons through the 1930s in large part because it was seen as a civilizing force for the material and moral improvement of indigenous peoples and cultures. In 1853, the politician Earl Grey had said, "The authority of the British Crown is at this moment the most powerful instrument under Providence, of maintaining peace and order in many extensive regions of the earth, and thereby assists in diffusing amongst millions of the human race the blessing of Christianity and civilisation."[4] The fact that Britain had abolished its own slave trade in 1807 under pressure from Christian humanitarians and the British public supported this view.

This casting of empire as benevolent was reinforced by how social anxieties were handled in Britain itself. Toward the end of the nineteenth century, as imperial efforts by other European powers increased, Britons were less and less sure of their place in the world. More and more they were encountering students, visitors, and emigrants from the periphery of the empire. Social Darwinism suggested that subjugated peoples had been conquered precisely because their societies and racial and ethnic "characters" were weaker than Britons'. Social Darwinism applied as well to the British working class and the poor, who were portrayed as degenerate, weak, and a potential source of threat to national stability. "Social imperialism" advocated not only pursuit of British interests abroad, but also aggressive action at home where the British state was cast as an "active agent of social good."[5]

The role of Christianity in the spread and maintenance of the British Empire was various, crucial, and irreducibly ambiguous. Christian teachings advocating care for the downtrodden assured Britons that their motives for imperial expansion were honorable: they were protecting the vulnerable, bringing the benefits of civilization, and overcoming ignorance and superstition. That empire enriched its purveyors simply indicated its overall beneficence. Widespread missionary societies at the end of the eighteenth century provided for the religious needs of British settlers and the conversion of non-Christian indigenous peoples. Protestant societies in particular tried to avoid "political" involvement with imperialism. Nevertheless, teaching Christianity was a major vehicle for increasing literacy and for advocating cultural and moral norms and practices. At the same time, there was a lively debate among missionaries and their supporters about whether the spread of Christianity would be more effective were the religious message separated as far as possible from British culture.[6]

It was often the missionaries who criticized colonial governments' corruption and disregard of the well-being and interests of indigenous populations, though most of their efforts failed to point to the fundamental injustices of colonial rule itself. Even so, Christianity was linked to the powers of conquest and colonization; and conversion provided indigenous people with one way to form strategic alliances with the colonizers. Yet Christianity's egalitarian message was not lost on colonialists or colonized: eighteenth-century slave owners attempted to keep slaves away from Christianity and its teachings. And nineteenth- and twentieth-century indigenous politicians and activists used Christian claims to press for greater self-determination and self-governance.[7]

By the beginning of the twentieth century, the British Empire was in decline; other European nations were expanding their empires; and Britain's domestic economy was depressed, perennially so in agricultural areas. In South Africa a costly war against the Afrikaaners had begun, and wars with the indigenous Xhosa continued. Some colonies had achieved "dominion" status and were largely self-governing. Others were the sites of uprisings (Ireland in 1916, India in 1919) and resistance movements in support of "home rule." By the 1920s, a redefinition of the relationships between Britain and its various territories was clearly needed.

Between the world wars, there was increasing consensus in Britain itself that colonial territories would gradually attain self-rule, though the modes and timetables for such change were constantly and often violently disputed. The worldwide depression of the 1930s increased tensions as colonial export prices fell and capital investments were withdrawn. Independence movements, such as those in India, broadened their appeal beyond the middle class to the poor and dispossessed. British responses to civil disobedience and other forms of resistance were often disproportionate and undercut official efforts to maintain good relations with the colonized. Those reforms that were enacted were often "too little, too late."[8] Yet even as colonial resistance grew, in Britain itself in 1937 the leftist George Orwell was still able to say that "at the bottom of his heart, no Englishman . . . does want [the empire] to disintegrate."[9]

Whereas the empire had rallied to Britain's support in 1914, in 1939 the response to threats in Europe was neither rapid nor certain. The dominions (Australia, New Zealand, and Canada) made their own declarations of war. In India the National Congress Party demanded a declaration that India was an independent nation in return for a declaration of war, provoking an internal crisis which increased antagonism between Hindus and Muslims. In 1942 Britain refused to respond to massive food shortages in India; 1.5 million lives were lost to famine and epidemic. Although Britain regained its former possessions upon the end of the war in 1945, colonial independence had become inevitable. India and Pakistan gained independence in 1947 while continuing as members of the commonwealth, with other colonies following suit in the 1950s and 1960s. In Britain itself, the will to empire had evaporated.

TEMPLE'S THEOLOGY AND SOCIAL ETHICS

During Temple's lifetime, Britain was the richest nation in the world, in large part because of its imperial holdings. At the same time, in Britain itself at about 1900, one-third of the population did not have enough to eat; the average life expectancy among the poor was about thirty; and perhaps 20,000 people died annually from diseases directly related to poverty.[10] Despite these realities, many European thinkers embraced a version of philosophical idealism influenced by Darwin's theory of development as evolution (with the uses noted above), by Platonic idealism, and by Hegel's understanding of history as progress toward an ideal. In such idealism, assessment of historical realities played a small role at best. Temple's philosophical theology is a solid example of such idealism. In his case, though, this theoretical idealism was the foundation for a strong theoretical and practical commitment to social change. The connection between theology and ethical practice is Temple's major legacy in the twenty-first century.

By his own account, Temple was a Christian who never experienced religious doubt. He was always confident that God's purposes are embodied and fulfilled in the incarnation of God in Christ, in which God enters into full fellowship with humanity so that humanity may be in communion with God.[11] Temple's focus on the incarnation continued a significant line of nineteenth-century Anglican thought that saw all things in light of God's dwelling in history in and through Jesus Christ. Focus on the incarnation provided a robust understanding of the established church as the instrument of God's mission. It also provided the basis for British Christian Socialism and its various efforts with the working poor. Outworkings of both concepts are found in Temple's theology.

Late nineteenth-century philosophical idealism gave Temple a way to use basic Christian presuppositions to build a coherent account of the universe as a fundamentally rational whole whose unity can be grasped in both principle and fact.[12] Rationality (or "Mind") develops over time in and through matter; and full unity gradually comes into being, rather than being given at the outset. Temple used Hegel's dialectics to explain the evolution of creation from one level to the next, with later levels (e.g., human rationality and fellowship) emerging from earlier levels (e.g., matter itself and its basic organization). Earlier levels are not surpassed, however. Rather, they find their fulfillment and purpose in that to which they give rise. This process of development has its source and its fulfillment in God its creator. All that is, is an expression of the character of God. Thus, there is an orderliness in creation intended by God, sustained by God despite human limitations and sin, and finally fulfilled by God eschatologically. Temple insisted that this divinely intended order stands in considerable contrast to the world as it presently is. Even so, there is a tendency to equate humanly constructed social orders with divine intentions, and to see ameliorating poverty (for example) as an easily implemented correction of course.

For Temple, the incarnation of Christ brings about the realization of the ideal and the real together in history. In the incarnation, the power that creates the world and sustains it enters the world in its own forms of matter and Mind. Because the incarnate one is also the creator, the incarnation is the natural culmination of the very processes of the world itself.[13] So Christianity is the most avowedly materialist of all the great religions; its own most central saying is: "The Word was made flesh," where the last term was, no doubt, chosen because of its specially materialistic associations. By the very nature of its central doctrine Christianity is committed to a belief in the ultimate significance of the historical process, and in the reality of matter and its place in the divine scheme.[14]

The incarnate Christ embodies God's determination to fulfill the divine purposes at the same time that the incarnation is an earnest of God's presence and activity in history, showing how God will fulfill or perfect creation. Because of the Word made flesh, hope in even the direst of social conditions is possible and richly warranted. In Christ, human persons and groups find their way from selfishness to fellowship. That, at least, is the ideal.

Humanity develops in community, where personality—what today we call full human dignity—is formed and supported and nurtured. To develop as intended, personality requires liberty, social fellowship, and the opportunity for service (through which persons recognize that they need and are needed by others).[15] Theologically, society is properly structured only insofar as it serves the purpose of fulfilling personality. Sin disrupts the divine purposes as persons misunderstand their true good and establish groups or societies based on selfishness and the privileging of some groups over others. That is, sin is manifest as social injustice as well as in individual behavior.[16]

The mission of the church, then, is not only to proclaim God's purposes and the place of human persons within them. The church is also called to continue the incarnation by manifesting, however partially and imperfectly, the fellowship for which humanity is created. Temple writes:

> The Church exists to be the chief and signal vehicle of the transforming Spirit, who steadily wins men [sic], so far as they open their hearts to [God], from self-seeking to self-giving, from the isolation of selfishness to the fellowship of the Holy Spirit. We are thus called to enter into the very activity of God whereby [God] is known to be God . . . . we are to plunge the nations in the cleansing tide of the Love which is to us the open secret of the universe. Nothing less than this is our vocation as members of the Church, which is the Body of Christ, the vehicle and medium of [the Holy] Spirit.[17]

Unlike some other theological idealists, Temple is clear that this fellowship is eschatological; the church itself is not the kingdom of God.[18] However, Temple did think that the church is the temporal goal of society in history: "Christendom is precisely the world no longer alien, but as seeking to conduct its affairs in the power of that life of which the Church is the channel and trustee."[19] At the same time, it is not only the church which is the "vehicle and medium" of the Holy Spirit: secular entities and movements and other biblical and nonbiblical religions also serve this purpose in history.

Temple cast the processes of God's involvement with the world as sacramental. For Temple, a sacrament is "God's spiritual self-utterance through created matter."[20] This is most evident in the Word of God made flesh, Jesus the Christ. By extension, the church is also a sacrament insofar as it proclaims and manifests the work of God in the world. So the sacrament of the Eucharist, for Temple, is the "perfect symbol of the economic life" humanity should share because the bread and wine are an "instance of God's gifts made available for the satisfaction of [human] needs."[21]

Temple's theology of a sacramental universe—a coherent whole created and sustained by a loving God, and manifesting God's love and purpose through its fundamental ordering and the course of history—has certain advantages and attractions. It literally *makes* sense of things: it gives meaning to ordinary events by placing them on a large, comprehensible canvas. It finds history purposive in claiming that it is, ultimately, God who reigns, not those who wield more immediately evident power. It inspires hope in those subjugated or marginalized by the prevailing socio-economic order by proclaiming an underlying and enduring benevolent order in which their deprivations and dehumanization are redressed.

But there are perennial problems with such an approach. One is the constant temptation to identify what ought to be with what is, to equate reality and the ideal—in theological terms, to see the eschaton as already realized "on earth as it is in heaven." This was one of the major problems of the theological liberalism of the late nineteenth and early twentieth centuries which saw the economic and imperial development of North Atlantic nations as inevitable progress that increasingly approximated the kingdom of God. Identifying human achievement in one sector of society with the outworkings of the divine will obscures the consequences of that achievement for those whose deprivation provides the resources needed for achievement. Thus, Temple could see imperialism as part of a positive movement from nationalism to the ideal of worldwide fellowship: "In this fact of the British Empire, then, we have 'the noblest project of freedom that the world has seen.'"[22]

South Africa's support of Britain in World War I and the British government's actions in New Zealand to protect the Maoris from Britain's own settlers led him to say, "Here already we see in the Imperial Government the germ of a World Government deriving its authority from a moral need. This Empire does not stand in the line of succession with Assyria, Babylon, Macedon and Rome; it is a new kind of fact."[23] The ongoing oppression of the Xhosa and others in South Africa and of the Maoris in New Zealand is not taken into account. Theology blesses empire.

A related problem with theological idealism is that it can give no satisfactory theoretical or practical account of the existence of evil. How are events of mass suffering, for example, part of the "purposeful unfolding" of the Mind of a loving God?[24] For that matter, how do they proclaim that it is God and not the existing structure of power that truly reigns? Temple attempted—unsuccessfully—to address this problem in both *Christus Veritas* and *Nature, Man, and God.* Later, in light of the Great Depression and the rise of European fascism in the 1930s, he seemed to move away from his fundamental theological idealism toward an ethical realism influenced by Reinhold Niebuhr, writing in 1940 that theologians and preachers

> must start from the fearful tension between the doctrine of the Love of God and the actual facts of daily experience. When we have eliminated war, it will be time to discuss whether its monstrous evil can then be seen as a "constituent element of the absolute good." Till then we had better get on with the job of eliminating it by the power of the Gospel, which we must present, not as the clue to a universal synthesis, but as the source of world-transformation.[25]

Whether Temple would have continued on this course after World War II, or returned to a chastened idealism cannot be known, given Temple's early death in 1944.[26]

That Temple's theological idealism could not satisfactorily address the problem of the manifest reality of evil did not in any way deter him from building a solid social ethics that would address the ills of the present world. In Temple's view, social injustice is an affront to God because it damages human persons and communities and blocks the development of personality (human dignity). A society that thrives on chronic unemployment and underemployment, perennial poverty, and systemic curtailing of persons' potential cannot be tolerated by Christians. "Why should some of God's children have full opportunity to develop their capacities in freely-chosen occupations, while others are confined to a stunted form of existence, enslaved to types of labour which represent no personal choice but the sole opportunity offered? The Christian cannot ignore a challenge in the name of justice."[27]

Instead, Christians could derive from their fundamental doctrinal stance a set of theological principles that apply to a wide range of social issues. The principles of liberty (respect for personality), social fellowship, and service provide the basis for a series of "middle axioms" or guidelines that "mediate between the fundamental principles and the tangle of particular problems."[28]

Temple developed his social ethics through the interaction of his theological understanding of the incarnation with his concrete involvement in a variety of movements aimed toward social transformation. From his university days he was involved with the Workers' Educational Association in which workers set the curriculum and scholars provided the teaching.[29] He was a regular speaker for years at summer conferences of the Student Christian Movement (important in a variety of progressive social causes, including the ecumenical movement). In 1924 he chaired the Conference on Christian Politics, Economics, and Citizenship (COPEC), the culmination of four years of study which was, at the time, "the most considerable effort made . . . anywhere in the world to focus Christian thought and action on the urgent problems of the day."[30] In 1926, as part of the Industrial Christian Fellowship, Temple sought to mediate the British coal miners' strike, an effort that failed in part because the church leaders were naïve about the willingness of employers to engage in arbitration. Temple and his colleagues were roundly criticized for "church interference" in economic affairs.

Temple's middle axioms and his work in support of laborers and the poor came to their fullest expression in his *Christianity and Social Order* (1942). Here he argued that Christians "are entitled to call upon the Government to set before itself the following objectives and pursue them as steadily and rapidly as opportunity permits": for all people, decent housing; education directed toward students' aptitudes; adequate income and meaningful work; effective "voice in the conduct of business or industry"; sufficient daily, weekly, and annual leisure time; and freedom of worship, speech, and assembly.[31] *How* the government ought to provide for such things Temple thought was beyond the church as a body to say: the work of qualified experts was necessary; and it is possible for Christians to disagree about the best policies to enact these proposals. But *that* the church had both the right and the duty to call for such reforms Temple did not doubt. The church "is bound to 'interfere' because it is by vocation the agent of God's purpose, outside the scope of which no human interest or activity can fall."[32]

Here we note two things in particular: First, Temple's critique of the economic practices of Great Britain (and, by extension, its empire) did not run deep enough to lead him to advocate more than significant reforms within existing economic structures. At the same time, his calls for reform were highly effective: within five years of the end of World War II, "many of the social and economic objectives advocated by Temple had been achieved" in the development of the British welfare state.[33]

Second, Temple is also widely regarded as one of the key figures of the ecumenical movement of the twentieth century. This movement grew in part out of Christian social movements that supported the justice claims of labor. These movements also saw Christian unity as a way of peace and reconciliation in a world increasingly fragmented by nationalist fervor. Toward the end of World War I, when efforts to convene a "genuinely international labour conference" failed, Temple took up the cause as a leader of what became the first Universal Christian Conference on Life and Work held in Stockholm in 1925.[34] The studies leading to COPEC served as the British contribution to this conference. Temple was also deeply involved in the work of the World Conference on Faith and Order, and chaired its 1937 meeting in Edinburgh. As these two ecumenical efforts converged to form the World Council of Churches, Temple was widely viewed as "its God-given leader."[35] His death meant that the mantle of leadership landed elsewhere, but he continues to be a major influence on worldwide ecumenism.

In sum, Temple's focus on Christ's incarnation and on the universe as a sacrament led directly to his involvement with multiple social movements and to his formulation of a social ethics that insisted that the church legitimately has a public voice in the affairs of the world. Some of his efforts reflect the failings of theological idealism. Even so, the effect of his work on twentieth-century Britain and on worldwide Christianity is significant and long-lasting.

IMPLICATIONS

What, then, are we to make of Temple's theology and social ethics more than sixty years after his death? Temple himself recognized in the last years of his life that philosophical idealism was no longer compelling to other theologians; nor could it meet the severe challenges of the rise of fascism, genocide, and global war.[36]

A simple appropriation of Temple's theological approach is no more satisfactory today. As noted above, theological idealism tends to disguise as divinely mandated those humanly created and maintained social, economic, and cultural systems that do violence to human dignity and to the natural world. Further, this approach to theology cannot give an adequate account of evil within the framework of a strong understanding of divine providence such as is necessary to support Temple's view of history as development or evolution. Minimally what is needed to address these concerns is much greater emphasis on eschatology and a recasting of incarnation as leading inexorably, in a world beset by systemic sin, to suffering, passion, and crucifixion. Some contemporary political, liberation, and postcolonial theologies take this approach. They achieve much of what Temple attempted, insofar as they make meaning of history on a larger scale than immediate local events, place that meaning both under the sovereignty of God and actual human conditions, and look toward eschatological fulfillment beyond history that can nevertheless be anticipated to some extent within history.

So it would appear that, of all Temple's work, it is his method for social ethics that has the greatest value in the twenty-first century, because it builds clearly from a coherent set of basic theological affirmations. Temple's middle axioms are a direct outgrowth of his fundamental theology: if human dignity is a central part of divine purposiveness, human social order must conduce to its formation and nurture not just for a few but for all. Resistance to social injustice and advocacy of social transformation are warranted directly by claims about the nature of God and the world, claims that themselves are richly and explicitly warranted by Scripture and significant strands of the church's tradition. In a time when mainline and global churches are contesting the relation of faith and practice (as in debates about global economics or human sexuality), thoroughly and clearly articulated theological arguments are needed. Further, Temple's insistence that the church can advocate certain outcomes but not the detailed policies that will produce them offers a way for disputants to identify common social goals without further polarizing those advocating different concrete practices.

But Temple's work is helpful in another, less evident, and perhaps counter-intuitive way. Temple's approach very much depends on the church's having a central role to play in public life, as the established Church of England certainly had in his time. The late twentieth and early twenty-first centuries are marked by the declining influence of liberal Christianity and its ecclesial embodiments around the North Atlantic. "Christendom"—a social, political, and cultural order built on Christian beliefs—is no more, and contemporary Christians both liberal and conservative must recognize this fact. However, the alternatives are not free of problems. To the extent that the Christian community is construed as a counterculture that must step back from public involvement and tend primarily if not exclusively to the formation of its own members, the privatization of religion characteristic of "the suburban captivity of the churches" continues, only with a postmodern rationale.[37] Temple's boldness in pointing to a view of the universe that entails a particular kind of society that can be described fairly concretely stands as a counterbalance to contemporary impulses to cultural relativism and to strict localization of Christian critiques and visions. The end of Christendom does not absolve Christians of the responsibility to advocate for more humane social structures and practices. Temple's insistence on making Christian claims in the public square reminds us that clarity and transparency about the reasons for our claims are needed if Christians today are to be effective in persuading others that the world is not the world that ought to be.

FURTHER READING

Primary Sources

Temple, William. *Christian Faith and Life*. New York, N.Y.: Macmillan, 1931.
_____. *Christianity and Social Order*. New York, N.Y.: Penguin Books, 1942.
_____. *Hope of a New World*. New York, N.Y.: Macmillan, 1924.
_____. *Nature, Man, and God*. The Gifford Lectures, University of Glasgow, 1932-33 and 1933-34. London: Macmillan, 1934. Reprint, 1949. See especially lecture 19.

Secondary Sources

Dackson, Wendy. *The Ecclesiology of Archbishop William Temple (1881-1944)*. Lewiston, Ont.: Edwin Mellen Press, 2004.
Lowry, Charles W. *William Temple: An Archbishop for All Seasons*. Washington, D.C.: University Press of America, 1982.
Suggate, Alan M. *William Temple and Christian Social Ethics Today*. Edinburgh: T. & T. Clark, 1987.
Spencer, Stephen. *William Temple: A Calling to Prophecy*. London: SPCK, 2001.

CHAPTER 24

Karl Barth

Cynthia L. Rigby

In August of 2004, the twenty-fourth Council of the World Alliance of Reformed Churches held a conference in Accra, Ghana. The theme of the conference was "That All May Live in Fullness."[1] In the course of describing how Christian believers are called to promote humanization by addressing global economic disparities, one document produced at the conference defined "empire" as follows:

> The convergence of economic, political, cultural, and military interests that constitute a system of domination in which benefits are forced to flow from the weak to the powerful. Centered in the last remaining superpower yet spread all over the world, Empire crosses all boundaries, reconstructs identities, subverts cultures, overcomes nation states, and challenges religious communities.[2]

The conference proceedings did not include focused consideration of how Karl Barth's theology can support working prophetically against the dehumanizing impact of empire. And yet surely the participants would agree that Barth—the most influential Reformed theologian since Jean Calvin—has specific wisdom to contribute to the shape of the World Alliance of Reformed Churches' vision for the promotion of the full humanity of all. In this chapter, I have the delegates at Accra in mind. I invite them (as imagined readers) to explore how Barth resisted empire, both as a Christian believer who took concrete historical risks and as a theologian who developed approaches and ideas in deference to a Kingdom that subverts all systems of domination.

Barth holds that to be a member of the Christian community is actively to oppose and work to remedy the dehumanizing impact of empire; in the terms of

337

the above-cited definition, to stop the "flow of benefits from the weak to the powerful." The way to do this, he believes, is to respond, ever-again, to the ever-new "command of God." Appeal to the command of God as justification for taking particular actions will rightly be greeted by raised eyebrows on the part of those who recognize the way in which the rhetoric of "divine command" has been and is being used to buttress empire. Barth insists, despite his shared concerns in this regard, that the divine command never serves to notarize the agendas of those who would dominate others, but rather subverts them. "The command of God," he says,

> is self-evidently and in all circumstances a call for counter-movements on behalf of humanity and against its denial in any form, and therefore a call for the championing of the weak against every kind of encroachment on the part of the strong . . . Christianity in the West has its main work cut out to comprehend the disorder in the decisive form [i.e., capitalism] still current in the West, to remember and to assert the command of God in face of this form, and to keep to the 'left' in opposition to its champions, i.e., to confess that it is fundamentally on the side of the victims of this disorder and to espouse their cause.[3]

This chapter has in mind, then, the question of how Barth's historical and theological contributions might facilitate our participation in humanizing counter-movements in the face of empire. What is it that he taught us, both historically and theologically, about the revolutionary character of submitting to the command of God? And, most important, how does such submission, on the part of those of us who are powerful, facilitate our standing in solidarity with those who are victimized?

The chapter is divided into three parts. First, it reflects on Barth in his historical context, highlighting concrete instances of his resistance to the drive toward empire and presenting the context for the development of his *crisis* theology in the time of the crises precipitated by the power struggles of the two world wars. Second, it delves deeper into the revolutionary character of Barth's theology by probing his understanding of the character and content of the Word of God, and how he thought it disarmed the hegemonic, ideological thinking on which empire feeds. Finally, it briefly considers the import of Barth's understanding of the Word of God for the task of theologians entering the twenty-first century, arguing that it supports the coming of a kingdom in which "all can live in fullness."

THE GERMAN CRISIS AND CRISIS THEOLOGY

Karl Barth lived from 1886-1968; the majority of his life was during the decades defined by the two world wars (1914-1918, 1939-1945).[4] Many significant Barth scholars have represented Barth's life as characterized by acts of resistance against attempts to establish empire.[5] As pastor of the Reformed Church in the industrial town of Safenwil, Switzerland (1911-1921), Barth was very involved not only in fulfilling his pastoral responsibilities but also in studying socialism and working with the trade unions. A member of the Swiss Social Democratic Party and known for giving controversial lectures, including "Jesus Christ and the Movement for Social Justice" (1911)[6] and "Religion and Socialism" (1915), Barth was commonly known as the "Red" pastor. He later expressed that it was through his exposure to the "class conflict" in the life of his congregation he was "touched for the first time by the real problems of real life."[7] In 1914, when he was 28 years old, Barth became disillusioned with his liberal theological training. Ninety-three German intellectuals had proclaimed their support of Kaiser Wilhelm II, proponent of German imperialism and commander-in-chief of the armed forces. "Among these intellectuals I discovered to my horror almost all of my theological teachers whom I had greatly venerated," Barth comments, adding that he "suddenly realized [he] could not any longer follow either their ethics and dogmatics or their understanding of the Bible and of history."[8]

His teachers' support of that which he understood to be antithetical to the command of God precipitated Barth's development of a theological method which he hoped would be less apt to confuse the Word of God with the world of culture.[9] Barth began working out this method in the writing of his commentaries on Romans (1919 and 1922, respectively), the second of which, he believed, was a vast improvement over the first because it more rightly represented the "otherness" of God. In short, Barth came to argue, in contrast to the theological approach of nineteenth-century liberalism, that theology cannot have an "anthropological starting-point," but must be grounded in the self-revelation of the God who is otherwise hidden to us. Instead of holding, as his teachers had, that culture and theology exist in a relationship that is in some way harmonious, Barth held that encounter with the Word of God precipitates crises in our understanding of ourselves and our world that provoke personal and societal transformation.

In 1921, Barth moved from being a pastor in Safenwil to being a professor of Reformed theology in Göttingen, Germany. Arriving in Göttingen shortly after the end of World War I, Barth found himself plunged into the malaise of a country that had lost both territory and identity and had been forced, via the Treaty of Versailles (1919), to bear all responsibility for starting the war. Globally, awareness was growing that more people had been killed, captured, or lost in World War I than in any former war (approximately fifteen million). Twenty to forty million additional people died between 1918 and 1920 of an influenza pandemic. Meanwhile, the Weimar Republic, which would govern the former German Reich until 1933, had emerged. Intellectual and artistic life and productivity were beginning, again, to flourish. It was during this period of personal and global transition that Barth and his colleagues Friedrich Gogarten, George Merz, and Eduard Thurneysen came together in founding a journal aptly titled *Zwischen den Zeiten* ("Between the Times"), not only in honor of the historical situation they faced, but in the recognition that the work of theological reflection always takes place between the now and the not yet—between the coming of Christ and the coming to fruition of the Kingdom. Committed to developing an approach to theology that came to be known as "neo-orthodoxy," Barth and his colleagues strove in their work to honor the complete otherness of God, who is at once both hidden from us and known to us in the divine self-revelation. Published from 1922 to 1933, *Zwischen den Zeiten* emerged as the primary theological voice in Germany against Nazism.

As Hitler and his supporters steadily rose to power in the early 1930s, Barth continued to oppose them as well as to speak prophetically against those professing Christians who strove to offer theological justification for the Nazi agenda. In 1931, after the Nazis had gained one-third of the seats in the Reichstag, Barth joined the Social Democratic Party (SPD) which would in 1933 be banned for voting against the "Enabling Act" that granted "extra constitutional powers" to the Third Reich.[10] While 1933 marked the forced end of *Zwischen den Zeiten,* it was also the year in which Barth published and distributed his pamphlet, "Theological Existence Today" (*Theologische Existenz Heute*). In this pamphlet, Barth spoke adamantly against the theology of the "German Christians," (*Deutsche Christen*), a party formed by the German National Socialists in 1932 for the purpose of promoting Christian unity and thereby national unity. At one point in his discourse Barth rails against the faulty perceptions of three prominent clergypersons[11] who had made a statement in support of the German Christian Church. "A mighty National Movement has captured and exalted our German Nation," they had declared. "An all-embracing reorganization of the State is taking place within the awakened German people. We give our hearty assent to this turning-point of history. God has given us this: to Him be the glory."[12] In contrast, Barth insists that "[t]he Church preaches the Gospel in all the kingdoms of this world. . . . She preaches it also in the Third Reich, but not *under* it, nor in *its* spirit." No one has privileged access to the Word of God, and no one is abandoned—all are subject to crisis!

Barth was also among those who renounced the teaching of the German Christians that one could not be truly German unless one were Christian, and one could not be truly Christian if one were ethnically Jewish.[13] By this insidious logic, of course, persons who were Jewish could not be German citizens; their very presence in Germany worked against the purity of the German nation. Condemning this way of thinking, Barth insisted that "[t]he fellowship of those belonging to the Church is not determined by blood . . . not by race, but by the Holy Spirit and Baptism."[14]

A more formalized and collaborative rejection of the theology of the German Christians is reflected in the 1934 Declaration of Barmen, authored primarily by Barth and signed by Reformed and Lutheran pastors who identified themselves as the "Confessing Church," in contrast to the German Christians. In the face of what Trevor Hart has identified as "increasingly heretical rhetoric from the German Christians,"[15] those who stood behind Barmen upheld the sovereignty of God and the lordship of Jesus Christ alone. The German Christians made statements such as the following:

> Christ, as God the helper and saviour, has, through Hitler, become mighty among us. . . . Hitler (National Socialism) is now the way of the Spirit and Will of God for the church of Christ among the German nation.[16]

The Confessing Church countered, via Barmen, with:

> We reject the false doctrine, as though the church could and would have to acknowledge as a source of its proclamation, apart from and besides this one Word of God [i.e., Jesus Christ], still other events and powers, figures and truths, as God's revelation.[17]

Clearly, crisis theology is in play, in the logic of Barmen, insofar as the lordship of Christ is understood to relativize all "other lords."[18]

In 1934, Barth refused to pledge allegiance to Hitler without adding a phrase qualifying that he could do so only to the degree that Hitler's leadership was consistent with his convictions as an "evangelical Christian." As a result, Barth was suspended from his teaching position in Bonn, where he had held a professorship since 1930. Many of his colleagues believed that this act of political resistance was unnecessary.[19] His books, including the first completed part-volume of the *Church Dogmatics,* were confiscated and not allowed to be sold. Barth was forced out of Germany in 1935, four years before the start of World War II.

According to Timothy Gorringe, Barth's return to Switzerland allowed him more freedom, and therefore, ultimately, more influence, than he would have had if he remained in Germany. He "intervened politically," in this period, "with increasing frequency and vehemence," "publishing yearly updates" on the German church struggle, writing a plethora of personal and open letters, and lecturing.[20] So effective were his efforts that Germany banned all of his work in 1938, issuing a diplomatic appeal to the war-neutral Swiss government to censor Barth. In addition to censoring some of his open letters and lectures, Basel University publicly rebuked him.[21] In 1940, when he was 54 years old, Barth joined the Swiss army and served as a guard at the German frontier.[22]

Ending in 1945, World War II was followed by the Cold War between the last remaining superpowers, the United States and the Soviet Union. The Marshall Plan (1947), conceived primarily by U.S. political leaders, was aimed at supporting reconstruction in Europe by way of the promotion of capitalism rather than communism. In the period between the world wars and his death in 1968, Barth remained committed to his conviction that theology was not in the business of promoting any particular ideology, believing that the Word of God throws all human agendas into crisis. He was consistently clear, to the disappointment of many loyal readers of his work, that it was historically and spiritually problematic to identify capitalism solely with "good," and communism solely with "evil." Along these lines, he challenged Western Christians to recognize the ways in which the drive to accumulate property (and, on a larger scale, territory) fed the dynamics of the wars. In the Darmstadt Statement of 1947, a document co-authored with Lutheran colleague Hans-Joachim Iwand, Barth not only named explicitly Germany's responsibility for the war, but also associated the national church's support of Hitler with its anti-communist ideology.[23] In 1949, Barth reacted vehemently to the tendency of the Barthians to apply his "Nein!" of the Nazi era to the communism of the day. While the national church's theological logic for supporting Hitler necessitated, in 1934, that even trace amounts of natural theology be utterly condemned, Barth believed the divine command in relation to communism was not "No!" but "maybe." "[E]verybody is rushing about today crying that same 'No' must be said again," he complained, ". . . As if such simple repetitions ever occurred in history! And as if the church were an automatic machine producing the same goods today as yesterday . . ."[24]

Barth firmly challenged Christian believers who assumed the success of the Western capitalistic agenda and the advancement of the kingdom of God go hand-in-hand. In 1948, in the opening session of the first meeting of the World Council of Churches, Barth argued that the mission of the global Christian Church is "not . . . something like a Christian Marshall plan" in which the goal is "the Christianization of all humanity."[25] Eleven years later he was still arguing that "[w]e must be . . . on our guard against regarding our *Western judgment* as the right and *Christian judgment*."[26] "Our Western 'No'. . . could only be a *Christian* 'No,'" he warned, ". . . if we . . . were attempting a more humane but no less energetic solution to this problem [i.e., of reconstruction]." [27] Barth even went so far as to comment that "the 'fleshpots' and 'complacency' of the West," which he equated with the "'American way of life,' represent a greater danger to the Christian soul than communism."[28] Again manifesting his conviction that the Word of God throws *all* human agendas into crisis, Barth insisted that "[t]he message from Christ is as repulsive and painful to the West as to the East." "Who knows," he added, "perhaps it is *more* painful and repulsive to the West than to the East."[29]

While a brief survey of Barth's life certainly uncovers a significant number of instances in which he countered developing hegemonies, and while it is clear that his theological logic for doing so was because he believed he was faithfully submitting to the command of God, what is less clear is whether Barth's engagement in the work of social justice was "integral" or "incidental" to Barth's theology.[30] Was Barth engaged in empire-defying work because he happened to be living, as a faithful Christian believer, in a period in history that cried out—especially loudly—for the taking of such responsibility?[31] Or is there also something inherent, in the content of his theology, that would always lead to the taking of such risks? Related to this, especially if it is held that Barth's revolutionary living is *incidental* to his theology, is an even more pressing question: Can Barth's theological approach be used just as readily to *support* empire as to *challenge* it, depending on what any particular person with power understands the command of God to be? Was Barth simply mistaken in speaking with such confidence that the command of God "is in all circumstances a call for counter-movements on behalf of humanity"?[32] These are the questions that drive the following sections.

THE COMMAND OF GOD AND COUNTER-MOVEMENT

Barth believes that what God commands is good because God has commanded it. The ordering of his logic is both crucial and controversial: he does *not* hold that, *because* something is good, and God is good, God must have commanded it. Our task, as Christian believers, is not to establish and apply a set of criteria in order to evaluate what is good (or just, or loving) and therefore the command of God. Rather, it is to recognize what God commands us to do and to do it.

One can see why Barth's approach is met with consternation by many Christian ethicists, who point out that, without a shared commitment to developing criteria for discerning the good, ethics—as such—is impossible.[33] There is a sense in which Barth would agree, arguing that Christian believers who do the work of public theology should not develop arguments with the goal of arriving at consensus, but should rather focus on bearing witness to what God is up to in the world. How distorted versions of Barth's approach have been co-opted and used for the promotion of empire can readily be seen in history. Too often, people have sought to gain an excess of power by representing themselves as "theologians" who have special access to the command of God that they are then charged to disseminate to the receiving masses, rather than as those who are genuinely open to themselves being transformed in the context of communal discussion and debate. Certainly, the steps from *recognizing that the theologian is called to bear witness to what God commands,* to *assuming that the theologian knows better than anyone else what God commands,* to *holding that what the theologian commands is what God commands* can be all too short. And if these steps are so readily taken, what is to prevent anyone with power, under the guise of thinking theologically, from leveraging his or her positions as the will of God?

Barth would argue that the guard against moving from the recognition of the divine command to mistakenly identifying human commands with God's command is the content of the command itself. And the content of the command is known always in relation to God's self-revelation to us in the person of Jesus Christ. For Barth, what prevents us from mistaking our own commands for God's, and what licenses us to speak prophetically against those who are leveraging their own abusive agendas in the name of God, is constant reference to the event of Jesus Christ as it has been made known to us in God's self-revelation. While all kinds of debates can be had about the specifics of what Jesus Christ said and did, it is clear that he sided with the marginalized, rejecting systems that disempower some for the benefit of others as antithetical to the kingdom of God. When the German Christians replaced the biblical witness to who Jesus Christ is with their own understanding they were simply wrong, Barth believed. And they were wrong, he thought, not because the supporters of Barmen could necessarily make a better argument for who God really is, but because they lost sight of who God *actually* is.[34]

All renderings of what God wills in any particular moment and context must, then, be checked against the "norming norm" of the Word revealed in Jesus Christ. It is in and through him, Barth thought, and not in accordance with some abstract principle or desire for what God *should* be like, that it is clear the command of God *always* supports counter-movements against injustice and for humanization. Any claims regarding the command of God that perpetuate empire are, simply, not the command of the God whom we know to stand always with the marginalized because Jesus Christ stood – and therefore God stands – always with the marginalized. Our job, according to Barth, is to ever point away from ourselves to the One who gives the command;[35] the One who—being free—always commands in a way consistent with God's being as it has become known to the world in God's acts.

Consistent with his Christocentric approach to the matter of the divine command is Barth's rejection of "casuistical ethics." Barth disdainfully describes casuistry as a "method or technique of fixat[ing]. . . the divine command in a . . . text of ethical law" which is then applied "to the plenitude of conditions and possibilities of the activity of all [people]" with the purpose of "deducing good or evil in the particular instance of human conduct."[36] The person who speaks about God's commandments in general terms

> does so by claiming that in a *summa* of ethical statements compiled by him and his like from the Bible, natural law and tradition, he can know the command of God, see through and past it, and thus master and handle it, i.e., apply it to himself and others, so that armed with this instrument he may speak as law.[37]

Casuistry is dangerous, Barth thought, because—following the dynamics of the fall in the Garden of Eden—it represents an attempt to "set [ourselves] on God's throne" with the purpose of "distinguishing good and evil."[38]

In his ethics, Barth himself worked to avoid casuistry. Where he was unsuccessful in this, the repercussions he feared are in evidence. For example, in the better portion of his discussion of "Man and Woman" in his *Church Dogmatics,* Barth insists that "we cannot and may not prejudge the issue with an abstract definition" of what it means to be one sex, rather than another.[39] Rather, we can only know what it means to be a man or be a woman in the particular moment and context in which one "hears and obeys the divine command."[40] Barth then goes on, however, to make the surprisingly definitive statement that "[m]an and woman are an A and a B. . . . A precedes B, and B follows A. . . . It means super- and sub-ordination."[41] The man's role, according to Barth's understanding of the command of God, is to "lead as the inspirer, leader and initiator in their common being and action."[42] For a woman to "wish" to replace the man in this role is, for Barth, a "wish not to be a woman."[43] Clearly, it is precisely when Barth forgets the wisdom of his own insight and begins to apply a *general* understanding of what God desires men and women to be that he reinforces oppressive power dynamics in which the power of some (men) is insured by the weakness of others (women).

Rather than investing in the formulation of a general ethics, Barth believed that Christian believers are called to address the challenges posed by the world by way of constant obedience to the command of the God we know in Jesus Christ. To live in obedience to the command of God, he insisted, is to decide "*not* to be obedient to power as power."[44] Rather, it is consistently and voraciously to live in the world as those who are with and for the world, intolerant of dehumanizing power structures. It is ceaselessly to ask the question, in relation to each situation in which we find ourselves, "What are we to do?" Famously, Barth held that pastors, as those called to the ongoing work of discerning the Word of God, should preach "with a Bible in one hand and a newspaper in the other."[45] This comment of Barth's is most often used to represent his controversial conviction that the Bible should be studied with an eye toward current events, and current events with an eye toward the Bible, if God's Word is to be rightfully discerned and proclaimed. This comment also counteracts superficial readings of Barth's work that mistakenly associate his insistence on obedience to God's command, and his corresponding rejection of natural theology, with passivity and myopia. As William Placher puts it in his recent book, Barth believed that "*from* a Christian perspective one can engage in conversation with anybody about anything—from Mozart to Nietzsche to Pure Land Buddhism, to cite the topics of a few of the lengthy excurses in the *Church Dogmatics*."[46]

To live in the world as those who consistently seek to discern and obey God's command is not, for Barth, to enjoy perfect clarity about what God's command is, apart from the particular moment and context in which it is revealed. On the contrary, Barth thought that consistently to ask the question, "What are we to do?" subjecting ourselves with every asking to the living Word of God, is never to become cavalier even in relation to our best insights. "The continuity of a life which steadily affirms itself from one decision to another," Barth argues, "can only be the continuity of disobedience."[47] Rather than showcasing our degree of "rightness," we are instead charged to live as those who are humbly aware of our constant need for correction and growth.

> We can never look back upon a genuine previous conversion and instruction without its necessarily compelling us to be more serious than ever in our present circumstances, to prepare ourselves for fuller openness to truth, to inquire more searchingly than ever before: *What* ought we to do?[48]

Barth was known to have practiced what he preached, in this regard. As was noted in his obituary, for example, Barth "was willing to reverse himself at times," and "insisted that even his own *Church Dogmatics* was tentative and written only to be revised and refined by his students."[49] One example of his own refining of his work in the *Church Dogmatics* came in the 1950s when Barth recognized that the inordinate amount of faith in human potential he had earlier criticized was now being replaced by unhealthy degrees of trust in structures of authority. His theological emphasis shifted, accordingly, in the final part-volumes of the *Church Dogmatics,* from the transcendence of God to the "genuine subjectivity" of human beings in the dynamics of reconciliation.[50]

It is in fact in these later part-volumes of his work that Barth most convincingly plays out his idea that obedience to the divine command propels counter-movements that defy the kingdom of this world by participating in the kingdom of God. Obedience to the command of God, as Barth understands it, is about always returning to who God is as "the One who loves in freedom"[51] and in this way being ourselves reoriented to our own freedom as those who are "righteous partners"[52] with God and "genuine subjects . . . in the great event of reconciliation."[53] Those who are guilty of the sin of pride, when they obey the divine command as it is known in the one who emptied himself, cease to disempower others.[54] Those who are guilty of self-deprecation, when they obey the divine command as it is known in the one who is exalted above every name, cease to remain complacent and begin to engage in revolutionary activity.[55] Obeying the command of the God who has not only demonstrated love but *is* love is, according to Barth, to enter into the freedom of our existence as those who are created and redeemed to be with and for one another, standing in solidarity with one another even as God, in Jesus Christ, stands in solidarity with us. In this posture of exercising our freedom in relationship to the God who loves us freely, our understanding of power shifts from thinking in terms of commodities to be exchanged to life and work to be shared.

IMPLICATIONS FOR DOING THEOLOGY IN THE TWENTY-FIRST CENTURY

What might be learned from the life and theology of Karl Barth that would support the 2004 delegates at Accra in their struggle against the dynamics of empire? What does Barth have to teach us about participating in humanizing counter-movements that "espouse the cause"[56] of those who have been victimized?

The documents produced at Accra reflect a deep yearning for global engagement in proactive prophetic work that recognizes and promotes the full humanity of all people, including—especially—those who have been marginalized. Coupled with this is the desire that all participate in the articulation and implementation of this prophetic vision, since a vision shared and promoted by only a few runs the risk of perpetuating yet another system in which some lord over others what they perceive to be right and true. What the participants at Accra desire is that Christian believers speak prophetically but not hegemonically; that they challenge empire without unwittingly perpetuating it in another form.

Barth offers, to twenty-first century theological discourse, an example of how this can be done by those who identify themselves as followers of Jesus Christ. Submitting themselves ever-again to the command of God—living in crisis rather than with complacency—Christian believers may speak prophetically as those whose fundamental posture is not to be "right," but to bear witness to a truth that de-centers and relativizes all other powers and perceptions of truth. Insofar as the prophet points her finger toward Jesus Christ and not at herself, according to Barth, she is herself open to personal revision and change. She needs not protect her position, since what she bears witness to needs no protection. She is open to conversation with others as she continues seeking to understand that which is beyond herself. On a corporate scale, according to Barth, the church, as the community of believers, does not possess the "right" answer in contrast to the world that needs this answer, and that therefore had better listen to the church. Rather, the church exists for the sake of the world as "a parable and promise of the Kingdom of God." Insofar as it is "Reformed and always reforming, according to the Word of God,"[57] the church can admit that it might be wrong—even when it believes it is right!—listening to the critiques and views of others in the global conversation.

What makes it possible to speak prophetically while still being genuinely open to the voices of others, according to Barth, is the fact that there exists behind the "divine command" a real God—a transcendent God who has made Godself known to us in the person of Jesus Christ. To Christ we appeal, he believes, in standing firmly for the marginalized. And through him we submit, as we listen to the voices of others in the work of ascertaining what new shape the command of God is taking in this particular moment and context.

If in Barth's theology we find a valuable way to speak prophetically but not hegemonically, we will need in the twenty-first century to revisit ways of speaking about the divine transcendence that take into account the important critiques made—by deconstructionist thinkers, feminist thinkers, and others—at the turn of the century. There is no question, again, that appeal to a transcendent God has been used to support the dynamics of empire. Too often, the powerful have controlled the weak by emphasizing God's transcendence, omnipotence, judgment, and command as means of fostering passivity and fear. Because God is transcendent and omnipotent, our proverbial hands are tied, the logic goes. We need, simply, to "trust and obey," waiting patiently for God to act, rather than ourselves exercising agency. But to dismiss all understandings of the divine transcendence as inherently flawed because of the abuses with which the concept has frequently been associated is also problematic. This is true for the simple reason that belief in a transcendent God has also, often, *promoted* humanization. The African American slaves of the nineteenth century, for example, appealed to God's transcendence and power in ways that empowered them to speak prophetically against the abuses of the slaveholder and to live as agents in relationship to the events of their lives.

Barth's theology helps parse out when the appeal to a transcendent God disempowers the marginalized, and when it empowers. What needs always to be taken into account, according to Barth, is the content of the appeal. When the transcendent God ostensibly referenced is actually a God of our own self-projection—a God who reinforces our own position and power—the appeal must be prophetically denounced on the basis of who God actually is. For Barth, again, it makes all the difference that the one whose command we obey is not just any old god, but the God born of Mary, a friend eating with tax collectors and sinners, a fellow-sufferer crying out on the cross, an embodied human being rising to new life. Such a

God—*this* God—pulls the rug out from under us and our hegemonic tendencies, challenging us to stay in conversation, to renounce disempowering powers, and to work for the humanization characteristic of the kingdom of God.

But Barth's Christocentric focus accomplishes more toward articulating what would constitute an empowering understanding of the divine transcendence than simply testifying that the omnipotent God is in touch with human frailty. It is not only that the omnipotent God, known to us in Jesus Christ, turns out to be nicer than we expected (and certainly nicer than the God projected by those German Christians!). While a God who is a benevolent dictator is certainly an improvement on a God who is not—while the command of such a God might entail that more hungry are fed and more wealthy are humbled—such a God is still a God of empire, a God whose rule is contingent on the subservience (and therefore disempowerment) of the weak. In contrast to this, Barth understands the command of God, always discerned through the event of God's self-revelation in Jesus Christ, fully to include the creative contribution of the human agent who is submitting to the command.[58] This is, admittedly, most obvious in his later work, where he explicitly develops the implications of the Chalcedonian dialectic between the full humanity and the full divinity of Jesus Christ.[59] Here it is startlingly evident (especially for those who have embraced Barth's emphasis on the otherness of God) that, whatever obedience to the command of the transcendent God is being recommended, it is not an obedience extrinsic to God's own exercise of agency. Rather, our obedience is itself included in the very life of God, in and through the person of Jesus Christ. And yet it is still *our* agency that is being exercised. In and through the fully human, fully divine one, divine and human agency are distinguished, but never separated. Human agents make an integral contribution to the work of God, exercising their agency in creative, humanizing acts of obedience.

Barth's argument at this point suggests that obedience to the command of a transcendent God is potentially humanizing when the actions of this God, and the actions of those obeying, are understood to be inseparable as well as distinguishable. This essay has discussed Barth's emphasis on distinguishing between our actions and God's. The convolution of human actions with God's actions is of course used by those with power to justify the perpetuation of empire. But dividing human actions from divine actions is also used to disempower.[60] Such a strategy, which inevitably includes appealing to a transcendent God whose actions merely *provoke* (rather than also *include*) our response, is used by those with power both to abdicate responsibility for the ultimate significance of their actions and to encourage the weak to see their actions as ultimately insignificant and therefore immediately pointless.

In Barth's understanding, obedience to the command of the "totally other" God fully includes us. Again, this is because God has revealed, in God's self-revelation in Jesus Christ, that humanity is included in the very life and work of God. Because our actions are not identical to God's, Barth thinks, we are called to live as those who are constantly open to conversation and critique, ever in process of listening, thinking, praying, and discerning the shape of God's Word for each particular moment. When we live in such a posture, we are drawn to participation in counter-movements that defy the workings of empire. "Can one ask God for something which one is not at the same moment willing and determined within the limits of one's own possibilities to bring about?" Barth once asked.[61] It is precisely because he believed human actions cannot be separated from the actions of God that Barth lived the way he did, exhorting others to participate in God's work of bringing the kingdom to earth, as it is in heaven.

FURTHER READING

Primary Sources

Barth, Karl. *Church Dogmatics*, 12 vols. Edited by Geoffrey and T. F. Torrance. Edinburgh: T. & T. Clark, 1956-1976.

_____. *The Humanity of God*. Nashville, Tenn.: John Knox Press, 1960.

Green, Clifford, ed. *Karl Barth: Theologian of Freedom*. Minneapolis, Minn.: Fortress Press, 1991.

Secondary Sources

DeGruchy, John. *Liberating Reformed Theology: A South African Contribution to an Ecumenical Debate*. Grand Rapids, Mich.: Eerdmans, 1991.

Gorringe, Timothy. *Karl Barth: Against Hegemony*. Oxford: Oxford University Press, 1999.

Hunsinger, George, ed. *Jesus Christ and Radical Politics*. Philadelphia, Pa.: Westminster Press, 1976.

Hart, Trevor. *Regarding Karl Barth*. Cumbria, UK: Paternoster Press, 1999.

CHAPTER 25

Hendrik Kraemer

Jan H. Pranger

"I have had to round up nine women and three children begging for mercy and had them shot. It was an unpleasant job, but it had to be done. The soldiers enjoyed spearing them to their bayonets."[1]

—*Hendrikus Colijn, 2nd Lieutenant, Royal Netherlands-Indies Army, CEO of Royal Dutch Shell, Prime Minister of the Netherlands*

In November 1916 the Dutch Bible Society decided to send a missionary to the Dutch East Indies to study the social and cultural developments among the nationalist and Muslim elites of Java.[2] The growing nationalistic consciousness among the Javanese elite had caught the attention of Dutch missionary leaders in the East Indies, the former Dutch colony that is now Indonesia. They were especially eager to engage the Islamic resurgence that threatened to deny their hopes to shape the future of Indonesia (which today remains the largest Muslim country in the world).[3] The proposal to undertake this mission came from a graduate student named Hendrik Kraemer. After completing his studies of Javanese Islam, Kraemer served between 1922 and 1936 as a missionary in colonial Indonesia.

Kraemer became an important figure in the world of mission and ecumenism, best known for his missionary approach to other religions. His ideas, especially as expressed in his 1938 publication *The Christian Message in a Non-Christian World*, wielded great influence well into the second half of the twentieth century, and continue to be a reference point in Christian debates about interreligious dialogue. Thus Kraemer remains a controversial figure. He is credited with helping to build ecumenical institutions and advocating the independence of Third World churches; for example, he strongly supported the independence and contextualization of Indonesian Christianity. Living amidst the transition from a colonial to a formally postcolonial world, Kraemer sought to dissociate Christian faith and mission from historical Western Christianity by arguing that Christian faith had a supranational character. Mission was equally necessary in East and West and was primarily a task of local churches within their own cultures and societies. At the same time, Kraemer's exclusivist ideas regarding other religions and religious syncretism remain deeply controversial and have made him a "symbol of missionary arrogance and intolerance."[4]

While Kraemer's work has been extensively discussed, little *critical* attention has been given to the impact of colonialism on his ideas. To be sure, colonial rule, nationalist movements, and postcolonial independence are explicit topics in Kraemer's work. Indeed, his support for the independence of Third World churches and for Christianity's supranational character make him in important ways an early advocate of postcolonial and global Christianity. But in this chapter we will not limit ourselves to Kraemer's explicit reflection on empire or church. Cultures of empire extend far beyond individual and conscious choices. They shape cultural representations of self and others in ways that enable the social and political conditions necessary for colonial rule.

As Edward W. Said has pointed out, the institutions that produce and disseminate knowledge of other peoples and societies, especially academic scholarship and missions, played a central role in the culture of empire by creating and legitimizing colonialist forms of knowledge.[5] Kraemer came of age in a colonizing society, served as a missionary to colonial Indonesia, and studied and later taught at the University of Leiden, an institution which played a central role in the education of colonial administrators. His personal and professional choices as missionary and scholar are thus all woven deeply into the historical reality of Dutch rule over Indonesia, and are embedded in institutions closely connected with the colonial enterprise.[6] Indeed, it can sometimes be difficult to distinguish between Kraemer's missionary interests and issues of concern to Dutch colonial policy. A particularly important illustration of this overlap is Kraemer's interest in Islamic nationalism, which was of clear significance to Christian missions but had also long been identified as a major threat to Dutch colonial rule, specifically by Kraemer's doctoral advisor, Christiaan Snouck Hurgronje.[7]

For these reasons, this article will take a postcolonial viewpoint and ask to what extent Kraemer's missiological and ecumenical vision was shaped by his colonial experience. Similarly we ask whether Kraemer's approach to other cultures and religions reflected or contributed to the culture of empire in the Netherlands. Colijn's quotation above serves as a reminder of the violent nature of Dutch colonialism, how deeply it permeated Dutch society, and the extent to which it felt itself fully justified. Obviously Kraemer had nothing to do with Colijn's atrocities, which took place when Kraemer was six years old. Indeed, Kraemer himself was never involved in military campaigns, and spoke out strongly against Dutch military actions in 1947-1948. However, colonial violence in its various forms was never absent from Indonesia, and much of that violence was made possible by the views of colonizing self and colonized others that circulated in Dutch society and Protestantism. As a prominent missionary and scholar Kraemer both mirrored and contributed to this culture of empire in the Netherlands. Taken together with his sympathy for Indonesia's independence and his advocacy of postcolonial Christianity, this makes Kraemer an intriguing study of the tensions and contradictions that arise from ideological captivity to empire.

Hence we do not raise postcolonial questions to assign moral blame in hindsight. The purpose of postcolonial studies is emancipatory. Kraemer was a person shaped by his culture, society, and history—as are we. Precisely for that reason we need to study the cultures and histories that shape us. Postcolonial studies retrace colonial history because past colonial significations continue to shape former colonizers and colonized both. Indeed, we revisit the past in the hope of a free and just future for all. Moreover, postcolonial studies can help us maintain a critical awareness toward the imperial contexts and structures of our own time. Specifically, Kraemer's Orientalist views of the relations between East and West, and his moral and theological defense of colonial relationships, can offer insight into the functioning of present day political, moral, and religious discourses that legitimize imperial domination.

In the following I will make three specific claims regarding Kraemer's work. First, his support for the independence of Indonesia's churches can be seen in part as a response to Kraemer's negative experience with Islamic nationalism in colonial Indonesia. Second, Kraemer's arguments for Christianity's supranational character and his related criticism of Third World churches' involvement in nationalistic movements stand in marked contrast to his nationalistic arguments favoring

Dutch colonialism. Third, Kraemer's Orientalist (and theological) views of religions and the East-West relationship stood in the way of a real encounter with religious others.

KRAEMER IN THE CONTEXT OF EMPIRE

Although we focus mainly on the Dutch empire in Indonesia we should recognize that Kraemer negotiated three different imperial configurations of power, namely pre-World War II colonial Holland, Nazi Europe, and the post-World War II period which saw Europe's former colonies emerge as independent nations. Of these, what most claimed Kraemer's attention was what he called the meeting between East and West that played itself out in colonial and postcolonial Asia. Kraemer himself first encountered the East in Dutch Indonesia.

For three centuries the Dutch colonial interaction with Indonesian society was primarily determined by aggressive pursuit of economic interests, but due to more activist and liberal policies of the colonial government the situation began to change around 1870. On one hand this activism led to the military "pacification" of the outer parts of the Indonesian archipelago. Kraemer's teacher Snouck Hurgronje was the government's main advisor during the violent campaign in Aceh. On the other hand the Dutch intensified their involvement in Indonesian society through education and other policies that sought to "civilize" its peoples. This so-called "ethical" policy was based on the idea of Dutch "guardianship" over Indonesia. One of its main proponents was theologian-politician Abraham Kuyper who in the late nineteenth century articulated the three-fold goals of Dutch colonial policy as "morally fostering the colony, steward its property to its best interests, and to prepare its future autonomy."[8] However, during Kraemer's years in Indonesia Kuyper's party was led by Colijn whose colonial policy instead aimed at a federalist relation between the Netherlands and its colonies. The colonial reality of the early twentieth century in which Kraemer worked was thus determined by the colonial administration wavering between policies advocating and rejecting autonomy as the eventual goal, and by emerging Indonesian nationalisms of secular and Islamic orientations that grew stronger as political reforms stalled.

KRAEMER IN COLONIAL INDONESIA

Born in Amsterdam in 1888 in a working-class milieu, Kraemer came under the care of a Protestant orphanage after the death of his parents. At the age of sixteen he entered a missionary training school in Rotterdam. Afterwards the Bible Society sponsored Kraemer to study Eastern languages at the University of Leiden. During his student years Kraemer was active in the Dutch Student Christian Association and came into contact with international missionary leaders such as John R. Mott. As leader of the Student Volunteer Movement, Mott inspired students to "evangelize the world in this generation," and it was he who, during a visit to Holland in 1913, pointed Kraemer and other Dutch missionaries to the importance of engaging the emerging Javanese elite before nationalism would alienate them from the Christian West.[9]

Kraemer arrived in Indonesia in 1922 with an ambivalent attitude toward colonialism and nationalism. He had been sympathetic to the goal of an autonomous Indonesia since his student days, yet he was also convinced that Dutch supervision was necessary to achieve this goal. His views would basically remain unchanged until after World War II. Accordingly, he saw the role of Christian mission during his early years in Indonesia in terms of the "positive criticism of nationalism," and his own task as the sympathetic engagement of the "earnestly striving movements of the Javanese people."[10]

Kraemer indeed developed relations with secular and Muslim movements in Java.[11] He became especially involved with Young Java, a Javanese student organization, and also struck up friendly relationships with the leader of Muhammadijah, Ahmad Dahlan. Yet Kraemer soon became critical of the anti-missionary character of Muslim-inspired nationalism, especially of Sarekat Islam led by Hadji Salim.[12] He criticized Sarekat for being overly political and insufficiently religious in character.[13] In this criticism we hear the clear echo of Kraemer's teacher Snouck Hurgronje, who as advisor to the Dutch colonial administration had sought to encourage Islam as a religion while trying to curtail its political aspirations.

Karel Steenbrink relates a conflict with Salim that sheds some further light on Kraemer's involvement.[14] Following lectures by Kraemer on Christianity for Young Java, Muslim students counseled by Salim proposed lectures on Islam. When this proposal was rejected Kraemer was seen as excluding Muslim influence from Young Java and the Muslim students established their own Young Muslim Society. It became a politically influential group with strong opposition against Christian missions.

Whether this incident was a cause or a symptom, it is clear that Kraemer was growing frustrated with Muslim resistance to Christian conversion and feared its turn toward nationalism. The early 1920s were years of intense missionary discussion—in Indonesia and internationally—about how best to approach Islam.[15] Though in Indonesia Kramer experienced Islam foremost as a public force, it was through personal faith that Kraemer knew religion and it was through this that he hoped to interact with others as a missionary. The politicized reality left him frustrated regarding the possibility of reaching Muslims. Kraemer expressed his powerlessness some years later: "the riddle of Islam is that, though as a religion it is shallow and poor in regard to content, it surpasses all religions in the world in the power by which it holds all those who profess it."[16] This comment also illustrates the largely negative attitude which Kraemer would continue to display toward Islam. Indeed, in an interesting projection onto Islam of his own fears as a colonial missionary Kraemer would speak of Islam as a "very consistent form of imperialism"—in a time when most of Islam was under colonial rule.[17] Kraemer thus came to fear Islam's growing influence on Indonesian nationalism; it does not seem far-fetched to argue that Kraemer's continued wariness of nationalistic movements related to other religions had its roots in his experiences with Islam in colonial Indonesia.

Another source of frustration for Kraemer was the policy of noncooperation with the colonial authorities to which Indonesian nationalism turned in the 1920s. Both the anti-missionary and the noncooperative stance of nationalist movements contradicted Kraemer's fundamental vision of the renewal of the East through the interaction with Christianity and the West, and thus constituted a crisis for his hope for a constructive critical relationship to Indonesian nationalism. Instead Kraemer turned his attention to supporting independent and indigenous Indonesian Christian churches. This he came to see as the priority of Christian mission amidst Indonesia's growing nationalism. Indonesia's Christians needed to be organized as independent churches: *free from* paternalistic European influences, and *free for* their missionary presence amidst their own culture and toward Islam. Such churches would be able to make a Christian contribution to independent Indonesia: shaped by their own Indonesian culture they were best equipped to renew their culture and society in light of the gospel. For European missions this new vision implied neutrality and independence toward the colonial administration. In Kraemer's emerging ecumenical vision, church and mission were "universal and supranational" in character: "the missions and all who serve her are fundamentally obligated to independence from the interests of one's own nation. The mission worker's being Dutch or being European is eclipsed by being a servant of Christ."[18]

We can thus see the fundamental missionary vision for which Kraemer's years in Indonesia have come to be known—and which was also central to his ecumenical contribution—namely the development of independent, indigenous, and missionary churches in part as a response to the crisis that Muslim activism created for his initial missionary vision. This realization is particularly interesting in light of Kraemer's own lack of attention to the way the East influenced and challenged the West.

KRAEMER AT TAMBARAM

After his time in Indonesia, Kraemer participated in the 1938 conference of the International Missionary Council in Tambaram, India. In preparation he wrote *The Christian Message in a Non-Christian World*, in which he emphasized the unique character of Christian faith and rejected comparisons with other religions based on shared moral or religious values. Kraemer presented Christian faith as "Biblical realism" to emphasize its biblical foundation and "objective" nature. Faith was a response to God's unique self-revelation in Jesus Christ, and thus radically different from human religions. While other religions reflected a desire for God they remained human, sinful strivings; in Christian faith alone human beings encountered divine revelation and absolute truth. *The Christian Message* also emphasized that God acted in human history and this, in Kraemer's view, set Christianity fundamentally apart from South and East Asian religions. These he characterized as "naturalistic," and "monistic," and in his judgment they failed to grasp the absolute distance between God and creature, God's involvement in history, and the idea of absolute moral and religious truth. By essentializing religions in terms of a foundational view of the God-world relationship unique to each religion, Kraemer further emphasized the fundamental differences between religions and closed the door to finding common ground in shared values or beliefs. In fact, in such comparisons Kraemer saw the danger of "syncretism," by which he meant "the illegitimate mingling of different religious elements."[19] For Kraemer syncretism was essentially a theological concept, which stood for a relativistic denial of absolute truth and Christian faith's uniqueness. Interestingly, Kraemer foremost identified relativism as the crisis of Western culture, but rearticulated as "syncretism" it became an effective barrier against Third World churches exploring relationships with other faiths.

The final report of the conference leaned heavily toward Kraemer's position, which often has been seen as Tambaram's unofficial outcome. Ironically the majority of the delegates in Tambaram came from the non-Western world, yet Kraemer's views drowned out many important Third World voices. Indeed, it is tempting to see Kraemer's views of other religions as the product of a colonial mindset. But Christian exclusivism is not unique to Kraemer and not conclusively linked to empire. Yet we can argue that interreligious relationships fell victim to Kraemer's ecumenical vision, which was in some important respects modeled after empire. Kraemer developed the idea of the supranational character of mission into a global vision for the church. He claimed that "the *sui generis* character of the church . . . consists in the fact that Jesus Christ is its primal and ultimate King and Lord, whose authority transcends and conditions all other authority and loyalty."[20] Kraemer's vision of such a global Christian community was not a universal, centralized monolith—here the analogy with empire may break down as Kraemer did not want a return to Christendom—but based on local churches with an indigenous character and witness. Grounded in their societies but bound together by their common obedience to Christ and loyalty to the universal church, Kraemer believed that such churches could give a common witness amidst the spiritual crises that affected the non-Christian world in East and West. However, in such a supranational entity there was no place for anything that claimed a comparable loyalty, e.g., nationalism, nor for anything that threatened its absolute character, e.g., the suggestion that Christianity was one religious path among many.

KRAEMER AND NAZI RULE

From 1937 until 1947 Kraemer served as professor of religion at the University of Leiden. This appointment placed Kraemer in Holland during the Nazi empire and afterwards during the struggle for Indonesia's independence. His primary involvement before, during, and after the war was the renewal of the Netherlands Reformed Church, and here Kraemer tried to implement the missionary ecclesiology that he had developed working with the churches in colonial Indonesia. Kraemer became the chairman of an influential national committee that sought to inspire the Netherlands Reformed Church to a missionary presence in Dutch society. Under the German occupation such a vision included the struggle with Nazi ideology and policies. Already before the war Kraemer had identified the Nazi ideology as an expression of the crisis of Western culture. In the terms of his missiological paradigm it was a pseudo-absolute that substituted absolute loyalty to nation and race for human obedience to God.

Kraemer became an important voice of opposition to the Nazis within the churches—which on an institutional level tended to operate with caution and often with a lack of clarity—and took a clear stance against anti-Jewish policies in church and academy.[21] Kraemer was instrumental in the rejection of the Aryan clause by the Reformed church board, and together with fifty-three colleagues stepped down from his teaching post in protest of the Nazification of the university. In the context of anti-Jewish policies he published a commentary on Romans that called the existence of the Jewish people a sign of God's work in the world that Christians need to respect. It was subsequently declared illegal by Nazi censorship.[22] Kraemer helped draft an urgent message to Nazi Commissioner Seyss-Inquart on behalf of the major churches to protest the deportations of the Jews from the Netherlands as the transports began in July 1942. Two days later, before writing a more comprehensive response, Kraemer was interned by the Germans and held captive until early 1943.[23]

INDONESIAN INDEPENDENCE AND THE POSTCOLONIAL WORLD

With the defeat of Germany and Japan in 1945 a radically different world emerged, especially in Asia. Japan had occupied the Dutch Indies in 1942, thus ending over three centuries of Dutch colonialism in the region. After Japan's surrender in 1945 the Republic of Indonesia proclaimed its independence. To Kraemer these events marked a watershed in the relationship between Holland and Indonesia.

Kraemer had supported Dutch leadership over Indonesia up to World War II. Co-editing a book on Dutch national identity in 1940, Kraemer called the "symbiosis with Indonesia" essential to Dutch identity and emphasized the need for a "living imperial awareness" on the part of the Dutch people.[24] He argued that as leader of a worldwide empire the Dutch people were called to help find answers to global moral challenges.[25] Regarding Indonesian nationalism Kraemer reminded his audience that the legitimate goal of Dutch governance of Indonesia was the welfare of its people. Immediate independence, he argued, ran counter to that goal as Indonesia's social structures were yet unable to cope with the global political realities and economic forces. For that reason continued Dutch leadership was "necessary and justified."[26]

These arguments from 1940 underscore how deeply Kraemer was inscribed in the Dutch colonial relationship with Indonesia, and demonstrate not only his captivity to the culture of empire but his encouragement of it. Indeed, they illustrate the contradictions in the colonial Kraemer, on the one hand advocating critical distance from nationalist causes for churches in the Third World, yet on the other hand advocating a colonial Dutch nationalism.

It is remarkable, then, to see Kraemer strongly advocate Indonesia's independence after the war. Based on the sympathy which Kraemer had always expressed for Indonesia's future independence, scholars often see continuity between his pre- and post-war position. Indeed, Kraemer himself observed that the principles of self-expression and responsibility had already guided his support for the independence of the Indonesian churches.[27] Yet before 1940 Kraemer had not applied those criteria to the Indonesian peoples as a whole, instead defending the colonial relationship. After the war, however, Kraemer believed that the time of Indonesia's rightful autonomy had come. Departing from his earlier paternalistic arguments he now argued that what mattered were not European criteria of "mature" or "immature," but the fact that a "group of people only can develop its own strengths and potentials when they can be fully themselves, and are solely responsible for their own actions and fate."[28] Kraemer thus for the first time gave priority to Indonesia's self-expression, and this marked an important shift in his position. Several factors may have contributed to this change, including Kraemer's own experiences of occupation in Holland, his continued exposure to the parochial and self-interested view which Dutch society held of Indonesia, and certainly his inside knowledge of the Indonesian situation, which made him see that the historical reality had fundamentally changed and that Dutch efforts to reestablish colonial control were futile.

This time around Kraemer's position was very different from the Dutch colonial and political elite. Contesting the legitimacy of the Republic of Indonesia the Dutch government in 1947-1948 initiated military actions against the republic that killed an estimated 100,000 or more Indonesians. Kraemer publicly protested against these actions, arguing that they were nothing short of a colonial war, immoral, un-Christian, as well as shortsighted and doomed to fail. Rather than conquer Indonesia the Dutch people should conquer their own pride, interests, and desire for power.[29] Taking on theological arguments Kraemer criticized Christian politicians who insisted upon the divinely instituted power of the Dutch government in the territories, as well as theologians like Arnold van Ruler who saw

God's revelation communicated through Christian cultures and thus defended continued European colonization. Instead, Kraemer argued that God's will for the Dutch people was to take responsibility for Indonesia as an equal partner. In 1949 international pressure forced the Netherlands to recognize Indonesia's independence.

Kraemer himself in 1948 took up the directorship of the newly established Ecumenical Institute near Geneva, where he helped build up the post-war ecumenical movement. He served in this position until 1956. Most interesting from our perspective are the tensions that emerged in the post-war years between Kraemer's supranational missionary paradigm and the needs of Christians in Europe's former colonies. The demands for nation building in postcolonial societies often brought churches in close alliance with nationalist and other social movements. Kraemer cautioned against these developments, just as he reiterated his warning against syncretism as Christians in the Third World began to engage their neighbors of other faiths in dialogue. In turn, many Asian theologians strongly criticized Kraemer's work and legacy.[30]

These tensions can be illustrated by the contributions of two important Indian theologians who followed Kraemer in leadership positions in the ecumenical movement. M. M. Thomas remained indebted to Kraemer's view of history but called for a "theology of values," which could help Christians communicate with their neighbors of other faiths and ideologies.[31] Kraemer had rejected shared human values as a point of contact between Christianity and other religions, but Thomas criticized Kraemer's approach and instead called for a "Christ-centered syncretism."[32] Similarly Stanley J. Samartha, the long-term director of the WCC's interreligious dialogue programs, directly challenged many of the fundamental theological assumptions in Kraemer's approach to other religions.[33] On the other hand, during these same years Kraemer's legacy was in important ways continued by his pupil Arend T. van Leeuwen, whose 1964 contribution *Christianity in World History* built on aspects of Kraemer's work by sketching a fundamental historical opposition between the anti-religious, secularizing force of the Christian gospel and the world's religions.[34]

KRAEMER'S WORK IN RELATION TO EMPIRE

Kraemer wrote frequently about issues related to nationalism and colonialism.[35] As we have seen, he was sympathetic toward Indonesia's moderate nationalist movements and saw Indonesia's autonomy as the goal of colonial politics. Yet he was also convinced that Indonesia's future independence required Dutch leadership, in which he saw God's calling. These beliefs marked Kraemer as an idealistic representative of the "ethical policy" especially as represented by Protestant Christianity, convinced of its paternal task and superiority.[36] Although Kraemer realized that European colonialism was often motivated by greed and desire for power, and he criticized it as such, he also believed that at its best it was inspired by a "vision of moral responsibility and renewal of life for certain parts of humanity," which had its roots in the French Revolution and was represented by people such as Edmund Burke and Conrad van Deventer.[37] As late as 1960 he saw in colonialism, "the synthesis of Christian sensitivity and humanitarian idealism and enthusiasm."[38] After the postwar emergence of the postcolonial world Kraemer argued that the West had to offer "loyal cooperation" to the East, which "as the result of forces, aspirations and motivations awakened by the West itself, was again taking responsibility for its own fate."[39]

Kraemer always held a positive view of the institutions in which he himself was involved. Although mission did play an important role in the impact of the West on the East, in Kraemer's view it was not part of colonialism, and self-sacrificial in nature. He held very similar views of Western academic scholarship of Eastern societies and religions.[40]

EAST AND WEST IN INTERACTION

Kraemer is mostly remembered for his contribution to the discussion about interreligious dialogue. Yet Kraemer's view of the colonial relationship was foremost cast in a historical and theological perspective on the interaction between East and West, an issue in which he had a lifelong interest and which also deeply influenced his perspective on other religions.[41]

Kraemer rejected both the unbridgeable difference between East and West and their fundamental sameness. East and West were deeply distinct, but they were also drawn together through their historical interaction and especially through the impact of Western colonization and Christian mission on the East. Through this interaction, which Kraemer saw as morally ambivalent but also as inevitable and necessary, the East was thrown into a crisis but also ultimately renewed:

> [We] must state the solemnizing fact of the material and spiritual meeting, the clash and intermingling of East and West, of which drama we are *nolens volens*

the fellow-spectators and fellow-players. The difficult point in it is that it is an occurrence of superhuman purport, driving at a hidden purpose, as well as a satanic conflict of power and weakness, egoism and helplessness.[42]

Kraemer's view of the relationship between East and West was basically a modified modernization thesis. He held that modernizing, social, political, economic, and technological forces ("the West") forced changes upon traditional societies ("the East") that caused a crisis for their social, cultural, and especially religious institutions. What further characterized Kraemer's take on modenization were, first, his Orientalist views which, after first dividing the world in these two contrasting poles, viewed the East as inherently incapable of change so that change that did occur was a reaction to Western initiative. The result was a binary opposition between West/modernity and East/tradition. Second, Kraemer's take on the global modernization process was that in its deepest essence the crisis was spiritual. Yet, unlike conventional views of modernization, which include Christianity among the traditions critically affected by social and other changes, Kraemer saw Christianity as uniquely capable of providing an answer to this spiritual crisis. In fact, not only did Christian faith provide the answer to the crisis, but Kraemer saw Western society, too, critically affected by the crisis provoked by the forces of modernization. As a result Christian mission had a vital contribution to make in East and West.

It is no coincidence that we can hear echoes of Christian motifs of cross and resurrection—and particularly neo-orthodox theology's emphasis on God's Word as both the crisis for and salvation of humanity—in this narrative of crisis and renewal, especially when it pertains to the impact of the West upon the East. Discussing the necessity of Christian renewal of Bali's culture amidst the crisis caused by Western influence, Kraemer referred to the New Testament notion of losing one's life to find it—thus expressing the religious significance of colonialism's impact.[43] Indeed, underlying Kraemer's assessment of colonialism was his conviction that the historical interaction between East and West had divine direction and purpose. The intercultural encounter between East and West drew the whole world into one shared and interdependent reality, which for Kraemer held great eschatological significance.

MISSION IN BALI

We can illustrate Kraemer's view of the encounter between East and West, and especially the way in which he brought this view to bear on the missionary task and other religions, by discussing the role of mission in Bali. After a military campaign Bali had come under Dutch control in 1908, yet the colonial authorities did not allow missions to operate on this predominantly Hindu island. In the 1920s the missions began to challenge this policy, and Kraemer contributed to this discussion with a book analyzing the importance of Christian mission for Bali.[44]

Peter van der Veer, who discusses Kraemer's intervention extensively, observes that his portrayal of the history of Dutch rule over the island followed the standard colonial narrative. Bali's rulers, portrayed as Oriental despots, provoked the legitimate Dutch response to occupy their territories, while their peoples, now protected from their rulers, welcomed the Dutch authorities.[45] The violent character of Dutch colonialism was sanitized. Kraemer then analyzed the impact of Dutch rule, which created a social and spiritual crisis for the "intricately structured society" of Bali.[46]

Turning to religion, Kraemer disagreed with opponents of missions on whether religion had a central integrative role in Bali's society. Rather than being "deeply religious," Kraemer considered Bali's religion the result of a superficial influence of Tantric Hinduism on the animistic and magical indigenous religion. He considered the internal renewal of this religion impossible, instead seeing it "defenselessly adrift amidst the internal and external influences of the modern period" (107). Whatever the integrative character of religion in traditional Balinese society, amidst the global forces of the modern world it was no longer able to provide its people with direction and meaning. Kraemer's missionary gaze also found Bali's religion lacking religious depth. He asserted that its religiosity was this-worldly rather than other-worldly: it centered on pleasing the gods in order to assure a good harvest, a long life, health, and happiness. The gods were not revered but used, which he saw as "the eternal threat to all religious people of all times and all stages of religious development" (109). Nowhere in Bali's religiosity did Kraemer find "real religious seriousness" that had struggled for light and truth through despair and found religious certainty (121). Kraemer saw the Balinese as caught in a social crisis and without sufficient spiritual resources, in need of Christian mission to help them find new religious and moral foundations that could help them work through the confrontation with the West "which the supernatural leadership of history had ordained" (133).

For our purposes most significant in Kraemer's assessment is how he used both his theological understanding of religion and his Orientalist missiological framework as a foil to interpret Bali's religiosity. The heart of Kraemer's missionary approach was the encounter with others, not as non-Christians or as objects for conversion, but as fellow human beings.[47] However, at least as far as Kraemer's writing is concerned, his Orientalist and theological perspectives usually got in the way of an encounter in which the religious other was heard on his or her own terms.

KRAEMER AND ORIENTALISM

As the discussion above clearly illustrates, Kraemer's thinking about other religions and the global cultural interaction was a form of the Orientalism critiqued by Said and others.[48] For a student and later professor at a university which offered scholarly support to the Dutch colonial administration, this is hardly surprising. Orientalism, while presenting itself as gathering and disseminating knowledge about the Orient, really constructed "the Orient" in accordance with Western interests and desires. Its discourse, which included not just academic knowledge but literature and theology as well, also helped legitimize colonial rule through its constructions of the Occidental self as superior and Oriental others as dependent.

Typically, Kraemer's discussions operated with a binary opposition between West and East, with the East covering everything between the Egypt and China, Islam and the South Asian religions. These opposite poles were characterized by different, hierarchically ranked essences. Kraemer spoke consistently of the dynamic and active character of the West versus the passive character of the East. Central differences between East and West, according to Kraemer, were social change, historical consciousness, and the idea of justice. Insofar as these notions did appear in the East, he considered them the result of, or reaction to, Western intervention. Kraemer in some ways even saw anti-colonial protest originate in the West, which has brought colonial domination but also "taught the Orientals to regard it [domination] as a *moral* issue, an entirely new way of viewing it."[49]

Kraemer's work lacks the obvious pejorative comments often characterizing European colonial discourse about the East. Nevertheless Kraemer described the world in terms directly derived from Eurocentric Orientalism, which arguably did the most damage when masked as objective, scientific, and moral knowledge. Most important, in Kraemer's case, Orientalist discourse fundamentally informed his Christian theology, including his view of other religions, Christian mission, and God's presence in the world.

BEYOND KRAEMER AND EMPIRE

The central question in this volume is how historically important Christian think-ers have related to the empires of their time. That question is raised to no small degree in order to learn from their struggles for our own lives, in contexts that con-tinue to be determined by political and economic empires, and the claims of those empires for moral and religious support. Kraemer's life and work show us the dif-ficulty and complexity of living in empire, as Christians or otherwise, and it is important that we learn both from his prophetic recognition and critique of mis-guided defenses of empire as well as from the problematic way in which central aspects of Kraemer's own thought were captive to colonial and Orientalist modes of thinking. Kraemer helped give voice to Christian protest against the Nazi occu-pation and its persecution of Jews, and after 1945 he came out unconditionally for Indonesian independence and against Dutch recolonization. At the same time, we have seen that much of Kraemer's missiological and ecumenical views were deeply embedded in ideological frameworks that supported European colonialism. Because Kraemer as an ecumenical thinker clearly sought to overcome Eurocentric and narrow nationalist identifications, his work serves as a strong reminder of the difficulty of escaping the hegemonic discourses of empire.

Because of this ideological captivity to the culture of empire, many of Kraemer's ecumenical and missiological perspectives are of limited use today. Yet we can still learn from the way in which Kraemer did not ignore empire but recognized the necessity to reflect on it theologically throughout his career, and attempted to do so from what he took to be a global ecumenical rather than a narrow Euro-centric orientation. And while his moral and theological justifications of European colonialism are deeply problematic, Kraemer was certainly not blind to the mate-rial reality of colonialism and empire, nor to the suffering they caused. Thus a continuing relevance of Kraemer's work lies in his attention to the social, economic, cultural, and religious consequences of the colonial interaction, which he consistently referred to as a crisis for the colonial society. Today, similar crises and sufferings are brought about by an important heir of European colonialism, the globalization of neo-liberal capitalism—now in important ways linked to America's empire—with its disregard for universal human dignity, economic jus-tice, and ecological sustainability.

We can use this continuity to illustrate how theological reflection in the postco-lonial world has moved beyond Kraemer by revisiting two central assumptions in his missiological vision in relation to today's crises of the global community. As we saw, Kraemer described the colonial interaction as a social and spiritual crisis for the colonized society that needed to be healed by Christian faith and ethics—as should the spiritual crises of the colonizing West. The global Christian community should thus be involved in the healing of the world, though not, in Kraemer's view, by cooperating with (religious) others but precisely by presenting Christian faith as an absolute and unique divine-human reality untouched by religious syncretism. Today, the proposal for a supranational Christian absolutism as the answer to the crises that threaten the global community seems not only inadequate but self-defeating, as these crises command building bridges between (religious) communities and a committed but nonabsolutist, communicative, and eschatological approach to our own religious identities and truths. Thus, many Christian theologians in the postcolonial world seek mutually enriching relations with other faiths, emphasize the historical interrelatedness of the religions, and argue for reading the Bible intertextually with other religious texts.

Similarly, Kraemer's view of the encounters between East and West—or in our time the processes of economic, political, and technological globalization—as somehow part of God's purpose for humanity hinged upon the critical assumption that through these encounters God was drawing humanity to greater unity and community. While Kraemer saw both human sin and God's saving activity at work in the historical process, his fundamental theological assumption was that overall global history expresses God's purpose—indeed, this assumption led him to affirm colonialism as a necessary historical instrument. Yet while Kraemer in the early twentieth century could perhaps still hope that the global cultural, economic, and technological interactions were drawing together still largely isolated human communities from around the world into greater networks of human communication, responsibility, and community, today we can no longer simply take such optimism about the future of global interaction on face value. Ours is a shrinking world for those who are privileged in terms of wealth, freedom to travel, and access to information, yet it is also a world of ever higher barriers for the majority of people who lack those privileges. Rather than share Kraemer's optimism that saw God's hand in processes of modernization and globalization, we need to look for God's presence first among the ever-larger groups of people in the postcolonial world who are victimized and left behind by globalization. Where Kraemer saw the crises brought by modernity as an opportunity for renewal, today many of the world's poor are excluded from the benefits of processes of globalization to such an extent that they face, historically speaking, a cross without resurrection. And precisely for people marginalized by globalization, religion—sometimes Christianity, sometimes another—is often one of the few sources of empowerment. Indeed, it is often religion's this-worldly capacity to help cope with the struggles of daily life for dignity, survival, and resistance that is of great significance to the victims of globalization. A theology for the postcolonial world should begin by affirming the central importance to God of those marginalized by historical processes of colonization, modernization, and globalization, and should theologically appreciate their religions—Christian or otherwise—as a potential source of divine empowerment.

Further Reading

Primary Sources

Kraemer, Hendrik. "Imperialism and Self-Expression." *The Student World* 28, no. 81 (1935): 328-48.

_____. *The Christian Message in a Non-Christian World*. London: Edinburgh House Press, 1947.

_____. "The Missionary Implication of the End of Western Colonialism and the Collapse of Western Christianity." *The Student World* 53, no. 1/2 (1960): 195-206.

Secondary Sources

Hallencreutz, Carl F. *Kraemer Towards Tambaram: A Study in Hendrik Kraemer's Missionary Approach*. English rev. ed. Studia Missionalia Upsaliensia 7. Lund: Gleerup, 1966.

Said, Edward W. *Orientalism*. New York, N.Y.: Vintage Books, 1978.

Steenbrink, Karel A. *Dutch Colonialism and Indonesian Islam: Contacts and Conflicts, 1596-1950*. Currents of Encounter 7. Translated by Jan Steenbrink and Henry Jansen. Amsterdam: Rodopi, 1993.

CHAPTER 26

Reinhold Niebuhr

Larry L. Rasmussen

Karl Paul Reinhold Niebuhr (1892-1971), a dramatist of theological ideas in the public arena, was a public intellectual who enjoyed a considerable following among secular as well as religious audiences. His thought centers in his dynamic understanding of human nature and human history as rooted in his theological anthropology. Every treatment of empire by Niebuhr reflects an understanding of society in light of human nature, its reach, and its powers.

Niebuhr's analysis and reflection are concrete and contextual, even when universal themes and patterns recur throughout in a consistent theory of power. The right beginning point, then, is Niebuhr's own context and the formative events that set the direction of his thinking.

Niebuhr's formative years were spent in the parish, with the thirteen years at Bethel Evangelical Church in Detroit (1915-1928) decisive for his theology. On the anvil of Detroit's harsh industrial reality, the trauma of World War I, and the onset of the Great Depression, Niebuhr tested the alternatives he would find wanting—religious and secular liberalism and Marxism—and began to put in place the baselines of the neo-Augustinian/neo-Reformation school later identified with him: Christian realism. Detroit also kindled the Christian indignation that would always fuel Niebuhr's activism, as well as his restless quest to illumine the day's events theologically. He found himself opposing both Henry Ford and the Ku Klux Klan, championing the labor movement, chairing the Mayor's Inter-Racial Committee, serving on the Detroit Council of Churches Industrial Relations Commission, joining the Fellowship of Reconciliation, and pastoring a growing congregation. In addition, Lydia Hosto Niebuhr, his widowed mother already long skilled in parish affairs, freed her son's week for a full speaking schedule and a steady stream of articles for the national church and secular press. Niebuhr would write later that the "convictions which dawned in my pastorate" were elaborated "in a teaching position in a theological seminary" (Union Seminary in New York, where he taught from 1928 until retiring in 1960).[1] But they were indeed convictions forged in a city pastorate.

Niebuhr is remembered, however, not for his parish ministry but his career as a social ethicist and theologian of public life. The 1930s, '40s, and '50s were the heyday of this career, years when a war consumed much of the world and the U.S. assumed a global imperial role in Cold War competition with the U.S.S.R. and its allies. Niebuhr, always the contextual theologian, thus turned his attention largely to global politics and the temptations and responsibilities of United States American power. Two volumes at the end of these decades speak most directly to empire, *The Irony of American History* (1952) and *The Structure of Nations and Empires* (1959). Other works are important as well.[2] With the exception of *Moral Man and Immoral Society*, all the relevant texts are theologically grounded in his Gifford Lectures and the theological *pièce de résistance* of this period, *The Nature and Destiny of Man* (1941, 1943).[3]

Yet Niebuhr's first thoughts on American empire surface even earlier in his career as a teacher and publicist, before any of the above-mentioned volumes and before his well-known treatment of the U.S. and U.S.S.R. as competing imperial powers. These, too, are postwar reflections. But the war is World War I, and Niebuhr's writing is a 1930 *The Atlantic Monthly* article entitled "Awkward Imperialists."

Neither the earlier nor later treatments are intelligible, however, apart from Niebuhr's understanding of "the self and the dramas of history" and his theory of power, group political power above all. We turn to these as the necessary segue to his treatment of empire.

Power and Empire

For Niebuhr, the structures of the self and the structures of society are analogous. Human nature makes history what it is *as* history. But how does human nature determine the character of history and the play of empire? Langdon Gilkey's volume, *On Niebuhr: A Theological Study*, together with his essay, "Reinhold Niebuhr's Theology of History," provide appropriate summaries of key themes, as does Niebuhr's own text, *The Structure of Nations and Empires*.[4]

The Structure of Nations and Empires begins with the observation that "the communities of mankind, like every human achievement and contrivance, are subject to endless variety and progression."[5] Tribe, city-state, nation, empires ancient and modern—all these are diverse forms in the ongoing human quest for community. For Niebuhr, our basic nature as creatures is social. Because love as "comm-union" is the very law of our being, we endlessly and necessarily seek the self's meaning and fulfillment in diverse, changing communities. In the course of this, persistent and perennial elements and patterns recur amid the contingent and novel ones— thus the "structure" of nations and empires. Still, neither the contingent nor the enduring elements are grounded in the nature of empire or the nature of tribe or state. Rather, they express the underlying nature of the human self as a history-making social creature. The nature of this history-making social creature can be sketched as follows, as that bears on the topic of empire.

Niebuhr spoke often of the "indeterminate possibilities" of history, empire among them. New cultural forms will arise, others will die. Endless levels of technical, social, legal, and political economic organization are possible, though all are only provisional. The reason? Human nature is "incurably creative," in Niebuhr's view. History is thus endlessly dynamic.[6] We are always breaking the mold, with no resting point.

This restless creativity and these indeterminate possibilities mean the triumph of human freedom over structure. That, in turn, meant that no "final" society, in the sense of permanent, is possible in history.[7] One implication is that among the "laws" of empire, a sure one is this: they fall. (The one thousand year empire of the Nazi Third Reich lasted twelve years. Rome did far better, but its ruins have long outlived its conquests.)

Yet Niebuhr's thought is paradoxical. While human nature is endlessly creative, and history knows novelty, at the same time human nature remains constant enough to guarantee that the future will show the same general dynamics as the past and present.[8] This includes the manifestation of persisting sinfulness. "Where there is history at all, there is freedom," says Niebuhr, and "where there is freedom, there is sin."[9] Niebuhr thus rejects any possibility of a perfect society in history. Not to be lost here is that the constancy of human nature lets Niebuhr make comparisons across diverse (and always imperfect) societies, exposing remarkable similarities where they may not be expected, at least not by those given to under-scoring differences and novelty. (Niebuhr's exposition of the Cold War protagonists, the U.S. and the U.S.S.R., as both "idealist" imperial powers will soon provide an example.)

These aspects of human nature and history mean the continuation of both sin and grace in old and new forms. They also mean that the possibilities of evil tend to develop apace with the possibilities of good. Advances in social structures, like technical advances, thus bring new possibilities for malevolence as well as benevolence.[10] In Niebuhr's words:

> Every human advance offers new possibilities of catastrophe and every virtue has the possibilities of a vicious aberration in it . . . The conclusion most abhorrent to the modern mood is that the possibilities of evil grow with the possibilities of good, and that human history is therefore not so much a chronicle of the progressive victory of the good over evil, of cosmos over chaos, as the story of an ever increasing cosmos, creating ever increasing possibilities of chaos.[11]

For Niebuhr no level of achievement and no concrete social order appear as "righteous" before God. That is, none perfectly reveal the rule and being of God. All history thus stands under divine judgment until its end. Still, all civilizations, social orders, and groups in history are not thereby rendered equal in virtue or worth for Niebuhr.[12] He never paints all empires with the brush of moral equivalence, even in the face of common imperial impulses. The moral differences of "less and more" can matter immensely, even when no community stands righteous before God.

The resolution of history's agonies is not in terms of the manifestation of divine power *over* evil—as sinners all, that would kill us all. Rather, it is in terms of the manifestation of the divine love and mercy *to* evil. God through Christ manifests the divine conquest of evil "through forgiveness and renewal rather than through power and sovereignty, that is, in and through human freedom and not over it."[13] This makes the play of human freedom and power central to Niebuhr's sociopolitical analysis, just as it makes clear why he sought to rally religious resources for the transformation of society in and through that freedom and power, precarious as it is.

These summaries linking Niebuhr's two consuming theological subjects, human nature and human history, set the stage for his treatment of power and empire in the period of his greatest attention, the post-World War II Cold War competition between the U.S. and the U.S.S.R.. His analysis follows.

In *The Irony of American History*, Niebuhr argues that neither protagonist, the

Soviet Union or the U.S.A., thought of itself as an empire, though each behaved like one. Each claimed an ideology that was officially nonimperial. Thus neither nation spoke of itself as imperial, though each found occasion to name the other "an evil empire" while identifying itself as *the* bulwark against the other's imperialism.

U.S. democratic capitalists and Soviet socialists did not fancy the global reach of their interests as imperial because both were "idealists," to use Niebuhr's term. Both were even utopian in their vision of a world rid of tyranny and marked by prosperity. The communists were "hard utopians" (Niebuhr's phrase). That is, they were ardent believers that the course of history was headed the same direction as they and that it was meet, right, and salutary to employ all means necessary to see the proper end of history realized: namely, a socialist society of genuine equality and a shared, common good. By way of contrast, the Americans were "soft utopians," confident that progressive elements around the world would align with the march of democracy and the free market as the combination that best meets basic human longings for freedom wed to prosperity. This utopianism is "soft," Niebuhr says, in that it wins by demonstration and cooperation rather than force and imposition. It has little taste for the sorrows of empire and prefers example, the example of an economically successful democracy open to all races and creeds. Force, including military force, may well be needed, but in order to contain communism and its hard utopianism, thereby making space for democratic capitalism. Niebuhr's point, to repeat, is that neither superpower conceived its designs as *imperial,* though each conceived the other in exactly those terms. Both also denied their own imperialism for idealistic reasons.[14]

Niebuhr's second point in the 1962 work is that both U.S. and Soviet utopianisms were doomed by the ironies of history. History rarely conforms to human dreams and restless human nature is always breaking its own molds, sometimes for better, sometimes for worse. History is thus inherently volatile and given to unplanned outcomes. "Our own nation," Niebuhr wrote, "always a vivid symbol of the most characteristic attitudes of a bourgeois culture, is less potent to do what it wants in the hour of its greatest strength than it was in the hour of its infancy. . . . The pattern of the historical drama grows more quickly than the strength of even the most powerful . . . nation."[15]

Yet Niebuhr's theology of history put him in touch with such pathos and irony well before this exposition in *The Irony of American History.* A passage penned two decades earlier, in 1943, might have been dated 2003, save for the reference to the Soviets: "Americans who imagine that they can establish a world order upon the basis of American conceptions of 'free enterprise' will be as certainly frustrated by the complexities of history as [the] Communists, because of those same complexities, will be disappointed in their hope for a world revolution."[16]

That passage found a companion piece as Niebuhr contemplated eventual victory by one side or the other in the Cold War. He foresaw a certain danger, no matter who emerged victorious. (Attending to moral differences and eschewing moral equivalence, he ardently hoped it would be the U.S. and worked toward that end.) This again from 1962: "The victors would . . . face the 'imperial' problem of using power in global terms but from one particular center of authority, so preponderant and unchallenged that its world rule would almost certainly violate basic standards of justice."[17] (I interject an aside that follows from this: Guantanamo, Abu Ghraib, tortuous endruns around international conventions on torture, literally unwarranted invasions of citizens' privacy, ideological tests for sorting friends and foes in government itself—none of these would have taken Niebuhr by surprise, whatever anger and outspoken opposition they would certainly have evoked. They confirm his worry that "basic standards of justice" will "almost certainly" be violated by those wielding imperial power.)

This Cold War analysis and these post-Cold War examples all conform to Niebuhr's theory of power, rooted in his neo-Augustinian and neo-Reformation doctrine of human nature and human history. Seven theses supply the stripped-down version of this critical element in Niebuhr's treatment of human community in all forms. We entertain them here. They draw largely, but not exclusively, from *Moral Man and Immoral Society* (1932).

"There is no ethical force strong enough to place inner checks upon the use of power if its quantity is inordinate."[18] Wherever power is excessively concentrated—political-economic power, social power, religious power—neither moral appeal nor sweet reason is a significant check, much less the means of transformation. Like Frederick Douglass, Niebuhr was convinced that "when collective power . . . exploits weakness, it can never be dislodged unless [countervailing] power is raised against it."[19]

Evil and injustice flow from imbalances of power. Abuse of power follows from its concentration. True, power is necessary for the organization and maintenance of human society and for social justice itself. Power is a requirement for achieving greater good even as it is also the means for greater evil. Powerlessness is certainly no virtue! It, too, can be a factor in exploitation (the powerless are the most vulnerable of all, and exploited because of that). But our attention, like Niebuhr's, is to power in the hands of those who hold it and benefit from it; and that power invariably generates injustice in the process of protecting privilege.

This propensity to injustice on the part of unchecked, reigning power put Niebuhr on the side of the underdog again and again, and led him to an important distinction: *the disinherited have more of a right to fight for their (violated) rights than the powerful have to extend their (protected) rights.* It is thus possible to distinguish between morally justified and morally unjustified self-interest and self-seeking. Differently said, all cases of self-assertion, even arrogance, are not the same. This point was never lost on Niebuhr as he measured disproportions of power and took the side of countervailing power.

The institutionalized power of privilege is often more covert than overt, giving it the appearance of nonviolence. This nurtures self-delusion on the part of those who wield such systemic power. They see overt opposition to their privilege as "a power move" on the part of dissidents, while their own daily institutional habits are perceived as a force for stability and tranquility. Niebuhr put it this way: "It is significant . . . that the middle-class Church which disavows violence, even to the degree of frowning upon a strike, is usually composed of people who have enough economic and other forms of covert power to be able to dispense with the more overt forms of violence."[20]

All this makes democracy and democratic power precious to Niebuhr, both as a check on the ever-present imperial impulses in human nature and as the matrix for achieving social good. But it is not democracy as the franchise alone. Votes mean little if influence can be bought or subtly coerced. Rather, democracy is genuine when two conditions exist: (1) when it is a form of government in which criticism of government, even resistance to government, is built into the principle of government itself, that is, when space is systematically created to organize countervailing power; and (2) when democracy is the means of sharing political, economic, and social power in the interests of social justice and the common good. Democracy is not, for Niebuhr, maximal liberty married to corporate-regulated markets in the interests of an ownership society. Democracy is a balance of all three of democracy's classic values—freedom, equality, community. More precisely for Niebuhr, freedom and equality in roughly equal measure are the regulative principles of justice in the interests of a more communitarian (or common good) democracy.

With such attention to power and human nature, we can understand why Niebuhr emphasizes both clauses of his famous defense of democracy: "Man's capacity for justice makes democracy possible; man's inclination to injustice makes democracy necessary."[21] In short, a Niebuhrian is always wary of inordinate concentrations of power, even under the banner of democracy and freedom (the inclination to injustice). Likewise, a Niebuhrian always seeks to make space for countering inordinate power in the interests of a common good that is not only desirable, but attainable (the capacity for justice).

Powerful democratic nations frequently suffer from a certain naïveté and self-delusion. They fail to recognize the sure imperialism which flows from disproportions of power between more powerful nations and less powerful, whether domestic polities are democratic or not. Indeed, the very moral idealism that bolsters the case for democracies often serves not only to justify their imperialism but intensify it. Power operating behind a screen of acclaimed ideal ends is frequently more self-delusory and sometimes more evil in practice than open and cynical defiance of moral ends. This is Niebuhr's parallel, for politics, of Luther's remark that oftentimes the curses of the ungodly are more pleasing to God than the alleluias of the pious! (Another aside: George W. Bush perfectly illustrates this naïveté and self-delusion when he says straightforwardly that the U.S. mission of global freedom is not imperial and ought not be viewed by others in that way.)

Lastly, *religion normally intensifies power dynamics.* Religious *humility* tends to check the headstrong exercise of power and hold it accountable to standards beyond itself. It recognizes that we are judged by transcendent standards not of our own making and that we belong to a community of responsibility and accountability which doesn't begin and end with our own ego and will, even our own collective ego and will. On the other hand, religious *pride* tends to foster extremism, fanaticism, intolerance, and absolutism. "Religion is humility before the absolute and self-assertion in terms of the absolute."[22]

This note on religion is important to imperial politics for two reasons. First, it means that politically conservative religious culture can powerfully bolster nationalist movements to unify society as a collective "we" vis-à-vis a threatening "they." Leaders sense this keenly, so now and again they attach divine sanction to their missions, sometimes opportunistically, sometimes with genuine conviction. Second, the play of religion and power also means that jihad and crusade may easily come to mirror one another. When the liberation cause of empire is conceived of as religiously pure and driven in a classic battle of good versus evil, all means are justified and even, given status in a divine mission.

Niebuhr's complex understanding of human nature and history had no patience with such collective illusions, wherever they appeared and under whatever auspices. But as the first-generation child of immigrants, he was especially keen to be an enthusiastic student of his own nation—thus his early and continuous attention to U.S. American culture and the events shaping it. This attention includes sensitivity to imperial impulses very early on, so we turn next to what appears to be his earliest treatment of empire. It not only anticipates later treatments, it adds to them. It also provides a fitting exposition of his working theology and theory of power.

In 1930 Niebuhr penned *The Atlantic Monthly* essay, "Awkward Imperialists."[23] While the theological anthropology assumed is the same as that forged just a few years earlier in Detroit and elaborated later in *The Nature and Destiny of Man*, the specific subject of American empire is provoked by the post-World War I emergence of the U.S. as a nation relatively untouched by the terrible destruction of "the Great War." The change of status for the nation was dramatic. Before the war, the U.S. was a debtor nation. After the war, North Atlantic nations were indebted to the U.S. The U.S. also emerged as a highly productive nation in the post-war years. Its exports exceeded its imports and "America" was on its way to becoming, quite suddenly, the world's wealthiest nation. For Niebuhr, that would mean imperial impulses and temptations.

Alerted to these impulses, Niebuhr next notes two historical novelties interlaced with the persisting elements of empire. First, while most past empires were established and consolidated by military power, "our" age is markedly an age of economic power. So it is quite natural "that our nation, the wealthiest in the world, should become the real empire of modern civilization. Our imperialism reveals ancient motives, but the technique is new. . . .We are the first empire of the world to establish our sway without legions. Our legions are dollars" (670). The primacy of economic power over military and priestly power and alliances leads to the second factor. "We are not prosperous because we are imperialists; we are imperialists because we are prosperous" (670). This empire is "economic overlordship through economic penetration" (671).

This significant shift of imperial means and underlying power—a prescient anticipation of post-Niebuhrian discussions of "neo-colonialism"—has far-reaching implications that Niebuhr does not pursue at the moment (though we will do so soon.) Instead, he moves directly from his description of the U.S. in the post-World War I world to the kind of moral reflection that became his signature. That it was rooted in his theological anthropology, yet eschewed explicit God-talk for a largely secular readership like *Atlantic Monthly*'s, bears the same signature. Here is his next paragraph, in full.

> It is inevitable that men should hate those who hold power over them. They may love the virtuous and admire the brilliant; but they hate the powerful. Hatred is compounded of envy and fear, and power breeds both. The fear is justified because powerful individuals and nations, even when they make benevolent pretensions, are not as generous as their pretensions or even their intentions. A defect in the human imagination obscures the mixture of motives which enters into human actions and social policies and makes honest self-analysis almost impossible; and lack of social intelligence prevents the holder of power from gauging the consequences of his actions in the lives of others, particularly if no direct contact is possible. If the envy is not as justified as the fear, it is at least as inevitable. Great power is usually accompanied by special privilege (a proof that it is not wielded as unselfishly as is imagined), and privilege incites envy. (671)

Niebuhr then addresses the resentment that imperial power inevitably creates and which every empire must counteract in some fashion. Before he goes to the English, Germans, and U.S. Americans as examples, he includes an aside that foreshadows his fuller treatment of democracy in *The Children of Light and the Children of Darkness:*

> Democracy is a device for making power sufferable in a community partly by making it derivative and responsible and partly by giving it the semblance of social responsibility and derivation. Since social intelligence in political communities has never been very high, the semblance of democracy has been almost as efficacious as the reality. (671)

(Recall the contention of *Moral Man and Immoral Society,* itself about to be drafted, that the power of democracy is often more covert than overt in democratic institutions, making such coercive power seem nonviolent. Further, while democracy as a polity is preferred, it is not exempt from imperious uses of its powers.)

But, Niebuhr continues, the techniques of democratic rule have not to date been developed in and for international relations. Imperial powers are thus left to their own resources in addressing resentment. Some have fared better than others, he says, again eschewing moral equivalence. The English have done better than most because of a certain genius for politics that usually gauges the interests and reactions of their subjects before they issue in social and political violence. Neither the Germans nor the Americans display such "political grace," Niebuhr goes on to say.

> If the Germans were too much the philosophers and therefore too much the absolutists to engage successfully in the relativities of politics, we are too much the engineers. Our power is derived from our engineering ability, and we erroneously assume that the same genius which created it can wield it. (672)

This sweeping insight, so typical of Niebuhr, is soon qualified and supplemented so as to uncover further reasons for our imperial disposition. U.S. wealth is hardly explained *solely* by native engineering acumen. "[W]e had a virgin continent to exploit"; "energetic and vigorous stocks of the European population came to our shores to supply the energy for its exploitation"; timely inventions such as the steam engine and telegraph hastened the continent's economic unity; and, if Weber and Tawney are right about the Protestant ethic, even "our religion contributed to our prosperity, [adding] moral self-respect to the more obvious incentives of commercial and industrial energy" (672).

As noted, this economic juggernaut made us imperialists less by deliberate design than by the power of both our virtues and vices in tandem with economic needs and incentives. "We were forced to conquer foreign markets to prevent the automatic machine from glutting our home markets; we needed foreign investment opportunities to get rid of our surplus wealth, particularly since we had not learned to distribute it more equitably at home; and our industry reached out into the world to feed the maw of the machine with raw materials" (672).

Only after this lengthy introduction about a new, economy-based imperialism with an American label do we arrive at Niebuhr's topic sentence: "Our resulting imperial power is administered with singular awkwardness" (672-73). The sources of awkwardness are numerous. We greet the rising tide of resentment against us "with a mingled feeling of incredulity and injured innocence." And because "we are a business people" who know little about the intricacies of politics, especially international politics, "we seek a businesslike rather than a political settlement of conflicts," little realizing this "leaves human and intangible factors out of consideration" (673). The lack of political imagination is worsened by the suddenness of

our coming into imperial power and by the fact that we are geographically too isolated from the world to enter intimately into the thoughts of others.

> It was only yesterday that we were a youthful nation, conscious of making an
> adventure in democratic government which the older nations did not quite
> approve, and we still imagine that it is our virtue rather than our power which
> the older nations envy. We cannot believe that any of them have outstripped
> us in the theory and practice of democratic government. We hold ourselves
> aloof from international councils because we feel ourselves too powerful to be
> in need of counseling with others, but we are able to practise the deception of
> imagining that our superior political virtue rather than our economic strength
> makes such abstention possible and advisable. (673)

To these defects rendering American imperialism so awkward—our naïve engineering and business problem-solving dispositions, our geographic isolation and
distance of mind and heart from other nations, and our political adolescence—
Niebuhr adds another, this one religio-cultural. While our prosperity has largely
dissipated the virtue of self-discipline that our puritanism inculcated, not all the
puritan *vices* have taken leave. We continue to have a puritan penchant "for over-
simplifying moral and social problems" (674). Niebuhr here cites with approval
a Mr. Garvin, who writes in *The London Observer* that "the man who wants to be
just and does not know how to be wise is dangerous. That is particularly true, since
self-interest is bound to color every conception of justice" (674). Niebuhr adds to
Garvin's commentary his own. "It has always been the habit of fortunate people to
ascribe their luck or their fortune to their own moral qualities rather than to any
inscrutability of history, and our fortune-favored nation has developed this habit
with the greatest possible consistency" (674). In other words,

> [O]ur puritan background has made us more than ordinarily naïve in deal-
> ing with the complexities of modern international life. We make simple moral
> judgments, remain unconscious of the self-interest which colors them, support
> them with an enthusiasm which derives from our waning but still influential
> evangelical piety, and are surprised that our contemporaries do not accept us
> as saviors of the world. (674)

All these 1930 reasons for imperial awkwardness foreshadow Niebuhr's better-
known treatment of American imperialism two decades later. Yet sometimes his
early analysis not only hints of what is to come, it bears the very same language. To

wit: "The fact is that our political naïveté betrays us into sentimentality, and sentimentality always looks like idealism from an inside perspective and like hypocrisy from an outside one" (675).

As Niebuhr finishes his essay with a look ahead, the prospects for American imperialism are, as always, qualified in the manner mandated by his understanding of human nature and history.

> We shall remain the economic overlords of the Western world and prove ourselves uncompromising on anything which touches the essentials of our empire. No one knows what the future may hold in store for us. The fate of imperialists is always uncertain, and awkward imperialists run a double hazard. Responsibility sometimes forces the development of latent capacities, and it may be that we shall learn political grace and acquire a technique adequate for the problems before us in time to be saved from disaster. A decade of world responsibility does not offer sufficient evidence for any bold generalizations. But such evidence as is available certainly does not encourage the faith that we shall develop a political genius equal to the responsibilities thrust upon us by our imperial power. (675)

COMMENTARY AND CRITIQUE

What is the evidence, seventy-five years later, of moral and political maturity appropriate to the vast power wielded by the U.S.? Recent history is not heartening. U.S. utopianism certainly lives on. The civil religion version was on full display at the memorial service for President Ronald Reagan in the National Cathedral. Reagan's favorite text, chosen years before, was read as Scripture itself: the Puritan vision of this nation as a city-set-on-a-hill and representing a new start for humankind. Puritan confidence, even language, marked the Clinton administration as well, with its talk of "The New Covenant." But the most blatant surge of utopianism issuing in imperialism came with the George W. Bush administration. The volume of two of its leading neo-conservatives, Richard Perle and David Frum, is entitled *The End of Evil*. The initial Pentagon name for the bombing of Afghanistan in pursuit of terrorists was "Operation Infinite Justice." And even with the Iraqi quagmire and the neo-conservative agenda of "benevolent global hegemony" of a "Pax Americana" in shambles, President Bush did not shrink from global freedom and democracy as the sacred mission of the U.S. in and on behalf of the world. His second inaugural address says straightforwardly: "It is the policy of the

United States to seek and support the growth of democratic movements and institutions in every nation and culture, with the ultimate goal of ending tyranny in the world."[24] American idealism and utopianism run deep as the ideology of an officially optimistic society.

How does this occur in a "soft utopian" imperial nation like the U.S.A.? Douglas John Hall, deeply immersed in Niebuhrian perspectives, outlines three succinct and successive moves. First, we dissociate evil from our own identity and essence, despite the fact we were a slaveholding nation, South and North, and a land-grabbing settler nation, East and West, across the formative centuries of our existence. Second, we believe evil can be eliminated. The historical optimism of a "can do" culture occupying the moral high ground is a recurring theme across U.S. history here, what Niebuhr cites as our identity as engineers and business people with a Puritan penchant for moral simplicity. Third, we often see our national role as the eliminators of evil. Evil is thus "out there," not "in here," and our national redeemer role is to rally the forces of good against the forces of evil in a mission laid upon us by God and history.[25]

This is the dynamic of set-high-on-a-hill American exceptionalism. It is the same exceptionalism that largely assumed the right of continental expansion, and, when needed, justified overt and covert interventions abroad, in keeping with the Monroe Doctrine and its several corollaries. Two tenets of the George W. Bush administration reinforce this, now in a world with a single superpower (though an increasingly challenged one). These tenets take the form of a fundamental objective and a fundamental faith. The fundamental objective is the prevention of any nation or group of nations from threatening America's dominance. Yet this "benevolent hegemony" of the neo-conservatives and hard-line conservatives is not theirs alone. It is the position of the government's official 2002 *National Security Strategy of the United States*, which speaks of "a distinctly American internationalism that reflects the union of our values and our national interests."[26] This union of values and interests belongs to the fundamental, largely bi-partisan, faith that the maximal use of American power is good for America and good for the world (the confluence of our interests and values with those to which other peoples aspire). Here Bush taps a stream that runs much deeper and broader than the conservatives and radicals at the core of his administration. This path trails back to the origins of the nation itself. That formidable stream is faith, freedom, and free markets as the creed of a redeemer nation "with the soul of a church" (G.K. Chesterton). Present conservative religion and politics taps into that stream whether neo-conservatives prosper or not.

But there is another, more critical element that will outlast the grim fate of the Bush years. This element was already captured by Niebuhr in his 1930 essay, though it was not elaborated. I will state it as a thesis. If you wish to understand U.S. domestic and foreign policy since World War II, even World War I, and if you wish to know why the U.S. will seek to exercise imperial power for the foreseeable future, no matter who is president, you need understand only one thing: the exacting requirements of U.S. American affluence. Both Presidents Bush have said exactly the same thing, the first at the Earth Summit in 1992, the second after September 11, 2001: "The American way of life is not up for negotiation." They were not aberrant in this, or partisan. We will do all we need and can to keep the American way of life *as American affluence* from the negotiating table. With our inordinate power, that means an imperial posture virtuously clad in an ideology of democratic capitalism, with freedom and prosperity the promise and the lure. Such prosperity is in fact the validation of faith, freedom, and free markets as the creed of a redeemer nation, indeed the creed of a righteous empire that does not understand its unrighteousness.

There is, however, another kind of American exceptionalism, and it, too, is possible among the "indeterminate possibilities" of history. Niebuhr himself worked tirelessly for it, not without effect. It is far from the moral vanity and idealist moral fantasy that has only made American power more dangerous in the Bush years. It is, in Peter Beinart's words, "our recognition that we are not angels that makes us exceptional. Because we recognize that we can be corrupted by unlimited power, we accept the restraints that empires refuse."[27] The Marshall Plan and post-World War II rebuilding of defeated enemy nations, rendering them friends and allies, is a noteworthy example. The exceptionalism of greatness, then, is humility and the sober realism that attends the morally hazardous decisions of wielding great power on the part of those who know they are not virtuous and whose way of life is always up for renegotiation. Reciprocity, with freedom and equality the regulative principles of justice, is the proper stance, rather than the righteousness of overweening power. Exactly this was Niebuhr's message throughout the years he watched American empire, from within and with a wary eye, as a prophet in the king's court.

It would be very un-Niebuhrian to close without a critique of his position. He always expected to learn from others, and change. His own doctrine of human nature insists that all views, his own included, are partial and tainted. A comparison with his fellow ethicist and colleague, John C. Bennett, exposes some shortcomings. Bennett, in *The Radical Imperative*,[28] resurrects sharp attention to economic issues and economic justice, whereas these had largely slipped from view in Niebuhr's Cold War critique of competing empires. There is some irony here in that Niebuhr was so far-seeing and insightful in his 1930 "neo-colonialist" analysis of economic power as the base and drive of emerging American empire. In any event, Bennett is more sensitive to the dynamics of colonialism and the voices of the "Third World," as well as the voices of women. And while Niebuhr maintained his attention to, and critique of, white racism vis-à-vis blacks in the U.S., there is no parallel attention to Native Americans and their experience of home-grown imperialism. Niebuhr's own language of a "virgin continent" awaiting European exploitation participates in the myths held by those same European immigrants and their progeny. Bennett's embrace of liberation theologies reflects a sharper sensitivity to these voices, their experience, and their critique of empire. (In fairness, it must also be said that Bennett, always a Niebuhrian, was still working during the years Niebuhr's health prevented that, and that these years were generative ones for liberation theologies at home and abroad as well as for the second wave of feminism.)

This criticism acknowledged, Reinhold Niebuhr remains to this day the single most incisive student of U.S. American power; and his insights flow from his theology of human nature and history.

FURTHER READING

Primary Sources

Niebuhr, Reinhold. *Moral Man and Immoral Society*. New York, N.Y.: Charles Scribner's Sons, 1932.

_____. *The Nature and Destiny of Man*. 2 vols. New York, N.Y.: Charles Scribner's Sons, 1941, 1943.

_____. *The Children of Light and the Children of Darkness*. New York, N.Y.: Charles Scribner's Sons, 1944.

_____. *The Structure of Nations and Empires*. New York, N.Y.: Charles Scribner's Sons, 1959.

_____. *The Irony of American History*. 1952. Reprint, New York, N.Y.: Charles Scribner's Sons, 1962.

Secondary Sources

Brown, Charles C. *Niebuhr and His Age: Reinhold Niebuhr's Prophetic Role and Legacy*. Harrisburg, Pa.: Trinity Press International, 2002.

_____, ed. *A Reinhold Niebuhr Reader: Selected Essays, Articles, and Book Reviews*. Philadelphia, Pa.: Trinity Press International, 1992.

Gilkey, Langdon. *On Niebuhr: A Theological Study*. Chicago, Ill.: University of Chicago Press, 2001.

Rasmussen, Larry L., ed. *Reinhold Niebuhr: Theologian of Public Life*. Minneapolis, Minn.: Fortress Press, 1991.

CHAPTER 27

Dietrich Bonhoeffer

David N. Field

Dietrich Bonhoeffer (1906-1945) lived within a nexus of imperial interactions. He was born during the German Wilhelminen Empire and spent most of his childhood in its capital, Berlin. He was fascinated by Mahatma Gandhi's struggle against British imperialism. With the rise of the Third Reich he became an active opponent of Nazism in the church. After the outbreak of World War II, Bonhoeffer became involved in a plot to assassinate Hitler and overthrow the Nazi regime. His major function within the plot was to establish communication with the government of the British Empire.

BONHOEFFER'S GERMANY AS IMPERIAL CONTEXT

During Bonhoeffer's life the globe was dominated by the great European empires, the largest of which was the British. The defeat of the German Empire in World War I and the Treaty of Versailles resulted in the reduction of Germany's territory, severe restrictions on its military power, the loss of its colonies, and the undermining of its economy. The majority of Germans viewed these measures as unjustly blaming Germany for the war, and they believed justice demanded revision of the treaty, including the return of all territory inhabited by Germans.

Hitler promised a return to the glories of the empire. The economic problems would be solved, Germany would regain its military power, German-speaking areas in other countries would be incorporated into the new Third Reich, and the nation's borders would be expanded to the east to provide living room for the expanding German population. All who were perceived as undermining German glory because of their racial "impurity," ideological differences, political opposition, or nonconformist behavior would be dealt with.

The reality of implementing such policies was the conquest of other countries, the totalitarian control of society and the suppression of all opposition. Political power was concentrated not only in the Nazi party but more particularly in the person of Adolf Hitler. In practice, the program of massive rearmament required the acquisition of financial and monetary resources, raw materials, industrial plants, and cheap labor. This in turn necessitated the conquest of surrounding states and the exploitation of people categorized as subhuman.

Hitler came to power through democratic means and initially depended on the support of the conservative parties in the *Reichstag* (parliament). Many of his policies initially found favor with supporters of traditional values, not only because they promised a return to German greatness but because the Nazis, in theory, affirmed these values. They rejected as degenerate the liberal culture that emerged in the Weimar Republic, promoted the traditional role of women as mothers and housewives, controlled and censored art, suppressed prostitution, and persecuted gay men. Further, they portrayed themselves as the force that could save Germany from the anti-Christian communists. The Nazi party proclaimed its support for "positive Christianity"—a Christianity which supported their nationalistic ideals. Hitler described the Nazi success in religious terms, appealing to the "Almighty" and claiming the support of "providence."

The decisive turning point in the shift from democracy to dictatorship came as a consequence of the burning of the Reichstag building on February 27, 1933. In response to this terrorist act, the Reich's President Von Hindenberg suspended the constitutional protection of individual freedoms. This legalized restrictions on the freedom of speech and association, and provided for the interception of post, telegram, and telephone communications. It permitted arbitrary searches, confiscation and restriction of property, and the detention of suspects without trial in concentration camps.

THE SHAPING OF AN ACTIVIST THEOLOGIAN

Dietrich Bonhoeffer was born in 1906 into an upper-middle-class family. He shared the opinion that the Versailles treaty victimized Germany. In his youth he experienced its economic consequences, which were exacerbated by the Great Depression. Despite being protected from its worst effects by his privileged family setting, Bonhoeffer developed a sensitivity to the plight of victims of imperial politics and economic exploitation.

Bonhoeffer studied theology at the universities of Tübingen and Berlin. In his doctoral thesis *Sanctorum Communio* and his *Habilitationsschrift*,[1] *Act and Being,* he developed a social understanding of theology which was to provide the theological basis for his struggle against Nazism.

In 1930 he was awarded a fellowship to study at Union Seminary in New York. While Bonhoeffer was unimpressed with American theology, the year proved fruitful as a source of significant friendships. One was with a French student Jean Lasserre, a committed pacifist who challenged Bonhoeffer to take seriously the Sermon on the Mount—and particularly Jesus' words on nonviolence—and apply them to the contemporary international tensions. Another was with an African American, Frank Fisher, through whom Bonhoeffer became aware of the realities of racism; this awareness was deepened by his involvement in the Abyssinian Baptist Church in Harlem.

In 1931 Bonhoeffer returned to Germany to teach at the University of Berlin. He taught a confirmation class in a poor area of Berlin and became involved in the ecumenical movement as a youth secretary for the World Alliance for Promoting International Friendship through the Churches. In his ecumenical work, he struggled to convince churches to become agents for peace, arguing that the ecumenical movement needed to understand itself as part of the church, called to clearly articulate God's concrete command for the time—world peace.

In 1933 Hitler came to power; unlike many Germans, Bonhoeffer recognized that Hitler was intent on establishing a militaristic dictatorship that threatened not only Germany but also world peace. He was well informed about plans for the legal implementation of Nazi policy and resulting atrocities by his brother-in-law, Hans von Dohnanyi, who was a senior official in the ministry of justice. The initial focus of Bonhoeffer's opposition to Nazism was, however, in the church.

The German tradition of theological support for nationalism took a radical turn in the 1930s with the emergence of the German Christian movement, which promoted a theological version of Nazi ideology. Nazi flags appeared in churches and many church leaders supported the Nazi party in its aim of "rebuilding" Germany and "protecting" it from its enemies. In parallel, the Nazi government was attempting to neutralize opposition from and to establish control over the church.

Bonhoeffer was a consistent opponent of the Nazification of the church. He saw Nazi ideology as incompatible with the gospel, and believed its theological form was heretical. In August 1933, Bonhoeffer took part in drafting the

Bethel Confession, which attempted to state this clearly. However, the draft was diluted when circulated to other theologians, notably in its paragraphs dealing with the Jews and the state. The situation reached a crisis when the synod of the Old Prussian Protestant Church decided that in the future no people with Jewish ancestry would be accepted for the ministry. In response, Bonhoeffer and others organized the Pastors Emergency League in 1933. Out of this emerged the Confessing Church in 1934, with the adoption of the Barmen Confession, which established a parallel church structure supported by many pastors and lay people. Three groups began to emerge in the German Protestant Church: the German Christians, who sought to transform the church into the religious wing of the Nazi state, the Confessing Church, which opposed the Nazification of the church but not necessarily the Nazi political program; and the neutrals, who saw the struggle as a political one which had nothing to do with the mission of the church. Bonhoeffer, disillusioned with the vacillation among opponents to the Nazification of the church, accepted a call to pastor two German congregations in London in October 1933.

Bonhoeffer continued to work in support of the Confessing Church, staying in constant touch with church leaders in Germany, motivating the German congregations in England to align themselves with the Confessing Church, and attempting to have the ecumenical movement recognize the Confessing Church as the authentic representative of the German Protestant Church, to take a stronger position on world peace, and to organize support for German refugees.

Bonhoeffer's theological pilgrimage through this time was shaped by three dynamics. The first was his interpretation of the Sermon on the Mount and its advocacy of nonviolence as applicable to the church in his context. The second was his understanding that the mission of the church included taking a clear stand on world peace, the persecution of the Jews and others, and opposition to Nazi tyranny. The church struggle, while having its own particular character, was related to the broader struggle against Nazism. Here Bonhoeffer's position contrasted sharply with many within the Confessing Church who rejected the Nazification of the church but were eager to assert their patriotism and support for the Nazi state and later the war. The third was his fascination with Gandhi. He planned to visit India to learn from him how the Sermon on the Mount could be translated into nonviolent resistance against Hitler. New developments in Germany prevented him from fulfilling this plan.

The Confessing Church called him to return to Germany to lead an illegal seminary. In Germany aspiring pastors studied at a university theological faculty. This was often supplemented by practical training at a church-run seminary. Students from the Confessing Church were excluded from the official seminaries and so the Confessing Church began to set up its own illegal seminaries. Bonhoeffer returned to participate in this movement, adding an intensive study of discipleship focused on the Sermon on the Mount to the normal curriculum. The seminary Bonhoeffer directed became an intentional community of disciples with a rhythm of meditation, prayer, worship, and study. Bonhoeffer and his students engaged in regular missions in support of Confessing Church congregations. His hope was that such communities of disciples would become the core of a renewed church. This church would reject the authoritarian and idolatrous claims of the Nazis, live in simple and direct obedience to the commands of Christ, provide for the victims of oppression, cry out for the oppressed, and oppose injustice. However, in 1937, the seminary was closed by the Gestapo.

In 1938, Hans von Dohnanyi brought Bonhoeffer into contact with the military-political resistance to Hitler, which was planning a coup against Hitler. Dohnanyi had taken up a position in the *Abwehr* (military intelligence), which was the center of the resistance, in 1939, and in 1940 he arranged for Bonhoeffer's employment as a confidential agent of the *Abwehr* (thus enabling him to evade conscription). Officially Bonhoeffer was to use his ecumenical contacts to obtain intelligence for the military. His undercover work was to use his contacts to communicate with the British government, to inform them of the conspiracy and to request a ceasefire when the planned coup took place. Bonhoeffer, an admirer of Gandhi, became the chief communicator with the British Empire in seeking its aid to end Hitler's rule. The idea of simple obedience to Christ's commands and the dream of open and direct action against the Nazis was subsumed by conspiracy, deception, and assassination plans. The incomplete manuscript of his book on *Ethics* provides clues to his theological interpretation of the conspiracy.

In 1943, Bonhoeffer was arrested as part of a Gestapo investigation into an *Abwehr* operation smuggling Jews into Switzerland. He was then interrogated on charges relating to his avoidance of military service. In prison, he engaged in new theological work focused on the meaning of Christianity in a nonreligious world. On July 20, 1944, there was an unsuccessful attempt to assassinate Hitler, and the subsequent investigation uncovered Bonhoeffer's role in the conspiracy. He was executed on April 9, 1945.

THEOLOGICAL MOTIFS

Bonhoeffer's theology is characterized by coherence and change in response to his context. Key motifs present in his earliest work are complemented, corrected, and enriched by others that emerge later as Bonhoeffer responded to new situations. Some of these motifs are explored below.

The Social Character of Human Personhood

Bonhoeffer's early writings developed his understanding of human personhood as constituted by the encounter with an "other" (the I-You relationship). The individual person only exists in relation to an "other." In an authentic "I-You" relationship, the other, the You, constitutes a boundary or limit for the I. The You makes an ethical claim that demands a response by the I. The person constituted as the I responds to the claim of the You. To be a person, then, is to act responsibly in relation to an "other." It is to be over-against-the-other, with-the-other, and for-the-other. This understanding is grounded theologically in three ways. First, God, the divine You, is revealed in Jesus Christ as the one whose freedom is freedom for us. Human relationships are an analogy of this. Second, God has willed that human persons be constituted through the encounter with the other. Third, the divine other is encountered in and through the human other so that the ethical claim of the human You is God's ethical claim on the I, yet it is simultaneously the genuine claim of the human other.

The I-You encounter takes place in the context of concrete social formations. Bonhoeffer distinguishes between societies (social structures which are a means to an end) and communities (social structures which are ends in themselves). He argued that communities act as persons. A community can be a You that demands an ethical response or it can be an I to whom an ethical claim is made. This ethical claim is heard by individuals who act on behalf of, in the place of, and for their communities.

God's intention in creation was for human beings to live in community with each other, with God, and in dependence on and dominion over the earth. Community with God is only possible within a human community characterized by respect for the otherness of the other, love, service, and mutual dependence. Relationships with God, with one another, and with the earth are simultaneous and interdependent; one cannot have one without the others.

Sin arises as human beings turn in on themselves and become isolated in their love of the self. They refuse to be with-the-other and for-the-other and become away-from-the-other and against-the-other. This turning in on oneself is expressed in the use of power in the service of oneself and in domination over others in all levels of human interaction. Individual human beings use and abuse each other to attain their own ends. Communities become means by which individuals seek their own ends. Societies become institutions "for the systematic exploitation of one by the other."[2] According to this understanding, Bonhoeffer saw the Third Reich as the embodiment of sin, as it sought the welfare of the German nation through violence, mass murder, tyranny, and war.

Due to the interdependence of the relationship between human beings, God, and the earth, human sin entails a break in all three relationships. We cannot have God without our fellow humans and we can only genuinely relate to the earth through the restoration of the relationships with God and our fellow humans. God has acted in Jesus Christ, who took responsibility for humanity and acted on its behalf, to bring human beings into genuine community with God and each other and to restore their relation with the earth. Salvation is the restoration of true humanity as a consequence of God's reconciliation of the world in Christ.

The Church

Bonhoeffer devoted himself to the struggle for the authenticity and renewal of the church. The church is that part of the world which is aware that God has reconciled the world to Godself and which gives expression to this reconciliation. In the church, God in Christ acts through the word and sacrament to redeem and restore human beings to full humanity in community with God and each other. As such, the church is the presence of Christ on earth; it is "Christ existing as church-community."[3] This does not deny the church's brokenness and failures, but affirms that Christ is really present in a state of humiliation to redeem human beings. Hence the church is an end itself; in its own life it manifests the community between human beings and between humanity and God. Yet it is also a means to an end, as it is God's instrument to restore human beings to genuine community with God and with each other in a renewed relation to the earth.

When a church becomes an expression of alienation rather than community between human beings, it ceases to be the church; it is no longer the presence of Christ on earth. Thus Bonhoeffer understood the official Protestant church in Germany had ceased to be the church. Any attempt to introduce or impose an ideology that contradicts God's reconciling purpose must be rejected. In his book *Discipleship*, Bonhoeffer argues three points in this regard. First, the church as the community of disciples follows only one Lord, Jesus Christ; no other leader can claim authority in the church. Second, the church must give visible expression to the community of humanity and God even when this leads to persecution. Third, in giving visible expression to God's reconciling purpose, the church stands in strong contrast to world—in this case a society dominated by Nazism. Bonhoeffer rejected as "cheap grace" the idea that God offers forgiveness without demanding radical obedience to Christ; this cheap grace was a comforting message which excused Christians from active opposition to Nazism. He argued that God's grace is "costly grace" which requires discipleship in opposition to the powers of evil, in this case Nazi tyranny. Grace, faith, and obedience are inseparably related.

However, when the church becomes so concerned about its own preservation that it is not prepared to take risky action on behalf of others, particularly the victims of society, it is no longer acting as God's instrument to establish genuine community. The concern for truth and the integrity of the church must always be linked to the mission of the church and never the preservation of the church for itself. The church's mission is one of self-sacrificial action for and on behalf of others regardless of whether they are Christians. In his prison writings Bonhoeffer puts it bluntly: "The church is the church only when it exists for others."[4] It ceases to be the church when it concentrates on its own preservation and neglects its responsibility for others.

The State

Bonhoeffer confronted a state that assumed absolute power, engaged in war and genocide, and brutally crushed all opposition. He responded by affirming that the state was intended to be a form of Christ's reign; not as an instrument of salvation but as an instrument for the conservation of life. Theologicaly the state is an order of preservation, that is, a social institution that God uses to restrain evil and establish order to preserve the fallen world for redemption in Christ. When it no longer functions to preserve the world for Christ, the state loses its validity. When the state understands itself as an order of salvation and its leader as a messianic figure, it has become idolatrous and must be rejected.

Bonhoeffer later replaced the concept of orders of preservation with the dynamic concept of mandates. A mandate is a divine commission grounded in the revelation of Christ for the ordering of human life, which finds expression in particular social institutions. Bonhoeffer identified four mandates: work or culture, marriage and family, government, and the church. None of these exists on its own; together, as they complement, interact with, and limit each other, they give expression to the divine command. The mandates must not be identified with particular historical forms; in different socio-historical contexts, they are expressed in varying degrees of adequacy in concrete forms. Further, "persistent, arbitrary violation" of the mandated task "extinguishes the divine mandate."[5]

Government—and not the state—is the divine mandate. The state comprises both the rulers and the ruled in a social structure: government refers only to the rulers. Government receives its authority from above, from God, not from below, from the people. This is not a reference to the historical means by which a government attained power but to its *being as government*, regardless of its historical origins. Once it is in power, its being as government is the consequence of the divine mandate, regardless of whether it recognizes this. As such, the government acts as God's representative. The mandate of the government is the implementation of justice through the punishment of the wicked and the promotion of the good. Even when a government is unjust it must be respected and obeyed. It may be disobeyed only on the points where its rule violates divine commands. There is no general right to revolution against an unjust state; however, individual Christians must act with responsibility in their own vocation in society. Such responsibility might, in extraordinary cases, include involvement in the overthrow of a government. It was because Bonhoeffer held such a high view of government that he reacted with costly commitment against a government that grotesquely abused the divine mandate.

This view of government does not demand a particular form of state. But certain things make for a "relatively best form of the state."[6] These include a form in which it is clear that its authority comes from God, which maintains justice, which respects the other mandates, which allows for the preaching of the gospel, and which exists in solidarity and mutual trust with its subjects.

Bonhoeffer recognized that the successful and the powerful make history at the expense of the weak and the vulnerable. States and empires have often arisen out of bloodshed, injustice, and exploitation. Yet, because governments are God's agents, God acts through them, in the course of history, to bring justice, peace, and prosperity. An empire founded on exploitation and self-interest may become an instrument bringing justice and prosperity to the conquered lands. This does not justify the injustice but affirms God's gracious action in history.

Relationship between Church and State

How does the church as God's instrument to establish genuine community relate to the state? Before the war, Bonhoeffer argued that the church should respond to an unjust state in three ways: First, it should critique the state, asking it to examine itself and the legitimacy of its actions. He also argued that the church must clearly and concretely proclaim God's command to the specific situation. This includes the denunciation of unjust political and economic systems, and annunciation of the command for world peace. Bonhoeffer was involved in protesting against the implementation of unjust laws and frustrated at the Confessing Church's failure to speak out for the Jews. Second, the church has an obligation to support and help the victims of the state regardless of their religion. Bonhoeffer took part in efforts to save elderly and handicapped people from enforced euthanasia and participated in a plot to smuggle Jews to Switzerland. Third, in extreme situations, the church can engage in direct political action to bring an end to a state's tyranny.

In general, Bonhoeffer drew a distinction between the role of the church and the responsibility of individual Christians. The task of the church was not to make detailed policy proposals; it was rather to equip Christians to act responsibly in their vocations on behalf of and for the good of others. The intention of the church was not to Christianize the state through implementation of specifically Christian laws, but rather that the state should promote justice. In prison he argued that there are activities which belong in the inner life of the church and not in society, the "disciplines of secret": they include worship, the sacraments, prayer, and the confession of faith. These are not to be imposed on society; however, action in society derives its strength from them and without them the church cannot impact society.

Responsibility and Reality

Bonhoeffer argued that ethics is about "how Christ may take form among us today and here."[7] This is grounded in a number of propositions. First, in Christ, God and the world are reconciled. Second, it is this world in all its complexity, brokenness and joy that God has reconciled to Godself. Third, as a consequence of God's reconciling action, Christ is taking form in this world. But what is this form of

Christ? As the incarnate one, the form of Christ is an affirmation of real human beings (in contrast to the Nazi idolization of Aryanism and its rejection of some people as subhuman); as the crucified one, the form of Christ is judgment on all human sin and evil and thus the rejection of social structures which embody evil; as the resurrected one, the form of Christ is the affirmation that God is creating new human beings in the midst of the old and thus the affirmation of all that works for justice and peace. The form of Christ will be realized in diverse ways in different contexts. Thus the task of ethics is to discern in a concrete socio-historical reality how the form of Christ is to be realized and to act in order to bring this about. In this task there are no abstract ideals or principles but rather careful decision-making that takes into account the context, our motives, the biblical commands, and most significantly the consequences of our actions. But primary importance is given to taking concrete action in a given situation.

Bonhoeffer characterizes such action as responsible action. It is responsible because it responds with the whole of who we are to the claim of our neighbor. We are to act for the good of, on behalf of, and in the place of our fellow human beings. In such action I take responsibility for my action. In a complex and fallen world such action is never a choice between right and wrong or good and evil; it is a choice between one right and another or one wrong and another. It is choosing the lesser evil to prevent the greater. It is being prepared to transgress accepted norms, even biblical ones, for the good of the other. In acting we take responsibility for the guilt entailed in engaging in activities which are wrong. Responsible action does not attempt to turn the world upside down but acts in the sphere in which a person has influence and opportunity. Such action is grounded in Jesus Christ who took responsibility for human beings, acting in their place and on their behalf; in doing so, he took upon himself our sin and guilt.

For Bonhoeffer responsible action meant going against the received tradition and becoming involved in the morally murky world of conspiracy and assassination. In order to end tyranny, he became involved in lying, deceit, and murder plots. Responsible action involved deciding between empires, against the Third Reich and for negotiation with the British Empire—not to further British imperial power, but to defeat Nazism. To seek to do the absolute right or good thing would mean to tell the truth, openly oppose Nazism, and not to try to kill anyone (including Hitler). In Bonhoeffer's view, the pursuit of such moral purity would result in doing nothing, or engaging in futile heroics which would permit the tyranny, war, and genocide to continue. This would constitute a rejection of responsibility and a failure to act on behalf of others.

This understanding of responsibility achieves a new focus in his prison writings. He argued that human beings had reached a stage of historical development which he described as having come of age. In this stage of moral responsibility and accountability, humans are no longer dependent upon a divine parent, and must make decisions for themselves and accept the consequences of these decisions, without expecting God to miraculously intervene and rescue them or change the situation. The Christian is called not to escape into pious enclave but to live passionately in the midst of earthly life with all its complexity, ambiguity, failures, suffering, and joy, and there to act responsibly for the good of the other. This is not to say that God is not present or active in the world; it is to recognize that God is present in weakness and suffering, and acts in response to and through the prayer and responsible actions of human beings.

Orientation to the Victims

For Bonhoeffer, who came from an affluent family, a distinguishing mark of Christianity is not merely the relationship with the other but the relationship with the suffering, excluded, and victimized other. In Bonhoeffer's case, the victimized other was the Jew. Bonhoeffer grounded this claim christologically in the fact that Jesus was God, incarnated in a rejected, despised, victimized, and crucified human being.

Today Christ continues to come to us in the person of the poor, the victimized, the suffering, and the excluded. What is done to them is done to Christ; our response to them is our response to Christ. This means that Christianity has an unavoidable bias in favor of the victims. A Christian must have "an irresistible love for the lowly, the sick, for those who are in misery, for those who are demeaned and abused, for those who suffer injustice and are rejected, for anyone in pain and anxiety."[8] It also means Christianity has a particular perspective on the world, one which views the world "from below, from the perspective of the outcast, the suspects, the maltreated, the powerless, the oppressed, the reviled—in short, from the perspective of those who suffer."[9]

BONHOEFFER AND CONTEMPORARY IMPERIALISM

Bonhoeffer's life and theology has been used and abused to support diverse political goals, including imperial ones. His theology is not always consistent and cannot be easily categorized in terms of contemporary theological models. Thus, for example, his theology of sociality is at its core egalitarian, yet other aspects of his thought are patriarchal and hierarchical. However, the core dynamics of his theology are persistently anti-imperial and stand in stark contrast to the policies of the American empire and its religious supporters. A "Bonhoefferian" response to contemporary empire would include the following six emphases.

First, nations are communal persons whose identity is shaped by their response to the ethical challenge posed by the other, whether this other is individual or communal. When a nation acts to ensure its own political and economic benefit through the exploitation, suppression, and domination of an other or seeks to impose its will on an other for its own purposes, it is an embodiment of sin. Imperialism in all its forms is sinful.

Second, if the church is to express its true nature as the manifestation of God's reconciling action in the world, it must reject any attempt to co-opt it in support of imperial goals, recognize that the theological justification of imperial power is heresy, and remove any symbolic identification with imperialistic nationalism. Rather it must engage in a journey of identification with the marginalized, the exploited, the oppressed, and the suffering.

Third, the church must constantly engage in a struggle to be—in all dimensions of its life and praxis—a community of human beings living in genuine communion with each other, with God, and in dynamic interdependence with the earth. It must struggle to remove expressions of domination, denigration, exploitation, segregation, paternalism, and other forms of injustice from its life.

Fourth, the church is only the church when it acts on behalf of others. In particular it has an obligation to stand with, cry for, and act on behalf of the good of victims of imperial power, regardless of their religious beliefs. Christians who seek to be "neutral," seeing no spiritual or theological significance in imperial politics, are no longer acting as Christians, regardless of their religious professions or practices.

Fifth, Christians need to view the world and evaluate imperial policies and practices from the perspectives of their victims and not from the benefits that they might bring to the powerful, in this case the American nation and its people.

Sixth, theological and ethical reflection must be accompanied by costly praxis on behalf of the victims. Individual Christians or churches are called to responsible action in opposition to imperial exploitation and oppression, and in promotion of an alternative just order in all areas where they have opportunity and influence.

Bonhoeffer summarizes his own challenge to imperial power thus:

> Christianity stands or falls with its revolutionary protest against violence, arbitrariness and pride of power and with its apologia for the weak. . . . Christianity is rather doing too little in showing these points than too much. Christianity has adjusted itself much too easily to the worship of power. It should give more offence, more shock to the world than it is doing. Christianity should . . . take a much more definite stand for the weak than to consider the potential moral right of the strong.[10]

FURTHER READING

Primary Sources

Bonhoeffer, Dietrich. *Dietrich Bonhoeffer Works*. Vol. 1, *Sanctorum Communio: A Theological Study of the Sociology of the Church*. Translated by Reinhard Kraus and Nancy Lukens. Minneapolis, Minn.: Fortress Press, 1998.

_____. *Dietrich Bonhoeffer Works*. Vol. 3, *Creation and Fall*. Translated by Douglas Stephen Baxter. Minneapolis, Minn.: Fortress Press, 1998.

_____. *Dietrich Bonhoeffer Works*. Vol. 4, *Discipleship*. Translated by Geffery B. Kelly and John D. Godsey. Minneapolis, Minn.: Fortress Press, 2003.

_____. *Dietrich Bonhoeffer Works*. Vol. 6, *Ethics*. Translated Reinhard Kraus, Charles C. West, and Douglas W. Stott. Minneapolis, Minn.: Fortress Press, 2005.

_____. *Dietrich Bonhoeffer Works*. Vol. 16, *Conspiracy and Imprisonment 1940-1945*. Translated by Lisa E. Dahill. Minneapolis, Minn.: Fortress Press, 2006.

_____. *Letters and Papers from Prison*. Enlarged ed. New York, N.Y.: Macmillan, 1972.

_____. *A Testament to Freedom: The Essential Writings of Dietrich Bonhoeffer*. Edited by Geffrey B. Kelly and F. Barton Nelson. San Francisco, Calif.: HarperSanFrancisco, 1995.

Secondary Sources

Bethge, Eberhard. *Dietrich Bonhoeffer: A Biography*. Minneapolis, Minn.: Fortress Press, 2000.

De Gruchy, John W., ed. *The Cambridge Companion to Dietrich Bonhoeffer*. Cambridge: Cambridge University Press, 1999.

Green, Clifford J. *Bonhoeffer: A Theology of Sociality*. Grand Rapids, Mich.: Eerdmans, 1999.

Kelly, Geffrey B., and F. Burton Nelson. *The Cost of Moral Leadership: The Spirituality of Dietrich Bonhoeffer*. Grand Rapids, Mich.: Eerdmans, 2003.

Rasmussen, Larry L. *Dietrich Bonhoeffer: Reality and Resistance*. Louisville, Ky.: Westminster John Knox Press, 2005.

CHAPTER 28

Simone Weil

Inese Radzins

One who is uprooted, uproots
One who is rooted does not uproot.[1]

SITUATING SIMONE WEIL: THE CONTEXT

Simone Weil's roots lie in the difficult period of European history between the two world wars, when France faced waning power in the midst of the struggle to maintain an empire. Weil was born in Paris in 1909 to an assimilated Jewish family and died in 1943, while working for the French resistance in London. From early on, Weil had two overlapping commitments. One was to the life of action, as shown by her year of factory work, support of various French labor organizations and the unemployed, and an attempt to fight in the Spanish Civil War. The other sphere was that of ideas or thought, evidenced by her ranking first in the entrance exams to the elite École Normale Supérieure (followed in second place by Simone de Beauvoir), teaching at girls' high schools and writing prolifically about subjects as diverse as politics, math, art, literature, philology, philosophy, and religion. Weil never thought of the two endeavors as separate: thinking for Weil was a type of labor and physical work a form of thinking.

Her own thinking, from a young age, was shaped by an acute attentiveness to those in society who were marginalized and experiencing suffering: the rural and urban poor, the unemployed, and any victims of war or famine. In 1915, during

World War I, she and her brother André, like many French children, "adopted" soldiers on the front line to whom they sent care packages. Weil's nanny reports that she found Simone, at the young age of eleven, attending a meeting of the unemployed that was occurring down the street from her home. Later, in high school and college, Weil would often take up collections for the dispossessed and the unemployed. Living in Marseille during the early years of World War II she aided Jewish refugees from Germany and distributed her meal ticket rations to Indochinese workers.[2]

After completing her *diplôme* at the prestigious *École Normale Supérieure* and passing the highly competitive French teaching examination, the *agrégation*, Weil requested teaching assignments in rural and industrial areas, so as to be closer to the working classes. Besides her teaching and syndicalist activities in the 1930s, she engaged in numerous other endeavors: she wrote intriguing analyses of Marx, traveled to Germany, where she examined the failure of the communist party to resist Hitler, worked for a year in various factories, briefly participated in the Spanish Civil War (against Franco), and intensified her commitment to Christianity.

Three distinct forces shaped her identity as both philosopher and activist: being born into a Jewish family, identifying herself as a French citizen/patriot, and defining her inspiration as Christian. Weil grew up in a close-knit and highly intellectual family. Throughout her life she remained close to her brother André and her parents.[3] The Weils were assimilated Jews and both Simone and her brother André claimed to have learned of their Jewish heritage around the age of ten. Somewhat ironically, for a thinker preoccupied with the idea of rootedness, she seems never to have fully engaged her Jewish origins. In fact, when she wrote about the Israelites and the Hebrew Bible, she often made gross anti-Jewish remarks and even anti-Semitic generalizations.[4]

What took precedence in Weil's self-identification were her French nationality and her Christian inspiration. However, her vision of both differed from traditional notions of either. For Weil, Christianity and the French Revolution of 1789 contained valuable, what she would even refer to as supernatural, ideals. The ideals of both involved what she called an "obligation" to the other human being. In *The Need for Roots*, a manuscript outlining the possibilities for renewing France after World War II, Weil explained:

> The notion of obligations comes before that of rights, which is subordinate and relative to the former. . . . Rights are always found to be related to certain con-

ditions. Obligations alone remain independent of conditions. . . . All human beings are bound by identical obligations, although these are performed in different ways according to particular circumstances. . . . The object of any obligation, in the realm of human affairs, is always the human being as such. There exists an obligation toward every human being for the sole reason that he or she is a human being, without any other condition requiring to be fulfilled, and even without any recognition of such obligation on the part of the individual concerned. . . . The fact that a human being possesses an eternal destiny imposes only one obligation: respect. The obligation is only performed if the respect is effectively expressed in a real, not a fictitious, way; and this can only be done through the medium of Man's earthly needs. On this point, the human conscience has never varied.[5]

There is a certain essentialism in Weil which some may find problematic: the idea that all human beings have, as a part of their core structure, a specific obligation toward any other human person. In Weil's estimation, the gospel expressed this obligation in terms of loving one's neighbor. The French Revolution also attempted to convey this obligation, but stumbled when it resorted to the language of rights.

Whereas rights are based on external conditions, conventions, customs, social structures, or historical heritage (for example, women did not have the "right" to vote for much of human history), obligations depend only upon the interior motivations of an individual. Weil is clear that obligation issues in respect toward others simply because they are human beings. The form this respect takes is two-fold. First and foremost it requires an attention to the physical needs of the other. In the face of a real physical need, one is obligated to give. The crucial point is that this decision to give cannot be forced; it must arise out of every individual.

Second, Weil is clear that this obligation issued in a real, rather than a "fictitious," respect toward the other. Respect for another person entails treating them as an end in themselves, as a human being, rather than as a means. "Fictitious respect" involves seeing the other person in terms of one's own self-interest. This false respect imposes ideas upon the other: for example, Christians have often thought that others *need* their religion, capitalists have asserted that others *need* free markets, and modern democracies have believed that other societies *need* democratic systems. The assertion of my perceived need onto the other does not respect the other person; rather, it sees the other as a means toward my own end. For Weil, respect means allowing my neighbor to be themselves rather than trying to impose my agenda or values upon them. What rooted Weil's Christianity and her nationalism was this idea of a universal obligation that not only characterized all human beings but also provided the foundation for true justice. However, Weil also believed that Western society had lost the true meaning of this obligation, because modern justice, in her estimation "dispense[s] him who possesses from the obligation of giving."[6]

It is also important to note the singularity of Weil's Christianity. She had a firm belief that her inspiration was Christian, even without the name of God.[7] For Weil, Christianity did not depend upon an affirmation of faith, dogma, adherence to doctrine, or membership in the church. She explicitly rejected baptism into the Catholic Church because she had a strong sense of her vocation being "outside the church."[8] Weil's calling to remain outside involved her relationship to what typically have been considered "unbelievers," people, ideas, and cultures beyond the purview of the church. She asserted that not being in the church allowed her to have a certain contact with those outsiders. As soon as one becomes an "insider" one differentiates: who is in and who is not. This type of differentiation, in her mind, violated the message of the gospel, whose central concerns are love, truth, and justice; three ideas that cannot be the sole property of any one culture or religion. Thus Weil's idea of Christianity involved any expression of truth—secular or sacred. For her, truth was found not only in other world religions, the Egyptian Book of the Dead, the Bhagavad Gita, the Cathars, but also in Plato, the French Revolution, Marx, and Kant's categorical imperative.

Weil spent her last year in New York and London, where she died of tuberculosis in August of 1943, having refused to supplement her diet more than the rations her countrymen in France were allowed. Questions remain as to whether this was the result of an anorexic condition or a form of solidarity with those suffering in the war; perhaps this is not a significant distinction. During this last period of her life the most systematic writings on France and Christianity appear. They can be found in *Waiting for God, Letter to a Priest, The Need for Roots,* and "On the Colonial Question" (in *Simone Weil on Colonialism*). Reading these works together reveals Weil's thoughts on the relationship between empire and the Christian tradition. This relationship is rooted, she argued, in a certain destructive tendency, exemplified in her time by the problem of colonialism.

UPROOTING: WEIL'S CRITIQUE OF EMPIRE AND CHRISTIANITY

Weil's engagement with colonialism began, as J. P. Little notes in *Simone Weil on Colonialism*, with two events in the early 1930s.[9] In her "Letter to the Indochinese," Weil explained her thinking at that time:

> At the Colonial Exhibition, I saw the crowd, many of whom read *Le Petit Parisien*, contemplating the reproduction of the temple of Angkor with foolish admiration, mindlessly indifferent to the sufferings caused by the regime thus represented. Since that time, I have never been able to think of Indochina without feeling ashamed of my country.[10]

This "shame" about her country reveals the spirit of Weil's nationalism. Although she defined herself as a patriot, Weil's nationalism involved shame, rather than triumph, over France's colonies. Instead of seeing the colonies as an asset to France's empire, she understood them as a huge liability. She explained: "Every time an Arab or an Indochinese is insulted without being able to answer back, beaten without being able to fight back, starved without being able to protest, killed without recourse to justice, it is France that is dishonored. And she is dishonored in this way, alas, every day."[11] Weil was pointing to a two-fold dynamic in colonialism: the destruction of the countries that suffer under it and that of the countries that practice it. They are different types of destruction to be sure, but destructions nevertheless.

In the first case, colonialism is a crime because it uproots other peoples and cultures (which in the French case concerned mainly the Indochinese and North Africans as well as workers from both countries in France). It deprived others of their distinctive roots—their history, culture, religion, land, and social structures. Christianity was not blameless in this endeavor; Weil observed that "missionary zeal has not Christianized Africa, Asia and Oceania, but has brought these territories under the cold, cruel and destructive domination of the white race, which has trodden everything."[12] In the second case, colonialism is a crime because it is France's own self-destruction. This is why Weil ironically accused the French government of "anti-French plots in north Africa."[13] She highlighted the paradox that although France claimed the universality of its ideals of citizenship for all persons, France refused to apply them to the colonies. Colonialism was for Weil antithetical to the true French spirit.

Weil's approach to social problems, including that of colonialism, was genealogical. Her interest lay in locating the conditions that produced the suffering of those dispossessed—the workers, the poor, the colonized. In the case of colonialism, Weil situated the causes in the failure of both Christianity and the state of France to live up to their ideals, their roots. What makes Weil's analysis of colonialism unique is that she grounded it in a strong critique of the relationship between Christianity and empire. (*Empire* here connotes Europe and the way in which its history—from the Roman Empire to twentieth-century nation-states—has been defined by imperial ambitions.) For Weil it was impossible to think of European politics without also thinking of Christianity and vice versa. The conjunction of these two forces determined that domination would define European history, a dynamic clearly seen, Weil argued, in the tragedy of colonialism.

The roots of this relationship lie in what I will refer to as an ideology of progress. Weil explained:

> The modern superstition in regard to progress is a by-product of the lie thanks to which Christianity was made the official Roman religion; it is bound up with the destruction of the spiritual treasures of those countries which were conquered by Rome, with the concealment of the perfect continuity existing between these treasures and Christianity, with an historical conception concerning the Redemption, making of the latter a temporal operation instead of an eternal one.[14]

Weil saw European history as grounded in a superstitious belief in progress that she claimed functioned as the guiding ideology of the West. The power of any ideology lies in its ability to mask a certain reality by privileging particular events or ideas over others. The idea of progress appeared to highlight the *possibilities* and *potential* of human beings and societies. For example, colonization was often undertaken to "civilize" and "Christianize" others—to help humanity progress toward a better future. However, Weil would argue that this idea of progress actually hides a deeper and more problematic reality: the destruction of other peoples and the concealment of any relationship to them. Colonialism, Weil argued, should be understood as the process that suppressed other peoples and cultures. It is this hidden reality—the destruction perpetrated in the name of an expanding Christianity and empire—that interested Weil. Her concern, in the words of Christine Ann Evans, was to "dismantle" this ideology of progress.[15] This proved to be incredibly difficult because it involved a complex structure composed of various forces—the uprooting, violent, and totalizing tendencies of Europe.

Weil located the roots of the ideology of progress in the collusion of ancient

Rome and early Christianity. This relationship was forged, she asserted, on the basis of a "lie."[16] It was an important conclusion for Weil that Christianity lies to itself about its own motives, about the reality that the church was seeking something—power and prestige—contrary to its own roots. In the fourth century, the Roman Empire and Christianity were each concerned with maximizing their power, growing their respective structures. What happened when the empire adopted Christianity as the official religion, according to Weil's analysis, was beneficial for both entities. The empire offered Christianity the material resources it lacked: political power and military might. In turn, Christianity offered the spiritual justification needed by the empire—divine sanctioning of the state's actions.

Christianity offered a spiritual logic for the empire's notion of conquest and expansion. Weil explained:

> There is no reason whatever to suppose that after so atrocious a crime as the murder of a perfect being humanity must needs have become better; and, in fact, taken in the mass, it does not appear to have done so. The Redemption is situated on another plane—an eternal plane. Speaking generally, there is no reason to establish any connection between the degree of perfection and chronological sequence. Christianity was responsible for bringing this notion of progress, previously unknown, into the world; and this notion, become the bane of the modern world, has de-Christianized it. We must abandon the notion. We must get rid of our superstition of chronology in order to find Eternity.[17]

Although one might contest her idea that Christianity brought the idea of progress into the world, Weil's emphasis is on the movement to make Christ the turning point, or lynchpin, of history. She suggested that the *idea* of the perfection of Christ was in some way transposed onto Christian identity. This resulted in a narrative that emphasized the perfection of time and human history through the Christian religion. What Weil called a "superstition of chronology" implied a belief that history was being perfected through Christianity. If Jesus was considered the perfection of history, and if the possibility of this perfection in some way accompanies Christianity, other religions are displaced as inadequate and unnecessary. I would suggest that the superstition regarding chronology fueled the idea of expansion upon which the notion of empire was based. In fact, it offered a more compelling reason for this expansion. Christianity, with its emphasis on temporal perfection, and empire, with its emphasis on physical expansion, colluded in defining the history of Europe in terms of an ideology of progress.

For Weil, this collusion of Christianity and empire was a devastating blow to the religion. She asserted that in becoming the religion of the empire Christianity joined forces with "the Beast of the Apocalypse."[18] The church, from Constantine through to the twentieth century, has worked in tandem with governments and thereby legitimized their actions. In this legitimization it has de-legitimized itself: trading its truth and its ideals for power. Weil concluded that in adopting imperial practices, Christianity lost its foundation: the crucial obligation to the other. However, some might suggest that the imperial practices so easily accepted by Christians were already somehow inherent in the early Christian movement (for example, the command to "make disciples" could be interpreted to imply the necessary growth of the movement). As we will see below, Weil locates this tendency toward power and control not in religion or in government, but rather in the necessary collective structure of existence. In Weil's estimation the only way to regain the soul of Christianity and that of France was to expose the way an ideology of progress functioned in the relationship between Christianity and empire.

The first component of Weil's critique of Christianity and empire concerns the dynamic of force, also referred to as power, might, or violence. Little notes that beginning with power is necessary because "[r]elationships between the colonizing power and the colonized are based, like other relationships in society, on force."[19] In her commentary on the *Iliad*, Weil explained that society would always be engaged in an almost never-ending cycle of violence. She observed:

> Human history is simply the history of the servitude which makes men—oppressors and oppressed alike—the plaything of the instruments of domination they themselves have manufactured, and thus reduces living humanity to being the chattel of inanimate chattels.[20]

Force was for Weil the proper subject of European history. This idea of force was not limited to its physical manifestations, but included also its more subtle, emotional or psychological, forms. Human beings are all—oppressed and oppressor alike—under the terrible yoke of force.

The cycle of violence depends upon a certain natural tendency, Weil observed, by every individual and entity, to extend its own power. In this regard, she was fond of quoting Thucydides who, in her paraphrase, observed that every person "exercises all the power at their disposal."[21] However, this extension is in reality an impossibility because it is insatiable. Weil wrote:

> There is in the very essence of power, a fundamental contradiction that prevents it from ever existing in the true sense of the word; those who are called the master, ceaselessly compelled to reinforce their power for fear of seeing it snatched away from them, are forever seeking a dominion essentially impossible to attain.[22]

For Weil, this inordinate desire for power resulted in the cruel dynamic of force that so clearly characterized European civilization. This desire was exemplified in the history of France which, Weil observed, "became a nation like any other, thinking only to carve out in the world her portion of Asiatic and black flesh, and to gain hegemony in Europe."[23] She also noted that Christianity was not immune to this power-seeking tendency:

> After the fall of the Roman Empire, which had been totalitarian, it was the Church that was the first to establish a rough sort of totalitarianism in Europe in the thirteenth century, after the war with the Albigenses. This tree bore much fruit. And the motive power of this totalitarianism was the use of those two little words: *anathema sit*.[24]

The need to exert force, by Christianity and empire, is accomplished through centralized structures and occurs in varying degrees through the police, the military, and, above all for Weil, through the use of the words *anathema sit*, "be ye cursed" or "be ye damned." Historically, the church used these words to exclude persons who did not adhere to church doctrine. For Weil this points to the way Christianity divides society into believers and nonbelievers: one is either with the church or against it. What the *anathema* does is conceal Christianity's deep affinities with other religions and cultures by invalidating them. This is apparent in the destruction wrought by events such as the crusades, the Inquisition, and more recently, colonial practices. It is this tendency toward power and this economy of violence, so prevalent in Christianity and empire, which an ideology of progress attempts to mask.

The violent nature of history can only be understood in light of another concept Weil discussed when criticizing Christianity and empire—the role of the collective. Regarding this she wrote:

> There is nothing more real in this world than war, including also under that name the conflicts of masked power, for it is this, as Heraclitus says, that makes slaves of some and freemen of others, men of some, gods of others—but

false gods, of course. This is the active principle of social life, whose fortune, success or failure, is almost entirely determined by this illusion. War is made up of prestige. It is this which permits the devil to say to Christ: "all this power and the glory of them is delivered to me." The supreme social value or rather the unique value, is prestige. That is indeed a shadow. That is a lie. The things which project this shadow are, according to Plato, puppets. Which means real but artificial things, fabricated like imitations of real and natural things. These puppets are the social institutions.[25]

Here Weil summarizes her concern: the desire for power and the ensuing violence of society is rooted in the social nature of existence. An ideology of progress not only masks violence, it also masks the ambiguity of our collective nature. Herein lies the crux of Weil's critique of Europe, what I will refer to as *the paradox of collectivism*. Although she acknowledged that human beings must live collectively and was herself often involved in communal action, Weil believed that collective existence was inherently problematic. It is both necessary and impossible. So she observed that the collective was "food for a certain number of human souls"[26] and also "something animal, which hinders the soul's salvation."[27] This applied also to Christianity: "what frightens me is the church as a social structure."[28] Social existence is significant because it is the only way that individuals can be rooted—in a particular culture, history, religion, family, or tradition. Insofar as they provide roots, collective structures are invaluable and even beautiful. What worried Weil was what she saw in her own time as the susceptibility of the individual to communal thinking, speaking, and acting: whether that be fascism (Mussolini, Franco, and Hitler), communism (Lenin and Stalin), or colonialism (practiced by most European powers).

As regards the individual, the problem with the collective is that it exerts a certain pressure—at times implicit, at others explicit—upon the individual to conform to group standards. There is, Weil observed, a crucial difference between the individual and the collective. She wrote:

> A man is sometimes moved by justice, even when it demands that he act against his own interest; a collectivity, whether it be nation, class, party or group, is hardly ever moved by justice, except when it is itself wronged.[29]

The problem with the collective is that it can prevent the individual from exercising their obligation toward the other. For Weil, the individual's capacity to take responsibility for their actions, to live by their conscience, can be easily altered by "group-think." In order to operate collectively, the group requires limitations on individuality. Often the constraints are minimal but as the group grows, the constraints increase. Weil had an almost inherent skepticism of any collective structure and herself refused membership in any organization, even ones with which she sympathized, like the communist party or the Catholic Church. Her skepticism came from her mentor, Alain (Émile Chartier), and from her readings of Marx and Plato. From the latter she adopts the term "great beast" to refer to collectives. Weil explained: "This great beast, which is the social animal, is by every evidence the same as the beast of the Apocalypse."[30]

Weil located the problem of collectives in their self-serving nature. Typically, the focus of any group is its own survival. Nations (and I would add churches) are judged, Weil remarked, by success rather than justice.[31] The problem is that success is defined by the entity itself and need not correspond to what is actually just. A state's definition of justice typically reflects its own self-interest. Weil insists that Christianity and France have lost their ideal of justice because they have been motivated solely by self-interest. Both put the desires of the collective above the respect due others. Thus France's success is couched in terms of extending its colonial power and Christianity's in terms of converts. Weil managed to expose the self-augmenting logic of collectives that an ideology of progress assumes as necessary or inevitable.

The third and final point Weil's analysis offers is that the cycle of violence perpetrated by various self-interested groups or societies always involves uprooting—the destruction of local traditions, peoples, cultures, histories, and religions. In this sense, the history of both Christianity and European empire is the extermination of various other peoples and cultures. What is dangerous is that this suppression is considered a necessary move in maintaining power. It is a vicious cycle: the group's identity—the growth of the nation-state—can only be asserted by suppressing various others. Presciently, Evans notes that for Weil the history of France has been one that "canonized a narrative of uprooting."[32] She observed that the state of France came into being only by destroying numerous others: "the inhabitants of Provence, Brittany, Alsace, and Franche-Comté."[33] Likewise, Christianity grew through various conquests by suppressing other religions, often through forced conversions. For Weil, this cultural and religious uprooting was an almost unforgivable crime that continued to define France in her time.

This destruction depends upon a certain concealment. One of the most brutal points Weil made is that an ideology of progress masks the actual humanity of others and thus our obligation to each other. She observed that the Roman Empire and Christianity were able to destroy others only by concealing "the perfect continuity existing between these treasures and Christianity."[34] The desire for self-preservation and the use of force this demands creates a barrier to seeing the other in human terms. Christianity and empire, I suggest, are structurally programmed to ignore the humanity of *others*. This blindness depends, Weil suggested, upon two ideas.

The first is that France and Christianity understand themselves as having a monopoly on the truth. She wrote: "The powerful, be they priests, military leaders, kings or capitalists, always believe they command by divine right."[35] This depends upon an attitude of superiority: If I have the truth, my life, values, culture, and religion are more meaningful than any others. Consequently, my truth should be shared with others, who could be enlightened by it. This develops the attitude of paternalism so prevalent in colonialism. The colonizers understand themselves as improving the lot of those colonized by *civilizing* and *Christianizing* them. Weil observed that Europe has historically been obsessed with making everyone else resemble it—forcing its religion, political and social systems, and even history, upon the colonized.[36] This is why Weil concluded that Europe tends to "civilize others by massacring them."[37] Behind this ideology of sameness lies a fear of difference and of dissent—both in the religious and political realms. Anything different is perceived as a threat and thus must be quelled, suppressed, and destroyed.

The second point Weil makes regarding concealment is that it depends upon a certain objectification. Colonialism treats humans as objects, rather than subjects. She explained: "By depriving people of their tradition, of their past, and thus of their soul, colonization reduces them to the state of matter, but matter that is human."[38] This occurs when France sees the colonized peoples in terms of a work force that could be exploited and when Christianity sees them as entities to be converted. In both cases, people are treated as means or objects, rather than as full human beings. This suppression of otherness is in direct contradiction to the idea of respect for the other that Weil saw as inherent in Christianity and the French Revolution. An ideology of progress depends upon concealing the humanity of other persons and masking the destruction perpetrated upon them.

CONSTRUCTIVE PROPOSAL: POSSIBILITIES FOR RE-ROOTING FRANCE AND CHRISTIANITY

> Over the last few years we have felt very deeply that the modern Western world, including our conception of democracy, is insufficient. Europe suffers from a number of maladies so severe that one hardly dares to think about it.[39]

Faced with the challenges of increasing globalization, many persons today might echo Weil's sentiment. To the extent that the West continues to wield tremendous power in the world and contribute to much of its destruction—be that social, political, environmental, economic, or cultural—many of Weil's insights remain valid. What she provides is a model for those living in the West (whether Europe, Canada, or the United States) of how to create a self-critique of the oppressor. Her writing addressed the dominant powers of Europe and not primarily those who were colonized. In this regard, I suggest that she offers Westerners three possibilities for thinking about the contemporary situation.

The first is found in her general approach: the assertion of a universal obligation to the other and a rigorous analysis and critique of one's historic situation. Weil's concern was locating the causes of the injustice she observed in her time. Her definition of injustice is rooted in her idea of a universal obligation to the other. Some may find this assertion—of a universal condition that applies to all persons—problematic and dismiss it as Weil's way of inscribing her own Western value system upon all human beings. For her, however, it is an important step in locating injustice; for injustice occurs where people deny this obligation (whether it is done overtly or covertly). Whereas she oriented her analysis of injustice around colonialism, today we might begin by exploring America's hegemonic position, the effects of modern global capitalism, the various forms of postcolonial oppression, or the numerous religious conflicts plaguing our world.

Yet Weil never offered a formula to apply to all situations. Instead, she encouraged an ongoing critical engagement with contemporary reality. This means that we begin, as Weil did, with a rigorous exploration of our context: asking what injustices are occurring, searching out their historic conditions, and exploring to what extent we ourselves might be implicated. The key to this approach lies in distancing ourselves—as much as possible—from any of our collective structures. Because our communities are structured around self-interest, Weil is clear that one must have the space to ask what those interests are and in what ways they might mask one's obligation to the other. Although some may criticize her call for distancing as an impossible attempt at objectivity, Weil asserted that it is only through a rigorous disengagement that one can be truly engaged. Thus she surmised that in order to love France "we must feel that she has a past; but we must not love the historical wrapper of that past."[40] For Weil this "historic wrapper of the past" was the ideology of progress that functioned in destroying much of Europe and the rest of the world. Weil challenges us to discover, through a rigorous analysis, what the historic wrapper, or the dominant ideology, of our contemporary situations might be. Weil suggested that without this rigorous analysis, change would be impossible.

Second, in exposing the endemic structure of the ideology of progress, Weil cautions us to be limited in our expectations for change. Her point was that it is almost impossible to extricate our modern understanding of institutions from the belief in and emphasis upon progress. To varying degrees, the survival of our institutions depends upon this ideology. Although the nature of the problem is no longer explicit colonialism, there are various postcolonial forms of domination that continue to plague the world. We might observe the way the West continues to insist upon exerting its power under the guise of progress (whether economic, military, cultural, or global). For example, we are accustomed to hearing about the importance of "growing" structures, whether those be markets, political institutions, or churches. One could ask if it is even possible to conceive of a social structure that does not promote its own self-interest, be it political, religious, or cultural.

Weil believed that renouncing this ideology was almost impossible for it required an impractical solution—a real revolution. She explained:

> Generally speaking, the sudden reversal of the relationship between forces which is what we usually understand by the term "revolution" is not only a phenomenon unknown in history, but furthermore, if we examine it closely, something literally inconceivable, for it would be a victory of weakness over force, the equivalent of a balance whose lighter scale were to go down.[41]

For Weil, the word *revolution* typically referenced events in history that transferred power from one group to another. Because they usually depended upon the use of force and some type of oppression, revolutions almost necessarily reinscribed an ideology of progress. Weil did not want to suggest that revolutions were unimportant, but rather to emphasize the difficulty of extricating oneself from the cycle of violence. And it was for this very reason that she was incredibly guarded in her proposals for change, calling for the "practical solution that is least bad."[42] She believed that the "reform or transformation of society can have no other reason-able object than to make it less evil."[43]

Third and finally, Weil offers the possibility of rethinking both Christianity and empire in terms of the concept of "weakness." She suggested that the only way of subverting the West's inordinate desire to extend its power under the guise of prog-ress was in emphasizing a renunciation of power in all its various forms, whether military, economic, political, cultural, or religious. Instead of asking "what can we do?", Weil challenges us to think about what we should not be doing. Weil locat-ed the resources for this type of thinking in various places: Prometheus, Job, Jesus, Joan of Ark, St. John of the Cross, the Occitanian civilization of the twelfth centu-ry and in the East, which she claimed remained rooted in a spiritual past. (A more recent example of this type of renunciation can be seen in the Civil Rights Move-ment exemplified and led by Martin Luther King, the power of which came spe-cifically from its rejection of force.) What characterized Weil's examples was a certain renunciation of force that would consequently allow a space for recognizing and respecting the *other*. Accordingly, her hope for France and Christianity was rooted in the idea of detachment.

She complicated matters when she suggested that this type of waiting should characterize not just individual life, but communal life as well. As regards the state of France, Weil argued that it must renounce its colonies and colonial mentality. She wrote: "Today it is possible that France will have to choose between attach-ment to her empire and the need once more to have a soul."[44] She also proposed that France "establish relationships with other countries on the basis of cultur-al exchange."[45] Weil believed that dialogue and exchange, rather than force, could foster a climate for respect. Although it appears too idealistic, one could ask how international relations would be altered if all countries took a similar approach. As regards domestic policy, Weil suggested that the state cultivate a society dedicated to the spirituality of work that would focus on the needs of the worker, rather than on their output. This, she believed, would help relieve the alienation and uproot-ing caused by modern industrialization.

Even more striking is Weil's vision of Christianity, whose transformation would entail a renunciation of what she referred to as the "superstition of chronology." Christianity would need to stop thinking of itself as the only source of truth in the world. She explained:

> In particular, the belief that a man can be saved outside the visible Church
> requires that all the elements of faith should be pondered afresh, under the

pain of complete incoherence. For the entire edifice is built around the contrary affirmation, which scarcely anybody today would venture to support.[46]

For Weil, Christianity had to be rethought in an effort to renounce its totalizing tendencies. First, the imperial theology permeating many Christian communities would have to be renounced, since it "invalidates the Gospel."[47] Second, Christianity would have to recognize the continuity between it and other sources of truth that have traditionally been considered "outside" the church. I would suggest that Weil is calling for a truly universal Christianity: one that could assert its own truth along with the truths of others.[48] Today, one wonders if Christian communities in the West are able to extricate themselves from this type of imperial theology, with its images of kingdom, metaphors of "ruling," supercessionist mentalities, triumphalist language, and hierarchical structuring.

Weil realized that asking France to renounce its colonies and Christianity to renounce its claim to having the *real* truth were risky proposals. Can France, or any nation, remain powerful without asserting its power? Can Christianity remain viable without its exclusive claim to truth? Weil believed that this risk had to be taken if either was to regain its soul and become firmly rooted. If the West and Christianity continue on their present course they remain uprooted, invalid. In relinquishing their power and their ideological natures, both risk their existence (as did Jesus, Joan of Ark, the Cathars, and Martin Luther King). In Weil's estimation the only hope for Christianity and empire lay in taking this risk—in a renunciation of power that could perhaps minimize some of the evil in the world and could possibly, but only possibly, help foster a humanity without force.

FURTHER READING

Primary Sources

Little, J. P. *Simone Weil on Colonialism: An Ethic of the Other*. Oxford: Rowman and Littlefield, 2003.

Weil, Simone. *Letter to a Priest*. New York, N.Y.: Penguin, 2003.

_____. *The Need for Roots*. London: Routledge, 2001.

_____. *Oppression and Liberty*. London: Routledge, 2001.

_____. *Waiting for God*. New York, N.Y.: Perennial, 2001.

_____. *Œuvres*. Paris: Quarto Gallimard, 1999.

Secondary Sources

Little, J. P. *Simone Weil: Waiting on Truth*. Oxford: Berg, 1988.

Pétrement, Simone. *Simone Weil: A Life*. New York, N.Y.: Panetheon Books, 1976.

Vetö, Miklos. *The Religious Metaphysics of Simone Weil*. Albany, N.Y.: State University of New York Press, 1994.

CHAPTER 29

M. M. Thomas

Sathianathan Clarke

Madathiparampil Mammen Thomas (1916-1996) theologized contextually and systematically. His extensive and engaging writings span more than fifty years through pre- and post-independence India. There can be no doubt that Thomas was the most prolific Indian Protestant theologian writing in the twentieth century. He wrote numerous books, several Bible expositions, and hundreds of articles in his lifetime. As an Indian theologian living during the age of internationalization, he found himself residing in and writing from multiple locations. He traveled widely and regularly all over India and across the whole world as a political activist, theological lecturer, and ecumenical leader. Thomas also had many opportunities to work with an array of local and international theological and political scholars in many regions of India, Asia, Europe, and the United States of America. M. M. Thomas was acknowledged by the church, both nationally and globally, as an influential and valuable theologian. Thus, unlike many who self-propel into the relational web of Western imperial privilege and who self-project as postcolonial representatives of an imaginary community within the crevices of modern academic discourse, Thomas was rooted in the faithful praxis of the Indian Church and the Indian working class in envisioning new possibilities for their future.

Any attempt to use "postcolonial" as a diagnostic tool with which to assess Thomas's theological contribution is riddled with complications. One set of these complications stems from the ambiguity of the field itself: is it the nationalist, nativist, or hybrid stream of postcolonial studies that will constitute the analytical optic in a critical study of Thomas's theology? Nationalism confronted colonialism by developing a Western-style entity of nation-state to dismantle the empire. Imitation was thus its forte as well as its weakness. Nativism was a reaching-inward-and-backward movement, which re-membered and set in motion originary cultural and religious resources that were alleged to have eluded capture and assimilation by the colonizer. Difference was its characteristic feature. Clearly between these two options exists a whole range of mediatory hybrid postcolonial stances.[1]

Another set of problems is built into compiling Thomas's own writings: the diachronic feature of his extended writing career, which began in the 1930s and ended in the 1990s, is unmistakable. The contextual shifts are fascinating and multiplex. Postcolonial markers appear dimly in the theological reflections of Thomas on pre-colonial India even while colonial inflections litter his ruminations in postcolonial (independent) India. Moreover, colonial and postcolonial mergers, in the most intimate and inchoate of ways, appear in his theology quite unannounced during the same time span while addressing different themes. Thus, a postcolonial stance in interpreting God may be operational alongside a much more colonial manner of viewing Christ while propagating a hybridized pre- and postcolonial conception of the world.

In this essay I shall set myself realistic and realizable objectives. I shall elaborate upon select theological themes associated with Thomas in his creative interpretation of the liberating potentialities of the Christian gospel in India. While stressing the learning points of this theologically substantive contribution of Thomas to the emergence of an authentic voice for Indian theology, I will also aim to critically assess its limitations and liabilities when viewed through the unfolding insights of postcolonialism. But first let me introduce Thomas in a bit more detail.

FOREGROUNDING THOMAS'S BACKGROUND

M. M. Thomas was born on May 15, 1916 into an ancient Christian family, which professes to go back to at least the fourth century C.E. in Kerala, a region on the southwest coast of India. His father was the secretary of a local cooperative society and his mother was a school teacher. Thus, although from the socially elite Syrian Christian community, which staked its claim to be equal to the Brahmin (highest in rank) in the Indian caste hierarchy, Thomas grew up in an economically middle-class family. M. M. Thomas was a faithful member of the Mar Thoma Malankara Syrian Church, which is a Reformed Syrian orthodox church established in the mid-nineteenth century. Thomas was a lay, self-educated theologian rooted in the energy of the nationalist movements in India and Asia (influenced by Gandhi) and carried forward by the ferment of the ecumenical movement all over the world. Somewhat implicitly, the popular appeal of the Marxist political agenda also drew his attention with the expansion of the Communist party in Kerala. He died on December 3, 1996.

Three further background comments are pertinent to the interpretation of Thomas's work. First, Thomas's theology has its origins in a profound experience of displacement. It is generated at the boundary between the church and communist party. In 1943, Thomas was disaffirmed by both the communities that he wanted to serve through a lifelong vocation. "Since he got convinced of his Christian vocation, he applied for entry into the ordained ministry of the Mar Thoma Church. But the ordination committee found his views on Christian social ethics with its leanings toward Marxian social insight unacceptable; his application was rejected. Around this time it appeared to him that his association with the Communist Party would provide him greater opportunities for social action and so he applied for membership. But this too was rejected since the Communist Party felt that his basic commitment was to the Christian faith and that it would weaken his allegiance to the Communist ideology."[2] Interestingly, the overall concerns of both the church and the communist party always showed up in his theological work: the salvation language of the church constantly coalesced with the humanization vocabulary of the communist party. Thomas's theological *topos* (place) was constituted out of being partially rejected from a couple of *topia* (concrete places). And yet these two collective entities always were part of Thomas's own theological passion and historical commitment.

Second, Thomas began theologizing within an ethos in which the Indian nationalist struggle against the British Empire was thriving, and continued writing through the sometimes-flourishing and sometimes-faltering development of the Republic of India. Through much of his reflection one can notice certain ambivalence: hopeful, at times tinged with unrealistic, aspirations mingled nebulously and intriguingly with skeptical, at times laced with pessimistic doubt in conceptualizing the role of the Indian nation-state. The nation-state represented one form of anti-colonial imagining. It symbolized a concrete corporate entity that would assemble and represent the native as a cohesive, even fused, collectivity. To comprehend the extent of the impingement of this phenomenon on Thomas as a theologian let us be clear that what was taking place in India was historically tied up with a host of other independence movements in Asia. Thomas interpreted these as "revolutionary movements," which were both resisting Western political and economic domination and carving out strategies and structures for forging independent nation-states. He discerned a common spirit behind a common movement in history.

Third, Thomas also served as a political statesman. He was, as it were, truly a public theologian. He sought to influence the framework and the functioning of the nation-state before India's independence from the British Empire in 1947 and thereafter as India, now a sovereign nation, worked toward living out its freedom beyond Western colonialism. Thomas was bestowed the honor of being made the governor of the state of Nagaland (1990-1992) in independent India. When one realizes that Christians consist of less than three percent of the population in India, this responsibility, of serving as a theologian-statesman in an increasingly Hindu fundamentalism-prone postcolonial situation, takes on added significance. In spite of this public persona, one must note that the constituency Thomas addressed in his theological writings was the Christian community. While the Indian Christian community was his primary addressee, there can be little doubt that the world Christian community was paying close attention to his "living theology." This gradual process of being incorporated as a representative of the promising nation and the hope-filled church may explain Thomas's reticence for unconstructive and uncompromising criticism as well as his propensity for generating negotiatory and expectant configurations of Indian theology.

LIVING THEOLOGY

Theology, for Thomas, cannot be confined to the universal plane alone because theologies are multiple and grounded upon specific peoples, worldviews, and locations. Abstract universalism is a feature of colonizing religious and ideological systems. The unitary and uniform projections of Christian theology, in Thomas's thinking, were connected with the anti-native and anti-contextual propensities of Western dominant theorizing. Historicizing and contextualizing such Western-inherited and domination-prone theologies was the objective of Indian theology. Thomas submitted that Indian theology could undertake this assignment by deliberately grounding thinking about God in the concrete and actual world of the native peoples: A "living theology" is always situational but "the context of theology [for Thomas] is not merely a religious or philosophical one; it is above all the context of the revolutionary, modern world."[3] This provoked Thomas to recast the definition of theology. "Indian Christian theology is understood here as reflections in an articulated form on God, Christ and the Church at the point of the meeting of the Christian faith with Indian people and their world-views, cultures and beliefs."[4] The stuff of theology involves reflection on God, Christ, and the church and yet this content becomes steeped within the socio-political and religio-cultural world of Indians.

This shift, somewhat of a precursor to the methodological reversal called for by liberation theology, clearly has postcolonial ramifications. Local communities and peoples' movements become, for Thomas, the crucial initial locus and focus of Christian theology. "Thus from the beginning his commitment to communicate Christian faith found expression in a theological-ideological dialectic and it has sprung up from his deep conviction that political and social changes developing in India provide the context for theological reflection."[5] At a time in which the empire was identified with Christianity, this relocation of the site of theology was potentially a subversive suggestion. In a radical methodological move, Thomas appeared to be positing anthropology rather than theology as the starting point for Christian reflection on faith. This is not to suggest that for Thomas anthropology subsumes theology. In fact, in Thomas's overall framework, theology relativizes anthropology. Methodologically we may infer that, for Thomas, anthropology and theology are dialectically related even as the local context of human living functions as the locus of reflection upon God. The theological warrant to acknowledge, scrutinize, and reflect upon the historical contexts of the native peoples as an invitation to do theology was an anti-imperialist maneuver. Preoccupation with discourse about God far-removed from the struggles of human beings was a well-established ploy of colonizing powers. Native peoples were incorporated into the discipline of directing their gaze outward and upward. As an act of divine faith and godly devotion they turned away both from the human subjugation that they fully experienced and from the human regimes that perpetuated such subjection. Thomas reversed this by encouraging a theological watch on the historical situation of contemporary human beings in India. This is what allows for the possibility of theology to become contextual, liberative, and anti-colonial in India.

Thomas further provided concrete theological substance to what was taking place among the peoples in India and Asia. In his reading of the historical context, Thomas identified a broad and influential spirit of social, economic, and political revolution at work among local communities, which Christian theology needed to recognize and integrate. Thomas noted that the overall situation through the mid-twentieth century in India was one of struggle for humanization. Theology, inasmuch as it desired to be living, was to take this historical situation and context as the basis of faith reflection. Thomas advanced an interesting theological rationale for this overall context in which Indians (Asian and African peoples as well) were striving for their own autonomy and liberation, primarily through nationalist movements. He connected the theological goal of Christian salvation with the native people's legitimate objective of humanization. Search for fuller humanity motivated these native collectives in their resistance against domination and advancement of liberation. Again it is important to reiterate that the historical context, which manifests these rampant and revolutionary movements toward humanization, is not to be categorically identified with the process of salvation. Salvation as the gift of God in Jesus Christ modifies and qualifies all humanization movements. Thus through a dialectical relationship salvation represented the ultimate activity of God that forms and informs penultimate strivings of humanization.

Besides the methodological reversal that Thomas initiated, his decision to interpret humanization through the concept of salvation also had important implications for an anti-colonial theological strategy. First, it construed possibilities for solidarity-formation among local peoples cutting across language, caste, religious, and ideological lines. By indicating that God's objective (salvation) is intricately and intimately tied up with subjugated peoples' goal (humanization) Thomas was able to urge Indian and Asian societies, which were historically divided by religion and ideology, to construe realizable and effective networks of solidarity. Second, it disengaged the uncritical relationship between the Western Christian community and the native Christian community. Indian Christian identity configurations were allowed to be at odds with their Western counterparts when it came to interpreting salvation through the lens of humanization. Indian theology thus tended to seek continuity not so much with the doctrinal and dogmatic traditions of historical Christianity, which purports to be one tight and unbroken unitary phenomenon preserved by the West. Rather it allowed for versions of Christian faith that are saturated by the historicity and the worldview of local and native communities, that is of Indians in his particular context. Finally, it judiciously retained salvation as the central category that fueled Western mission intervention, which was ambivalently linked with the colonial project, and shrewdly transfigured this to include the native need for humanization, which in turn garnered legitimacy for the resistance and liberation movement of colonized peoples. The movement of peoples' struggle against domination was intrinsically theological since it brought together the forces of humanization, which in a qualified way was a manifestation of God's promise of salvation for all God's children. Thomas's agenda for Christian soteriology was both context-situated and liberation-centered. It is within the context of the quest for humanization, which was spreading all over India and other previously colonized nations in the world, that the working of God's salvation may be located and interpreted.

Dilemmas of Thomas's Indian Theology

What Thomas offered as an incredibly useful approach to disrupt Indian Christians' preoccupation with Western theology was, however, compromised by the manner in which he packed his anthropological reading of the contextual human situation with modern Western meta-categories. Thomas conceptualized time from within a modern, Western metaphysical framework, which quite easily and naturally led to christological affirmations and commitments, which in turn reinforced his God-directed linear construction of history. Thomas believed that this Christian idea of history was indeed a gift of colonial rule to India since it presented Hinduism with an alternative to its unhelpful and traditional ahistorical viewpoint.[6] Thomas is explicit about this matter:

> [I]t remains largely true that the religious culture of India never came to distinguish radically between nature and history. Nature is the realm of necessity and knows no freedom to make history possible. And Hinduism, popular Hinduism at any rate, accepts the cycle of nature as the pattern of man and the cosmos. Higher Hinduism with its emphasis on mysticism made self-realization totally spiritual, with no relation to nature, so that the tension between spirit and nature never became the essence of human selfhood; and without that tension the idea of finite freedom cannot have substance, and spirituality becomes ahistorical; so that both Hindu naturalism and Hindu mysticism [are] unable to make man aware of life as historical destiny.[7]

Thus, even as theologies were posited as multiple, history was constructed to be unitary, linear, and moving toward a purposive end. Moreover, colonial categories of history within the logic of "manifest destiny" rightfully trumped Indian conceptions of time.

It is within this template of Christian (Western) history that Jesus Christ takes on universal meaning for all peoples of the world. History, as interpreted by Thomas, manifests the restless, but purposive, creative, and redemptive struggles of peoples all over the world in search of humanization. This rendering of history also makes meaningful the Christian proclamation that the resistive and liberative dynamic is founded in and funded by Jesus Christ. The anthropological reading of anti-colonial struggles in India was soaked in the Christian affirmation that "Jesus Christ and the New Humanity offered in Him are presented as the spiritual foundation, the source of judgment, renewal and ultimate fulfillment of the struggle of mankind for its humanity."[8] Having universalized history and made Christ its lynchpin and directive force toward humanization of all peoples, Thomas explicitly enunciates that such a messianic Jesus Christ is deliberately anti-colonial.

> In fact Christianity itself has often in its history succumbed to the Messianism of the Conquering King rather than of the crucified servant Christ. Christian communalism is an expression of it in India. . . . Unless the Crucified Jesus is emphasized as the central symbol of Christian messianism, the contribution of Christianity to Indian philosophy may be the intensification of a philosophy of history which posits totalitarian statism of a religious or secularist kind as its goal.[9]

The ambivalence of Thomas's theological assertion is obvious. He posits a colonial construction of history in conjunction with an anti-imperialistic Christ. Cruciform humanity as symbolized by the cross is the model that energizes human history toward fuller humanity. Jesus Christ as suffering crucified servant lures and galvanizes human beings in their struggle toward humanization. This model of cruciform humanity also judges and redeems all religious philosophies (including Christianity) and secular ideologies (including Marxism, capitalism, and modernism) from their conquering and colonizing pathways.

For Thomas, the colonial gift of Christ to India became the foundation for the anti-colonial quest for fuller humanity. Surprisingly he does not discern this impact on India within pre-Western colonial Christian activity. I point to this because M. M. Thomas comes from a Syrian Christian tradition that claims to date back to the fourth century of the Common Era, if one disregards the quite commonly assumed, and certainly plausible, myth that the Apostle Thomas arrived to evangelize India in 52 C.E.. It seems quite legitimate to ask Thomas the question, "What was this Syrian Christian Christ doing before the Western missionaries unleashed his power in India during the British colonial era?" Having said this, when one analyzes the impact of Jesus Christ on India in the colonial period we must admit that Thomas's assertion was not a vacuous or fanciful faith declaration. He demonstrates comprehensively and convincingly that both prominent Hindu thinkers[10] and preeminent secular (nationalist, humanist, and Marxist) leaders[11] were influenced by the relevance of Jesus Christ in reinterpreting the concept of humanization. He theorizes that Christianity introduced into Indian religious and secular philosophy the idea that history is heading toward an ultimate destiny in which fuller humanity is an objective and that the *Gestalt* of this humanization seems also connected with Jesus Christ.

Of course, the colonial influence on knowledge production was ignored by Thomas. No doubt many important religious and secular Indian thinkers interrogated and interpreted this central Christian figure; but we cannot underestimate the contrived knowledge-generation potential of Jesus Christ within an unequal colonial power configuration. The onus on Indian, native, non-Christian thinkers to deal with Jesus Christ, inasmuch as this symbol unified and animated the imagination of their Western colonial masters, must be interpreted within the power dynamics set in motion by the British Empire. This may explain why much of the Hindu and secularist engagement with the figure of Jesus that Thomas lifts up in his work wanes (one could even argue that it almost dies out) after India's independence from the British in 1947. Furthermore, while Thomas deals with the ways in which Indian progressive thinkers assimilated Jesus for the objective of humanization of all peoples, he does not accentuate the manner in which they debunk the Christian assertion that Christ is the key to human salvation.

There is a certain methodological trap that Thomas unsuspectingly lays for himself. On the one hand, his theology takes off from the anthropological movement of the resistive and liberative struggles of colonized peoples. The activity of local communities' struggle for fuller humanity takes on authentic meaning and theological value. On the other hand, by crediting the source and sustenance of this liberation activity to the power of Jesus Christ, Thomas allows for the colonization of the differentiated and variegated bases and authorities that ground and bolster peoples of other faiths and ideologies in their struggle against political and economic domination. Christ takes on universal significance by incorporating even the struggles of the natives that do not know him or do not want to be identified with him. One wonders whether Christocentrism was Thomas's undoing. While

it extends the working of God to the humanizing goals of marginalized and subjugated peoples it also confines and controls the plurality of such workings to fit
into the saving activity of one unitary and universal divine agent. Jesus Christ nar-
rows and constricts the fullness of God appropriated in the public domain. To put
this in the language that Thomas introduces, God risks losing God's plethora at the
hand of the concrete Christian Christ. What is designed as a move to free Christ
from the imprisonment of the Christian community also functions as a scheme to
contain other manifestations of the divine that do not fit the Christ mold. In other words, decolonizing Christ for Christians functions to colonize the God-expres-
sions of a majority of Indians. Perhaps a theocentric proposal could have made
room for more God outside of Christ while also legitimizing various models of
being human beyond Jesus!

Of course one must be cognizant of the fact that Thomas was addressing his
theology to the Christian community. He was decolonizing Christ from the confinement of the church. Salvation offered by this divine-human being spilled over
beyond the individual lives of Christians and outside of boundaries of their churches. For Thomas, the working of God in the incarnational presence of Christ must
be seen in the social, economic, and political currents of the world. The surge of
colonized peoples toward their own fuller humanity was also an expression of the
dynamic of God as symbolized in the revelation of Jesus Christ. If the Christian
community is unable to discern this sign of the times then it is bound to miss the
opportunity to cooperate in God's purposive work in the world. From this angle,
Jesus Christ is made broader for Christians since Thomas expands this concrete
symbol into a public dynamic. Thus even that which does not bear Christ's name
can be accepted as containing its effects. This is why Christians are challenged by
Thomas to "risk Christ for Christ's sake."

One specific area in which this push to de-center and dismantle Christian exclu-
siveness can be seen in Thomas's pluralistic ecclesiological thought. Clearly the
boundaries between the "Church of Christ" and the "Common Humanity in
Christ" are reimagined. On the one hand, the church as community in Christ
was identified not so much with participation in baptism or sharing of certain
doctrinal affirmations or belonging to a separated-from-the-world holy people; rather
the hallmark of the church had to do with it being part of the collective struggle
for fuller humanity. Christ's energy bursts the seams of the manifest church. On
the other hand, the church was construed as an open community. It embraced

more than the self-confessed Christian community. The interconnected community was somewhat amorphous and fluid and thus reeked with native Indian affectation. The church was reconceived with leaky boundaries so that Christ extends the kingdom beyond the domain of the Eucharistic community. The new wine overflows the earthen cup. The following is Thomas's explication:

> First, the koinonia of the Eucharistic community of the church, itself a unity of diverse peoples acknowledging the **person** of Jesus as the Messiah; second, a larger koinonia of dialogue among people of different faiths inwardly being renewed by their acknowledgment of the ultimacy of the **pattern** of the servanthood as exemplified by the crucified Jesus; third, a still larger koinonia of those involved in the power-political struggle for new societies and a new world community based on secular or religious anthropologies **informed** by the agape of the cross.[12]

Reflections on Thomas's Living Theology

A few thoughts, influenced by my engagement with postcolonial writing, come to mind when reflecting on the theological work of M. M. Thomas. Thomas did not share the premise of postcolonial thinkers in general that the encounter with Western colonialism did have profound pathological effects on Indian peoples, which must be probed and unmasked to identify unproductive amnesia among the colonized. This necessary stocktaking of various colonial encounters aids in native self-assessment that is crucial to wholesome self-actualization. This conscious analysis of the colonial encounter enables Indian people to sort out what is authentic self-expression from what is merely imitation of the valorized colonial other. While the former self-imaginings are surely laced with several power determinants, the latter self-projections primarily stem from the distortions produced by unequal power relations between the colonized and colonizer. Undertaking this self-reflective process of self-knowing, especially for previously colonized peoples, has many therapeutic benefits. Furthermore, honestly facing concrete colonial encounters also equips colonized peoples to identify such colonizing structures and strategies in the future on their way toward fuller humanity. This can be thought of as the proactive tactical benefit of critical analysis of colonial effects. Thomas seems unable to meticulously register and methodically dissect the Western colonial regimes that distort native humanizing imaginings.

The humanizing momentum anchored in Christ, which works through the progression of unfolding history, hardly warrants that we look backward critically. Rather, in Thomas's schema, the present is salvaged through theological discernment of the liberation activities surrounding local resisting communities and the future is constituted by political realignment of striving humanity as it goes about fulfilling God's future, which has been proclaimed and promised by Jesus Christ. Perhaps Thomas can be said to be performing one important role that is necessary in postcolonial scholarship: he lifts up the fertile, liberation-poised, present formations of local communities, which have future humanizing promise, instead of focusing upon the debilitating knowledge-based, politically-funded, and economically-driven Western colonial strategies, which—while being rooted in the past—have devastating present effects. There is an unwillingness to become preoccupied with the agents that arrive from the West through the colonial mechanism. Instead, local agency and collective peoples' power become the subjects of discernment and discourse.

More important, one can make the argument that in Thomas's theological work the subjectivity of the native agents was not predominantly represented as a counter-being and an oppositional-becoming. This drift to construe colonized communities as the sum total of object anti-bodies countering the colonizing subjects is an unconscious liability even among postcolonial intellectuals. Thomas partially overcomes this through a theological move. Because the agency of humanization is centered in the dynamic of Jesus Christ, for Thomas, communities of struggle are infused more with the energy and will of striving with Christ toward fuller humanity rather than merely wresting this away from other human colonial subjects. The colonizer-colonized binary is dislocated. A new subject (Christ), which is founded in history with present affectation and future benefits for the humanization of all peoples, is posited. Human subject-object will to power is circumvented into an open future beyond these competing and colliding entities. Thomas recommits scholarship to the native agents of theology. He promotes a theology that "views the Indians who were subject to Christian missions neither simply as victims nor simply as resistors (against Hinduism or Islam, as was once argued for those who did convert, or against the Christians, said of those who did not convert), but rather as active agents."[13] Such native and local Christian agents are taken to be articulators and enactors of deep human subjectivity even if fragmentarily worked out in a world of power configurations that attempt to thwart and re-engineer their overall subjectivity.

In spite of this generous reading of Thomas's theology, two questions do remain. First, by deciding not to bring systematic attention to the Western agents of over-reaching, dominating, exploiting, self-expanding imperial power, has Thomas denied empowerment for the subjugated peoples, which would arise from the power to name and shame the colonizers? Second, by choosing not to study the complex mechanism of knowledge/power of colonialism, has Thomas curtailed access to authentic native self-knowing, which may be an important resource in overcoming future forms of domination on the way toward humanization?

Thomas must surely be given credit for foregrounding theology without equating religion with the amorphous and elastic field of culture. There exists a propensity in postcolonial thought to be reductionistic. Religion is subsumed into politics, economics, or literature. Thus, a serious problem from a theologian/religionist's viewpoint is that postcolonialism highlights the political, ideological, cultural, and economic dimensions at the expense of the religious aspect. Thomas initiates a trajectory for postcolonialism that rejects the (modernist/Enlightenment's and postmodernist/secularists'?) prejudice that religion can be reduced to politics, economics, and culture. This trajectory deliberately brings back religion as a means of subjugation, survival, and liberation. This does not mean that religion is everything; neither does this mean that religion is nothing.

Finally, setting up a bifocal analytical framework for doing theology is a significant contribution. Thomas pays attention to the capitalistic global expansion of Western modernity. This he interprets to be a distortion in which "fuller humanity" equals maximally satisfying one's insatiable media-stimulated and West-imitating human appetite. On the other hand, he also takes into account the power usurpation mechanisms of the Indian nation state. He interprets this as a perversion in which "fuller humanity" equals optimally sharing in the tyrannical erection of a muscular and authoritarian imagined political collectivity. Thus, Thomas was able to deal with all aspects of contemporaneous forms of domination and imperial power that contribute to dehumanization. In this sense Thomas again proves that he is uninterested in dwelling upon the Western colonial encounters and consequences of the past, but rather wishes to move from the present situation of competing regimes of power configurations to the future work of advancing humanization for all.

BROADENING THE ANTI-IMPERIAL ANALYSIS

Let me conclude by making two basic (even simplistic) observations on Thomas's theological methodology.[14] I believe that addressing these limitations will strengthen the anti-imperial objectives of theologies committed to resisting regimes of domination and enhancing structures of freedom and justice. There appears to be a blind spot in Thomas to the fundamental, destructive, and overwhelming impact of patriarchy in Asian and Indian liberative movements toward humanization. While feminist or womanist voices may not have been a conscious part of theological and political discourse through his early days of writing, there appears to be no justification for ducking this crucial analytical resource for understanding and overcoming a notorious native dimension of domination (colonization) in India during the latter decades of his writing career. Whether this neglect was influenced by his masculine construction of Jesus Christ as the source, inertia, and goal of humanization or by his Indian patriarchal chauvinism that dovetailed on male-centered Western theological neo-orthodoxy (since Thomas was deeply influenced by Barth, Brunner, and the Niebuhrs) will remain an unanswered question in this essay. Of course, using postcolonial terminology one could say that it could well be a hybrid of both these factors with the provision that one can identity several more substantive contributory elements that abetted this neglect.

In a similar vein, there have been many critical voices that have pointed to Thomas's lack of attention to another major feature of "internal colonialism" that was distinctly, prevailingly, and intrinsically part of systematic dehumanization of Indian society. The ejection of Dalits (outcast communities that constitute about 15 percent of the Indian population) by the caste community was a systematic, comprehensive, and hegemonic practice of indigenous colonization of one collective by another based on religious and cultural sanctions and economic and social strictures. For Thomas, who was a member of the dominant Syrian Christian (caste) community, to have missed this in some analytical (theological and anthropological) depth makes one wonder whether he deliberately undercuts particular human beings and their concrete debilitation in valorizing the much more abstract notion of humanization. Simon de Beauvoir was right when she warns that one needs to label as "totalitarian" and oppose all such "doctrines which raise up beyond [hu]man the mirage of [Hu]Mankind."[15] Any anti-imperial theological analysis ought to be acutely aware of both the internal and external forms of domination and subjugation. The future of living theology in India depends upon a comprehensive (both past and present) analysis of the historical context, an inclusive understanding of the God experiences of all its interfaith and multi-ideological constituencies, and a commitment to overcome all (both external and internal) structures and agencies of colonization.

FURTHER READING

Primary Sources

Thomas, M. M. *Religion and the Revolt of the Oppressed*. Delhi: ISPCK, 1981.
_____. *Man and the Universe of Faiths*. Bangalore: CISRS, 1975.
_____. *Acknowledged Christ of the Indian Renaissance*. London: SCM Press, 1969.
_____. *The Christian Response to the Asian Revolution*. London: SCM Press, 1966.

Secondary Sources

Philip, T. M. *The Encounter between Theology and Ideology: An Exploration of the Communicative Theology of M. M. Thomas*. Madras: CLS, 1986.
Thomas, T. Jacob, ed. *M. M. Thomas Reader: Selected Texts on Theology, Religion and Society*. Tiruvalla: CSS, 2002.
Wolters, Hielke. *Theology of Participation: M. M. Thomas' Concept of Salvation and the Collective Struggle for Fuller Humanity in India*. Delhi, ISPCK, 1996.

CHAPTER 30

Juan Luis Segundo

Roger Haight, S.J.

Juan Luis Segundo (1925-1996) formed part of the first wave of liberation theologians in Latin America. He was a Roman Catholic Jesuit priest from Uruguay who flourished after the Second Vatican Council (1962-1965) and died before the end of the century. During the course of his theological career he generated a distinctive theological perspective in a large number of books that were read around the world. In this representation of his thought, I will first sketch his Latin American context and some of the sources that helped shape his theology. I will then represent his "utopian vision" in five seminal ideas or sets of ideas around a specific topic. The last section will draw out some of the relevance of this liberation theologian for our contemporary situation.

THE LIFE AND TIMES OF JUAN LUIS SEGUNDO

Latin America after World War II was a distinctive continent, poised between Europe and the United States on the one hand and the so-called Third World on the other. Since it had been colonized for centuries by the nations of the Iberian Peninsula, it shared in European culture and had strong ties of culture and trade with Europe. But it was also a continent in which the majority of the population lived in poverty and in many areas destitution. When people made a distinction between European or Western nations and the poor nations of the South, Latin American found itself somewhere in the middle. Unlike the nations of Africa, the revolutions for independence in Latin America occurred during the nineteenth century, but many countries remained tied to Europe and increasingly the United States in patterns of economic dependence. The wave of nationalism and independence movements after World War II, however, was also experienced in Latin America as a desire for a better distribution of wealth. In the 1960s and 1970s, democracy failed in many countries and one saw the rise of the national security state.

Juan Luis Segundo was born in Montevideo on March 31, 1925. The fact that Uruguay is a small, largely middle-class country, whose population is predominately descended from Europeans and lives in and around the capital city, has a bearing on Segundo's theology. In 1941 at the age of sixteen he joined the Jesuits, and continued his education in Jesuit schools in Argentina, until in 1953 he traveled to Louvain in Belgium for his seminary level training in theology. After ordination as a priest in 1955 and two more years of Jesuit formation, he took up the study of theology at the University of Paris. In 1963 Segundo was awarded the highest classification for the *Doctorat ès Lettres* in theology on the basis of two theses.[1]

Segundo never held a position as a professor of theology in Uruguay. In 1965 he began and directed the Peter Faber Center for the training of the laity in matters relating to theology, society, and culture. He also edited the monthly organ of the center, *Perspectivas de diálogo*. In 1975 the journal was suppressed by the rightwing Uruguayan government, and Segundo's religious superiors under pressure closed down his center. Thereafter Segundo continued his theological career by writing and lecturing and teaching widely outside of Uruguay. While at home, he wrote in connection with two or more groups of friends, acquaintances, and other interested parties which he animated. The continual dialogue with these circles and the authors he read nurtured his thought until his death in 1996.

These bare facts of his career do not explain Segundo's role in the rise of liberation theology. Liberation theology flourished after Vatican II largely because the "Pastoral Constitution on the Church in the Modern World" fired theologians around the world to turn to the social and cultural situations in which they lived and to take up the concerns of the poor in their theology.[2] In 1968 the Latin American Bishops Conference met in Medellín, Columbia, and as a conference committed the church to attend to the structures of violence which held the poor in a form of socioeconomic captivity. Shortly thereafter the phrase "liberation theology" was coined and it helped to solidify a movement. But the roots of liberation theology in Latin America reach back to the period before the council. In the 1950s and early 1960s considerable energy in the church was directed toward social issues through various church agencies working with workers and students.

Segundo himself sees the origins of liberation theology as fermentation among university students in the early 1960s who began to grasp the repressive "anti-Christian elements hidden in a so-called Christian society."[3] Others read work among the poor themselves as the catalyst of liberation theology. But in works published in 1962, "Segundo was already presenting basic theological ideas along liberation lines that were prior to and independent of both Vatican II and European political theology."[4]

Before moving to an account of some of the seminal ideas of Segundo's distinctive vision, it will be helpful to raise up three motifs or themes that pervade all his thinking. They function like the presuppositions of his writing that provided its consistent shape and direction. They can be linked to three distinct sources which he held in a synthetic tension.

The first derives from Segundo's first doctoral thesis which engaged the thought of Nicholas Berdyaev.[5] It was not the first time that Segundo had encountered existentialist philosophy and theology. During his earlier studies in philosophy he had authored a brief work examining existentialist and poetic approaches to reality.[6] Fairly early in his intellectual development, therefore, Segundo was drawn away from the objective Aristotelianism that structured the scholastic syntheses of Roman Catholic philosophy and theology. In his work on Berdyaev he formulated the lifelong conviction that the essential characteristic of the human is freedom.

Second, Segundo was also influenced by Marxian thought, the values of socialism, the impact of society on perception and knowing, and hence the need to have recourse to the social sciences. In an early work on Christian anthropology he entered into a dialectical conversation between existentialism and Marxism in an effort to preserve the values of both in an integral Christian concept of the human.[7] The work shows a concern for social structures, the function of the church in society, the role of Christianity in human history, and a recognition of the degree to which culture and society influenced human thinking.

Sometime in the course of the 1960s Segundo read Teilhard de Chardin extensively and internalized his evolutionary view of reality. Segundo was captivated by the dual love of Teilhard for God and for the earth: God and world, spirit and matter, were not antithetical. This profound insight, its attendant implications, and the encompassing commitment that it entailed united to provide a cosmological framework for Segundo's thinking. The following remarkable image typifies Segundo's embrace of Teilhard's perspective:

Up to now human beings have lived apart from each other, scattered around the world and closed in upon themselves. They have been like passengers who accidentally met in the hold of a ship, not even suspecting the ship's motion. Clustered together on the earth, they found nothing better to do than to fight or amuse themselves. Now, by chance, or better, as a natural result of organization, our eyes are beginning to open. The most daring among us have climbed to the bridge. They have seen the ship that carries us all. They have glimpsed the ship's prow cutting the waves. They have noticed that a boiler keeps the ship going and a rudder keeps it on course. And, most important of all, they have seen clouds floating above and caught the scent of distant islands on the horizon. It is no longer agitation down in the hold, just drifting along; the time has come to pilot the ship. It is inevitable that a different humanity must emerge from this vision.[8]

In the years that followed his founding of the Peter Faber Center, Segundo began to elaborate a theological vision of Christianity that put conceptual flesh on these seminal ideas.

FIVE GENERATIVE IDEAS DRIVING SEGUNDO'S THEOLOGY

Segundo's writing spans five decades, from the 1950s into the 1990s. His career consisted in reading, thinking, writing, and interacting with interlocutors. His two most elaborate and significant works were multivolume projects. The first carried as its general title in English *A Theology for Artisans of a New Humanity*; it included treatises on the church, the theology of grace, God, sacraments, and sin and grace in a context of social history and evolution. Christology was conspicuously missing in this series, and Segundo filled the void with a five-volume work published in the 1980s. The general title of this work is *Jesus of Nazareth Yesterday and Today*, and it included significant volumes on faith and ideology, Jesus, Paul, spirituality, and Christ in an evolutionary framework. Segundo published other works on method and fundamental theological themes that add breadth and depth to these works, but I will draw a portrait of his theology mainly from these two works. I will represent his theology in a holistic manner around five constitutive ideas. When these interrelated conceptions are gathered together, they will provide a sketch of his thinking, surely something of a caricature, but one that will fairly accurately differentiate a distinctive contribution to theology.

Human Freedom

One can often locate in thinkers of a systematic or constructive bent a fundamental idea or value, or a knot of them pulled tightly together, that provides the premises of his or her thinking and suffuse all that is said. Segundo's theology offers several candidates for this position, but the freedom of the human person seems to underlie them all. Freedom, or what he qualifies further as liberty, defines the human person. "A man without freedom would not be a human person."[9] Segundo's anthropology is rooted in the willing and acting side of the person, and knowledge is oriented to this end.

Segundo forcefully insists that the freedom that he prizes cannot be reduced to free choice, the power of deliberation leading to a particular decision. In fact, the reduction of freedom to choice leads to deleterious consequences because it tends to reduce the value of human freedom to the objects that are chosen. Following an existentialist lead, Segundo finds the value of freedom in human commitment: in the inner spontaneity that overcomes various inner and outer constraints, and in the deliberate directing of human energy in action that creates or fashions new relationships and new reality.

Since Augustine, Catholic dogmatics has considered the dynamic relationship between human beings and God in terms of the theology of grace, that is, God's gracious approach to the human. As in Augustine, this discussion became aligned with the practical doctrine of the Holy Spirit, that is, God at work in the human person, and it results in a Christian anthropology. For Segundo, God's grace, or God as spirit, opens up a freedom that is turned in upon itself, tied by inner bonds of self-concern or egoism, or by more external bonds such as habit, routine, or internalized social and cultural restraints. Grace consists in God's personal presence to and empowerment of the human subject enabling it to break through these determinisms in self-transcending love or attraction for value beyond the self. Somehow in the course of Augustine's fight with Pelagius and subsequent history the discussion of the fundamental dynamism of God's grace got derailed: the problem became conceived as grace *versus* freedom. In Segundo, the logic of God's grace pits it against the dehumanizing bondage and constraint of sin. Grace in its turn liberates human freedom.

In a later work Segundo overhauls his theology of grace and freedom in dialogue with Paul.[10] He conceptualizes Paul's classic description of the divided self in terms of a conflict between creative freedom and the mechanisms of the world that suppress liberty. The physiological and psychological determinisms that constitute our flesh are compounded by the "second nature" of internalized social, political, and cultural restraints that should be a platform for freedom but in fact strangle freedom and creativity. Sin has its roots in the gap or distance between the original intentionality of freedom and its inability to perform; egoism is a kind of surrender to and passivity before the entropic forces of mechanism and control. The spirit or grace of God allows freedom to break out of the enclosed and impacted self.

These foundational concepts lead to a dynamic view of Christianity and provide a stimulus for an active Christian life. God's grace cannot be reconciled with a passive, quietist, or merely contemplative Christianity. Grace awakens freedom to its intended potential; grace empowers rebirth, vitality, activity, creativity, novelty. Passive Christianity for Segundo describes an inner contradiction; it is no ideal; it cannot exist authentically. God's grace moves in the direction of liberating the human and thus humanization, and this process is designed to extend into the social and political arenas.

God: Transcendent and Immanent

Segundo's approach to God veers away from the question of God's existence. He felt it was far more important to examine the image of God, the conception of God that people constructed. We have a tendency to construct a God in our own self-image, to project self-serving idols. On the one hand the transcendence of God prophetically shatters all human constructions of God. On the other hand, the immanence of God in Jesus and as spirit at work in the human subject gives one biblical and experiential leverage to form an idea of God. I will turn to Segundo's Christology in the following section, and I have already spoken of the manifestations of God as spirit in the world and the human subject. These are the sources for Segundo's idea of God.

Segundo depicts God as personal, loving, and creatively supportive of the processes in history that subvert dehumanization and promote the increase of human liberty.

First of all, God is personal love. This evangelical characterization of God cannot be proven, but can be encountered in the symbols of nature or the signs of history. There is no rational demonstration of a God of love. But human beings can encounter God as a "Thou," a force that self-communicates as love through this-worldly mediations. One has to find God in the world not outside it.[11] The prime example of this for Christians is Jesus of Nazareth. One encounters God in his historical words and gestures.

God stands against objective structures that are destructive of human subjectivity. God unmasks idolatry. Segundo holds "that our conception of God, which views God solely as some immutable, self-sufficient nature without any real interest in what God brought about is nothing but the rationalization of our own alienated societal relationships." What if, he asks, "we conceive God as being universal, not because God is the keystone of a mechanism in which one or more groups dominate other groups, but because God turns each individual human being and each human community into an absolute and thus poses a radical obstacle to any and all use of people as mere tools?"[12]

God as creator and as spirit provides the power and energy within evolution and the positive vectors of history. Segundo sees the universe driven by the two forces of entropy and negentropy. Negentropy names the positive creative energy leading to further complexity and higher forms of life. Christianity has its place within this large vision of reality and must not be conceived as detached from the world or secular history as a parallel and competitive force. For example, instead of seeing secularization as loss of religion's control over society, the church should turn to the world to find God at work "in the task of liberating human beings from 'any and every servitude.'" "At bottom secularization means that everything in the church, absolutely everything, must be translated from 'religious' terms into tasks in history."[13] I will return to this theme under the title of a theology of history and eschatology to show how these ideas are part of a still larger conception of reality.

Jesus Christ

Segundo's formal Christology is contained in two volumes of the series entitled *Jesus of Nazareth Yesterday and Today*, the whole of which provides an expansive Christian vision.[14] In the first of these two volumes, Segundo presents an interpretation of the historical Jesus; in the first part of the other volume, he provides an interpretation of classical christological doctrine. What follows represents each of these formal dimensions of Segundo's Christology.

Segundo defends a simultaneously religious and political interpretation of Jesus because these two dimensions of Jewish society and culture interpenetrated each other: it could not have been otherwise, especially in a time of political occupation.

Segundo backs up this premise with some of Jesus' overtly political sayings and actions, not least of which is the language of the kingdom of God.

Segundo defends the proposition that "the kingdom of God" refers to the reversal of the situation of poor and marginalized sinners and is to be achieved on earth. This social change will not depend of the virtue or the goodness of those marginalized, but will be effected absolutely gratuitously by the power of God. "Jesus' listeners understood one thing perfectly: while the force behind the kingdom was the force of God, the reality of the kingdom was something to be achieved on earth, so that society as a whole would reflect the will of God."[15]

This message of Jesus, however, was geared in different ways to three different groups: members of the political religious establishment who were its opponents, the poor themselves who were its beneficiaries, and Jesus' disciples. Relative to the first group, Jesus' preaching was a sharp critique; it contradicted the inner values of religious control and empire; it looked to conversion, but in fact stirred up antagonism and conflict. Relative to the second group, the poor, Segundo reads Jesus' preaching less in terms of conversion and more as an external or objective emancipation for their benefit. Jesus' preaching intended a situation of humanization in which the poor would be released from the captivity of deprivation and want; it is a restoration of humanity prior to sin and virtue. To the third group, those who would be his disciples, Jesus communicated "the religio-political task of unmasking the mechanisms of ideological oppression, giving them an assignment as hazardous as his own."[16]

As a conclusion to the argument, Segundo proposes that Jesus preached the kingdom of God as a historical process with a religio-political goal, namely, to bring social conflicts out into the open and to unmask their premises as contradictory to God because oppressive of the poor. Jesus "is doing *something more* than proclaiming a future event. He is *generating a historical conflict*." "Jesus is seeking *to place historical causality in the service of the kingdom*."[17] In other words, the kingdom of God enlists the cooperation and co-causality of human agents.

The classical christological doctrines declare that Jesus is truly human and truly divine. But, Segundo asks, how can one predicate a divinity that we do not know upon a human being about whom we know a good deal insofar as he is truly one of us and his basic values are preserved in the synoptics? This dilemma forces Segundo to interpret the classical doctrine of Jesus' divinity from the epistemological perspective of Jesus being a medium of the revelation of God. According to the logic of revelation and a response of faith, "Jesus is divine" really responds to the quest for knowledge of God: it says "God is Jesus," or "God is like Jesus," or "God is truly revealed in the person and actions of Jesus." In the statement that Jesus is God, "the known term shedding light on the other is *Jesus*, his history, and his activity." The equivalent of "Jesus is God" in the performance of faith is that "Jesus, with the values iconically represented in his life, constitutes the *Absolute* for me . . . " or "that the ultimate reality was manifested to us in him."[18] Segundo thus offers a dynamic Christology and a revelational and exemplary soteriology. These aim at mediating a way of life, a spirituality of following Christ. "The thing being opposed, then, is first and foremost any and every absolutization of values other than those manifested by Jesus in his human history. The target, then, is the absolutization of what is false: i.e., idolatry."[19] The thing promoted is a salvation that becomes actual in and through the historical and worldly following of Jesus.

The Church

Segundo's picture of the church coheres with the ideas thus far presented. He introduces his ecclesiology with the question of why, if it is so important for human salvation, did the church appear so late in human history? What constitutes the necessity of the church?[20] Segundo's response to these questions defines the distinctive character of the church. This appears in the mission, the character, and the ministerial activity of the church.

The question of when the church appeared in history really applies to Christ: in the course of evolution and history, the time was right. For the role of the church is to continue to make real and actual the gesture of God in history that was Jesus Christ. The mission, purpose, and task of the church lies in its being the visible communitarian sign of the event of Jesus Christ. The church's necessity should not be understood as a requirement for the salvation of individual people. Its necessity rests in the reality of the communication of God with humanity in Jesus Christ. If that communication fails to be actualized in a community, it will cease to exist. Jesus Christ revealed an explicit awareness of the power of God's love in history and this awareness created a new level of human existence in the evolutionary scale. "It is ...something new and definitive, creating a new balance upon which everything else will depend from now on." In response to this Christ event, "there must be a people who know the mystery of love, who will meet and dialogue with those who are moving toward the gospel and confronting the questions raised by love."[21]

This mission of the church is played out very broadly speaking in negative and positive ways. The church as part of society has an intrinsic task to be a critic of society and culture when their systemic behavior contradicts fundamental human values. More positively, the church is called to be a leaven in society. No other institution is so specifically charged with preserving the human values that should motivate and sustain technological and political reason in the running of society. The public role of the church consists in holding up before society and government the humane values of the kingdom of God revealed by Jesus Christ.

For the church to be itself and to perform its mission it must be a small but active community. First of all, it is a community and not an objective institution. As a community, it is charged with the role of being a sign or standard in history. But this implies that it cannot be a "church" in Troeltsch's sense of being coextensive with society and still be an active sign over-against society. Just as passive Christian faith is contradictory on the level of the person, so too, a church of the masses conformed to society contradicts the church's nature and mission. Given its mission, for the church to be the sign and sacrament of the values of Jesus requires that it be a small, active community. All people do not have a vocation to be a Christian; in fact, few do. The universality of the church does not consist quantitatively in gaining large numbers of members, but in actualizing a message that has implications for all human beings. The church is the corporate symbol of God's love for the world, of God's "Yes" to the world; it should communicate that the response of love on the part of human beings is ultimately worthwhile. "The 'little flock' may remain such, but it can recapitulate the universe and thus be the most decisive and substantial factor in human history."[22]

Finally, this activist conception of the church with a mission to the world and human history has implications for ministry. Segundo looks upon ministries of mass appeal, that encourage passivity in the Christian life without awakening engaged activity in the world that reflects the values of Jesus, as fundamentally misguided. Church ministry should be oriented to nurturing the lives of Christian agents who are active in the world.[23]

Continuous Eschatology

Segundo's eschatology shows the expansive character of his worldview. His eschatology mixes a strong theme of teleology with a biblical sense of resurrection and the end time. One can see a certain parallelism between the individual life mov-

ing toward resurrection and all of history moving toward an eschatological kingdom of God. Three major components of Segundo's eschatology are his sense of
Christian spirituality, his theology of history, and the continuity of the end time
with history.

I begin with Segundo's conception of human spirituality from a Christian perspective as a project in history. Segundo strongly argues against a conception of
human freedom that reduces it and hence Christian spirituality to doing good
things or bad things. This depicts the whole of life as a test or a trial by free choice.
This in turn diminishes the value of freedom to the objects chosen. In contrast
to this, Segundo views the world as being in the process of creation, and human
beings as having been commissioned to take part in this process. "God fashions
this world into a system of signs . . . through which God leads us to shoulder the
task of freeing all its dynamisms for the service of love and the construction of
the world."[24] God's creative energy in the cosmos has become conscious as human
beings become its agents.

Segundo's theology of history extrapolates from God at work in human freedom
and evolutionary theory. Segundo is an Augustinian anti-Pelagian. Only grace can
open human freedom up in self-transcending love. But this means that wherever authentic self-transcendence occurs, there the spirit of God is at work in history. With the emergence of the human, God works in the world through human
agents. Broadening out this basic Christian conception, Segundo depicts history being driven forward by the dialectics of two vectors of energy. In this scheme
the entropy and negentropy of nature appear as sin and graced freedom in human
history. "From Christian revelation we know that a divine force carries individual
human beings, the human race, and the whole universe toward their recapitulation
in Christ." In the process of history, "love, grace, life, and God's gift make up the
positive vector of evolution." By contrast, "deliberate opposition to God's grace has
always been called 'sin': and its ultimate motivating force, which leads to the denial and rejection of love, has been called egotism." This "egotism, sin, enslavement
to the world and the flesh make up the negative vector of evolution."[25] The dialectical interaction of these two forces fuel a process that moves toward the goal of
the final kingdom of God. "This goal, this utopia that founds history, is made up
of the elements of history itself no matter how far it is projected into some future
age. But there these elements are arranged in such a way that violence, domination
by force, and external control are excluded from them."[26]

Segundo insists that the process of history must be understood in a way that overcomes a dualism that would drain human freedom of its significance. He insists that "the Christian image of eternal life can only be fashioned with the materials, that is, the values of this one."[27] Grace and resurrection mean the transformation of material fashioned by or through human freedom into something permanent and everlasting. "Hence it is the *earth* that we are looking forward to and that is identical with eternal life. It is our earth and our history and our effort transformed by the gift of God's grace. Through this gift our transient and mortal earth acquires perduring incorruptibility and immortality, the qualities that come from on high. Grace elevates the human earth and human history."[28]

Finally, Segundo insists quite strongly that human freedom cooperates in the fashioning of the eschatological kingdom of God. If this were not the case, the creative aspect of human freedom would be a deception and an illusion. God opens up freedom to transcend the self; God then bestows upon that which loving freedom creates the status of eternal reality in the end time. Segundo quite explicitly uses the language of cooperation and synergism, not as two equal partners, but in terms of grace liberating and sustaining freedom. "In the building up of God's kingdom, not even God will supply the results that were not procured in a creative, realistic way by God's co-workers seeking to be *as effective as they could be.*"[29]

SEGUNDO IN NORTH AMERICA

Juan Luis Segundo lived in a highly secularized country with a largely middle-class population. These contextual data may mean that his liberation theology will resonate in some sectors of a North American audience. But before making this constructive move, it might be helpful to distinguish Segundo from other Latin American liberation theologians and relate him to feminist liberation theology.

Commentators usually locate Juan Luis Segundo within the group of Latin American liberation theologians, Protestant and Catholic, who defined the movement in the 1960s and the 1970s. In fact Segundo collaborated with many of these theologians at various conferences that helped solidify the movement. But during the 1970s, at least two factors began to differentiate Segundo from several other liberation theologians: the first had to do with the level of his writing, the second with his constituency and perhaps his audience.

Regarding the first, Segundo's was a thoroughly intellectual project; he sought to reinterpret the fundamental doctrinal beliefs of Christians. And to do this he appealed to a variety of disciplines. More than many liberation theologians Segundo commented on the thought of Karl Marx; he appealed to science and the philosophy of science; he was well grounded in philosophy; he appealed to the social sciences. Whereas much of the work of liberation theologians consists in occasional articles, Segundo wrote many monographs. He brought a broad erudition across several disciplines to the project of constructing a large theoretical and theological synthesis.

The second point has to do with Segundo's audience. There is no doubt that Segundo composed his theology on behalf of the poor, but his writing does not address the poor. Segundo worked with and spoke to the middle class. No doubt the society and culture of Uruguay partly account for this aspect of his thought. But it is also due to his own conviction. While other liberation theologians pointed to the eruption of the poor and envisaged the power of the poor in history, Segundo believed that the middle class provided the dynamism of society; social liberation was needed precisely because the poor lacked power. He did not easily relate to the idea of the organic intellectual who learned from the poor by insertion and participant observation.[30] These dimensions distinguished his work from that of many of his peers.

In 1985 Segundo had a chance to explicitly reflect upon feminist liberation theology.[31] Generally Segundo agreed with the feminist critique of androcentrism and hierarchy in the church: "there is an imbalance here that is not only completely unjust, but also greatly damages the church. It deprives the church of a dimension that is complementary in every functioning of human society, every human being." Regarding the role of women in the church Segundo believed that "there is no theological reason why women should not be ordained and, therefore, exercise authority. Whether it is women or men exercising authority, however, it should not be exercised in a merely vertical manner."[32] Segundo was generally supportive of North American feminist liberation theology but added a conditional critique in terms of the dimensions of the international system of market economics. Women should be wary of seeking power in an unjust system: "the liberation of the society in which we live is a precondition for truly posing the question of the oppression of women within that society." "If women in the rich countries are not critical of the overall system, they do not realize that their struggle for liberation presupposes the slavery of women in poor countries."[33]

I turn now to the question of whether Segundo might be of particular relevance to North American theology today. I will explore that possibility within the framework of spirituality. After defining more exactly what the term "spirituality" intends, I will open up three areas in which Segundo's implicit spirituality may find purchase among members of the mainline churches.

The terms "spirituality" as it is used here refers simultaneously to two levels of the Christian life. On the most fundamental level it designates the way Christians actually live their lives. Spirituality in this concrete sense means the sum total of the activities of a Christian. In many respects all persons define themselves by their activity. When human activity is not reduced to blind action but includes deliberately passive appreciation, quiet contemplation, and active reflection along with our decisions and actions, it readily appears that we are what we do. This formula should not be read as reductive. On the contrary, it precisely aims at being holistic and inclusive. By using human action as a category, I am attempting to find a way to encompass the complexity of both the individual person and the group, insofar as identity resides in a maze of dimensions and relationships.

The first definition of spirituality presupposes that the individual and corporate activity of Christians correlates in some measure with their set of beliefs. All human activity carries and is carried by human intelligence even when a conscious reflective awareness does not catch up with hidden motives and vague desires. To be human is to be reflectively conscious and in that measure liberated from the raw mechanism of stimulus and response. Therefore, where distinctly human activity is concerned, one expects to find some level of human thought, whether critical or otherwise, reflected in the behavior. When ministerial agents or theologians raise up the implied theory or rationale of Christian action, these understandings, and the principles and axioms that flow from them, represent spirituality on a second critical and reflective stage or level. Spirituality on this second level consists in Christian self-understanding that reflects or elicits and empowers a Christian way of life. In its elaborated form it points the direction for Christian action.

Within the framework of spirituality understood in this way, I believe that the theology of Segundo that has been schematically outlined in the second part of this essay could connect and empower North American Christians. Because North American Christianity ranks among the most pluralistic of any church in the world, this correlation would apply more specifically for that segment of Christians who are active, educated, and perhaps somewhat dissatisfied with the spirituality of their own mainline churches. Segundo's view of Christianity as a dedicated minority cuts through various aspects of the "established" character of the mainline churches. In any case, three aspects of the spirituality implicit in Segundo's theology point in the direction of a certain relevance for North America: it is pragmatically activist, prophetically critical, and provides an empowering vision.

The spirituality contained in Segundo's theology has its foundation and source in the freedom that defines what it means to be human. Freedom qualifies the defining spiritual element that constitutes a human person. Freedom becomes most fully itself when the self-transcending potential of the human is fully activated. In Christian language, this occurs when the power of love that comes from an immanent God as spirit urges and carries human freedom beyond itself in recognition, decision, commitment, and continuous loyalty to a value or cause beyond the self. Segundo's is an activist spirituality because freedom happens and only fully exists when it becomes activated and actualized in action. Human beings are united with God in a variety of ways whether or not they intentionally direct their minds and actions to God. But conscious response to God in action turns an otherwise feeble Christian spirituality into a robust union and mutual indwelling of wills. Practical action converts empty desire into participation in reality. As John's gospel makes clear, people are truly united with God existentially when they act out their faith commitment in love.

I just described how Segundo's liberation theology differs from other liberation theologians in directly addressing a dynamic middle class whom he believed supplied the power and energy of history. The poor in Segundo's view will benefit from changes in the social, economic, and political structures that dehumanize by strangling their potential to develop and exercise their freedom. But in modern societies the engine of change lies in an educated middle class which in democratic industrial nations collectively runs the apparatus of history. Segundo's theology launches an appeal to the Christian values of the kingdom of God against the background of a severe critique of the systems in place that literally contradict American religious values and hold whole groups of people down. He speaks to technicians and professionals, to teachers and managers, to the single and the partnered who are fully employed and want to contribute to a better world. There can be no social amelioration without severe social critique that convinces people that individualist, materialist, racist, sexist, and imperialist structures can be changed by significant social involvement. The individual, in the end, gains his or her freedom not by the results of action, but by participation in the project.

Segundo's theology, therefore, also empowers a Christian life with a conception of human action and especially work that infuses it with spiritual value. The wedding of love of God and love for the world in Teilhard converts to love of God and love of history and social-historical processes. Segundo refuses a bifurcated restriction of spiritual value to the sphere of the preached word or the supernatural sacrament that leaves secular engagement a neutral or negative area of life. Segundo raises up work, constructive action in the world, creative risk, and entrepreneurship to a genuinely spiritual level as that which most fully shapes persons in themselves through their active relationships. More explicitly, formal spiritual activities should fold into themselves secular activities and relationships and integrate them into the self-constituting action that constructs human relationships with God. In Segundo's conception particular, finite, limited human actions and careers become part of the pool of self-transcending love that finally constitutes the kingdom of God. The sustaining empowerment of God's love thus gives human action in history an absolute value.[34]

FURTHER READING

Primary Sources

Segundo, Juan Luis. *Theology for Artisans of a New Humanity*. Vol. 1, *The Community Called Church*. Vol. 2, *Grace and the Human Condition*. Vol. 3, *Our Idea of God*. Vol. 4, *The Sacraments Today*. Vol. 5, *Evolution and Guilt*. Maryknoll, N.Y.: Orbis Books, 1973-1974.

_____. *The Liberation of Theology*. Maryknoll, N.Y.: Orbis Books, 1976.

_____. *Jesus of Nazareth Yesterday and Today*. Vol. 1, *Faith and Ideologies*. Vol. 2, *The Historical Jesus of the Synoptics*. Vol. 3, *The Humanist Christology of Paul*. Vol. 4, *The Christ of the Ignatian Exercises*. Vol. 5, *An Evolutionary Approach to Jesus of Nazareth*. Maryknoll, N.Y.: Orbis Books, 1984-1988.

_____. *Signs of the Times: Theological Reflections*. Edited by Alfred T. Hennelly. Maryknoll, N.Y.: Orbis Books, 1993.

Secondary Sources

Ching, Theresa Lowe. *Efficacious Love: Its Meaning and Function in the Theology of Juan Luis Segundo*. Lanham, Md.: University Press of America, 1989.

Stefano, Frances. *The Absolute Value of Human Action in the Theology of Juan Luis Segundo*. Lanham, Md.: University Press of America, 1992.

CHAPTER 31

John S. Mbiti

James W. Perkinson

In so short an essay, wrestling with a general question of theological production under conditions of imperial domination, much must be stipulated and much merely hinted. Here the exercise involves an African theologian, John Mbiti, who first came to attention through publication of his *African Religions and Philosophy* in 1969 and *Concepts of God in Africa* in 1970. Mbiti quickly established the character of his distinctive contributions to modern theology with the 1971 Oxford University Press publicaton of his dissertation research under the title *New Testament Eschatology in an African Background: A Study of the Encounter between New Testament Theology and African Traditional Concepts.* John Mbiti, reputed "father of contemporary African theology," offers a corpus of writing and a personal history of teaching and pastoring that exhibit marked ambivalence in the theater of post-independence African struggle that has shaped the context of his career.

Born in Kenya in 1931, between the two world wars, Mbiti grew up in a traditionalist context, often enough—in the midst of his early years working in the fields, herding sheep, goats, and cattle, and going to school—witnessing the mystical powers of the indigenous practices he would later theorize in his academic work.[1] Already a novelist in high school, he studied English and geography at Makere University College in Kampala, Uganda, just after it had been absorbed under the umbrella of the University of London, and began his affiliation with the Anglican tradition in activities on campus. Upon graduation, after a brief stint collecting stories and proverbs of his own Akamba people, he traveled to the U.S. to earn A.B. and Th.B. degrees in theology at Barrington College in New England. He returned to Kenya to work at the Teacher Training College at Kangundo for two years, before heading off to Cambridge University where he completed doctoral studies in 1963. After ordination to Anglican orders the same year, Mbiti returned to Makere as a lecturer/professor in New Testament studies, theology, African religion, and world religions until 1974. He then served as director and professor at the Ecumenical Institute of the World Council of Churches in Geneva until 1980, and engaged in full-time pastoral ministry in Burgdorf with the Reformed Church of Bern, Switzerland from 1981 until he retired in 1996. He peppered those activities with part-time theology teaching at the University of Bern, numerous visiting professor roles in schools in Africa, Australia, Britain, Canada, Germany, Switzerland, and the U.S., and a prolific record of book and article publications (including *Love and Marriage in Africa* in 1973, *The Prayers of African Religion* in 1975, and *Bible and Theology in African Christianity* in 1986). Clearly, his is a life and ministry stretched across much of the geography historically hosting imperial relations in central Africa, reflecting both serious challenge to those relations and partial complicity with some of their operative assumptions and normative practices.

Western imperial aggression in Africa culminates (most visibly) in the 1885 Berlin Conference whose deliberations carved up much of the continent between England, France, Portugal, and Belgium. Only with the late 1950s–early 1960s independence movements did national elites in many African countries emerge as the tenants of their own (largely one-party) political systems, pursuing modern visions of development and power. In the wake of independence, however, European political control merely gave way to Western-initiated neo-liberal economic predation across much of the continent, which continues to morph into a plethora of postmodern paradoxes on the ground: extraordinarily high birth rates coupled with progressive disintegration of the family, "dictatorial regimes functioning under the cathartic name of democracy," the breakdown of religious traditions accompanied by the rise of syncretic churches, etc.[2] Here I can only note debates about the exact character of imperialism and its relationship to colonialism in the last five hundred years of European takeover of the globe without either reviewing or adjudicating them.

Suffice it to say that what V. Y. Mudimbe calls at one point "colonial imperialism"—however parsed out into "before" and "after," "cause" and "effect"—implements an imperial power of the (European) Same whose result remains the production of an "intermediate cultural space" that will exercise Mbiti's most controversial claim. This zone of marginality and diffusion, in which "vestiges of the past" (tribal ties, for instance) hide new structures based on class position or access to capital, emerges as irreducibly hybrid—neither traditional nor modern.[3] And of course, now, closer in to the present moment, a philosopher like Bernard-Henri Lévy can track the appearance of a new form of "hauntology"—wars grinding on over decades, like perpetual-motion machines, the forgotten eddies of a now defunct East-West struggle—three of which the author investigates in Africa.[4] Characteristic of these conflicts is their gradual warping of local economy into a military enterprise between protagonists launching their terrors at each other through interposed populations. And finally the AIDS crisis—the new theological touchstone, against which any current soteriological claim must now be measured in much of Africa—discloses the latest "warp" of imperial power.[5] In the losing struggle with transnational pharmaceuticals—over pricing and availability of the drug cocktail that, in the West, so obviously "stays" the disease's "execution" of its victims—entire African demographies are being ravaged. This complex landscape of "colonial/imperial" ruptures forms the backdrop and foreground alike in terms of which to contextualize the work of a globalized scholar like Mbiti.

THE FOCUS OF MBITI'S WORK

Mbiti himself begins his career as one invited by his milieu to view African traditional culture as demonic and anti-Christian; subsequent research conducted back in Africa after theological studies in England and the U.S. causes him to revise that inherited valuation and become a careful investigator, and sometime champion, of indigenous practices and spirituality.[6] By no stretch of the imagination a pluralist in the mix of interreligious encounter (on the order of a John Hick or a Paul Knitter), Mbiti nonetheless labors intensively against operative Western colonial notions of African peoples as "primitive" and their practices as "backward" (9). In his earliest publication, he ranges through the history of European description, interpretation, and explanation of African religions in particular, staking out his own distinctive terrain of calling for serious dialogue between Christianity and African religiosity, and exploring the degree to which the latter can be understood to represent a *praeparatio evangelica* for the former.[7]

Part of his argument—and indeed, part of the motive force for his own work—is his concern for a distinctive African theology.[8] As of 1968 when Mbiti began his doctoral work, evangelistic activity had grown dramatically across the continent, but that wide-spread preaching had not yet issued in serious theology responsive to the uniqueness of African religiosity. While contending that Christianity and Islam alike, as well as African traditional religions (ATRs), can claim to be "indigenous" to Africa, he underscored the allergic reactions and annihilatory intentions of the missionary orientation shared by the former two with respect to the latter (344). Both Islam and Christianity, he asserted, have rabidly sought to reduce the presence of ATRs to mere anachronism. Nevertheless, Mbiti is also insistent that neither of the two world religions has made more than a shallow penetration into the African *persona*. Rather, in its historical-cultural roots, social dimensions, self-consciousness, and expectations, the latter remains traditionalist and anchored in the older spiritual orientation. And it is this conviction—and the investigations it gives rise to in Mbiti's work—that gives him his particular angle in the mix of postcolonial political struggle and spiritual warfare taking place, post-independence, on the African continent.

African Religions and Philosophy set the tone and mapped the agenda for his later work. The range of topics covered—under a somewhat abstractly conceived and problematically asserted generalization of "Africa"—is more beholden to anthropology for its focus than to the typical loci of theological reflection. Not "God," "Jesus," "Church," etc., but themes such as "Time," "Spiritual Beings, Spirits, and the Living Dead," "Ethnic Groups, Kinship, and the Individual," "Initiation and Puberty Rites," "Specialists: Medicine-Men, Rainmakers, Kings and Priests," and "Mystical Power, Magic, Witchcraft and Sorcery," populate the table of contents and drive the apology for dialogue. It is these more traditionally conceived indices of spirituality—and indeed, of "reality"—that Mbiti insists must be accorded attention and respect in moving toward an ecclesial practice and theological reflection in Africa that is more than merely a surface phenomenon.

But it is not merely Christianity that exercises Mbiti's concern (though he does accord that religion a unique and "terrible" responsibility to point the way in humanity's search for the Ultimate and he does articulate Jesus Christ as the unique goal and standard for individuals and communities, "whether they attain that goal religiously or ideologically") (363). As traditional religious practice is more and more relegated to invisibility and unconscious influence—with no scholarly champions to advocate its case or modernize its expression—Mbiti anticipates a continued erosion of traditional ritual and ceremonial *form* (359). But he is also clear that this is accompanied by a lingering half-life of *belief* (at the level of emotion) and *practice* (in everyday recourse to things like magic and witchcraft, work with the spirits, and attention to the living-dead) underneath the social surfaces upon which modernity etches its relentless rubrics of change. And the resilience of these "unconscious religious depths" portends a peculiar future and far-reaching influence. Not only is Mbiti convinced that the older religious traditions of Africa afford the "only lasting potentialities for a basis, a foundation, and a direction of life for African societies" (362-63). But he will even go so far as to deem religious coexistence, cooperation, and even competition in Africa (between Christianity, Islam, and ATRs) as perhaps necessary for the survival of humanity itself. The ultimate test of such is not which religion "wins in the end," but whether humankind as a whole "benefits or loses" from allowing religiousness a prominent place in the ongoing search for meaning and being (363). Writing at the other end of his career, in a book chapter in 2001, he has not changed his opinion, but asserts, for African religions, a particular role of humanization and celebration, communalization of endeavor and preservation of nature—now in the globalizing world order.[9]

AFRICAN TRADITIONAL RELIGION AND IMPERIAL CHRISTIANITY

Against such a general background, the concerns of this essay find particularly suggestive allusion in an internet exchange generated in 2004, discussing Mbiti's work on Runoko Rashidi's Global African Presence e-Group. In that dialogue, a voice self-identified only as that of a newly initiated priest of Orisa (after fourteen years as a devotee), writes:

> Mbiti's writings have fueled many a traditionalist devotee's journey. On the other hand, Runoko's writings do nothing to guide us back to our traditional spirituality . . . Mbiti has done more as a Christian minister to share the realities and the past of traditional settings than Runoko has. His book *Introduction to African Religions* alone has helped many Afrocentric people begin their studies.[10]

Indeed, the exchange begins with an assertion that whereas most of the academic methodologies used to describe African religion have tended to "(a) Christianize (b) Islamize (c) demystify (d) demonize or otherwise harm our traditions," Mbiti—though not innocent of such charges—has generally been more clear than others about what is African and what is neo-colonial in his descriptions.[11]

Such a discussion at once highlights the continuing impact of Mbiti's ideas beyond Christianity proper and at the same time exhibits the kind of issues—such as what is "African" and what "neocolonial" in contemporary spiritual practice on the continent or in the diaspora—that form the subtext of our inquiry here. That Mbiti's own work should serve to animate a *quest into* traditional religion, and not merely "conversion of" or "away from" such, is a prime theological datum that goes to the heart of the question of Christianity and empire. At first glance, the question that Mbiti's work raises is one of identification of the precise dividing line—or alternatively, sympathetic conjuncture—between traditional religion and Christianity. But part and parcel of that already immensely complex conundrum is the historically inextricable issue of the degree to which Western imperial power is interwoven with Christian mission and Christian identity itself, even after a measure of African indigenization of the gospel. The conviction of a Christian "duty to share"—of having a religious truth or vision or way of living that is held as "universal" in relevance a priori and necessary for human wholeness historically—is only inchoately separable from the question of an imperial conviction of cultural superiority or economic entitlement or political "right" (!) to conquer. Inside the contemporary fascination with interreligious dialogue, the issue of power asymmetries, cultural presuppositions, and epistemic (and real) violence remains fraught.

The question that emerges is one of theoretical standpoint and practical location. At this point in the late capitalist process of globalization, how would one gain concrete perspective on the precise place where "Christianity" can be distinguished from "imperial violence" or "colonial hubris"? Or on the flip side, just what is "African" in African traditional religions, and how might an anti-imperial "African Christianity" even be imagined, much less realized? Long-term "immersion" ("baptism") in the subtext and infrastructure of traditional religious practice—however compromised already by imperial invasion and missionary imposition—might itself constitute one of the necessary practices for genuine "Christian" interrogation of the historical relations between Christianity and the imperium. Such an immersion is at least one meaning of the theological orientation going by the name of indigenization, often associated with Mbiti (though hardly claimed by him as a watchword).

INDIGENIZATION AND LIBERATION

Mbiti certainly intended that his research and writing should contribute to the emergence of a genuine African Christianity, nurtured by an indigenous African theology. Shortly after surfacing as a major new voice in African theology with his first three publications, Mbiti was invited to Union Theological Seminary in 1972-73 to teach a year-long course with the reputed "father" of newly emergent Black Theology, James Cone. After many conversations articulating their respective positions, the debate went public in print.[12] Mbiti emphasized a vision of African theology arising out of the joy of being Christian that distinguished it from American and South African Black Theologies. Suspicious of what he called the latter's "mythologizing of liberation" and its fetishization of "Blackness" to the detriment of attention paid to other theological issues, Mbiti urged a basic "live and let live" relationship between the two. Willing to concede a certain admirable relevance of Black Theology's concerns for the American context, he sharply repudiated its import for Africa. Against what he perceived to be an over-emphasis on painful oppression, Mbiti held that African theology had no ideology to propagate.[13] The issue for Cone, on the other hand, was not to separate the two emphases or seek to fight shy of ideology, but rather to clarify, for any given theological initiative, which ideology, serving whose interests, articulated from what social a priori, a theological initiative should provisionally embrace.[14]

The friction between indigenization initiatives and liberation agendas has recurred in African theological debate ever since. The search for "African" authenticity is itself an ideology in the eyes of an African liberationist like Jean-Marc Ela, giving rise to various rhetorics of indigenization and theories of adaptation that can easily hide the realities of domination.[15] Too often, for him, Roman ecclesiastic models have been merely Africanized without pushing beyond the question of culture to the politics of subordination.[16] Engelbert Mveng and others similarly cite the priority of the cry from poverty that forms the counterpoint and subtext of civilized discourse about, and imposition upon, Africa.[17] In Mveng's view, religion is the opiate of the poor—often the only consolation they have—and thus one of the resources liberation must mobilize in pushing the agenda of indigenization, beyond merely liturgical innovation, toward a concern for the entirety of what he calls "anthropological impoverishment."[18]

In reviewing this history of options (between liberation and indigenization), Luke Lungile Pato solicits Sri Lankan theologian Aloyius Pieris to the effect that the two agendas, rightly understood, are specifications of the same process—"indigenization" naming the course of liberation in the domains of culture and religion and "liberation" underscoring the meaning of indigenization in relationship to political, economic, and social concerns.[19] Pato's ultimate critique, however, circles the discussion back around to Mbiti and empire in relationship to the theme that will occupy the rest of our exploration in this writing. And that is the theme of time. Pato argues that part of the problem at the heart of the indigenization/liberation debates is a common reification of the notion of culture, and a search, or repudiation of such search, for a static, pre-colonial past.[20] The African traditional worldview and symbology has never been merely immutable and self-referential, however, but dynamic and praxiological. The trick is to refuse false dichotomies in the effort to engage the real suffering and concrete possibilities awaiting theological explication and political mobilization—whether working as a liberationist organizer or an ecclesial innovator. Mbiti certainly stands on the horizon of each as a conundrum and cipher, "good to think with" in an age of imperial reach that grows daily more difficult to discern in all of its capillaric force inside economic infrastructure and cultural subtext.[21] And without question the articulation of Mbiti that is most compelling and troubling for subsequent theorists, whether secular or religious, is his construction of "African time."

THE FUTURE OF EMPIRE IN THE TIME OF AFRICA

In his first attempt to delineate an "African ontology" that would facilitate a deeper penetration of Western Christianity "into the religious world of traditional African life," Mbiti identifies temporality as the key concept necessary to grasp African beliefs, attitudes, practices, and general way of life (19, 21). In the late 1960s when Mbiti was first writing, the question of a distinctive notion of time among African peoples had not yet received theoretical attention, and Mbiti sought to pioneer the discussion. His examination of East African languages (Kikamba and Gikuyu in particular, backed up by Kiswahili and a sprinkling of Luganda) and of African calendars confirmed his experientially-informed perception that Africans largely conceive of time as two-dimensioned, focused on past and present (21). Rather than the linear model of movement found in much of the West, in which the temporal flow is perceived as leading from the past through the present to a future that can be plotted with the same set of coordinates, time in most of Africa, Mbiti argues, flows from present to past and admits of very little conceivable "future."

Among the Ankore of Uganda, for instance, the "day" is largely a function of cattle herding, in which there is "milking time," "resting time," "water drawing time," "grazing time," "return-to-the-kraal time," "sleep time," and so forth (25). Likewise, monthly demarcations partake of certain experiential conditions, as can be observed among the Latuka, where cyclical changes are referenced by names like "The Sun" (for October when it is quite hot), "give your uncle water," (for December when water grows scarce), "let them dig" (for the February planting preparations just before the rains return).

The movement of time in such an experience, Mbiti argues, is actually the inverse of the West—from the present toward the past as its centripetal fulfillment, rather than a cantilevering of anticipation out toward a meaning coming in from the horizon of the future. Such future as there is, in African languages and experience, takes its form from the present as its immediate progenitor, a projection already discernible in the present as an event in gestation. Beyond a few months (or at most a couple of years), the future is entirely opaque, outside the present rhythms whose structure could give predictable shape to what is emerging (23). Lacking any "eventful" characteristics, such a "future" is invisible and essentially nonexistent. In consequence—once again according to Mbitian logic—there is a marked lack of planning or concern for any notion of "progress" in traditional African societies (30).

Mbiti hypostatizes this two-fold temporal structure in terms of the Swahili words for present and past, respectively: *Sasa* and *Zamani*. Sasa covers some seven verb tenses parsing present experience among Akamba and Gikuyu between a "present" future extending only as far as six months (or sometimes even two years) hence, and the "present" that is "yesterday"(22, 28). *Zamani* covers a past divided between what is still specifiable and distinctly remembered, and what is in the indefinite past, the "graveyard of time," the final storehouse into which all events and phenomena congeal in a halting of temporal flow (29). Both Sasa and *Zamani* admit of quantity and quality and overlap each other. *Sasa* feeds *Zamani* with the events realized and lived in community in the micro-intensities of individual experience that are gradually relinquished to the macro-time. In this "backward" flow, conscious living in the vividness of now is relentlessly absorbed into the oceanic remembering of myth. Neither messianic hope nor final destruction are indigenous to such a scheme, but only the long, slow "fade out" of the *Zamani*, itself still harboring activity and happening. Here there is no myth of an end of time, but only the ceaseless rhythm of events and lives disappearing into the event-horizon of the deep past, a back-flow carried forward only in mythic narration, as incorrigible as the endless cycle of birth, marriage, procreation, and death (31). This conception also gives rise to the African idea of the "living-dead," of ancestors yet remembered by someone living, who—as long as that organic connection with the community remains intact—are also deemed "living" members of the *Sasa*-present, still likely to intervene in current affairs. Such are considered guardians of morality and practice, active agencies demanding attention and care by way of libation and honor. Once no one living has any experiential memory of the dead one, however, the ancestor "disappears" into the deeper recesses of *Zamani*, shifting from material presence toward spiritual resonance. They are eligible, perhaps, for mythic embodiment as a new hero or spirit-*persona* in the possession cult (to the degree he or she gained notoriety and importance while alive), but otherwise are in the process of becoming insubstantial and nameless (except in the monotones of recited genealogies), part of the general opacity of *Zamani* "eternity" (32–34).

While there are many other nuances fleshed out in this distinctive traditional structure, its basic difference from the West also serves to underscore the way Mbiti sketches out the upheavals of the last two centuries. Mission Christianity, in his analysis, introduces not merely a new content to African traditional religions, but even more fundamentally, a profound rupture of the African temporal orbit. In both *African Religions* and *New Testament Eschatology,* he comprehends the phenomenon of African Independent Churches (AICs) as the most likely seedbed of a potential African theology. But he laments the way the narrow register of traditional conceptions of the future (as extending at most six months to two years from the present) have been exploited by fundamentalist eschatologies (especially in relationship to the preaching of the Africa Inland Mission) at the expense of what he would assert as genuine Christian eschatology.[22] He sees a ready articulation between the "thin" (immediate) future of the ATRs and the immediacy and materiality and solely futuristic substance of AIM expectations of the (so-called) "second coming" that undercuts both this-worldly engagement with social problems and a more complex embrace of eschatology (as simultaneously "realized" in personal interiority and ecclesial "love" practices and "not yet" in final consummation). Within such an analysis, mission Christianity ruptures traditional mentality with a more robust future that ends up only teasing poor people with hope of an immediate release from pain and struggle. When that promised change does not readily occur, the result is disillusionment and sectarian separatism, in a self-fissioning AIC movement, in which the anticipated paradisal deliverance is unconsciously refocused as "partially realized" in the new charismatic leaders, who break away and command a following (307).

More broadly, the advent of European colonialism and American neo-liberalism have revolutionized African cultural rhythms, imposing a new beat carried by missionary eschatologies and syncopated by science and technology, mass urbanization and modern medicine, detribalization of the community, individualization of the economy, and nationalization of politics. The traditional solidarity articulated in the aphorism, "I am because we are and since we are, therefore I am," is being ground under in such a scenario. The modern onslaught produces profound alienation from traditional moorings without providing a credible and compelling substitute for the self-consciousness torn by such a radical rupture. The result is often a rabid search for rootage in the eroding "cultural *Zamani*"—a fetishism of the past that animates even elite movements like *Négritude*, African Personality, and the artistic focus on recovery of traditional music, dance, and folk stories (297). But it is also a search seeking to shift the mythic riches of that African *Zamani* toward a modern emphasis on *Sasa* and the future that Mbiti finds operating in the new ideological movements and in Christian ecumenism and messianism and Muslim brotherhoods and nationalism (357). And it is just here, in Mbiti's manner of posing modernity as, at root, a rupture and reconfiguration of African time-signatures, that empire and resistance place perhaps their most intriguing question marks on his work.

WILL THE REAL FUTURE PLEASE STAND UP?

Critical reception of Mbiti's African time construction has been quite mixed. There are those who take Mbiti to task for what they regard as his misplaced African exceptionalism. Souleymane Bachir Diagne, for instance, challenges Mbiti's argument for a distinctive African ontology of time by asserting that the issue can not be solved merely by examining verb tenses in the languages involved, but rather demands attention to the actual *use* of words (and, for that matter, calendars), and that any comparative examination of actual usage reveals African societies imagining and planning for future outcomes not all that differently from Western societies.[23] David Smith's article on Ugandan Ernest Beyaraza's *The African Concept of*

Time: A Comparative Study of Various Theories reiterates the latter's charge that Mbiti's notion of "African time" reinforces colonial ideas of Africa as primitive and seeks to combat such by pointing out the pervasive emphasis on children and (thus) the long-term future (not just ancestry and the past) so evident among Africa's various societies.[24] And Moses Òkè recasts Mbiti's analysis (of African time as futureless) as more accurately pointing to a "time-discipline problem" with respect to *planning* that he says should have occasioned from Mbiti, as a critical philosopher, not mere patronizing description but advocacy for a more progressive commitment to development and social improvement.[25]

Each of the three criticisms of Mbiti does, however, underscore a basic ambivalence present in his "African" notion of time (however its distinctiveness is conceived or reframed) that offers a suggestive counterpoint for the concern for empire exercising this essay. As already noted, for many scholars, the question of empire in our day cannot be separated from the question of neo-liberal globalization and privatization. Imperialism waxes wily in its symbiosis with transnational corporate culture, mass-marketed imagery, digitalized consumption patterns, and Western financial underpinning. No longer limited to the nation-state form, in the new millennium, empire must be discerned and challenged in its "micro-logic" cultural powers as well as its international political militancy.[26] For a Christian theology compelled by its own origins in movements as disparate as slave liberation (Moses' Exodus "maroon-walk"[27]), peasant resistance (Jesus' rural organizing) and urban anti-imperialism (the "outlaw" culture of Paul[28]), African temporal novelty demands careful scrutiny. Without question, distinctive work with time and timing has been an irrepressible feature of African and Afro-diasporic struggles to survive European colonialism, American slavery, and Western racism.[29]

In the Americas alone, the long history of rhythmic innovation resulting in hybrid musical cultures like those of the spirituals, the blues, jazz, gospel, soul, dub, reggae, soca, mambo, samba, and hip-hop gives trenchant witness to the fact that time can be differently deployed than simply "chronologically." In music, black cultures have regularly explored the open intervals between the beats in syncopated forms of "off-timing"[30] that train artist and audience alike to create pleasure and explore freedom outside the regularities of a merely uniform rhythm. As with the ear, so with the body—a dissonant aesthetic can train for a dissenting politics. It is no accident that disparate black political struggles (e.g., the Haitian Revolution, abolition in the U.S. and the Civil War, the populist movement, the Civil

Rights Movement) have co-existed with, and been deeply informed by, distinctive black musics (voudou drumming, the spirituals, the blues, soul). Resistance to colonialism on the continent likewise innovated hybrid political movements combining ideals of Western nationalism, the ecological sensibility of African traditional religions (such as employed in Kenya's own Mau Mau revolt or the ZANLA guerilla movement in Zimbabwe[31]), and rhythmic recapitulations of indigenous identities in the art accompanying those independence initiatives. While not the same claim as Mbiti makes, nor a simple matter of cause and effect, this pan-African "politics of off-timing" nonetheless partakes of a peculiar orientation toward the temporal order that refuses merely Western chronologies. Contra the capitalist ordering of time into uniform homogenous units, measured solely by labor output, this time-sensibility works time up into multiple pleasures of "working it" in the club, on the street corner, or in the bedroom—and in so doing gives an alternative perspective on, and valuing of, labor itself.[32] Not surprisingly, in contemporary hip-hop, it is also a sensibility now rupturing Euro-American cultural imperialism from within.

Whether Mbiti's *Sasa/Zamani* construct will stand up to inspection over the long haul, it remains for the short term "gyroscopic" in effect—an idea whose turns simultaneously twist back on the assumptions of anyone holding it up to scrutiny. In a world just beginning to face into the patent unsustainability of the capitalist frenzy to accumulate, what is the value of an alternative approach that does not simply routinize time toward an ever-more ruthless exploitation in service of production and consumption? The orientation of development schemes answering only to short-term profitability and short-lived competitive advantage has yet to meet its ultimate evaluation in the longer time frame of evolutionary history. Certainly relentless planning has become an integral part of the will-to-control embedded in contemporary science and corporate management that may well constitute a step toward "playing God" from which it is virtually impossible for human hubris to retreat. But given the dystopian scenarios (rapid depletion of fossil fuels, global warming, rampant desertification, and soil loss, along with the prospect of nuclear conflict) increasingly emerging as the after-effect of our drive toward one or another version of technological totalitarianism, it may be that the Western notion of the "future" itself needs to be interrogated as an imperial construct.

The likely disappearance in our own lifetimes of the last hunter-gatherer cultures devoted to a more present-oriented existence may well stand as a quintessential sign of the times. Such cultures—like the San of southern Africa or the Huaroni of South America—represent the last vestiges of a way of organizing human social life that focuses not on economic "progress" and ever-greater consumption of the environment, but rather on sustainable reciprocity and deep intimacy with other life forms. Such cultures do not generally elaborate the future in terms of an anticipation of "more and better," and in some cases do not even have words for ideas like "time," "take," "want," or "worry."[33] Far from existing in a constant struggle with hunger (as popularly imagined in the typical Western mindset), these societies are largely, in the words of anthropologist Marshall Sahlins, humanity's "original leisure societies."[34] And the anarcho-primitivist theories[35] attempting to articulate the inchoate questions about prediction and control such cultures pose toward our "civilized" achievements are perhaps the postmodern equivalent of Abel's anti-imperial "blood-groan" against city-founder Cain recorded in Genesis. At the very least, the alternative time orientations of hunter-gatherer and African traditional societies invite "developed" social orders to come clean about the imperial enslavements, genocides, and extinctions that have everywhere been their condition of possibility (ever since the first turn to settled agriculture and progressive urbanization more than five millennia ago).

Ironically, Òkè's final challenge to Mbiti's uplift of African temporal distinctiveness is a three-fold choice for African societies. In the face of what Òkè calls the "debilitating effects [of] a poor time orientation," such societies must anticipate either recolonization, early extinction, or embrace of a developmentalist future in kind.[36]

But must Africa become Europe or America to survive? The African comeback might well be its own insistent inquiry whenever faced with malaise and demise: not "what" is wrong, but *who* is really "eating" whom and what is the antidote for the out-of-control appetite?[37] One must ask, has Africa ever really been decolonized since Europe carved up the continent in 1885—or only subjected to ever-renewed "consumption" by Western-style development schemes and economic interests (however they might be expressed politically)? It may be—in view of the longest-term future—that ultimately the most debilitating concept of the future is modernity's own. And African traditional religion's "presentist" orientation represents a summons to global Christian practice, from the deep ancestral past of all of us, to turn from embrace of the imperial will-to-control, toward an actual trust in a God willing to die resisting empire's savagery.

Further Reading

Primary Sources

Mbiti, John S. *African Religions and Philosophy*. Garden City, N.Y.: Anchor Books, 1969.

_____. *Concepts of God in Africa*. New York, N.Y.: Praeger Publishers, 1970.

_____. *New Testament Eschatology in an African Background: a Study of the Encounter between New Testament Theology and African Traditional Concepts*. Oxford: Oxford University Press, 1971.

_____. "An African Views American Black Theology." In *Black Theology: A Documentary History, 1966–1979*. Edited by Gayraud S. Wilmore and James H. Cone, 477–82. Maryknoll, N.Y.: Orbis Books, 1979.

Secondary Sources

Cone, James. "A Black American Perspective on the Future of African Theology." In *Black Theology: A Documentary History, 1966–1979*. Edited by Gayraud S. Wilmore and James H. Cone, 492–502. Maryknoll, N.Y.: Orbis Books, 1979.

Diagne, Souleymane Bachir. "On Prospective: Development and a Political Culture of Time." *Africa Development* 29, no. 1 (2004): 55–69.

Òkè, Moses. "From an African Ontology to an African Epistemology: A Critique of J. S. Mbiti on the Time Conception of Africans." *Quest: An African Journal of Philosophy* 18 (2004): 25–36. See http://www.quest-journal.net.

Smith, Daniel. "Time and Not the Other Time in Africa: On Ernest Beyaraza: The African Concept of Time: A Comparative Study of Various Theories." *Forum for Intercultural Philosophy* 3, 2001, http://lit.polylog.org/3/rsd-en.htm (September 2007).

CHAPTER 32

Mercy Amba Oduyoye

Kwok Pui-lan

Mercy Amba Oduyoye is a pioneer of African women's theology and a tireless promoter of Third World feminist theology.[1] A Christian educator, theologian, great African storyteller, and leader of the ecumenical movement, Oduyoye was the first woman president (1996-2001) of the Ecumenical Association of Third World Theologians (EATWOT). In her several books and more than eighty published articles, Oduyoye has written on numerous subjects, such as the doctrine of God, feminism, the Bible, women's rituals, the church, mission, and spirituality.

Born as Amba Ewudziwa on a cocoa farm of Amoanna in 1934, when Ghana was still a British colony, Oduyoye is a third-generation Christian, whose family members are prominent leaders of the Methodist Church.[2] She has lived through a tumultuous period of African history—the struggle against colonial domination, political instability following independence, the widening economic gap between the northern and southern hemispheres, famines and ecological disasters, the overthrow of apartheid, violent religious and ethnic strife, and the tortuous road to democracy. Educated in Ghana and at Cambridge University in England, Oduyoye was active in the Student Christian Movement (SCM) through which she met her future husband, the Nigerian SCM General Secretary Modupe Oduyoye. Her sensitivity to gender issues began when she moved to teach theology at the University of Ibadan in Nigeria in the 1970s, where all her colleagues were male. This was her first exposure to the subjugation of women in patrilineal Africa, because she has come from a matrilineal heritage. Her initiative to identify and recommend other African women theologians led to the formation in 1989 of the Circle of Concerned African Women Theologians, which has organized several assemblies and promoted African women's theological scholarship.[3] Oduyoye writes, "African women's theology is developing in the context of global challenges and situations in Africa's religio-culture that call for transformation."[4]

Her long ecumenical journey began in 1966, when she served as Education Secretary of the World Council of Churches (WCC). She was one of the notable women leaders, when the WCC pushed for greater inclusion of women in leadership and the life of the church. She served on the Central Committee and the Faith and Order Commission before assuming the position as Deputy General Secretary (1987-1994). Instrumental in the WCC's study on "Community of Women and Men in Church and Society," Oduyoye played a crucial role in the Ecumenical Decade of the Churches in Solidarity with Women (1988-1998) and wrote the book *Who Will Roll the Stone Away?* to explain the decade's rationale and process.[5] Oduyoye has been a speaker and guest professor in numerous universities and seminaries in Africa, Europe, and North America and currently serves as director of the Institute of African Women in Religion and Culture in Accra, Ghana. A trailblazer who has left a rich legacy for African women's theology, Oduyoye has inspired the upcoming generation of women theologians from the Third World. Her colleague Elizabeth Amoah notes that Oduyoye's theological work has several foci: "1) reflections on post-colonial Christianity in Africa; 2) women, tradition and the gospel in Africa; and 3) global issues from African perspectives. These themes form the pivot around which many current African women theologians do their theologizing."[6]

GENDER, CULTURE, AND COLONIALISM

In *Orientalism*, Edward W. Said argues that colonialism involves not only political and military domination, but also cultural hegemony in terms of the production of knowledge about the other and representation of the colonized.[7] Labeled variously as the "primitive" and "uncivilized" "dark continent," Africa has had its unfair share of racist and colonialist myths projected onto its cultures and peoples. To counteract such colonial misrepresentations, anti-colonial struggles in Africa began with the affirmation of the dignity of black people and the positive elements of their cultures. Frantz Fanon analyzed the wounds inflicted by insidious myths and stereotypes upon the psyches of black men and women, as well as the complex psychodynamics developed under the conditions of colonialism.[8] Leaders of the *négritude* movement, such as Aimé Césaire and Léopold Senghor, advocated a return to traditional African culture and insisted that cultural independence was a prerequisite to other independences.

The development of African theology must be seen within this larger matrix of the struggle to define African cultural identity and autonomy. Since the regaining of national independence, progressive church leaders and theologians in Africa have called for the abolition of the colonial trappings of Christianity and for the building of a church of African color, a Christianity with an African face. As a result, there have been two major thrusts in the development of African theology: inculturation and liberation.[9]

Inculturation entails proclaiming the gospel using the languages, worldviews, and thought patterns of African cultures. Culture is seen by some African theologians as the foundation of their identity, their historical path to salvation, and the best African vehicle for the gospel.[10] Liberation refers to Africans' urgent need to strive for economic and political freedom from neo-colonialism. The black-consciousness movement and the struggle against apartheid in South Africa formed backdrops for the development of theologies of liberation. Although inculturation and liberation are not mutually exclusive, the emphases of the two approaches are quite different and often seen in tension with one another: the former focuses more on culture, identity, and religion, while the latter highlights the need for social and political transformation.

The issue of gender featured prominently in the cultural debates between the colonizers and the colonized. The encounter between Western colonizing culture and indigenous cultures raised thorny issues pertaining to women's roles and sexuality, polygamy, child marriage, veiling, female circumcision, and widowhood. The subordination of women was often cited as symptomatic of the inferiority of indigenous cultures, and saving colonized women from their oppression, ignorance, and heathenism became an integral part of the colonialist discourse. Shuttled between tradition and modernity, indigenous women were seen either as victims of male aggression or as pitiful objects of Westerners' compassion.[11] To reclaim that they are subjects in charge of their own destiny, African women have to fight against patriarchy in their traditions, on the one hand, and the complex legacy of colonialist feminism, on the other.

As her woman's consciousness developed, Oduyoye became painfully aware that the male theologians who were developing theology with an African face had a male face in mind. She became convinced that there could not be a comprehensive and integrated Christian anthropology if a feminist perspective were left out. In a 1982 article entitled "Feminism: A Pre-Condition for a Christian Anthropology," she defined feminism as follows:

> Feminism has become the shorthand for the proclamation that women's experiences should become an integral part of what goes into the definition of "being human." It is to highlight what the world and the world view of the woman looks like as she struggles side by side with the man to realize her full potential as a human being by shedding all that hampers her. . . . Feminism then is an emphasis on the wholeness of the human community as made up of beings some of whom are male and others female. It seeks to express what is not so obvious, that is, that *male-humanity has a partner in female-humanity*, and that both expressions of humanity are needed to shape a balanced community within which each will experience a fullness of Be-ing.[12]

Oduyoye challenges those theologians who attempt to inculturate Christianity into the African soil for failing to take into account patriarchal elements found in African cultures. She defines culture in a very comprehensive way, as "a people's world-view, way of life, values, philosophy of life, the psychology that governs behavior, their sociology and social arrangements, all that they have carved and cultured out of their environment to differentiate their style of life from other peoples."[13] Within African cultural traditions, beliefs and practices such as stereotypical sex roles, the ritual impurity of menstruating women, and the exclusion of females from certain rituals marginalize women and render them second-class citizens.

Simultaneously, Oduyoye decries the fact that those theologians arguing passionately for liberation are talking about the liberation of only half of the African people if they overlook the abject poverty of women, who still "grind and pound their hours away."[14] Arguing that African women have always worked and provided for their families, she says, "The question is what kind of work [they do], and how is it valued by society as a whole."[15] She insists that feminism is central to the discussion of both inculturation and liberation, and attempts to link the two together. At the same time, her understanding of feminism is not separatist, as she always tries to involve men as equal partners to build a just and peaceful African society in the midst of interethnic strife and abject poverty.

Oduyoye does not see women's struggle for economic and political liberation as separated from their determination to overcome religio-cultural oppression:

"Socio-political and even economic participation is governed by religious beliefs of the primal religion of Africa."[16] The social status of women and their culturally prescribed roles directly affect the range of women's economic participation. As Carol S. Robb has observed, the ways a society structures women's sexuality have direct bearings on economic justice: "[W]omen's experiences of sexuality compromise our access to the economy to an extent that is not true for men."[17] Oduyoye illustrates vividly how true Robb's analysis is in her context: "African men carry none of the life-giving burdens that African women carry. Women with babies on their backs and yams, firewood, and water on their heads [are] the common image of African women in real life as in art."[18] While some of Oduyoye's statements at times present a generalized picture of African women, she hopes to arouse the consciousness of gender imbalance that causes so much pain and suffering in many particular African societies.

Oduyoye often laments that people outside Africa, including many Western feminists, tend to focus on the religio-cultural oppression of African women, without paying equal attention to African women's suffering under economic injustice. The latter would require these outside commentators to examine their own complacency in maintaining a global economic order that keeps many African women living on a subsistence level. With memories of colonialism fresh in their minds, Oduyoye notes, African women resist the patronizing attitude of women in the northern hemisphere: "Northern women (feminists) took it upon themselves to describe to African women the nature of their oppression, which they named polygyny. . . . They facilely undertook to save us from genital mutilation with the stroke of a pen, while we knew all along that such liberation would involve a long struggle with religious beliefs and age-old conventions."[19] Northern women's condescending and patronizing attitudes may easily reinscribe the colonialist feminism[20] of an earlier time.

While Oduyoye condemns patriarchy in African societies, which is reinforced by myths, rituals, and teachings of Christianity, Islam, and African traditional religions, she avoids presenting African women only as victims. Born of the matrilineal Akan heritage and married into the patrilineal Yoruba system of western Nigeria, she is sensitive to the different social statuses and expectations of women in Africa. For example, Akan women are the center of kinship, and even marriage does not change their economic involvement. Market women can exert great influence at home and in their local communities. Even in extreme poverty, most

African women assume the enormous burden of feeding their families and taking care of their children.

Oduyoye consistently places issues surrounding African women's sexuality and rituals in the wider socioeconomic context of Africa, thereby challenging some of the cultural assumptions of her audience. For example, Oduyoye knows that polygamy sometimes arises out of dire economic conditions, and she does not condemn the practice outright. When there is a change of attitude toward procreation and a growing understanding of mutuality and partnership in marital union, she believes, polygamous marriages will become less attractive. Stern condemnation alone will not stamp out this deep-rooted practice.[21] Interpreting the birth, puberty, and marriage rituals of women, Oduyoye urges us to place the concept of human sexuality within the total enterprise of struggling to understand our humanity. For African women, human sexuality does not just designate the love and bonding of two individuals but has deep religious dimensions as well. Oduyoye is aware that some rituals reinforce the primacy of the mothering role of women, while others, such as the mourning rituals of widows, subscribe to the notion of impurity and pollution of women. But she is careful to point out that there are also liberatory elements in Africans' traditional religions, which should not be overlooked.[22]

CROSSROADS CHRISTIANITY AND HYBRIDIZATION

Oduyoye regrets that people often forget that Christianity has a long history in Africa and did not arrive on African soil in the modern period. She points out that there have been different waves of African Christianity: the indigenous forms making up the Coptic and Ethiopian Orthodox churches, the arrival of Catholic missionaries since the fifteenth century, the expansion of Protestant missions during the colonial era, the establishment of African Independent Churches, and newer religious movements that are spreading like mushrooms all over the continent. From early on, Oduyoye expressed interest in how these divergent expressions of Christianity interacted with African culture. For example, she discussed the relation of African religious beliefs and practices to Christian theology in a paper delivered at a gathering of African theologians in Accra, Ghana, in 1977.[23] For her, Africans do not need to give up their cultural identity to become Christians, and it is not uncommon to see African Christians pour libations, offer incantations, follow widows' rites, and practice naming and funeral ceremonies in their indigenous cultures. Oduyoye calls this phenomenon "crossroads Christianity" to encompass the fluid interface and interaction between African culture and Western forms of Christianity.[24]

Although Oduyoye does not draw explicitly from the theoretical framework of postcolonial theory, we can discern similarities between her arguments and postcolonial thought, especially in the area of cultural criticism. This is because Oduyoye is analyzing the same cultural phenomena facing many newly independent countries, though she may not use the jargon employed by postcolonial theorists. My point is not to claim Oduyoye as a proto-postcolonial critic but to situate her work within the larger context of intellectual debates today. In this way we can better appreciate the significance of her work and her implicit challenge that theory can be expressed in more than one way.

For example, Oduyoye's analysis of crossroads Christianity, with its fluidity and border crossing, shows affinity with the concept of hybridization in postcolonial thought. Hybridity refers to the gray area of the in-between, defying easy categorizations and boundaries. Vietnamese cultural critic and filmmaker Trinh T. Minh-ha describes the prevalence of hybridity in cultures shaped by many political and cultural forces: "[N]ever has one been made to realize as poignantly as in these times how thoroughly hybrid historical and cultural experiences are, or how radically they evolve within apparently conflictual and incompatible domains, cutting across territorial and disciplinary borders, defying policy-oriented rationales and resisting the simplifying action of nationalist closures."[25]

Echoing the critique of postcolonial cultural critics, Oduyoye questions the construction of a generalized and universalized cultural identity for the whole African continent. Such a construction collapses differences into sameness because it does not consider the diversity of African cultures and development over time:

> Looking at contemporary Africa, one cannot use the word culture in the singular. Not even in pre-colonial Africa would such a use have been appropriate, for the communal way of life had a variety of manifestations on the continent. . . . In today's Africa, as one moves from country to country, one senses a change in way of life. . . . It is therefore neither helpful nor realistic to speak in terms of African culture, except in the broadest way. Culture is historical, it develops, it changes, [and] there are continuous aspects as well as innovative ones.[26]

In her own works Oduyoye has increasingly paid attention to the diversity within African cultures and the different languages, worldviews, and folkways of

African women. This is most evident in her later works, such as *Daughters of Anowa*, a work to which I will return.

Postcolonial critic Homi Bhabha has pointed out that myths of homogeneous national or cultural identity have been created to benefit those who are in the majority or who are in power. The postcolonial perspective, he insists, forces us to rethink the limitations of a consensual sense of cultural community, because it tends to exclude minorities and women, as well as migrant, diasporic, and refugee populations.[27] In a similar vein Oduyoye asks the question: Who are the people who benefit from the notion of a pan-African identity, especially when such an identity is defined by male norms? "[W]hy do I cringe every time I read African self-identity or African authenticity? . . . [I]t is the male writers who make me cringe. . . . When they acknowledge that the past is not all golden, are they saying that these 'ungolden' aspects include the dehumanization of women, and that these should be eliminated?"[28]

Oduyoye's critique of the male construction of African identity is most evident in her lengthy and careful discussion of Kenyan theologian John Mbiti's view on love and marriage in Africa.[29] Mbiti's writings on African religions, philosophy, and cultural customs have enormous influence both in Africa and abroad. For Mbiti, marriage is foundational in African society, and marriage and procreation are a unity in African communities. Mbiti points out that women who are childless are condemned as outcasts, and homosexual relationships are considered immoral, unnatural, and dangerous to society. Elaborate marriage ceremonies, rites of passage, and socialization of the young ensure the perpetuation of these cultural values. Oduyoye, who is childless, questions whether the sole aim of marriage and sex is procreation, and she is horrified by the demonization of homosexuals. She asks whether there is mutuality and reciprocity in marital relationships when the wife is required to complement the husband's needs, and not vice versa. In the end Oduyoye challenges Mbiti's presentation of the African perspective on love and marriage as arising from a singularly male point of view: "He is presenting a man's concerns for marriage. That the whole issue of the contemporary struggles of married women in the modern sector is not discussed is related to the factor of perspectives and experience."[30]

While Oduyoye criticizes constructions of African identity that fail to take note of diversity and hybridity, she is equally adamant in her challenge of the superiority complex of some Western Christians. If Christianity can interact with Jewish, Greek, Russian, and European cultures, Oduyoye does not see why it can't learn something through its interchange with African culture.[31] While the inculturation process has often been labeled "syncretistic," Oduyoye notes that African Christians are not prone to seeing syncretism negatively. She writes: "Syncretism is accepted as a concept that is applied to 'difference seeking arbitration' in the context of a Christianity that presents itself as intolerant of difference. Such Christianity employs the language of the powerful, seeking to control diversity and achieve conformity with their own standpoint."[32]

It is clear to Oduyoye that African Christianity cannot resort to a nativistic mode of returning to traditional culture, nor can it simply mimic Western colonial forms. Instead it must be an organic development that involves genuine intercultural dialogue, with openness toward "creating space for shared thinking, partnerships, a conscious effort to maintain self-determination, and the development of collaboration."[33] She rejects the colonial idea that cultures are fixed and so tightly bound that mutual exchange and interaction are not possible. Yet she is wary of the liberal position of cultural pluralism, which assumes that all cultures are equal and can compete with one another on a level playing field. She insists that the dialectic between the powerful and the powerless cannot be overlooked in our cultural analysis.

CULTURAL HERMENEUTICS, FOLKTALK, AND THE BIBLE

Cultural hermeneutics is an important tool that African women theologians have developed to analyze their culture, religion, and the Christian heritage. Since African women's cultural traditions are multilayered, their cultural hermeneutics has to be multidimensional as well, analyzing different aspects of culture at the same time. Kenyan theologian Musimbi Kanyoro points out that cultural hermeneutics in the African context involves the critique of colonial and white myths about African women; an analysis of the rituals and ceremonies that define a woman's life journey and the social institutions that support those rituals; an examination of cultural ideologies regarding gender roles and power in society; and the recovery of sources and data that provide information about women's diverse experience and the gender struggles defined by history, culture, race, and class structure.[34]

Oduyoye describes the importance of cultural hermeneutics at the beginning of her book *Introducing African Women's Theology*. She argues that cultural hermeneutics enables women to interpret their experiences and realities and to see that culture is dynamic and evolving and not something given. One important aspect of cultural hermeneutics, Oduyoye points out, is a hermeneutics of liberation, which allows African women to identify and promote life-affirming aspects in their culture. An important criterion is that these cultural elements promote women's full humanity and participation in society. This self-affirmation is necessary today because the African continent is marginalized in the globalization process, and people from outside have used the excuse of culture to underrate Africans. But African women also need to engage in a hermeneutics of suspicion, which entails challenging inhuman and domesticating customs and traditions while recovering their historical memory. Because of Africa's peripheral role in the world and the negative stereotypes imposed on its peoples, African women have felt pressure to keep silent about their oppression. This subtle coercion must be exposed so that African women can feel free to voice their opinions and to struggle for greater justice. Moreover, the hermeneutics of suspicion must go hand in hand with a hermeneutics of commitment, as African women must take up the responsibility to change and transform those oppressive customs in order to bring about a fullness of life.[35]

Oduyoye applies the insights of cultural hermeneutics to the scrutiny of the oral traditions in Africa, which she has called "folktalk" in her work. Oral traditions are prevalent throughout Africa, yet African male theologians have seldom paid sufficient attention to this important dimension of their culture. Academic theologians have been preoccupied with the study of theological and historical texts, predominantly handed down from the West, without paying much attention to the oral folk tradition. They are therefore primarily interested in inculturation from above, and neglect inculturation from below.[36] In *Hearing and Knowing*, Oduyoye draws attention to the oral sources of theology, giving examples of songs and impromptu lyrics that Africans sing to interpret biblical events, call people to worship, and teach the young.[37] Unfortunately, this oral theology has not yet been systematically collected and analyzed by African theologians.

In *Daughters of Anowa*, Oduyoye includes a whole section of analysis of folktalk, which includes myths, folktales, and proverbs shared among all the people, not just the learned or the elderly. Folktalk is an integral part of the "religio-cultural corpus" of Africa, because it is "dynamic and malleable, [and] interplays with the changing conditions of life to direct individual self-perception and to shape the entire community."[38]

One can discern several hermeneutical principles in Oduyoye's detailed exegesis of the folktalk among the masses. First, she is interested in how the corpus of folktalk reflects or is used to actually shape women's lives. For example, in myths of origins, she pays close attention to the roles of male and female actors, the depiction of female power, and the relationship between women and primacy of life (21–29). In the exegesis of proverbs, she examines the making of women and prescriptions for the feminine (58–63). Oduyoye finds that in general the folktalk reinforces the subordinate position of women and perpetuates their stereotypical roles as mothers, wives, caretakers, and self-sacrificial persons who put others' needs first. The folktalk also censors women who seek equal power with their spouses, who do not tolerate polygamy, and who are too demanding.

The second principle is to ask for whose benefit these myths, folktales, and proverbs are told from generation to generation. Using insights gleaned from rhetorical criticism, Oduyoye argues that comments in the folktalk do not reflect historical reality but are rhetorical devices aimed at shaping communal values and changing behaviors: "For me, African myths are ideological constructions of a by-gone age that are used to validate and reinforce societal relations. For this reason, each time I hear 'in our culture' or 'the elders say' I cannot help asking, for whose benefit? Some person or group or structure must be reaping ease and plenty from whatever follows" (35).

The last principle Oduyoye suggests is to have the courage to discard some of the folktalk that is harmful and no longer relevant, and to continue to develop a new tapestry of meanings for women. Although myths, folktales, and proverbs are still influential in African culture and among Africans in diaspora, Oduyoye believes that culture is not static and is constantly open to transformation. She calls upon women to use their creativity and insights to weave new patterns of meaning for their lives. The resulting new tapestry will be multi-stranded, vibrant, and colorful, reflecting the equal values of women and men and the mutual dependence and reciprocity of the human community (74–76).

Oduyoye's cultural critique of folktalk adds to the richness of oral hermeneutics emerging from Third World women and minorities in the United States. Renita Weems, an African American biblical scholar, has pointed to the importance of oral and aural hermeneutics for black people in America, especially for black women, the majority of whom were illiterate for a long time.[39] Womanist scholars have looked to spirituals and other songs as resources for understanding the ethical val-

ues and God-talk of black women.[40] In my study of Asian women's biblical interpretation, I have also pointed to the centrality of the oral medium in the transmission of Asian classical texts and religious scriptures. Asian women do not write
commentaries on the Bible; instead they talk about it and devise skits for discussion, dramatizing, and performing the Bible. Like Oduyoye, I have noted that few
Asian male theologians have regarded these oral resources as important for theology.[41] Oduyoye's critique of myths, folktales, and proverbs that shape the communal
perception of womanhood is significant, because few feminist scholars worldwide
have looked into these important resources and developed ways to do exegesis of
them. Her hermeneutical principles will be important references for women in
other cultures to use to debunk the androcentric biases of their own folktalk.

African women theologians have also applied cultural hermeneutics to examining the Bible from their standpoints and to scrutinizing the multicultural layers embedded in biblical narratives. Just as not all African cultures are inclusive
and liberating for women, Oduyoye warns that we must exercise caution when
approaching the Bible, because not everything said in the Bible is good news for
women.[42] Musimbi Kanyoro offers a concrete example in her reading of the story
of Ruth. She observes that the practice of requiring a widow to marry the brother
of her dead husband can be found in many parts of Africa and that the church and
women themselves have used the story of Ruth to endorse this cultural practice.
While Western feminists have either praised the friendship between Naomi and
Ruth or highlighted the courage of these women to make decisions for their survival, Kanyoro focuses on Orpah and asks how we can support women like Orpah
who do not follow cultural expectations. While Ruth, who succumbs to the cultural expectations of her time, has her share of blessing, what is the blessing for
Orpah, who decides to be different? How can Orpah stand up against communal
criticism and mobilize support?[43] Reading the story of Ruth against the realities of
African culture enables Kanyoro to pose new questions to the biblical text and to
go beyond the usual feminist recuperation of the female protagonists of the story. Kanyoro points out rather sharply that the women in the Ruth story are positioned in different ways vis-à-vis their culture and that there is more than one way
of responding. Reading the text through both a cultural lens and a gendered lens
may enable us to see the multiple layers of the text.

Cultural hermeneutics also encourages African women to pay attention to the
use of African cultural resources as critical tools for interpreting the Bible. In her

introduction to a collection of essays on African women and the Bible, Musa Dube outlines the different approaches African women theologians are pursuing. Given that African women themselves are reading the Bible, which has been translated into their vernacular languages, some researchers have documented and exposed colonial and patriarchal translations to develop a gender-neutral and decolonizing reading. Others have examined methods of storytelling, because storytellers have told and retold Bible stories to address the needs of the community, sometimes adding new characters or including the responses of the listeners or comparing the Bible stories with African stories. Dube herself has looked at divination, a practice common in southern Africa, in which the biblical text is used as a tool. For example, in the African Independent Churches, people ask diviner-healers to interpret certain biblical passages in order to diagnose troubled relationships and offer solutions for healing. To understand how African women use the Bible, women theologians have to read the Bible with ordinary readers, nonacademic women interpreters, and document their feminist methods of resistance.[44]

GLOBAL ISSUES AND WOMEN'S SOLIDARITY

Oduyoye is aware that the old form of colonialism has been replaced by the exploitation of the neo-liberal market economy. She describes this exploitation as a form of "neo-slavery" that makes "nations replace food crops with cash crops, receive a pittance for their labours, [and] use that pittance to pay 'debts' owed to their trading partners."[45] The unhealthy economic conditions and the dire need for survival have fueled racial, cultural, and religious conflicts worldwide. She notes that with some exceptions, the majority of the armed conflicts have taken place in the South, while the North exploits the situation in order to keep their arms industry flourishing. Thus, theological reflection must give justice and peace issues critical attention. Oduyoye decries that theologians who are well away from these conflicts often jump straight to just war theory and pacifism, violence and nonviolence when they discuss peace issues, while neglecting to address the root causes of war and conflicts. In contrast, Third World theologians have spoken about seeking the reign of God and the need for continuous struggles to eradicate injustice and violence so that the world can have sustainable peace. The liberation of women from patriarchy and other forms of violence is an inseparable part of pursuing peace, and so is the protection of the environment and the habitat for life to flourish.[46]

Oduyoye is also keen on addressing other global issues that are affecting the African continent, such as HIV/AIDS, which has ravaged many African nations, particularly in sub-Sahara. Today, the AIDS epidemic has a feminine face, as women in Africa infected and affected by HIV/AIDS far outnumber men, and the victims of AIDS have left behind millions of orphans. Members of the Circle of Concerned African Women Theologians have taken bold steps in discussing issues of sexuality in the context of the HIV/AIDS epidemic, thereby breaking the silence of cultural taboos and stereotypes. They have also addressed the stigma associated with the disease and produced resources for the churches.[47] Facing the daunting situation of extreme poverty, chronic hunger, HIV/AIDS pandemic, and the social injustices of globalization, Nyambura J. Njoroge of Kenya writes: "the whole Africa cries out for a life-giving theology that can bring healing, transformation, and hope."[48] She credits Oduyoye's life and ministry as setting a model for others to emulate.

Oduyoye has always been interested in making connections among women's situations in the Third World. At the second assembly of EATWOT, in New Delhi, India, in 1981, Oduyoye described the intervention of women in the proceedings as an "irruption within the irruption" and named sexism as a grave concern.[49] Because of the persistence and hard work of its female members, EATWOT has taken the slow and painful steps to recognize the gender divide and to make room for women's leadership.[50] For Oduyoye, EATWOT is an important forum for Third World women to share their experiences and to develop methodologies for feminist theology from Third World perspectives. She notes that Africans and Asians share similar multireligious contexts and can learn from one another how to use those immense religio-cultural resources in doing theology. She also finds that African women have much to discuss with women in Latin America, because there are Africans in diaspora in the Americas. The social and class analysis of Latin American theology and the movement of Christian base communities are helpful lessons for those fighting crippling poverty in society. African women also share commonalities in their religious beliefs and worldviews with Pacific and Native women. Oduyoye notices that in many Third World countries charismatic movements and new religious movements are on the rise, presenting new challenges to women.[51] Third World women theologians need to continue to exchange ideas, learn from one another, and share strategies against oppression.

Over the years Oduyoye has had ample opportunities to listen to debates on global feminist issues and the solidarity of women among Western feminists. She cautions that Western feminists cannot take from Africa what they want or seem to lack, without reciprocity. They also should not naïvely think that by their goodwill they could change the plight of African women, who must shape their own destiny and future. To her Western feminist colleagues, Oduyoye issues this important charge:

> Western women rightly yearn for a coalition of "strong women around the world." In their search they have turned their attention to Africa's matrilineal (mother-centered) cultures, to African goddesses and market women, and those in the front line of the struggle against apartheid and other imposed structures of oppression in Africa. As academics they have a right to do research. But as women who would be sisters, they have a responsibility to relate to African women in a way that expresses genuine solidarity. On their own, they cannot liberate us.[52]

Oduyoye has always displayed cultural sensitivity in negotiating differences, as well as a tremendous sense of pride, dignity, humor, and wit in her struggle as an African woman. Since dialogue across racial, religious, and class backgrounds is still difficult, we can learn to practice hospitality in our encounter with others. Oduyoye identifies hospitality as an important African value as well as a significant theme in the Bible. Hospitality in the African context has much to do with the affirmation of life and the care for the needy, refugees, and strangers among us. "Hospitality," Oduyoye writes, "is built on reciprocity, openness and acceptance, but to open one's self to the other is always a risk."[53] Only when we learn to offer and receive hospitality can women and men collaborate with one another to work toward a new creation and a new community.

Today, when the majority of the Christian population is living in the South, we have to pay increasing attention to how theologians such as Oduyoye are reinterpreting Christian faith. She points to a postcolonial trajectory for a future history of Christian theology that is dialogical, uses narrative genres, respects all cultures, and addresses gender dynamics in complex ways. While she has left a rich legacy, there are issues that will need further elaboration, such as the development of a cultural hermeneutics that accounts for the cultural and religious diversity in African feminist theology, the conceptualization of a healthy sexual theology, and the need to promote women's leadership in church and society. As women in poor communities of Africa and other parts of the world have borne disproportionally the burden of globalization, we will need to articulate a transnational feminist theology that will work for the empowerment of women and foster solidarity across differences and boundaries.

FURTHER READING

Primary Sources

Oduyoye, Mercy Amba. *Beads and Strands: Reflections of an African Woman on Christianity in Africa.* Maryknoll, N.Y.: Orbis Books, 2004.

_____. *Daughters of Anowa: African Women and Patriarchy.* Maryknoll, N.Y.: Orbis Books, 1995.

_____. *Hearing and Knowing: Theological Reflections on Christianity in Africa.* Maryknoll, N.Y.: Orbis Books, 1986.

_____. *Introducing African Women's Theology.* Cleveland, Ohio: The Pilgrim Press, 2001.

Secondary Sources

Phiri, Isabel Apawo, and Sarojini Nadar, eds. *African Women, Religion, and Health: Essays in Honor of Mercy Amba Ewudziwa Oduyoye.* Maryknoll, N.Y.: Orbis Books, 2006.

Oduyoye, Mercy Amba, and Musimbi R. A. Kanyoro, eds. *The Will to Arise: Women, Tradition and the Church in Africa.* Maryknoll, N.Y.: Orbis Books, 1992.

Oduyoye, Mercy Amba, and Virginia Fabella, eds. *With Passion and Compassion: Third World Women Doing Theology.* Maryknoll, N.Y.: Orbis Books, 1988.

NOTES

CHAPTER 1   CHRISTIAN THEOLOGY AND EMPIRES

1. Joerg Rieger, *Christ and Empire: From Paul to Postcolonial Times* (Minneapolis, Minn.: Fortress Press, 2007); the conceptual background of the term "surplus" is discussed in the book's introduction.

2. This definition is developed in my book *Christ and Empire*.

3. To be sure, this is no rehash of vulgar embodiments of the "base vs. superstructure" discussion, according to which either material and economic conditions or the world of ideas determine the course of events. Empire is located not just in material and economic conditions: it promotes its own world of ideas. Likewise, a "theological surplus" is not just an invention of the world of ideas but is tied to alternative ways of life and production.

4. See Rieger, *Christ and Empire*, chapter 1.

5. See, for instance, the report on the history of effects of Las Casas's work by Benjamin Keen, "Introduction," in *Bartolomé de Las Casas in History: Toward an Understanding of the Man and His Work*, ed. Juan Friede and Benjamin Keen (DeKalb, Ill.: Northern Illinois University Press, 1971).

6. See Susanne Zantop, *Colonial Fantasies: Conquest, Family, and Nation in Precolonial Germany, 1770–1870* (Durham, N.C.: Duke University Press, 1997).

7. Friedrich Schleiermacher, *The Christian Faith*, ed. H. R. Mackintosh and J. S. Stewart (Edinburgh: T. & T. Clark, 1986), 450.

8. See Edward W. Said, *Orientalism* (New York: Random House, 1979), and Walter Mignolo, *Local Histories/Global Designs: Coloniality, Subaltern Knowledges, and Border Thinking* (Princeton, N.J.: Princeton University Press, 2000).

9. For the notion of ambivalence, see Homi Bhabha, *The Location of Culture* (London: Routledge, 1994), 86. Bhabha connects this term with his more famous notion of "mimicry": "the discourse of mimicry is constructed around an *ambivalence*" (emphasis in original). By repeating colonial images with a slight difference, rather than representing them accurately, mimicry establishes a challenge to the colonial narcissism and fiction of self-identity (*Location*, 88).

10. Bhabha, *Location,* 88. While Bhabha sees this ambivalence of mimicry as a surface effect and does not want to see this as too closely related to the Freudian notion of the "return of the repressed," I do not think that these matters are mutually exclusive. For an effort to read Bhabha's work in relation to the notion of repression see my essay, "Liberating God-Talk: Postcolonialism and the Challenge of the Margins," in *Postcolonialism and Theology*, ed. Catherine Keller, Michael Nausner, and Mayra Rivera (St. Louis, Mo.: Chalice Press, 2004).

11. For a more detailed account of the councils of Nicaea and Chalcedon see Rieger, *Christ and Empire*, chapter 2.

12. Revenue is first used to pay the company—sometimes at inflated cost—and then split 60/40, 60 percent for the state, 40 percent for the company. The contracts last for twenty-five to forty years, which is the life expectancy of an oil field; Iraq has the third-largest oil reserves in the world, after Saudi Arabia and Canada (*People's Weekly World* [January 7-13, 2006], 13).

13. The initial scenario of empire developed by Michael Hardt and Antonio Negri in their book, *Empire* (Cambridge, Mass.: Harvard University Press, 2000) still seems to me to capture these moves better than their more recent book, *Multitude: War and Democracy in the Age of Empire* (New York, N.Y.: Penguin Books, 2004).

14. David Bosch, *Transforming Mission: Paradigm Shifts in Theology of Mission* (Maryknoll, N.Y: Orbis Books, 1991); for a more critical assessment of mission in a postcolonial situation see my essay, "Theology and Mission in a Postcolonial World," *Mission Studies: Journal of the International Association for Mission Studies* 21, no. 2 (2004): 201–27.

CHAPTER 2   THEOLOGY AND SOCIAL THEORY

1.   Michel Foucault, *The Order of Things: An Archaeology of the Human Sciences* (New York, N.Y.: Vintage Books, 1973).

2.   See for example, A. James Reimer, ed., *The Influence of the Frankfurt School on Contemporary Theology: Critical Theory and the Future of Religion* (Lewiston, N.Y.: Edwin Mellen Press, 1992); Don S. Browning and Francis Schüssler Fiorenza, eds., *Habermas, Modernity, and Public Theology* (New York, N.Y.: Crossroad, 1992); Paul Lakeland, *Theology and Critical Theory: The Discourse of the Church* (Nashville, Tenn.: Abindon, 1990).

3.   Juan Luis Segundo, *The Liberation of Theology*, trans. John Drury (Maryknoll, N.Y.: Orbis Books, 1976), 116.

4.   Hent de Vries, *Philosophy and the Turn to Religion* (Baltimore, Md.: Johns Hopkins University Press, 1999); Creston Davis, John Milbank, and Slavoj Žižek, eds., *Theology and the Political* (Durham, N.C.: Duke University Press, 2005).

5.   Gustavo Gutiérrez, *A Theology of Liberation: History, Politics, and Salvation*, rev. ed., trans. Sister Caridad Inda and John Eagleson (Maryknoll, N.Y.: Orbis Books, 1988), 5.

6.   Gustavo Gutiérrez, "Theology and the Social Sciences," in his *The Truth Shall Make You Free: Confrontations*, trans. Matthew J. O'Connell (Maryknoll, N.Y.: Orbis Books, 1990), 58.

7.   Segundo, *The Liberation of Theology*, 40.

8.   Segundo, *Liberation*, 48–57.

9.   Clodovis Boff, *Theology and Praxis: Epistemological Foundations*, trans. Robert R. Barr (Maryknoll, N.Y.: Orbis Books, 1987), 31. Emphasis in original.

10. Boff, *Theology and Praxis*, 57–59.

11. Boff, *Theology and Praxis*, 56–57.

12. John Milbank, *Theology and Social Theory: Beyond Secular Reason*, 2nd ed. (Malden, Mass.: Blackwell, 2006), 52. Hereafter page references will be given in parenthesis in the text.

13. See the chapters by Elina Vuola, Mayra Rivera, and Mary Grey in *Interpreting the Postmodern: Responses to "Radical Orthodoxy,"* ed. Rosemary Radford Ruether and Marion Grau (New York: T. & T. Clark, 2006), and especially Marcella María Althaus-Reid, "A Saint and a Church for Twenty Dollars: Sending Radical Orthodoxy to Ayacucho," in *Interpreting the Postmodern*, 107–18.

14. Richard King, "Cartographies of the Imagination, Legacies of Colonialism: The Discourse of Religion and the Mapping of Indic Traditions," *Evam: Forum on Indian Representations* 3 (2004): 273.

15. Marcella Althaus-Reid, *Indecent Theology: Theological Perversions in Sex, Gender and Politics* (London: Routledge, 2000), 30.

16. Rey Chow, *The Protestant Ethnic and the Spirit of Capitalism* (New York, N.Y.: Columbia University Press, 2002), 2.

17. Catherine Keller, Michael Nausner, and Mayra Rivera, eds., *Postcolonial Theologies: Divinity and Empire* (St. Louis, Mo.: Chalice Press, 2005).

18. Dipesh Chakrabarty, *Provincializing Europe: Postcolonial Thought and Historical Difference* (Princeton, N.J.: Princeton University Press, 2000).

19. Edward W. Said, *The World, the Text, and the Critic* (Cambridge, Mass.: Harvard University Press, 1983), 39.

20. Nicholas Harrison discusses these issues with reference to Conrad's *Heart of Darkness* in his *Postcolonial Criticism* (Cambridge, U.K.: Polity Press, 2003), 22–61.

21. See the chapters on Augustine and Julian of Norwich in this volume.

22. Edward W. Said, *Culture and Imperialism* (New York, N.Y.: Knopf, 1994).

23. See the chapters on Søren Kierkegaard, Hendrik Kraemer, and Simone Weil in this volume.

24. Homi Bhabha, *The Location of Culture* (London: Routledge, 1994).

25. Wonhee Anne Joh, *Heart of the Cross: A Postcolonial Christology* (Louisville, Ky.: Westminster John Knox Press, 2006), 54.

26. C. S. Song, *Theology from the Womb of Asia* (Maryknoll, N.Y.: Orbis Books, 1986), 16.

27. See the chapter on M. M. Thomas in this volume.

28. Gayatri Chakravorty Spivak, "Subaltern Studies: Deconstructing Historiography," in her *In Other Worlds: Essays in Cultural Politics* (New York, N.Y.: Routledge, 1998), 197–221.

29. Chow, *The Protestant Ethnic*, 103–8.

30. Michael Hardt and Antonio Negri, *Empire* (Cambridge, Mass.: Harvard University Press, 2000), xii. Emphasis in the original.

31. Noam Chomsky, *Hegemony or Survival: America's Quest for Global Dominance* (New York, N.Y.: Metropolitan Books, 2003), 11. See also David Harvey, *The New Imperialism* (Oxford: Oxford University Press, 2003).

32. Arjun Appadurai, "Grassroots Globalization and the Research Imagination," in *Globalization*, ed. Arjun Appadurai (Durham, N.C.: Duke University Press, 2001), 1–21.

33. Ibid., 6.

34. Milbank, *Theology and Social Theory*, 13.

35. Carter Heyward, *The Redemption of God: A Theology of Mutual Relation* (Washington, D.C.: University Press of America, 1982).

36. Catherine Keller, "Preemption and Omnipotence: A Niebuhrian Prophecy," in her *God and Power: Counter-Apocalyptic Journeys* (Minneapolis, Minn.: Fortress Press, 2005), 31.

37. See the discussion of violence in the Christian tradition in Oliver McTernan, *Violence in God's Name: Religion in an Age of Conflict* (Maryknoll, N.Y.: Orbis Books, 2003), 52–66.

38. Peter J. Haas, "The Just War Doctrine and Postmodern Warfare," in *Strike Terror No More: Theology, Ethics, and the New War*, ed. Jon L. Berquist (St. Louis, Mo.: Chalice Press, 2002), 236–44.

39. Dorothee Soelle, *Suffering*, trans. Everett R. Kalin (Philadelphia, Pa: Fortress Press, 1984); and Rita Nakashima Brock, *Journeys by Heart: A Christology of Erotic Power* (New York, N.Y.: Crossroad, 1988), 56.

40. Julia Kristeva, "Holbein's Dead Christ," in her *Black Sun: Depression and Melancholia*, trans. Leon S. Roudiez (New York, N.Y.: Columbia University Press, 1989), 105–38.

41. Slavoj Žižek, *The Fragile Absolute, or Why Is the Christian Legacy Worth Fighting For?* (London: Verso, 2000), 157–60.

42. Rita Nakashima Brock and Rebecca Ann Parker, *Proverbs of Ashes: Violence, Redemptive Suffering and the Search for What Saves Us* (Boston, Mass.: Beacon Press, 2001).

43. Rita Nakashima Brock, "The Cross of Resurrection and Communal Redemption," in *Cross-Examinations: Readings on the Meaning of the Cross Today*, ed. Marit Trelstad (Minneapolis, Minn.: Fortress Press, 2006), 250.

44. Emilie M. Townes, *Womanist Ethics and the Cultural Production of Evil* (New York: Palgrave Macmillan, 2006), 5.

45. Townes, *Womanist Ethics*, 21.

46. See the Global Issues that Affect Everyone Web site, http://www.globalissues.org/TradeRelated/Facts.asp#fact1.

47. Leonardo Boff, *Cry of the Earth, Cry of the Poor* (Maryknoll, N.Y.: Orbis Books, 1997), 112–14.

48. Ivone Gebara, *Longing for Running Water: Ecofeminism and Liberation* (Minneapolis, Minn.: Fortress Press, 1999), 173–92.

49. Marcella Althaus-Reid, *From Feminist Theology to Indecent Theology* (London: SCM Press, 2004), 4.

CHAPTER 3   THE CHRISTIAN TRADITION AND EMPIRES

1.   *Of the Laws of Ecclesiastical Polity*, Book 2, in *The Works of that Learned and Judicious Divine Mr. Richard Hooker*, arranged by John Keble, 7th ed. (1887; repr. Ellicott City, Md.: Via Media, 1994), 286–336.

2.   For a clear summary of the case, see Diarmaid MacCulloch, *The Reformation: A History* (New York: Penguin Books, 2003), especially 106–15. See also the essays in this volume by Anthony J. Chvala-Smith, Deanna A. Thompson, and Don H. Compier.

3.   F. D. E. Schleiermacher, *The Christian Faith* (Edinburgh: T. & T. Clark, 1928). Also, see Joerg Rieger's chapter on Schleiermacher in this volume.

4.   Von Harnack's views are summarized in *Outlines of the History of Dogma* (Boston, Mass: Beacon Press, 1893).

5.   See George A. Lindbeck's influential critique of the "experiential-expressive model" in *The Nature of Doctrine: Religion and Theology in a Postliberal Age* (Philadelphia, Pa: Westminster Press, 1984).

6.   Adolf von Harnack, *What is Christianity?* (New York: Harper & Row, 1957). The original German title was *The Essence [Wesen] of Christianity*. Students of von Harnack

must also ask how his presuppositions could lead him to unquestioning support for German imperial ambitions.

7.   See especially Hall's three-volume systematic theology, *Christian Theology in a North American Context*, vol. 1, *Thinking the Faith;* vol. 2, *Professing the Faith;* and vol. 3, *Confessing the Faith* (Minneapolis, Minn.: Fortress Press, 1989, 1993, 1996). For a fuller version of my critique of his work, see "Review Article," *Anglican Theological Review* 81 (Winter 1999): 133–143.

8.   The reflections in this paragraph are inspired by Jean-François Lyotard's analysis of "metanarratives" in *The Postmodern Condition: A Report on Knowledge* (Minneapolis, Minn.: University of Minnesota Press, 1984).

9.   See Anthony J. Chvala-Smith's comments on Augustine's rhetoric in this volume. See also Kathy Eden, *Hermeneutics and the Rhetorical Tradition: Chapters in the Ancient Legacy and Its Humanist Reception* (New Haven, Conn.: Yale University Press, 1997).

10.   Aristotle, *On Rhetoric*, 1.2.1 (New York: Oxford University Press, 1991), 36.

11.   See Augustine's description of the goal of Christian persuasion in *On Christian Doctrine* (New York: Macmillan, 1958). See also David Cunningham, ed., *To Teach, to Delight, and to Move: Theological Education in a Post-Christian World* (Eugene, Oreg.: Cascade Books, 2004).

12.   As in Foucault's *Discipline and Punish: The Birth of the Prison* (New York, N.Y.: Vintage, 1979), 23, 26, 29.

13.   Foucault declared: "a topological and geological survey of the battlefield—that is the intellectual's role." See *Power/Knowledge: Selected Interviews and Other Writings, 1972–1977*, ed. Colin Gordon (New York, N.Y.: Pantheon, 1980), 62.

14.   Compare Lyotard's critique of "consensus" in *The Postmodern Condition*, 65–66. In the book's last sentence he says: "let us activate the differences" (82).

15.   This metaphor is inspired by Foucault's approach.

16.   This fact is obscured by the all-too-common practice of simply citing volumes and pages of Luther's works without any reference to the specific context of the particular declaration. Studies of Calvin suffer from the same malady.

17.   Compare Michelle A. Gonzalez's reflections on *lo cotidiano* in chapter 15.

18.   Foucault, *Discipline and Punish*, 31.

CHAPTER 4   PAUL AND EARLY CHRISTIANITY

1.   Robert Payne, *Ancient Rome* (New York, N.Y.: Idbooks, 2001). On the topics mentioned, see 193–94, 159, 189, and 182–84, respectively.

2.   For a comprehensive social history of the Jesus movement and ministry of Paul in the context of the Roman Empire, see Ekkehard W. Stegemann and Wolfgang Stegemann, *The Jesus Movement: A Social History of Its First Century*, trans. by O. C. Dean Jr. (Minneapolis, Minn.: Fortress Press, 1999). On Jesus, see Gerd Theissen and Annette Merz, *The Historical Jesus: A Comprehensive Guide* (Minneapolis, Minn.: Fortress Press, 1998).

3.   H. Jagersma, *A History of Israel from Alexander the Great to Bar Kochba*, trans. John Bowden (Philadelphia, Pa.: Fortress Press, 1986), 98.

4.   On kinds of Jewish resistance to imperial domination, see Richard A. Horsley, *Jesus and Empire* (Minneapolis, Minn.: Fortress Press, 2003), 35–54. In postcolonial theory, the works of Frantz Fanon are especially relevant for the matter of resistance to colonialism. While postcolonial theory has arisen as the analysis of modern European nations and societies they colonized, the dynamic of postcolonial thinking and resistance occurs in ancient empires, too.

5.   "I want you to understand that Christ is the head of every man, and the husband is the head of his wife, and God is the head of Christ" (1 Cor. 11:3).

6.   Antoinette Clark Wire, "1 Corinthians," in *Searching the Scriptures*, vol. 2, *A Feminist Commentary*, ed. Elisabeth Schüssler Fiorenza (New York, N.Y.: Crossroad Publishing Co., 1994), 153-95; 156.

7.   These statements are from Mary C. Boys, *Has God Only One Blessing?* (New York, N.Y.: Paulist Press, 2000). On the historical development of Christian anti-Judaism, see John T. Pawlikowski, "The Christ Event and the Jewish People," in *Thinking of Christ: Proclamation, Explanation, Meaning,* ed. Tatha Wiley (New York, N.Y.: Continuum International, 2003), 103–21.

8.   Catholic Good Friday Prayer, cited in Boys, *Has God Only One Blessing?*, 203.

9.   Martin Luther, *Jews and Their Lies* (1542), cited in Dan Cohn-Sherbok, *The Crucified Jew: Twenty Centuries of Christian Anti-Semitism* (London: HarperCollins, 1992), 73.

10. Martin Noth, *The Laws in the Pentateuch and Other Studies* (Edinburgh: Oliver and Boyd, 1966), 63.

11. Gustavo Gutiérrez, *A Theology of Liberation* (Maryknoll, N.Y.: Orbis Books, 1973), 92.

12. Leonardo Boff, *Passion of Christ, Passion of the World* (Maryknoll, N.Y.: Orbis Books, 1987), 130.

13. Boff, *Passion of Christ,* 3.

14. The conclusions noted here are characteristic of those biblical scholars associated with the "new perspective," a shift generated by the work of Krister Stendahl. A major figure and work in the recovery of Paul in his social and historical context is E. P. Sanders, *Paul and Palestinian Judaism* (Philadelphia, Pa.: Fortress Press, 1977). The work of James Dunn has been central as well. See James D. G. Dunn, *The Theology of Paul the Apostle* (Grand Rapids, Mich.: Eerdmans, 1998). Works by Richard Horsley, Neil Elliott, and others put Paul specifically in the imperial context.

15. See, for example, Richard A. Horsley and Neil Asher Silberman, *The Message and the Kingdom: How Jesus and Paul Ignited a Revolution and Transformed the Ancient World* (Minneapolis, Minn.: Fortress Press, 1997).

16. *Postcolonial* may refer to a critique of or resistance to political oppression by foreign rule, as here, or to a type of method. On the emergence of postcolonialism as critical discourse, see R.J. Sugirtharajah, *Postcolonial Reconfigurations: An Alternative Way of Reading the Bible and Doing Theology* (St. Louis, Mo.: Chalice Press, 2003), 13–16.

17. See the postcolonial theorist Homi K. Bhabha, *The Location of Culture* (New York: Routledge, 1994) on Bhabha's concept of mimicry. A text can mimic a dominant discourse as a means of critique but end up reinforcing the status quo at the same time.

The discourse of mimicry may appear to reverse structures but without questioning the underlying hierarchy that gives rise to the original structure of domination or power.

CHAPTER 5   ATHANASIUS OF ALEXANDRIA

1. For a summary of negative and positive evaluations of Athanasius, see Duane W. H. Arnold, *The Early Episcopal Career of Athanasius of Alexandria* (Notre Dame, Ind.: University of Notre Dame Press, 1991), 9–24.

2. For a summary of the history of this interpretation among Protestants, including contemporary theologians such as John Howard Yoder and Stanley Hauerwas, see Daniel H. Williams, *Retrieving the Tradition and Renewing Evangelicalism: A Primer for Suspicious Protestants* (Grand Rapids, Mich.: Eerdmans, 1999), 101–31.

3. Timothy Ware, *The Orthodox Church* (London: Penguin Books, 1987), 26–50. On the spiritual unity of Eastern Christianity, see Peter Brown, *The Cult of the Saints* (Chicago, Ill.: University of Chicago Press, 1981).

4. Peter Brown, "Eastern and Western Christendom in Late Antiquity: A Parting of the Ways," in *Society and the Holy in Late Antiquity* (Berkeley, Calif.: University of California Press, 1982), 166–95.

5. Peter Garnsey and Caroline Humfress, *The Evolution of the Late Antique World* (Cambridge, U.K.: Orchard Academic Press, 2001), 83–91.

6. Garnsey and Humfress, *The Evolution*, 19–23.

7. Ibid., 27.

8. Elizabeth De Palma Digeser, *The Making of Christian Rome: Lactantius and Rome* (Ithaca, N.Y.: Cornell University Press, 2000), 91–111; William H. C. Frend, *Martyrdom and Persecution in the Early Church* (New York, N.Y.: Anchor Books, 1967), 351–92.

9. Richard Paul Vaggione, *Eunomius of Cyzicus and the Nicene Revolution* (Oxford: Oxford University Press, 2000), 150.

10. Peter Brown, *Power and Persuasion: Towards a Christian Empire* (Madison, Wis.: University of Wisconsin Press, 1992); Hal Drake, *Constantine and the Bishops* (Baltimore, Md.: Johns Hopkins University Press, 2000), 482; Claudia Rapp, *Holy Bishops in Late Antiquity* (Berkeley, Calif.: University of California Press, 2005), 274f.

11. Christopher Haas, *Alexandria in Late Antiquity: Topography and Social Conflict* (Baltimore, Md.: Johns Hopkins University Press, 1997).

12. Vaggione, *Eunomius*, 30–34.

13. Michael Gaddis, *There Is No Crime for Those Who Have Christ: Religious Violence in the Christian Roman Empire* (Berkeley, Calif.: University of California Press, 2005), 277–79; Drake, *Constantine*, 407–408.

14. Haas, *Alexandria*, 245–316; Timothy Gregory, *Vox Populi: Violence and Popular Involvement in the Religious Controversies of the Fifth Century* (Columbus, Ohio: Ohio State University Press, 1979).

15. Glenn Bowersock, "From Emperor to Bishop: The Self-Conscious Transfiguration of Political Power in the Fourth Century," *Classical Philology* 81 (1986): 298–307; Neil McLynn, "The Transformation of Imperial Churchgoing in the Fourth Century," in

Approaching Late Antiquity, ed. Simon Swain and Mark Edwards (Oxford: Oxford University Press, 2004), 235–70.

16. The most current narrative is Vaggione, *Eunomius*. See also Michel Barnes, "The Fourth Century as Trinitarian Canon," in *Christian Origins: Theology, Rhetoric, and Community*, ed. Lewis Ayres and Gareth Jones (London: Routledge, 1998), 47–66.

17. Lewis Ayres, *Nicaea and Its Legacy: An Approach to Fourth-Century Trinitarian Theology* (Oxford: Oxford University Press, 2004).

18. Compare Timothy D. Barnes, *Athanasius and Constantius: Theology and Politics in the Constantinian Empire* (Cambridge, Mass.: Harvard University Press, 1993), 13–14, to Sara Parvis, *Marcellus of Ancyra and the Lost Years of the Arian Controversy, 325–345* (Oxford: Oxford University Press, 2006), 141 n. 31.

19. Athanasius, *On the Incarnation*, 54; on dating of his works see Parvis, *Marcellus*, 60–65.

20. *Apol. Sec.* 9.4. While Arnold tries to defend Athanasius against charges of violence, most scholars accept them.

21. Parvis, *Marcellus*, 192; Haas, *Alexandria*, 276

22. This is the astute evaluation of Vaggione, *Eunomius*, 104.

23. Maurice Wiles, "Attitudes to Arius in the Arian Controversy," in *Arianism after Arius: Essays on the Development of the Fourth Century Trinitarian Conflicts*, ed. Michel Barnes and Daniel Williams (Edinburgh: T. & T. Clark, 1993), 31–44.

24. Rebecca Lyman, "A Topography of Heresy: Mapping the Rhetorical Creation of Arianism," in *Arianism after Arius*, 45–64; Virginia Burrus, "The Heretical Woman as Symbol in Alexander, Athanasius, Epiphanius, and Jerome" *Harvard Theological Review* 84 (1991): 229–48.

25. *History of the Arians*, 77; Barnes, *Athanasius*, 121–35.

26. Lyman, "Topography," 45–64; Barnes, *Athanasius*, 135.

27. Annick Martin, *Athanase d'Alexandrie et l'Eglise d'Egypte au IVe Siecle* (Roma: Ecole française de Rome, 1996), 637–706, 822.

28. David Brakke, *Athanasius and the Politics of Asceticism* (Oxford: Clarendon Press, 1995), 336–42.

29. Brakke, *Athanasius*, 201–45; Robert Gregg and Dennis Groh, *Early Arianism: A View of Salvation* (Philadelphia, Pa.: Fortress Press, 1981), 131–59.

30. Averil Cameron, "How to Read Heresiology," in *The Cultural Turn in Late Antique Studies*, ed. Dale Martin and Patricia Cox Miller (Durham, N.C.: Duke University Press, 2005), 193–212.

31. Harry Maier, "Heresy, Households, and the Disciplining of Diversity," in *Late Ancient Christianity*, ed. Virginia Burrus (Minneapolis, Minn.: Fortress Press, 2005), 213–33.

32. Richard Lim, "Christian Triumph and Controversy," in *Late Antiquity: A Guide to the Postclassical World*, ed. G. W. Bowersock, Peter Brown, Oleg Grabar (Cambridge, Mass.: Harvard University Press, 1999), 196–218.

33. Drake, *Constantine*, 438.

34. Hal Drake, ed., *Violence in Late Antiquity: Perceptions and Practices* (London: Ashgate Publishing, 2006).

35. Gaddis, *There Is No Crime*, 339. See also Ramsey MacMullen, *Voting about God in Early Church Councils* (New Haven, Conn.: Yale University Press, 2006).

36. Gaddis, *There is no Crime*, 332.

37. Richard Hingley, *Globalizing Roman Culture: Unity, Diversity and Empire* (London: Routledge, 2005), 30–49.

38. Hingley, *Globalization*, 47; 53.

39. Hingley, *Globalization*, 63.

40. Hingley, *Globalization*, 111.

41. Michel Foucault, *Discipline and Punish: The Birth of the Prison*, trans. Alan Sheridan (New York, N.Y.: Vintage Books, 1995), 30. See my larger discussion in "Ascetics and Bishops: Epiphanius on Orthodoxy," in *Orthodoxie Christianisme Histoire: Orthodoxy Christianity History*, ed. S. Elm, E. Rebillard, A. Romano (Rome: Ecole Française de Rome, 2000), 149–61.

42. Robin Furneaux, *William Wilberforce* (Vancouver: Regent College Publishing, 1974), 99.

43. Edward W. Said, *Culture and Imperialism* (New York, N.Y.: Knopf, 1993), 26f.; William D. Hart, *Edward Said and the Religious Effects of Culture* (Cambridge, U.K.: Cambridge University Press, 2000), 101.

44. Virginia Burrus, *"Begotten, Not Made": Conceiving Manhood in Late Antiquity* (Stanford, Calif.: Stanford University Press, 2000).

45. On the shifting definitions of Arianism, see Maurice F. Wiles, *Archetypal Heresy: Arianism through the Centuries* (Oxford: Clarendon Press, 1996).

46. Philip Jenkins, *The New Faces of Christianity: Believing the Bible in the Global South* (Oxford: Oxford University Press, 2006), 2–17.

47. Emmanuel Levinas, "Peace and Proximity," in *Emmanuel Levinas: Basic Philosophical Writings*, ed. Adriaan T. Peperzak, Simon Critchley, and Robert Bernasconi (Bloomington, Ind.: Indiana University Press, 1996), 166.

CHAPTER 6   AUGUSTINE OF HIPPO

1.   William C. Placher, *A History of Christian Theology: An Introduction* (Philadelphia, Pa.: Westminster Press, 1983), 108.

2.   The classic biography of Augustine is Peter Brown's *Augustine of Hippo: A Biography*, 2nd ed. (Berkeley, Calif.: University of California Press, 2000).

3.   Virgil, *The Aeneid*, in *Virgil's Works: The Aeneid, Eclogues, and Georgics*, trans. J. W. MacKail (New York, N.Y.: Modern Library, 1934), 126.

4.   Augustine, *The City of God*, trans. Marcus Dods, introduction by Thomas Merton (New York, N.Y.: Modern Library, 1993), V. 15.

5.   Williston Walker, *A History of the Christian Church*, 3rd ed., rev. Robert T. Handy (New York. N.Y.: Charles Scribner's Sons, 1970), 111.

6.   Brown, *Augustine*, 14.

7.   Possidius, *The Life of Saint Augustine,* trans. Matthew O'Connell, ed. John E. Rotelle, O.S.A., The Augustinian Series, vol. 1 (Villanova, Pa.: Augustinian Press, 1988), 28.4.

8.   Possidius, *Life,* 28.6.

9.   James J. O'Donnell, *Augustine: A New Biography,* 1st ed. (New York, N.Y.: Harper Collins, 2005), 115–17.

10. Augustine, *Confessions*, trans. Maria Boulding, O.S.B., ed. John E. Rotelle, O.S.A. I/1 (Hyde Park, N.Y.: New City Press, 1997), II.3.5–6 .

11. See Mark Ellingsen, *The Richness of Augustine: His Context and Pastoral Theology* (Louisville, Ky.: Westminster John Knox Press, 2005), 8–10. Ellingsen cites Augustine's noteworthy riposte to Julian of Eclanum, "Don't out of pride in your earthly ancestry dismiss [me] just because I am Punic."

12. Peter Brown, *Religion and Society in the Age of Saint Augustine* (New York, N.Y.: Harper & Row, 1972), 288.

13. *City of God*, V. 25–26.

14. Walker, *History*, 106.

15. Augustine, *Letters* 211–270, 1*–29*, trans. Roland Teske, S.J., *The Works of Saint Augustine: A Translation for the 21st Century*, ed. Boniface Ramsey, II/4 (Hyde Park, N.Y.: New City Press, 2004), 220.3.

16. Brown, *Augustine*, 222; Henry Chadwick, *Augustine: A Very Short Introduction* (Oxford: Oxford University Press, 1986), 81.

17. Brown, *Augustine*, 210–11.

18. See Peter Brown, *The Body and Society: Men, Women, and Sexual Renunciation in Early Christianity* (New York, N.Y.: Columbia University Press, 1988), 313–17.

19. Brown, *The Body and Society*.

20. Augustine, as will be seen shortly, rejects this view in Book III of *The Literal Meaning of Genesis*.

21. Augustine, *The Literal Meaning of Genesis*, trans. and notes Edmund Hill, O.P., general intro., and other introduction M. Fiedrowicz, trans Matthew O'Connell, *The Works of Saint Augustine: A Translation for the 21st Century*, ed. John E. Rotelle, O.S.A., I/13 (Hyde Park, N.Y.: New City Press, 1991), IX.5.9. Again, Augustine's speculation must be seen in a social context in which male friendship was considered a higher good than even family relationships.

22. A key point of Brown's book, *The Body and Society.*

23. On this point, I have been helped by Ellingsen, *Richness*, 140–1 and Chadwick, *Augustine,* 93–4.

24. On Augustine's relationship with and dismissal of this woman, see Wills, *Saint Augustine* (New York, N.Y.: Viking, 1999), 15–18, 40–41.

25. Augustine, *The Excellence of Marriage*, trans. Ray Kearney; ed. with introductions and notes David G. Hunter, *The Works of Saint Augustine: A Translation for the 21st Century*, ed. John E. Rotelle, O.S.A., I/9 (Hyde Park, N.Y.: New City Press, 1999), 3.3; 4.4; 7.7. See also Augustine's *The Literal Meaning of Genesis,* IX.7.12.

26. Augustine, *The Excellence of Marriage*, 8.8.

27. Augustine, *The Trinity*, introduction, translation, and notes Edmund Hill, O.P., *The Works of Saint Augustine: A Translation for the 21st Century*, ed. John E. Rotelle, O.S.A., I/5 (Brooklyn, N.Y.: New City Press, 1991), 12.12.

28. Augustine, *The Literal Meaning of Genesis*, X.1.2, IX.3.6

29. *Confessions,* I.16.26; Brown, *Augustine*, 23.

30. Possidius, *Life*, 4.1–3.

31. Augustine, *Letter* 2*.14; Peter Brown, *Power and Persuasion in Late Antiquity: Towards a Christian Empire* (Madison, Wis.: University of Wisconsin Press, 1992), 75.

32. Augustine, *Letter* 220.4–5.

33. Augustine, *Letters* 100–55, trans. Roland Teske, S.J., *The Works of Saint Augustine: A Translation for the 21st Century*, ed. Boniface Ramsey, II/2 (Hyde Park, N.Y.: New City Press, 2003), *Letters* 113–16.

34. *Letter* 113.

35. *Letter* 114.

36. *Letter* 114.

37. *Letters* 152–53.

38. *Letter* 152.2.

39. *Letter* 153.3.

40. *Letter* 153.14.

41. *Letter* 153.3.

42. Brown, *Augustine,* 236; W.H.C. Frend, *The Rise of Christianity* (Philadelphia, Pa.: Fortress Press, 1984), 672.

43. Possidius, *Life,* 10.6.

44. Possidius, *Life,* 10.6.

45. Possidius, *Life,* 12.1.

46. Chadwick, *Augustine,* 83.

47. Augustine, *Letter* 133.1

48. *Letter* 134.2.

49. *Letter* 134.4.

50. Augustine, *Letters* 156–210, trans. Roland Teske, S.J., *The Works of Saint Augustine: A Translation for the 21st Century*, ed. Boniface Ramsey, II/3 (Hyde Park, N.Y.: New City Press, 2004), *Letter* 185.18, 25–28.

51. Frend, *Early Church,* 672.

52. *Letter* 185.

53. Augustine outlines his biblical hermeneutics in *On Christian Doctrine.*

54. *Letter* 185.18.

55. Jaroslav Pelikan, *The Excellent Empire: The Fall of Rome and the Triumph of the Church,* The Rauschenbusch Lectures, New Series, I (San Francisco, Calif.: Harper & Row, 1987), 23.

56. Chadwick, *Augustine,* 85.

57. *City of God,* 14.28

58. *City of God,* 1.35.

59. *City of God,* 1.35.

60. Gary Wills, *Saint Augustine,* 115–116.

61. *City of God,* 4.4.

62. Chadwick, *Augustine,* 106.

63. Chadwick, *Augustine,* 106.

64. Gerard O'Daly, *Augustine's City of God: A Reader's Guide* (Oxford: Oxford University Press, 1999), 9.

65. *Letter* 138.3.

66. Hill, "Introduction," in Augustine, *The Trinity,* 20.

CHAPTER 7   WYNFRITH - BONIFACE

1. Peter Brown, *The Rise of Western Christendom: Triumph and Diversity, A.D. 200–1000*, 2nd ed. (Malden, Mass: Blackwell, 2003), 420.

2. Herwig Wolfram, *The Roman Empire and Its Germanic Peoples* (Berkeley, Calif.: University of California Press, 1990), 247, 11.

3. Dates given for the migrations vary quite widely. This is the wave relevant to us here. Other migrations are dated later and at times are considered in some places to have continued into early medieval times.

4. See Augustine's designation of the invading Arian Visigoths in the *City of God Against the Pagans*.

5. Brown, *Rise*, 137.

6. Brown, *Rise*, 408.

7. Lutz E. von Padberg, *Christianisierung im Mittelalter* (Darmstadt: Wissenschaftliche Buchgesellschaft, 2006), 67.

8. Brown, *Rise*, 429.

9. Assumptions vary as to whether Boniface or a local, Frankish bishop crowned Pippin. von Padberg argues for a Frankish bishop loyal to the king doing so and makes the case that the aging Boniface had become frustrated and withdrew from the Carolingians after Pippin had put on the back burner the ecclesial reforms Boniface had pushed. von Padberg, *Christianisierung*, 68–69. Pippin is the first "king" of the Franks, previous rulers in his line had the title of "*maior domus*, the mayor of the palace." Theodor Schiefer, *Winfrid-Bonifatius und die Christliche Grundlegung Europas* (Freiburg: Herder, 1954), 258.

10. Willibald, "The Life of Saint Boniface," in *Soldiers of Christ: Saints and Saints' Lives from Late Antiquity and the Early Middle Ages*, ed. Thomas F.X. Noble and Thomas Head (University Park, Pa.: Pennsylvania State University Press, 1995), 121.

11. Noble, "Life of Saint Boniface," 110.

12. For an English edition of his letters see Saint Boniface, *The Letters of Saint Boniface*, introduction by Thomas F.X. Noble, transl. by Ephraim Emerton (New York, N.Y.: Columbia University Press, 2000).

13. Brown, *Rise*, 420.

14. Noble, "Life of Saint Boniface," 121.

15. The terms Wessex, Sussex, and Essex refer to Westsaxon, Southsaxon, and Eastsaxon regions in Britain.

16. von Padberg, *Christianisierung*, 66.

17. Letter IX, Boniface, *Letters*, 20.

18. Nikola Proksch, "The Anglo-Saxon Missionaries to the Continent," in *Monks of England: The Benedictines in England from Augustine to the Present Day*, ed. Daniel Rees (London: SPCK, 1997), 47.

19. Gert Haendler, "Bonifatius," in *Mittelalter* (Gestalten der Kirchengeschichte), ed. Martin Greschat (Stuttgart, Germany: Kohlhammer, 1983), 78.

20. Compare Nicholas Howe, "Rome: Capital of Anglo-Saxon England," *Journal of Medieval and Early Modern Studies* 34, no.1 (Winter 2004): 147–72.

21. Noble, "Life of Saint Boniface," 126.

22. John Seville Higgins, "The Ultramontanism of Saint Boniface," *Church History* 2, no. 4 (December 1933): 203.

23. John Michael Wallace-Hadrill, "A Background to Boniface's Mission," in *England Before the Conquest* (Cambridge: Cambridge University Press, 1971), 38.

24. Schiefer, *Winfrid-Bonifatius*, 57.

25. Noble, "Life of Saint Boniface," 127.

26. Later missionaries and teachers attempted to harness this mindset and produced texts like *The Heliand*, and the *Dream of the Rood*, which depicted Christ as a tribal leader and the disciples as a loyal group of brothers in arms. Others tried to remake feuding warriors into Christian knights, with highly problematic outcomes, such as the crusades.

27. Proksch writes: "A common feature of the mission to the Germanic peoples—whether in Merovingian Gaul, Anglo-Saxon England, or in Northern Germany—was the initial acceptance of Christianity by leading figures of high social standing. Often their entire clan-group would follow them in the new allegiance." Proksch, "Anglo-Saxon Missionaries," 49.

28. Gregory the Great, Epistle LXXVI. To Mellitus, Abbot. NPNF 213. Found online at http://www.ccel.org/ccel/schaff/npnf213.ii.vii.cccvi.html.

29. Brown, *Rise*, 427.

30. Letter XV (23), Boniface, *Letters*, 27–28. Ironically, this remark was written at the time when the Iberian Peninsula had only recently been lost to Christian rule.

31. von Padberg, *Christianisierung*, 65.

32. Brown, *Rise*, 421.

33. The Germanic deity referred to here may have been Odin or Tyr. Noble, "Life of Saint Boniface," 126.

34. Noble, "Life of Saint Boniface," 126–27.

35. Von Padberg, *Christianisierung*, 64.

36. Simon Schama, *Landscape and Memory* (New York: Alfred E. Knopf 1995), 217.

37. Large-scale deforestation, however, likely did not occur until the late Middle Ages and the beginning of the transformation towards capitalism and industrialism.

38. Von Padberg, *Christianisierung*, 67–68.

39. Letter XXII, Boniface, *Letters*, 38–39.

40. Other clan members include Willibald and Hugeburc. von Padberg, *Christianisierung*, 65.

41. Rudolf, "The Life of Saint Leoba," in *Soldiers of Christ*, 272–73. See also Proksch, "Anglo-Saxon Missionaries," 45.

42. Thomas F. X. Noble and Thomas Head, "Introduction," in *Soldiers of Christ*, xxxv.

43. Boniface, *Letters*, 135.

44. Lutz E. von Padberg and Hans-Walter Stork, *Der Ragyndrudis-Codex Des Hl. Bonifatius* (Fulda: Verlag Parzeller, 1994), 17 and images throughout.

45. See Schiefer, *Winfrid-Bonifatius*, 59.

46. http://www.bonifatius-musical.de/go.php It appears that the growing together of Europe does not always erase local traditions and specificities but in fact oftentimes revives local traditions in a search for one's own particularity.

47. Kai Uwe Schierz, ed., *Von Bonifatius Bis Beuys - oder: Vom Umgang mit Den Heiligen Eichen* (Erfurt: Druckhaus Gera, 2004).

48. See Friedrich Wilhelm Graf, "Germanisierung Des Christentums," in *Religion in Geschichte und Gegenwart*, 3rd ed., Hans Dieter Betz et al. (Tübingen: Mohr Siebeck, 1998), 754; and James C. Russell, *The Germanization of Early Medieval Christianity: A Sociohistorical Approach to Religious Transformation* (Oxford: Oxford University Press, 1994).

49. John Lindow, *Norse Mythology: A Guide to the Gods, Heroes, Rituals and Beliefs* (Oxford: Oxford University Press, 2001), 10, 17, 23.

50. For an excellent exploration of the Nazi obsession with finding the manuscript of Tacitus's *Germania* in the last days of the war, see Schama, *Landscape and Memory*, 76 ff.

51. Patrick Geary's excellent exploration of Middle European tribal cultures demonstrates amply the hybrid histories and intermingling of these peoples and their migrations, as well as the futility of delineating them by tribal, national, or racial designations in a misled search for essential national or racial identities in more recent times. See Patrick J. Geary, *The Myth of Nations: The Medieval Origins of Europe* (Princeton, N.J.: Princeton University Press, 2002).

52. For an account of the shift of understandings of center and periphery in Anglo-Saxon mission, see Howe, "Rome: Capital of Anglo-Saxon England," 152 et passim.

53. See http://speakingoffaith.publicradio.org/programs/plantingthefuture/transcript.shtml.

Chapter 8   Theodore the Studdite

1. See the Quinisext Council, Canon 82, in Mansi, 11:977E-980B; cited in Paul J. Alexander, *The Patriarch Nicephorus of Constantinople: Ecclesiastical Policy and Image Worship in the Byzantine Empire* (Oxford: Clarendon Press, 1958), 45.

2. Most famously, Eusebius of Caesarea had responded with ridicule to a request for a picture of Christ from a member of the imperial family; and a generation later Epiphanius of Salamis had condemned the liturgical use of images as idolatrous.

3. See Judith Herrin, "The Context of Iconoclast Reform," *Iconoclasm: Papers Given at the Ninth Spring Symposium of Byzantine Studies, University of Birmingham, March 1975*, ed. Anthony Bryer and Judith Herrin (Birmingham: John Goodman & Sons, 1977), 20.

4. See Hélène Ahrweiler, "The Geography of the Iconoclast World," in *Iconoclasm: Papers given at the Ninth Spring Symposium of Byzantine Studies, University of Birmingham, March 1975*, ed. Anthony Bryer and Judith Herrin (Birmingham: John Goodman & Sons, 1977), 25.

5. St. John of Damascus, *Three Treatises on the Divine Images* (Crestwood, N.Y.: St. Vladimir's Seminary Press, 2003), I.8; cf. III.40.

6. John, *Three Treatises*, I.17; cf. I.44-47; III.11, 23.

7. John, *Three Treatises*, I.8; cf. I.16, 51; II.5; III.2, 6, 8, 26

8. See especially John, *Three Treatises*, I.16; cf. II.14. John concedes (in *Three Treatises*, II.10 and III.9) that some images remain idols, but such a determination can only be made based on consideration of what is depicted and the use made of it.

9. "Symbol of Chalcedon" (DS 301), in *The Christian Faith in the Doctrinal Documents of the Catholic Church*, revised ed., ed. J. Neuner and J. Dupuis (New York, N.Y.: Alba House, 1982), 154.

10. The Iconoclast Council of 754 concluded: "From those . . . who think that they are drawing the icon of Christ, it must be gathered either that the divinity is circumscribable and confused with the flesh or that the body of Christ was without divinity and divided." Mansi, 13:260A, cited in Daniel J. Sahas, *Icon and Logos: Sources in Eighth-Century Iconoclasm* (Toronto: University of Toronto Press, 1986), 90.

11. See Roman Cholij, *Theodore the Stoudite: The Ordering of Holiness* (Oxford: Oxford University Press, 2002), 164.

12. See, e.g., Mansi, 13:340D (in Sahas, *Icon and Logos*, 156-57): "For the name 'Christ' implies two natures, the one being visible and the other invisible. Thus this Christ, while visible to people by means of the curtain, that is his flesh, made the divine nature—even though this remained concealed—manifest through signs. Therefore it is in this form, seen by people, that the Holy Church of God depicts Christ" (translation slightly altered).

13. Theodore was exiled for five months in 797 by Emperor Constantine VI for condemning the latter's divorce and remarriage; he was exiled again from 809-811 by Emperor Nicephorus for objecting to the reinstatement of the priest who had performed Constantine's second marriage.

14. Theodore the Studite, Epistle 478.69; cited in Cholij, *Theodore the Stoudite*, 146.

15. In stressing the distinction between the Eucharist as the one legitimate "icon" and painted images, the iconoclasts argued that Christ "commanded that the substance of bread be offered which does not yield the shape of a man's form, so that idolatry may not be introduced indirectly." Mansi,13:264B, in Sahas, *Icon and Logos*, 93–96.

16. See, e.g., Mansi, 13:2767C-E, in Sahas, *Icon and Logos*, 105.

17. See St. Theodore the Studite, *On the Holy Icons* (Crestwood, N.Y.: St. Vladimir's Seminary Press, 2001), III.A.10, 32, 43.

18. " . . . the same hypostasis of the Word is uncircumscribable according to the nature of His divinity but circumscribed according to His essence like ours. This human nature does not have its existence . . . apart from the hypostasis of the Word, but has its existence in that hypostasis . . . and in it is contemplated in an individual manner and is circumscribed." Theodore, *On the Holy Icons*, III.A.22.

19. Theodore, *On the Holy Icons*, III.A.34.

20. Theodore, *On the Holy Icons*, I.17.

21. "The image of Christ is nothing else than Christ, except obviously for the difference of essence. . . . It follows that the veneration of the images is veneration of Christ." Theodore, *On the Holy Icons*, III.C.14.

22. Theodore, *On the Holy Icons*, III.D.10: "the failure to go forth into a material imprint eliminates his existence in human form."

23. Theodore, *On the Holy Icons*, III.C.1–2.

24. Theodore, *On the Holy Icons*, I.10.

25. Theodore, *On the Holy Icons*, II.15; cf. III.C.5.

26. Theodore, *On the Holy Icons*, III.D.8.

27. "... the disciples first saw the Lord and later wrote out the message," so that "if the sight of Christ is removed, the written word about him must be removed first; and if the second is sketched out, the first must be sketched beforehand." Theodore, *On the Holy Icons*, III.A.2.

28. Theodore, *On the Holy Icons*, III.D.12.

29. See the criticism of orthodox iconography in Alain Besançon, *The Forbidden Image: An Intellectual History of Iconoclasm* (Chicago, Ill.: University of Chicago Press, 2000), especially 134–44.

30. Hans Urs von Balthasar, *Seeing the Form*, vol. 1 of *The Glory of the Lord: A Theological Aesthetics*, ed. Joseph Fessio and John Riches (San Francisco, Calif.: Ignatius, 1982), 41.

31. Ibid.

32. See especially Peter Brown, "A Dark Age Crisis: Aspects of the Iconoclastic Controversy," *English Historical Review* 346 (1973): 1–34.

CHAPTER 9   ANSELM OF CANTERBURY

1. Among the important Anselmian innovations I will not be able to consider in this brief essay are what might be called an inward turn in devotional practice, as well as Anselm's ethical theory, which creatively combines the teleological eudaimonism of Plato and Aristotle with a deontological argument which is usually assumed to begin only later, with Duns Scotus. See Jeffrey E. Brower, "Anselm on Ethics" in *The Cambridge Companion to Anselm,* ed. Brian Davies and Brian Leftow (Cambridge: Cambridge University Press, 2004), 222–56. For an overview of the inward turn, which Benedicta Ward describes as constituting a "revolution in devotional practice" that informed the shape of piety for "the whole of the later Middle Ages," see Ward, "Anselm of Canterbury and His Influence" in *Christian Spirituality: Origins to the Twelfth Century,* ed. Bernard McGinn and John Meyerdorff (New York, N.Y.: Crossroad, 1987), 196–205; see also R.W. Southern, *Saint Anselm and His Biographer: A Study of Monastic Life and Thought, 1059–c.1130* (Cambridge: Cambridge University Press, 1966), 36–47.

2. Anselm, *Monologion* in *St. Anselm: Basic Writings*, trans. S.N. Deane (La Salle, Ill.: Open Court Publishing Company, 1962), 139.

3. For a discussion of how this metaphor, and Neoplatonism more broadly, shaped the lives of medieval women, see chapter 3 of my *Christic Imagination: An Ethic of Incarnation and Ingenuity* (Minneapolis, Minn.: Fortress Press, forthcoming).

4. Ibid. See also R.W. Southern, *Saint Anselm: A Portrait in a Landscape* (Cambridge: Cambridge University Press, 1990).

5. Clifford R. Backman reminds us that "feudalism as a coherent, conscious, and cogent plan for how to model society never existed." Rather, what existed in Northern Europe was a society "characterized by *feudal relations*." Backman, *The Worlds of Medieval Europe* (New York, N.Y.: Oxford University Press, 2003), 176.

6. Ibid., 178.

7. As G. R. Evans notes, Anselm "treated the feudal framework of the society in which he had lived in northern France and England throughout most of his adult life as something more than a convenient image. Its structures appealed profoundly to his sense

of 'right order.'" See his "Anselm's Life, Works, and Immediate Influence" in *The Cambridge Companion to Anselm,* 18.

8. Joerg Rieger, *Christ and Empire: From Paul to Postcolonial Times* (Minneapolis, Minn.: Fortress Press, 2007).

9. Backman, *Worlds of Medieval Europe,* 151.

10. A key turning point came in 1059, when an ecclesial synod at Rome condemned lay investiture—according to which secular authorities invested clergy with the authority of their offices—and endorsed the Papal Election Decree, which made the papacy independent from secular power by decreeing that popes would thenceforth be freely elected by the College of Cardinals. By 1076, Pope Gregory VII and King Henry IV "declared each other excommunicated and deposed from office." Backman, *The Worlds of Medieval Europe,* 217–18.

11. Southern, *Saint Anselm,* 4.

12. "Armed with this new title," says Southern, "the way was clear for the full exercise of power in the name of the 'King of Kings and Lord of Lords to whom every knee shall bow'." A key to the shift toward papal power was the growth of canon law, "which attracted all important disputes to the papal court." *Western Society and the Church in the Middle Ages* (London: Penguin Books, 1990), 104–105, 212.

13. Southern, *Western Society,* 304.

14. Sally Vaughn, *Anselm of Bec and Robert of Meulan: The Wisdom of the Dove and the Innocence of the Serpent* (Berkeley, Calif.: University of California Press, 1987).

15. As Anselm says in the *Proslogion,* "The believer does not seek to understand, that he may believe, but he believes that he may understand: for unless he believed he would not understand." In *St. Anselm: Basic Writings,* 49.

16. In refusing to ground his arguments in appeals to ecclesiastical authority, Anselm raised the ire of his contemporaries, including his own mentor, Lanfranc. That said, we should also recognize that Anselm was not intentionally searching for an alternative authority to Scripture or tradition; rather, he sought to demonstrate that reason arrives at the same destination as faith.

17. Marilyn McCord Adams, "Anselm on Faith and Reason" in *The Cambridge Companion to Anselm,* 36–44.

18. Southern admits to one exception: Boso in the *Cur Deus Homo. Saint Anselm,* 114–15, 203.

19. Southern, *Anselm and His Biographer,* 48.

20. This definition is prefigured by both Seneca and Augustine. Anselm, *Proslogion,* 54.

21. Anselm, *Monologion* in *Saint Anselm: Basic Writings,* 132.

22. Anselm, *Monologion* in *Saint Anselm: Basic Writings,* 98.

23. Anselm, *Proslogion,* 57.

24. When considering the Neoplatonic valences of Anselm's concept of God we should not overlook the fact that Anselm appears to think of God as the ideal form and of all other beings as participating to greater or lesser degrees in that form. See especially the portrayal of God in the *Monologion.*

25. Quoted in Backman, *The Worlds of Medieval Europe,* 217–18.

26. R.W. Southern affirms that the church's main objective was to replace "the uni-

tary authority of the Empire" with "the unitary authority of the papacy." The church sought, in other words, to "[recreate] the Roman Empire on a religious basis." *Western Society and the Church in the Middle Ages*, 24.

27. Southern, *Saint Anselm*, 221.

28. Rieger, *Christ and Empire*, chapter 3.

29. The restoration of order is a primary concern for Anselm. As G. R. Evans notes, Anselm has a "continuing assumption that there is a rightness to things, a *rectitudo*, a divine harmony, which is divinely ordained and cannot ultimately fail. This gives an emphasis (characteristic of the period but particularly marked in Anselm) to the notion of fittingness (*convenienta; decentia*). For 'fittingness' is powerful in his frame of reference." Evans, "Anselm's Life, Works, and Immediate Influence," 21.

30. Rieger, *Christ and Empire*, chapter 3.

31. The clearly Neoplatonic assumption here is that human beings participate in the perfect "form" of human nature actualized by Christ, thus making his meritorious death efficacious for all humans. For further discussion, see David Brown, "Anselm on Atonement" in *The Cambridge Companion to Anselm*, 288–90.

32. For a thorough discussion of this earlier interpretation and its relation to the Anselmian construal of atonement, see my *Deceiving the Devil: Atonement, Abuse, and Ransom* (Cleveland, Ohio: The Pilgrim Press, 1998).

33. As Southern notes, the feudal notion of satisfaction "stood for rationality prevailing against the inroads of self-will and chaos." *Saint Anselm*, 227.

34. Gerd Althoff, "Satisfaction: Amicable Settlement of Conflicts" in *Ordering Medieval Society: Perspectives on Intellectual and Practical Modes of Shaping Social Relations*, ed. Bernhard Jussen, trans. Pamela Selwyn (Philadelphia, Pa.: University of Pennsylvania Press, 2001), 271–72.

35. Anselm envisions a complementary relationship between divine justice and mercy, but ultimately it is an eschatological vision. In recognition of the fact that justice takes precedence over mercy, he admits: "I do not deny that God is merciful. . . [but] we are speaking of that exceeding pity by which he makes man happy *after this life*" (emphasis added). *Cur Deus Homo*, 250.

36. One can turn to any number of places in the *Monologion* and the *Proslogion* where Anselm lists the divine attributes.

37. Charles Hartshorne, "father" of process theology, recognized this in 1962. See his introduction to the second edition of *St. Anselm: Basic Writings*.

38. Anselm, *Proslogion*, 72.

39. Anselm, *Monologion*, 107.

40. See Brown, "Anselm on Atonement," 292.

Chapter 10   Mechthild of Magdeburg

1. Mary Jeremy Finnegan, *Women of Helfta: Scholars and Mystics* (Athens, Ga.: University of Georgia Press, 1991).

2. *The Cambridge Medieval History*, vol. 6 *Triumph of the Papacy*, ed. J. R. Tanner, C. W. Previte-Orton, and Z. N. Brooke (New York: Macmillan, 1936), 109. For Mech-

thild's own reflection on war, see *The Flowing Light of the Godhead,* trans. Frank Tobin (New York, N.Y.: Paulist Press, 1998) 6:37 and 7:28.

3.   *Triumph of the Papacy,* 112–14.

4.   This general summary is indebted to Bernard McGinn, *The Flowering of Mysticism: Men and Women in the New Mysticism (1200–1350)* (New York: Crossroad, 1998), 2–4; Eric Christiansen, *The Northern Crusades: the Baltic and Catholic Frontier, 1100–1525,* (Minneapolis, Minn.: University of Minnesota Press, 1980), 87–88; Saskia Murk-Jansen, *Brides in the Desert: The Spirituality of the Beguines* (London: Darton, Longman and Todd, 1998), 15–17.

5.   Sara S. Poor, *Mechthild of Magdeburg and her Book: Gender and the Making of Textual Authority* (Philadephia, Pa.: University of Pennsylvania Press, 2004), 20, 30; *Church and City 1000–1500: Essays in Honour of Christopher Brooke,* ed. David Abulafia, Michael Franklin, and Miri Rubin (Cambridge: Cambridge University Press, 1992), 140–41.

6.   Christiansen, *The Northern Crusades,* 48.

7.   Christiansen, *The Northern Crusades,* 51.

8.   Christiansen, *The Northern Crusades,* 95.

9.   Murk-Jansen, *Brides in the Desert,* 23; McGinn, *Flowering of Mysticism,* 13.

10.   In addition to those listed for further reading, books on the beguine movement include: Jennifer Ward, *Women in Medieval Europe 1200–1500,* Emilie Zum Brunn and Georgette Epiney-Burgard, *Women Mystics in Medieval Europe,* Ulrike Wiethaus, *Maps of Flesh and Light: The Religious Experience of Medieval Women Mystics* and *The Reality of Mystical Experience: Self and World in the Work of Mechthild of Magdeburg,* Ernest W. McDonnell, *The Beguines and Beghards in Medieval Culture,* Caroline Walker Bynum, *Holy Feast and Holy Fast* and *Fragmentation and Redemption: Essays on Gender and the Human Body in Medieval Religion.*

11.   Elizabeth Alvilda Petroff, *Body and Soul: Essays on Medieval Women and Mysticism* (New York, N.Y.: Oxford University Press, 1994), 7; McGinn, *The Flowering of Mysticism,* 25–30.

12.   Malcolm Lambert, *Medieval Heresy: Popular Movements from the Gregorian Reform to the Reformation,* 3rd ed. (Oxford: Blackwell, 2002), 100.

13.   Walter Simons, "Staining the Speech of Things Divine: The Uses of Literacy in Medieval Beguine Communities," in *The Voice of Silence: Women's Literacy in a Men's Church,* ed. Therese de Hemptinne and Maria Eugenia Gongora (Turnhout, Belgium: Brepols Publishers, 2004), 87.

14.   Mark D. Jordan, *The Invention of Sodomy in Christian Theology* (Chicago, Ill.: University of Chicago Press, 1997), 92; see also Jessalyn Bird, "The Construction of Orthodoxy in *Pastoralia,*" in *Texts and the Repression of Medieval Heresy,* ed. Caterina Bruschi and Peter Biller (York, England: York Medieval Press, 2003), 49.

15.   McGinn describes the "positive, pastoral side [which] is especially evident in the numerous manuals for confessors that began to be produced around 1200," *The Flowering of Mysticism,* 11. By contrast, Jordan tracks with painstaking care the way in which this system subjected sexual practices of Christians to close scrutiny and rendered every "emission outside of the natural vessel, however it is brought about . . . a vice against nature and anyone who commits such an act is to be considered a Sodomite," *The Invention of Sodomy*

in Christian Theology, 102. Jordan's particular emphasis is the way this process creates the theological category and condemnation of sodomy and by extension homosexuality, but it is almost equally chilling as an account of the relentless and thorough condemnation of pleasure and eroticism in any form.

16. McGinn, *The Flowering of Mysticism,* 11.

17. Given, "The Beguins in Bernard Gui's *Liber Sententiarum,*" in *Texts and the Repression of Medieval Heresy*, 161.

18. Patschovsky, "Heresy and Society: On the Political Function of Heresy in the Medieval World," in *Texts and the Repression of Medieval Heresy*, 27. Richard Kieckhefer gives an example of financial motivations that could underlie inquisition in *Repression of Heresy in Medieval Germany* (Philadelphia, Pa.: University of Pennsylvania Press, 1979), 17. Murk-Jansen notes the use of inquisition against those who resisted sexual advances in *Brides in the Desert,* 26.

19. Bruschi and Biller, "Introduction," in *Texts and the Repression of Medieval Heresy*, 5.

20. "Introduction," *Texts and the Repression of Heresy,* 6. These authors point out the "very real sense contemporaries had of the awesome power and danger of these pieces of parchment," 6. See also Lambert, *Medieval Heresy,* 108.

21. Given, "The Beguines in Bernard Gui's *Liber Sententiarum,*" 153.

22. McGinn, *The Flowering of Mysticism,* 11.

23. Grace Jantzen, *Power, Gender, and Christian Mysticism* (Cambridge: Cambridge University Press, 1995), 2.

24. Poor, *Mechthild of Magdeburg and Her Book,* 20. For Mechthild's own view, see *The Flowing Light of the Godhead,* 6:32, in which she associates the Dominican tasks of preaching and hearing confessions with her own work.

25. Murk-Jansen, *Brides of the Desert,* 48–49; McGinn, *The Flowering of Mysticism,* 201–11, 235–38.

26. Justice complains that God has allowed mercy to take "from me what was rightfully mine . . . the true Son of God . . . robbed me of my strictest justice with his mercy" (*The Flowing Light of the Godhead,* 7:62).

27. See endnote 5, page 339, *Flowing Light of the Godhead.*

28. Poor, *Mechthild of Magdeburg and Her Book,* 3.

29. Alfred North Whitehead, *Process and Reality: An Essay in Cosmology,* Corrected Edition, ed. David Ray Griffin and Donald W. Sherburne (New York, N.Y.: Free Press, 1978), 342.

CHAPTER 12   JULIAN OF NORWICH

1. All textual references to Julian's *Showings* are taken from the Long Text in Julian of Norwich, *Showings,* trans. Edmund Colledge, O.S.A., and James Walsh, S.J. Classics of Western Spirituality (Mahwah, N.J.: Paulist Press, 1978). The first number refers to the Long Text chapter, and the second page number.

2. Grace Jantzen, *Julian of Norwich: Mystic and Theologian,* 2nd ed. (New York, N.Y.: Paulist Press, 2000), 90.

3. Lynn Staley, "Julian of Norwich and the Late Fourteenth-Century Crisis of Authority," in David Aers and Lynn Staley, *The Powers of the Holy: Religion, Politics, and*

Gender in Late Medieval English Culture (University Park, Pa.: Pennsylvania State University Press, 1996), 132.

4.   Although we have no record of Julian's contact with the bishop, the dates of his term (1370–1406) would have corresponded with her years at the Church of St. Julian. Richard Allington-Smith speculates about the possible contact between Julian and her bishop. He writes: "Did she and Henry Despenser ever meet? It is possible that he presided over the ceremony of her enclosure, whenever that was, for it called for the Bishop's attendance; but as Episcopal orders were not needed to validate the ceremony one of his vicars-general may have taken his place. But if they ever communicated what might they have said to each other? Would Henry, with his pragmatic, legal mind, have been able to understand her insights? . . . Sadly history has no time for such speculations," 139. See Richard Allington-Smith, *Henry Despenser the Fighting Bishop* (Dereham, Norfolk: Larks Press, 2003).

5.   The crusade was part of the ongoing period of the divided papacy, known as the Great Schism of the Western Church (1378–1417). Loyalty to the papacy generally fell along national lines; England supported the Roman-appointed pope, Urban VI, and France supported Clement VII, the pope seated in Avignon. For a good discussion of the crusade in the context of the Schism, see George M. Wrong, *The Crusade of 1383* (London: James Parker and Co., 1892).

6.   Given the physical seclusion of the anchoritic vocation, it is often assumed that Julian was entirely cut off from worldly affairs. Recent studies on the anchoritic life resist this depiction and reveal the degree to which many anchorites were engaged with the world. See Linda Georgianna. *The Solitary Self: Individuality in the "Ancrene Wisse"* (Cambridge, Mass.: Harvard University Press, 1981). Staley, "Julian of Norwich," 107–78.

7.   Cf. 22:216 to Anselm's *Cur Deus Homo* to see Julian's bold alternative understanding of redemption.

8.   See Lynn Staley's excellent reading of Julian's parable and its historical implications in "Julian of Norwich," 158–78.

9.   Christopher Abbott, *Julian of Norwich: Autobiography and Theology* (Woodbridge, Suffolk: D.S. Brewer, 1999), 119.

10. Jantzen, *Julian of Norwich: Mystic and Theologian*, 142.

11. Joan Nuth, *Wisdom's Daughter: The Theology of Julian of Norwich* (New York, N.Y.: Crossroad, 1991), 113.

12. Lynn Staley points out Julian's references to Parliament in the Middle English versions of both the Short and Long Texts. In the Short Text, the word is *parliamente*; in the Long Text, the word is *perlement*. See Staley, "Julian of Norwich," 158. For the Middle English texts, see Julian of Norwich, *A Book of Showings to the Anchoress Julian of Norwich*, ed. Edmund Colledge, O.S.A., and James Walsh, S.J. Vol. 2., *Studies and Texts* (Toronto: Pontifical Institute of Medieval Studies, 1978), 270, 648.

13. Staley, *The Powers of the Holy* 158.

14. Julian writes: "And I did not understand what they said, but all this, it seemed, was to move me to despair, and they seemed to be mocking us when we say our prayers lamely, lacking all the devout attention and wise care which we owe to God in our prayer," (69:315-316).

15. In the chapters following the final vision, Julian repeatedly references the Johannine admonition "You will not be overcome," recalling Jesus' words to the disciples at the time that he promises them the Paraclete-Spirit. With the presence of this spirit, they will have the strength to hold firmly to their faith. Julian tells us that the Lord wants his words to remain with us and to abide in us (71:318, 86:342); this parallels the Johannine instruction to abide and remain in love, both possible with the gift of the Paraclete-Spirit.

16. Summarizing the visions, she writes: "Know it well, love was his meaning. Who reveals it to you? Love. What did he reveal to you? Love. Why does he reveal it to you? For love. Remain in this, and you will know more of the same" (86:342).

17. Robert Jay Lifton, *Superpower Syndrome: America's Apocalyptic Confrontation with the World* (New York, N.Y.: Thunder's Mouth Press, 2003), 193.

18. Michael Hardt and Antonio Negri, *Multitude: War and Democracy in the Age of Empire* (New York, N.Y.: Penguin Press, 2004), xiii.

19. Lifton, *Superpower Syndrome,* 129.

20. President of the United States of America, *The National Security Strategy of the United States of America,* September 2002 <http://www.whitehouse.gov/nsc/nss.pdf>

CHAPTER 13   MARTIN LUTHER

1. Francis Fukuyama, "American Policy after Iraq: A Post-Bush Agenda," Speech at the Commonwealth Club of California, May 10, 2006, http://www.commonwealthclub.org/archive/index.php.

2. Francis Fukuyama, *America at the Crossroads: Democracy, Power, and the Neoconservative Legacy* (New Haven, Conn.: Yale University Press, 2006), 77.

3. While an in-depth analysis of bin Laden's type of resistance is beyond the scope of this paper, we can trace in his life the gradual rejection of virtually all kinds of temporal authority. Many temporal authorities have also rejected him, as his native Saudi Arabia did when they canceled his citizenship in 1994, and the Sudanese government forced him out of Sudan in 1996 after offering him a safe haven in 1992 (see Robert F. Worth's article, "Al-Qaeda's Inner Circle" in the *New York Review of Books* 53, no. 16, October 19, 2006). As James Turner Johnson suggests in his article on "Jihad and Just War," bin Laden's version of jihad continues to radicalize itself to the point of rejecting the actual history of Muslim societies and the Muslim faith. Indeed, "bin Laden's jihad not only pits Islam against America, the West as a whole, and ultimately the rest of the Islamic world," Johnson writes, "it also seeks to overthrow the contemporary Muslim states and mainstream views of Islamic traditions among the great majority of contemporary Muslims." See Turner's article "Jihad and Just War," in *First Things,* 124 (June/July 2002): 12–14.

4. C. Scott Dixon, *The Reformation in Germany* (Oxford: Blackwell, 2002), 17.

5. Martin Brecht, *Martin Luther: His Road to Reformation: 1483–1521,* trans. James L. Schaaf (Minneapolis, Minn.: Fortress Press), 387, as quoted in Dixon, 26.

6. Martin Luther, *Three Treatises,* trans. Charles M. Jacobs, A. T. W. Steinhauser, and W. A. Lambert (Philadelphia, Pa.: Fortress Press, 1978), 13–4.

7. For more on Luther's distinction between a theology of the cross and a theolo-

gy of glory, see chapter 1 in my book, *Crossing the Divide: Luther, Feminism, and the Cross* (Minneapolis, Minn.: Fortress Press, 2004).

8. Martin Luther, *Luther's Works,* American Edition, 55 vols. (St. Louis Mo.: Concordia Publishing; and Philadelphia, Pa.: Fortress Press, 1955–1986), 31:344. Hereafter *LW.* Here: *LW* 31:344.

9. *LW* 31:365.

10. Dixon, *The Reformation,* 30.

11. Dixon, *The Reformation,* 32.

12. *LW* 32:123.

13. Walter von Loewenich, *Martin Luther: The Man and His Work,* trans. Lawrence Denef (Minneapolis, Minn.: Fortress Press, 1986), 195.

14. See Heiko Oberman's useful chapter, "The Gospel of Social Unrest: 450 Years After the So-Called 'German Peasants' War' of 1525," in *The Dawn of the Reformation: Essays in Late Medieval and Early Reformation Thought,* ed. Heiko Oberman (Grand Rapids, Mich.: Eerdmans, 1992), 155–78.

15. Martin Luther, "Temporal Authority: To What Extent It Should Be Obeyed," *Martin Luther: Selections from His Writings,* ed. John Dillenberger (Garden City, N.Y.: Anchor Books, 1961), 371.

16. *LW* 45:91.

17. I'm helped in understanding Luther's opposition to theocracy by conversations with Gary Simpson, Luther Seminary, St. Paul, Minnesota. Dr. Simpson's perspective on these issues is laid out in his forthcoming book *War, Peace, and God* (Minneapolis, Minn.: Fortress Press, 2007).

18. Luther, *Selections from His Writings,* 385.

19. Cynthia Grant Schoenberger, "Luther and the Justifiability of Resistance to Legitimate Authority," *Journal of the History of Ideas* 40, no. 1 (1979): 3.

20. *LW* 45:106.

21. *LW* 45:6.

22. Luther, *Selections from His Writings,* 397.

23. Oberman, "The Gospel of Social Unrest," 156.

24. Oberman, "The Gospel of Social Unrest," 161.

25. *LW* 46:17–46.

26. *LW* 46:48.

27. *LW* 46:54.

28. Robert Schultz, Introduction to "On the Robbing and Murdering Hordes of Peasants," in *LW* 46:59.

29. *LW* 46:69.

30. Peter Matheson, *The Imaginative World of the Reformation* (Minneapolis, Minn.: Fortress Press, 2001), 97.

31. Matheson, *The Imaginative World,* 77.

32. *LW* 45:111.

33. Jürgen Moltmann, "Reformation and Revolution," in *Martin Luther and the Modern Mind: Freedom, Conscience, Toleration, Rights,* ed. Manfred Hoffmann, Toronto Studies in Theology, vol. 22 (New York, N.Y.: Edwin Mellen Press, 1985), 186.

34. Hans Hillerbrand, *The Reformation: A Narrative History Related By Contemporary Observers and Participants* (New York, N.Y.: Harper & Row, 1964), 375.

35. Dixon, *The Reformation*, 114.

36. Dixon, *The Reformation*, 110.

37. In the sixteenth century, the term "evangelical" referred to those who were dedicated to the rediscovery of the gospel, and those who held to the tenets of Scripture alone and justification by faith alone.

38. *LW* 34:xii.

39. *LW* 34:5.

40. *LW* 34:xii.

41. Preserved Smith and Charles M. Jacobs, eds. and trans., *Luther's Correspondence and Other Contemporary Letters,* vol. 2 (Philadelphia, Pa.: Lutheran Publication Society, 1918), 522.

42. Robert Bertram, "Confessio: Self-Defense Becomes Subversive," *Dialog* 26, no. 3 (1987): 204.

43. *LW* 46:185.

44. *LW* 46:171.

45. *LW* 46:171. Here Luther insists that before the emperor goes to war with the Turks, he must "begin with repentance," and that the empire itself must be reformed.

46. Gary Simpson references *LW* 13:49 and *LW* 46:226-7 when he discusses the pastor's admonitory role. See Simpson, "Toward a Lutheran 'Delight in the Law of the Lord': Church and State in the Context of Civil Society," in *Church & State: Lutheran Perspectives,* ed., John Stumme and Robert W. Tuttle (Minneapolis, Minn.: Fortress Press, 2003), 38.

47. Hillerbrand, *The Reformation: A Narrative History*, 376.

48. Dixon, *The Reformation*, 133.

49. *LW* 47:30.

50. *LW* 47:20.

51. *LW* 47:19.

52. *LW* 47:35.

53. *LW* 47:51.

54. Again I'm indebted to Gary Simpson for this qualification.

55. *LW* 3:94, 96.

56. See "Jesus Christ was Born a Jew," *LW* 45:200–6.

57. *LW* 47:138–9.

58. Sees Mark Edwards's discussion of this point in Mark U. Edwards Jr., *Luther's Last Battles: Politics and Polemics, 1531–1546* (Ithaca, N.Y.: Cornell University Press, 1983),128–33.

59. Dixon, *The Reformation*, 138.

60. Edwards, *Luther's Last Battles*, 66.

61. *LW* 46:162.

62. George Lindbeck, "Modernity and Luther's Understanding of the Freedom of the Christian," in *Luther and the Modern Mind*, 19.

63. Gary Simpson, "Hope in the Face of Empire: Failed Patriotism, Civil International Publicity, and Patriotic Peacebuilding," *Word & World* 25, no. 2 (Spring 2005): 135.

64. *LW* 46:165.

65. Jim Wallis, "Dangerous Religion: George W. Bush's Theology of Empire," *Sojourners Magazine*, September-October 2003, http://www.sojo.net/index.cfm?action=magazine.article&issue=soj0309&article=030910.

CHAPTER 14   BARTALOMÉ DE LAS CASAS

1. José Saramago, "Chiapas, a Name of Pain and Hope," in *Our Word is Our Weapon: Selected Writings*, Subcomandante Insurgente Marcos, ed. Juana Ponce de León (New York, N.Y.: Seven Stories, 2000), xx–xxi.

2. George Sanderlin, *Witness: Writings of Bartolomé de Las Casas*, trans. George Sanderlin (Maryknoll, N.Y.: Orbis Books, 1971), 2.

3. David M. Traboulay, *Columbus and Las Casas: The Conquest and Christianization of America, 1492–1566* (Lanman, Md.: University Press of America, 1994), 48.

4. Sanderlin, *Witness*, 3–4.

5. Enrique Dussel, "Beyond Eurocentrism: The World-System and the Limits of Modernity," in *The Cultures of Globalization*, ed. Fredric Jameson and Masao Miyoshi (Durham, N.C.: Duke University Press, 1998), 4.

6. Walter D. Mignolo, *The Darker Side of Renaissance: Literacy, Territoriality, and Colonization* (Ann Arbor, Mich.: University of Michigan Press, 1995), xi.

7. Alan Munslow, *The Routledge Companion to Historical Studies* (London: Routledge, 2000), 163.

8. Albert Memmi, *The Colonizer and the Colonized* (Boston, Mass.: Beacon Press, 1965), 149.

9. Luis Rivera Pagán, "Violence of the *Conquistadores* and Prophetic Indignation," in *Essays from the Diaspora* (Mexico: Publicaciones El Faro, 2002), 76.

10. Rivera Pagán, "Violence," 75.

11. Rivera Pagán, "Violence," 74.

12. Lewis Hanke, *All Mankind is One: A Study of the Disputation Between Bartolomé de Las Casas and Juan Ginés de Sepúlveda in 1550 on the Intellectual and Religious Capacity of the American Indians* (De Kalb, Ill.: Northern Illinois University Press, 1974), 5.

13. Paul S. Vickery, *Bartolomé de Las Casas: Great Prophet of the Americas* (New York, N.Y.: Paulist Press, 2006), 13.

14. For detailed analyses of Sepúlveda's argument see Juan Ginés de Sepúlveda, *Tratados Políticos de Juan Ginés de Sepúlveda*, trans. and ed. Ángel Losada (Madrid: Instituto de Estudios Políticos, 1963).

15. Gustavo Gutiérrez, "The Indian: Person and Poor, The Theological Perspective of Bartolomé de Las Casas," in *Witness: Writings of Bartolomé de Las Casas*, ed. and trans. George Sanderlin (Maryknoll, N.Y.: Orbis Books, 1971), xiv.

16. A discussion regarding the details of the *encomienda* system lies beyond the scope of my argument, but for further information see Luis Rivera Pagán, *Evangelización y Violencia: La Conquista de América* (San Juan: Editorial CEMI, 1990), 189–219.

17. Rivera Pagán, "Violence," 87.

18. Bartolomé de Las Casas, *The Devastation of the Indies: A Brief Account*, trans. Herman Briffault (Baltimore, Md.: Johns Hopkins University Press, 1992).

19. Las Casas, *Devastation,* 31–32.

20. Rivera Pagán, "Violence," 87.

21. Las Casas, *Devastation,* 129.

22. See Bartolomé de Las Casas, *Los Indios de Mexico y Nueva España,* ed. Edmundo O'Gorman (México: Editorial Porrua, 1971); Bartolomé de Las Casas, *Los Tesoros del Perú,* trans. Angel Losada (Madrid: Consejo Superior de Investigaciones Científicas, 1958).

23. Gutiérrez, "The Indian: Person and Poor," xv.

24. Bartolomé de Las Casas spoke against the existence of two humanities since he did not believe in the enslavement of Amerindians. This topic is controversial because while he spoke directly against the enslavement of Amerindians, he did not do so against the enslavement of Africans. Although he later regretted this position, Las Casas suggested that Africans should be used to help Spaniards in the sugar mills because that would liberate the Amerindians from that hard labor. Still today, this is the major critique of Las Casas by scholars.

25. Sanderlin, *Witness,* 99.

26. Sanderlin, *Witness,* 97.

27. Hanke, *All Mankind Is One,* 77.

28. Hanke, *All Mankind Is One,* 75.

29. Sanderlin, *Witness,* 100.

30. Sanderlin, *Witness,* 100.

31. Sanderlin, *Witness,* 97.

32. Bartolomé de Las Casas, *Obras Escogidas,* vol. 3, ed. Juan Pérez de Tudela (Madrid: Biblioteca de Autores Españoles, 1958), 430–34.

33. Bartholomé de Las Casas, *The Only Way,* ed. Helen Rand Parish, trans. Francis Patrick Sullivan (New York, N.Y.: Paulist Press, 1992), 83.

34. Las Casas, *The Only Way,* 127.

35. Gutiérrez, "The Indian: Person and Poor," xvi–xvii. It is important to acknowledge here that while I am pursuing a dialectical perspective on Las Casas, as he is both against and in favor of the empire, some other scholars such as Gustavo Gutiérrez will not see Las Casas in this perspective. See Gustavo Gutiérrez, *Las Casas: In Search of the Poor of Jesus Christ,* trans. Robert R. Barr (Maryknoll, N.Y.: Orbis Books, 1993).

36. Rivera Pagán, *Evangelización,* 105.

37. Sanderlin, *Witness,* 152.

38. Rivera Pagán, *Evangelización,* 105. This conceptualization of Las Casas as an *indigenista* only makes sense in the context of his romanticizing of the Amerindians. This romanticizing, which is open to critique in the present indigenous discourses, was the attitude that moved him to confront the colonial discourse and speak and act against war and in favor of indigenous rights. So it is important to acknowledge that the term *indigenista* should not be taken as an absolute.

39. Sanderlin, *Witness,* 176.

40. Sanderlin, *Witness,* 16.

41. See Gutiérrez, *Las Casas.*

42. Stephen P. Judd, "The Indigenous Theology Movement in Latin America: Encounters of Memory, Resistance, and Hope at the Crossroads," in *Resurgent Voices in Latin*

America: Indigenous Peoples, Political Mobilization, and Religious Change, ed. Edward L. Cleary and Timothy J. Steigenga (New Brunswick, N.J.: Rutgers University Press, 2004), 215.

43. Edward L. Cleary and Timothy J. Steigenga, "Resurgent Voices: Indians, Politics, and Religion in Latin America," in *Resurgent Voices in Latin America*, 1.

44. Judd, "The Indigenous Theology Movement," 227.

45. Judd, "The Indigenous Theology Movement," 228.

46. Christine Kovic, "Mayan Catholics in Chiapas, Mexico: Practicing Faith on Their Own Terms," in *Resurgent Voices in Latin America*, 198.

47. Kovic, "Mayan Catholics", 198.

CHAPTER 15   JEAN CALVIN

1. For a concise and readable survey of the relevant scholarship, consult Alister E. McGrath, *A Life of John Calvin* (Oxford: Blackwell, 1990), 105–28.

2. Trans. Talcott Parsons (New York: Scribners, 1958).

3. McGrath, *A Life of John Calvin*, 219–245, and William C. Innes, *Social Concern in Calvin's Geneva* (Allison Park, Pa.: Pickwick Publications, 1983).

4. For a thorough treatment, see Philip Benedict, *Christ's Churches Purely Reformed: A Social History of Calvinism* (New Haven, Conn.: Yale University Press, 2002).

5. For a thorough recent overview of the period, see Diarmaid MacCulloch, *The Reformation: A History* (New York, N.Y.: Penguin Books, 2003).

6. In our ecumenical era scholars often avoid the term Counter-Reformation, preferring to speak of the Catholic Reformation. It is certainly true that we should not lose sight of positive reform efforts by members of the established church. The spirituality of Teresa of Avila, John of the Cross, and Ignatius of Loyola was definitely not motivated solely by the desire to combat Protestantism. Nor were all the decrees of the Council of Trent (1547–48, 1551–52, and 1562–63), which also sought to improve the morals of the clergy. Nonetheless, the historical record clearly demonstrates that a concerted effort was being made on multiple fronts to contain and if possible destroy the manifestations of religious dissidence. No one pursued this international campaign more energetically than Philip II.

7. Geneva would not formally join the Swiss confederation until long alter Calvin's death. In practice, however, the independent city's authorities sought the protection of powerful cantons and strove to act in consort with them as much as possible. Bern was particularly influential in Genevan affairs.

8. Bernard Cottret, *Calvin: A Biography*, trans. M. Wallace McDonald (Grand Rapids, Mich.: Eerdmans, 2000), 8.

9. Christopher Elwood, *The Body Broken: The Calvinist Doctrine of the Eucharist and the Symbolization of Power in Sixteenth-Century France* (Oxford: Oxford University Press, 1999).

10. Once during Henry II's reign, his exasperation with the perceived intractability of papal policy led him to seriously contemplate following the example of Henry VIII of England in creating a French Catholic Church independent of Roman authority. Cooler

heads soon prevailed, however, and compromises prevented a breach. As the English precedent demonstrates, even a break with Rome would not necessarily have implied sympathy for Protestant notions of reform, which could only become predominant after the death of Henry VIII.

11. John T. McNeill, ed., *Calvin: Institutes of the Christian Religion*, The Library of Christian Classics 20–21, trans. Ford Lewis Battles (Philadelphia, Pa.: Westminster, 1960), 9–31.

12. Significantly subtitled "In the Name of All Who Wish Christ to Reign," in Henry Beveridge, ed. and trans., *Selected Works of John Calvin: Tracts and Letters* (rep. Grand Rapids, Mich.: Baker Book House, 1983), 1:121–234.

13. *Commentary on the Book of Isaiah*, trans. William Pringle (repr. Grand Rapids, Mich.: Eerdmans, 1958), 1: xv–xvii. Calvin says that he wrote the preface on January 15, 1559, the date he understood to have been set for Elizabeth's coronation. The earlier edition of 1550 had been dedicated to her half brother Edward VI.

14. See Calvin's letter to Cecil in *Letters of John Calvin*, 211–13. On the general question of Calvin's views of women, see Jane Dempsey Douglas, *Women, Freedom and Calvin: The 1983 Annie Kinhead Warfield Lectures* (Philadelphia, Pa.: Westminster Press, 1985).

15. Jean-Francois Gilmont, *John Calvin and the Printed Book*, trans. Karin Maag (Kirksville, Mo.: Truman State University Press, 2005).

16. On this subject, I highly recommend Heiko A. Oberman's *The Two Reformations: The Journey from the Last Days to the New World* (New Haven, Conn.: Yale University Press, 2003), especially 147–50. One may well ask why pastoral comfort required the affirmation of both preordained salvation *and* damnation. The answer seems to be that Calvin believed he was following Scripture and heightening the sense of God's absolute majesty.

17. All references taken from "On Shunning the Unlawful Rites of the Ungodly and Preserving the Purity of the Christian Religion" (1537), in Henry Beveridge, ed. and trans., vol. 3, 372, 379, 385–87, 393. Victorian translators generally softened the vulgarity of the original French.

18. William R Stevenson Jr., *Sovereign Grace: The Place and Significance of Christian Freedom in John Calvin's Political Thought* (Oxford: Oxford University Press, 1999), 155, lists references in the *Institutes*.

19. The most thorough study of Calvin's rhetorical authorship is Olivier Millet's *Calvin et la dynamique de la parole: Etude de rhétorique réformée* (Paris: Librairie Honoré Champion, 1992). See also my *John Calvin's Rhetorical Doctrine of Sin* (Lewiston, N.Y.: Edwin Mellen Press, 2001).

20. See Oberman, *The Two Reformations*, 130–34, who ably summarizes the content of the first book of the *Institutes*.

21. Max Engammare, "Calvin monarchomaque? Du soupçon l'argument," *Archiv für Reformationsgeschichte* 89 (1998): 207–25. See also Stevenson, *Sovereign Grace,* especially 34. For other examples of Calvin's political use of the pulpit, see William G. Naphy, *Calvin and the Consolidation of the Genevan Reformation* (Philadelphia, Pa.: Westminster John Knox Press, 1994).

22. Benedict, *Christ's Churches Purely Reformed*.

23. Jürgen Moltmann's *Theology of Hope* (New York, N.Y.: Harper & Row, 1967) pioneered eschatological reconceptualizations. For a particularly creative recent approach, see

Catherine Keller, *Apocalypse Now and Then: A Feminist Guide to the End of the World* (Boston, Mass.: Beacon Press, 1996).

CHAPTER 16   SOR JUANA INÉS DE LA CRUZ

Some of the material for this chapter has been drawn from Michelle A. Gonzalez, *Sor Juana: Beauty and Justice in the Americas* (Maryknoll, N.Y.: Orbis Books, 2003). Used with permission.

1.   A *criollo/a* is an individual of Spanish descent born in the Americas.

2.   Don Antonio Sebastián Toledo and the Vicereine Doña Leonor Carreto would leave a few years after Sor Juana took the veil. In 1673 a new viceroy was named, Don Pedro Nuño Colón de Portugal, who died four days after entering office. Fray Payo Enríquez de Rivera was named viceroy the following year. As a cleric his viceroyalty was characterized by the institutional joining of church and state. He retired after holding the position for six years. The following viceroy was Don Tomás Antonio de la Cerda, the Marquis de la Laguna, and his wife, María Luisa Manrique de Lara y Gonzaga, Countess of Paredes de Nava (1680–1688). Count de Galve replaced them in 1688. Octavio Paz, *Sor Juana, Or, The Traps of Faith* (Cambridge, Mass.: Harvard University Press, 1988), chapter 1.

3.   Sor Juana wrote various poems dedicated to María Luisa. Some modern scholars have hypothesized that Sor Juana's poetry to María Luisa, which at times uses the language of lovers, implies that Sor Juana was in fact a lesbian. At the same time, all of Sor Juana's poetry must be understood in light of the body of literature from which it emerges. Sor Juana often assumed a 'male' voice in her writing, and one cannot discern whether Sor Juana's use of loving language with regards to María Luisa was the result of rhetorical convention or motivated by erotic love. I mention this debate, for it is a conversation in contemporary Sor Juana scholarship. However, because of the uncertainty surrounding this matter, I leave this question open and unanswered. Also, I find it problematic to label a seventeenth-century figure with the contemporary label of lesbian. See Alicia Gaspar de Alba, "The Politics of Location of the Tenth Muse of America: An Interview with Sor Juana Inés de la Cruz," in *Living Chicana Theory*, ed. Carla Trujillo (Berkeley, Calif.: Third World Woman Press, 1998), 136–65; Gaspar de Alba, *Sor Juana's Second Dream* (Albuquerque, N. Mex.: The University of New Mexico Press, 1999); Paz, *Sor Juana*; Nina M. Scott, "'Ser mujer ni estar ausente, / no es de amarte impedimento': las poemas de Sor Juana al la contesa de Paredes," in *Y Diversa de Mí Misma en Vuestras Plumas Ando: Homenaje Internacional a la Sor Juana Inés de la Cruz*, ed. Sara Poot Herrera (Mexico City: El Colegio de México,1993), 159–70.

4.   A *villancico* was a poem set to music that was sung on religious holidays, usually in an ecclesial setting; a *sarao* is a celebratory song accompanied by a dance.

5.   Short of marriage or convent life, there were very few options for *criollas* in New Spain. For an excellent overview of the culture and daily life of women in New Spain, see Pilar Gonzalbo Aizpura, *Las Mujeres en la Nueva España: Educación y Vida Cotidiana* (Mexico City: El Colegio de México, 1987).

6.   Until recently the hypotheses surrounding these events assumed that Sor Juana's critique was in fact directed toward Vieira's sermon. However, today this is being contested. Elias Trabulse has put forth a theory based on the discovery of *La Carta de Serafina de Cristo*, dated February 1, 1691, directed at Fernández de Santa Cruz. In this letter, which Trabulse attributes to Sor Juana, the author ironically and defiantly states that the true object of *Atenagórica* was actually Núñez de Miranda. The author was in fact refuting his book entitled *Comulgador Penitente de la Purísima* (1690). In this book, Núñez de Miranda argues that Christ's greatest *fineza* (demonstration of love) was the Eucharist. The author of *Serafina de Cristo* contests this. In refuting him, however, the author also rejects a foundational rule of the *Congregación de Purísima*, a powerful group of clergy and political laity. Trabulse interprets this move as political suicide on Sor Juana's part. Sor Juana is not only refuting a powerful Jesuit, she is also contesting this group of elite people, who include the current viceroy. Elías Trabulse, *Los años finales de Sor Juana: una interpretación (1688–1695)* (Mexico: CONDUMEX, 1995), 18–20. Trabulse's interpretation has been contested recently by other *sorjuanistas*. See Marie-Cécile Bénassy-Berling, "Actualidad del sorjuanismo (1994–1999)," *Colonial Latin American Review* 9:2 (December 2000): 279. *Sorjuanista* is the term for a Sor Juana expert.

7.   A *mestizo/a* is an individual of Spanish and indigenous descent. A *mulato/a* is of African and Spanish descent.

8.   Irving A. Leonard, *Baroque Times in Old Mexico: Seventeenth-Century Persons, Places, and Practices* (Ann Arbor, Mich.: University of Michigan Press, 1959), 31.

9.   Yolanda Martínez San Miguel, *Saberes Americanos: Subalternidad y epistemología en los escritos de Sor Juana* (Pittsburg, Pa.: University of Pittsburg, 1999), 31–33.

10.   The viceroy was unable to bring his children to New Spain, and a royal inspector who visited the court monitored him. Octavio Paz, *Sor Juana*, 21–23.

11.   José Carlos González Boixo, "Femenismo y Intelectualidad en Sor Juana," in *Sor Juana Inés de la Cruz*, ed. Luis Sáinz de Medrano (Rome: Bulzoni Editore, 1997), 34.

12.   Electa Arenal and Amanda Powell, "Preface," in *The Answer / La Respuesta*, ed. and trans. Electa Arenal and Amanda Powell (New York, N.Y.: Feminist Press at the City University of New York, 1994), ix.

13.   Arenal and Powell's edited text offers an excellent introduction to those works that emphasize gender in Sor Juana's corpus.

14.   Martínez-San Miguel, *Saberes Americanos*, 13–14.

15.   Martínez-San Miguel, *Saberes Americanos*, 51.

16.   As Stephanie Merrim writes, "Sor Juana militantly defends a woman's right to education and, by implication, participation in the male order. All of this together, added to the example of her own literary life, substantiates the obvious: that—as is entirely natural in view of the context in which she wrote—rather than asserting or projecting women's 'difference,' both ideologically and literally, Sor Juana sought to *negate* their difference, to introject or appropriate the masculine realm for the feminine and to place them on the same continuum. For Sor Juana, to write with the words of the ruling order may well have entailed claiming the woman's equal rights to write in that world." Stephanie Merrim, "Toward a Feminist Reading of Sor Juana Inés de la Cruz: Past, Present, and Future Directions in Sor Juana Criticism," in *Feminist Perspectives on Sor Juana Inés de la Cruz*, ed. Stephanie Merrim (Detroit, Mich.: Wayne State University Press, 1991), 22–23.

17. Sor Juana Inés de la Cruz, *Obras Completas de Sor Juana Inés de la Cruz*, vol. 4, ed. Alfonso Mendez Plancarte and Alberto G. Salceda (México: Instituto Mexiquense de Cultura; Fondo de Cultura Económica, 1995), 444–45. For English translation see Sor Juana, *The Answer/La Respuesta*, 47.

18. Kathleen A. Meyers, "Sor Juana's *Respuesta*: Rewriting the *Vitae*," *Revista Canadiense de Estudios Hispánicos* 14, no. 3 (Spring 1990): 459–69.

19. Meyers, "Sor Juana's *Respuesta*," 463.

20. Pamela Kirk, *Sor Juana Inés de la Cruz: Religion, Art, and Feminism* (New York, N.Y.: Continuum, 1998), 50.

21. Pamela Kirk, "Christ as Divine Narcissus: A Theological Analysis of 'El Divino Narciso' by Sor Juana Inés de la Cruz," *Word & World* 12:2 (Spring 1998): 153.

22. Marie-Cécile Bénassy-Berling, *Humanisme et Religion chez Sor Juana Inés de la Cruz: La Femme et la Culture au XVIIe Siècle* (Paris: Editions Hispaniques, 1982), 298–99.

23. *Obras Completas*, 3:105.

24. *Obras Completas*, 2:14–17.

25. *Obras Completas*, 39–42.

26. Kirk, *Sor Juana Inés de la Cruz*, 71.

27. *Obras Completas*, 2:182.

28. *Obras Completas*, 2: 209.

29. Jean Franco, *Plotting Women: Gender and Representation in Mexico* (New York: Columbia University Press, 1989), 51.

30. Trabulse, *Los años finales de Sor Juana*, 28–31.

31. Trabulse thanks historian Teresa Castelló Yturbide for copying the ledger of the contents of Sor Juana's cell at the time of her death, thus giving scholars today this information. *Los años finales*, 37.

32. As collections such as *Untold Sisters: Hispanic Nuns in Their Own Works* demonstrate, Sor Juana must be understood within the literary canon of women religious writing in the Americas. Electa Arenal and Stacey Schlau, *Untold Sisters* (Albuquerque, N. Mex.: University of New Mexico Press, 1989). For an account of Sor Juana in light of early modern women's writings see Stephanie Merrim, *Early Modern Women's Writing and Sor Juana Inés de la Cruz* (Nashville, Tenn.: Vanderbilt University Press, 1999).

33. Pamela Kirk, "Sor Juana Inés de la Cruz: Precursor of Latin American Feminism," *Journal of Hispanic/Latino Theology* 5:3 (1998): 17.

34. This emphasis on *lo cotidiano* mirrors contemporary Latina theological concerns. Since their earliest work, Latina theologians María Pilar Aquino and Ada María Isasi-Díaz have emphasized the daily life of Latinas as *the* starting point for their theologies. See Aquino, *Our Cry for Life: Feminist Theology from Latin America* (Maryknoll, N.Y.: Orbis Books, 1993) and Isasi-Díaz, "*Lo Cotidiano*: Everyday Struggles in Hispanas/Latinas' Lives," in *La Lucha Continues: Mujerista Theology* (Maryknoll, N.Y.: Orbis Books, 2004), 92–106.

35. Kirk, *Sor Juana Inés de la Cruz*, 65.

36. Dale T. Irvin, *Christian Histories, Christian Traditioning: Rendering Accounts* (Maryknoll, N.Y.: Orbis Books, 1998), xi–xii.

37. Irvin, *Christian Histories*, 88.

38. Albert J. Raboteau, "Africans in the Diaspora," *Princeton Theological Seminary Bulletin* 7, no. 2 (1986): 115.

39. *Obras Completas*, 4:440; *The Answer/La Respuesta*, 139.

40. *Obras Completas*, 4:441; *The Answer/La Repuesta*, 41, 83.

Chapter 17 Jonathan Edwards

1. Standard biographies of Jonathan Edwards are by George Marsden, *Jonathan Edwards: A Life* (New Haven, Conn.: Yale University Press, 2003) and Patricia Tracy, *Jonathan Edwards, Pastor: Religion and Society in Eighteenth-Century Northampton* (New York, N.Y.: Hill and Wang, 1980).

2. See for instance, Robert Jenson, *America's Theologian: A Recommendation of Jonathan Edwards* (New York, N.Y.: Oxford University Press, 1988).

3. Jonathan Edwards, *Apocalyptic Writings: Works of Jonathan Edwards*, vol. 5, *Apocalyptic Writings*, ed. by Stephen J. Stein (New Haven, Conn.: Yale University Press, 1977), 173–74.

4. Marsden, *Jonathan Edwards*, 258.

5. The description of Edwards's metaphysics and his understanding of God's relationship to the world given here and at the end of this chapter are drawn from Sang Hyun Lee, *The Philosophical Theology of Jonathan Edwards* (Princeton, N.J.: Princeton University Press, 1988), 170–241.

6. Edwards, *Apocalyptic Writings*, 188.

7. Alan Heimert, *Religion and the American Mind* (Cambridge, Mass.: Harvard University Press, 1966), 14.

8. C.C. Goen, "Jonathan Edwards: A New Departure in Eschatology," *Church History* 28 (1959): 25–40.

9. Avihu Zakai, *Jonathan Edwards's Philosophy of History* (Princeton, N.J.: Princeton University Press, 2003), 250–52.

10. Jonathan Edwards, *The Works of Jonathan Edwards*, vol. 16, *Letters and Personal Writings*, ed. George Claghorn (New Haven, Conn.: Yale University Press, 1998), 442.

11. Jonathan Edwards, *The Works of Jonathan Edwards*, vol. 8, *Ethical Writings*, ed. Paul Ramsey (New Haven, Conn.: Yale University Press, 1989), 602.

12. Kenneth Minkema, "Jonathan Edwards's Defense of Slavery," *The Massachusetts Historical Review* 4 (2002): 10.

13. Edwards, *Apocalyptic Writings*, 136.

14. Edwards, *Apocalyptic Writings*, 136.

15. Minkema, "Jonathan Edwards's Defense of Slavery," 9.

16. Marsden, *Jonathan Edwards*, 426.

17. Minkema, "Jonathan Edwards's Defense of Slavery," 11.

18. Richard Bushman, *From Puritan To Yankee* (Cambridge, Mass.: Harvard University Press, 1967), 143.

19. Mark Valeri, "The Economic Thought of Jonathan Edwards," *Church History* 60 (1991): 37–54.

20. Kenneth Minkema and Harry Stout, "The Edwardsean Tradition and the Anti-Slavery Debate, 1740–1865," *The Journal of American History* 92 (June 2005): 57.

21. Paul Tillich, *The Socialist Decision* (Lanham, Md.: University Press of America, 1983), 110–12.

22. Edwards, *Apocalyptic Writings*, 136.

CHAPTER 18   JOHN WESLEY

1. Franz Hinkelammert, "Las condiciones económicos-sociales del Metodismo en la Inglaterra del Siglo XVIII," in *La tradición protestante en la teología latinoamericana: Primer intento: lectura de la tradición metodista,* ed. José Duque (San José, Costa Rica: DEI, 1983), 21–30.

2. See Randy Maddox, "Nurturing the New Creation: Reflections on a Wesleyan Trajectory," in *Wesleyan Perspectives on the New Creation*, ed. M. Douglas Meeks (Nashville, Tenn.: Kingswood Books, 2004), 21–52.

3. See, for example, Musa Dube, *Postcolonial Feminist Interpretation of the Bible* (St. Louis, Mo.: Chalice Press, 2000).

4. The case is different, however, when Wesley finds it necessary to contest deist assertions about the sufficiency of the natural light of reason for the attainment of the marks of faith. When this is the issue, Wesley is all too ready to produce illustrations of the negative character of those nations that live without the light of the gospel. Even here, however, he will generally have to admit that Christian nations are not in a significantly better state, as we shall see.

5. John Wesley, *The Works of John Wesley*, 3rd ed. (1872), 14 vols. (Grand Rapids, Mich.: Baker Book House, 1979), 12:38–39. All Wesley citations unless otherwise noted are from this edition, hereinafter cited as *Works* with volume and page numbers.

6. Sermon on the Mount no. 8 in *Works* 5:365. It is important to note that Wesley is not repeating a sort of "noble savage" ideology. In this sermon he has been quite clear about what he takes to be the viciousness of some aspects of Native American life. This is why he has said at the outset: "it is not easy to say . . . where the advantage lies" in a comparison of European and American customs.

7. *Works* 11:61.

8. *Works* 11:62.

9. *Works* 11: 64–65.

10. *Works* 11:65. Emphasis in original.

11. Sermon xxxviii (of 1750) in *Works* 5:479–92

12. Sermon xxxviii (of 1750) in *Works* 5:482.

13. Sermon lxix (of 1784) in *Works* 6:337–49.

14. Sermon lxix (of 1784) in *Works* 6:345.

15. Sermon lxix (of 1784) in *Works* 6:345.

16. Sermon lxix (of 1784) in *Works* 6:345.

17. Hinkelammert, "Las condiciones económicos-sociales," 26.

18. *Works* 4:89.

19. "Mystery of Iniquity" in *Works* 6:265. Emphasis in original.

20. *Works* 11:125–26.

21. Journal entry of Feb. 23, 1776, in *Works* 4:68.

22. Sermon lxix (of 1784) in *Works* 6:337–49.

23. *Works* 11:65.

24. *Works* 11:67.

25. *Works* 11:68.

26. *Works* 11:70.

27. *Works* 11:77.

28. *Works* 11:78.

29. *Works* 11:73.

30. *Works* 11:77.

31. "A Seasonable Address" in *Works* 11:125.

32. "A Seasonable Address" in *Works* 11:126.

33. *Works* 13:153.

34. See the journal entry for April 18, 1785, in *Works* 4:302. Nearly a century later, Karl Marx in his articles on imperialism in India published in the New York Daily Tribune of 1853 will also lament the carnage that resulted from England's policies in India but will provide a sort of secular theodicy for this suffering by supposing that it is a necessary stage in the ultimate preparation of India to participate in the coming revolution of the proletariat. Fortunately Wesley offers no such theodicy, secular or otherwise.

35. Sermon lxiii, *Works* 6:277–87.

CHAPTER 19   FRIEDRICH SCHLEIERMACHER

1.   One of the pioneers of reading Schleiermacher in light of the power struggles of his day is Frederick Herzog, "Schleiermacher and the Problem of Power" in his *Justice Church: The New Function of the Church in North American Christianity* (Maryknoll, N.Y.: Orbis Books, 1980), 55–69. More recently Kwok Pui-lan has addressed some of the colonial connotations of Schleiermacher's work in her book *Postcolonial Imagination and Feminist Theology* (Louisville, Ky.: Westminster John Knox Press, 2005), 189–93. See also my chapter on Schleiermacher in Joerg Rieger, *God and the Excluded: Visions and Blindspots in Contemporary Theology* (Minneapolis, Minn.: Fortress Press, 2001), 17–41.

2.   For a more detailed account of Schleiermacher and empire along similar lines see chapter 5 in Joerg Rieger, *Christ and Empire: From Paul to Postcolonial Times* (Minneapolis, Minn.: Fortress Press, 2007).

3.   James M. Brandt, *All Things New: Reform of Church and Society in Schleiermacher's Christian Ethics* (Louisville, Ky.: Westminster John Knox Press, 2001), 109–34, tracks Schleiermacher's involvement in political matters; like the Romantics, Schleiermacher was not always supportive of the political powers of his day and critiqued the government of Prussia's King Friedrich Wilhelm III. Theodore Vial, "Schleiermacher and the State," in *The Cambridge Companion to Friedrich Schleiermacher*, ed. Jacqueline Mariña (Cambridge: Cambridge University Press, 2005), 275, mentions Schleiermacher's undercover work against the French.

4.   In the late seventeenth century, Prussia briefly established forts on the coast of West Africa and leased part of the West Indian island of St. Thomas from Denmark. In 1751, Frederick the Great established the unsuccessful Asiatic-Chinese Merchant Society. See the introduction to *The Imperialist Imagination: German Colonialism and Its Legacy,*

ed. Sara Friedrichsmeyer, Sara Lennox, and Susanne Zantop (Ann Arbor, Mich: University of Michigan Press, 1998), 9.

5.   See Susanne Zantop, *Colonial Fantasies: Conquest, Family, and Nation in Precolonial Germany, 1770–1870* (Durham, N.C.: Duke University Press, 1997), 22, 29.

6.   Günter Meckenstock in his introduction calls it *gewichtig;* Friedrich Daniel Ernst Schleiermacher, *Schriften aus der Berliner Zeit 1800–1802*, ed. Günter Meckenstock, Kritische Gesamtausgabe, Hans-Joachim Birkner et al, abt. 1, vol. 3 (Berlin: Walter de Gruyter, 1988), lxxxv.

7.   Edward Said, *Orientalism* (New York, N.Y.: Vintage Books, 1979), 19, observes that German scholarship about the Orient and other non-European places was based on materials gathered first-hand by imperial Britain and France.

8.   This helps us better understand scholars such as Friedrich Max Müller who became one of the top authorities on Indian language and religion without ever traveling to India. See Peter van der Veer, *Imperial Encounters: Religion and Modernity in India and Britain* (Princeton, N.J.: Princeton University Press, 2001), 106.

9.   For the term "Occidentalism" see Walter Mignolo, *Local Histories/Global Designs: Coloniality, Subaltern Knowledges, and Border Thinking* (Princeton, N.J.: Princeton University Press, 2000), 18–21. See also Zantop, *Colonial Fantasies*, 10, who coins the phrase "German Occidentalism" in contrast to Said's notion of Orientalism.

10.   For the term "colonial fantasies" and an interpretation of particular German colonial fantasies see Susanne Zantop, *Colonial Fantasies,* 4; the term links "the individual subconscious and the political subconscious of a society."

11.   Friedrich Daniel Ernst Schleiermacher, letter of March 1, 1799, in *Briefwechsel 1799–1800*, ed. Andreas Arndt and Wolfgang Virmond, *Kritische Gesamtausgabe*, ed. Hans-Joachim Birkner, et al., Abt. 5, vol. 3 (Berlin: Walter de Gruyter, 1992), 24.

12.   Schleiermacher, "Materialien zur Siedlungsgeschichte Neuhollands (Australiens)," in *Schriften aus der Berliner Zeit 1800–1802*, ed. Günter Meckenstock, *Kritische Gesamtausgabe*, ed. Hans-Joachim Birkner, et al., Abt. 1, vol. 3 (Berlin: Walter de Gruyter, 1988), 251; these insights are from his translation of a 1789 report by Arthur Phillip, "The voyage of Governor Phillip to Botany Bay."

13.   Schleiermacher, "Zur Siedlungsgeschichte Neuhollands (Australiens)," in *Schriften aus der Berliner Zeit: 1800–1802*, 269, 271.

14.   Schleiermacher, "Zur Siedlungsgeschichte," 253.

15.   Schleiermacher, "Zur Siedlungsgeschichte," 270–71.

16.   Schleiermacher, "Zur Siedlungsgeschichte," 278.

17.   Schleiermacher, "Zur Siedlungsgeschichte," 279.

18.   Said, *Orientalism*, 117.

19.   See Hans Peter Herrmann, Hans-Martin Blitz, and Susanna Mossmann, *Machtphantasie Deutschland: Nationalismus, Männlichkeit und Fremdenhass im Vaterlandsdiskurs deutscher Schriftsteller des 18. Jahrhunderts* (Frankfurt: Suhrkamp, 1996), 125–27. See also Jonathan M. Hess, *Germans, Jews, and the Claims of Modernity* (New Haven, Conn.: Yale University Press, 2002).

20.   Zantop, *Colonial Fantasies*, 7.

21.   See Zantop, *Colonial Fantasies*, 8.

22. Mary Louise Pratt, *Imperial Eyes: Travel Writing and Transculturation* (New York, N.Y.: Routledge, 1992), 115.

23. For a brief introduction to Schleiermacher's famous notion of "feeling of absolute dependence" see Rieger, *God and the Excluded*, 21–23.

24. Stephen Prickett, "Coleridge, Schlegel and Schleiermacher: England, Germany (and Australia) in 1798," in *1798: The Year of the Lyrical Ballads*, ed. Richard Cronin (New York, N.Y.: St. Martin's Press, 1998), 181–82. Prickett is mistaken, however, when he claims that the challenge was to include the Aboriginals "within the fold of Christianity." Schleiermacher's notion of religion was broader.

25. Schleiermacher, *The Christian Faith*, ed. H.R. Mackintosh and J.S. Stewart (Edinburgh: T. & T. Clark, 1986), 439, notes that the three offices display "new and intensified forms of those through which in the old covenant the divine government was revealed."

26. Schleiermacher, *On Religion: Speeches to Its Cultured Despisers*, trans. John Oman (Louisville, KY.: Westminster John Knox Press, 1994), 239. Nevertheless, Schleiermacher considers Judaism a matter of the past, *On Religion*, 238. As a childlike religion, "it could only work on a narrow scene, without complications, where the whole being simple, the natural consequences of actions would not be disturbed or hindered," *On Religion*, 240.

27. Schleiermacher, *The Christian Faith*, 37. Nevertheless, the trajectory of Schleiermacher's argument is the same as the more polite language of the *Speeches*.

28. See Kurt Nowak, *Schleiermacher: Leben, Werk und Wirkung*, 2nd ed. (Göttingen: Vandenhoeck & Ruprecht, 2002), 95–97.

29. Schleiermacher, *The Christian Faith*, 440; in this case "harmony between the old covenant and the new."

30. Schleiermacher, *The Christian Faith*, 425, 426, 427.

31. Schleiermacher, *The Christian Faith*, 427.

32. Schleiermacher, *The Christian Faith*, 31; he explicitly rejects the view that "Christian religion (piety) should adopt towards at least most other forms of piety the attitude of the true towards the false."

33. Schleiermacher, *The Christian Faith*, 556–57.

34. Schleiermacher, *The Christian Faith*, 449.

35. Schleiermacher, *The Christian Faith*, 450.

36. See Schleiermacher's typology of religion, which takes for granted states of religious development, *The Christian Faith*, 31–52.

37. This role of language is noted by Gunther Pakendorf, "Mission as Gewalt. Die Missionsordnung im 19. Jahrhundert" in *Mission und Gewalt: Der Umgang christlicher Missionen mit Gewalt und die Ausbreitung des Christentums in Afrika und Asien in der Zeit von 1792–1918/19*, ed. Ulrich van der Heyden and Jürgen Becher (Stuttgart: Franz Steiner Verlag, 2000), 240. For the concept of the panopticon, first suggested by Jeremy Bentham, see Michel Foucault, *Discipline and Punish: The Birth of the Prison*, trans. Alan Sheridan (New York: Pantheon Books, 1977), 195–228.

38. Homi Bhabha, *The Location of Culture* (New York, N.Y.: Routledge, 1994), 111.

39. Schleiermacher, *The Christian Faith*, 433. Schleiermacher calls this a "mystical" perspective as opposed to a magical and empirical one: *The Christian Faith*, 434.

40. "In our view, the suffering of Christ has nothing to say," says Schleiermacher, *The Christian Faith*, 435. At best, it is "an element of secondary importance," 436.

41. Schleiermacher, *On Religion*, 245.

42. Schleiermacher, *On Religion*, 236–37.

43. Schleiermacher, *On Religion*, 251.

44. Schleiermacher, *On Religion*, 252.

45. Schleiermacher, *Die Christliche Sitte nach den Grundsätzen der evangelischen Kirche im Zusammenhang dargestellt* (Waltrop: Spenner, 1999), 291–92; the basis is God's grace, ibid., 317. Since Schleiermacher identifies a relation between the Holy Spirit and the human spirit, he is able to appreciate human achievements. At the same time, the Holy Spirit is clearly a higher form of the human spirit, ibid., 313.

46. Schleiermacher, *Christliche Sitte*, 370–71. The Christians experience a "*religiöse Lust*" and the non-Christians desire to receive "*den wahren Gegenstand ihres Verlangens.*"

47. Schleiermacher, *Christliche Sitte*, 383. This argument is developed in contrast to the Roman Catholic Church, because it assumes that the church is already perfected, *Christliche Sitte*, 384.

48. Schleiermacher, *Christliche Sitte*, 388–89.

49. Schleiermacher, *Christliche Sitte*, 394. This contradicts George Lindbeck's claim that Schleiermacher is an experiential expressivist; Schleiermacher is much closer to Lindbeck's own "cultural linguistic" approach. See Lindbeck, *The Nature of Doctrine: Religion and Theology in a Postliberal Age* (Philadelphia, Pa.: Westminster Press, 1984).

50. Schleiermacher, *Christliche Sitte*, 396.

51. For the notion of hybridity see Bhabha, *Location of Culture*. Bhabha would agree that the hybridized embody the greatest diversity of experience and the broader horizon.

52. Schleiermacher, *Christliche Sitte*, 666–67.

53. Brandt, *All Things New*, 129.

54. Schleiermacher, *Christliche Sitte*, 514.

55. Zantop, *Colonial Fantasies*, 100–101.

CHAPTER 20   G. W. F. HEGEL

1. G. W. F. Hegel, *Philosophy of Right*, trans. T. M. Knox (Oxford; Clarendon Press, 1942), 11.

2. For the classic discussion of Orientalism, see Edward W. Said, *Orientalism* (New York, N.Y.: Pantheon Books, 1978). Although Said focuses on Anglo-French Orientalism, he does note that the common element of Orientalisms of all sorts "was a kind of intellectual *authority* over the Orient within Western culture" (Said, *Orientalism*, 19).

3. *Hegel: The Letters*, trans. Clark Butler and Christiane Seiler (Bloomington, Ind.: Indiana University Press, 1984), 451.

4. Joachim Ritter, *Hegel and the French Revolution*, trans. Richard Dien Winfield (Cambridge, Mass.: MIT Press, 1982), 43.

5. H. S. Harris, "Hegel's Intellectual Development to 1807," in *The Cambridge Companion to Hegel*, ed. Frederick C. Beiser (Cambridge: Cambridge University Press, 1993), 26.

6. Gayatri Chakravorty Spivak, *A Critique of Postcolonial Reason* (Cambridge, Mass.: Harvard University Press, 1999), 7.

7. G. W. F. Hegel, *The Philosophy of History*, trans. J. Sibree (New York: Willey Book Co., 1944), 341, 344, 416, 417, 416.

8. G. W. F. Hegel, *Phenomenology of Spirit*, trans. A.V. Miller (Oxford: Oxford University Press, 1977), 360.

9. *Hegel: The Letters*, 307.

10. Terry Pinkard, *Hegel: A Biography* (Cambridge: Cambridge University Press, 2000), 228–29.

11. Hegel, *The Philosophy of History*, 446.

12. G. W. F. Hegel, *Lectures on the Philosophy of Religion*, vol. 1, ed. Peter C. Hodgson (Berkeley, Calif.: University of California Press, 1984), 84.

13. Ibid., 233 n. 191.

14. Peter C. Hodgson, ed., *G. W. F. Hegel: Theologian of the Spirit* (Minneapolis, Minn.: Fortress Press, 1997), 7. Hodgson provides another helpful description of Hegel's panentheistic vision when he states that "[w]ith respect to God and the natural world, we can say that the divine is natural and human to the extent that God is *not*, or does not *remain*, merely essential being (*Wesen*); while nature and humanity are divine precisely *in* their essential being, as distinct from their determinate and finite being (*Dasein*)" (Hodgson, *Theologian*, 9).

15. For a discussion of metanarratives and the problem of the Other, see Paul Lakeland, *Postmodernity: Christian Identity in a Fragmented Age* (Minneapolis, Minn.: Fortress Press, 1997), 30–36.

16. Hegel, *The Philosophy of History*, 63.

17. Hegel, *Lectures on the Philosophy of Religion*, vol. 1, 318, 318 n. 120, 197 n. 32.

18. Hegel, *The Philosophy of History*, 99, 139, 111, 112.

19. Hegel, *Lectures on the Philosophy of Religion*, vol. 2, 234, 250.

20. Hegel, *The Philosophy of History*, 138, 144.

21. For a critique of Hegel's view of Indian culture, see Spivak, *A Critique of Postcolonial Reason*, 37–67.

22. Hegel, *The Philosophy of History*, 173, 174, 175, 221.

23. See Hegel, *Lectures on the Philosophy of Religion*, 3:242–43.

24. Hegel, *The Philosophy of History*, 360.

25. Hegel, *Lectures on the Philosophy of Religion*, vol. 2. Besides Africa, Hegel associates this lowest form of religion with "Eskimos," "Mongols," and some Chinese (ibid., *Lectures*, 272–78).

26. Hegel proposes a "geographical basis" for the character of world history. "In the Frigid and in the Torrid zone the locality of World-historical peoples cannot be found." Africa, the "Gold-land," is just too hot, so he suggests, to emerge from "childhood" or "the dark mantle of Night" (Hegel, *The Philosophy of History*, 91, 80).

27. Hegel, *The Philosophy of History*, 93. I am indebted to an excellent overview of the role of Africa in Hegel's thought by Shannon M. Mussett, "On the Threshold of History: The Role of Nature and Africa in Hegel's Philosophy," in *Tensional Landscape: The Dynamics of Boundaries and Placements*, ed. Gary Backhaus and John Murungi (Lanham, Md.: Lexington Books, 2004). As Mussett points out, Hegel affirms that "Man is implicitly rational; herein lies the possibility of equal justice for all men and the futility of a rigid

distinction between races which have rights and those which have none." G. W. F. Hegel, *Philosophy of Mind: Being Part Three of the Encyclopaedia of the Philosophical Sciences,* trans. William Wallace and A.V. Miller (Oxford: Clarendon Press, 1971), 9. Spiritual differences between peoples are not to be associated, in other words, with biological differences. Rather, spiritual differences are related to the ways in which climate and geography can affect spirit's development (see Mussett, "On the Threshold of History," 12). Hegel, however, is hardly consistent about this. In a curiously pathetic twist, Hegel describes indigenous peoples in the Americas as inferior to Europeans and African slaves "in all respects, even in regard to size." He goes on to observe that the "weakness of the American [Indian] physique was a chief reason for bringing the negroes to America, to employ their labor in the work that had to be done in the New World." Moreover, "negroes are far more susceptible to European culture than the Indians, and an English traveler has adduced instances of negroes having become competent clergymen, medical men, etc. . . . while only a single native was known to him whose intellect was sufficiently developed to enable him to study, but who had died soon after beginning, through excessive brandy-drinking" (Hegel, *The Philosophy of History,* 81, 82).

28. Peter Hodgson comments that "by the end of his career he had a broad mastery of the available materials, a mastery won by extensive study during the 1820s. At the beginning of the decade his primary competence was in Egyptian, Greek, Roman, and Christian religion, based on earlier studies; the significant changes occurred in his knowledge of the non-Western religions: the 'religion of magic' (African and Eskimo), Chinese religion (including Zhou religion, Daoism, Confucianism), Buddhism, Lamaism, Hinduism, and Persian religion (Zoroastrianism). Significant changes also occurred in his assessment of Judaism. . . . Islam remained a major lacuna in his knowledge and treatment." Peter C. Hodgson, "Logic, History, and Alternative Paradigms in Hegel's Interpretation of the Religions," *Journal of Religion,* 68 (1988): 2.

29. Molefi Kete Asante, *Kemet, Afrocentricity, and Knowledge* (Trenton, N.J.: Africa World Press, 1990), 33. See also, Mussett, "On the Threshold of History," 13–14.

30. A now classic critical treatment of metanarratives is Jean François Lyotard, *The Postmodern Condition: A Report on Knowledge,* trans. Geoff Bennington and Brian Massouri (Minneapolis, Minn: University of Minnesota Press, 1984).

31. Hodgson suggests that "Hegel's philosophical history of religion is not evolutionary or developmental; rather it is *typological.*" This may be a plausible reading of Hegel given that he "almost playfully" experimented with the categorization of the religions in his lectures on the philosophy of religion over the years (Hodgson, "Logic, History, and Alternative Paradigms," 9, 20). However, when viewed in relation to his philosophy of history, it is difficult not to draw the conclusion of a deep developmentalism in Hegel's account of spirit.

32. William David Hart, "Slavoj Žižek and the Imperial/Colonial Model of Religion," *Nepantla: Views from South* 3, no. 3 (2002): 555. This reading of Hegel is consistent with the observation by other critics that "Hegel's drama of the Other . . . could not but take place against the historical backdrop of European expansion and the enslavement of African, American, and Asian peoples." Michael Hardt and Antonio Negri, *Empire* (Cambridge, Mass.: Harvard University Press, 2000), 82.

33. Hegel, *Philosophy of Right,* 126.

34. For a discussion of Hegel's progressive liberalism, see Kenneth Westphal, "The Basic Context and Structure of Hegel's *Philosophy of Right*," in *The Cambridge Companion to Hegel*, ed. Friedrich C. Beiser (Cambridge: Cambridge University Press, 1993), 234–69.

35. Hegel, *Philosophy of Right*, 40, 42, 57, 126.

36. Shlomo Avineri argues that the problem of Hegel's account of civil society is rooted in "basing his definition of personality on property" (*Hegel's Theory of the Modern State*, [Cambridge: Cambridge University Press, 1972], 137).

37. These class divisions are reminiscent of the gradation of religions and cultures we have already examined. At the bottom one has the "substantial or immediate" class, which is associated with nature and uses "comparatively little" reflection and independence of will, relative to the other two classes. The "reflecting" or "business" class is noted for its "reflection," "intelligence," and "industry." Finally, there is the "universal class" or the "class of civil servants" which has for its labor not the production of goods and services but "the universal interests of the community" (Hegel, *Philosophy of Right*, 131, 132).

38. Hegel, *Philosophy of Right*, 149, 150.

39. Hegel, *Philosophy of Right*, 150, 151.

40. Hegel, *Philosophy of Right*, 213, 297, 219.

41. Hardt and Negri, *Empire*, 82.

42. Hegel, *Philosophy of Right*, 151.

43. Tsenay Serequeberhan, "The Idea of Colonialism in Hegel's Philosophy of Right," *International Philosophical Quarterly* 29, no. 3 (1989): 312.

44. See, for example, Emmanuel Lévinas's classic critique of Hegel on this point in *Totality and Infinity* (Pittsburgh, Pa: Duquesne University Press, 1969).

45. I agree with Hodgson when he observes that "Hegel did not regard his own philosophy as the final philosophy but only as the philosophy in which the thoughts of his own age were most adequately apprehended" (Hodgson, "Logic, History, and Alternative Paradigms," 7).

46. Hegel, *Phenomenology of Spirit*, 19.

47. Edward Said captures this point nicely when he observed that "[t]he irony is that Hegel's dialectic is Hegel's, after all: he was there first, just as the Marxist dialectic of subject and object had been there before Fanon of *Les Damnés* used it to explain the struggle between colonizer and colonized." Edward W. Said, *Culture and Imperialism* (New York, N.Y.: Vintage Books, 1994), 210.

48. Hegel, *The Philosophy of History*, 86.

CHAPTER 21   SØREN KIERKEGAARD

1. See Bruce H. Kirmmse, "'Out with It!': The Modern Breakthrough, Kierkegaard and Denmark" in *The Cambridge Companion to Kierkegaard*, ed. Alastair Hannay and Gordon D. Marino (Cambridge: Cambridge University Press, 1998), 15–47.

2. See Roland Ruppenthal, "Denmark and the Continental System," *Journal of Modern History* 15, no.1 (March 1943): 7–23.

3. N. A. T. Hall, Maritime Maroons, " 'Grand Marronage' from the Danish West Indies," *The William Quarterly*, 3rd. series, 42 no. 4 (October 1985): 476–77.

4.   Albert G. Keller, "Notes on the Danish West Indies," *Annals of the American Academy of Political and Social Sciences* 22 (The United States and Latin America) (July 1903): 99–100.

5.   For a discussion of the role of these countries in European imperialism, see Glyndwr Williams, *The Expansion of Europe in the Eighteenth Century Overseas Rivalry, Discovery and Exploitation* (New York, N.Y.: Walker and Company, 1967).

6.   Robert L. Perkins, "Power, Politics, and Media Critique: Kierkegaard's First Brush with the Press," in *International Kierkegaard Commentary: Early Polemical Writings*, ed. Robert L. Perkins (Macon, Ga.: Mercer University Press, 1999), 27–28.

7.   Steven Best and Douglas Kellner, "Modernity, Mass Society and the Media: Reflections on the *Corsair Affair*," in *International Kierkegaard Commentary: The Corsair Affair*, ed. Robert L. Perkins (Macon, Ga.: Mercer University Press, 1990), 23.

8.   *The Corsair Affair*, 167–68.

9.   *The Corsair Affair*, 172.

10.   See the essay in Bibliotheca Kierkegaadiana by Karstein Hopland, "Passion (Lidenskab)," in *Some of Kierkegaard's Main Categories*, Marie Mikulová Thulstrup (Copenhagen: C.A. Reitzels Forlag, 1988), in *Bibliotheca Kierkegaadiana: Edenda Curaverunt*, Vol. 16, ed. Niels hgulstrup et, 80–93.

11.   Søren Kierkegaard, *The Two Ages: The Age of Revolution and the Present Age, a Literary Review*, Kierkegaard's Writings 14, ed. and trans. Howard V. Hong and Edna H. Hong (Princeton, N.J.: Princeton University Press, 1978), 61ff.

12.   *The Two Ages*, 68. Italics in the original.

13.   *The Two Ages*, 68–70.

14.   *The Two Ages*, 81–82.

15.   *The Two Ages*, 66.

16.   *The Two Ages*, 74–75.

17.   *The Two Ages*, 74.

18.   *The Two Ages*, 74.

19.   *The Two Ages*, 74.

20.   Alongside Kierkegaard's own explication in *Two Ages*, a fuller discussion of the role of envy in his thought can be found in Robert L. Perkins, "Envy as Personal Phenomenon and as Politics," in *International Kierkegaard Commentary: Two Ages*, ed. Robert L. Perkins (Macon, Ga.: Mercer University Press, 1984), 107–32.

21.   Perkins, "Envy," 81.

22.   Perkins, "Envy," 72ff.

23.   Perkins, "Envy," 84–85.

24.   Perkins, "Envy," 85.

25.   Søren Kierkegaard, *Works of Love: Some Christian Reflections in the Form of Discourses*, ed. and trans. Howard V. Hong and Edna H. Hong (New York, N.Y.: Harper and Brothers, 1962), 34–40.

26.   Kierkegaard, *Works of Love*, 46–57.

27.   Kierkegaard, *Works of Love*, 81–98.

28.   On this view of love see H. M. Kuitert, *Everything Is Politics but Politics Is Not Everything: A Theological Perspective on Faith and Politics*, trans. John Bowden (London: SCM Press, 1986), 128.

29. Søren Kierkegaard, *Attack Upon "Christendom,"* trans. Walter Lowrie (Princeton, N.J.: Princeton University Press, 1968).

30. Good background on this can be found in the two introductions by Walter Lowrie and Howard A. Johnson to their edition of the *Attack Upon "Christendom."*

31. Søren Kierkegaard, *The Point of View,* ed. and trans. Howard V. Hong and Edna H. Hong (1859; repr., Princeton, N.J.: Princeton University Press, 1998).

32. Kierkegaard, *The Point of View,* 463.

33. I do not have the space here to discuss in detail Kierkegaard's prescriptions for how one becomes a Christian in Christendom. The reader can find that in the last sections of *Concluding Unscientific Postscript to Philosophical Fragments,* Kierkegaard's Writings 12, ed. and trans. Howard V. Hong and Edna H. Hong (Princeton, N.J.: Princeton University Press, 1992) as well as in other writings such as his *Practice in Christianity,* Kierkegaard's Writings 20, ed. and trans. Howard V. Hong and Edna H. Hong (Princeton, N.J.: Princeton University Press, 1991).

34. Kierkegaard, *Attack,* 164–65.

35. Remarkably, a good example of this occurred in Denmark itself in 2005 when the Danish newspaper, the *Jyllands-Posten,* published twelve editorial cartoons depicting the Islamic prophet Muhammad. Islam forbids depictions of the prophet. The paper defended its actions by appealing to freedom of the press and claimed that it had sparked the debate in order to test Islam's capacity for self-criticism. The incident became an international crisis as major European newspapers reprinted the cartoons.

36. Kierkegaard, *Attack,* 132–33.

37. Kierkegaard, *Attack,* 128–29.

38. Kierkegaard, *Attack,* 172–73.

39. See Samuel P. Huntington, *Clash of Civilizations and the Remaking of the World Order* (New York, N.Y.: Simon and Schuster, 1998).

CHAPTER 22   FREDERICK DOUGLASS

This chapter has drawn material from Reginald F. Davis, *Frederick Douglass: A Precursor of Liberation Theology* (Macon, Ga.: Mercer University Press, 2005). Used by permission of the publisher.

1. Frederick Douglass to Thomas Auld, September 3, 1848, in *Anti-Slavery Bugle,* September 29, 1848.

2. Frederick Douglass, *My Bondage and My Freedom* (New York, N.Y.: Arno Press, 1969), 320.

3. Frederick Douglass, *The Life and Times of Frederick Douglass* (New York, N.Y.: Pathway, 1941), 139.

4. Frederick Douglass, "The Meaning of July 4th for the Negro," in *The Life and Writings of Frederick Douglass,* ed. Philip S. Foner (New York, N.Y.: International Publishers, 1972), 2:199.

5. Frederick Douglass, *Narrative of the Life of Frederick Douglass, an American Slave* (New York, N.Y.: Penguin Books, 1982), 153.

6. Douglass, *The Life and Times*, 285.

7. Benjamin E. Mays, *The Negro's God* (New York, N.Y.: Atheneum, 1969), 155.

8. "The Ladies," *North Star*, August 10, 1848 in Philip S. Foner, *Frederick Douglass on Women's Rights* (New York, N.Y.: Da Capo Press, 1992), 49. Address before Woman Suffrage Convention, n.d. in *Frederick Douglass on Women's Rights*, 125.

9. Foner, *Frederick Douglass on Women's Rights*, 159.

10. Foner, *Frederick Douglass on Women's Rights,* 41.

11. *Douglass' Monthly*, July 1859.

12. *North Star*, July 14, 1848.

13. James H. Cone, *A Black Theology of Liberation* (New York, N.Y.: Lippincott, 1970), 44.

14. James H. Cone, *God of the Oppressed* (New York, N.Y: Seabury Press, 1975), 268.

15. Cone, *God of the Oppressed*, 192.

16. William R. Jones, *Is God a White Racist? A Preamble to Black Theology* (Garden City, N.Y.: Anchor Press, 1973), 8.

17. Jones, *Is God?* 187.

18. James H. Cone, *Black Theology & Black Power* (1969; repr., Maryknoll, N.Y.: Orbis Books, 1997), 130.

19. Cone, *God of the Oppressed*, 51.

20. Gayraud S. Wilmore and James H. Cone, *Black Theology: A Documentary History, 1968–1979* (Maryknoll, N.Y.: Orbis Books, 1979), 136.

21. Cone, *Black Theology of Liberation*, 6.

22. Douglass, *The Life and Times*, 139.

CHAPTER 23 WILLIAM TEMPLE

1. Alan M. Suggate, *William Temple and Christian Social Ethics Today* (Edinburgh: T. & T. Clark, 1987).

2. P. J. Marshall, "1783–1870: An Expanding Empire," in *The Cambridge Illustrated History of the British Empire*, ed. P. J. Marshall (Cambridge: Cambridge University Press, 1996), 32.

3. Dane Kennedy, *Britain and Empire, 1880–1945* (London: Pearson Education Ltd., 2002), 9.

4. Marshall, "1783–1870: An Expanding Empire," 30.

5. On "Social imperialism" see B. Semmel, *Imperialism and Social Reform: English Social-Imperial Thought 1895–1914* (New York, N.Y.: Anchor Books, 1968).

6. Andrew Porter, "Empires in the Mind," in *The Cambridge Illustrated History of the British Empire*, 205–6.

7. Ibid., 206–9.

8. Roy Douglas, *Liquidation of Empire: The Decline of the British Empire* (New York, N.Y.: Palgrave Macmillan, 2002), 160.

9. George Orwell, *The Road to Wigan Pier*, 148, quoted in Douglas, *Liquidation of Empire*, 1.

10. Stephen Spencer, *William Temple: A Calling to Prophecy* (London: SPCK, 2001), 9.

11. Spencer, *William Temple*, 35.

12. See Temple's major philosophical-theological books, *Mens Creatrix* (1917), *Christus Veritas* (1924), and *Nature, Man, and God* (1934). See also John Macquarrie, "William Temple: Philosopher, Theologian, Churchman," in *Experiment of Life: Science and Religion*, ed. F. Kenneth Hare (Toronto: University of Toronto Press, 1983), 5.

13. Robert Craig, *Social Concern in the Thought of William Temple* (London: Victor Gollancz Ltd., 1963), 63.

14. William Temple, *Nature, Man, and God*. The Gifford Lectures, University of Glasgow, 1932–33 and 1933–34. (1934; repr., London: Macmillan, 1949), 478.

15. William Temple, *Christianity and Social Order* (New York, N.Y.: Penguin Books, 1942), ch. 5.

16. William Temple, *Christus Veritas* (1924; repr., London: Macmillan, 1954), 212.

17. William Temple, *Fellowship with God* (London: Macmillan, 1920), 141–42.

18. Wendy Dackson, *The Ecclesiology of Archbishop William Temple (1881–1944)* (Lewiston, Ont.: Edwin Mellen Press, 2004), 70ff.

19. William Temple, *Mens Creatrix* (London: Macmillan, 1917), 326.

20. Dackson, *The Ecclesiology*, 113.

21. William Temple, *Hope of a New World* (New York, N.Y.: Macmillan, 1924), 69.

22. Quoted in Charles W. Lowry, *William Temple: An Archbishop for All Seasons* (Washington, D.C.: University Press of America, 1982), 98.

23. Lowry, *William Temple*, 98.

24. Spencer, *William Temple*, 28–9.

25. William Temple, *Thoughts in War-Time* (London: Macmillan, 1940), 103; internal quotation, *Christus Veritas*, 254.

26. See Suggate, *William Temple and Christian Social Ethics Today*.

27. *Christianity and Social Order*, 15. Temple broadly practiced this belief throughout his life. See especially Spencer, *William Temple*.

28. William Temple, "The Chairman's Opening Address," in *Malvern, 1941: The Life of the Church and the Order of Society, Being the Proceedings of the Archbishop of York's Conference*. (London: Longmans Green, 1941); quoted in Spencer, *William Temple*, 69.

29. Spencer, *William Temple*, 5–6.

30. Nils Karlström, "Movements for International Friendship and Life and Work, 1910–1925," in *A History of the Ecumenical Movement, 1517–1948*, 4th ed., ed. Ruth Rouse and Stephen Charles Neill (London: SPCK, 1954); 540.

31. Temple, *Christianity and Social Order*, 75.

32. Temple, *Christianity and Social Order*, 16.

33. Spencer, *William Temple*, 104.

34. Karlström, "Movements for International Friendship," 523.

35. Willem Adolf Visser 't Hooft, "The Genesis of the World Council of Churches," in *A History of the Ecumenical Movement, 1517–1948*, 713.

36. See especially Temple's 1942 letter to philosopher Dorothy Emmett in F. A. Iremonger, *William Temple, Archbishop of Canterbury: His Life and Letters* (London: Oxford University Press, 1948), 537–38; and William Temple, "Theology To-Day," *Theology* 42 (November 1939), 326–33.

37. Cf. Kathryn Tanner, *Economy of Grace* (Minneapolis, Minn.: Fortress Press, 2005).

Chapter 24   Karl Barth

1. I am indebted to my colleague, Professor Ellen Babinsky, for guiding me to information related to the Accra conference, where she served as a delegate.

2. This citation is from the "mission session plenary report" of the conference. The full text of this report can be found at http://warc.jalb.de/warcajsp/news_file/doc-180-1.pdf.

3. Karl Barth, *Church Dogmatics*, 12 vols., ed. Geoffrey Bromiley and T. F. Torrance (Edinburgh: T. & T. Clark, 1956–1976), 3:4, 544. Hereafter abbreviated as "*CD*."

4. A wonderful chronology of Barth's life, with major events set in columns alongside his publications, corresponding historical events, and notable cultural occurrences and publications can be found in an appendix to Timothy Gorringe's *Karl Barth: Against Hegemony* (Oxford: Oxford University Press, 1999), 292–301.

5. For example, see George Hunsinger, ed., *Karl Barth and Radical Politics* (Philadelphia, Pa.: Westminster Press, 1976); Clifford Green, ed., *Karl Barth: Theologian of Freedom* (Minneapolis, Minn.: Fortress Press, 1991); John DeGruchy, *Liberating Reformed Theology: A South African Contribution to an Ecumenical Debate* (Grand Rapids, Mich.: Eerdmans, 1991); and Gorringe, *Karl Barth*. Agreeing that Barth's life was dedicated to the work of humanization, some American theologians have asked whether or not Barth's anti-hegemonic actions were "integral" or "incidental" to Barth's theology (see Joseph Bettis, "Political Theology and Social Ethics: The Socialist Humanism of Karl Barth," in *Jesus Christ and Radical Politics*, ed. George Hunsinger [Philadelphia, Pa.: Westminster Press, 1976], 159–79). We will revisit this matter later in the chapter.

6. The text of this lecture is printed in Hunsinger, *Jesus Christ and Radical Politics*, 19–45.

7. Gorringe, *Karl Barth*, 30–31, citing *K. Barth – R. Bultmann, Letters 1922–1966*, trans. G.W. Bromiley (Grand Rapids, Mich.: Eerdmans, 1981), 154.

8. Edward Fiske, "Karl Barth Dies in Basel; Protestant Theologian, 82," *New York Times*, December 11, 1968, 1.

9. I draw this last phrase from Paul Louis Metzger's helpful book, *The Word of Christ and the World of Culture* (Grand Rapids, Mich.: Eerdmans), 2003.

10. Wikipedia, "Social Democratic Party of Germany," at http://en.wikipedia.org/wiki/Social_Democratic_Party_of_Germany.

11. "Dr. Kapler, President of the Central Board of the German Evangelical Churches; Bishop Marahens (Lutheran) of Hannover; and Pastor Hesse of Elberfeld," cited in Trevor Hart, *Regarding Karl Barth* (Cumbria, U.K.: Paternoster Press, 1999), 144.

12. Hart, *Regarding Karl Barth*, 145. Citing *Theological Existence To-day*, trans. R. Birch Hoyle (London: Hodder and Stoughton, 1933), 23.

13. There were, of course, various approaches and proposed solutions to this so-called "Jewish question," ranging from assigning Jewish persons residing in Germany noncitizen status to annihilating them (the so-called "final solution").

14. Hart, *Regarding Karl Barth*, 146. Citing *Theological Existence To-day*, 52.

15. Hart, *Regarding Karl Barth*, 148.

16. Hart, *Regarding Karl Barth*, 148. Citing Eberhard Jüngel, *Christ, Justice, and Peace: Toward a Theology of the State in Dialogue with the Barmen Declaration*, trans. D. Bruce Hamill and Alan J. Torrance (Edinburgh: T. & T. Clark, 1992), 22.

17. For a full text of the Barmen Declaration, see *The Presbyterian Book of Confessions* (Louisville, Ky.: Office of the General Assembly, Presbyterian Publishing Corporation, 1999), 8.01-8.28, 247–50. Hart compares the preceding quotation from Jüngel with this same quotation from the Barmen Declaration, but uses a different translation.

18. Barmen Declaration, in *The Presbyterian Book of Confessions*, 8.15.

19. See "Barth Unsupported by Friends on Oath," *New York Times*, December 18, 1934, 8.

20. Gorringe, *Karl Barth*, 121.

21. Gorringe, *Karl Barth*, 121.

22. Fiske, "Karl Barth Dies," 1.

23. Matthew D. Hockenos, "The German Protestant Church and its Mission to the Jews after the Holocaust," June 2003, http://www.calvin.edu/academic/cas/akz/akz2306.htm.

24. Karl Barth, "The Church Between East and West," in Green, *Karl Barth*, 311.

25. Karl Barth, "No Christian Marshall Plan," *Christian Century*, December 8, 1948, 1330–33. *The Christian Century* here reprinted Barth's address, changing the title from "The World's Disorder and God's Design" (which was the theme of the conference). I am indebted to Don Compier for reminding me of Barth's influential role in the formative period of the World Council of Churches.

26. Green, *Karl Barth*, 309.

27. Green, *Karl Barth*, 313.

28. Sydney Gruson, "Karl Barth Tells Germans the 'American Way' Perils Souls More Than Reds Do," *New York Times*, January 19, 1959, 8. Gruson is here citing from Barth's "Letter to a Pastor in the German Democratic Republic," a pamphlet circulating in Germany at the time the article is written.

29. Gruson, "Karl Barth Tells," 8, emphasis added.

30. Joseph Bettis poses the question in these terms in his "Political Theology and Social Ethics," 161.

31. Bettis himself argues that Barth's radical life follows from his theology, but recognizes his argument as a minority view among "American theologians," who would understand Barth's political activities "as incidental to Barth's theological work." "Most . . . would say that Barth's theology has no direct political content," writes Bettis. "Or, they would say that Barth's social ethic is an absolutistic ethic, an eschatological ethic, suited for 'between the times,' but unsuited for providing any help in the hard political decisions of everyday life, " see ibid., 161.

32. *CD* 3:4, 544 (as cited earlier).

33. Reinhold Niebuhr went so far as to argue that Barth, in "protecting the truth of the gospel by separating it from all the disciples of culture and all the common experiences of our ethical life . . . has become irrelevant to all Christians in the Western world who believe in accepting common and collective responsibilities without illusion and without despair" (cited by Thomas E. McCollough in "Reinhold Niebuhr and Karl Barth on the Relevance of Theology," *Journal of Religion* 43, no. 1 [January 1963]: 49).

34. Here, Barth's realist conceptuality should be noted. His theological understanding all hinges on his conviction that there is a subject God who exists behind our reference to "God," a subject who reveals Godself to us.

35. Famously, Barth had a painting by Grünewald hanging above his office desk that

features John the Baptist pointing to Jesus, hanging on the cross. Barth said he hung the painting there to remind him that the focus of his theological work was not to direct others to himself, but to Christ.

36. *CD* 3:4, 4.

37. *CD* 3:4, 10.

38. *CD* 3:4, 10.

39. *CD* 3:4, 150.

40. See *CD* 3:4, §54, especially 149ff.

41. *CD* 3:4, 169.

42. *CD* 3:4, 170.

43. *CD* 3:4, 171.

44. William Werpehowski, "Command and History in the Ethics of Karl Barth" *Journal of Religious Ethics* 9 (Fall 1981): 302.

45. While the original source of this statement cannot here be documented, the statement is well-known and commonly cited among Barth scholars.

46. William C. Placher, *The Triune God: An Essay in Postliberal Theology* (Louisville, Ky.: Westminster John Knox Press, 2007), 23.

47. *CD* 2:2, 647.

48. *CD* 2:2, 647. Quoted by Werpehowski, "Command and History," 306.

49. *The New York Times*, 1968. Along the same lines, John H. Yoder dedicated a critical reading of Barth's ethics to Barth himself, commenting that the work should be "seen as a grateful tribute to the stature of a teacher who was above the need to want those who learned from him to become his disciples." See John H. Yoder, *Karl Barth and the Problem of War* (Nashville, Tenn.: Abingdon Press, 1970), 7–8.

50. See *CD* 4:2, 10.

51. See *CD* 2:1, §28.

52. *CD* 4:2, 6.

53. *CD* 4:2, 8.

54. See *CD* 4:1 and Philippians 2:7.

55. See *CD* 4:2 and Philippians 2:9.

56. As quoted earlier from Barth, *CD* 3:4, 544.

57. "*Ecclesia reformata, semper reformanda.*" The Reformed church has claimed this way of understanding itself since the sixteenth century.

58. For more on this, see Cynthia L. Rigby, "Mary and the Artistry of God," in *Blessed One: Protestant Perspectives on Mary*, ed. Beverly Roberts Gaventa and Cynthia L. Rigby (Louisville, Ky.: Westminster John Knox Press, 2003), 145–58.

59. See, in particular, *The Humanity of God* (Nashville: John Knox Press, 1960) and *CD* 4:1 (for discussion of why it matters that Christians confess that the fully divine one is fully human) and 4:2 (for discussion of why it matters that the fully divine one is fully human). Earlier in the writing of the *Church Dogmatics,* theologians had wondered if Barth would be successful in his plan to articulate the human side, as well as the divine side, of the divine/human dialectic. For example, see Paul Lehmann's *Forgiveness: A Decisive Issue in Protestant Thought* (Ann Arbor, Mich.: University Microfilms, 1941), written shortly after the publication of *CD* 1:1.

60. Helmut Gollwitzer makes this point well in "Why Black Theology?" *Union Seminary Quarterly Review* 31, no. 1 (Fall 1975): 54.

61. Ibid., 54, citing *Theologische Studien*, Heft 104 (1970): 44–45.

CHAPTER 25   HENDRIK KRAEMER

1. H. Colijn about his role in the "pacification" of Lombok in a letter to his wife in 1894. Cited in Geert Mak, *De Eeuw Van Mijn Vader* (Amsterdam: Atlas, 1999), 127. Unless otherwise indicated translations from Dutch to English are mine. After serving in the KNIL Colijn became CEO for Royal Dutch Shell, and succeeded Abraham Kuyper as leader of the (Christian) Anti-Revolutionary Party in 1922. He served as prime minister of the Netherlands five times between 1925 and 1939.

2. Carl F. Hallencreutz, *Kraemer Towards Tambaram: A Study in Hendik Kraemer's Missionary Approach*, English rev. ed., Studia Missionalia Upsaliensia 7 (Lund: Gleerup, 1966), 70–72.

3. Hallencreutz, *Kraemer Towards Tambaram,* 43–44.

4. M. R. Spindler, "Inleiding," in *Hendrik Kraemer: Bibliographie En Archief*, ed. Retnowinarti, M. Dirkzwager (Leiden, Netherlands: Interuniversitair Instituut voor Missiologie en Oecumenica, 1988), 4.

5. Edward W. Said, *Culture and Imperialism* (New York, N.Y.: Vintage Books, 1994).

6. We can already see this in the decision to send Kraemer to Java. The voices which shaped Kraemer's mission were not simply missionary leaders. Kraemer was supported by Alexander W. F. Idenburg, former governor-general of the East Indies and vice chairman of the Bible Society. Kraemer had beforehand consulted his mentor at Leiden University, the influential theologian Pierre D. Chantepie de la Saussaye, while the supervisor of his thesis on Javanese Islam was Leiden's professor of comparative religion Christiaan Snouck Hurgronje, the main architect of Dutch colonial policies regarding Islam in Indonesia. See Hallencreutz, *Kraemer Towards Tambaram*, 70–72.

7. Said already discusses Snouck Hurgronje's work as an example of Orientalism. See Said, *Orientalism*, 209–10. For a more extensive discussion of C. Snouck Hurgronje's involvement in Indonesia and Dutch colonial politics see Peter Van der Veer, *Modern Oriëntalisme Essays over De Westerse Beschavingsdrang*, Meulenhoff Editie (Amsterdam: Meulenhoff, 1995), 167–86.

8. Abraham Kuyper, *Ons Program* (Amsterdam: 1879). Quoted in Hallencreutz, *Kraemer Towards Tambaram*, 25.

9. Hallencreutz, *Kraemer Towards Tambaram*, 43.

10. Here I rely on Hallencreutz who refers to Kraemer's positive attitude towards Indonesian independence in a book review from his student days. See ibid., 155. The review is Hendrik Kraemer, "Soembangsih," *Eltheto* 73, no. 4 (1919): 112–19. Kraemer uses this phrase in a letter to L. J. van Wijk dated March 6, 1924, and quoted by Hallencreutz.

11. Hallencreutz, *Kraemer Towards Tambaram*, 161–64. See also Arend Theodoor Van Leeuwen, *Hendrik Kraemer: Dienaar Der Wereldkerk* (Amsterdam: W. ten Have, 1959), 25–30.

12. Hallencreutz, *Kraemer Towards Tambaram*, 130.

13. Hallencreutz, *Kraemer Towards Tambaram,* 130, n. 6. Hallencreutz quotes extensively from Kraemer's report on Sarekat Islam's program.

14. Karel A. Steenbrink, *Dutch Colonialism and Indonesian Islam: Contacts and Conflicts, 1596–1950,* Currents of Encounter, vol. 7, trans. Jan Steenbrink and Henry Jansen (Amsterdam: Rodopi, 1993), 111–12.

15. See Hallencreutz, *Kraemer Towards Tambaram,* 140–44.

16. Quoted in Steenbrink, *Dutch Colonialism,* 112.

17. Hendrik Kraemer, "Imperialism and Self-Expression," *The Student World* 28, no. 81 (1935): 334.

18. Hendrik Kraemer, Preface to *De Zending En Het Indonesisch Nationalisme,* J. A. Verdoorn (Amsterdam: Uitgeverij Vrij Nederland, 1945), ix.

19. Hendrik Kraemer, *The Christian Message in a Non-Christian World* (London: Edinburgh House Press, 1947), 203.

20. Kraemer, *The Christian Message,* 417.

21. Van Leeuwen, *Christianity in World History,* 137–40.

22. Hendrik Kraemer, *Het Raadsel Der Geschiedenis: Gedachten Uit Romeinen 9–11* ('s-Gravenhage: D.A. Daamen, 1941).

23. Johan M. Snoek, *De Nederlandse Kerken En De Joden, 1940–1945* (Kampen: J. H. Kok, 1990), 90.

24. Hendrik Kraemer, "Indië Een Nederlandse Waarde," in *Nederland, Erfdeel En Taak,* ed. Jacob van Gelderen (Amsterdam: Wereldbibliotheek, 1940), 115. This text was commissioned by the Central Board of Advice concerning the Education and Relaxation of Mobilized Soldiers, but the German defeat of the Netherlands in May 1940 prevented the completed text from being published until 1945.

25. Kraemer, *"Indië Een Nederlans Waarde,"* 126

26. Kraemer, *"Indië Een Nederlans Waarde,"* 135.

27. Kraemer, Preface to *De Zending En Het Indonesisch Nationalism,* ix.

28. Kraemer, *De Zending,* ix. Kraemer did not extend his argument to Africa, where he considered Western leadership a continued necessity.

29. Hendrik Kraemer, "Nederland in De Waagschaal," *Wending* 2, no. 7 (1947): 380.

30. For instance, the Sri Lankan theologian Ariarajah has accused Barth and Kraemer of causing an isolationist attitude among the churches of India. See Christine Lienemann-Perrin, "Catholicity and Inculturation," in *Reformed and Ecumenical: On Being Reformed in Ecumenical Encounters,* ed. Christine Lienemann-Perrin et al., Currents of Encounter, vol. 16 (Amsterdam: Rodopi, 2000), 77.

31. See M. M. Thomas, "An Assessment of Tambaram's Contribution to the Search of the Asian Churches for an Authentic Selfhood," *International Review of Mission* 77 (1988): 390–97. See also the chapter on M. M. Thomas in this volume.

32. M. M. Thomas, "The Absoluteness of Jesus Christ and Christ-Centered Syncretism," *Ecumenical Review* 37 (1985): 387–97.

33. See Jan Hendrik Pranger, *Dialogue in Discussion,* IIMO Research Publication (Utrecht-Leiden: Interuniversitair Instituut voor Missiologie en Oecumenica, 1994), 101–16.

34. Arend Theodoor Van Leeuwen, *Christianity in World History: the Meeting of the Faiths of East and West* (New York, N.Y.: Scribner, 1964).

35. For instance see Hendrik Kraemer, "Een Gewichtig Probleem," *Eltheto* 69, no. 20 (1915): 151–57; "Het Boek Van De Kat Angelino," *De Opwekker* 77, no. 3 (1932): 86–179; Review of *Het Nationalisme Als Zedelijk Vraagstuk* by E. A. A. Vreede, *De Opwekker* 77, no. 8 (1932): 388–400.

36. For instance, see "thus the superiority of Westerners cannot be a narcotic to drug themselves with, nor a banner to fly in one's own honor, but a categorical imperative that inspires and admonishes," in Hendrik Kraemer, *Rede, Uitgesproken in De Algemeene Vergadering Van Het Nederlandsch Bijbelgenootschap Op Donderdag 21 Juni 1928 in De Doopsgezinde Kerk Te Amsterdam* (Amsterdam: Nederlandsch bijbelgenootschap, 1928), 15.

37. Kraemer, "Imperialism and Self-Expression," 330–31.

38. Kraemer, *World Cultures and World Religions: the Coming Dialogue*, 74.

39. Kraemer, "Oost En West," 145.

40. Kraemer wrote of Oriental scholarship that "in the future . . . there will no doubt be admiration for this restless study of the languages, literatures, religions and cultures of the East, for these determined attempts to disinterested understanding of these alien spiritual worlds." Kraemer, "Oost En West," 141–42.

41. Kraemer's interest in this issue dated back at least to 1914 when he first read an analysis of the Christian influence on the nineteenth-century Hindu reformers by the German missionary Hilko Schomerus. See Hallencreutz, *Kraemer Towards Tambaram*, 68.

42. Kraemer, "Imperialism and Self-Expression," 335–36.

43. Hendrik Kraemer, "Het Eenig-Toelaatbare Experiment," *De Stuw* 3 (1932) 18: 219–23. Quoted in Van der Veer, *Modern Oriëntalisme Essays*, 193.

44. Hendrik Kraemer, *De Strijd over Bali En De Zending: Een Studie En Een Appèl* (Amsterdam: H. J. Paris, 1933).

45. Van der Veer, *Modern Oriëntalisme Essays*, 194–95.

46. Kraemer, *De Strijd over Bali En De Zending: Een Studie En Een Appèl*, 61–62. Hereafter page references will be given in parenthesis in the text.

47. Kraemer, *The Christian Message*, 140.

48. Said, *Orientalism*.

49. Kraemer, "Imperialism and Self-Expression," 333.

Chapter 26   Reinhold Niebuhr

1. Reinhold Niebuhr, "Ten Years That Shook My World," *The Christian Century* 56, no. 17 (April 26, 1939): 542.

2. *Moral Man and Immoral Society* (1932), *The Children of Light and the Children of Darkness* (1944), *Faith and History* (1949), and *The Self and the Dramas of History* (1955).

3. Materials for this section, "Context," are drawn freely from my introduction to Niebuhr in Larry L. Rasmussen, ed., *Reinhold Niebuhr: Theologian of Public Life* (Minneapolis, Minn.: Fortress Press, 1991), 1–41.

4. Langdon Gilkey, *On Niebuhr: A Theological Study* (Chicago, Ill.: University of Chicago Press, 2001); Langdon Gilkey, "Reinhold Niebuhr's Theology of History," in Nathan A. Scott, *The Legacy of Reinhold Niebuhr* (Chicago, Ill.: University of Chicago

Press, 1975), 36–62; Reinhold Niebuhr, *The Structure of Nations and Empires* (New York, N.Y.: Charles Scribner's Sons, 1959).

5. Niebuhr, *The Structure of Nations and Empires*, 1.

6. Gilkey, "Reinhold Niebuhr's Theology of History," 45.

7. Gilkey, "Reinhold Niebuhr's Theology of History," 45.

8. Gilkey, "Reinhold Niebuhr's Theology of History," 46.

9. Reinhold Niebuhr, *The Nature and Destiny of Man*, vol. 2 (New York, N.Y.: Charles Scribner's Sons, 1943), 80.

10. Gilkey, "Reinhold Niebuhr's Theology of History," 46.

11. Reinhold Niebuhr, *An Interpretation of Christian Ethics* (New York, N.Y.: Meridian Books, 1963), 97–98.

12. Gilkey, "Reinhold Niebuhr's Theology of History," 55–56.

13. Gilkey, "Reinhold Niebuhr's Theology of History," 52.

14. Reinhold Niebuhr, *The Irony of American History* (1952; repr., New York: Charles Scribner's Sons, 1962), passim.

15. Niebuhr, *The Irony of American History*, 3.

16. Reinhold Niebuhr, "Russia and the West," *Nation* 156, January 16 and 23, 1943, 82–83, as exerpted in Charles C. Brown, *Niebuhr and His Age: Reinhold Niebuhr's Prophetic Role and Legacy* (Harrisburg, Pa.: Trinity Press International, 2002), 11.

17. Niebuhr, *The Irony of American History*, 2.

18. Reinhold Niebuhr, *Moral Man and Immoral Society* (New York, N.Y.: Charles Scribner's Sons, 1932), 164.

19. Niebuhr, *Moral Man*, xxiii.

20. Niebuhr, *An Interpretation of Christian Ethics*, 114.

21. Reinhold Niebuhr, *The Children of Light and the Children of Darkness* (New York, N.Y.: Charles Scribner's Sons, 1944), xiii.

22. Niebuhr, *Moral Man*, 64.

23. Reinhold Niebuhr, "Awkward Imperialists," *Atlantic Monthly* 145 (May 1930): 670–75. Page references to this essay are given in parentheses in the text. Readers can locate the full text on the following website: www.theatlantic.com/ideastour/idealism/niebuhr-full.mhtml.

24. Text cited from *The New Mexican*, October 15, 2006: B2.

25. Douglas John Hall, *Lighten Our Darkness: Toward an Indigenous Theology of the Cross* (Philadelphia, Pa: Westminster Press, 1976). See especially chapter 3, "The Official Religion of the Officially Optimistic Society," 73–106.

26. As cited by George Packer in "Fighting Faiths," *New Yorker*, July 10 and 17, 2006, 97.

27. Peter Beinart, as cited by Joe Klein in "The Truman Show," *New York Times Book Review*, June 11, 2006, 12. Klein is reviewing Peter Beinart, *The Good Fight* (San Francisco, Calif.: HarperCollins Publishers, 2006).

28. John C. Bennett, *The Radical Imperative: From Theology to Social Ethics* (Philadelphia, Pa.: Westminster Press, 1975).

CHAPTER 27   DIETRICH BONHOEFFER

1. The postdoctoral dissertation required by German universities to qualify for a permanent teaching position.

2. Dietrich Bonhoeffer, *Dietrich Bonhoeffer Works*, vol. 1, *Sanctorum Communio: A Theological Study of the Sociology of the Church*, trans. Reinhard Kraus and Nancy Lukens (Minneapolis, Minn.: Fortress Press, 1998), 118.

3. Dietrich Bonhoeffer, *Dietrich Bonhoeffer Works,* 1:189.

4. Dietrich Bonhoeffer, *Letters and Papers from Prison*. Enlarged ed. (New York, N.Y.: Macmillan, 1972), 382.

5. Dietrich Bonhoeffer, *Dietrich Bonhoeffer Works*, vol. 6, *Ethics*, trans. Reinhard Kraus, Charles C. West, and Douglas W. Stott (Minneapolis, Minn.: Fortress Press, 2005), 70.

6. Dietrich Bonhoeffer, *Dietrich Bonhoeffer Works*, vol.16, *Conspiracy and Imprisonment 1940–1945*, trans. Lisa E. Dahil (Minneapolis, Minn.: Fortress Press, 2006), 527.

7. Bonhoeffer, *Ethics*, 99.

8. Dietrich Bonhoeffer, *Dietrich Bonhoeffer Works*, vol. 4, *Discipleship*, trans. Geffrey B. Kelly and John D. Godsey (Minneapolis, Minn.: Fortress Press, 2003), 106.

9. Bonhoeffer, *Letters and Papers from Prison*, 17.

10. Dietrich Bonhoeffer, *Dietrich Bonhoeffer Werke*, vol. 13, *London 1933–1935* (Gütersloh: Kaiser, 1994), 411.

CHAPTER 28   SIMONE WEIL

1. This is my translation of the French text, "Qui est déraciné déracine. Qui est enraciné ne déracine pas." Simone Weil, *L'enracinement* (Paris: Gallimard, 1950), 49.

2. Weil used the term Annamites or Indochinese to refer to the Vietnamese. For biographical information see Simone Pétrement, *Simone Weil: A Life* (New York, N.Y.: Pantheon, 1976) and J. P. Little, *Simone Weil: Waiting on Truth* (Oxford: Berg Women's Series, 1988).

3. This is asserted by her biographers (ibid.) and evidenced in their correspondence (see Richard Rhees, *Simone Weil: Seventy Letters* [London: Oxford University Press, 1965]). André became a famous mathematician and for many years worked at the Institute for Advanced Studies at Princeton. He also took great care in supervising the translations of his sister's work (see Desmond Avery, "Simone Weil, philosopher, according to André Weil, mathematician, in 50 unpublished letters to Richard Rees, editor," *Cahiers Simone Weil* 29:3 [September 2006], 309–12).

4. The issue of her relationship to Judaism has been a longstanding concern in Weilian scholarship. See Thomas Nevin, *Simone Weil: Portrait of a Self-Exiled Jew* (Chapel Hill, N.C.: University of North Carolina Press, 1991); Florence deLussy "L'antijudaïsme de Simone Weil," *Simone Weil Œuvres* (Paris: Quarto Galllimard, 1999), 957–1016; and Emmanuel Levinas, "Simone Weil contre la Bible," *Évidences* 24 (1952), 9.

5. Weil, *Need for Roots*, 3–6.

6. Simone Weil, *Waiting for God* (New York, N.Y.: Perennial Classics, 2001), 85.

7. Weil, *Waiting for God*, 22 and 24.

8. Weil, *Waiting for God,* 6.

9.   The first was an article she read by Louis Roubaud in *Le Petit Parisien* that exposed the Yen Bay massacre in Indochina. The second was her experience of the 1931 "Colonial Exhibition" in Paris, a type of "World's Fair," the purpose of which was to highlight the achievements of France's colonies. J. P. Little, *Simone Weil on Colonialism: An Ethic of the Other* (Oxford: Rowman and Littlefield, 2003), 7.

10.   Little, *Simone Weil on Colonialism*, 29–30.

11.   Little, *Simone Weil on Colonialism*, 48.

12.   Simone Weil, *Letter to a Priest* (New York, N.Y.: Penguin, 2003), 32.

13.   Little, *Simone Weil on Colonialism,* 46.

14.   Weil, *Need for Roots,* 229.

15.   Christine Ann Evans, "The Nature of Narrative in Simone Weil's Vision of History: The Need for New Historical Roots," in *The Beauty that Saves*, ed. John M. Dunaway (Macon, Ga.: Mercer University Press, 1996), 56.

16.   Weil, *Need for Roots*, 229.

17.   Weil, *Letter to a Priest*, 47.

18.   Weil, *Letter to a Priest*, 78.

19.   Little, *Simone Weil on Colonialism*, 63.

20.   Simone Weil, *Oppression and Liberty* (Amherst, Mass.: University of Massachusetts Press, 1973), 69.

21.   Simone Weil, *Œuvres Complètes 6 2 Cahiers* (Paris: Gallimard, 1997), 255, 285. Thucydides's words are the following: "For of the gods we believe, and of men we know, that by a law of their nature they rule wherever they can. This law was not made by us, and we are not the first who have acted upon it; we did but inherit it, and shall bequeath it to all time, and we know that you and all mankind, if you were as strong as we are, would do as we do." (Thucydides, *History of the Peloponnesian War* [Oxford: Clarendon Press, 1900], 5.105.2.)

22.   Weil, *Oppression and Liberty*, 67.

23.   Weil, *Need for Roots*, 96. I use the newer translation by Little, *Simone Weil on Colonialism*, 125.

24.   Weil, *Waiting for God*, 37.

25.   Simone Weil, *Intimations of Christianity among the Ancient Greeks* (London: Routledge, 1987), 136.

26.   Weil, *Need for Roots*, 7.

27.   Ibid., 132.

28.   Weil, *Waiting for God*, 11.

29.   Little, *Simone Weil on Colonialism*, 63.

30.   Weil, *Intimation of Christianity,* 86.

31.   Little, *Simone Weil on Colonialism,* 94.

32.   Evans, "The Nature of Narrative," 63.

33.   Weil, *Need for Roots,* 144.

34.   Weil, *Need for Roots,* 229.

35.   Weil, *Oppression and Liberty*, 73.

36.   In this regard, Weil noted the absurdity of having Indochinese children learn the history of France as if it were their own (Little, *Simone Weil on Colonialism*, 78, 94).

37. Little, *Simone Weil on Colonialism*, 52.

38. Little, *Simone Weil on Colonialism*, 111.

39. Little, *Simone Weil on Colonialism*, 115.

40. Weil, *Need for Roots*, 232.

41. Weil, *Oppression and Liberty*, 78.

42. Little, *Simone Weil on Colonialism*, 112.

43. Weil, *Intimations of Christianity*, 86, and *Oppression and Liberty*, 103.

44. Weil, *Need for Roots,* 168. I have used the newer translation by Little, *Simone Weil on Colonialism*, 124.

45. Little, *Simone Weil on Colonialism*, 115.

46. Weil, *Letter to a Priest,* 46.

47. Weil, *Letter to a Priest,* 33. She elaborated: "The missionaries—even the martyrs amongst them—are too closely accompanied by guns and battleships for them to be true witnesses of the Lamb."

48. A more recent example of this type of theology may be found in the thinking of the Dalai Lama or Mother Teresa. The latter characterized the task of the Christian as helping "a Hindu become a better Hindu, a Muslim become a better Muslim, a Catholic become a better Catholic." EWTN Global Catholic Network http://www.ewtn.com/motherteresa/words.html.

Chapter 29   M. M. Thomas

1. For a creative discussion on the differences between nationalism, nativism, and hybridism in the Asian context see Kuan-Hsing Chen, "The Decolonization Question," in *Trajectories: Inter-Asian Cultural Studies*, ed. Kuan-Hsing Chen, Hsiu-Ling Kuo, Hans Hang, and Hsu Ming-Chu (London: Routledge, 1998), 1–53.

2. T. M. Philip, *The Encounter Between Theology and Ideology: An Exploration of the Communicative Theology of M. M. Thomas* (Madras: CLS, 1986), 8–9.

3. Robyn Boyd, *An Introduction to Indian Christian Theology* (Madras: CLS, 1969), 330.

4. M. M. Thomas, "Introduction" in M. M. Thomas and P. T. Thomas, *Towards an Indian Christian Theology: Life and Thought of Some Pioneers* (Tiruvalla: New Day Publications of India, 1992), 1.

5. Philip, *The Encounter between Theology and Ideology,* 30.

6. For an interesting though limited appraisal of M. M. Thomas's uncritical acceptance of the divine providence that undergirds some aspects of British imperialism in India, see R. S. Sugirtharajah, *Postcolonial Reconfigurations: An Alternative Way of Reading the Bible and Doing Theology* (London: SCM Press, 2003), 154–56.

7. T. Jacob Thomas, ed., *M. M. Thomas Reader: Selected Texts on Theology, Religion and Society* (Tiruvalla: CSS, 2002), 44.

8. M. M. Thomas, *Salvation and Humanization* (Madras: CLS, 1971), 4.

9. M. M. Thomas, ("The Christian Contribution to an Indian Philosophy of Being and Becoming Human,") *The Church's Mission and Post-Modern Humanism* (Tiruvalla: CSS, 1996).

10. M. M. Thomas, *Acknowledged Christ of the Indian Renaissance* (London: SCM Press, 1969).

11. M. M. Thomas, *Man and the Universe of Faiths* (Bangalore: CISRS, 1975); and *The Secular Ideologies of India and the Secular Meaning of Christ* (Bangalore: CISRS, 1976).

12. M. M. Thomas, *Risking Christ for Christ's Sake* (Geneva: World Council of Churches, 1987), 119.

13. Wendy Doniger, "A View from the Other Side: Postcolonialism, Religious Syncretism, and Class Conflict," in *Popular Christianity in India: Riting between the Lines*, ed. Selva J. Raj and Corinne G. Dempsey (Albany, N.Y.: State University of New York Press, 2002), xii and xiii.

14. For an excellent critical summation of M. M. Thomas's writings see Hielke Wolters, *Theology of Participation: M. M. Thomas' Concept of Salvation and the Collective Struggle for Fuller Humanity in India* (Delhi, ISPCK, 1996).

15. Simone de Beauvoir, *The Ethics of Ambiguity* (1948; repr., Secaucus, N.J.: Carol Publishing Group, 1997), 156.

Chapter 30 Juan Luis Segundo

1. Alfred Hennelly, *Theologies in Conflict* (Maryknoll, N.Y.: Orbis Books, 1979), 2. These biographical data are also drawn from Theresa Lowe Ching, *Efficacious Love in the Theology of Juan Luis Segundo* (Lanham, Md.: University Press of America, 1989). The two theses were *Berdiaeff: Une réflexion chrétienne sur la personne* (Paris: Montaigne, 1963) and *La cristiandad, una utopia?: I. Los hechos; II. Los principios* (Montevideo: Mimeográfica "Luz," 1964). The second of the theses was directed by Paul Ricoeur.

2. "Pastoral Constitution on the Church in the Modern World," *Vatican Council II: Constitutions, Decrees, Declarations,* ed. by Austin Flannery (Northport, N.Y.: Costello Publishing Company, 1996), 163–282.

3. Juan Luis Segundo, *Signs of the Times: Theological Reflections*, ed. Alfred T. Hennelly (Maryknoll, N.Y.: Orbis Books, 1993), 69.

4. Hennelly, *Theologies in Conflict*, 50.

5. Segundo, *Berdiaeff*.

6. Juan Luis Segundo, *Existentialismo, philosofia y poesia: Ensayo de sintesis* (Buenos Aires: Espasa-Calpe, 1948).

7. Juan Luis Segundo, *Concepción Christiana delhombre* (Montevideo: Mimeográfica "Luz," 1964).

8. Pierre Teilhard de Chardin, *Activation of Energy* (New York, N.Y.: Harcourt, Brace, 1971), 73–74, cited by Juan Luis Segundo, *The Community Called Church* (Maryknoll, N.Y.: Orbis Books, 1973), 121.

9. Juan Luis Segundo, *Grace and the Human Condition* (Maryknoll, N.Y.: Orbis Books, 1973), 44.

10. Juan Luis Segundo, *The Humanist Christology of Paul* (Maryknoll, N.Y.: Orbis Books, 1986).

11. Juan Luis Segundo, *Our Idea of God* (Maryknoll, N.Y.: Orbis Books, 1974), 92–

93. Note that the world also conceals God's presence, veils it beneath negative forces of death. One needs at this point an analysis of negative experiences of contrast that in their reaction against negativity also point to a source that validates such resistance.

12. Segundo, *God*, 133, 130, respectively.

13. Segundo, *God*, 76, 78.

14. The two volumes are *The Historical Jesus of the Synoptics* (Maryknoll, N.Y.: Orbis Books, 1985) and *The Christ of the Ignatian Exercises* (Maryknoll, N.Y.: Orbis Books, 1987). The relevant section in the second volume is chapter 1 entitled "Jesus and God: Approach to the Council of Chalcedon."

15. Segundo, *Jesus*, 88.

16. Segundo, *Jesus*, 139.

17. Segundo, *Jesus*, 148–149. The emphasis is Segundo's.

18. Segundo, *Christ*, 24, 26, 27, respectively.

19. Segundo, *Christ*, 40.

20. Segundo, *Church*, 3. This ecclesiology is supplemented by Segundo, *The Hidden Motives of Pastoral Action: Latin American Reflections* (Maryknoll, N.Y.: Orbis Books, 1978).

21. Segundo, *Church*, 60. The Teilhardian evolutionary worldview is evident in this formula.

22. Segundo, *Church*, 53. When charged with "elitism," Segundo does not completely reject the idea. But this is not an elitism in the ordinary sense of privilege, nor one based on esoteric knowledge. If it be elitism, it is one open to all who commit themselves to gospel values.

23. Segundo, *Hidden Motives*. Segundo's theology of the sacraments proposes an ecclesiological understanding closely linked to the mission of the church; the sacraments nurture Christian life engaged in society. Juan Luis Segundo, *The Sacraments Today* (Maryknoll, N. Y.: Orbis Books, 1974).

24. Segundo, *God*, 44. See also, for example, Segundo, *Grace*, 43–46, and 82–86. For a larger account of this spirituality as the project of freedom in history see Segundo, *Christ*, 44–124; Juan Luis Segundo, "Ignatius Loyola: Trial or Project?" in *Signs of the Times: Theological Reflections*, ed. Alfred T. Hennelly (Maryknoll, N. Y.: Orbis Books, 1993), 149–75.

25. Juan Luis Segundo, *Evolution and Guilt* (Maryknoll, N.Y.: Orbis Books, 1974), 126–27.

26. Segundo, *God*, 23. The process as Segundo characterizes it is neither automatic nor progressive, because it is in the hands of freedom; nor is it visible. But it transpires where love is efficacious and will appear in the end time.

27. Segundo, *Grace*, 71. "To put it in other words, we must reunite eternal life and the construction of history. Eternal life is *the new earth*." Ibid., 72.

28. Segundo, *Grace*, 73.

29. Segundo, *Paul*, 124. Also, 157.

30. See Segundo, *Signs of the Times*, 73–80.

31. In an interview with Elsa Tamez found in *Against Machismo*, ed. Elsa Tamez (Oak Park, Ill.: Meyer Stone Books, 1987), 3–10.

32. Tamez, *Against Machismo*, 6–7.

33. Tamez, *Against Machismo*, 4–5. In Tamez's view, the main contribution that Segundo makes to feminist liberation theology lies in the area of hermeneutical theory, but in fact he adds little to the work of Elisabeth Schüssler Fiorenza.

34. This is the thesis of Frances Stefano, *The Absolute Value of Human Action in the Theology of Juan Luis Segundo* (Lanham, Md.: University Press of America, 1992).

CHAPTER 31   JOHN S. MBITI

1. John S. Mbiti, *African Religions and Philosophy* (Garden City, N.Y.: Anchor Books, 1969), 253–54. Hereafter page references to this book are given in parentheses in the text.

2. V. Y. Mudimbe, *The Invention of Africa: Gnosis, Philosophy, and the Order of Knowledge* (Bloomington, Ind.: Indiana University Press, 1988), 5.

3. Ibid., 3, 20, 4; Samir Amin, *L'Accumulation à l'échelle mondiale* (Paris: Anthropos, 1974). Translated as *Accumulation on a World Scale: A Critique of the Theory of Underdevelopment*, trans. Brian Pearce (New York: Monthly Review, 1974), 377.

4. Bernard-Henri Lévy, *War, Evil, and the End of History*, trans. C. Mandell (Hoboken, N.J.: Melville House Publishing, 2004), 3–6.

5. Indeed, the disease complex can be theologically imagined as a kind of demonic force raging uncontained inside the late capitalist forces of globalization that have shattered traditional village networks into an impossible two-step, in which nomadic male workers gravitate to cities in search of jobs while trying to support rural families living long distances away. In such a situation of separation, infection rates sky-rocket as males seek out urban prostitutes and then spread the disease in periodic visits home.

6. John S. Mbiti, "The Encounter of Christian Faith and African Religion," *Christian Century*, August 27-September 3, 1980, 818; Mbiti, *African Religions*, 253–54.

7. Mbiti, *African Religions*, 8–19, 363; John S. Mbiti, *New Testament Eschatology in an African Background: A Study of the Encounter between New Testament Theology and African Traditional Concepts* (Oxford: Oxford University Press, 1971), 189.

8. Mbiti, *New Testament Eschatology*, 188.

9. John S. Mbiti, "African Religion and World Order," in *Toward a Global Civilization? The Contribution of Religions*, ed. Patricia M. Mische and Melissa Merkling (New York N.Y.: Peter Lang Publishing, Inc., 2001), 370.

10. Cf. comments under the name of NeterHeru, in Assata Shakur Forum entitled "Role of Women in African Traditional Religion," 8-20-2004, http://www.assatashakur.org/forum/showthread.php?t=78.

11. NeterHeru, "Role of Women."

12. Luke Lungile Pato, "Indigenization and Liberation: A Challenge to Theology in the Southern African Context," *Journal of Theology for Southern Africa* 99 (November 1997): 41; John S. Mbiti, "An African Views American Black Theology," in *Black Theology: A Documentary History, 1966–1979*, ed. Gayraud S. Wilmore and James H. Cone (Maryknoll, N.Y.: Orbis Books, 1979), 481; James H. Cone, "A Black American Perspective on the Future of African Theology," in ibid., 494.

13. Pato, "Indigenization and Liberation," 41.

14. James Cone, *God of the Oppressed* (New York, N.Y.: Seabury Press, 1975), 95.

15. Jean-Marc Ela, *African Cry* (Maryknoll, N.Y.: Orbis Books, 1986), 148; Pato, "Indigenization and Liberation," 42.

16. Ela, *African Cry,* 102.

17. Engelbert Mveng, "Third World Theology—What Theology? What Third World?: Evaluation by an African Delegate," in *Irruption of the Third World: Challenge to Theology,* ed. Virginia Fabella and Sergio Torres (Maryknoll, N.Y.: Orbis Books, 1983), 220; Pato, "Indigenization and Liberation," 42.

18. Mveng, "Third World Theology," 220; Pato, "Indigenization and Liberation," 43.

19. Pato, "Indigenization and Liberation," 43.

20. Pato, "Indigenization and Liberation," 43.

21. The reference here is to critical theories seeking to develop concepts that pay attention to very subtle, "micrologic" structures of domination.

22. Mbiti, *New Testament Eschatology,* 57; Mbiti, *African Religions,* 35, 283, 306–7.

23. Souleymane Bachir Diagne, "On Prospective Development and a Political Culture of Time," *Africa Development* 29, no. 1 (2004): 62.

24. Daniel Smith, "Time and Not the Other Time in Africa: On Ernest Beyaraza: The African Concept of Time: A Comparative Study of Various Theories," *Forum for Intercultural Philosophy* 3 (2001): http://lit.polylog.org/3/rsd-en.htm, 2.

25. Moses Òkè, "From an African Ontology to an African Epistemology: A Critique of J. S. Mbiti on the Time Conception of Africans," *Quest: An African Journal of Philosophy* 18 (2004): 25–36. See http://www.quest-journal.net.

26. Cf. critical theory concepts like Antonio Gramsci's "hegemony," underscoring the way power seeks to secure consent by co-opting gestures of resistance or amalgamating diverse political orientations and class interests; in Antonio Gramsci, *Prison Notebooks* (New York, N.Y.: Columbia University Press, 1992), 12–13, 53–56, 80, 128. Cf. also Stuart Hall's "articulation theory," highlighting the way different discourses and practices are brought into a reciprocal, though often oblique, operation, in Stuart Hall, "Race, Articulation, and Societies Structured in Dominance," in *Race Critical Theories: Text and Context,* ed. Philomena Essed and David Theo Goldberg (Malden, Mass.: Blackwell Publishers, 2002), 42–44.

27. A play on the idea of New World escaped slaves in the Caribbean called "maroons" (from the Spanish word, *cimaroon,* for domesticated animals or slaves that have gone free) and Michael Jackson's famous "moon-walk" dance step.

28. Cf. the work of scholars like William Herzog on readings of Paul in his Roman imperial context—a context that frequently imprisoned him and his followers and by 64 C.E. had outlawed Christianity itself—in a talk quoted in James W. Perkinson, *Shamanism, Racism, and Hip-Hop Culture: Essays on White Supremacy and Black Subversion* (New York, N.Y.: Palgrave Macmillan, 2005), 208.

29. Perkinson, *Shamanism,* 85–116.

30. Cf. Kristin Hunter Lattany, "'Off-timing': Stepping to the Different Drummer," *Lure and Loathing: Essays on Race, Identity, and the Ambivalence of Assimilation,* ed. Gerald Early (New York, N.Y.: Penguin Books, 1994), 163–74.

31. Cf. David Lan, *Guns & Rain: Guerillas and Spirit Mediums in Zimbabwe* (Berkeley, Calif.: University of California Press, 1985), xiii, 3, 128, 146.

32. Cf. especially chapter 5 in Paul Gilroy, *There Ain't No Black in the Union Jack: The Cultural Politics of Race and Nation* (London: Hutchinson, 1987; Chicago: University of Chicago Press, 1991).

33. Cf. the *New York Times* account of the Moken—the hunter-gatherer "sea gypsies" off the coast of Thailand and Burma who survived the 2004 tsunami by reading the behavior of the sea and fleeing to high ground in "Sea Gypsies See Signs in the Waves," *New York Times*, December 25, 2005, section A.

34. Cf. Marshall Sahlins, "The Original Affluent Society," in *Limited Wants, Unlimited Means: A Reader on Hunter-Gatherer Economics and the Environment,* ed. John Gowdy (Washington, D.C.: Island Press, 1998), 5–41.

35. Cf. works like those of Sahlins, Daniel Quinn, *Ishmael* (New York, N.Y.: Bantam/Turner Books, 1992); Paul Shepard, *The Tender Carnivore and the Sacred Game* (Athens, Ga.: University of Georgia Press, 1998); *Coming Home to the Pleistocene,* ed. Florence R. Shepard (Washington, D.C.: Island Press/Shearwater Books, 1998); and John Zerzan, *Elements of Refusal* (Columbia, Mo.: C.A.L. Press/Paleo Editions, 1999).

36. Òkè, "From an African Ontology to an African Epistemology," 31.

37. A reference to the politics of witchcraft discourse in many African societies that "explains" harm as resulting from human conscious or unconscious intentionality to consume the substance of others, often through mobilizing a toxin, poison, or curse. See also the work of Elias Kifon Bongmba, *African Witchcraft and Otherness: A Philosophical and Theological Critique of Intersubjective Relations* (New York, N.Y.: State University of New York Press, 2001), 20, 26–29; and Cécé Kolié, "Jesus as Healer?" in *Faces of Jesus in Africa*, ed. Robert J. Schreiter (Maryknoll, N.Y.: Orbis Books, 1991), 136, 138, 145–46.

CHAPTER 32   MERCY AMBA ODUYOYEE

1. This is a revised version of an article that was first published as "Mercy Amba Oduyoye and African Women's Theology," *Journal of Feminist Studies in Religion* 20, no. 1 (2004): 7–22.

2. For Oduyoye's life history, see Mercy Amba Oduyoye, *Beads and Strands: Reflections of an African Woman on Christianity in Africa* (Maryknoll, N.Y.: Orbis Books, 2004), xi–xiv.

3. Musimbi R. A. Kanyoro, "Beads and Strands: Threading More Beads in the Story of the Circle," in *African Women, Religion, and Health: Essays in Honor of Mercy Amba Ewudziwa Oduyoye*, ed. Isabel Apawo Phiri and Sarojina Nadar (Maryknoll, N.Y.: Orbis Books, 2006), 19–42.

4. Mercy Amba Oduyoye, *Introducing African Women's Theology* (Cleveland, Ohio: The Pilgrim Press, 2001), 38.

5. Mercy Oduyoye, *Who Will Roll the Stone Away? The Ecumenical Decade of the Churches in Solidarity with Women* (Geneva: World Council of Churches, 1990)

6. Elizabeth Amoah, Preface, in *African Women, Religion, and Health*, xxi.

7. Edward W. Said, *Orientalism* (New York, N.Y.: Vintage, 1978).

8. Frantz Fanon, *Black Skin, White Masks*, trans. Charles Lam Markmann (New York, N.Y.: Grove, 1967).

9. Emmanuel Martey, *African Theology: Inculturation and Liberation* (Maryknoll, N.Y.: Orbis, 1993).

10. See "African Report," in *Third World Theologies: Commonalities and Divergences*, ed. K. C. Abraham (Maryknoll, N.Y.: Orbis Books, 1990), 44.

11. See Kwok Pui-lan, "Unbinding Our Feet: Saving Brown Women and Feminist Religious Discourse," in *Postcolonialism, Feminism, and Religious Discourse*, ed. Laura E. Donaldson and Kwok Pui-lan (New York, N.Y.: Routledge, 2002), 64–69.

12. Mercy Amba Oduyoye, "Feminism: A Pre-Condition for a Christian Anthropology," *Africa Theological Journal* 11, no. 3 (1982): 193 (Oduyoye's emphasis). This article appears as chapter 10 of Oduyoye's *Hearing and Knowing: Theological Reflections on Christianity in Africa* (Maryknoll, N.Y.: Orbis Books, 1986), 120–37.

13. Mercy Amba Oduyoye, "Contextualization as a Dynamic in Theological Education," *Theological Education* 30, supp. 1 (1993): 109.

14. Oduyoye, "Feminism," 196.

15. Oduyoye, "Feminism," 196.

16. Mercy Amba Oduyoye, "Christian Feminism and African Culture: The 'Hearth' of the Matter," in *The Future of Liberation Theology: Essays in Honor of Gustavo Gutiérrez*, ed. Marc H. Ellis and Otto Maduro (Maryknoll, N.Y.: Orbis Books, 1989), 443.

17. Carol S. Robb, *Equal Value: An Ethical Approach to Economics and Sex* (Boston, Mass.: Beacon Press, 1995), 1.

18. Mercy Amba Oduyoye, "Feminist Theology in an African Perspective," in *Paths of African Theology*, ed. Rosino Gibellini (Maryknoll, N.Y.: Orbis Books, 1994), 174.

19. Mercy Amba Oduyoye, "African Culture and the Gospel: Inculturation from an African Woman's Perspective," in *On Gospel—Many Cultures: Case Studies and Reflections on Cross-Cultural Theology* (Amsterdam: Rodopi, 2003), 56–57. Oduyoye has in mind Northern women's writings, such as Mary Daly, *Gyn/Ecology: The Metaethics of Radical Feminism* (Boston, Mass.: Beacon Press, 1978), 153–77.

20. Leela Gandhi refers to this as "the colonialist deployment of 'feminist criteria' to bolster the appeal of the 'civilising mission.'" See her *Postcolonial Theory: A Critical Introduction* (New York, N.Y.: Columbia University Press, 1998), 83.

21. Mercy Amba Oduyoye, "A Critique of Mbiti's View on Love and Marriage in Africa," in *Religious Plurality in Africa: Essays in Honour of John S. Mbiti*, ed. Jacob K. Olupona and Sulayman S. Nyang (Berlin: Mouton de Gruyter, 1993), 362.

22. Mercy Amba Oduyoye, "Liberative Ritual and African Religion," in *Popular Religion, Liberation, and Contextual Theology: Papers from a Congress (January 3–7, 1990, Nijmegen, the Netherlands) Dedicated to Arnulf Camps OFM*, ed. Jacques Van Nieuwenhove and Berma Klein Goldewijk (Kampen, Neth.: Uitgeversmaatschappij J. H. Kok, 1991), 79.

23. Mercy Amba Oduyoye, "The Value of African Religious Beliefs and Practices for Christian Theology," in *African Theology en Route: Papers from the Pan African Conference of Third World Theologians, December 17–23, 1997, Accra, Ghana*, ed. Kofi Appiah-Kubi and Sergio Torres (Maryknoll, N.Y.: Orbis Books, 1979), 109–16.

24. Mercy Amba Oduyoye, "Christianity and African Culture," *International Review of Mission* 84 (1995): 80–81.

25. Trinh T. Minh-ha, "An Acoustic Journey," in *Rethinking Borders*, ed. John C. Welchman (Minneapolis, Minn.: University of Minnesota Press, 1996), 1.

26. Oduyoye, "Christianity and African Culture," 78–79.

27. Homi K. Bhabha, *The Location of Culture* (New York, N.Y.: Routledge, 1994), 175.

28. Oduyoye, "Christianity and African Culture," 86–87.

29. Oduyoye, "A Critique of Mbiti's View," 341–65.

30. Oduyoye, "A Critique of Mbiti's View," 360–61.

31. Oduyoye, "Christianity and African Culture," 89.

32. Oduyoye, "African Culture and the Gospel," 46–47.

33. Mercy Amba Oduyoye, "The Impact of Women's Theology on the Development of Dialogue in EATWOT," *Voices from the Third World* 19, no. 1 (June 1999): 12.

34. Musimbi R. A. Kanyoro, "Cultural Hermeneutics: An African Contribution," in *Other Ways of Reading: African Women and the Bible*, ed. Musa W. Dube (Atlanta, Ga.: Society of Biblical Literature, 2001), 101–13. See also her *Introducing Feminist Cultural Hermeneutics: An African Perspective* (Cleveland, Ohio: The Pilgrim Press, 2002).

35. Oduyoye, *Introducing African Women's Theology*, 11–14.

36. Following Laurenti Magesa, Oduyoye differentiates between inculturation from above, with the permission and advice of authorities, from inculturation from below, which reflects popular praxis and spirituality. See Oduyoye, "African Culture and the Gospel," 45–47.

37. Oduyoye, *Hearing and Knowing*, 45–50.

38. Mercy Amba Oduyoye, *Daughters of Anowa: African Women and Patriarchy* (Maryknoll, N.Y.: Orbis Books, 1995), 20. Hereafter page references will be given in parenthesis in the text.

39. Renita J. Weems, "Reading *Her Way* through the Struggle: African Women and the Bible," in *Stony the Road We Trod: African American Biblical Interpretation*, ed. Cain Hope Felder (Minneapolis, Minn.: Fortress Press, 1991), 57–77.

40. See, e.g., Cheryl A. Kirk-Duggan, "African-American Spirituals: Confronting and Exorcising Evil through Song," in *A Troubling in My Soul: Womanist Perspectives on Evil and Suffering*, ed. Emilie M. Townes (Maryknoll, N.Y.: Orbis Books, 1993), 150–71.

41. Kwok Pui-lan, *Discovering the Bible in the Non-Biblical World* (Maryknoll, N.Y.: Orbis, 1995), 44–56.

42. Oduyoye, *Introducing African Women's Theology*, 11–12.

43. Kanyoro, "Cultural Hermeneutics," 105–6.

44. Musa W. Dube, introduction to Dube, *Other Ways of Reading*, 1–19.

45. Mercy Amba Oduyoye, *Beads and Strands*, 40.

46. Oduyoye, *Beads and Strands,* 41–42.

47. Musa W. Dube and Musimbi R. A. Kanyoro, ed., *Grant Me Justice! HIV/AIDS and Gender Readings of the Bible* (Pietermaritzburg, South Africa: Cluster Publications, 2004).

48. Nyambura J. Njoroge, "Let's Celebrate the Power of Naming," in *African Women, Religion, and Health*, 64.

49. Mercy Amba Oduyoye, "Reflection from a Third World Woman's Perspective: Women's Experience and Liberation Theologies," in *Irruption of the Third World: The*

Challenge to Theology, ed. Virginia Fabella and Sergio Torres (Maryknoll, N.Y.: Orbis Books, 1983), 246–55.

50. Oduyoye gives a detailed account of the struggle for inclusion of women in EAT-WOT in "Impact of Women's Theology," 11–34.

51. Mercy Amba Oduyoye, "Commonalities: An African Perspective," in Abraham, *Third World Theologies*, 102.

52. Oduyoye, "Feminist Theology," 168.

53. Oduyoye, *Introducing African Women's Theology*, 93.

INDEX

Created by Eileen Quam